Advanced Human Resource Management

Strategic Perspective

(Revised & Updated)

Advanced Human Resource Management

Strategic Perspective

(Revised & Updated)

Prof. S. C. Gupta

Senior Visiting Professor
and Management Consultant

Ane Books Pvt. Ltd.

New Delhi ♦ Chennai

Advanced Human Resource Management: Strategic Perspective

S.C. Gupta

First Edition : 2008
Revised & Updated : 2011
Reprint : 2018, 2019 , **2020**

Published by

Ane Books Pvt. Ltd.
4821, Parwana Bhawan, 1st Floor, 24 Ansari Road, Darya Ganj, **New Delhi** - 110 002, India
Tel.: +91(011) 23276843-44, Fax: +91(011) 23276863
e-mail: kapoor@anebooks.com, anebooks@vsnl.net
Website: www.anebooks.com

Branch Office:

- Avantika Niwas, 1st Floor, 19 Doraiswamy Road, T. Nagar, **Chennai** - 600 017, Tel.: +91(044) 28141554, 28141209 e-mail: anebookschennai@gmail.com, rathinam@anebooks.com

ISBN : 978-81-8052-193-5

Printed at: Repro Knowledgecast Limited, Thane.

Dedicated
to
my wife Rukmani
and to my daughters
Archana, Sharmila and Geetanjali

Preface to the Revised Edition

This book on Advanced Human Resources has been revised and updated in the light of increasing pace of globalization and changes in the global economy affecting organizations.

A thorough look has been taken on questions and student assignments. An annexure has been added to provide students with basic knowledge of HRM required to understand and follow this advanced version.

Prof. S. C. Gupta

Preface to the First Edition

How much HR function has transformed in the last two decades is unimaginable; from compliance and union management it has become a function to lead people. In today's turbulent global environment and knowledge-based economy, the major challenge faced by any organization is not only to continuously add value to its products and services but to learn new ways of doing business and unlearn old ways as suggested by Tom Peters and others.

This requires a paradigm shift in the minds of management and employees. This requires the belief that people are the most precious assets and the real core competency of any organization. And people have changed too. They have high aspirations of career growth and the need for participation in management. This requires that people who share the vision and culture are recruited, retained and trained to achieve organisational goals. This also requires redesigning the organization structure and creation of the organisational culture of sharing knowledge and instilling teamwork apart from an appropriate set of HR processes and policies that are in sync with corporate policies.

This book explains precisely how HR processes can be integrated and designed to drive corporate strategy and successfully implement it too. This book is different because it explores the strategic and contextual variables that drive the HR strategy, philosophy, policies, programmes, practices and processes to deliver performance, duly supported by appropriate models, research and corporate examples and case studies.

I have been teaching Strategic Human Resource Management (SHRM), Organization Behaviour, Business Policy and Strategic Management for the last 10 years and also guiding research projects in these areas. To my surprise, I found that there is hardly any book which deals in depth with the emerging field of strategic and international human resource management and covers the design of HR processes, structure and culture in an integrated manner. In short, they are about improving HRM efficiency rather than its effectiveness. It is critical that these basic HR processes are designed in tune with the company's overall strategy, type of labour markets and prevailing macro environment including legal framework and national culture so as to match the nature of the industry, its life cycle stage and many other factors. This type of analysis is attempted in this book.

This book provides a practical approach to investment and flexibility perspective, HR audit and balance scorecard, outsourcing, competency management, labour markets, diversity and strategic retention. It deals with HR practices of multinationals and their role in cross-border mergers, acquisitions and joint ventures. The emerging areas of e-HRM and HR's role in fostering quality and innovation are covered as well.

The main issues before academics and industry are: How can human resource function add value to a company and enhance its sustainable competitive advantage? How can this function inculcate creativity and innovation in the organization? How can it increase employee satisfaction, commitment and loyalty? How can it build human values of good ethics and corporate governance? What can this function do to increase employee retention and solve other problems? What is the right structure that fits with the strategy? How can HR strategy influence corporate strategy? How can employee behaviour and organization culture be changed? And, in short, how can an organization become a learning organization? These are some of the questions and topics that I have tried to address in this book.

The book has three parts. The first deals with strategic perspective of HRM, focusing mainly on the relationship of HR strategy and corporate strategy, and its implementation and various themes. Part 2 deals with HR processes, their integration and alignment with each other and external alignment. Part 3 deals with current issues in HRM like e-HRM and HR's role in MNCs.

The book is basically developed for senior students of Human Resource discipline but is equally useful for HR executives in industry who are struggling to make their organization a competitive and dynamic one. I hope that this book will serve their purpose. The field of SHRM is still evolving and its boundaries are not yet settled. This book is authored comprehensively to bring out the critical role SHRM is playing in this flat world.

Prof. S. C. Gupta

Acknowledgements

At the outset, I would like to express my gratitude and thanks to the Almighty for providing me the energy, insights and inspiration to write a book on this fascinating subject. I would like to thank Mr. Sunil Saxena, Jai Raj Kapoor and his dedicated team of my publishers Ane Books Pvt. Ltd., for constantly urging me to write and providing excellent editorial support. I place on record my thanks to fellow academicians and to my students.

Finally, I would like to thank my wife, Rukmani, who inspired me to finish this work, even at the cost of sacrificing our social life.

I place this work at the feet of Lord Shiva, as my humble offer to HIM.

Prof. S. C. Gupta

Contents

Part 1: Strategic HRM

Part 1

STRATEGIC HR

1 Evolution of SHRM

Learning Objectives

After studying this chapter, you will be able to:

- Understand why HRM has become such a crucial function for business success.
- Know the evolution of HRM over time.
- Understand the concept of HRM and differences between Personnel Management.
- Learn the concept of Strategic HRM.
- Distinguish between HRM and SHRM.

INTRODUCTION

The growth of the knowledge-based society, along with the pressures inherent in opening up emerging markets, has led cutting-edge global companies to recognise now, more than ever before that Human Resources (HR) and intellectual capital are as significant as financial assets in building sustainable competitive advantage. To maintain the lead position, the corporate sector is gradually bridging the gap between its human resource rhetoric and reality.

The strategic issues before the global leaders are to demonstrate how organizations create value from their human capital. Whether they compete for business in the market place, for cost-leadership or differentiation strategies, their effective implementation demands strategizing and leveraging their human resources. Some companies, in fact, are competing entirely on the basis of their human resources alone. Effective HR management in any organization comes down to getting the right people at the right place and at the right time and at the right cost. These knowledge workers must then mesh into a cohesive network in which they share their knowledge and ideas with each other and at the same time create new knowledge, which in turn leads to competitive advantage.

We explore the concept and evolution of HRM and SHRM (Strategic Human Resource Management), learning what distinguishes them from each other.

EVOLUTION OF THE HRM FUNCTION

The importance of people management in increasing production was realized very early during the days of F. W. Taylor, Henry Fayol, Chester Bernard and others during the age of classical management. Legal recognition and governmental support to provide basic amenities to people, however, started during the war years only. What was born then was Personnel Administration with the appointment of 'Welfare Officers' in mines and factories. The need to contain the influence of unions was also appreciated. However, it remained a reactive administration department handling workers' complaints and grievances and assisting in appointments, transfers and retirement of employees. It is in this context that Peter Drucker commented:

> Personnel Administration is largely a collection of incidental techniques without much internal cohesion. It is partly a file clerk's job, partly a house keeping job, partly a social worker's job and partly fire-fighting to head off union trouble or to settle it. The things they do like....are necessary chores. I doubt that they should be put together in one department for they are a hodge-podge. They are neither one function by kinship or skills required to carry out the activities, nor are they a function by being linked together in the work process by forming a distinct stage in the work of managers or in the process of business.

A further fillip to personnel management was seen in the 1960s when companies went into an expansion mode. The need was felt for a specialist function to organize recruitment and selection processes properly, to minimize shortages of skilled personnel in production processes and in the marketing department. Unions were also getting more organized and stronger the world over and a need was felt to structure employee compensation by proper 'job evaluation' and 'wage surveys'. Some training was also considered necessary. These activities were organized under the function called 'human resource management' or 'personnel management', which also included labour management to handle compliance of various acts like the Industrial Disputes Act and Factories Act amongst others.

HRM DEFINED

We are now in a position to define and explain HRM more comprehensively. Walton, while explaining HRM (1985), stressed mutuality between employers and employees. He defined HRM as: 'Mutual goals, mutual influence, mutual respect, mutual rewards and mutual responsibility". The theory is that policies of mutuality will elicit commitment which, in turn, will yield both better economic performance and greater human development. Therefore, 'HRM is the set of functions and activities that are designed to bring the employees and organisations together, so that goals of both are met.'

Jucious (1975) defines this function in the following manner:

> 'HRM is the field of management which has to do with planning, organising, directing and controlling the functions of procuring, developing, maintaining and utilising employees such that:

A. Objectives of the company are attained;

B. Objectives of all levels of personnel are served to the highest possible degree; and

C. Objectives of society are duly considered and served.

Figure 1.1 shows major HR organizational processes, common to all organizations. These processes are all interrelated and all are influenced by external environment facing the organization.

The important processes are related to acquisition, maintenance, development and motivation of people to ensure their commitment, creativity, best effort and cooperation in achieving

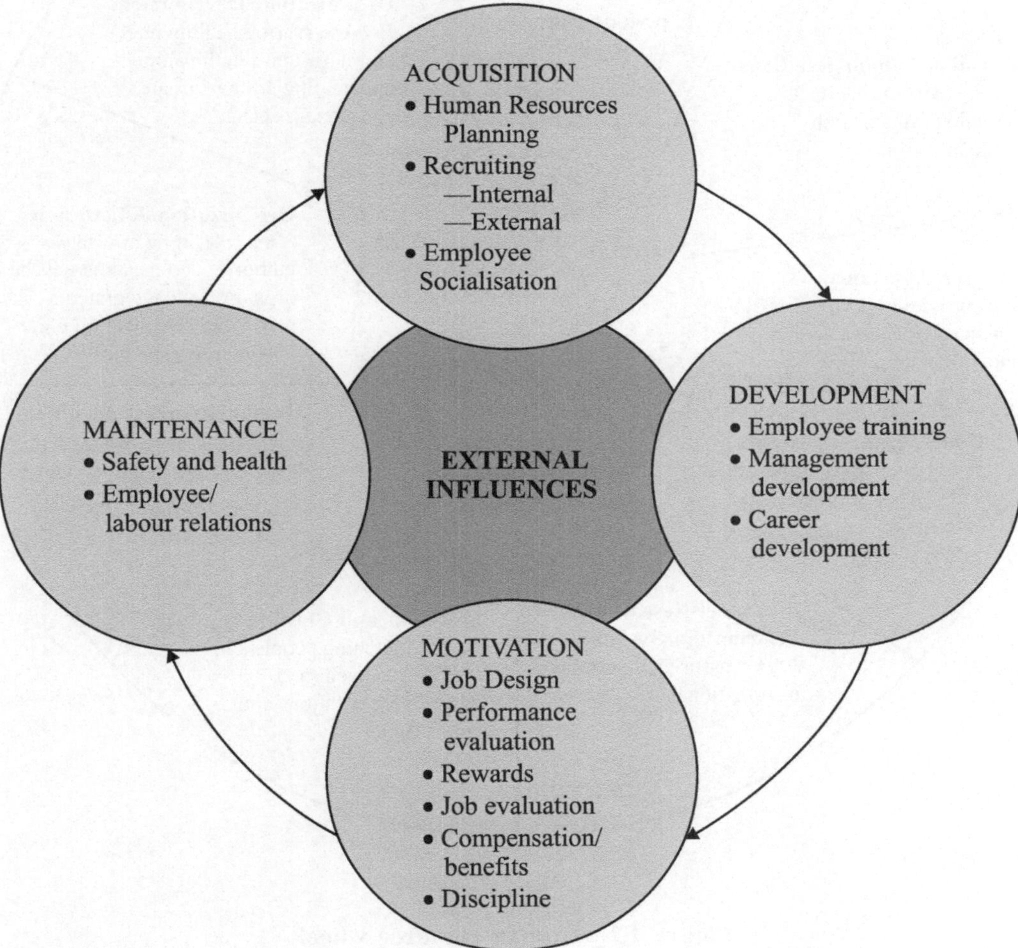

Figure 1.1. HRM components

Source: Adapted from Meg Isaac Sternberg, 'Organisational Model for Human Resource Planning'. Unpublished paper, Baltimore, U.S.A., 1984.

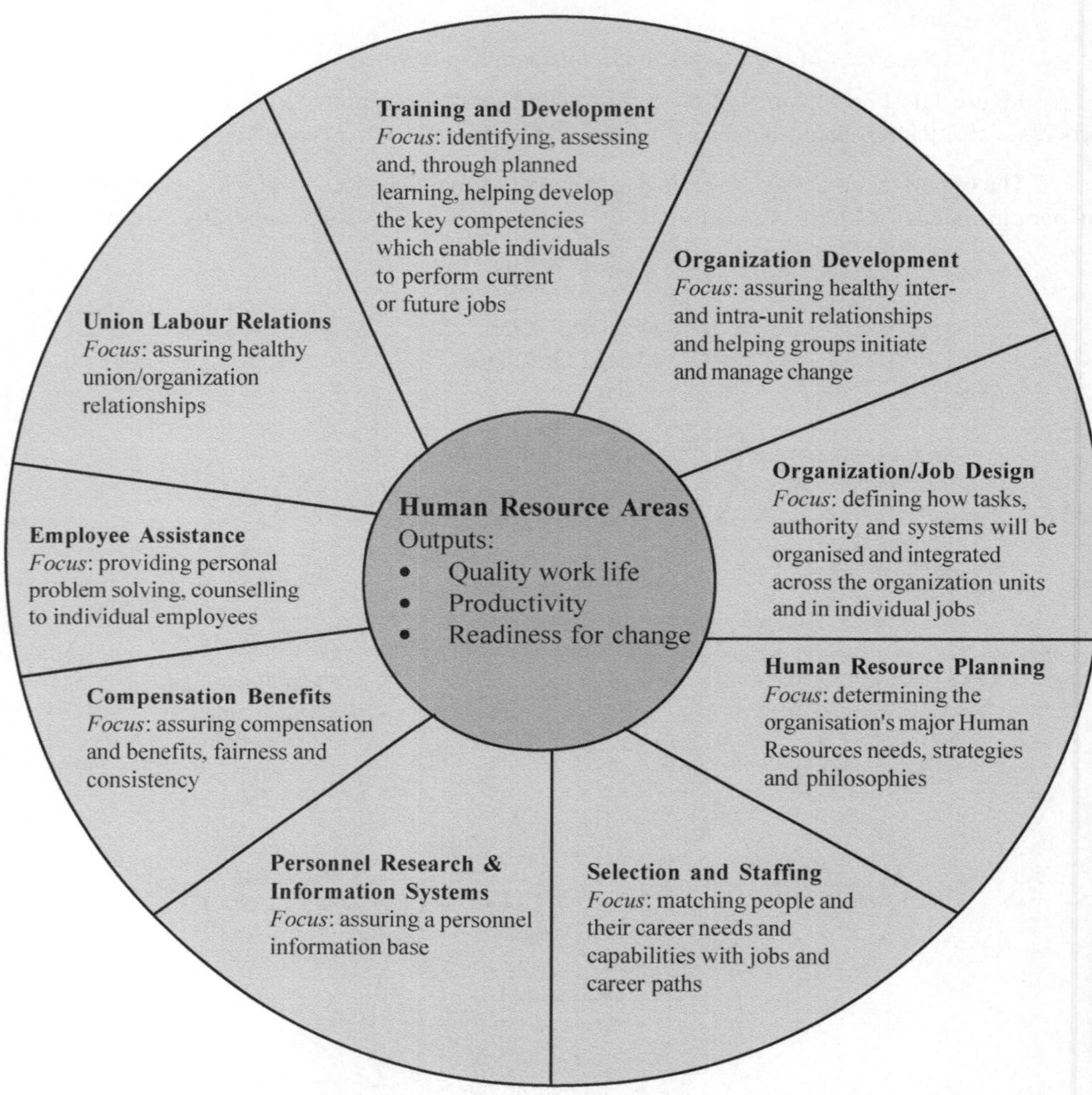

Figure 1.2. Human resource wheel

Source: American Society for Training and Development, *Models for Excellence* (ASTD, 1983) p. 23, reproduced with permission.

organizational objectives. The American Society for Training and Development has identified nine human resource areas that constitute the field of HRM. These areas are:

1. Selection and staffing,
2. Training and development,
3. Compensation, benefits and rewards,
4. Organization development,
5. Human resource planning,
6. Union labour relations,
7. Personnel research and information system,
8. Employee assistance, and
9. Organization/job design.

These areas are shown in Figure 1.1.

Differences Between HRM and Personnel Management

There is considerable overlap and confusion in two words—HRM and Personnel Management— as most books have a common title on the subject. Further, there is no clear transition from one stage to another. Different companies facing different types of competition and environment are in the process of change. Table 1.1 shows the differences between them:

TABLE 1.1

Differences Between SHRM and Traditional Personnel Management Approach

Dimension	SHRM Approach	Traditional Personnel Management Approach
Planning and Strategy Formulation	Involved in formulating overall organisational plan and aligning human resources function with the company's strategy	Involved in operational/tactical planning of HR function only within the organisational strategy
Authority Level	HR function head is part of top management team. Often, HR head is member of Board	Medium status and authority at manager's level, often reports to operation's functional head
Scope	Concerned with all employees including top managers and also external stakeholders, government officials, etc.	Concerned primarily with temporary, casual and contract labour, or only with workers
Decision-making	Involved in making all decisions pertaining to human capital	Works under the guidance of senior managers and decides only routine matters

Continued ...

...*Continued*

Dimension	SHRM Approach	Traditional Personnel Management Approach
Integration	HR function is fully integrated with other organisational functions like marketing, finance, operations and material management. Attends all inter-departmental meetings and participates in problem solving. Shares responsibility. Makes suggestions and is consulted	Moderate to small integration with other functions or departments. Focuses primarily on HR processes
Coordination	Coordinates all human resource activities, vertically and horizontally across all units and departments	Limited coordination within the HR function and with other line managers
Prized Management Skills	Negotiation, leadership and team-building	Facilitation to keep things going. Communicates upwards and downwards effectively
Beliefs and Assumptions:		
—Contract	Aim to go beyond contract	Careful delineation of written contracts
—Rules	'Can Do' outlook, impatient with rules	Clear rules/mutuality
—Guide to management action	Business needs	Procedures
—Behaviour referent	Values/Mission/Vision	Norms/Customs/Vision
—Managerial task *vis-a-vis* labour	Nurturing	Monitoring
—Nature of relations	Unitarist	Pluralist
—Conflict	De-emphasised	Institutionalised
Strategic Aspects		
—Key relations	Customer and 360°	Labour management
—Initiatives	integrated	Piecemeal
—Corporate plan	Central	Marginal
Speed of decisions	Fast	Slow
Line Management		
—Management role	Transformational leadership	Transactional leadership

Continued ...

...Continued

Dimension	SHRM Approach	Traditional Personnel Management Approach
—Key managers	General/departmental heads/ line managers	Personnel/IR specialists
—Communication	Direct	Indirect
—Standardisation	Low (parity not seen as relevant)	High (parity an important issue)
Key Levers		
—Selection	Integrated, key tasks	Separate, marginal tasks
—Pay	Performance-related	Job related (fixed grades)
—Conditions	Harmonisation	Separately negotiated
—Labour management	Maintaining peace, solving individual grievances as per situation	Collective bargaining contracts. regular interface with unions to make them partners
—Job categories/grades	Few	Many
—Communication	Increased flow	Restricted flow
—Job design	Team work	Division of labour
—Conflict handling	Manage climate and culture	Reach temporary truces
—Training and development	Controlled access	Learning companies
—Foci of attention for interventions	Wide-ranging cultural, structural and personnel strategies	Personnel procedures

Source: Storey, J. (1989). *New Perspectives on HRM.* London, U.K., Routledge.

VARIABLES THAT INFLUENCE HRM

Why do people in some companies contribute more by way of increased productivity, commitment and creativity than others? To answer this, one has to analyse the major variables/ factors that influence people management functions in all organizations. These factors can be broadly grouped into

1. human capital and its characteristics,
2. group dynamics and team culture,
3. the organization's vision, core values and human resource policies, and
4. the external environment including characteristics of labour markets.

These variables are discussed in later sections. The first three factors constitute the core of 'organization behaviour (OB)' which forms the bedrock of human resource management. There are many excellent books available on OB, and it is presumed that the students have adequate knowledge of it. Human resource management is about how OB is applied to management of people within the organisation's constraints to achieve its objectives. A model can be developed to show inter-relationship amongst these independent factors to depict that they, together, drive the organisation's effectiveness.

The dependent variables are listed below. If the independent variables are successfully managed and processes designed properly the resultant outcome, of course, would be, sustainable competitive advantage, increased market value of the firm and employee satisfaction and retention. The strengths and weaknesses of these factors can be researched for any one company or industry or used to identify if there are other factors that also influence the outcome. Longitudinal studies can be done to see how these factors change with other environmental factors.

Dependent Variables

1. Long-term profitability and market share.
2. Job satisfaction.
3. Commitment.
4. Productivity.
5. Quality of products and services.
6. Management of change and innovation.
7. Low turnover and low absenteeism.
8. Consumer satisfaction.

HR Practices that Distinguish Successful Firms

Pfeffer enumerates 13 human resource practices that seem to distinguish between high-achieving firms and poor performers. Out of these 13 management practices, seven are particularly interesting because they can be implemented in ways that make them fit the unique business enviroments companies must face. The proper mix of HRM practices depends on how work processes are organised. These seven processes are as follows: (Universalism concept of HRM):

1. Selectivity in Recruiting the Best

Hiring the right people means more than just securing employees who possess the knowledge, skills and abilities required to perform a particular job; these people must also be able to acquire new knowledge and skills as jobs and environment change. In addition, employees must find the work satisfying and that the overall organisational climate and reward structure meets their needs. Organisations spend large amounts of resources and effort in selecting the best. They select people for their values and culture compatibility too. This is their core competency and in labour markets where there is shortage it results in a 'war for talent' which they always win.

2. Incentive Pay

If employees are expected to perform in extraordinary ways and add value to the firm, sharing gains achieved with the employees meets the needs of workplace justice and fairness. Some form of performance-contingent pay is required if employees are expected to be consistent in their efforts to add value to the firm. If employees believe that their contributions are instrumental in enhancing firm performance and increasing profitability, they will want to share in the benefits. How this is done, again is strategic and important (individual level, group level, unit level or company level and in what proportion?). We believe the key is to link rewards to the particular performance parameters required of employees and to make sure that all relevant characteristics—like dependability, quality and quantity of output, generation of new ideas or cooperation are encouraged.

3. Employee Ownership

Employees can share the ownership of the firm by holding the company's stock. By making employees shareholders the company reduces the conflict between capital and labour. This puts the performance-pay contingency at the organisational level.

4. Training and Skill Development

High–performing firms display a greater commitment to training and skill development than their counterparts. This core HRM activity is related to 'Kaizen'. However, knowledge and skill acquisition will not lead to improved firm performance unless employees are allowed and encouraged to use job-related knowledge and skills when performing their job. Thus, firms must take care to select people who are willing to learn and adapt and also establish rewards that encourage employees to participate in training.

5. Cross-utilisation and Cross-training

Training and development should also allow 'flexibility' so that employees are utilized even during production slowdowns. When people are able to perform multiple jobs, or are multi-skilled, they represent a reserve of talent and are more likely to appreciate how their work and output levels affect the work of other employees in jobs related to their own.

6. Symbolic Egalitarianism

If the goal is to increase communication between and across organisational levels, a case can be made for reducing sub-divisions in job grades and other areas of inequality. Firms must signal through practices and policies that all are equal.

7. Wage Compression

The relative pay differences between people at various organization levels can have profound effects on employee perceptions. These perceptions, in turn, can result in a wide variety of employee attitudes and behaviours. Current theory and empirical evidence suggest that if the goal is to increase the level of cooperation and team orientation, pay differences between jobs should be reduced. Note that this concerns pay distinctions at the level of the job, not at the level of the individual. That is, incentive pay is distinguished from pay hierarchy compression. This, of course, depends on the HR strategy to be adopted.

The other six management practices constitute the common characteristics or motivational factors displayed by excellent companies as researched by Robert Waterman and Tom Peters. They argue that top performing companies provide employees with:

8. Something to believe in (Vision/Mission)
9. A feeling of control (Empowerment)
10. Job challenge
11. The opportunity to engage in lifelong learning
12. Recognition for achievement
13. Working in teams

According to Waterman (1998) what makes the best firms the best cannot be attributed to such things as technology, a bright idea, a masterly strategy...the best firms are better organised to meet the needs of their people, so that they attract better people than their competitors do and their people are more greatly motivated to do a superior job, it is what they do. (Waterman. *What American Does Right: Learning from Companies that Put People First*. New York, U.S.A.: W.W. Norton and Company, 1999, p.17).

Evolution of SHRM Thought

The success of Japanese firms in the 1980s was attributed mostly to their human resource practices and organisational and national cultures. This realisation attracted attention to the crucial role of the HR function in providing sustainable competitiveness. There is growing fusion of personnel management, industrial relations, human resource development and knowledge management which combinedly constitutes the field of Strategic Human Resource Management (SHRM). Its key characteristics are best summarized by Sission (1989):

1. A stress on the integration of personnel policies both with one another and with corporate planning more generally;
2. The locus of responsibility for personnel managers no longer resides with specialist managers but is now assumed by senior line managers;
3. The focus shifts from management-trade union relations to management-employee relations, from collectivism to individualism; and
4. There is stress on commitment and the exercise of initiative, with managers donning the role of 'enablers', 'coaches' and 'facilitators'.

Hendry and Pettigrew (1986) describe SHRM as follows:

1. The use of planning;
2. A coherent approach to the design and management of the personnel system based on an employment policy and manpower strategy, and often underpinned by an employment 'philosophy';

3. HRM activities and policies that match some explicit strategy; and
4. Seeing the people of an organization as a strategic 'resource' for achieving competitive advantage.

Growing Importance of People at the Boundary

In the current scenario of competitive globalisation, dynamic business environment, mass customisation and short product life, strategic response of companies is more shaped by people at the boundary of the organization rather than people at the core. Because they are in constant interaction with customers, competitors and other stockholders, they observe trends, understand requirements, perceive changes and interpret events faster for the company as a whole and also for themselves. They identify opportunities and anticipate likely threats as well as being aware of their company's strengths and weaknesses. What decides a final response or corporate strategy is the degree of openness, trust and degree of interaction between core and boundary. Such an internal environment in the firm defines its organization culture, encompassing how much there is of open discussion and debate, how much such differences in opinion are appreciated and whether every one supports the final decisions. While the quality of decision-making depends on organization culture, speed of response and implementation depends largely on the organization structure.

The open system of SHRM, therefore, declares that there is no one best way. The strategic approaches are contingent to situations. HR strategy should be suitable to a given situation and in accord with the firm's needs. The HR strategy and corporate strategy influence each other and are in a circular relationship with each other to obtain the desired outcomes in a given environment.

Key Themes of SHRM

As we have seen, the field of SHRM is still emerging and therefore, to bring clarity and focus on further research in this field, Guest (1987) has suggested that some themes that create SHRM and result in strong integration of people are as under:

1. Investment perspective, which means that for major HR policy decisions there must be some cost benefit analysis to justify investment.
2. Performance management perspective means that HR policies and programmes should result in achievement of organizational, divisional, unit level and individual goal achievement.
3. Strategic integration means that all the HR processes are integrated with each other such that they increase the effectiveness of each function and synergise with each other to ensure overall effectiveness.
4. Flexibility is seen as being primarily concerned with what is sometimes called the functional flexibility but also with an adaptable organizational structure with the capacity to manage innovation and to respond to 'change'.
5. High quality; refers to all aspects of managerial behaviour, including management of employees and investment in high quality employees which, in turn, will bear directly on the quality of goods and services provided.

6. Diversity management refers to growing diversity at today's work-place, requiring new approaches to understand differences in cross-cultural, gender, religious and ethnic oriented behaviour. Thus, diversity is valued and used as a valuable resource in managing people.

The subsequent chapters in this book mostly discuss the key levers of SHRM and how they can be integrated.

Progress Towards SHRM

In spite of the rhetoric that people are our best assets, many organizations are not able to realize the full benefits that the SHRM function can provide. The barriers to SHRM are discussed in the next chapter. To ascertain the status of SHRM in organizations, we give below some of the key questions which need to be explored to assess strategic content of their approach that confirms that they are practising SHRM.

1. Is there a formal mission statement? Were employees involved in formulating the mission statement? Is it shared by them? Is it reflected in their attitude and behaviour?
2. Is corporate and business strategy linked to the mission? Is it known and understood by the HRM functionaries at different levels.
3. Are the HRM strategic objectives and goals derived from and linked to corporate business strategy and plans?
4. How have training and development policies been framed? Have their costs and benefits been assessed?
5. Is there an evaluation and feedback system? What is the philosophy of performance evaluation? Is it effective and acceptable? Have indicators of performance been established?
6. How much leadership is displayed at different levels?
7. How is collaboration with line managers obtained in implementing HRM plans? Who takes personnel decisions: line managers or HR managers?
8. What are current major HRD initiatives like TQM, BPR, Six Sigma, etc?
9. Are HR strategy, organization structure, organization culture, and compensation structure and work systems including decision-making styles in sync with each other?
10. How much flexibility exists in the system and how is diversity managed?
11. To what degree does the HR function contribute to designing work processes of the future?
12. Do HR people possess information about labour markets and organisational capability to inform decision makers who are formulating business strategy?

The Map of HRM Territory

SHRM has a much wider periphery today. It encompasses all the HR areas and is practised by 'all employees.' This is due to decentralisation and development of all employees and their empowerment. This facilitates deeper communication, involvement and commitment of middle management and other employees within the organization, thus integrating structure, strategy and culture with HR policies to gain organisational outcomes. A more flexible model was developed by Beer and his associates (1984) at Harvard University. In this model, the concept of HRM is widened to include situational factors like workforce characteristics, management philosophy, labour markets and concerns of shareholders and community, government role and unions' attitude.

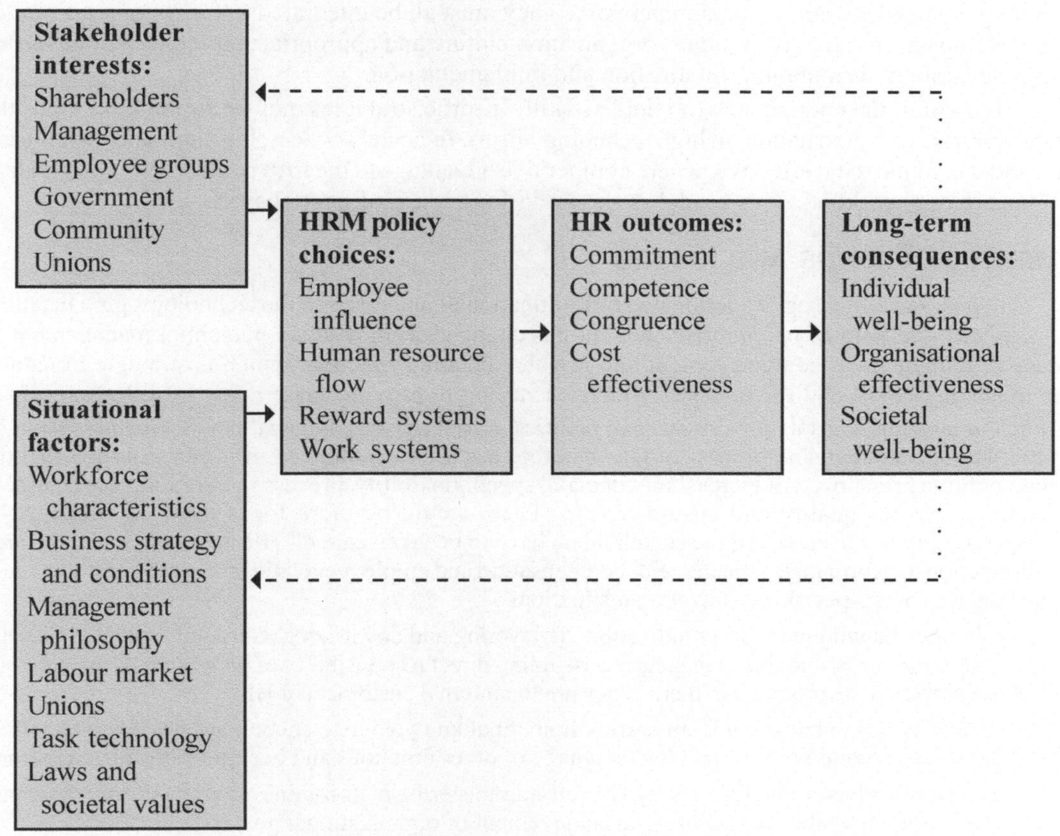

Figure 1.3. The map of the HRM territory

Source: Beer *et al.* (1984:16).

The Open System of SHRM (Hendry and Pettigrew); Salman and Maybey Model

In today's flat world and knowledge economy, competitive advantage is delivered increasingly by knowledge workers. In such firms strategy is emerging rather than being formulated (Mintzberg). People at the boundary are playing a significant role in generating creative ideas and implementing them in innovative ways. The role of top management is to support them. The organization pyramid is now inverted.

Hendry and Pettigrew support the view that there is no one best way of doing things. Their model of open SHRM starts with an analysis of the environment within which organisations exist, and which they seek to control or survive in, through certain strategies. These strategies, once tentatively decided, require certain kinds of behaviour if they are to be achieved. These desired behaviours will be produced by certain HR strategies, supported by the organization culture to sustain it and certain types of organization structure, which will facilitate clarity of roles and goals, including the needed communication network. They must all be integrated to function in unison for synergic impact. In turn, HR policies, organization culture and appropriate structure will influence corporate strategy formulation, finalization and implementation.

To exploit the competency of people's skill, specific strategies may be formulated. Thus the relationship is circular in nature. In high technology firms, financial services, hospitals and institutions, this model is found to be effective, where competitive advantage to the firm comes from 'information and knowledge workers'. This model is shown in Figure 2.8 of next chapter.

Emerging Trends and Issues

In post-industrial society dominated by multinationals and information technology, globalization, and services, the field of people management has changed from reactive personnel management to proactive human resource management and to value creating function, which is strategic in nature. The trends in SHRM and the issues to which it is trying to provide answers are as follows:

1. Each organization has its own situational realities, characteristics and challenges. Business strategy and the role, strategy and process of HR therefore has to be customized. It is generally felt that the competitive pressures will increasingly demand speed, flexibility, process integration, team building and concern for quality and customer care. There would be more focus on results and social responsibility of business. All the stakeholders have to be taken care of. HR interventions in the area of selection, performance management, compensation and employee relations have to be strategically managed to meet specific organizational situations.
2. HR roles are changing with decentralization, de-layering and downsizing. Corporate and HR roles are changing to advisory and line managers are assuming direct responsibility of people under their charge. HR is a service to be provided to them. They are the internal customers of HR.
3. HR capability has to come out from narrow functional knowledge to encompass business capability. HR has to understand the concerns and language of other functions and become their trusted partner.
4. More and more reliance on IT is making HR self-administering in its routine aspects. HR has, therefore, to be more direct, visibly contributing to achievement of organizational goals.
5. Upgrading employees, preparing them for change, modernization of mind, leading to collaboration and innovation is another important role emerging for SHRM.
6. Management of redundancy due to upgradation of technology is another area. In this context transparency, communication, redeployment, retaining and rightsizing are being emphasized.
7. Internationalization and training of people in cross-cultural operations is gaining added importance and HR has to prepare organizations for expatriate management.
8. Employee burnout, work-life balance and management of stress have become prime responsibilities of HR because people are the most vital resource.
9. Building unions as strategic partners of business and to make business a joint partnership between unions and management is a challenge. How organizations listen to the 'voice' of employees and act on it is the responsibility of SHRM as unions are losing their hold in MNCs.
10. Finally, the role of HR in business restructuring, acquisitions, mergers and joint ventures has become the most important strategic responsibility of HR function.

All these issues have been explored, discussed and analyzed in this book in great depth, illustrated with cases and theoretical models.

Questions and Assignment

Q.1. Explain the concept of HRM and how it is different from personnel management.

Q.2. What do you understand by Strategic Human Resource Management? How is it different from HRM?

Q.3. What are the main characteristics of SHRM?

Q.4. State the HR policies that distinguish successful organizations.

Q.5. Explain the main themes of SHRM. Explore any one theme in detail.

Q.6. Discuss the current issues being faced and the trends that are emerging in the field of SHRM.

Assignment

In groups of three, study any one organization for its HR practices and people and interview some employees to identify where it stands in its transformation towards becoming truly strategic. Present your findings to the class.

CASE

TATA STEEL is a role model global company in HR

It believes in total transparency between the employers and customers, unions, government and the community, resulting in 90 years of industrial peace, business-led strategies and many transformations. It has continuously improved productivity, reduced cost and manpower by upgrading technology through involvement of employees and unions.

Corporate philosophy: Humanization of technology—We Make Men To Make Steel. It speaks about its people orientation in management. Focus—'modernisation of technology along with modernisation of mind.'

Vision: Jamshedji wanted every member of the management to whole-heartedly cultivate and exhibit an unflinching consideration for the people and harmonise the objectives of business with the needs, hopes and aspiration of the people. It has grown entirely through Indian know-how used from the beginning. The owners view the organization as a public institution of which they are trustees.

Vision is sought to be attained by maintaining employee relations, developing people, and modernising technology. Union leaders are progressive and believe in 'joint consultations' which started in 1956. It has a three tier formation: JDC (Joint Departmental Council at unit level); JWC (Joint Works Council at works level and JCM (Joint Council of Consultative Management) at the apex level.

The company has successfully adopted and implemented the following Human Resource strategies:

- Rightsizing the organization.
- Continuous training and development.
- Increasing flexibility and versatility of workers.
- Maintaining harmonious relations.
- Selecting, retaining and career development of human capital.
- Performance-based reward system.
- Continuous improvement of processes.

In the field of Employee Welfare, Tata Steel was responsible for several firsts. Among them

- 8-hour working day (1912)
- Free medical aid (1915)
- Creation of welfare department (1917)
- Schooling facilities for employees' children (1917)
- Formation of works' committee (1920)
- Workers' provident fund (1920)
- Worker's accident compensation scheme (1920)
- Technical institute for apprentices, craftsmen and engineering graduates (1928)
- Maternity benefits (1928)
- Profit-sharing bonus (1934)
- Retirement gratuity (1937)
- *Ex gratia* payment for workers who are victims of road accidents while coming to work (1937)
- Tata Steel completely modernised its operations leading to a many-fold rise in production (from 0.5 to 3.2 million tonnes), reducing labour by a third and increasing productivity 10-fold, and is today producing the lowest-cost steel in the world.

The corporate objectives that guide the company's executives are:

- Satisfied customers,
- Industry leadership, and
- Profitable growth.

The following strategies led to the achievement of these goals:

- Focusing on people.
- Commitment to total quality.
- Leadership in technology.
- Acting as an ethical and responsible corporate entity, subserving modernisation to increasing obsolescence through timely upgrading.
- Alliances with Thyssen of Germany, Nippon Steel of Japan, Hoovegovens of The Netherlands and Voest Alpine of Austria. The organization believes that petals alone are never as fragrant as the flowers. Hence every unit in the group complements the other.
- Staying at the top by innovating at the bottom.

Strategy for Growth: Tata Steel has consistently made continuous investment in:

- Technology
- People
- Welfare
- Collaborations
- Consolidation
- Innovation
- Community development—The management has all along practised what its founder said: 'It is not enough to improve the quality of our own life, if we cannot improve the quality of life of those around us' (Tata).

Modernisation of the Mind: This company realised that to succeed in global competition, it has to continuously modernise its plant and technology. But to achieve it, it has to continuously enhance the competencies of its employees. For this, it has set up one of the best training centres in the world. The training objectives and strategies are listed in Table 1.2.

MANAGEMENT OF REDUNDANCY

The modernisation of technology needed massive adjustments and readjustments in the surplus manpower resulting from closure of units, skill obsolescence and rationalisation of environmental constraints and compulsions to meet government guidelines.

TABLE 1.2

HRD Objectives	Modernisation of Mind
• Recognise human beings as assets	• Modern training and development facilities
• Create achievement oriented culture	• Concept of training executives
• Enhance professional abilities	• Formation of training strategies and policies
• Inculcate wisdom through collective wisdom	• Widening of managerial horizons through external programmes
• Create environment of respect and trust	• Employees' awareness programme
• Create sense of belonging	• Person of the Month award
• Sustain and improve climate of industrial relations	• Performance evaluation system
	• Survey of employees' attitude, morale, satisfaction
	• Community policy and resources for it
	• Productivity enhancement through employee-involvement
	• Training of employees' wards
	• Innovative approaches to rightsizing the workforce
	• On-the-job training, pre-employment training, process-operation training
	• HRD committee headed by MD, technical education and advisory committee and strategic training and review committee headed by vice-presidents

The historical agreement of 1956 has been a major constraint. This agreement demanded cooperative relations between management and labour for modernisation and expansion. It stipulated that there will be no retrenchment of existing employees. Those employees who are shifted to other jobs will be trained for those jobs and their existing salary will be protected. A permanent placement committee was set up to decide the manner of filling vacancies. It maintains statistics such as age, designation, grade, skills, qualifications, etc. and decides using the following criteria:

1. Matching of skills and vacant posts.
2. Training and deployment for mismatched skill-post situations.
3. Deploying personnel two or three levels below existing grades while protecting salaries.

4. Employees in excess of the standard force are placed against likely future vacancies.
5. Plan deployment in line with technology in use.
6. Training and retraining
7. Separation of surplus staff through voluntary retirement or early separation schemes. The benefits of VR and ESS are:
   - Payment of 1.25 times monthly salary as pension up to the age of 60 years
   - Medical facilities and refundable loans up to Rs. 2,00,000 or 50 per cent of total pension benefit, whichever is less.
   - Other benefits like house rent, education grant and payment of normal gratuity, encashment of leave, etc.

About 8,000 persons opted out under these schemes.

TABLE 1.3

Category of Employees		Cluster Classification	Number of Grades
Workers	Unskilled and Skilled	A	2
	Skilled	B	3
	Highly Skilled	C	3
	Super Skilled	D	2

RESULTS

- No wonder, Tata Steel's performance for over 70 years has been outstanding and the Tata spirit can be seen and felt when one visits the plant.
- Evidence of urge to assume more responsibility, improved team spirit.
- Encouragement towards creativity and innovativeness and desire for self-development.
- Employee willingness to accept change—new technology and new methods of working.
- All expectations surpassed in the areas of production, productivity, cost and profits.
- Targets of 3 million tonnes crude steel production exceeded in the very first year of plant capacity upgrade.
- Improvement in quality of both work and personal life.
- Creation of many world records in the areas of steel production, iron production, equipment life, etc.
- Many innovative breakthroughs in processes, utilisation of resources and energy conservation.
- Sustained industrial peace and prosperity.
- Winners of several corporate and individual national and international recognitions and awards.
- In the recent acquisition of Corus, the Tata management brought the union leaders of the target company to see for themselves how employees participate in decision making at Jamshedpur and that helped very much to clinch the deal.

Question

Q.1. What are the main strengths of Tata Steel and how has this organization been able to ensure long industrial peace with modernisation?

TABLE 1.3

Category of Employees		Cluster Classification	Number of Grades
Workers	Unskilled and Skilled	A	2
	Skilled	B	3
	Highly Skilled	C	3
	Super Skilled	D	2

4. Employees in excess of the standard force are placed against likely future vacancies.
5. Plan deployment in line with technology in use.
6. Training and retraining
7. Separation of surplus staff through voluntary retirement or early separation schemes. The benefits of VR and ESS are:
   - Payment of 1.25 times monthly salary as pension up to the age of 60 years
   - Medical facilities and refundable loans up to Rs. 2,00,000 or 50 per cent of total pension benefit, whichever is less.
   - Other benefits like house rent, education grant and payment of normal gratuity, encashment of leave, etc.

About 8,000 persons opted out under these schemes.

Results

- No wonder, Tata Steel's performance for over 70 years has been outstanding and the Tata spirit can be seen and felt when one visits the plant.
- Evidence of urge to assume more responsibility, improved team spirit.
- Encouragement towards creativity and innovativeness and desire for self-development.
- Employee willingness to accept change—new technology and new methods of working.
- All expectations surpassed in the areas of production, productivity, cost and profits.
- Targets of 3 million tonnes crude steel production exceeded in the very first year of plant capacity upgrade.
- Improvement in quality of both work and personal life.
- Creation of many world records in the areas of steel production, iron production, equipment life, etc.
- Many innovative breakthroughs in processes, utilisation of resources and energy conservation.

- Sustained industrial peace and prosperity.
- Winners of several corporate and individual national and international recognitions and awards.
- In the recent acquisition of Corus, the Tata management brought the union leaders of the target company to see for themselves how employees participate in decision making at Jamshedpur and that helped very much to clinch the deal.

Question

Q.1. What are the main strengths of Tata Steel and how has this organization been able to ensure long industrial peace with modernisation?

2 Corporate and HR Strategy—Relationship & Implementation

Learning Objectives

After studying this chapter, you will be able to learn:

- The concept of corporate strategy and corporate planning.
- The concept of HR strategy and HR planning.
- The concept of 'fit' and degree of fit between corporate and HR strategies.
- Theoretical models that explain these concepts and their usefulness.
- Detailed explanation of the 5 Ps of HRM, that is, HR Philosophy, HR Policies, HR Programmes, HR Practices and HR Processes.
- The concept of 'core competency' and how HR architecture can contribute to a sustainable competitive advantage to firms.
- The organisational examples for the above theoretical framework.

INTRODUCTION

Organizations are increasingly looking towards HRM interventions to survive and compete in the global markets. What are these interventions and how are they to be selected and designed to deliver the desired results? This is a critical question before top management and senior HR executives. A search for the answer leads to the concept of integration of corporate and HR strategies. In fact, Fombrun *et al.* (1984), developed the concept of linking business strategy and HRM and organization structures to create a 'tight fit' between them. The HR interventions adopted by some successful firms include amongst others: empowerment, trust, learning organization, leadership, excellence, career planning, quality circles, performance related pay and de-layering. These were *ad-hoc* interventions which yielded mixed results. Since then, the approach has become more structured and all these HR processes and policies, organization culture and structure need to 'fit' dynamically with corporate strategy for optimum results.

This chapter explores this aspect of 'fit' between corporate and HR strategies. Further, what really constitutes the HR strategy? How is it different from HR policies or HR planning for that matter? How does it provide the 'core competency' and thus sustainable competitive advantage to any organization? And, finally, can it be industry-specific or organization-specific in the same industry? These are the questions we will deal with in this chapter.

THE CONCEPT OF CORPORATE STRATEGY

Corporate strategy refers to the set of perspective management measures taken with a view to ensuring the survival and long term success of an enterprise in a competitive environment. Kenichi Ohmae, a world renowned authority on management, observes in his book, *The Mind of the Strategist*:

> "What business strategy is all about,—what distinguishes it from all other kinds of business planning—is, in a word, competitive advantage. Corporate strategy thus implies an attempt to alter a company's strength relative to that of its competitors in the most efficient way".

Gary Hammel and C. K. Prahalad, in their best-seller, *Competing for the Future*, observe:

> 'Substantial challenges face any organization intent on getting to the future first. The first challenge, how to navigate from here to there, arrives as both public and private institutions struggle to plot a course through an increasingly inconsistent environment, where experience is rapidly devalued and familiar landmarks no longer serve as guideposts. Never before has the institutional terrain been changing so quickly or have industry boundaries been so malleable. Never before have competitors, partners, suppliers and buyers been so indistinguishable. How, then, does one get to the future first even when there is no map?"

> As Peter Drucker warns, management has no choice but to anticipate the future, to attempt to mould it, and to balance short-range and long-range goals. The future will just not happen if one wishes hard enough. It requires decisions—now. It demands allocation of resources—now. It imposes risk—now. It requires action—now. It requires work—now. And the tasks of strategic management include these.

The ultimate objective of corporate strategy is to identify the new and different businesses, technologies and markets which the company should try to create long-range. But the work starts with the question: what is our present business? Which of our present businesses should we abandon? Which should we play down? Which should we push and supply new resources to? Where do we want to be five years from now and how?

THE EFFECTIVE STRATEGIES

In the early 1980s, Hershey Foods' senior management defined a long-term gap between their desired performance of the firm and what its strategic plan projected. The gap was in terms of size: sales and income. Acquisitions could fill the gap. One of the staff's major undertakings was to highlight a list of the top 50 acquisition candidates. The analysis was carefully crafted and utilised a scan of the entire Compustata data set. First, companies that were too large or too small were eliminated. The next set of parameters related to historical profitability, sales growth, leverage and stock price performance. Management participated in setting the parameters of the screening process, every step along the way. The effort was completed, a list of the top 50 acquisition candidates was compiled and presented to senior management. At the top of the list, the number one acquisition candidate for Hershey Foods was Cross (as in Cross pens). Management sat in silence, until someone asked the question, "what does Hershey know about running a pen company?" The answer, of course, was nothing. Forty-eight of the fifty companies were outside the food industry and outside Hershey's area of expertise.

Although at the time, it seemed like a wasted effort, that exercise helped senior management focus on strategy, not just filling a 'gap' in a strategic plan. It began a keen self-assessment by senior management that culminated in understanding that. Hershey's key strengths and core competencies centre around manufacturing a quality confectionery product, selling that product and delivering the product anywhere in the United States and Canada. From these core competencies, Hershey's general acquisition strategy was formed.

Strategy involves continued reassessment of the firm's political, economic, financial and technological environments. These must be related to the changing characteristics of the firm's industry and its competitive environment. The purpose of environmental reassessment is to reassess the broad forces for change. In this framework, the firm must determine whether its current policies and performance are appropriate in relation to its opportunities and threats. The firm then formulates strategic alternatives to achieve its goals. The firm must judge whether the managerial, technological and financial resources it possesses are sufficient to achieve a competitive superiority. The goal is to develop a bundle of capabilities that will enable the firm to achieve an advantage over its competitors. The advantages should be reflected in superior growth and superior returns to shareholders. The literature of strategy emphasises that these capabilities cannot be readily imitated by competitors. M&A activities can also contribute in developing an organization system with superior performance with proper HR planning.

A model for competition analysis is depicted in Figure 2.1 outlining the various factors that need to be evaluated in a systematic manner to evaluate and decide which industries to enter and which ones to quit. This evaluation and analysis is done by people and hence influenced by their perceptive vision and mutual relationships.

An example of successful strategies is provided in Box 2.1

These questions and quotes amply explain the fields of corporate strategy. It is necessary to state that the strategy is formulated in the minds of people; it is evaluated by them and implemented by them. This is where the HR processes of managing people come in.

Porter, Hammel and Prahalad emphasise that the essence of strategy is "being distinctively different from competitors." Japanese companies which triggered the global revolution in the 1980s pioneered such processes as TQM, Quality Circle, Kaizen, etc. through their HR policies, practices and organization culture.

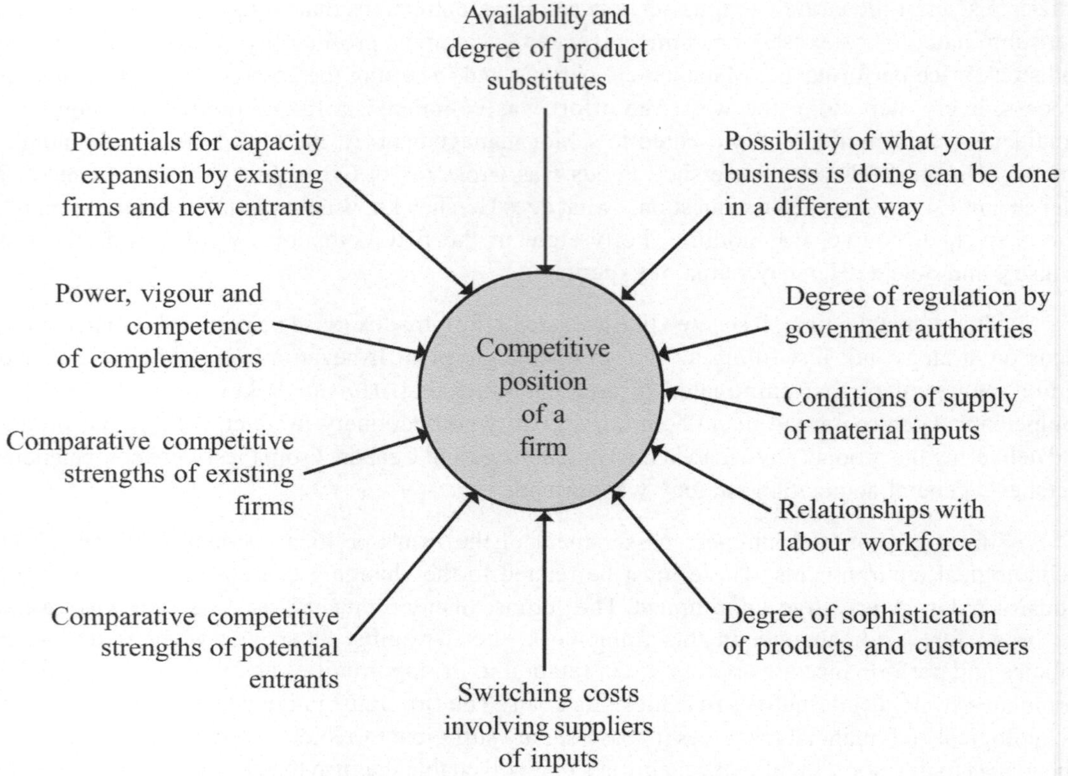

Figure 2.1. Dimensions of Competitive analysis

The Concept of Human Resource Strategy

Human resource strategy involves a central philosophy of the way that people in the organization are managed, and translation of this philosophy into personnel policies and practices. It requires HR processes and practices to be integrated so that they make a coherent whole and also that this whole is integrated with the business and organizational strategy. These themes of integration and central management have been studied by a number of writers, such as Handy *et al.*, 1989; Hendry & Pettigrew, 1986, and others. Baird *et al.*, 1983, went one step beyond this to suggest that there can be no organizational strategy without inclusion of human resources.

Human resource strategy in general is behaviour based. In the traditional approach there would be analysis of employee behaviour required to achieve organizational objectives and then modifying HR processes of recruitment, compensation and performance management, etc. This is shown in Table 2.1. In this table, the three types of Poster's corporate strategies: Cost leadership, Differentiation and Innovation or Focus are shown alongwith the required employee role/behaviour for their successful implementation with corresponding HRM policies that promote such behaviour.

BOX 2.1
Effective Strategies

To illuminate the preceding, examples of effective strategies may be summarised. Mechael Dell formulated the vision of selling made-to-order computers by mail. From this basic concept, the vision expanded to a broad supplier system to maximise choice and quality, minimising investment in inventory and warehouses to achieve cost and prices that competitors could not match.

Amazon early recognised the potential of e-commerce for providing convenience in the purchase of books. Warehouse and other inventory costs were reduced. Investments in retail facilities and receivables were avoided. Much information about the books was provided using the potential of the Internet. From books, Amazon has expanded into a wide range of products such as music, CDs and electronics.

Starbucks reflected the concept that the consumption of premium coffee could take place in an attractive setting with facilities for relaxing, reading, and perhaps socialising. Mergers facilitated expanding nationally and internationally.

Borders provided a superstore in which to browse for books in a pleasant environment including coffee. Its strategic vision has to be adjusted to meet the competition of the Internet bookstores.

Mcdonald's formulated the concept of supply of high-quality beef for its hamburgers sold in a clean environment at low prices. The Golden Arches symbolise its quality assurance.

Wal-Mart began with the concept that less populated areas made it possible to establish department stores within a broader geographic business operation that could achieve economies of inventory control, warehousing and logistical support. Greater variety at lower prices could be achieved. Sam Walton implemented a friendly welcome back to shoppers by helpful employees. From regional beginnings Wal-Mart has moved worldwide, expanding in to a broader range of products including groceries.

In 1984, Intel found that Japanese companies were producing higher-quality memory chips at lower costs and prices. Memories were key to Intel's early strategy. Intel developed and refined new technologies on memory products where they were easier to test. But it shifted its strategy from memory to processors. Its mix of employees shifted from hardware to software programmers.

Cisco began selling basic network routers to corporate customers. From a single product company, Cisco evolved into a complete data networking solution provider. Between 1993 and 1999, Cisco engaged in more than 50 acquisitions. Its underlying strategy was to acquire the technology and people to provide Cisco with the capabilities to perform an expanded role in the data networking industry.

The above represents a small sample of strategic visions that guided firms to success. They represent important innovations in thinking and implementation. There are no simple formulas for innovation and creativity, but the strategy literature has developed a number of approaches for achieving competitive superiority.

TABLE 2.1
Corporate Strategy, Associated Employee Role Behaviour and HRM Policies

Corporate Strategy	Employee Role Behaviour	HRM Policies
Cost Leadership	Relatively repetitive and predictable behaviour	Relatively explicit and fixed job descriptions and allow little room for ambiguity
	A rather short term focus	A mix of individual and group criteria for performance appraisal that is mostly short term and result oriented
	A modest concern for quality of output	Close monitoring of market pay levels for use in making compensation decisions
	Primarily autonomous or individual activity	Narrowly designed jobs and narrowly defined career paths that encourage specialisation, expertise and efficiency
	High concern for quantity of output	Minimal levels of employee training and development
	Primary concern for results; low risk-taking activity; high degree of comfort with stability	
Differentiation or quality enhancement	Relatively repetitive and predictable behaviours	Relatively fixed and explicit job description
	A more long term or intermediate focus	High levels of employee participation in decisions relevant to immediate work conditions and the job itself
	A moderate amount of cooperative, inter-dependent behaviour	A mix of individual and group criteria for performance appraisal that is mostly short-term and results oriented
	A high concern for quality of output	A relatively egalitarian treatment of employees and some guarantees of employment security
	A modest concern for quantity of output	Extensive and continuous training and development of employees

Continued...

...Continued

Corporate Strategy	Employee Role Behaviour	HRM Policies
	High concern for process; low risk-taking activity; commitment to goals of the organization	
Innovation/Focus	A high degree of creative behaviour	Jobs that require close interaction and coordination among groups of individuals
	Longer-term focus	Performance appraisals that are more likely to reflect longer-term and group-based achievements
	A relatively high level of cooperative, interdependent behaviour	Jobs that allow employees to develop skills that can be used in other positions of the firm
	A moderate degree of concern for quality	Compensation systems that emphasise internal equity rather than external parity. Pay rates that tend to be low, but allow employees to be stockholders and have more freedom to choose the mix of components that make up their pay
	A moderate concern for quantity; an equal degree of concern for process and results	Broader career paths to reinforce the development of skills
	A greater degree of risk-taking, a higher tolerance of ambiguity and unpredictabilty	

Source: Schuler & Jackson, 1987.

The Concept of 'Fit' Between Corporate and HR Strategy

In most books on Business Policy and Strategic Management, the traditional strategic process starts with analyses of the company's vision, mission, core values and stakeholders, followed by analysis of external environment including industry analysis to identify opportunities and threats. Next, an internal analysis is done of resources to identify strengths and weaknesses and value chain analysis. Based on this basic work at the corporate level, different SBUs (strategic business units) finalise their product-market strategies to gain sustainable competitive advantage.

Once this is worked out, various functional strategies are formulated in the areas of HRM, marketing, finance and R&D. This is the traditional method depicted in Figure 2.2, which presents the traditional way of depicting corporate strategy driving HR strategy, which results in business outcomes. In this model, HR systems appropriately take into account business strategy and other contextual factors that affect the firm's performance by changing the composition of the firm's internal labour market and by influencing the behaviours of individuals making up this internal talent pool.

For example, if the firm is pursuing a cost-based strategy, it will employ labour with just needed competencies paying the same or below industry level wages, employing more temporary and casual labour, spending the minimum on training and development.

Performance in such firms is rated on quantity of goods produced or sold, jobs are well defined and delegation of authority is minimum, controls are strong, union activity is discouraged and so on. On the other hand, if the firm's strategy is to compete on differentiation, innovation and quality, the firm employs individuals with high levels of competencies and pays higher wages to retain and motivate them.

Control is exercised through organization culture, which is more open; employees are encouraged to take risks, training and development is given high priority and the structure is relatively flatter. Performance criteria stress quality, customer orientation and innovation. Work is organised through teams. Leadership is exercised at all levels.

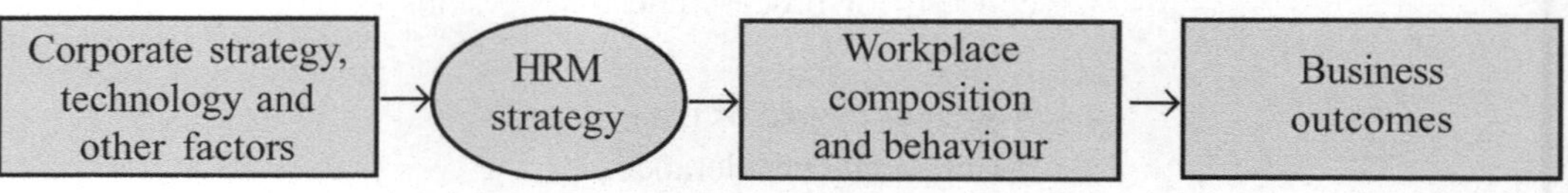

Figure. 2.2. Traditional system

Traditional System Changes

With globalisation and liberalisation, business competition has become stronger emphasizing the need for customer orientation. In this changing scenario, the need was felt to give more importance to job related competencies in relation to its strategic and business contexts. Infusion of high technology and automation has further emphasized the requirement of multi-tasking and team working. This led to changes in the traditional approach of SHRM as shown in Figure 2.3, reflecting a closer relationship between corporate strategy, HRM systems and business outcomes. Jackson, Schuler and Riverio developed this model after a study of 267 firms. Here the connection between strategic context and HRM strategy passes through the behavioural/role requirements of targeted job classes. Work processes and their associated role requirements are directly influenced by strategy, technology and other factors embedded in the business environment. HR systems can be designed to maximise the likelihood that the right people accept job offers and that these employees contribute to meet business objectives. It may be added that the knowledge and skills required to perform jobs at a high level of proficiency vary greatly within and across companies. The main variables for relative contribution, however, remain organization culture and structure and HR policies mix.

HR Architecture for Process Design

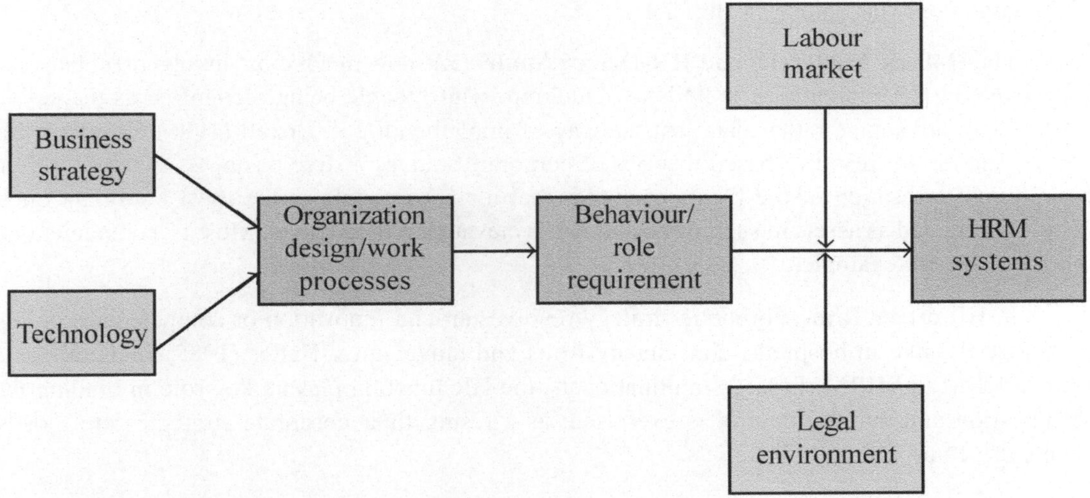

Figure 2.3. Jackson, Schuler & Riverio model

Degree of Integration

The degree of integration between corporate strategy and human resource strategy differs considerably between different organisations, as shown in Figure 2.4 In the **Separation Model (A)** there is no integration at all. Some firms are so occupied with the problems or issues of manufacturing, financial matters or others that HRM is run in an *ad-hoc* manner. Such companies are small outfits, owner-driven or in decline. However, some large public sector units can also be spotted, where HR decisions are mostly forced by unions or government on the firm. This was the case some 25 years back when labour was cheap and inter-firm competition was not so fierce.

The **Fit Model (B)** represents growing recognition of the importance of people to the achievement of organisational strategy. Employees are seen as the key in implementation of the declared organisational strategy and human resource strategy is designed to fit the requirements of the organisation's strategy. Some early models of HR, like the one proposed by Schuler and Jackson (see Figure 2.3) present this approach (see Table 2.1 also). Here, HR strategy is assumed to be a top-down and rational process. Goals are set in corporate strategy for each function including HR and functions have to take steps to achieve the same. Most manufacturing organisations, big and small, are characterised by this approach. Here HR is functioning as a staff function and the HR head is at the 'General Manager's level.

The **Dialogue Model (C)** takes the relationship one step further, as it recognises the need for two-way communication and some debate. There is no one clear corporate strategy visible and several alternatives are examined, for example, a mining company may be deciding about introduction of capital intensive technology which will replace unionised labour force. Clearly the decision requires support of unions and the role of HR becomes crucial. The debate, however, is limited to such matters only, as shown in Box 2.1

The **Holistic Model (D) and HR-Driven Model (E)** show much more involvement between corporate and HR strategies. The holistic model represents people being recognised as the key to comparative advantage rather than just the way of implementing it. Boxall (1996), develops this idea in relation to 'resource based theories of corporate strategy'. Here business strategy is based on optimum utilisation of the firm's resources that includes people as the most important ones. People are treated as assets in such firms and HR is elevated to board level. Most IT companies and services firm are examples.

In HR driven firms, corporate strategy revolves around innovation or competencies of key professionals, like in hospitals, consultancy firms and universities. Butler (1988) finds this as a shift of HRM to SHRM. In large multinationals, the HR function plays a key role in binding the organization and cultural control is exercised; as a result, their corporate strategies are mostly people driven as well as holistic.

FORMAL MODELS EXPLAINING THE CONCEPTS

Formal models have been presented by various authors over the last 20 years to explain the concept of integration and interdependence between corporate and HR strategies. These models help us to understand how HR strategies are developed, and also to understand them better. We can isolate various variables influencing HR strategies and study their relative impact in a given environment for an organization. We can even better analyse why some strategies of some companies are more effective than others. The important models are explained below.

Fombrun, Tichy & Devanna's Matching Model

They proposed the basic framework shown in Figures 2.5 and 2.6. It represents the location of HRM in relation to corporate strategy. It validates the I/O (input–output) model of corporate

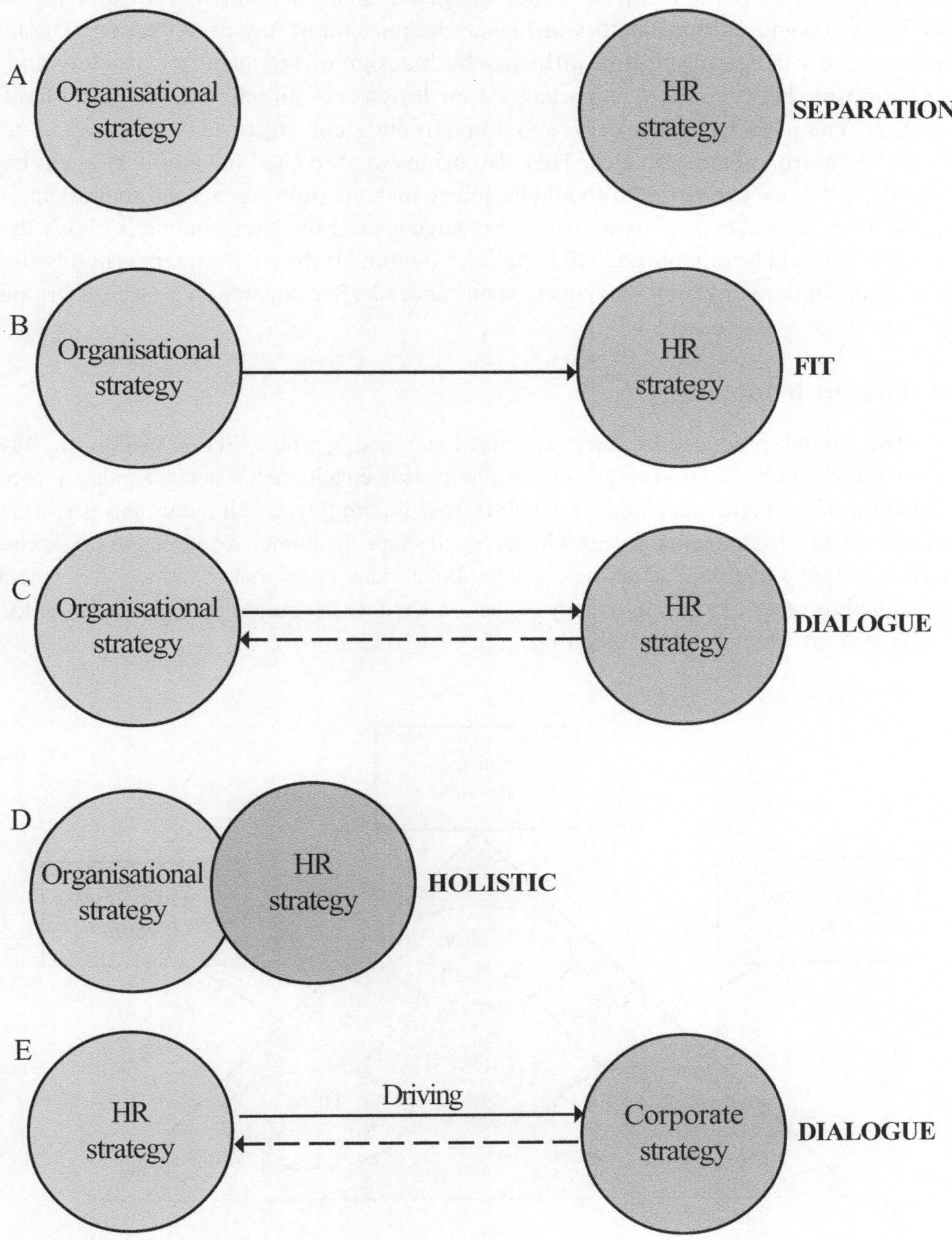

Figure 2.4. Potential relationships between organisational strategy and HR strategy

strategy, which rests on primacy of environmental fit for organisational strategy and success. The elements of the environment, both local and global, in the domain of political, technological, economic and socio-cultural factors influence the mission of any organization. The mission, objectives and strategy of the firm influence both design of organization structure and HRM. The relationship between HRM and organization design is bi-directional, that is, both influence each other. The learning is that firms should restructure and adjust their HRM architecture in the light of environmental changes. This also brings out the need for monitoring environment constantly by HR executives, who should be able to pick the right signals and suggest appropriate changes. They should be able to manage the change also. If the environment is highly dynamic, the structure should be organic and HRM policies flexible. If the environment is highly turbulent, only the learning organization will survive and succeed. (See chapter on Learning Organization and Knowledge Management.)

The Harvard Model

This model, produced by Beer, Spector, Lawrence, Quinn Mills & Walton in 1984, is an analytical model rather than a prescriptive one and has been adopted in the U. K. also. It recognises the interests of different stakeholders which impact on employee behaviour and performance. It also emphasises environmental forces which help to shape the human resources strategic choices—identified in the 'situation' factors box. Poole (1990), also notes that the model has potential for international or other comparative analysis, as it takes into account different sets of philosophies and assumptions which may be operating.

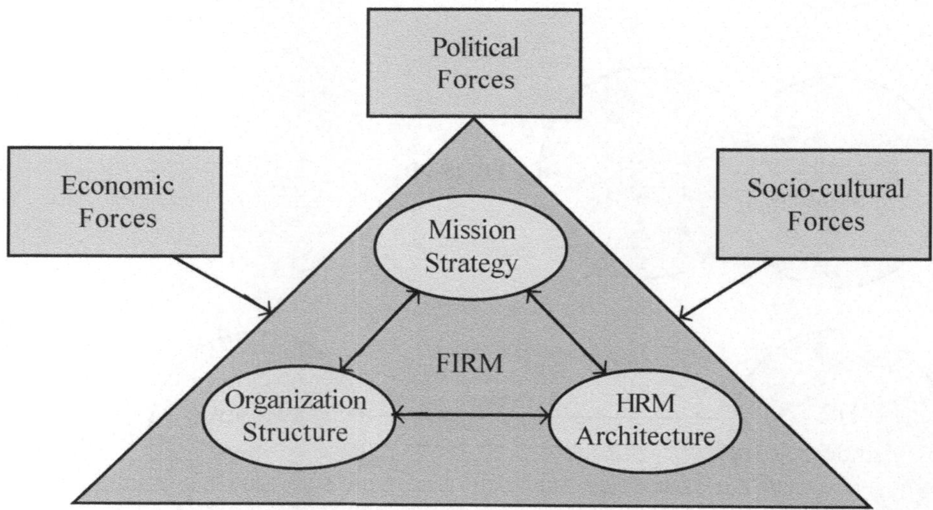

Figure 2.5. Strategic management and environment pressures

The Warwick Model-(Figure 2.7)

This model, based on the Harvard Model, emanates from the Centre for Strategy and Change at Warwick University (Hendry & Pettigrew). Here the prescriptive elements of the Harvard model are absent and there is greater emphasis on an analytical approach to human resources strategy. The model gives full importance to the external context of human resource strategy; and also identifies two-way rather than a one way relationship with organisational strategy. There is also the important recognition of the impact of the role of the personnel function on human resource content.

In a key statement Hendry & Pettigrew warn against 'treating the design of HRM system in an orderly rational way' and note the importance of learning to the formation of strategy. The authors of this model recognise Mintzberg's perspective of emergent strategy rather than a purely rational, top-down planned approach.

Upstream

First order:	1. Long-term direction of the firm 2. Scope of activities, markets, locations, etc.
Second order:	Internal operating procedures, relationship between parts of the firm
Third order:	Strategic choice in human resource management

Downstream

Outcomes; style, structure, conduct of human resource management

External factors (feeding into each level): capital market; produce market; technology; labour markets; workforce characteristics and values; public policy; law; Regular

Figure 2.6. Three levels of strategic decision-making (by John Purcell)

Note: Purcell analyses different corporate strategies and structures to see how they influence HRM practices. The model is derived from the work of Chandler (1960).

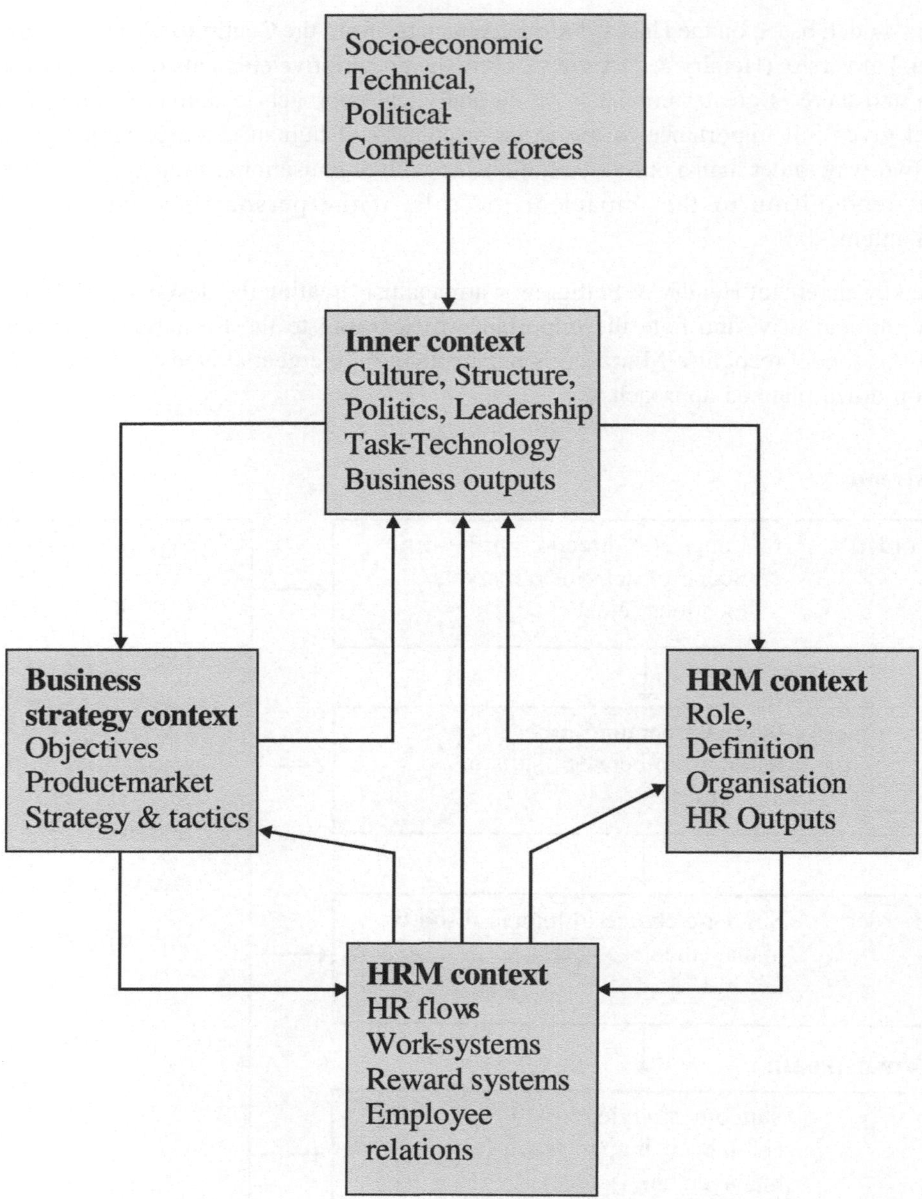

Figure 2.7. Model of strategic change and HRM by Hendry & Pettigrew

TABLE 2.2
HRM Processes to Support Corporate Strategy

Strategy	Structure	Selection	Appraisal	Rewards	Developments	Example
Single-product firm	Functional	Functionally oriented: Subjective criteria used	Subjective measures via personal contact	Unsystematic and allocated in a paternalistic manner.	Unsystematic Largely job experience	Small firms
Single product vertically integrated	Functional	Functionally oriented. Standardised criteria used	Impersonal. Based on productivity data	Related to performance and productivity	Functional specialists with some generalists. Largely rotation	Bata
Growth by acquisition–holding company of unrelated products	Separate self-contained businesses	Functionally oriented but varies from business to business	Impersonal. Based on return on investment and profitability	Formula-based return on investment and profitability	Cross-functional but not cross-business	Piramal Group . Leyman Brothers
Related diversification through internal growth and acquisition	Multi-divisional	Functionally and generalist oriented; systematic criteria used	Impersonal. Based on ROI, productivity and subjective assessment of contribution to company	Large bonuses based on profitability and subjective assessment of contribution to overall company	Cross-functional and cross-corporate. Formal	Tata Group HUL
Multiple products in multiple countries	Global organization. Geographic centre and worldwide divisions and subsidiaries	Functionally and more of generalist orientation: Systematic criteria used	Impersonal. Based on multiple goals such as ROI, profit tailored to country and products	Bonuses. Based on multiple planned goals with moderate top management discretion	Cross-divisional cross subsidiary to corporate. Formal and systematic	All MNCs

Source: Storey and Sission (1983).

TABLE 2.3
Life Cycle-related HRM Strategies
(Organisations pass through different life cycle stages and each stage has its own challenges which require different HRM strategies)

HR Strategies	Start-up	Growth	Maturity	Decline
Recruitment, selection and staffing	Attract best technical and professional talent. Recruit for new activities Recruit entrepreneurial style	Recruit adequate number and mix of qualified workers. Management succession planning. Manage rapid internal and external labour markets. Recruit for future business	Encourage adequate turnover to minimise future lay-offs. Provide new openings Encourage cross-functional . mobility Reorganise shift jobs. around	Plan and implement workforce reduction and reallocation. Transfer to different businesses. Outplacements Early retirements, VRS, golden handshake
Compensation and benefits	Meet or exceed labour market rates to attract needed talent	Meet external market but consider equity effects. Establish formal compensation structure	Compensation to be linked to achievement of targets. Control compensation	Tighter cost control
Employee training and development	Define future skill requirements and begin establishing career ladders. Minimum training until critical mass of people in business than job-related	Job skills. Interpersonal skills Mould effective mgmt team through MDP and OD	Emphasis on job training. Supervisory development and MDPs. Maintain and focus on development of flexibility, skills of an ageing workforce	Implement retraining and career consulting services. Provide support to people transferred to other jobs/departments
Employee relations	Set basic employee philosophy and organization	Maintain labour peace, encourage pro-management unions and maintain employee morale and motivation	Control labour costs and maintain labour peace. Introduce workers' participation in management. Improve productivity and multi-skilling based contracts with union	Negotiate job security and employment adjustments. Encourage productity and maintain peace but not at any cost. Divest unit
Performance appraisal	Appraise milestone linked criteria, flexible initiative and high value addition	Linked to growth, market share, unit cost reduction	Evaluate efficiency and profit margin performance linked to market share increase	Linked to cost reduction and efficiency

Continued ...

...Continued

HR Strategies	Start-up	Growth	Maturity	Decline
Rewards	Salary + equity position	Salary + bonus for target + equity for key people	Incentive plan linked to efficiency and profit. Performance related pay	Incentive plan linked to cost reduction
Dominant values	Entrepreneurship	Selling, sales	Competitiveness	Cost control
CEO style	Risk-taking, young, team builder. High initiative. Visionary leadership	Young, competitive, dynamic, relationship builder and market oriented	Experienced, mature, good reader of external environment and able to maintain favourable relations with government and regulators	Efficient, charismatic to turn around the business. Caring, mature.

Five Ps of HRM

HR Philosophy

The HR philosophy is a sub-set of the management philosophy of any organization. Management philosophy is about how best to manage and control all resources including people. It is about relative focus on short-range or long-range goals. It is about degree of empowerment and delegation to lower levels. It is about relative focus on profits or customer satisfaction. HR philosophy, on the other hand, focuses on treating people either as cost or investment and how to control and reward them. Management philosophy is reflected in the mission statement and organization structure. HR philosophy is reflected through the statement of core values and organization culture and climate. HR philosophy is reflected through the management style of key executives. The HR philosophy of Tata Steel 'We Make Men To Make Steel' reflects abundantly its approach for managing people. Human resource philosophy is a statement of how the organization regards its human resources, what role the resources play in the overall success of the business, and how they are to be treated and managed. Statements like 'we recognize that teamwork, cooperation, and a clean, safe, well maintained workplace are essential to fulfilling our customer commitments'. And again, 'our work environment is based on mutual respect, personal satisfaction and growth opportunities for every one. Mere statements do not constitute the philosophy. It must be breathed and lived by everyone.'

HR Policies

Policies are guidelines for thinking and action. They are not rules. HR policy does not mean HR policy manual; while the manual may contain the guidelines, people perceive them as a rule book prescribing very specific actions permitted in very specific situations. HR policies are guidelines about various people related to issues. For example, the promotions policy which may specify preferences to be given to seniority or competence or preference for internal promotions or open competition, etc. Policies can be explicit or implicit. Most of them are implicit and guided by traditions and past practices.

HR Processes

Processes are how things get done in organizations, the method for arriving at results. Tasks are what the group is working on to achieve, processes are 'how' they are accomplishing those tasks. Important HR processes have been mentioned in Chapter 1, like recruitment and selection, performance appraisal, training and development, compensation and rewards management and employee relations. Each process is interlinked with the others and any change in one is reflected in all other processes. The purpose of this book is to focus more on this interconnectivity rather on the processes themselves. Other important organizational processes are communication, problem-solving and decision-making, resource allocation, conflict management, etc. which are equally if not more important.

HR Programmes

Shaped by HR policies, HR programmes represent coordinated efforts specifically intended to initiate, disseminate, and sustain strategic organizational change necessitated by strategic business needs. They may begin from the top or simultaneously at two levels or units. These programmes have human resource issues in their perspective and objectives. Programmes formulated to bring about change emanate by asking the following questions and are called strategic HR programmes:

- What is the nature of the corporate culture? Is it supportive of the business?
- What kind of people and how many will be needed?
- Are performance levels high enough to meet demands for increased profitability, innovation, higher productivity, better quality and improved customer service? What is the commitment to the company?
- Are there any potential constraints such as skill shortages or HR problems?

HR programmes have definite objectives, budgets and action plans and should be reviewed periodically. For example, MNC runs a programme of diversity training and education.

HR Practices

Jeffrey A. Mello, in his book *Strategic Human Resources*, suggests that HR practices can be best analysed in terms of 'roles'. Generally the roles that individuals assume in organizations fall into three categories: leadership, managerial and operational. In each case, behaviours associated with a given role should support strategic needs. Leadership roles include establishing direction, aligning people, motivating and inspiring individuals, and causing radical and useful change. The leader lives by the basic values of the firm and demonstrates honesty and ethical behaviour in business transactions. He shows concern for others and leads by example. He demonstrates confidence in himself and strives for continuous improvement.

Managerial roles are traditional roles of planning, directing, delegating, organizing and coordinating activities. Operational roles are needed to deliver services or make products. They are 'doing' roles and as such their content is far more specific than for other roles. Roles can move. Although these roles are labelled leadership, managerial and operational they can be performed by anyone; in fact, all roles need to be performed by all at times. However, the higher the hierarchy, more leadership and managerial roles are required to be performed. At the middle level, more managerial roles are required to be performed. In strategic change situations, roles often shift.

Once the role behaviours are identified, HR practices can be developed to reinforce role performance. While many HR practices are used in organizations without regard to organizational strategy, some practices tie role behaviour directly to strategic needs, for example, when the company has defined a need to improve the quality, practices like group participation in problem solving and training in statistical measures can be introduced.

In conclusion, the 5 Ps of HR need to be matched with organizational strategic needs to formulate a coherent HR architecture of a firm to achieve the mission of the organization.

LEVERS OF HR STRATEGY—OPEN SYSTEM APPROACH

The concept of strategic HRM and HR strategies can be best summarised through the Mabey & Salman model as shown in Figure 2.8. This model is also the basis of this book in dealing with the subject of strategic HRM. The required outcomes or desired employee behaviours for the needed corporate mission and strategy are to be pursued through HR systems (architecture) which is supported by key levers of organizational structure and organisational culture. These variables are inter-related and influence each other. Hence for the desired change all three must be used in concert and harmony. These three factors are driven by corporate strategy which itself is linked to organizational environment. Mabey & Salman believe that the desired employee behaviours will be developed, except where the intended HR system is beyond the organisation's resource capabilities. This open model is based on the contingency approach and every organization must analyse its situation to select what is best for it in the given situation.

Figure 2.9 represent the eight HR processes that can be strategically aligned with the corporate strategy of the company for achievement of its mission and objectives. These critical eight processes are depicted as spokes of a SHRM wheel in Figure 2.9 and have been discussed in depth in subsequent chapters. These are:

1. Performance management (Chapter 10)
2. Recruitment and Selection (Chapter 15)
3. Training and Development (Chapter 12)
4. Compensation and Reward Management (Chapter 11)
5. Employee Relations (Chapter 13)
6. Restructuring and Downsizing (Chapter 14)
7. Organization Culture Change (Chapter 7)
8. Management of Change (Chapter 13)

It may again be emphasized that these processes are highly interrelated and must be integrated keeping the desired behaviours and mission of the firm in focus. Along with these levers and 5 Ps of HR, it is expected that the HR function can provide leadership and guide the corporate strategy of the firm as shown by the upward arrows in Figure 2.8.

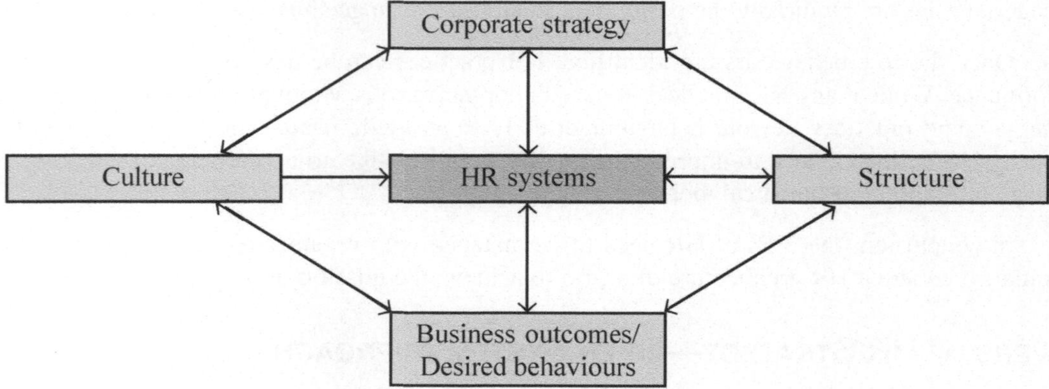

Figure 2.8. Open system of SHRM—A model

BOX 2.2

ABB faced the following HR challenges: Labour unrest, Low productivity, Old demotivated employees, Aggressive unions; Loss making business.

An attitudinal survey was conducted focusing on self introspection, team building, interpersonal relationship, attitudinal change, creativity.

Organizational culture diagnostic survey assessing organizational support; achievement motivation; controls and roles in implementing TQM.

Key areas of improvements identified were: reduced control orientation; cross functional team building; transparency in communication process; flexibility of operations and enhanced organizational support; empowerment.

Total employee alignment was attempted through: shared vision, personnel development programmes, building teams, enhanced internal customer orientation and focus on continuous improvement in cost, quality and service. Open communication system upward, downward and horizontal was strengthened

Results: revenue tripled in three years, material cost as per cent of revenue dropped by 27 per cent; drop in manpower by 19 per cent, revenue per employee increased by 340 per cent. Salaries were increased by 17 per cent.

Source: ABB in India from 1993 to 1996.

BARRIERS TO STRATEGIC HR

In spite of the success of many companies like HP, Tata Steel, and others, a large number of organizations still have not learnt to value their employees as assets and have not introduced SHRM strategies. The reasons for the same are enumerated in the following paragraphs:

1. Focus on current performance and short-term approach in corporate planning. Peter Drucker made a statement that 'managers work with both hands.' What he was trying to say was that corporate strategy is balancing the long-term goals with short-term performance. It is observed that compensation and performance management is based on current goals. Even training and development is oriented to meet current needs. This is not surprising given the emphasis by most firms and their shareholders on 'quarterly results.' There are few incentives for managers to think long-term.
2. Focusing on 'part and neglecting the whole.' Many HR managers are unable to think strategically given their segmented understanding of the entire business. HRM is a complex and ever changing function, requiring a tremendous amount of technical knowledge. HR managers often have inadequate general management training to understand the entire organization and issues and challenges being faced in the finance, marketing or operations side of the company. Unless senior HR managers can appreciate these functional issues and speak the language of these disciplines, they cannot fully contribute to the organization in a strategic manner nor gain the support of managers in these areas.
3. Most senior managers lack appreciation of the value of HR and its ability to contribute to the organization from a strategic perspective. Many simply understand the traditional or operational function of HR and fail to realize the contributions HR can make as a strategic partner. Managers throughout the organizations often see the organization function as adding unnecessary bureaucracy to their work, deemed to be more of an adversary than ally. Their perception of HR is that it is rule oriented (You can do this...you have to do that) and that it delays their ability to do a job or provide the service in time and in sufficient measure.
4. Role of Line Managers. Few functional managers see themselves as HR managers as well and are concerned more with technical aspects of their areas of responsibility than the human aspects. Regardless of the function or technical speciality of a manager, any individual who has responsibility for people is an HR manager. The role of HR as a strategic partner involves line managers assuming more responsibility for day-to-day issues, with HR providing internal support and advice for employee relations rather than assuming full and sole responsibility for it.
5. HR's inability to quantify the results in money terms. With competitive pressures making organizations more bottom-line oriented, programmes that may not have direct quantifiable benefits, such as team-building, face resistance and may be shelved. Senior HR managers consistently find resistance towards resources being allocated to programmes that have less tangible, measurable benefits than those that do.
6. Human assets are riskier than capital assets. Another barrier to strategic HR is the fact that human assets are not owned by the organisations and therefore, perceived to be a higher risk investment than capital investment. Particularly in high competitive industries where key executives may be recruited from competitors, there is an incentive to invest

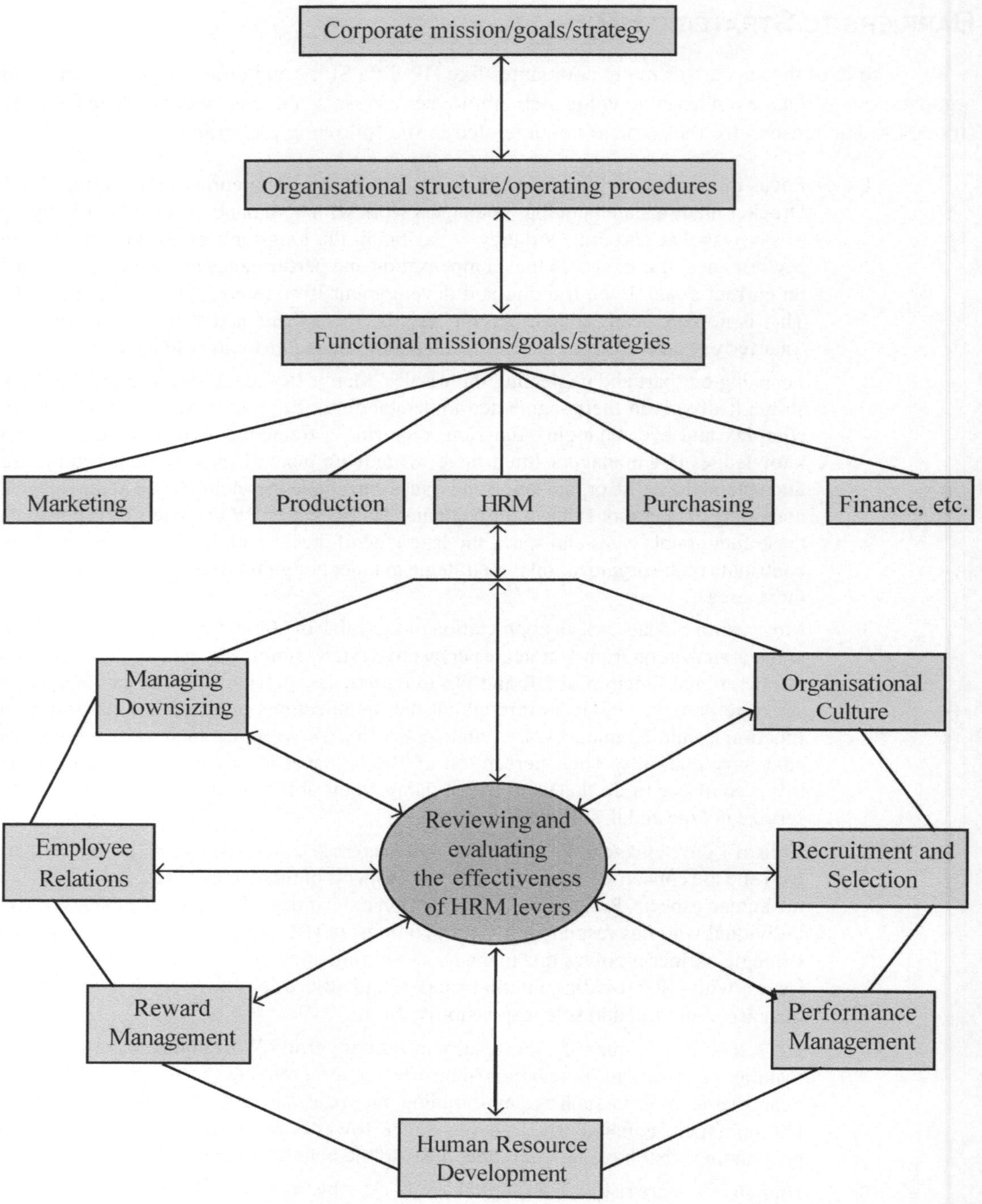

Figure 2.9. Levers of HR strategy

less in employees than in technology and information, which are more proprietary. They fail to realize that it is the people who utilize technology and information which provide the competitive advantage. Although technology and information constantly need to be replaced due to depreciation in their value, an organisation's human resources hold their value and this value can be enhanced by minimal investment in them.

7. Resistance to change. A strategic approach may require drastic changes in how work is organized; how employees are hired, trained and developed; how performance is measured and compensated, etc. Such significant changes can be risky for those responsible to implement them if their efforts fail. Hence, change efforts are delayed or kept in abeyance for other urgent tasks.

8. Ignoring the national culture. All management practices that have a bearing on human behaviour are conditioned by national culture. Practices that have succeeded in other countries or in other organizations may not give the same results if blindly aped. For example, quality circles did not succeed in many Indian companies.

Implementation Of HR Strategy

> It was exciting stuff. We could see how employee attitudes drove not just customer service but also turnover and the likelihood that employees would recommend Sears and its merchandise to friends, family and customers. We discovered that an employee's ability to see the connection between his or her work and the company's strategic objectives was a driver of positive behaviour...We were also able to establish fairly precise statistical relations. We began to see exactly how a change in training or business literacy affected revenues.
>
> *Anthony J. Rucci, Steven P. Kirn and Richard I. Quinn*

This quotation in the box captures the energy that can be created when an organization aligns its HR architecture with its larger plan for strategy implementation—and devises a way to measure that alignment. If we take a closer look at Sear's transformation experience, we can see that the company's effort centred on telling the 'story' of how value is created within the organization. Specifically, Sears executives clarified how their employees drive customer satisfaction and how that satisfaction, in turn, fuels overall firm performance. They have reinforced the story by involving a broad cross-section of senior managers, providing developmental opportunities for those supervisors who lacked the leadership skills needed to implement the new strategy, and realigning the HR system to support the strategy.

Equally important, they designed a measurement system that let them test their hypotheses about how employee behaviours, customer satisfaction and financial performance are all linked. In other words, Sears moved beyond the hypothetical and devised ways to demonstrate objectively HR's contribution to implementation of the company's new strategy. Human resource managers could now cite hard evidence that a "5-point improvement in employee attitudes will drive a 1.3-point improvement in customer satisfaction, which in turn will drive a .5 per cent improvement in revenue growth".

To achieve the kind of strategy alignment that Sears accomplished, a company must engage in a two-step process. First, managers have to understand fully the 'story' of how value is created in their firm. Once they achieve this understanding, they can then design a measurement system based on that story. We can think of this process in terms of two general questions.

First, how should strategy be implemented in our firm. This is another way of asking how the firm generates value. Asking this question focuses the organization on two dimensions of the strategy implementation story.

Second, what performance measures capture this broadly defined strategy implementation process? This question encourages managers to attach metrics to the conceptual foundation that they envisioned after understanding their firm's value-creation story.

Once HR managers have addressed these two questions, they must then communicate it to middle managers and front-line employees. This way, every member of the organization knows how to support the firm's success. These questions also help the organization decide how to allocate resources so as to breathe life into the value-creation story. Finally, and most important, the insights generated by the questions guide the decisions that every employee makes, every day.

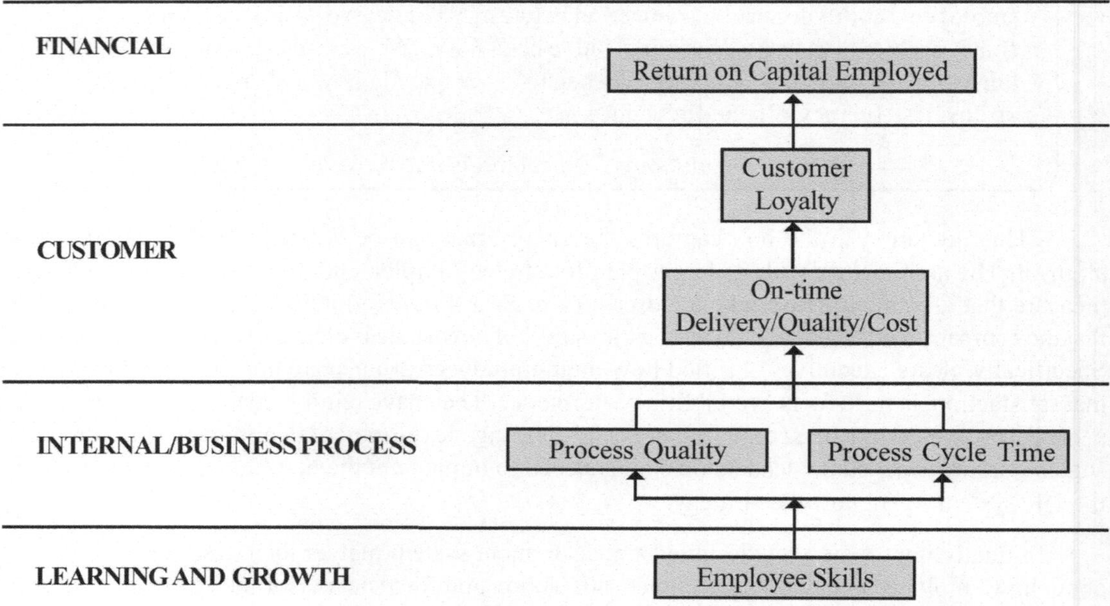

Figure 2.10. A simple illustration of value creation

Source: Robert S. Kaplan and David P. Norton, *The Balanced Scorecard.* Boston, Mass., U.S.A., Harvard Business School Press, 1996, p. 31.

INTEGRATING HR INTO BUSINESS PERFORMANCE MEASUREMENT: UNDERSTANDING HR DELIVERABLES

Grasping the relationships among key success factors is essential for measuring HR's traditionally elusive role in driving organisational performance. Once a company firmly anchors HR in its strategy implementation system, it can then see the connections between HR and the company's success drivers. By measuring HR's effect on these drivers, the firm can quantify HR's overall strategic impact.

To integrate HR into a business-performance measurement system, managers must identify the points of intersection between HR and the organisation's strategy implementation plan. We can think of these points as *strategic HR deliverables*, namely, those outcomes of the HR architecture that serve to execute the firm's strategy. This is in contrast to HR 'doables' that focus on HR efficiency and activity counts. These deliverables come in two categories: performance-drivers and enablers. HR *performance drivers* are core people-related capabilities or assets, such as employee productivity or employee satisfaction. Even though these may seem so important as to be generic, there is actually no single correct set of performance drivers. Each firm custom-identifies its own set based on its unique characteristics and the requirements of its strategy implementation process.

Enablers reinforce performance drivers. For example, a particular change in a company's reward structure might encourage preventive maintenance rather than reactive maintenance. An emphasis on preventive maintenance might in turn 'enable' a performance driver called "on-time delivery." Any performance driver may have several enablers. The enablers, themselves, in isolation, may seem mundane, but—as we'll see—their cumulative effect can have strategic importance.

Let's look at these two categories of HR deliverables in greater detail.

HR Performance Drivers

The credibility of HR measures is particularly important when financial and non-financial performance measures conflict. Inevitably, there comes a time when people measures are up, but financials are down. Naturally, the CEO objects to paying bonuses when 'performance' does not warrant it. However, such reactions miss an essential point: Balanced performance measurement means paying attention to *both* lagging and leading indicators. And, it is the *leading* indicators—such as HR measures—that really drive value creation in the organization. The hesitation to reward managers when people measures are up and financial measures are down reflects a lack of agreement among executives that HR measures in fact drive the entire company's performance. In this example, the reward system has been 'balanced' to address some vague concern about 'people issues,' but no one can articulate how these measures reflect value creation in the firm.

Identifying key HR performance drivers can be challenging, because they are unique to each firm. The experience at Quantum Corporation offers an apt example. At Quantum, a leading manufacturer of hard disks and computer peripherals, executives emphasise something they call "time-to-volume." In Quantum's view, being first to market does not mean being first to announce or demonstrate a new product. Rather, it means that customers actually get the new products they want, when they want them, and in the quantities they require. Time-to-volume hinges on rapid product development—without the sacrifice of quality—plus the ability to ramp up production fast enough to meet customers' needs. Quantum identified a set of *value behaviours*, such as staying flexible and adaptable, taking initiative for one's own development and resolving issues in an objective manner, as one time-to-volume driver. There is nothing ad hoc or symbolic about the importance of these behaviours to the success of the company. Quantum integrates them directly into its performance criteria and gives them equal weight with more traditional performance measures. Indeed, one half of bonus and merit pay is based on financial results, and one half on an employee's adherence to the value behaviours. As one senior executive observed, "You can't simply 'get results' too often while leaving a pile of dead bodies behind you."

HR Enablers

As we mentioned, HR enablers reinforce core performance drivers. To provide another example, if a firm identifies employee productivity as a core performance driver, then "re-skilling" might be an enabler.

Our experience with a major money-centre bank illustrates what can happen when managers do not connect HR enablers with various performance drivers in the broader organization. This particular bank had decided to shift the focus of its retail business from service to sales. The bank identified a set of performance drivers that included increase cross-selling to existing customers, teller product knowledge, and sales skills. However, its HR enablers still emphasised service. For instance, the organization still had the following:

- training programmes that focused on service rather than sales;
- performance appraisal and merit pay that rewarded service rather than sales;
- hiring practices based on service competencies rather than sales competencies;
- turnover rates that undermined relationship building between tellers and retail customers; and
- low pay and benefits for tellers, who were considered overhead rather than a source of revenue growth.

Because of the disconnect between its new goals and outdated HR enablers, the bank failed to achieve its sales and profitability targets. Without the properly aligned enablers, it was simply unable to implement its new sales strategy. The lesson here is that the entire HR *system* influences employee behaviour from many points. Thus HR has that many more opportunities to enable—or impede—the firm's key performance drivers.

Another example from the banking industry illustrates how easy it is to overlook the power of HR enablers. When the Wells Fargo Online Financial Services (OFS) group implemented a Balanced Scorecard to measure the firm's overall progress towards its goals of growing revenue and maximising profits, it identified three key strategic drivers:

1. add and retain high-value and high-potential-value customers;
2. increase revenue per customer; and
3. reduce cost per consumer.

Figure 2.11 articulates the 'story' of how OFS expected to achieve those goals. OFS also identified several HR performance drivers that it felt would play an important part in the success of its strategy, shown in the Learning and Growth section of the figure.

- attract and retain key OFS players and staff;
- enhance OFS bench strength and succession planning;
- increase managerial competency and functional competency at all levels;
- continue development of the OFS organization and culture; and
- deploy the Scorecard and embed it in OFS.

According to Mary D'Agostino, VP of Strategy at OFS, acknowledging these HR drivers signalled an important step for Wells Fargo, in which the culture "embraces financial measures." But OFS managers never achieved consensus on *how* these HR drivers directly affected the three strategic goals. As a result, while the company agreed to monitor these drivers yearly, it neglected to formally build them into its Scorecard.

In short, human resources managers should evaluate the degree to which their firm's entire *system* of enablers—from employee selection to development and rewards—support the *non*-HR drivers outlined in the firm's Scorecard. For example, one common performance driver is to "develop superior service quality." But if line managers are struggling with high staff turnover and insufficient rewards for service quality, how can they achieve their targeted service quality levels? As another example, suppose an organisation's R&D unit contributes to the firm's larger strategy implementation process, this organisation's HR manager could readily generate ideas for enabling the R&D unit's success. Specifically, she might suggest a reward system that encourages marketable innovations, a timely sourcing function that provides technological expertise and incentives to encourage a low level of employee turnover among key R&D talent. This kind of synergy makes for true business partnering between HR and the rest of the organization.

A Seven-Step Model for Implementing HR's Strategic Role

How can HR formalise this kind of strategic role? Figure 2.12 illustrates how HR can link its deliverables to the firm's strategy for implementation process. While we elaborate on various components of this model in the chapter, we summarise it for you in the following seven steps:

Step 1: Clearly Define Business Strategy

At the strategy-development 'table', senior HR leaders provide an essential perspective. By focussing on how to *implement* the strategy rather than solely on what the strategy consists of, they can facilitate a discussion about how to communicate the firm's goals throughout the organization. When strategic goals are *not* developed with an eye towards how they will be implemented and communicated throughout the organization, they tend to become very generic—for example, "maximise operative efficiency" or "increase present in international markets", or "improve productivity". These goals are so vague that individual employees simply cannot know how to take action to achieve them. Worse, employees cannot recognise them as unique to their firm.

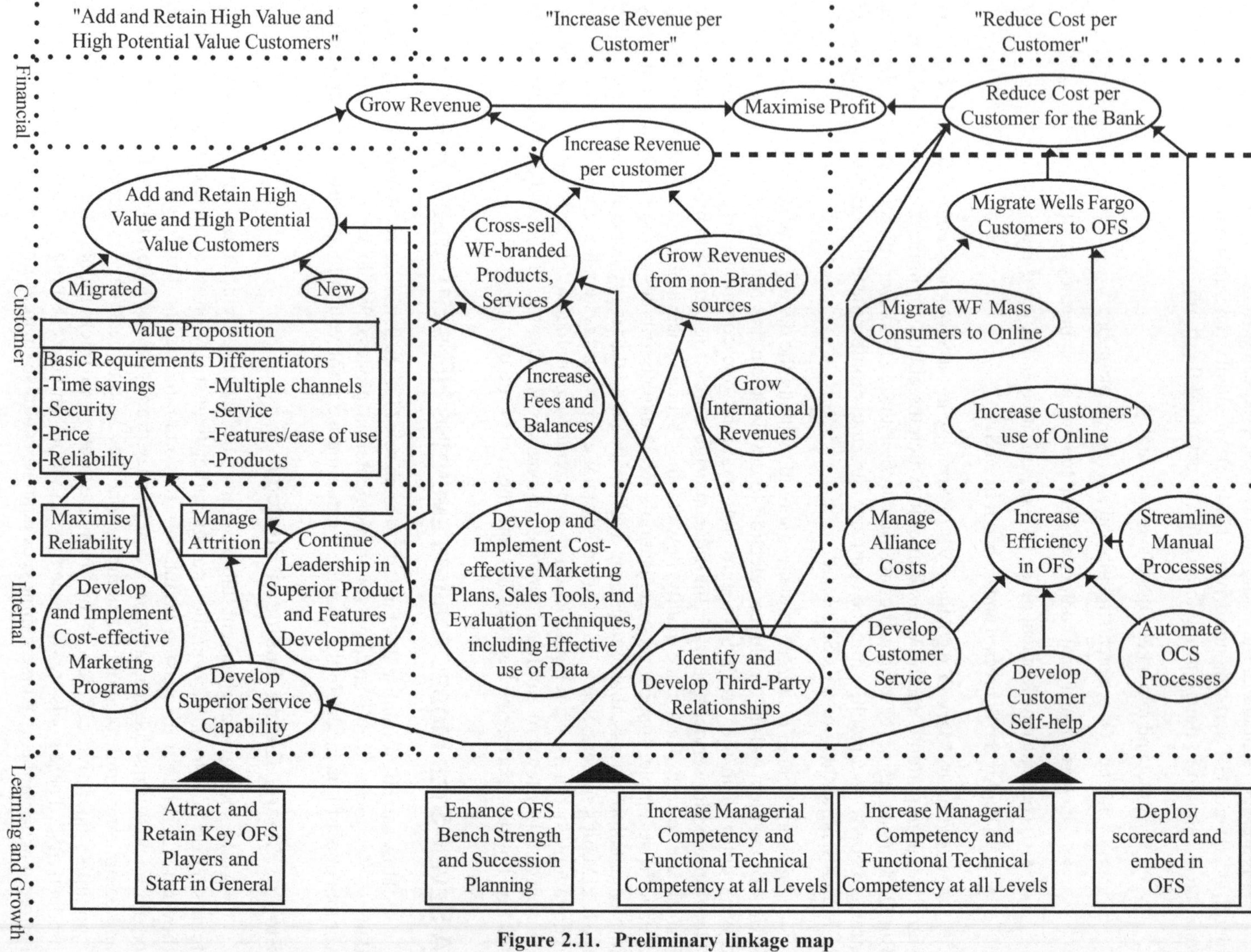

Figure 2.11. Preliminary linkage map

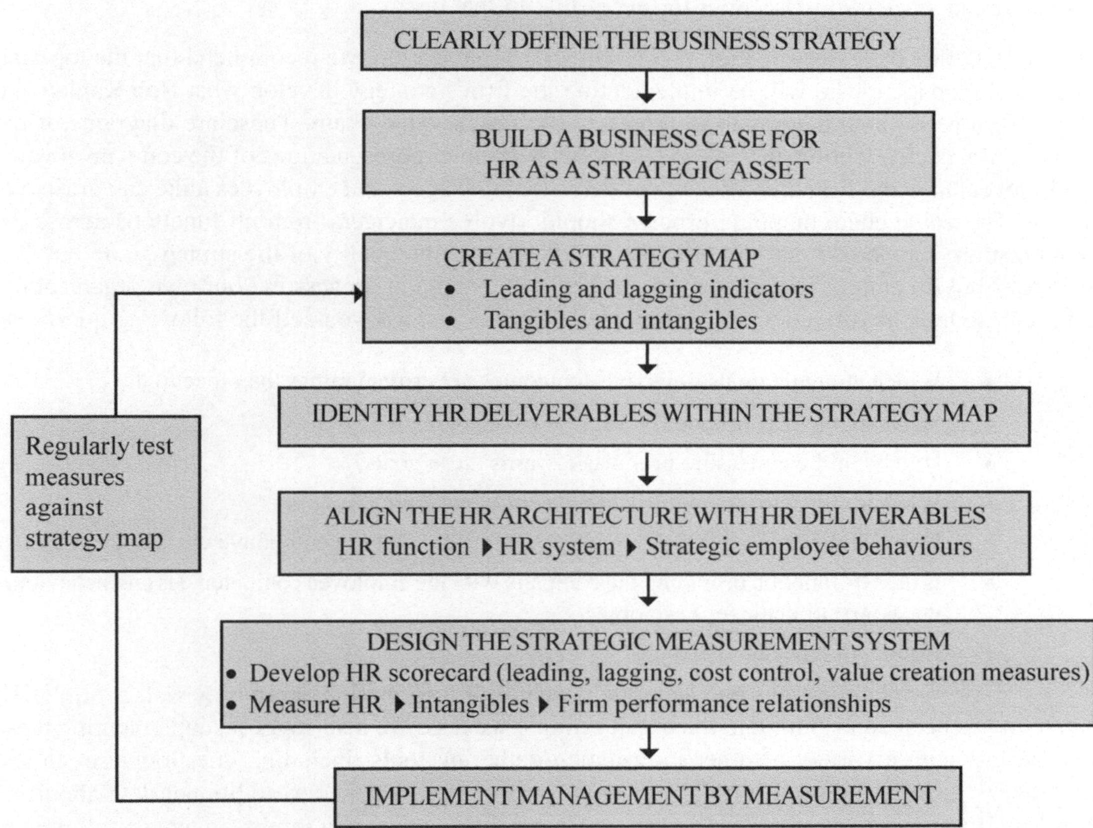

Figure 2.12. Transforming the HR architecture into a strategic asset

Step 2: Build a Business Case for HR as a Strategic Asset

Once a firm clarifies its strategy, human resource professionals need to build a clear business case for *why* and *how* HR can support that strategy. In making this business case, you have the benefit of a decade of systematic research to support your recommendations. While a comprehensive review of this research is beyond the scope of this book, we can highlight the key results. First, evidence gathered from four national surveys and more than 2,800 firms strongly suggests that a high-performance work system has a distinct, positive influence on a firm's financial performance. (Source: Mark A. Huselit and Brian E. Baeker, 1995).

Clarifying a firm's strategy sets the stage for implementing that strategy. But it is the first step. In most organisations, the customer value embodied in the firm's products and services is the result of a complex, cumulative process—what Michael Porter refers to as the firm's *value chain.*

All firms have a value chain—even those that have not articulated it—and the company's performance measurement system must account for every link in that chain.

To define the value-creation process in your organization, we recommend that the top- and mid-level managers who will be implementing the firm's strategy develop what Bob Kaplan and Dave Norton call a strategy map to represent the firm's value chain. These are diagrams of the value chain, such as shown in 2.13 and 2.14. Such graphic representations of the company's value chain reveal *how* the firm creates value in terms that managers and employees alike can grasp and act on. The value chain mapping process should involve managers from all functions across the organization. This broad participation not only improves the quality of the strategy map but also increases buy-in among critical players. To begin the mapping process in your own organization, take a close look at your company's strategic objectives and ask yourself the following questions:

- Which strategic goals/objectives/outcomes are critical rather than nice to have?
- What are the performance drivers for each goal?
- How would we measure progress towards these goals?
- What are the barriers to the achievement of each goal?
- How would employees need to behave to ensure that the company achieves these goals?
- Is the HR function providing the company with the employee competencies and behaviours necessary to achieve these objectives?
- If not, what needs to change?

These simple questions can generate a wealth of information about how well a firm's HR function has been contributing to the organisation's success. We also suggest supplementing these discussions with a variety of other information-gathering tools, including questionnaires to test employees' understanding of the firm's goals, and surveys to generate additional data about the firm's performance drivers and organisational capabilities. Once you think you have a full picture of your firm's value chain, translate the information that you have gathered into a conceptual model using language and graphics that make sense in your organization. Then test for understanding and acceptance in small groups of opinion leaders and thought leaders throughout the firm.

A strategy map of the value-creation process contains *hypothesis*, or predictions, about which organisational processes drive firm performance. Normally a company validates these hypotheses only after achieving targets on performance drivers and observing the impact of these results on firm performance. However, the organization can graphically depict the balanced performance measurement system. The linchpin of successful strategy implementation is a strategically focused workforce, which we could consider the ultimate HR performance driver. Finally, a balanced performance measurement system, in tandem with an aligned HR system and effective knowledge management, is the foundation for a strategically focused organization.

We mentioned earlier that HR creates much of its value at the points of intersection between the HR system and the strategy implementation system. Maximising that value requires an understanding of both sides of that intersection. Historically, HR managers lacked the requisite knowledge of the business side of the intersection, and general managers did not fully appreciate the HR side. While this gap has narrowed in recent decades, human resource managers should take primary responsibility for depicting both HR performance drivers *and* HR enablers on the strategy map.

This process can be difficult. On the one hand, human resource performance drivers such as employee competence, motivation and availability are so fundamental that it may be virtually impossible to know where to locate them on the map. To perform this step, we recommend asking yourself which HR deliverables (again, both performance drivers and enablers) support the *firm-level* performance drives depicted in the strategy map. Try to focus on the kinds of strategic behaviours that are broadly a function of competencies, rewards and work organization. For example, your firm may decide that employee stability (that is, low turnover) improves R&D cycle time (a firm-level performance driver). Employee stability is thus a key HR enabler. Seeing this connection would prompt you to design policies—such as above-market salaries or bonuses—that would encourage lengthy tenure among experienced R&D staff.

Figure 2.14 represents results one might expect from following Steps 1 through 4 at the

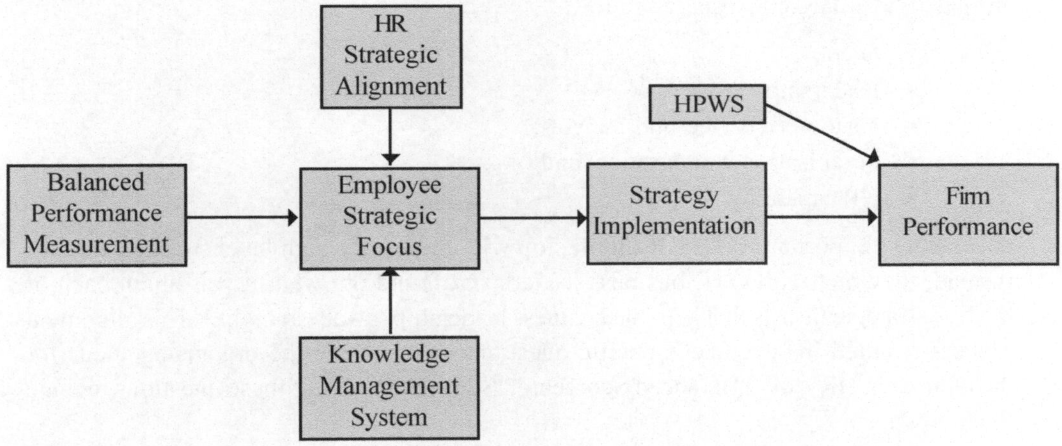

Figure 2.13. HR and strategic implementation

SBU level. Implementing Step 5 means developing a competency model and development programme to provide the HR deliverable specifically by this strategy.

Step 5 brings your firm's value-creation story to life by aligning the HR system with the firm's larger strategy-implementation system. But to do this, you need to think about how the component *within* your HR systems fit together (internal alignment) as well as how the HR system aligns with other elements in the firm's value chain (external alignment).

Steps 1 through 5 guide the development of the HR architecture and lay the groundwork necessary to measure the HR-firm performance relationship. In Step 6, you actually design that HR measurement system. This requires not only a new perspective on measuring HR performance,

BOX 2.3
Linking HR to Strategy at GTE

Steps 1 through 3 in the model described in this chapter are much more straightforward if the company has implemented, or is in the process of implementing, a wider Balanced Scorecard. In some cases, however, HR managers have to approximate Steps 1 through 3 without the benefit of the more systematic analysis that would have been part of a large Balanced Scorecard effort. The experience at GTE is a good illustration of how, when the larger organization has not participated in the 'creation of a strategy map' linking leading and lagging indicators of strategic performance, HR can begin to link its measurement system to the enterprise strategy.

At GTE, HR initially developed the firm's 'people imperatives' as part of a top leadership planning process called 'Leadership 2000.' These imperatives focused on the new behaviours and capabilities required to drive business results over the next five to ten years. This, in turn, was the foundation for a new HR strategy that was organised around five strategic thrusts, as follows.

- talent;
- leadership;
- customer service and support;
- organisational integration; and
- HR capability.

Most important, GTE HR didn't stop with these very high level strategic thrusts. Instead, they met with GTE business leaders and found out what it was about each of the five strategic thrusts that kept the business leadership 'awake at night.' This alignment process resulted in seventeen specific questions that became the organising focus for the metrics in HR's own Balanced Scorecard. Some examples of these questions include the following:

- Do we have the talent that we need to be successful in the future?
- How is HR helping GTE position itself to meet the needs of external customers?
- Is HR viewed as an enabler to attracting and retaining top talent at GTE?
- Are we managing the cost of turnover/churn?
- Are we managing financial risk?
- What is GTE's return on investment in people?

Source: Garrett Walker, HR director at GTE, interview with Mark Huslid, August 2000; and *Measure what Matters: Aligning Performance Measures with Business Strategy* (American Productivity and Quality Centre, 1999).

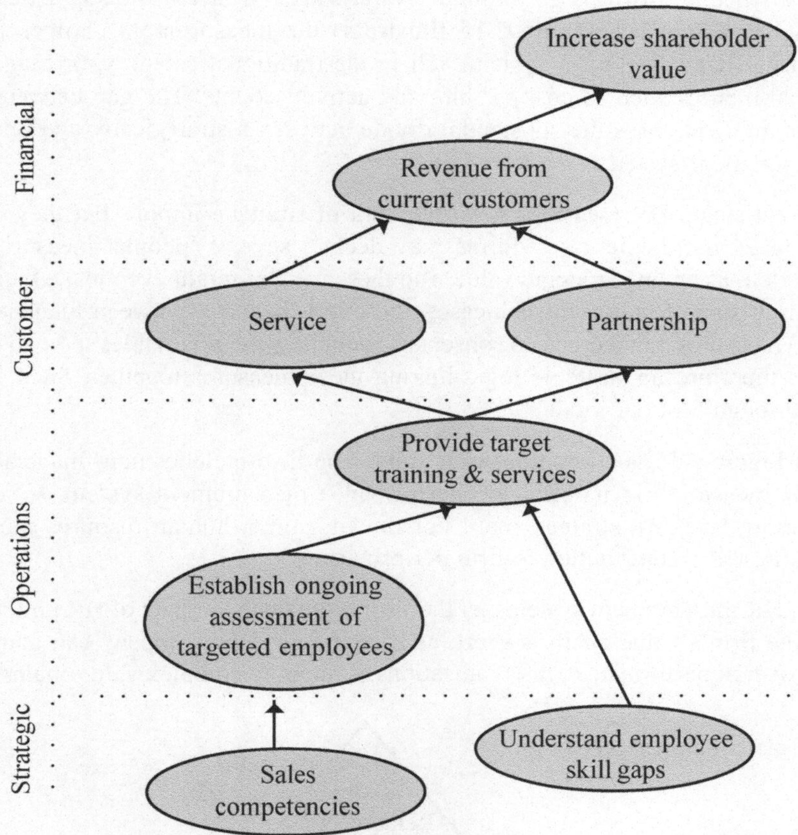

Figure 2.14. Strategy map: competency skill attainment focus

but also the resolution of some technical issues that many HR professionals may not be familiar with.

To measure the HR-firm performance relationship with precision, you need to develop valid measures of HR deliverables. This task has two dimensions. First, you have to be confident that you have chosen the correct HR performance drivers and enablers. This requires that you clearly comprehend the causal chain for effective strategy implementation in your organization. Second, you have to choose the correct *measures* for those deliverables. For example, the HR deliverable is senior staff employment stability, but there are several ways this concept could be measured. Developing the actual measure would require that you precisely define who constitutes the senior staff (for example, those with five to fifteen years of professional experience) and what you mean by employment stability. Does the latter include all turnover or just voluntary? Does it include individuals who have been promoted to management responsibilities? Finally, you need to measure those variables accurately.

In our experience, most firms go through several stages of increasing sophistication when they develop an HR Scorecard. Figure 2.15 illustrates the measurement choices facing HR professionals. Most HR measurement systems fall in the traditional category, or Stage 1. These include operational metrics such as cost per hire and activity counts. The gap between Stages 1 and 2 in the diagram symbolises the substantial divide between a strategically and operationally focused HR measurement system.

In the second stage, HR measures have the aura of strategic import, but they do little to validate HR's role as a strategic asset. Firms may declare several 'people' measures, such as employee satisfaction, as having strategic value, and these metrics might even make their way into the reward system in some fashion. In such cases, there is a 'balance' between financial ($$) and nonfinancial (NF) measures, but there is no consensus about how these variables serve to implement strategy. There is therefore no strategic logic linking these measures together. Such firms have skipped Steps 2 through 5 in our model.

Stage 3 in Figure 2.15 is a key transition point. The firm includes non-financial measures (among them HR measures) in its strategic performance measurement system. In addition, it locates each measure within a strategy map. For the first time, human resource measures are legitimately tracking HR's contribution to firm performance.

In Stage 4, HR measurement systems let the firm estimate the impact of HR policies on firm performance. If the firm's value chain is short, as it is at Sears, the company can gauge the full impact of HR on overall performance. In organisations, with more complex value chains, estimates

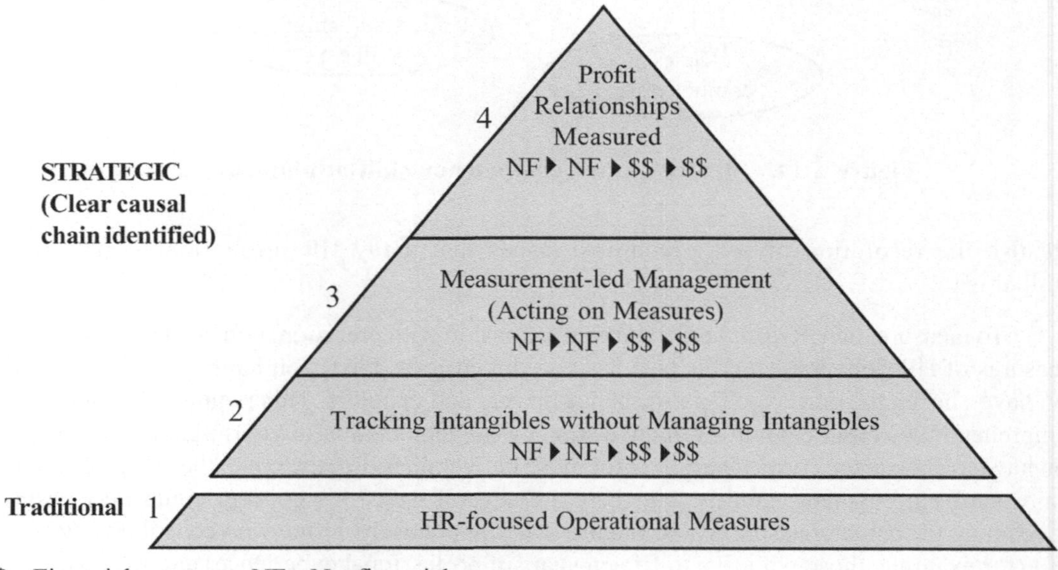

Figure 2.15. The creation of employee strategic focus through increasing measurement sophistication

of HR's influence may be limited to segments within the chain. Just because you cannot capture the full impact of HR on firm performance, that does not mean that you should not measure part of the impact. For example, consider the example of an imaginary company called Petro Pipeline in Figure 2.16. This describes a very small portion of a larger strategy map depicting Petro's strategy implementation system. It would be reasonably straightforward to measure the influence of the HR deliverables (improved employee focus on preventive maintenance) on "repair down time" and subsequent effects on customer perceptions of Petro as a reliable provider.

Clearly, measuring the HR-firm performance relationship is not an all-or-nothing proposition. Any progress beyond traditional measurement approaches is likely to yield substantial improvement later in the value chain. The more sophisticated the measurement system, the greater the eventual benefits.

Step 7: Implement Management by Measurement

Once the HR Scorecard is developed along the principles described in our model, the result is a powerful new management tool. Actually implementing this tool is much more than just "keeping score" of HR's impact on firm performance. If the Scorecard is aligned with the imperatives of the firm's strategy, HR professionals will have a new insight into what it takes to actually manage HR as a strategic asset.

For example, GTE HR has always measured the turnover rates in its businesses, but prior to the development of its HR Scorecard, there had been little effort to understand the underlying dimensions of the turnover rates and their consequences for organisational profitability. In other words, although GTE HR measured turnover in the past, it really did not manage it as a business problem in its respective business units. As the HR Scorecard was implemented, these turnover rates were more closely analysed indicating substantial increases among new hires and the most experienced employees. The result was new HR interventions for both groups that addressed these problems with associated benefits for the performance of the business units involved.

HR leaders must regularly review the HR deliverables they have defined in order to be sure that these drivers and the enablers remain strategically significant. This is particularly true for HR enablers that have direct links to specific business objectives. Skilled HR managers understand when an enabler is no longer playing a strategic role and needs to be replaced.

Corporate Example of Strategic HR Practices

Hindustan Unilever (HUL) is India's largest fast moving company in the FMCG industry. R&D and marketing are the key thrust areas in HUL. Yet it has accorded highest importance to HRM. Its HR philosophy is reflected in its mission statement (in part):

- People first and every thing is next. Ring of trust and confidence critical.
- Review and revise continuously.
- Don't hesitate to over-resource when called for or when finding worthy people.
- Continue to recruit quality resources for the organization rather for the job perspective only.

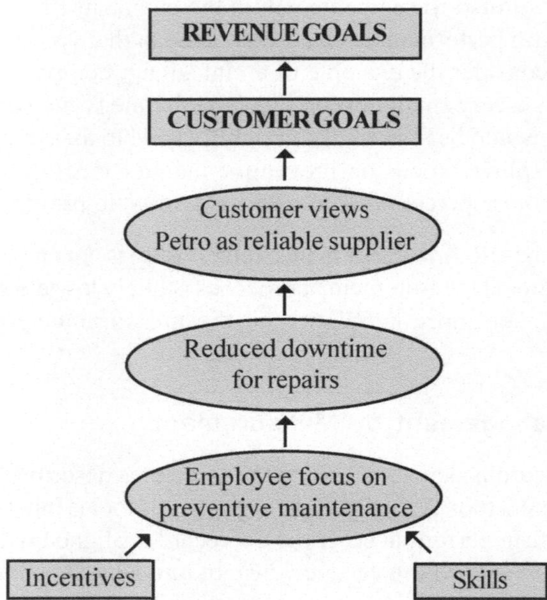

Figure 2.16. Influence of HR enablers at Petro Pipeline

- Planning for speed is very important. Closely monitor and be vigilant about expected synergies.
- Communicate, communicate and communicate.
- Top management is seen to be fair and equitable in dealing with people issues.
- Reward system to recognize efforts as much as possible.

Questions and Assignments

Q.1. What do you understand by corporate strategy? Support your answers with appropriate corporate examples. At what level do HR strategies fit into corporate strategy making? And why?

Q.2. What constitutes HR strategy? Explain the 5 Ps of HR.

Q.3. Discuss the degree of 'fit' in corporate and HR strategy that you see in practice in different companies.

Q.4. What are the barriers to SHRM? And how can they be overcome, if you face them as an HR executive?

Q.5. Discuss the Salman & Mabey Model of HR strategy, explaining the relationship with corporate culture and HR policy.

Q.6. What are different levers of SHRM? Discuss the integration between them.

Strategic Decision-making Categories

	Resourcing	Performance Management	Rewards	Management Development	Employee Relations
	Including all those activities related to internal movement of people across positions must match jobs and external hiring of people must match both organization and job. Hire from most prestigious institutions and groom their career	It contributes to two processes: 1). human resource planning 2) develop current pool of talent. Development process varies in form, like promotion, recognition, opportunities to learn, responsibility, security, respect from peer groups, co-employees, etc.	Rewards in relation to performance, financial, non-financial	Activities to ensure that individuals are properly equipped with knowledge to perform jobs	Activities oriented towards estab-lishing a degree of participation and collaboration between management, unions and employees
Strategic issues	Promotion system. Flow of people to match business strategies	Designing an appraisal system supportive of the corporate and business strategies	Designing a reward system to provide balance support to short term and long term goals	Job improvement. Career planning. Succession planning. Women managers. Expatriation. Career templates	Development of an HR policy. Flow of people to match business strategies. Match key executives to business strategies

Continued...

...Continued

Resourcing		Performance Management	Rewards	Management Development	Employee Relations
Strategic choices	Make vs. buy. Little recruiting above entry level vs sophisticated recruiting at all levels. Assessment centre approach	Process-oriented system. Identification of training needs vs. staffing needs. Individual/group	Compensation oriented towards performance, external competitiveness Cash vs. non-cash	Formal vs. informal. Extensive vs. limited. Skills building. vs. skills identification. Multiple career paths.	Individual vs. group representation. Employee involvement process. Strict regulatory compliance and go above it. Ethical conduct Continuous
all round learning					

Assignments

1. Compare and contrast SHRM in any two organizations, preferably one in manufacturing and the other in services. What are the differences?
2. Which of the models and approaches to Human Resource Strategy most clearly fits your organization (where you have taken training)?. Why did you come to this decision.

CASE

HEWLETT PACKARD (HP)

Stanford University classmates Bill Hewlett and Dave Packard founded Hewlett Packard (HP) in 1939. The company's first product, built in a Palo Alto garage, was an audio oscillator supplied to Walt Disney Studios. HP is a company unlike any in terms of its reach to consumers across different regions of the world and its leadership in a technology rich portfolio. It is the largest manufacturer of test and measurement instruments and computers.

From the beginning, HP has pursued a strategy that brings the products of scientific research into industrial application while maintaining the collegial atmosphere of a university laboratory (organization culture). The firm has concentrated on advanced technology and offers mostly state-of-the art products to a variety of industrial and consumer markets. HP's strategy is to pursue actively a given product line and market as long as the company has a distinctive technology or design advantage. But when products reach the stage when success depends primarily on low costs and highly competitive prices, HP typically moves out of the market and turns its attention to new design or entirely a new product.

Thus, HP's strategy of technological innovation, is supported by a highly flexible organization structure. It is organised around integrated self-contained product divisions that are given a great deal of independence. New divisions arise when a particular product line becomes large enough to support its continued growth out of the profits it generates. New divisions are also created when single divisions get to about two thousand people. HP has found that above this number, people start to lose identification with the product.

HP has been very effective in identifying and hiring competent scientists and engineers and creating a corporate culture that fosters innovation and high performance. The firm was committed early on to give meaning to work as well as to making a profit. Part of the commitment is to provide long-term employment and establish a generous profit sharing plan. The HR policy is not to lay-off employees. For example, in the 1970s when there was a recession, everyone at HP took a 10 per cent cut. Management also downplays authority and strongly supports group decision-making. HP employees meet weekly to resolve production problems. Pay increase in HP is based on merit and seniority. Performance appraisals are conducted four times a year, and evaluations are based on teamwork and targets. Managers and operatives alike are addressed on a first-name basis.

The work areas are open and machines are set to allow people to work at their own pace. If employees have a problem, they are encouraged to air it openly. They can take their grievances to any level. Stories circulate that some employees have even called HP's president with a problem.

Independent divisions formulate their own strategy and also implement it. The role of top management is to coordinate and maintain HP's unique culture.

There are many other companies that are following the open HR system prevailing in HP, to gain global competitiveness. More and more companies are changing and modifying their HR systems.

3 Human Resource Audit and Balance Scorecard

Learning Objectives

After studying this chapter, you will learn to:

- carry out a systematic HR audit of an organization.
- prepare a checklist for HR audit.
- Prepare an audit report.
- Understand the concept of Balance Scorecard.
- Understand HR Scorecard.
- Create HR Scorecard.
- Learn about high performance work systems—HR systems, alignment and HR deliverables.
- Construct the HR Scorecard.

INTRODUCTION

HR audit is the systematic assessment of an organisation's HR service excellence. A good HR audit helps an organization to achieve its strategic long-term and short-term goals. Firms are investing heavily in the 3 Cs—competencies, commitment, and culture. Competencies are not restricted to individuals but are spread over teams, departments, divisions, SBUs. They provide the lead and competitive advantage to the firm.

The commitment to the firm is a complex factor dependent upon several factors like reward and recognition, developmental and learning opportunities, etc. Culture is represented by the values and norms articulated and practiced by the organization. It improves motivational levels and the commitment of employees and helps in instilling pride amongst the employees. The various instruments used for culture building include climate survey, value clarification exercises and vision/ mission workshops.

An HR audit helps to assess its current position. It helps in transforming the organization.

HR Audit

HR audit is an offshoot of the accounting system that tells the management what changes have been occurring in the HR department of the business over a period of time. HRA also involves accounting for investment in people, their replacement costs and the economic value of people in an organization.

Organisations can assess how much they can earn from an individual. The intellectual assets of the company are often worth three or four times the tangible assets. Human capital provides valuable expert services, such as consulting, financial planning and assurance services which are in great demand. Many leading companies like Infosys, BHEL, TCS, and NIIT are using HRA.

HR Audit Process

It is a comprehensive process which begins with an understanding of the future business plans and corporate strategies of the company. Some of the questions being raised and answered during the process are:

1. What is the 5 year plan of the company?
2. What competencies are needed to actualise these plans?
3. What is the current level of organisational efficiency in terms of productivity and profitability of the company?
4. Does the organization have a learning culture? If not, how does it intend to build it?
5. What are the various HR systems and subsystems geared to meet these requirements?

Challenges in HR Audit

1. Building and improving quality consciousness and culture of continuous improvement.
2. Striving to recruit and retain competent, creative, and committed employees.
3. Aligning the business processes with the technology, infrastructure, and leveraging it for competitive advantage.
4. Nurturing a creative and supportive work culture which inculcates professionalism and motivation among employees.
5. Retaining flexibility of organization in spite of growth and development.
6. Training and developing the people through various interventions such as training, mentoring, 360-degree feedback.
7. Promoting learning culture among the employees and facilitating the formation of informal networks to create a learning organization.

Methodology of Audit

- Individual interviews. The consultants begin their evaluation by means of one-to-one interviews with the top management and senior managers. This enables the auditors to understand the future plans, opportunities available and current problems being faced. These interviews help auditors to understand the capability and style of top management. It provides an overview of HR policy objectives.
- Group interviews. The purpose is to obtain feedback from various segments of employees through group interviews. These groups are selected on stratified sampling basis. In some cultures, individuals may not speak up and there group interviews are quite helpful.
- Workshops. In some cases, large scale interactive processes with 30 to 300 participants may be useful. Participants work in groups to give feedback on important topics and then present it to all for discussion.
- Questionnaires can be prepared on career planning, work allocation, learning and developmental systems and quality orientation. The aim is to capture the real picture about all HR processes. Typically, some of the questionnaires are designed with OCTAPAC (openness, confrontation, trust, autonomy, pro-action, authenticity, collaboration parameters). The questionnaires address the competence of HRD staff, style of line managers, efficacy and user friendliness in implementing various HR systems. These questionnaires can be used to benchmark the system and practices.
- Observations. Auditors must visit the workplace, plant, canteen and other welfare amenities to see for themselves. These visits help the auditors to assess the environment and welfare orientation of the organization.
- Secondary analysis. The analysis of secondary data gives much insight into the state of affairs. The areas covered under regulatory compliance audit include 1) personal files and record keeping, 2) job description, and 3) compliance with statutory requirements such as Compensation Act, rules regarding ESI, PF, Gratuity, etc.
- Review of all personal grievances and legal cases filed against the management by employees and trade unions.

HR Audit Checklist

Conducting an audit of HR function can be a valuable exercise that can lead to a better understanding of the important role human resource management plays in your company.

The following checklist can get you started.

The Purpose of the Audit

- To look for potentially serious problems (land mines)
- To find areas needing improvement
- To document processes for use in merger or reorganization
- To address compliance issues.

Sources of Data

- What do the written policies and procedures say?
- What do the HR managers say?
- What do the line managers say?

Basics

- How many employees are there in HR (and related departments, for example, training)?
- What is the organization chart for the HR department?
- What is the HR budget?

Recruitment

- How are candidates sourced?
- How are candidates selected?
- Are legal requirements met?
- Are the same processes used for all jobs, all locations?
- Are processes followed consistently?

Compensation and Benefits

- What are the different policy groups (for example, management, clerical, union)?
- How is the base pay policy set?
- What are the grading/job evaluation systems that are used?
- Are there up-to-date job descriptions?
- What variable pay practices are in place?
- How are pay increments decided?
- What is the benefit plan?
- Are the same processes used for all jobs, all locations?
- Are processes followed consistently?

Workforce Review

- Are there any critical skills shortages?
- Are there any critical succession issues?
- Is there anything unusual in the distribution of worker age, gender, etc.?
- What are the processes that are used for workforce planning?
- What are the processes that are used for succession planning?
- Are the same processes used for all jobs at all locations?
- Are processes followed consistently?

Training and Development

- How much training is given?
- How is the training programme managed?
- Are there any staff development programmes?
- Are the same processes used for all jobs, all locations?
- Are processes followed consistently?

Industrial Relations

- What unions exist and what jobs are covered?
- What collective agreements are in place? When do these expire?
- How many grievances are there per year?
- Are there any outstanding grievances?

Legal

- Are processes in place to manage compliance issues for all relevant jurisdictions?
- Is there any outstanding litigation?
- Are the same processes used for all jobs, all locations?
- Are processes followed consistently?

HR Technology

- What technology is installed?
- How up-to-date is the technology?
- Is the data clean?
- Are there any important technology projects in process?

Strategic HR

- Whom does the most senior HR person report to?
- How much interest does the top management have in HR issues?

Some other Audit Techniques to Consider

- Audit of the corporate culture.
- Competency of the audit staff.
- Metrics based audit, using metrics such as those proposed by the Saratoga Institute.
- Audit of customer satisfaction with HR.

MODULES OF HR AUDIT

Recruitment and Selection module will examine the following:

1. The existence of updated and accurate written policies and procedures to support the requirement and selection processes.
2. Its periodicity of review and changes made from time to time.
3. Its communication to all concerned.
4. The budget and timeframe for recruitment of different positions.
5. The methods adopted to maintain quality in the selection process.

Performance Management Module

1. The maintenance and update of clearly defined performance plans.
2. The extent of documentation about performance standards and actual results about various positions.
3. The communication of performance policy to employees.
4. The methodologies for identification of high performance employees.
5. The training and feedback provided—related details and systems.

Compensation Management Module

1. The existence of clearly defined compensation plans and administrative procedures.
2. Documentary support for salary actions relating to promotions, increases and demotions.
3. Written procedures addressing the statutory compliance requirements.
4. The procedure for examining compensation equity, external and internal.
5. Documented incentives—award or compensation programmes and implementation plans including the role of managers.

HR audit does not give an evaluation of individuals, but it essentially focuses on units and systems.

HR audit report is to be prepared and submitted on completion of the audit exercise to the sponsors for their consideration and necessary action. The profile of report is presented below:

STRUCTURE OF HR AUDIT REPORT

1. Introduction

How the brief description of the organization and its objectives and purpose of the audit, various methodologies employed, description of the HR practices, systems, framework and future plans of the organization are covered.

2. Current Status of HR Function

This part of the report deals with structure and staffing of HR function, its objectives, policies and programmes, its strengths and weaknesses, opportunities and challenges it is encountering.

3. General Observation

In the lights of facts gathered and analysed, it reviews general strengths, weaknesses and opportunities of the organization in relation to its present competencies, future potential and competitors and various factors affecting the organisational structure, culture, competence and commitment building activities.

4. HR Systems

In this part, the audit report covers the findings and recommendations pertaining to HR planning, recruitment and selection, compensation, performance appraisal practices, training and development effectiveness, and various other HR efforts to enhance organisational competitiveness and employee satisfaction. The contents should emerge out of the data collected and analysed.

5. Recommendations and Suggestions

In conclusion, the report should present its findings and suggestions outlining the steps required for improvement of HR development policies, programmes and practices and strategies for the organization. It can point to such successful strategies being followed in other similar organisations.

BALANCE SCORECARD

In the old economy, companies added value primarily by investing in tangible assets: plants, machinery, sales office and technology. Till 20 years ago, nearly two-thirds of the market value of the company came from tangible assets it owned. Today, an analysis of the Fortune 500 companies in the USA shows that 85 per cent value comes from intangible assets. If value—whether seen from the point of customer or the markets—has shifted to intangibles, companies need to understand the underlying factors that deliver better customer or shareholder value. The solution lies in implementing the technique of Balance Scorecard.

By the 1980s, many executives were convinced that traditional measures of financial performance didn't let them manage effectively and wanted to replace them with operational measures. Arguing that executives should track both financial and operational matrices, Robert Kaplan and David Norton suggested four sets of parameters.

First, how do customers see your company? Find out by measuring lead times, quality, service, performance and costs. Second, what must your company excel at? Determine the processes, and competencies that are most critical, and specify measures, such as cycle time, quality and employee skills and productivity. Third, can your company continue to improve and create value? Monitor your ability to launch new products, create more value for customers, and improve operating efficiencies. Fourth, how has your company done by your shareholders? Measure cash flow, quarterly sales growth, operating income by division and increased market share by segment and return on equity.

The balance scorecard lets executives see whether they have improved in one area at the cost of another. Knowing that, say the authors, will protect companies from sub-optimal results.

A balance scorecard (BSC) provides a framework for organisations to manage the implementation of strategy in an organization by linking the objectives, initiatives and corresponding measures for evaluating success in the organisations. In brief, it provides an overall performance measurement system by integrating financial measures, along with key performance indicators, that is perspective of customers, internal business processes, organisational growth, learning and innovation.

The BSC is a management system that enables organisations to clarify their vision and strategy and translate them into action. It provides a feedback around both the internal business processes and the external outcomes in order to continuously improve the strategic performance and results. It captures both the financial and non-financial aspects of a company's strategy and discusses the cause and effect relationship that drives business results. It is primarily a technique to implement the strategy and not to develop the strategy. In other words, it is a technique for operationalizing the vision/mission/strategy of the organization.

The Financial Perspective

The financial perspective includes the operating income, ROCE and EVA. The financial measures tell the results of actions already taken and it complements the financial measures with operational measures on customer satisfaction, internal processes and innovation perspective. Kaplan & Norton do not disregard the traditional need for financial data. Timely and accurate funding data will always be a priority, and managers will do whatever is necessary to provide it. In fact, often there is more than enough handling and processing of financial data. With the implementation of the corporate database, there is apprehension that more emphasis on financial data analysis is resulting in an unbalanced situation.

This perspective measures the ultimate results that the business provides to its stakeholders, through:

- Return on investment
- Revenue growth
- Sales growth and profitability
- Asset utilisation
- Economic value addition (EVA).

The Customer Perspective

Today, companies have realised the importance of customer focus and customer satisfaction in any business. These are: if customers are not satisfied, they will eventually find other suppliers that will meet their needs. Poor performance from this perspective is thus a leading indicator of future decline, even though the current financial picture may look good. Major dimensions affecting customer response and profitability are product and service attributes, customer relations, image and reputation. Key parameters in this perspective to be analysed are:

- Customer acquisition
- Customer retention
- Customer satisfaction
- Customer profitability

The customer perspective is measured through customer satisfaction, retention and market share in target segments.

The Business Process Perspective

This perspective refers to the internal business process. This perspective allows the managers to know how well their businesses are running, and whether the products and services conform to customer requirements. The main focus of this perspective is in defining the critical business processes in which the organization seeks to excel and that drive the business. Improvement in internal processes now is a lead indicator of financial success in the future:

- Cost
- Quality
- Delivery time
- Services
- Product performance.

These are required for business processes such as procurement, production and order fulfilment.

The Learning and Growth Perspective

This perspective includes employee training and corporate cultural attitudes related to both individual and corporate self-improvement. In the knowledge economy, human resources are the main recourse. In the current climate of rapid technological change, it is becoming necessary for knowledge workers to be in continuous learning mode. The organization has to identify the infrastructure that must be built in order to create long-term growth and improvement. The objective is to build up a mechanism to fill the existing gaps in knowledge and processes and be continually innovative. Adequate investment in these areas is crucial to long-term success:

- Training and Development
- Reward and Recognition
- Employee Satisfaction
- Employee Productivity
- Employee Retention
- Competencies to deliver required results

Employee learning and growth is measured through employee satisfaction, employee retention, skill sets, etc.

THE BALANCE SCORECARD LINKS PERFORMANCE MEASURES

What any organization measures strongly influences the behaviour of managers and employees. Executives also understand that traditional financial accounting measures like return-on-investment and earnings per share can give misleading signals for continuous improvement and innovation activities that today's competitive environment demands. Further, no single measure can provide a clear performance target or focus attention on the critical areas of business. Managers want a balanced presentation of financial and operational measures. It is therefore necessary that a firm's overall performance is planned, monitored and controlled in an integrated manner on all the four perspectives. Goals are set in key result areas in all four perspectives. It is not enough to set goals, there must be specific measurement criteria or standards set for these goals. The standards may require both objective and subjective assessment and accordingly information and accounting systems should be designed to provide timely data about these measures. Further, goals in one perspective may require supportive goals in other perspectives also. For example, in Table 3.1 the goals and their measures are depicted for a computer manufacturing firm, ECI.

STEPS IN CREATION OF BALANCE SCORECARD

Figure 3.1 shows a very general example of a scorecard. Where are we going? The vision: 'we should dominate the market.' How? By focusing on cost efficiency, high quality and by

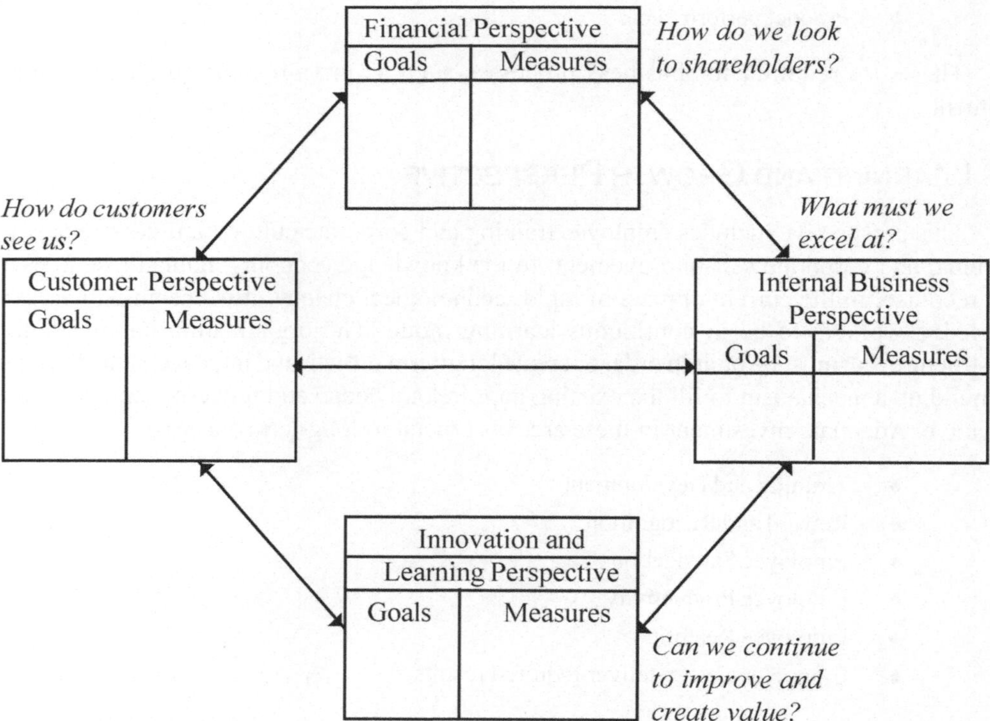

Figure 3.1. The balanced scorecard links peformance measures

TABLE 3.1
Goals and Measures of Computer Manufacturer, ECI

Financial Perspective		Customer Perspective	
Goals	**Measures**	**Goals**	**Measures**
Survive	Cash flow	New products	% age of sales from new products
Succeed	Quarterly sales growth division-wise		% sales from proprietary products
Prosper	Increased market share and ROI	Responsive supply	On time delivery defined by customer
		Preferred suppliers	Share of key account's purchase
		Customer partnerships	Number of cooperative engineering efforts
Internal Business Perspective		**Innovation and Learning Perspective**	
Technology capability	Performance of key technology parameters against competition	Technology leadership	Time to develop next generation
Design productivity	Silicon efficiency Engineering efficiency	Manufacturing	Process time to maturity Learning
New product introduction	Actual introduction schedule vs. plan	Product focus	% age of products that equal 80 % sales
		Time to Market	New product introduction vs. competition

investing on new technologies. In which perspectives should we excel at what? Responsibilities and action plans for achieving targets are set and defined.

The framework for the balance scorecard can be created with the following steps:

1. Create a vision statement and build the case for a balanced scorecard.
2. Identifying strategies.
3. Identifying critical successful factors and tactical activities.
4. Identifying performance measurements.
5. Identifying data sources for calculating measurements.
6. Creating a data warehouse to supply data.
7. Selecting information technology to create a data warehouse.

8. Creating a balanced scorecard report.
9. Managing the strategy using balanced scorecard.
10. Defining the tactical objective in support of strategy

Action Plans: Responsibility and action plans to reach the goals set out in different perspectives.

HR Scorecard

Traditionally, HR functions have struggled with appropriate and meaningful measures to quantify their value, or that of people engaged with business. The biggest problem faced by the HR department is communicating and reinforcing the linkage between HR action and business results. The business has a clear strategy and business results. The HR strategy is directly linked to the needs of business. The job of the HR department is to effectively communicate, motivate and track performances against organization and business goals, and to align HR action with business results.

The concept of HR Scorecard has been proposed by Becker, Huselid & Ulrich, who outline a powerful measurement system that highlights the indisputable role HR can play, as both a prime source of sustainable competitive advantage, and a key driver of value creation.

The emergence of the HR scorecard concept has taken its core design from the established balanced scorecard measurement framework applied in businesses in the Indian perspective: Glaxo Smithkline, Bharti Cellular, are using the scorecard as are Johnson and Johnson India Ltd. (2003), Coca-Cola India Ltd. (2004).

While there is no standard scorecard, the HR Scorecard includes four intellectual perspectives shown in Figure 3.2.

HR Financial Perspective

A central part of HR is supporting the business. HR needs to know that it is doing the right things.

Business Measures

Revenue per head (productivity) and customer satisfaction are examples of business performances that are significantly influenced by the quality of people management practices.

Strategic Contribution

Is HR capable of playing the role of strategic partner? Have they the necessary skills, outlook and the ability to raise HR and take a broader business perspective? These questions can be answered by combining the views of the senior executives responsible with a review of HR's strategic skill set.

HR Scorecard addresses how HR adds measurable financial value to the institution. This perspective measures ultimate results that the business provides to its stakeholders, through:

- Recruiting cost—external
- Training delivery
- Administering compensation
- Induction cost
- ROI on training
- Cost of service delivery.

HR Customer (Internal) Perspective

This includes measures of how HR is viewed by the internal customer, that is, by the employees of the company. Survey results are used for assessing the overall employee engagement, competitive capabilities and productivity.

Employee Engagement

HR needs to track the degree to which employees are contributing and feel a sense of involvement with the organization.

Retention

Some degree of employee turnover is healthy but excessive turnover is both disruptive and costly. Comparing the results of engagement with the turnover figures can shed light on the cause of turnover. Of particular importance is the turnover of high performers, the real talent of organization. In addition to actual turnover, HR should also seek to understand how the organisation's management practices affect the recruitment and retention of talent.

Competency

Many businesses struggle because they lack the skills they need. As the businesses grow and change, the skills they need shift. The introduction of computer based competency and performance systems enable organisations to aggregate skills availability and compare these with the profiles of skills needed. Understanding the gaps enables companies to better plan recruitment and training investment.

HR Learning and Growth Perspective

This perspective measures the success of the HR department in achieving its key goal of providing the organization with a large pool of talented employees by coaching and developing them to enhance their competencies and skill sets. Key parameters in this perspective to be analysed:

- Training programmes
- Motivation
- Leadership
- Talent management
- Competency development.

HR Internal Process Perspective

This perspective measures HR's success in operational excellence. Delivering effective HR services requires sound management of the function itself. The focus here is primarily on three basic areas: staffing, HR processes and traction.

HR Service

Is HR a customer-focused operation delivering satisfaction to its internal customers?

Key Transaction Event Management

How well does HR perform on key transactions such as payroll processing, pension administration, healthcare scheme changes or responding to queries? Measuring the effectiveness and quality of these transactions can provide useful process improvement information.

Creating an HR Scorecard

As we have seen, an HR Scorecard lets you do two important things: (1) manage HR as a strategic asset, and (2) demonstrate HR's contribution to your firm's financial success. Although each firm will depict its Scorecard in its own way, a well thought out Scorecard should get you thinking about four major themes: the key human resource deliverables that will leverage HR's role in your firm's overall strategy, the High Performance Work System, the extent to which that system is aligned with firm strategy, and the efficiency with which those deliverables are generated.

To begin an understanding what building an HR Scorecard requires, let us look at that process in a company we will call HiTech. For the sake of illustration we will focus on HiTech's R&D function and explore HR's potential role in this unit's strategy implementation model. As in many business units, R&D at HiTech has profitability goals that hinge on both *revenue growth* and *productivity improvement*—two important performance drivers. To build an HR Scorecard for just this unit, we need to understand the role that HR plays in these two dimensions of the R&D strategy map. We could describe this role as follows:

- *Revenue growth* ultimately derives from increased customer satisfaction, which in turn is boosted by product innovation and reliable delivery schedules, among other things.
    - Product innovation largely depends on the presence of talented staff with significant company experience. Through competency-based selection methods and retention programmes, HR contributes to stable, high-talent staffing in R&D.
    - Reliable delivery schedules in part hinge on maintenance of optimal staffing levels in manufacturing. Even if turnover in manufacturing is low, the company must fill vacancies quickly. By reducing recruiting cycle time, HR supports optimal staffing levels.
- *Productivity improvement* has links to the maintenance of optimal production schedules, which in turn depends on the maintenance of appropriate staffing levels. Again HR recruiting cycle time drives staffing levels.

DEVELOPING AN HR MEASUREMENT SYSTEM

Now let us 'walk through' a few steps in the HR Scorecard approach in order to illustrate how HiTech might begin developing its human resource measurement system.

Identifying HR Deliverables

There are two HR deliverables in this example. The first is *stable, high-talent staffing in the R&D function.* This deliverable has several dimensions. For one thing, the R&D staff must have the unique competencies defined by HiTech and must demonstrate those competencies at the highest levels. These competencies combine cutting-edge technical knowledge with the specialised product demands found in HiTech. Thus, they are not influenced by in-house professional-development efforts. Moreover, because these competencies are specific to HiTech and require several years of firm experience to develop, the company must keep its R&D staffing turnover very low.

The second HR deliverable is *optimal staffing levels in the manufacturing unit.*

Both of these deliverables have clear implications for HiTech overall performance. One contributes to revenue growth, while the other influences productivity growth.

HIGH-PERFORMANCE WORK SYSTEM

Once the HR deliverables have been clearly defined, we can begin to identify and measure the foundational High-Performance Work System elements that help to generate those deliverables. We term these elements a High-Performance Work System to represent the fact that they have been selected specifically with the intent of implementing strategy through the HR deliverables. In the case of HiTech, this means designing and implementing a validated competency model linked to every element in the HR system, and providing regular performance appraisals to all employees. As with all of the other elements of the HR scorecard, there are a variety of ways that these data can be represented. The most common approach is to present the proportion of achievement on each element, although it is also possible to indicate whether or not each element is either up to standard or below standard with a toggle indicating red (below standard), yellow (marginal) or green (meets standard).

Identifying HR System Alignment

What HR system elements need to reinforce one another so as to produce the two HR deliverables? In the case of stable, high-talent staffing in R&D we can assume that the firm has developed a validated competency model. At HiTech, selection into these positions must correspond to the existing competency model, and the quality of the lures should be at the highest levels. These alignment goals would strongly influence the particular sourcing decisions needed to produce those results. However, the sourcing decisions do not have to be part of the HR Scorecard. The assumption is that since you are measuring the outcomes of those sourcing decisions and since "what gets measured gets managed", then sourcing decisions will be guided by the need to achieve these outcome goals.

HiTech also needs to enact the kinds of retention policies that build experience in the R&D unit. Note, that retention policies as a key leading indicator is more important than the actual selection of policies, which are unique to each firm. At HiTech, a carefully chosen range of HR activities and policies, from supervisory training to unique benefit packages, might be in order. The key thing is that seemingly irrelevant HR "doables" have a clear strategic rationale.

To achieve optimal staffing in manufacturing, HR must keep its recruiting cycle time short. The appropriate alignment measure—for example, a fourteen-day recruiting cycle time—would reflect progress towards that objective.

Identifying HR Efficiency Measures

In this simple example, HiTech could identify cost per hire as a strategic efficiency measure. For both deliverables, cost per hire will probably be higher than average. But the benefits of those hiring processes will also be well above average. The HR scorecard that Hitech develops should highlight these links between important costs and benefits.

Figure 3.2 gives you a basic idea of how HiTech's HR Scorecard might look. Of course, an HR Scorecard for the entire company would include many more entries. This diagram represents a concise but comprehensive measurement system that will both guide HR strategic decision making and assess HR's contribution to R&D's performance. More important, the scorecard is presented in such a way that it reinforces the "causal logic" or strategy map of how HR creates value at HiTech.

THE THINKING BEHIND THE HR SCORECARD

Why have we chosen the identification of HR deliverables, the use of the High-Performance Work System alignment, and HR efficiency measure as essential elements of the HR Scorecard? We believe that this arrangement reflects a balance between the twin HR imperatives of cost control and value creation.

Cost control comes through measuring HR efficiency. Value creation comes through measuring HR deliverables, external HR system alignment, and the High-Performance Work System. These last three essential elements of the HR architecture trace a value chain from function to systems to employee behaviours.

In the following two sections, we outline a way of thinking about cost control and value creation. Again, it is more important that managers understand the reasoning behind the Scorecard that narrowly follow the particular format we have selected.

The value of the Scorecard diagram itself lies in the thinking that goes into it and its power as a decision-making tool since it is constructed.

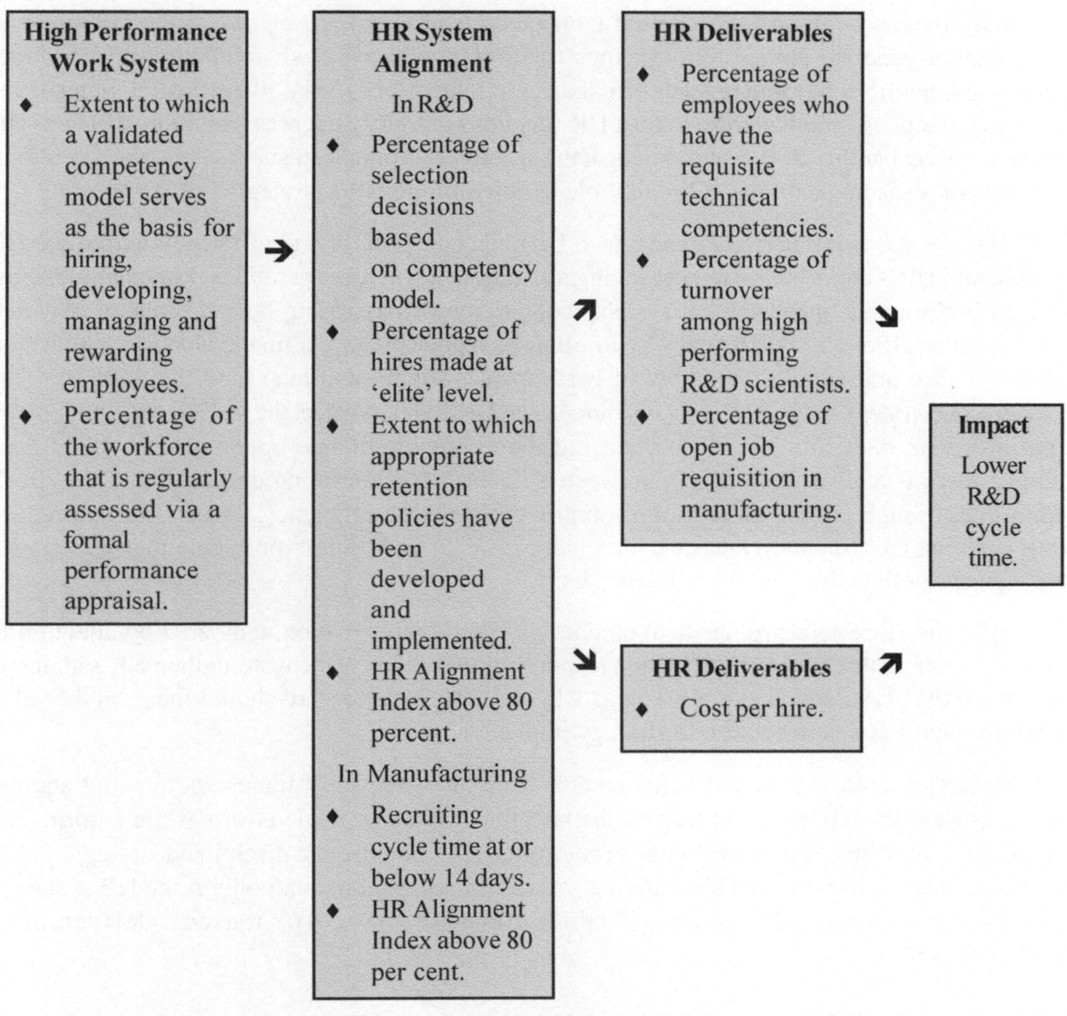

Figure 3.2. HR scorecard for HiTech's R&D function

The Bottom-Line Emphasis: Balancing Cost Control and Value Creation

Like most HR managers, you are probably under constant pressure to help your organization "drive out costs." Indeed, many line managers consider much of what HR does as overhead. In many instances, these managers are correct, which puts even more responsibility on HR to find efficiencies wherever possible.

We acknowledge these demands and believe that every HR Scorecard should include a dimension that captures the efficiency of the HR function. The problem is that in organisations that view HR as nothing more than a cost centre, efficiency of the HR function tends to be the only bottom-line metric in the HR measurement system.

Why have we put so little emphasis on this theme? First, efficiency in the HR function simply cannot generate enough cost savings to substantially affect shareholder value. Second, whatever competitive advantage such efficiencies might offer is very likely lost as other firms adopt such practices. In other words, most HR functions are fairly adept at providing efficient HR processes: this capability does not distinguish the successful from the unsuccessful firm. Therefore, these sorts of measures will play a limited role in determining HR's strategic influence.

There is a crucial difference, however, between cost control and efficiency within the HR function, and HR's contribution to cost saving and efficiency in line operations. For example, most balanced performance measurement systems contain metrics assessing both revenue growth and productivity or efficiency. "Efficiency" will often be represented by a financial lagging indicator, such as "reduce unit costs". A number of performance drivers will map onto that indicator (the arrows in your strategy map), but many will not. When HR enablers affect the "efficiency" component of those drivers, they are actually influencing the efficiency of line operations. In the HiTech example, there is a clear line of sight between efficiency HR recruiting processes and the firm's bottom line through HR's contribution to improved operating efficiency. Their efforts to reduce hiring cycle as an efficiency measure ultimately resulted in business problems that were much more significant than the original efficiency gains.

Still, the HR Scorecard needs to emphasise HR's value creation, tempered by attention to efficiency. Only in this way can the human resource management system strengthen HR's strategic influence in the organization overall. That is why most of the Scorecard should focus on the value created through HR's contribution to strategy implementation.

Balancing cost control and value creation measures helps HR managers to avoid another mistake as well: the tendency to focus on the benefits of HR's strategic efforts while ignoring the costs of those benefits. The highest rates of return for HR come from a disciplined strategic focus. HR deliverables, rather than doables, are the source of these benefits, but only if the HR system is managed efficiently. Remember, doables tend to be cost-focused: deliverables, benefits focused.

The Architectural Emphasis: Which HR Value Chain Elements go into the Scorecard?

Since the primary focus of HR's strategic role is value creation, thinking about HR architecture means taking the broad view of HR's value chain. Just as a corporate scorecard contains both leading and lagging indicators, the HR Scorecard must do the same. Of the four HR architecture elements that we recommend including in the Scorecard—High-Performance Work System, HR system alignment, HR efficiency and HR and deliverables—the first two are leading indicators and the second two are lagging indicators.

Measuring the High-Performance Work System lays the foundation of building HR into a strategic asset. A High-Performance Work System maximises the performance of the firm's employees. The problem is that the performance dimension tends to get lost in the attention most firms give to issues of efficiency, compliance constraints, employee relations, etc.—none of which is part of HR's strategic role. This is a mistake. The performance dimension needs to be prominent if a firm wants to enjoy the financial benefits that the Scorecard approach makes possible. Therefore, every firm's HR measurement system should include a collection of indicators that reflects the "performance focus" of each element in the HR system.

As we have seen, measuring HR system alignment means assessing how well the HR system meets the requirements of the firm's strategy implementation system, or what we have called "external" alignment. We have also mentioned "internal" alignment, defined as the extent to which each of the elements worked together rather than in conflict with one another. We do not give equal emphasis to internal alignment in our measurement system because, if the HR system is uniformly focused on strategy implementation, the elements should tend towards internal alignment. In other words, if HR managers can manage external alignment, then internal misalignments will tend to disappear. A focus on internal alignment becomes more appropriate as an initial diagnostic for those firms that have not adopted a strategic HR perspective. Internal misalignment, therefore is much more likely to be a symptom of an operationally focused HR system.

HR efficiency reflects the extent to which the HR function can help the rest of the firm to generate the needed competencies in a cost-effective manner. This does not mean that HR should try to simply minimise costs without attention to outcomes, but neither should they "throw money off the balcony". The metrics included in this category should reflect that balance.

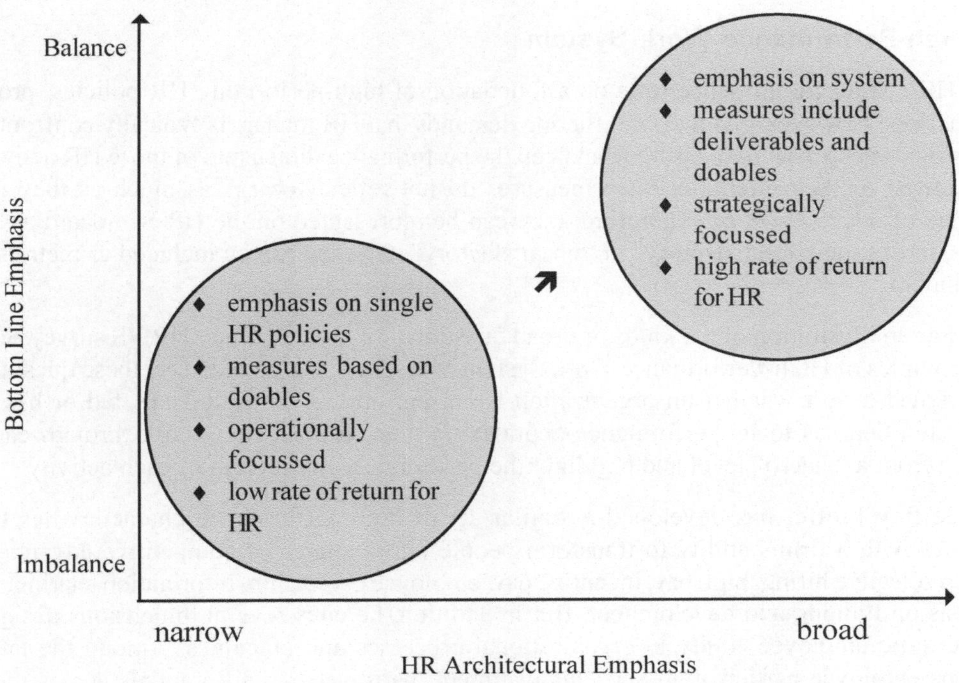

Figure 3.3. The synergy of measurement structure

And finally, HR deliverables are the key human-capital contributors to implementation of the firm's strategy. They tend to be strategically focused employee behaviours, such as the low turnover rates in the HiTech example.

How does this simple illustration in Figure 3.3 help us in understanding the appropriate structure of an HR Scorecard? While we will develop these ideas in more detail later, there are some organising principles to keep in mind. The structure of a strategic HR measurement system depends on striking the current balance between efficiency and value creation, while being guided by a broad strategic rather than a narrow operational perspective on HR.

It is important to understand the proper positioning on both dimensions provides the basis for synergies between the HR management and the measurement system. In other words, for HR to be able to demonstrate a significant impact on firm performance, the HR architecture should be designed as a strategic asset and the HR measurement must be designed to guide the management of that strategic asset.

Constructing The HR Scorecard

Now that he have talked about the four dimensions—HR deliverables, the High-Performance Work System, external HR system alignment, and HR efficiency—that should go into the HR Scorecard and the reasoning behind including them, let us move on to how you might actually use them to construct your Scorecard. First, we will take a closer look at each dimension.

The High-Performance Work System

HR's strategic influence rests on a foundation of high-performing HR policies, processes and practices. However, given the conflicting demands that HR managers typically confront, these professionals need a set of measures that keep the performance dimension of those HR activities at the forefront of their attention. Such measures do not reflect *what is* as much as they remind managers of *what should be*. Therefore, they can be represented on the HR Scorecard as simple toggles, indicating "unsatisfactory" or "unsatisfactory". Or, they can be included as metrics along a continuum.

For an illustration of the kinds of broad questions we include in our HPWS survey, see Box 3.1 "Examples of High-Performance Work System Measures". As you can see, these questions are not designed to test whether an organization is current on the very latest HR fad or has added another ten degrees to its performance-appraisal system. Rather, they work through each HR function from a "macro" level and highlight the performance orientation of each activity.

Jeffrey Pfeffer has developed a similar set of high-performance characteristics that he associates with a firm's ability to transform people into a source of competitive advantage. He includes selective hiring, high pay, incentive pay, employee ownership, information sharing, and an emphasis on training and development. But in addition, he cites several dimensions designed to provide more employee equity in organisational processes and outcomes. Among the latter, he mentions employee participation and empowerment, narrower pay differentials across the firm, symbolic egalitarianism and greater employment security. For your reference, we have listed more High-Performance Work System metrics in Table 3.2.

BOX 3.1
Examples of High-Performance Work System Measures

- How many *exceptional* candidates do we recruit for each *strategic* job opening?
- What proportion of all new hires have been selected based primarily on *validated* selection methods?
- To what extent has your firm adopted a professionally developed and validated competency model as the basis for hiring, developing, managing and rewarding employees?
- How many hours of training does a new employee receive each year?
- What percentage of the workforce is regularly assessed via a formal performance appraisal?
- What proportion of the workforce receives formal feedback on job performance from multiple sources?
- What proportion of merit pay is determined by a formal performance appraisal?
- If the market rate for total compensation would be the fiftieth percentile, what is your firms' current percentile ranking on total compensation?
- What percentage of your exempt and nonexempt employees is eligible for annual cash or deferred incentive plans, or for profit sharing?
- What percentage of the total compensation of your exempt and nonexempt employees is represented by variable pay?
- What is the likely *differential* in merit pay awards between high-performing and low-performing employees?

HR System Alignment

The next component in the HR Scorecard encourages you to gauge the alignment of the HR System with drivers of the firm's strategy implementation process. To transform a generic High-Performance Work System into a strategic asset, you need to focus that system directly on the human-capital aspects of those drivers.

Choosing the correct alignment measures is relatively straightforward. This process helps you understand the exact HR deliverables required to create value in the organization, which in turn indicates specific elements of the HR system (leading indicators) that must reinforce one another, in order to produce those deliverables. Therefore, specific alignment measures will be linked directly to specific deliverables in the Scorecard. Connecting them in this way highlights the cause-and-effect relationships needed to support HR's contribution to firm performance.

To select the appropriate alignment measures, focus on those elements of your HR system that make a definable and significant contribution to a particular HR deliverable. These differ for each firm. Identifying these measures requires you to combine a professional understanding of HR with a thorough knowledge of the value-creation process in your own firm. Remember that the

TABLE 3.2
High-Performance Work System Measures

Average merit increase granted job classification and job performance	Percentage of employees whose pay is performance-contingent
Backup talent ratio	Percentage of employees with development plans
Competency development expense per employee	Percentage of total salary at risk
Firm salary/competitor salary ratio	Quality of employee feedback systems
Incentive compensation differential (low versus high performers)	Range (distribution) of performance-appraisal ratings
Number and quality of cross-functional teams	Range in merit increase granted by classification
Number and type of 'special projects' to develop high-potential employees	
Number of suggestions generated and/or implemented	

alignment measures will follow directly from the "top-down" process. Based on the larger "strategy map" (Step 3 in our seven-step model), you will identify your HR deliverables, which in turn will point to certain elements of the HR system that require alignment. Therefore, there are no standard alignment measures that can be provided as examples. Instead, we emphasise the need for a standard process by which each firm will develop its own set of alignment measures.

Much like the High-Performance Work System measures, the external HR system alignment measures are designed largely for use within a firm's HR department. They too can be represented as toggles on the Scorecard, indicating alignment or non-alignment. The key issue is that they prompt HR managers to routinely think about alignment issues and highlight areas requiring action.

HR Efficiency: Core versus Strategic Metrics

As an HR professional, you doubtless have access to a wide range of benchmarks and cost standards by which you can measure HR's efficiency. We show a number of these models in Table 3.3. All of these metrics encourage cost savings and are the kinds of measures you would find in the first level of our measurement pyramid. But unless you want HR to be treated like a commodity in your organization, you should beware of building your measurement system unthinkingly on these generic benchmarks. Instead, separate out the costs associated with HR commodities such as employee benefits transactions and policy compliance, and the unique investments required to create HR's strategic value in your organization. (These choices will differ for each organization. Part of our rationale for including such a long list of potential metrics is to highlight the importance of choosing key metrics carefully using the process we have described. Otherwise, it is possible to

TABLE 3.3
HR Efficiency Measures (Doables)

Absenteeism rate by job category and job performance

Accident costs

Accident safety ratings

Average employee tenure (by performance level)

Average time for dispute resolution

Benefits costs as a percentage of payroll or revenue

Benefits costs/competitors' benefits costs ratio

Compliance with federal and state fair employment practices

Compliance with technical requirements of affirmative action

Comprehensiveness of safety monitoring

Cost of HR-related litigation

Cost of injuries

Cost per grievance

Cost per hire

Cost per trainee hour

HR department budget as a percentage of sales

HR expense per employee

HR expense/total expense

Incidence of injuries

Interviews-per-offer ratio (selection ratio)

Lost time due to accidents

Measures of cycle time for key HR processes

Number of applicants per recruiting source (by quality)

Number of stress related illnesses

Number of training days and programmes per year

Offer-to-acceptance ratio

OSHA audits

Percentage of and number of employees involved in training

Percentage of correct data in HR information system

Percentage of employee-development plans completed

Percentage of employees with access to appropriate training and development opportunities

Percentage of new material in training programmes each year

Percentage of payroll spent on training

Percentage of performance appraisals completed on time

Response time per information request

Sick days per full-time equivalent per year

Speed of salary action processing

Time needed to orient new employees

Time to fill an open position

Total compensation expense per employee

Total HR investment/earnings

Total HR investment/revenues

Turnover by recruiting source

Turnover costs

Continued ...

...Continued

Number of hires per recruiting source (by quality)	Turnover rate by job category and job performance
Number of courses taught by subject	Variable labour costs as percentage of variable revenue
Number of recruiting advertising programmes in place	Workers' compensation costs
Number of safety training and awareness activities	Workers' compensation experience rating

Source: Adapted from Dave Ulrich, "Measuring Human Resources: An Overview of Practice and a Prescription for Results," *Human Resources Management* 36 (Fall 1997), pp. 303-320.

become overwhelmed by the potential choices). Benchmarking is fine for the HR commodity activities, but it has no significant influence on your firm's ability to implement its strategy.

We thus recommend that HR managers divide their key efficiency metrics into two categories: core and strategic. *Core* efficiency measures represent significant HR expenditures that make no direct contribution to the firm's strategy implementation. *Strategic* efficiency measures assess the efficiency of HR activities and processes designed to produce *HR deliverables.* Separating these two helps you evaluate the net benefits of strategic deliverables and guides resource-allocation decisions. To see how this works, consider the following efficiency measures:

- benefit costs as a percentage of payroll;
- workers' compensation cost per employee;
- percentage of correct entries on HR information system;
- cost her hire;
- cost per trainee hour; and
- HR expense per employee.

The first three measures on the list would typically go in the core efficiency category. While certain benefit costs might give a firm an edge in recruiting high-talent employees, above-average benefit costs or workers' compensation payments are legitimately considered expenses rather than human capital investments. Likewise, transactional accuracy marginally improves employees' work experience, but it has little strategic significance.

Now look at the last three measures. Notice that these expenditures can each be thought of as investments that would yield considerable strategic value. To determine their value, one would have to go through the seven-step process tracing the links between the strategic efficiency measure and the subsequent elements in the HR value chain. Again, the HiTech example of reducing recruiting cycle time applies. Tightening this cycle may well raise "cost per hire" but in fact this practice is the first step in producing an HR enabler (stable staffing in R&D) that is essential to a key performance driver (R&D cycle time) in the firm's strategy implementation process. This is a good illustration of how a firm might attend to both the benefits and costs of an HR deliverable (see the upper right box in Figure 3.2).

HR deliverable measures help you identify the unique causal linkages by which the HR system generates value in your firm. They are not necessarily expressed in terms of firm performance or dollars, but they should be understood broadly to influence firm performance. The test of their importance is that senior line managers understand their significance and are willing to pay for them.

One challenge in measuring the impact of such "upstream" drivers is to avoid measure proliferation. It is easy to think that everything is important, but if you do this soon nothing is important. For measurement to matter, you have to measure only what matters. HR deliverable metrics that cannot be tied directly to your firm's strategy map should not be included in the HR Scorecard.

Choosing the appropriate HR deliverable measures depends on the role that HR will play in strategy implementation. At one extreme, HR deliverables could be characterised as *organisational capabilities*. Such capabilities would combine individual competencies with organisational systems that add value *throughout* the firm's value chain.

Note, though, that a capability is so central to successful strategy implementation that it cannot be linked to just one performance driver. We know of a major international consumer products firm that wanted to dramatically restructure its leadership capabilities. In the management's view, the firm with the best leadership talent would win in the marketplace, and this company intended to cultivate the best leadership talent in its industry. To achieve this goal, the management team developed its own competency model, which it considered proprietary. Next, it brought the executive search function in-house so that executive sourcing would reflect the proprietary competency model. Finally, the team added a powerful staff information system that would enable managers throughout the world to rapidly and effectively identify available managerial talent. No single element of this effort would constitute a strategic asset by itself, but taken together, these elements helped the firm develop a new organisational capability that senior line managers consider a key to the organisation's future success.

Thinking about HR deliverables in terms of organisational capabilities has a distinct appeal for human resources managers interested in underscoring HR's strategic value. This is because such capabilities seem to offer a competitive advantage so compelling that other managers cannot help but acknowledge their strategic value. The problem is that without clear validation of their strategic value from the senior executive team, HR managers will have a difficult time making the case post hoc. Viewing HR deliverables as organisational capabilities is thus an appropriate but limited measure of HR's strategic value. Identify this potential where possible, but also recognise that much of HR's strategic value lies elsewhere. Most important, do not try to puff up every HR initiative as a potential organisational capability. This kind of posturing will only undermine HR's legitimate strategic contribution.

In short, we are talking about taking a different perspective on HR's influence on firm performance. One approach is to focus on comprehensive people-related capabilities (such as leadership and organisational flexibility). It is easy to imagine how such capabilities contribute to organisational success in general, and perhaps even in your own organization. They are also appealing because they immediately allow HR managers to review what they are doing in "strategic" terms. While we do not dismiss this approach out of hand, we encourage HR managers to understand its limitations as well. Most important, an approach that thinks only of HR deliverables in terms of organisational capabilities tends not to link those deliverables concretely to the strategy implementation process. In other words, the valuation of those deliverables requires much the same leap of faith that has historically underlined HR's link to firm performance.

In contrast, with our seven-step model, measuring HR's contribution does not require a direct leap from HR deliverable to firm performance. Instead there is a "causal logic" between HR and other non-HR business outcomes (such as R&D cycle time in HiTech), which line managers consider credible.

For this reason, as you structure the "HR deliverables" section of your Scorecard, you should focus more on HR performance drivers and HR enablers than on potential organisational capabilities. These measures represent the human capital dimensions of discrete performance drivers in the firm's strategy map. Their individual effects on firm performance are much smaller than that of an HR capability, but there are so many of them that, cumulatively, they represent a significant source of value creation. Table 3.4 shows a list of potential HR performance-driver measures for purposes of illustration. However, we would never recommend selecting a measure without following the earlier steps in our model.

Ideally, the "HR deliverables" section of your Scorecard will include some measure of the strategic *impact* of the deliverables you have identified. This could include estimates of the relationships between each deliverable and individual firm-level performance drivers in the strategy map. Or, in a more elaborate system, you could link the effects of the deliverables through the performance drivers and ultimately to firm performance.

At this point, you will have defined the constituent elements of HR's strategic impact in your organization. Yet, even the HR deliverables represent just the *hypothetical* strategic influence of HR. Where possible, we encourage human resource managers to try to establish the *actual* impact of these deliverables on firm performance. This is the last piece of the sophisticated HR measurement system. It allows you to confidently make precise statements such as "HR deliverable *a* increased *x* by 20 per cent, which reduced *y* by 10 per cent, which in turn increased shareholder value by 3 per cent'.

Basing the HR Scorecard on the HR Function

Our approach to HR performance measurement has been to adopt as comprehensive a definition of HR as possible, hence our emphasis on what we call the HR architecture. This has involved both a somewhat different perspective on "HR" in the firm and some new ideas about the important dimensions of HR's performance. Making the leap from little or no performance measurement for HR to the concept of measuring the performance of the HR architecture can be daunting. Some firms may be more comfortable developing a Scorecard for the HR function as an interim step in this process. While we believe that the benefits of a more broadly focused Scorecard

TABLE 3.4
HR Performance-Driver Measures

Access to business information to facilitate decision making

Adherence by the workforce to core values such as cost consciousness

Average change in performance-appraisal rating over time

Change in employee mind-set

Climate surveys

Consistency and clarity of messages from top management and from HR

Customer complaints/praise

Customer satisfaction with hiring process

Degree of financial literacy among employees

Degree to which a "shared mind-set" exists

Diversity of race and gender by job category

Effectiveness of information sharing among departments

Effectiveness of performance appraisal processes for dealing with poor performers

Employee commitment survey scores

Employee competency growth

Employee development/advancement opportunities

Employee job involvement survey scores

Employee satisfaction with advancement opportunities, compensation, etc.

Employee turnover by performance level and by controllability

Extent to which HR is helping to develop necessary leadership competencies

Extent to which HR does a thorough job of pre-acquisition soft-asset due diligence

Extent to which HR leadership is involved early in selection of potential acquisition candidates

Extent to which HR measurement systems are seen as credible

Extent to which information is communicated effectively to employees

Extent to which the average employee can describe the firm's HR strategy

Extent to which the average employee can describe the firm's strategic intent

Extent to which the firm shares large amounts of relevant business information widely and freely with employees

Extent to which the firm has turned its strategy into specific goals/objectives that employees can act on in the short or long run

Extent to which top management shows commitment and leadership around knowledge-sharing issues throughout the firm

Percentage of employees making suggestions

Percentage of female and minority promotions

Percentage of intern conversion to hires

Continued ...

...Continued

Extent of cross-functional teamwork	Percentage of workforce that is promotable
Extent of organisational learning	Percentage of repatriate retention after one year
Extent of understanding of the firm's competitive strategy and operational goals	Percentage of employees with experience outside their current job responsibility or function
Extent to which employees have ready access to the information and knowledge that they need	Percentage of retention of high-performing key employees
Extent to which required employee competencies are reflected in recruiting, staffing and performance management	Percentage of consistent and equitable treatment of all employees
Extent to which employees are clear about the firm's goals and objectives	Performance of newly hired applicants
Extent to which employees are clear about their own goals	Planned development opportunities accomplished
Extent to which hiring, evaluation and compensation practices seek out and reward knowledge creation and sharing	The ratio of HR employees to total employment
	Requests for transfer per supervisor
	Retention rates of critical human capital
	Success rate of external hires
	Survey results on becoming "the" employer of choice in selected critical positions

Source: Adapted from Dave Ulrich, "Measuring Human Resources: An Overview of Practice and a Prescription for Results," *Human Resources Management* 36 (Fall 1997), pp. 303-320.

are compelling, some very good examples of HR Scorecards in practise have been organised around the HR function.

Figure 3.4 illustrates a graphical depiction of GTE's HR Scorecard. Here the HR function is viewed as an organisational unit that can be analysed in terms of the leading and lagging indicators associated with a Balanced Score. In this approach the "Operations" and "Customers" are not the larger operations or customers of GTE, but rather the operations or customers of GTE's HR function. This choice makes it more difficult to explicitly link HR to strategy implementation through the Scorecard but it is a reasonable decision given that, at the time, the larger organization had not developed a strategy map as part of a corporate-wide "balanced" performance management system.

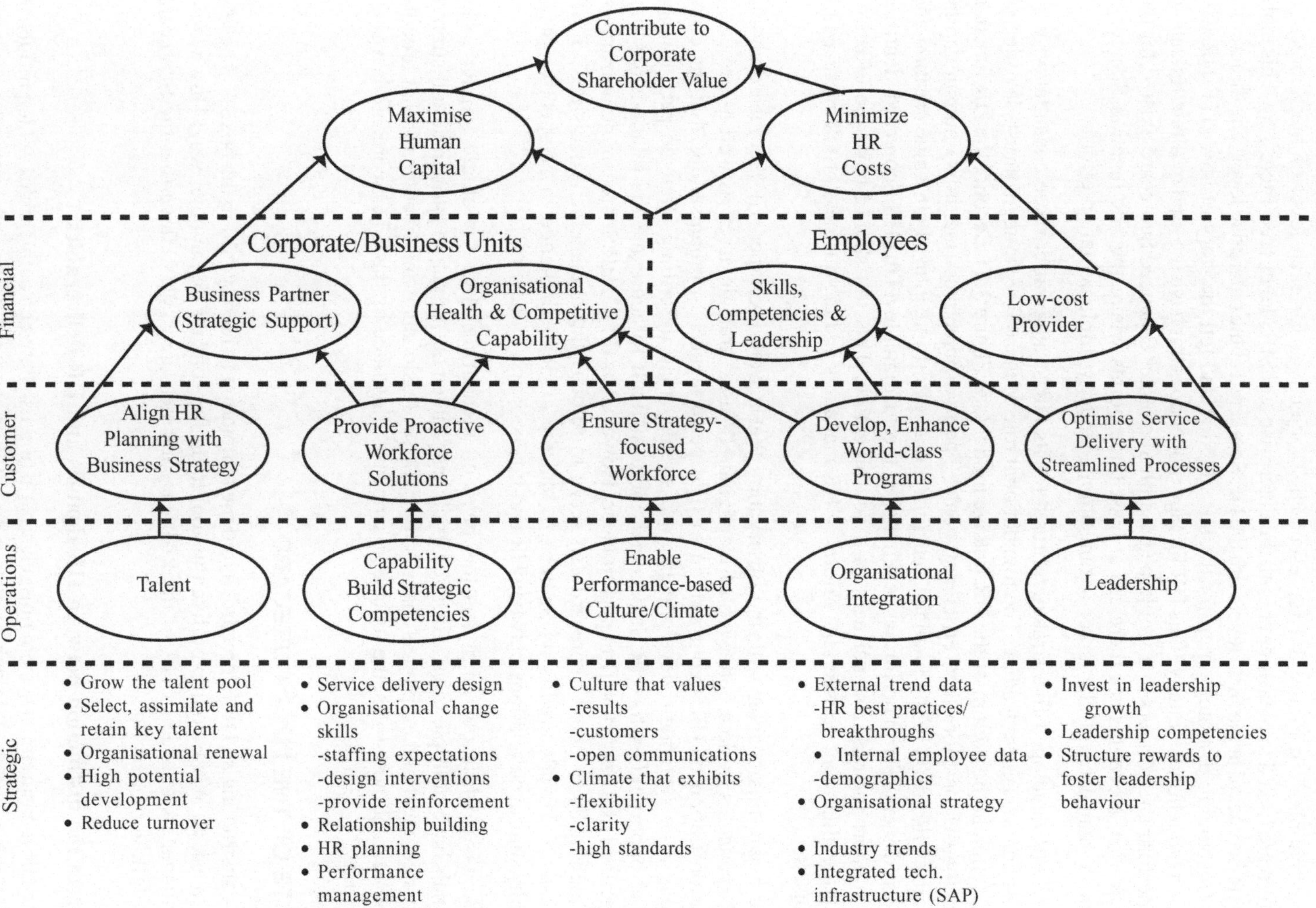

Figure 3.4. GTE HR linkage model

The "bubbles" in Figure 3.4 represent HR's objectives for each level of the Scorecard. These in turn are linked to measures at both the enterprise and SBU level {see Table 3.5). This table links the HR Scorecard at the SBU level with the HR Scorecard at the enterprise level. The directional arrows correspond to a strategy map for the HR function and tell the story of how GTE HR will implement its functional strategy. This HR linkage model does not have the kind of direct linkage to strategic performance drivers that would be possible if a larger Balanced Scorecard existed for the entire enterprise. Nevertheless, there are at least three points where the HR function Scorecard would tend to connect with the larger organisation's strategy implementation efforts.

GTE HR developed five strategic thrusts for its HR strategy after close consultation with the organisation's business leaders. The foundational role of these five strategic thrusts is reflected by their location at the bottom of the HR linkage model (see Figure 3.4). Second, the HR function Scorecard focuses on more than efficiency goals. The two objectives (maximise human capital and minimise HR costs) in the financial category are an effort to capture both value creation and efficiency as drivers of firm performance. Finally, at the customer level the HR Scorecard identifies strategic support for business partners as a key objective. This too should have the effect of improving the alignment between the efforts of HR managers and the business problems faced by line managers.

We began this chapter with the observation that a well-developed HR Scorecard should allow HR managers to do a better job of managing HR as a strategic asset, as well as provide a better demonstration of HR's contribution to firm performance. In organisations that have not gone through the systematic development of a strategy map describing strategic performance drivers and opportunities for HR, it becomes more difficult to aggregate the relationships that easily describe HR's impact on firm performance. However, as GTE's HR Scorecard demonstrates, even a functionally oriented Scorecard can serve to refocus the management decisions of HR professionals. GTE HR credits its Scorecard, and the associated change in perspective, with dramatically improved relations between HR and business unit managers.

Likewise, while our emphasis has been on measuring HR's "strategic impact", HR professionals have multiple roles, as Dave Ulrich has pointed out: strategic partner, administrative expert, change agent and employee champion. If HR professionals want a Scorecard that broadly touches on each of these roles, the functional emphasis illustrated by the GTE Scorecard is a good starting point.

BENEFITS OF THE HR SCORECARD

In constructing an HR Scorecard, avoid the temptation to merely "fill in the boxes". The key question to ask is: What would you like this tool to do for you? Or, put another way: How would you like managers outside of HR to think about your measures? We believe that the Scorecard offers the following benefits:

It reinforces the distinction between HR doables and HR deliverables

The HR measurement system must clearly distinguish between deliverables, which influence strategy implementation, and doables, which do not. For example, policy implementation is not a

TABLE 3.5
HR Performance-Driver Measures

Objectives	Enterprise Measures (Lagging Measures)	SBU Measures (Leading Measures)
Financial		
FI — Maximum shareholder value	◆ Total shareholder return ◆ Revenue per employee	◆ Human capital value added
F2 — Maximise human capital performance	◆ HR ROI (Index) ◆ Total HR cost employee	◆ Total labour cost percentage ◆ Competitive capability index
F3 — Minimize human resource costs	◆ Budget variance	
Customer		
C1 — Business partner (strategic support)	◆ Rating on corporate service agreements	◆ Employee engagement index
C2 — World-class standards	◆ Ranking of HR practice development/ audit (vs. benchmark)	◆ Comparative analysis results—Hi-Tech, RBOC's, IT peer groups
C3 — Responsive quality service	◆ Employee satisfaction survey results ◆ Benefit centre satisfaction percentage	◆ Hewitt—Average time to resolve ◆ Fidelity percentage resolved time
C4 — Low-cost provider	◆ HR cost factor indices	◆ Cost of service vs. benchmark
Operations		
O1 — Align HR planning with business priorities	◆ % of HR strategic plans implemented	◆ Time spent with executives
O2 — Provide quality consultative advice	◆ % of HR customised recommendations implemented	◆ % service coverage/client

Continued...

...Continued

Objectives	Enterprise Measures (Lagging Measures)	SBU Measures (Leading Measures)
O3 — Ensure a strategy based workforce	♦ % productivity improvement goals established ♦ % compensation schemes aligned to strategy	♦ % participation in goal setting processes linked to strategy
O4 — Develop and enhance world-class programmes	♦ Benchmarking ranking ♦ % programmes executed	♦ Programme development cycle time ♦ Key initiative tracking vs. milestones
O5 — Optimize HR services through alternative delivery channels	♦ Cost per delivery channel—HR interaction, automation, outsourcing ♦ Cycle time to fill ♦ Cost per transaction	♦ HR technology ROI and payback period ♦ % training delivered—CBT
Strategy		
S1 — Capability (build strategic competencies)	♦ LD participation	♦ Critical skill attainment
S2— Telent (select, assimilate & train)	♦ Voluntary separation rate/separation cost	♦ % new hires retention, 6 monthly/1 year ratio
S3 — Performance based culture/ climate	♦ Rating on viewpoints survey ♦ Organisational health index	♦ Internal promotion rate
S4 — Organisational integration (information for decision making)	♦ Reporting % accurate first request ♦ Turnaround time for ad hoc request	♦ Data availability
S5 — Leadership	♦ LDP bench strength ♦ Diversity ♦ Executive coaching	♦ High potential retention ♦ Offer acceptance rates ♦ Executive retention

deliverable until it creates employee behaviours that drive strategy implementation. An appropriate HR measurement system continually prompts HR professionals to think strategically as well as operationally.

It enables you to control costs and create value

HR will always be expected to control costs for the firm. At the same time, serving in a strategic role means that HR must also create value. The HR Scorecard helps human resource managers to effectively balance those two objectives. It not only encourages these practitioners to drive out costs where appropriate, but also helps them defend an "investment" by outlining the potential benefits in concrete terms.

It measures leading indicators

Our model of HR's strategic contribution links HR decisions and systems to HR deliverables, which in turn influence key performance drivers in the firm's strategy implementation. Just as there are leading and lagging indicators in the firm's overall balanced performance measurement system, there are both drivers and outcomes within the HR value chain. It is essential to monitor the alignment of those HR decisions and system elements that drive HR deliverables. Assessing this alignment provides feedback on HR's progress towards those deliverables and lays the foundation for HR's strategic influence.

It assesses HR's contribution to strategy implementation and, ultimately, to the "bottom line"

Any strategic performance measurement system should provide the chief HR officer (CHRO) with an answer to the question: "What is HR's contribution to the firm's performance?" The cumulative effect of the Scorecard's HR deliverable measures should provide that answer. Human resource managers should have a brief, credible, and clear *strategic* rationale for all deliverable measures. If that rationale does not exist, neither should the measure. Line managers should find these deliverable measures as credible as HR managers do, since these metrics represent solutions to business problems, not HR problems.

It lets HR professionals effectively manage their strategic responsibilities

The HR Scorecard encourages human resource managers to focus on exactly *how* their decisions affect the successful implementation of the firm's strategy. Just as we highlighted the importance of "employee strategic focus" for the entire firm, the HR Scorecard should reinforce the strategic focus of human resource managers. And because HR professionals can achieve that strategic influence largely by adopting a systemic perspective rather than fiddling with individual policies, the Scorecard further encourages them to think systematically about HR's strategy.

It encourages flexibility and change

A common criticism of performance measurement systems is that they become institutionalised and actually inhibit change. Strategies evolve, the organization needs to move in a different direction, but outdated performance goals cause managers and employees to want to maintain the status quo. Indeed, one criticism of management by measurement is that people become skilled at achieving the required numbers in the old system and are reluctant to change their management approach when shifting conditions demand it.

The HR Scorecard engenders flexibility and change because it focuses on the firm's strategy implementation, which constantly demands change. With this approach, measures take on a new meaning. They become simple indicators of an underlying logic that managers accept as legitimate. In other words, it is not just that people get used to hitting particular sets of numbers; they also get used to thinking about their own contribution to the firm's implementation of strategy. They see the big picture.

We believe that larger focus make its easier for managers to change direction. Unlike in a traditional organization, in a strategy-focused organization, people view the measures as means to an end, rather than ends in themselves.

Summary Tips for Managing with the HR Scorecard

Building an HR Scorecard should not be considered a one-time or even an annual event. To manage by measurement, human resource leaders must stay attuned to changes in the downstream performance drivers that HR is supporting. If these drivers change, or if the key HR deliverables that support them change, the Scorecard must shift accordingly. In building an HR Scorecard for your company, you therefore may want to include a component indicating how up to date the HR deliverables are.

The same strategic perspective that guides the construction of the HR Scorecard should also guide the management of HR. In particular, human resource staff should keep line managers continually informed of the status of HR deliverables. Feel free to also invite line managers to identify potential deliverables on their own. This is all part of forging a powerful new partnership.

Prerequisite for a Successful Scorecard

1. **CEO commitment:** The Scorecard works best if the CEO/top management shows personal commitment in implementing it.
2. **Selecting an effective Scorecard coordinator:** Typically, companies must choose a person who enjoys widespread trust and respect in the organization. His authority must also be expressly articulated.
3. **Implementation in a phased manner:** It has been seen that if the number of measures are increased over a period of time, it is easier for employees to adapt. It reduces the time spent on the initial phase and speeds up implementation.
4. **Commitment to simplicity, not perfection:** It is easy to get carried away by identified scores of objectives. About 10-15 objectives are enough to run a successful scorecard operation: it makes both the communication and implementation easy.
5. **Structuring of information system according to scorecard:** It is necessary that the organisational database is structured so as to provide the required timely information about various standards and their measures.

Utility of HR Scorecard

- It is helpful to executives as it provides an insight into the critical drivers of organizational success. The management can use the knowledge to better implement the strategy. It improves the bottom line by reducing process cost and improving productivity and mission effectiveness.
- By developing this technique, the management can ensure that everyone in the organization is focusing on aligned goals and objectives.
- Measurement of process efficiency provides rational basis for selecting what business process improvement to make first.
- It allows managers to identify best practices in the HR department and expand their usage elsewhere.
- The visibility provided by the HR Scorecard supports better and faster budget decisions and control of processes in the organisations.
- Visibility provides accountability and incentives based on real data. This allows for reinforcement and the motivation that comes from competition.
- It permits benchmarking of process performance against outside organisations.
- The HR Scorecard allows an organization to align its strategic activities to the strategic plans. It permits real deployment and implementation of the strategy on a continuous basis.

Limitations of HR Scorecard

- An HR Scorecard must be balanced. If it does not include both financial goals as well as non-financial goals, it will lose its utility. So if correct measures are not included in the HR Scorecard, the companies will find it difficult to deploy it into action.
- If the HR Scorecard becomes too functionally oriented, then too many measures and too many numbers will come into the picture and, therefore, the effectiveness of the tool will be lost.
- The HR Scorecard needs continuous review by the department. It should be updated regularly because the main drivers keep on changing. A static HR Scorecard will result in measuring the wrong things.
- It should be remembered that the Scorecard is not a strategy development tool. It is a tool for HR strategy implementation and overall control.

Questions and Assignments

Q.1. Explain the scope of HR audit and why is the audit necessary?

Q.2. You have been appointed as HR consultant to carry out the HR audit of a firm. Describe the methodology and broad contents of your report.

Q.3. Explain the benefits of HR audit and challenges that need to be faced in carrying out such an audit.

Q.4. What are the objectives of an HR Balance Scorecard and steps required in creating the same?

Q.5. What aspects are covered in an HR Balance Scorecard with regard to:

(i) Financial perspective

(ii) Customer perspective

(iii) The learning and growth perspective

Assignments

1. Carry out and compare the HR Audit of any two organisations. Bring out the main differences and try to explain the reasons for them.

2. Interview senior executives of a few firms where an HR Balance Scorecard is regularly used and find out its contribution and reasons for successes or failures in its application.

CASE

TESCO TAKES THE STEERING WHEEL

The icon that drives the world's third largest retailer, Tesco, motivates its employees to exceptional performance, influences the reduction and elimination of the mediocre and second-rate, and is more responsible for the company's success than any executive, employee, idea or initiative, as a steering wheel!

It all started in 1997, when Sir Terry Leahy took over as CEO of Tesco. Leahy dreamed of making Tesco a 'value retailer' by adopting 'The Tesco Way'. Under his leadership, Tesco implemented Kaplan & Norton's balanced scorecard concept. The balanced scorecard system aims to change organisations from financially driven to mission driven using four business perspectives: financial performance, internal processes, customer knowledge and learning and growth. Tesco adopted the Balanced Scorecard approach to meet its own requirements renaming it the Steering Wheel. Leahy has even credited Kaplan with inspiring the explosion in growth at the supermarket chain.

Tesco's Steering Wheel lies at the heart of the company's business planning strategy. It has four quadrants: People, Finance, Operations and Customer with each quadrant subdivided into segments. The Steering Wheel decides the key deliverables to achieve goals in each segment, providing a balanced approach to assess business performance, by being customer focused, striving for efficiency in operations and keeping people at the heart of all that the company does. Each segment is driven and monitored by Key Performance Indicators (KPIs), which set demanding but achievable targets for the business, and are backed by a sound business case quantifying the benefits. Where KPIs are not on track, the Steering Wheel puts in place action plans. Performance is reported quarterly to the Board, and a summary is sent to the top 2,000 managers in the company to cascade it on to the staff.

At the end of each year, every KPI in the Steering Wheel is reviewed to determine whether the business has met its objectives, and this shapes the level of remuneration for senior management. This is a clever way of linking strategy to day-to-day work. After all, there is more to running a business than financial matrixes. Bonuses are based on a sliding scale according to the level of achievement on the Corporate Steering Wheel. The Corporate Responsibilities KPIs are reported, measured and reported within the responsible and safe segment of the Operations Quadrant. This means that, rather than having a separate bolt-on corporate responsibility system, the management of corporate responsibility issues is embedded in the day-to-day running of the company.

Every store also has its own individual Steering Wheel, which is linked to every person's objectives, relating strategy to day-to-day work. International businesses which operate locally also have their own Steering Wheels. And that includes Bangalore-based Tesco Hindustan Service Centre, the 2,000 strong Global Services Arm of Tesco, which provides IT and business services to the retailer's operations across Europe and Asia.

"The Steering Wheel is a diagnostic management tool that helps decide when adjustments need be made to stay responsive to our customers and to our people. It is linked to every person's objectives, linking strategy to their day to day work and so making it meaningful," explains Sudesh Venkatesh, HR head, Tesco Hindustan Service Centre. (Source: www.humancapitalonline.com).

4 Investment Perspective—HR Decision Making

Learning Objectives

After studying this chapter you will learn:

- People in an organization are the most precious resources, not cost.
- The need for evaluation of HRM projects in terms of investment analysis.
- The technique of carrying out cost-benefit analyses.
- The technique of carrying out marginal cost analyses.
- The usefulness of carrying out benchmarking for HRM processes.

INTRODUCTION

Many CEOs and senior line executives often make the claim that: 'People are our most precious assets'. But they do not understand how the HR function can make the vision and mission of the organization a reality. They cannot explain how HR architecture helps their company to excel in the market place. The HR architecture is composed of three components—HR function, the HR system or processes, and resulting employee behaviour. This requires knowledge of 'strategic' HR drivers and how they are measured, monitored and controlled. This chapter attempts to explain the rationale or justification of various HR policies and processes in terms of their economic implications to the organisational performance. It tries to explain the investment perspective in decision-making about selecting particular HR systems for any organization or simply how HR adds value to the firm.

INVESTMENT PERSPECTIVE

Adopting a strategic view of HR involves considering an employee as human 'asset' and developing appropriate policies and programmes for investment in these assets to increase their value to the firm and the market place. The characterisation of employees as human assets has important implications for the strategic management of human resources in that it allows HRM to be viewed from an investment perspective. It aims at assessing the impact of HR architecture on business performance. For this to happen, the HR function has to play a central role in formulation and implementation of corporate strategy. Again, this means that HR is practised not only as a staff function but all the line managers take responsibility for people and people-management processes like other assets management.

Physical and capital assets in organisations such as plant, property, machinery and technology are acquired and subsequently managed most effectively by treating them as investments; the organization determines, after proper investment appraisal, the optimal mix of high-performance and high-return assets to attain its strategic objectives. Analysis is made of the cost and benefits of certain expenditures and judgements made concerning the risk and potential returns of such expenditures. Viewing human resources from the investment perspective, as other physical assets are viewed (rather than as variable costs of production), allows an organization to decide how to invest in HR architecture. This also means assessing risk and return on possible expenditures related to acquisition or development of human assets, allowing an organization to decide on meeting long-term performance goals.

Taking an investment perspective towards human resources/assets is critical considering that other physical assets such as facilities, products and services, technologies and markets can be readily imitated by competitors. Human assets cannot be duplicated and, therefore, become the base of competitive advantage that an organization holds in its markets. This is becoming increasingly important as the skills required for most jobs become less manual and more cerebral and knowledge-based in nature. Thought and decision-making processes as well as skills in analysing complex data are not owned by an organization but by individual employees. Technology is changing at a rapid pace and labourers are being replaced by knowledge workers. Thus, more and more human capital is getting inducted into today's workplace. Figure 4.1 illustrates some of the value employees bring to an organization.

FACTORS DETERMINING INVESTMENT ORIENTATION

There are many firms that do not have strategic HR architecture and therefore do not have an investment perspective. There are five factors that indicate the level of investment orientation of the HR architecture of any organization. As Jeffrey A. Mello puts it, the first of these factors is 'management values'. By answering the following questions regarding management values, some insight can be obtained.

- Does the organization see its people as being central to its mission or strategy?
- Do the company's mission statement and strategic objectives at corporate level and at each SBU level espouse the value of human assets in achieving its goals?
- Does the management philosophy stress the role of developing employees through training?

Please see Box 4.1 where the value proposition of Dana Corporation is illustrated. Senior management's style of actions will show how much they value their employees and whether they consider them as assets or costs.

BOX 4.1
Dana Corporation's Policy Statements Reflect Management Philosophy

Earnings

The purpose of the Dana Corporation is to earn money for its shareholders and to increase the value of their investment. We believe the best way to do this is to earn an acceptable return—by properly utilising our assets and controlling our cash.

Growth

We believe in steady growth to protect our assets against inflation.
We will grow in our selected markets by implementing our market strategies.

People

We are dedicated to the belief that our people are our most important asset. Wherever possible we encourage at Dana people within the entire world organization to become shareholders, or by some other means, own a part of their company.

We believe people respond to recognition, freedom to participate and the opportunity to develop.

We believe that people should be involved in setting their own goals and judging their own performance. The people who know best how the job should be done are the ones doing it.

We believe Dana people should accept only total quality in all tasks they perform.

We endorse productivity plans, which allow people to share in the rewards of productivity gains.

We believe that at Dana people should identify with the company. This identity should carry on after they have left active employment.

We believe facilities with people who have demonstrated a commitment to Dana will be competitive and thus warrant our support.

We believe that wages and benefits are the concern and responsibility of managers. The Management Resource Programme is a worldwide matter—it is a tool that should be used in the development of qualified Dana people. We encourage income protection, health programmes and education.

We believe that on-the-job training is an effective method of learning. A Dana manager must prove proficiency in at least one of our company's work—marketing, engineering, manufacturing, financial services, etc. Additionally, these people must prove their ability as supervisors and be able to get work done through other people. We recognise the importance of gaining experience both internationally and domestically.

We believe our people should move across product, discipline and organisational lines. These moves should not conflict with operating efficiency.

Continued ...

...Continued

We believing in promoting from within. Dana people interested in other positions are encouraged to discuss job opportunities with their supervisor.

Managers are responsible for the selection, education and training of all people.

All Dana people should have their job performance reviewed at least once a year by their supervisors.

We believe in providing programmes to support the Dana Style. We encourage professional and personal development of all Dana people.

Planning

We believe in planning at all levels.

The Policy Committee is responsible for developing the corporate strategic plan.

Each operating unit within its regional organization is responsible for a detailed five-year business plan. These business plans must support the corporate strategic plan and market strategies. These plans are reviewed annually.

Commitment is a key element of the Dana Management Style. The commitment and performance will be reviewed on a monthly basis by the appropriate regional operating committee and on a semi-annual basis during Mid-Year Reviews.

Organization

We discourage conformity, uniformity and centralisation.

We believe in a minimum number of management levels. Responsibility should be pushed as far into the organization as possible.

Organization structure must not conflict with doing what is best for all of Dana.

We believe in an organisational structure that allows the individual maximum freedom to perform and participate. This will simulate initiative innovation, and the entrepreneurial spirit that is the cornerstone of our success.

We believe in small, highly effective support groups to service specialised needs of the Policy Committee and the world organization at large as requested. We believe in task forces rather than permanent staff functions.

We do not believe in company-wide procedures. If an organization requires procedures, it is the responsibility of the manager to create them.

Customers

Dana is a global company focused on markets and customers. We compete globally by supplying products and services to meet the needs of our customers in our selected markets.

We are dedicated to the belief that we have a responsibility to be leaders in our selected markets.

Continued ...

...Continued

We believe it absolutely necessary to anticipate our customers needs for products and services of the highest quality. Once a commitment is made to a customer, every effort must be made to fulfil that obligation.

It is highly desirable to outsource a portion of our production needs. Outsourcing increases our competitiveness and protects the stability of employment to our people. It also protects our assets and assures performance to our customers.

Dana People throughout the organization are expected to know our customers and their needs.

Communication

We will communicate regularly with shareholders, customers, Dana people, general public and finance communities.

It is the job of all managers to keep Dana people informed. Each manager must decide on the best method of communication. We believe direct communication with all of our people eliminates the need for a third party involvement. All managers shall periodically inform their people about the performance and plans of their operation.

Citizenship

The Dana Corporation will be a good citizen worldwide. All Dana people are expected to do business in a professional and ethical manner with integrity.

Laws and regulations have become increasingly complex. The laws of propriety always govern. The General Counsel and each General Manager can give guidance when in doubt about appropriate conduct. It is expected that no one would wilfully violate the law and subject themselves to disciplinary action.

We encourage active participation of all of our people in community action.

We will support worthwhile community causes consistent with their importance to the good of Dana people in the community.

The Policy Committee
Dana Corporation

Approved by the Board of Directors
Dana Corporation

Source: Dana Corporation, Toledo, Ohio, U.S.A.

The second factor is attitude towards risk. Investments in human assets are generally more risky than investments in other physical assets. Unlike other assets, human beings are not owned by the organization. Hence, a risk-averse organization will make far less investment in people. But the returns from them over a long period are far higher than from other assets since, in a proper environment and culture, they appreciate greatly while other assets depreciate over time. There are

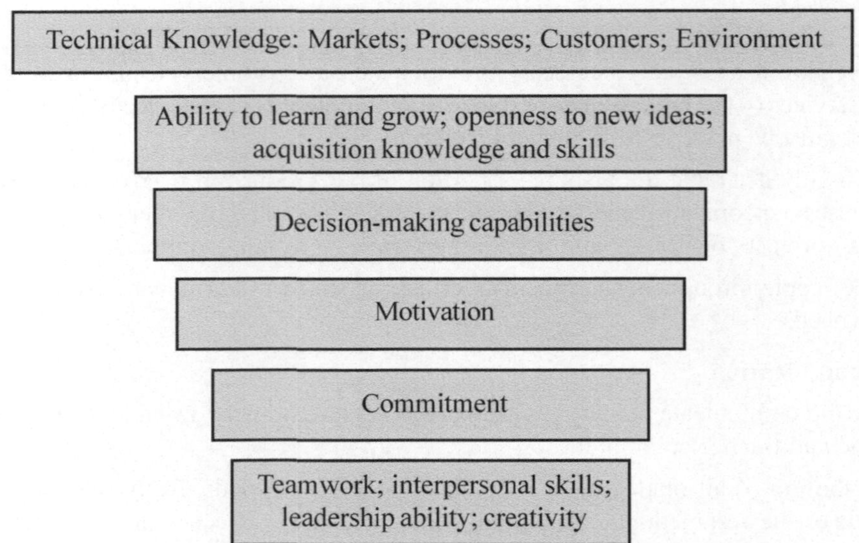

Figure 4.1. Sources of employee value

Source: Jeffrey A. Mello, *Strategic Human Resources Management,* p. 4.

sets of HR policies which can help to retain the assets and thus minimise the risk of losing investments, like stock-option, long term contracts, career advancement and additional professional opportunities.

The third factor is the employee's skills, whether they are organization specific or firm specific. This depends upon the nature of the industry and technology utilised, which may be generic or specific.

Some job skills like office management and accounting are commonly used. Another example is software used by the firm, which may be customised or popular-branded like Tally. If the employee skills are marketable, investment in such employees is highly risky.

In such cases, the firm has to formulate either a strong retention strategy, for example, by linking advancement and pay rise to the years of service.

The fourth, factor is 'utilitarian' or profit orientation. Firms with high profit orientation use a cost-benefit analysis approach for investment decisions.

This approach should use all aspects of costs, both direct and indirect, and benefits over a longer time horizon, as described in the next paragraph. The main difficulty that arises in estimating benefits is to quantify them in terms of money value.

The final factor impacting on an organisation's willingness to invest in its people is the availability of 'outsourcing'. An investment-oriented approach will determine whether its investment will produce sustainable competitive advantage over time. When specialists are available who can perform the tasks more efficiently, any internal programmes will be challenged and have to be evaluated relative to such a standard. This is true for all functions, be they accounting or information management.

Finally, every organization will evaluate the priorities in investments in other areas like product promotion or mergers and acquisition. Here, the investment in people being a long-term return is at a discount to short-term profitable propositions. Hence, this balance is another factor that can be observed.

Cost-Benefit Analysis—Selection of Projects

HR managers requesting funds from corporates encounter much tougher roadblocks than their peers in manufacturing or marketing because other disciplines have a long tradition of quantifying the potential benefits of their programmes and presenting them in a language that all can understand—money.

Cost-benefit analysis for the HR function can be divided into two parts: operational and strategic. Operational analysis describes how to improve the activities that the firm already performs. By costing such activities, the organization can explore ways to lower recruiting-related expenses, compare the advantages of outsourcing the benefits function versus keeping it in-house, etc. In contrast, strategic cost-benefit analysis derives from the firm's strategy and operational goals and thus focuses on questions such as: how can we best enhance employee strategic focus? HR Balance Scorecard, if the organization is preparing one, can best answer such questions. In both cases, data is not easily available in the firm's financial accounting system and therefore data-collection has to be custom-designed. This itself requires cost and effort.

Thus it is important to define what types of HR activities should be 'costed' and why? For example, is it important to know precisely what the ROI is for training activities or is it enough to know that the benefits of the firm's training activities exceed their cost? What is a more worthwhile activity: calculating your firm's cost per hire or determining the most effective way to increase employee competencies in a certain area, say decision-making skills. Should one be required or both? Cost-benefit analysis to be meaningful should be for activities having the following attributes:

1. Strategic importance. The activities should have a direct link to the implementation of the firm's strategy. This can be found from a study of value-chain or value-driven analysis.
2. Financial significance. An effective HR project addresses an area of HR that involves significant and on-going investments—for example, overall training and development, as opposed to a one time training session.
3. Widespread impact. The most important costing projects have the potential to affect a significant proportion of the workforce. Alternatively, they target categories of employees in strategic areas like R&D who have close links with the success of business.
4. Variable impact activities. For example, if some development programmes are successful in one unit and fail in others. Here CB analysis will help to understand why.
5. Focus on a key issue or problem. For example, should we introduce a new software for HRIS? or, introduce a new selection method?

Cost-benefit Analysis Examples

Example 1

Calculation of ROI on outsourcing the benefits programme that saves $1.2 million of 'in-house' costs, while incurring $ 800,000 on consulting fees. In addition, $ 100,000 is spent in transition from one system to another.

$$\text{ROI} = \frac{\$\ 1{,}200{,}000 - (\$\ 800{,}000 + \$\ 100{,}000)}{\$\ 800{,}000 + \$\ 100{,}000}$$

= 33 per cent

Pay back period = say current benefit costs are currently $ 1.2/12 = $ 100,000 per month.

The cost of transitioning to the outsourcing vendor is $ 100,000. Therefore, the vendor will save the firm the following per month in benefit and administration costs:

$$\frac{\$\ 1{,}200{,}000 - \$\ 800{,}000}{12}$$

= $ 33,333

Pay-back period = $ 100,000/33,333 = 3 months

Example 2

Breakeven cost analysis

The number of participants who must attend the programme to break even.

Suppose expenditure on advertising, room rental and staff salary = $ 20,000, which are fixed costs, whether one candidate or 100 candidates attend.

Say participants pay registration costs as $ 400 each. From this to be deducted are the variable costs on lunch, tea, study materials, etc., say $ 100 per participant.

Number of candidates required for breaking even is = $ 20,000/$ 300
= 67 participants.

Example 3

Net Present Value (NPV)

NPV analysis draws together all these factors—costs and benefits over multiple time periods, and compensation for uncertainty, opportunity costs, and the firm's cost of capital to assess the overall potential value of a proposed HR programme.

Most HR programmes show benefits over a number of years and therefore the time value of money is to be taken into account including opportunity cost analysis.

Suppose the cost of development and implementation of a new integrated performance management and incentive compensation is = $ 250,000.

Suppose this will increase the firm's cash flow or profit by $270,000 per year for the next five years. But incentives payout will be $ 130,000 per year for the 5 year period.

Suppose the firm's marginal cost of capital is 14 per cent. We can now calculate net present value of the investment.

Year	Particulars	Amount * Discount Factor	Present Value
1	Programme development cost	– $ 250,000 * 1	– $ 250,000
1–5	Increased wages	– $ 130,000 * 3.4-33	– $ 446,290
1–5	Increase in profit	+ $270,000 * 3.4-33	+ $926,910

Net Present Value = $ 280,620. The programme should be developed and implemented.

Note: 3.4-33 is the present value factor that can be found in any financial textbook.

Example 4

Suppose a firm has 1,000 employees; out of them 400 are high performers, 30 per cent amongst them leave every year (120). As a result, every year 120 people are newly recruited, trained and inducted, causing a loss. Suppose it is decided to reduce this to 15 per cent by providing extra incentives, promotions to 120 people every year. Work out the justification.

Table 1. Cost estimates of replacing 120 high potential managers

Year 1 (Hire 120 managers)	
Separation costs	$ 60,000
Recruiting costs	$ 900,000
Selection costs	$ 900,000
Training and induction costs	$ 600,000
Lower productivity—acculturation	$ 1,200,000
Lower productive long run	$ 300,000
Total	$ 6,660,000

Table 2. Cost estimates of reducing turnover from 30% to 15%

Year 1	
Increased variable pay for high performers	$ 1,200,000
Enhanced promotional opportunities	$ 360,000
Additional training competency development	$ 600,000

Year 2	
Increased variable pay for high performers	$ 1,200,000
Enhanced promotional opportunities	$ 360,000
Competency development training	$ 600,000
Year 3	
Increased variable pay for high performers	$ 1,200,000
Enhanced promotion opportunities	$ 360,000
Competency development training	$ 600,000
Present value costs (3 years at 10% cost of capital	$ 5,858,381

Table 3. Benefits of reducing turnover from 30% to 15%

Year 1 (60 employees)	
Enhanced productivity and lower induction replacement cost	$ 3,000,000
Year 2 (120 employees)	
Enhanced productivity and lower replacement costs (Current and prior year's retained employees)	$ 6,000,000
Year 3 (180 employees)	
Enhanced productivity and lower replacement costs	
Current and prior year's retained employees	$ 9,000.000
Present value benefits (3 years @ 10% cost of capital)	$ 13,320,929

Table 4. Net present value of reducing turnover from 30 percent to 15 percent

Present value of benefits	$ 13,320,929
Present value of costs	$ 5,858,381
At net present value, benefits	$ 7,462,548
	say $ 7.5 million

Hence the programmes are to be implemented.

Marginal Utility Analysis

The marginal utility model takes into account both costs and financial returns associated with changes in HRM practices. This approach takes into account present and future costs of HRM practices and future streams of revenue associated with improved levels of employee behaviour that can be attributed to the change in HRM practice. For an investment in HRM system to add value to the firm, it must generate an acceptable rate of return—which exceeds the cost of capital. An example from recruitment and selection is illustrated.

It takes into account the money invested into system improvements, the relative level of improvement, positive return associated with hiring and retention of more proactive employees, and the hiring context. The cost and revenue streams associated are then adjusted to take into account the time value of money and the cost of capital, variable costs associated with the improvements brought about by making better hiring decisions, and marginal taxes.

Let us assume that a retailer will be hiring 250 sales personnel during the year. This is a company with 65 stores nationwide. It pays 10 per cent of the retail sales value to the sales persons. High-performance sales persons can make well above the industry average of $ 41,000 per year in base pay and commissions. The average sales associate earns $ 33,000 in base pay and commission and the average yearly pay level for a below standard performer (15th percentile) is $ 25,000. After taking into account that all sales personnel are paid a base rate of $ 7.5 per hour, this means that the top performers are selling approximately $ 259,200 worth of merchandise per year, the average performer is selling approximately $ 179,200 worth of merchandise and the below standard performer only $ 99,200 worth per year.

The company currently uses a resume review, a paper-and-pencil personality test, and an informal selection interview when hiring new sales persons. This current selection system costs the company approximately $ 100 per applicant in processing fees. A consulting firm wants to sell the company a much more costly selection system that it claims is more 'valid' than the existing system. Statistical validity refers to the degree to which scores on a weighted average of predictor scores correlate with a measure of job performance. The consulting firm has provided evidence showing that in previous studies the correlation between applicant ratings made with the use of their systems and job performance was typically in the 0.45 range. Past studies of the company's current system has shown that when resume ratings, personality test scores and interview ratings are used to predict job performance, the resulting multiple correlation was approximately 0.30 while the new selection process will accurately predict the likely sales performance of job candidates to a higher degree (0.45 versus 0.30). Before the company decides to purchase the consulting firm's product and related services, it must determine if the higher degree of selection system accuracy is worth the additional price. To answer this key question, the company must collect and estimate some additional information to be used in conjunction with the marginal utility model (discussed in a following section of this chapter). The new selection system will cost the company nearly $ 400 per applicant.

The return associated with improving a selection system depends on the degree of improved accuracy and also upon a variety of other factors. For instance, it does not make much sense to invest in a selection system improvement if the labour market is so tight that the company will have to hire virtually all applicants meeting minimal hiring standards. The positive pay-off comes from being better able to identify the best applicants and then selecting only the best of the best. Therefore, the degree of selectivity the company can exercise and the overall quality of the labour market will affect this type of investment decision. The decision-making model must also take into account the time value of money. Cost incurred to hire new applicants is spent in the present but the returns will be realised only after some time in future.

Finally, gains associated with an improved selection system will go partly in taxes and increased variable costs brought about by increased sales from the new, improved group of employees. Let us assume 30 per cent are taxes and 65 per cent are the variable cost portions that will have to be incurred. Also, assume that the labour market will provide 5 applicants for each position. Should it hire a new system to select 250 salesmen?

N = 250
t = the time period in which the benefits occur
i = assume a current discount rate of 6 %
r_1 = 0.45
r_2 = 0.30
SD_y = \$ 80,000
ë/p = 1.40
T = assumed average tenure for this job class at 3 years
C_1, C_2 = \$ 400 and \$ 100
V = –0.65
Tax = 0.30
P = 0.20

$$CU = (N) * \{\sum_{t=1}^{T} [1/(1+i)^t] (r_1 - r_2)(SD_y)(9/p)(1 + V)(1-Tax)\} - [(N) \frac{\overline{(C1-C2)}}{p}] [1-Tax]$$

U = the increase in dollar pay-off, realised over the tenure of the new employees which results from selection of N employees by employing the new system
N = the number of employees selected
t = the time period in which the benefits occur
i = the current discount rate
r_1 = validity of new selection system
r_2 = validity of existing system
SD_y = the standard deviation of dollar pay-off, what a one standard deviation difference in job performance is worth in annual revenue to the firm
9/p = the estimated average score on the predictor among the group hired (in standard score form) (see table below)
T = average tenure of new employees
C1 and C2 = the cost per applicant of using the new C1 and old C2 procedure
V = the proportion of service value (attributable to improved selection) represented by variable costs. It will be negative if costs increase with increased revenue and show a positive value when costs decrease with increased revenue
Tax = the marginal tax rate
P = the selection ratio

U= N* {Summation of t=1 to T $[1/(1+I)^t]$ (R1-R2)* SD *X/q * (1+V) (1-Tax)}

U= 250*[(2.67) (0.15) (80.000)(1.4)(0.35)(0.70)]-[250*0.35*0.70]

U=$2,484,930 this positive return is realised for hiring 250 employees

X = (Selection Ratio)	X/q = Estimated Mean z Score
0.05	2.05
0.10	1.75
0.20	**1.40**
0.30	1.16
0.40	0.96
0.50	0.80
0.60	0.65
0.70	0.50

Hierarchy of Cost Benefit Analysis

A study by the authors of HR Balance Scorecard has brought out that most firms do not rigorously evaluate either the costs or the benefits associated with HR policies and programmes. In fact, a range of cost-benefit analyses exists. This range starts at its low end with simple cost and progresses to benefit estimates and cost-benefit-index calculation. Firms showing the highest quality of cost benefit analysis engage in these calculations in a regular, disciplined manner. This is shown below:

Level 3
Benefits estimates. Good cost estimates good calculations. NPV analysis. Marginal costing regularly and frequently.

Level 2
Benefits estimates, intuition cost estimates. Good calculations. Pay back calculations, breakeven costing, frequency irregular.

Level 1
Benefits estimates, intuition cost estimates, intuition calculations. Frequency none.

TABLE 4.1
What Firms Say they are Measuring and How
(Sample: 968 firms)

No.	Data in Percentages	Don't Determine	Subjective Estimates	Formal Calculations
1.	Turnover costs	43.7	43.1	13.1
2.	Employee replacement costs	38.2	48.8	13.0
3.	Economic value of the employees to the organization	67.4	26.6	6.0
4.	Cost of various employee behaviours like absenteeism, etc.	48.3	38.2	13.5
5.	Economic value of developing superior selection tests	79.4	17.1	3.5
6.	Economic costs of various training levels	79.4	17.1	3.5
7.	Economic benefits of additional recruiting`	57.3	35.4	7.3
8.	Economic benefits of increasing job satisfaction, commitment or job attitudes	54.9	42.3	6.1
9.	Economic benefits of low, medium, high performance on particular jobs	54.2	39.7	6.1

Role of Benchmarking

Any discussion of the CB analysis of HR investment raises the issue of benchmarking, or the process of collecting data on various aspects of the firm's architecture from a variety of firms and then using these data to evaluate one's own firm.

Benchmarking studies can be grouped into those that focus on specific levels of a particular variable or attribute (for example, what is our cost per hire relative to another firm in our industry?) and those that focus on specific processes (for example, how does Wal-Mart operate its world class logistics and distribution system?).

Studies about benchmark levels of an attribute are often conducted via surveys and include a large number of firms. Studies that benchmark processes generally include only a few firms and tend to be conducted via site visits or telephone interviews. The studies of benchmark processes can provide a rich source of information, understanding and often inspiration. Observing exemplary processes *in situ* can be a very important learning experience for teams that have responsibility for designing and implementing new processes within their own organisations. In contrast, the studies of benchmark attributes or variables are not as useful.

BOX 4.2
Can Benchmarking Ever be Strategic?

For benchmarking to help an organization create a long-term source of competitive advantage, the information derived from this process would have to be rare, difficult to imitate, and valued by the firm's internal or external customers. Yet almost by definition, if firms are readily willing to share such data, then it probably won't have much strategic value. Consider the case of HP. HP is one of the most widely benchmarked companies in the world, and its business processes (especially its HR management philosophies and practices) have been widely reported in the business press and many academic books and articles. Why is HP willing to share such information, which will surely be available to its customers? We believe that there are two important reasons. The first is that even if a firm is completely forthcoming about what they do, it does not help unless you know how they generated the solution, and the difficulties in the process of its implementation. Second, HP's management infrastructure relies heavily on leveraging employees' competencies and talents in new and different solutions. In this context, the firm is continuously improving its intellectual capital, and by the time your firm has replicated what is learned in the benchmarking process HP will have created new competencies to allow it to meet a new situation. In many industries, the firms that can learn the fastest are the winners. HP is a good example of just such a firm.

Our 'bottom line' is that benchmarking of key processes can be very helpful, especially if it can help you learn about new processes and ways of doing things. And if the process to be benchmarked comes from industries other than one's own, they have the potential to grant even more useful insights.

Source: Jay B. Barney. 'Firm Resources and Sustained Competitive Advantage'.

There are problems in benchmarking studies that focus on 'levels' of HRM practices and outcomes. The first is that there is a shortage of competent HR personnel in most companies and the second is that HR activities are being handled by line executives in increasing numbers and they are too busy to spare their time.

HR Costing Model of Rutgers University

Charles Fay, Steve Director, Paul Hampbel and Mark Husfield of HRSP and Rutgers University developed an integrated, spreadsheet-based costing model to evaluate the true economic costs and benefits associated with HR. In their methodologies they have divided costs into:

- Baseline Operating Costs: These are annual costs associated with HR processes and activities. These are the starting point and serve as the benchmark against which proposed changes in HR processes and activities will be compared.
- Adjustment Costs: These are recurring costs associated with implementation of human resource management activities.

- Steady-State Costs: These are recurring costs associated with implementation of the HR initiative plus those unrelated to the new initiative.
- Administrative Costs: These are the costs associated with designing, piloting, implementing, administering and evaluating an HR initiative or ongoing HR activity.
- Direct Costs: These are additional costs incurred as a result of a HR initiative or ongoing activity.

These costs are further divided into personnel, supplies, capital and outside services. Based on their consultancy and research they conclude the following:

1. The true costs associated with a firm's investment in people were not apparent in the budgeting and accounting systems of most HRM departments. Indeed, the HR department budget underestimates the firm's true value of investment in people, because 1) they are not well captured by the accounting system in general, and 2) much investment in people is distributed throughout the firm in the operating budgets of line managers. Most accounting systems are very imprecise in how they allocate costs for investments in people. As a result, nearly 50 per cent investment in people is underestimated in the HR department's budget.
2. The discipline imposed by a movement from considering only investments in the HR function as tracked by the accounting function to thinking about the economic investments in people can be very helpful in the process of cost-benefit analysis.
3. It is possible to determine the firm's true level of people-related investments, but it requires considerable resources. Before embarking on such a project, the firm should have a very good reason for doing so, as the process is very labour intensive.

Conclusion

Both CB analysis and HR Balance Scorecard development are important; indeed, they are complementary. Most firms use them sequentially. However, they are different in their width and their longevity of use. CB analysis is used by decision makers mostly, while Scorecard lays out a theory about how people create value throughout the organization. It is used to monitor the progress of strategy implementation. CB analysis is used for selecting the strategy.

Questions

Q.1. As an HR executive of a large firm, you are required to submit a budget for your department justifying the revenue and capital expenditure requested. Prepare an outline of the same. What difficulties are experienced in preparing such a budget?

Q.2. Carry out a hypothetical CB analysis for starting a management development programme for top management personnel. Assume your own data.

Q.3. How is marginal utility analysis used? Give an example.

Q.4. Why do most firms not carry out CB analysis? How will you select the activities for detailed analysis.

Q.5. What do you understand by investment perspective ? Why is it strategic in nature?

5 Labour Markets and Labour Flexibility

Learning Objectives

- To present competitive theories of labour markets.
- How labour markets operate in practice (concept of unemployment and wage rigidity).
- Analyse labour markets in relation to Human Resources Management.
- Understand the concept of labour flexibility, its evolution in the 1980s and 1990s.
- Learn about a Flexible Firm, different types of labour flexibility and its limits.
- Attitudes of unions and workers.
- Current management approaches to gain flexibility through team work.
- See how both domestic and international labour markets can influence business decisions.
- Understand the trends in workforce diversity for designing effective HR systems.
- Become acquainted with the number of levels at which labour markets can be analysed.
- Learn how labour markets take into account differences in factors such as values, need for achievement, strength of work orientation, individualist versus collectivist orientation and reward preference.

INTRODUCTION

In designing HR systems for competitive advantage, a powerful contextual factor to consider is the market for labour. There is a market for labour that can be distinguished from product and financial markets. Knowledge of the changing characteristics of labour markets influences the strategic decision-making process. For example, a certain strategic option may be ruled out if sufficient talent in key job classes is not available either from within or outside the firm. Often, worker shortage relates directly to labour costs because shortages in a particular labour market tend to drive up wages.

Studying labour-market characteristics goes well beyond studying simple supply and demand. An analysis of a particular labour market also needs to include a look at such things as the knowledge, skill, ability and interest profile of its members. Thus, labour markets can differ with respect to quality, quantity and diversity. Labour markets are somewhat unique, but do not operate much like product and financial markets. The uniqueness is due to the fact that 'people' cannot be bought and sold: they can only be rented for specific periods of time. Further, labour markets tend to be more heavily regulated than their product or financial counterparts. They also resist change and are capable of exerting influence through unionisation.

In view of this rigidity in managing labour, the induction of 'flexibility' in managing them has acquired the utmost importance to achieve a competitive advantage.

Types of Labour Markets

As workers, our chief aim is to earn income to finance our consumption of goods and services. But that income itself carries a cost in the form of leisure that we have to give up in order to earn it. As rational economic maximisers, we will allocate our time between work and leisure in such a way as to maximise the amount of satisfaction we can obtain given our preference as consumers. This combination will be different for different individuals, since some of us may be money-driven, while others may have a high leisure preference.

Employing organisations are also assumed to operate as maximising individuals. This means identifying a level of output and a combination of inputs to produce that which results in the maximisation of total revenues relative to total costs. Private firms operate in two sets of markets: markets for output and markets for inputs, the chief ones being labour and capital.

The theory of competitive markets states that the greater the degree of competition in both sets of markets, the greater is the pressure for cost minimisation. While in output markets, it is possible to raise price, the same is not possible in input markets. However, the efficiency of the latter can be increased.

Competitive Model of Labour Market

The characteristics of perfectly competitive labour markets are as follows:

1. There are a large number of small independent employers competing for labour and also a large number of workers competing for jobs.
2. New firms and new workers can enter the labour market at any time.
3. All jobs in the same market require the same skills, and all workers possess the same level of skills.
4. There are no non-wage benefits attached to any job which might alter their preference for any particular job.
5. Workers are perfectly mobile geographically. There is no advantage in working at any particular place.

6. The only cost to employer in hiring labour is wage. There are no fixed costs to employment that may lead employers to retain existing workers rather than replace them with new ones.
7. There is perfect information with employers about labour and with labour about employers.

In such labour markets, there will be a single, uniform wage in the labour market across all firms. Individual employers and labour have no power to influence the wage. This means that:

- The condition for profit maximisation in the short run is that wage is determined by the marginal product of labour.
- The number of workers employed will vary inversely with the wage. As wages rise; quantity of labour employed will fall.
- The amount of labour offered will vary positively with the wage.
- There should be equilibrium between supply of labour and wages paid by employers.
- There will be no unemployment in such markets.

However, in the long run, organisations can vary the amount of capital they can employ to replace labour by adopting new technologies. Such substitution will take place in response to changes in relative cost of capital against labour. The optimum ratio will be that where the ratio of marginal product to marginal cost for each factor is the same.

LABOUR MARKETS IN PRACTICE

There is unemployment and one reason for it is that there is wage rigidity. Employers should immediately reduce wages as their demand for labour falls. However, rather than adjusting the wage, employers do not immediately reduce wages but first cut back on recruitment, leave vacancies unfilled, cut overtime working, introduce short-time working and ultimately lay off workers. When their demand for labour rises, the initial response is not to raise the wages, but to demand increased overtime, outsource and intensify recruitment. Even in a severe recession, wages do not become flexible. Further when they do move, they move up more readily than down. Thus *wage rigidity* is the main reason for unemployment.

The other assumption that workers with same skills will be paid similar wages by all firms also does not hold in practice. A study of engineering workers undertaken by Nolan & Brown (1983) found that there was a wage differential of more than 50 per cent between the highest and lowest paying firms. Nor do these differences even out over time. Actually who you work for is the most critical variable in your pay.

Where skills are acquired from outside the firm and where wages are decided by external parity by the firm, it is called the external labour market. In practice, many firms develop their own structured internal labour markets by the following measures:

- External recruitment is confined to junior and trainee positions; most other positions are filled by internal promotion and transfer. Current job-holders are thus shielded from external competition.

- Jobs are designed and arranged to provide for career progression paths by gaining experience in lower positions.
- Rates of pay attach to jobs rather than to individual workers, contrary to competitive models.
- Pay structures are rigid and unresponsive to pressure from the external labour market.

Internal labour markets are more developed in large Japanese corporations.

Characteristic features of labour markets are as under:

- It is assumed that all jobs are the same and all workers are the same. This is also not true. In reality, there is not one homogenous labour market but a number of sub-markets for different jobs and occupations. Worker mobility is restricted between sub-markets by differences in skills. This also explains differences in wage rates.
- The size of employing organisations is important as large firms pay higher wages for the same skills than smaller ones. This is because large workplaces are more bureaucratic, impersonal and more productive of stress.
- There is never perfect information available. Workers search for jobs with some minimum in their mind and as soon as they get it they accept it, because there is a cost attached to job search. This also explains why unemployment coexists with unfilled vacancies. Further, workers do not select or reject jobs, firms do it.
- Labour is a quasi-fixed cost. It means that there are some fixed costs associated with employment (capital is all fixed in the short run). These are recruitment, selection, training, loss of output, etc. This means labour turnover is costly to employers. This also means that employers will try to retain workers for some time at least. To achieve this, they adopt deferred benefits like gratuity, pension, avoidance of lay off, seniority pay, etc.
- Government policies and unions exert influence or push wages upwards and government laws prevent hire-and-fire policies.
- Organisational decisions are also important. The market does not consist of many small firms, but of a few large companies. Their pricing, advertising and marketing policies influence the market.
- In the real world, workers can exercise considerable control over their effort. There is a gap in potential and actual performance. This brings in the role of management. Further, in large teams, some will try to reduce their contribution; hence there is a need for supervision. Workers like and need supervision. But supervision is costly and there is a limit to what it can do. Hence the need for individual incentives to workers.

Radical Approach

The radical version of the labour market takes the class nature of society as the starting point. Capitalists are motivated not by the search for efficiency, but by the need to generate surplus profits with which to finance further accumulation of capital. The source of such profits is an exploited workforce which is paid less than the value of what it produces. Workers' resistance to exploitation threatens the accumulation of capital and management attempts to weaken this resistance by adopting new technologies, work organisations and systems for managerial control and dividing the workforce. Also by keeping a pool of cheap labour (through contractors) and by bringing in disciplinary devices. Comparing their lot with contract labour, permanent employees reconcile themselves to the situation. Radical theory also emphasises the role of state in the labour market.

HRM Approaches and Labour Market Conditions

1. Promotion ladders and rigid job descriptions strengthen internal labour market which runs counter to the need for flexibility in deploying labour. Similarly, rigid pay structures also counter flexibility. Provision of incentives, job security and promotion ladders may not eliminate workers' exercising their power and opposing exploitation by resorting to strikes, etc.
2. Decentralisation and performance related pay is an attempt to obtain flexibility in deployment. Team working is also a major step in this direction. Quality control circles also help in gaining flexibility.
3. Selection procedures which emphasise a job applicant's personal values and attitudes as much as technical skills seek to ensure that selected employees are amenable and responsive to the system of incentives and control.
4. Policies aimed at individualising the employee relationship seek to divide the workers internally and weaken collective resistance to management.
5. Policies aimed at restructuring the workforce by reducing the proportion of 'core' workers and expanding the periphery, are attempts to divide and rule.

Flexibility Debate

What is Flexibility?

Flexibility has been discussed in relation to the adaptability of wages, versatility of workers within the production process, ease of engaging and dismissing employees, working-time adjustments, transfers to different locations and, in general, managing labour in response to the changing business environment. This need arises mainly from the following factors:

- Market volatility and uncertainty.
- Acceleration of technological change.
- Intensification of international competition.
- Mergers and acquisitions.
- Liberalisation and privatisation.

Four types of flexibility are desired:

1. Numerical flexibility.
2. Functional flexibility (ability of the firm to adjust and deploy the skills of employees to match task requirements).
3. Distancing, replacing permanent workers with contract labour, casual labour, temporary hands.

4. Pay flexibility: the extent to which pay supports the above three types of flexibility and performance.

The Flexible Firm

To attain flexibility, reorganisation of firms is taking place in which workers are differentiated into 'core' groups and 'peripherals' (Atkinson & Gregory, 1986, p. 13).

The core workers deliver flexibility through training, retraining and re-deployment across tasks. The size and composition of the core will depend on the type of the firm and design of jobs, since they supply firm specific skills. As firms invest in them in training, they are involved in long-term service contracts. This long tenure is also necessary for development of skills and experience which form the basis of flexibility. Policies for gaining their cooperation and commitment are necessary. Hence they are managed with 'soft' HR policies.

Peripheral workers supply numerical flexibility as per variation in production levels. They can be laid off and rehired as required. Again, their size will reflect the nature of skills required. Such skills should be easily available in the external labour markets. They consist of various types as shown in Figure 5.1. Peripheral workers will be exposed more and more to market forces. They act as a buffer between core group and the products' market. The benefits are:

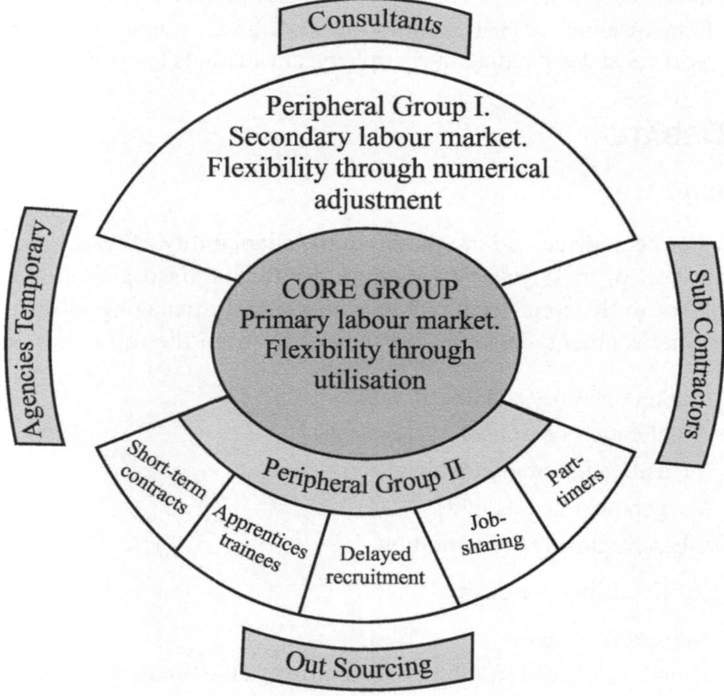

Figure 5.1. The flexible firm
Source: IMS

TABLE 5.1
Hours Worked, Wages and Vacation Days in Germany, France, Britain, Japan and the USA

	Britain	France	Germany	Japan	USA
Average weekly hours worked in manufacturing	38.8	39.0	37.6	41.5	4.0
Average total hourly compensation for production workers (US$)	14.24	17.34	26.23	18.75	15.49
Average annual vacation days	27	25	30	11	12

Source: Benjamin, D. 'Losing its Edge: Germany', *Wall Street Journal* B.1., (1972, July 30).

- Reduced labour cost.
- Savings in cost of carrying extra labour force or from shortage of labour and lost production.
- Increased productivity from core group.
- Helps in divide and rule, more exploitation, and better control from a radical perspective.

This flexible model of a firm suggests that different sets of HR policies are formulated and implemented. Hard HR policies are for peripherals. There are problems in this model. First, on what basis is the division made between core and peripherals? Unions will have a larger say in this matter than managerially defined skill-sets.

The dual set of HR policies at the same workplace will create tension and stress in workers. There are also costs to employing peripherals in terms of quality and productivity and commitment. But this is the trend as the percentage of peripherals is rising in every firm over the years. But there is a limit to flexibility as all workers cannot be at peripherals.

Supporters of flexibility argue that it reduces unemployment and improves the firm's as well as national competitiveness. But radicals see it as exploitation of the poor by the rich. Unions are slowly accepting this concept, though reluctantly. 'Therisim' has helped this to become acceptable in Europe. Even in China, in their SEZ areas, this is being largely practised.

Achieving Working-Time Flexibility

- By adjusting the number and timing of hours worked.
- Overtime.
- Shift working.

- Annual hours. Here employees are contracted to work a given number of hours over 12 months, rather than a specified number of hours per week; hours can be varied from week to week or even from season to season—in accordance with business requirements.
- Flexible working hours—or 'flexitime' employees may vary their daily start and finish times as long as they work total hours agreed upon for an accounting period—usually a month or week. Originally developed in Germany, flexitime helps to balance their personal and work lives. Women are more likely to favour flexitime.
- Part-time is defined as 30 or less hours per week. There is a growing trend for this arrangement.
- Temporary work.

Conclusion

Wage rates and unemployment rates can vary greatly across national boundaries. These indexes can be important factors for companies when making decisions about where to locate new plants and when evaluating the likely financial returns associated with investing in HR system improvement. These rates also can vary greatly within countries over time—at the level of local markets for labour. Something is true about skills availability across different countries and type of work culture that prevails across different societies.

Labour-market information needs to be current and accessible if it is to be of use to decision makers.

Questions and Assignment

Q.1. What are the grounds for arguing that the labour market is different from the markets for capital and goods and services?

Q.2. What are the main labour market issues that HRM seeks to address?

Q.3. What features of their labour market might lead many organisations to decide not to adopt an HRM approach to the management of their workers?

Q.4. Identify the tensions and possible contradictions contained within the concept of flexibility.

Q.5. Explain (a) how labour flexibility is an aim of HRM, and (b) how labour flexibility might conflict with HRM.

Q.6. Imagine you are in a management team setting up a factory or office for the first time in Haryana or any other place of your choice. You are aware that a range of wages and salaries is paid in the local labour market. Decide whether you should pitch your pay-levels at the higher or lower end of the range.

Q.7. Explain the weaknesses and strengths of competitive and radical perspectives on labour markets.

Assignment

A large retail store is planning to set up 500 stores in the NCR region of India. Prepare a detailed report about the nature of the labour market for its employees. Based on this study, suggest to the company about its likely recruitment, compensation and training policies.

CASE

FLEXIBLE FRIENDS

The increasing emphasis on part-time and temporary work has changed the job market beyond recognition. But while this trend has improved the productivity and flexibility of many businesses, it has raised difficult issues for managers.

How do companies find high-calibre staff prepared to work unconventional hours, often for relatively low pay? And how do they combat the widespread perception that these workers, who often have an important role in dealing with customers, are poorly trained and undervalued

Recent research by the Roffey Park Management Institute in Sussex concluded that businesses that are successful at managing part-time and temporary employees have put more efforts into meeting their needs.

The Burton Group, which replaced 1,000 full-time staff with 3,000 part-time jobs in 1993, has responded to recruitment problems by allowing store managers to write contracts to suit individual employees. At one Topshop outlet, a job is shared by a student who works in the vacation and a woman who works during the school term.

Asda, the retail group where 80 per cent of the workforce work part-time, has also felt the need to be more flexible towards part-time workers. Consultations showed that one reason for staff turnover reaching 30 per cent a year was that many wanted a longer working week.

'Employees who work very short hours, below the National Insurance threshold, are very cheap employees', says David Smith, employee relations manager at Asda. 'But we found people were leaving. So we are going against the trend and offering longer hours'. With the help of longer contracts and other measures, such as improved maternity leave, career breaks and the ability to swap shifts, staff turnover fell by 2 percentage points.

The issues concerning flexible workers are nothing new for Oxfordshire County Council where more than two-thirds of the 16,000 strong workforce work part-time. That partly reflects the need to cover round-the-clock services, such as in residential homes and fire fighting, but offering flexible working is also a way to attract professional employees, such as legal staff who might be paid more in the private sector. Valued staff may want time off for childcare, further education and other part-time jobs or may want to continue part-time after taking early retirement.

But much of the debate about flexible working concerns the other end of the spectrum, the poorly paid and lowly valued employees who do not qualify for National Insurance, for employment protection and for statutory benefits. Attention has particularly focused on zero-hour contracts, introduced by companies such as Burger King, in which individuals are only paid when dealing with customers. More than half the part-timers interviewed in a 1995 TUC study said employees regarded them as 'second class staff'.

The tendency to treat flexible workers as poor relations is creating a dilemma for employers, according to Christina Evans, a research associate at Roffey Park Management Institute. 'In many organisations, it is those who work "flexibly" who have the most responsibility for customer service, at peak trading periods. In other words, it is the "flexible" employees who are the ones who have the most impact on sales', she says.

Her research uncovered many positive aspects of flexible working. Companies often commented that part-time workers were more disciplined in their time management and more productive.

Nonetheless, the research highlighted a number of barriers to making the best use of flexible employees. Managers are often unenthusiastic about supervising them since it complicates scheduling and rota arrangements.

The assumptions that part-time employees are less career-minded can be self-fulfilling. Unless companies examine their promotion policies, there may be unintended barriers to the promotion of part-time workers. For example, at First Direct, the telephone banking service, the Roffey Park study noted an assumption that an employee could not be rated 'very good' unless they worked a full shift and were exposed to all the trading activities.

Training is a particularly vexed issue for flexible workers. Most companies would agree that part-time staff need at least as much training as full-time staff; yet few provide that.

The widespread practice of offering flexible workers worse pay, training and conditions than the full-time workforce could backfire, says the Institute of Management. It warns that the current attitude towards flexible workers could 'lead to the development of two-tier work forces—with all the difficulties inherent in managing them'.

More effort is needed to integrate flexible employees into the company's core workforce. 'What is needed is a new approach to managing flexible workers which acknowledges the needs of this group of employees to be valued, included and invested in', she says.

Source: Vanessa Houlder, *Financial Times*, 29 January 1977.

Questions

Q.1. What type of flexibility have employers in the retail sector in Britain sought to achieve through the use of part-time contracts?

Q.2. In what ways has their approach to the use of part-time labour complemented, and come in conflict with their broader business objectives?

Q.3. How might retail employers construct part-time contracts to meet their requirements for flexibility and quality customer service?

6 Changing Workplace and Managing Diversity

Learning Objectives

After studying this chapter you will be able to comprehend:

- The importance of managing diversity at the workplace.
- The concept of diversity and its various dimensions.
- Different organisational approaches in dealing with diversified work groups.
- The legal framework to ensure compliance.
- The model and process of diversity management.
- How organisational mind-set can be changed for effective management of diversity.

INTRODUCTION

Walk into Malik's Bakery in New York and you might think you have entered the United Nations building. In the kitchen are bakers: Hoans from Vietnam, Ideleso Oliver from Cuba, Joe Vigh from Rumania. Workers on the front counters are two women from Germany and the Czech Republic. The popular bakery is owned and operated by Lea Malik, a native of Hungary. Like Malik's Bakery, most companies in the U. S. have a multicultural workforce and most international organisations are becoming highly diversified and multicultural.

Diversity is a challenge that has the potential to be a positive or negative influence on an organization. Ignoring the issue will drain an organization of its most vital resources. In order that diversity is valued and utilised, its knowledge must be combined to change the mind-set and organisational policies and practices. While it is a fact that diversity will become increasingly present, it becomes all the more important to capitalise it as an organisational asset.

Minorities represent over one quarter of the American workforce and this is projected to increase substantially in the future. The Hispanic population is one of the fastest growing groups in the U.S.A. and is replacing African-Americans as the second largest ethnic group. Within the next

50 years, one in four Americans, 14 per cent, will be African-Americans, and 8 per cent will be Asian-Americans. By 2060, non-Hispanic whites will be a minority. Further, women now represent 50 per cent of the paid workforce compared to just 20 per cent a few decades ago. Similarly, the percentage of aged people (above 50 years) is increasing in every country.

There are many other dimensions of diversity existing in organisations. Managers need to understand how the social environment affects an employee's beliefs about work and they must know the communication skills and self esteem in members of diverse work groups.

The Concept of Diversity

We discriminate between people in many aspects of our life and work and this leads to 'stereotyping'. Stereotypings tend to become rigid judgements about others that ignore the specific person and the current situation. Stereotyping can lead to prejudices, which are judgements about others that reinforce beliefs about superiority and inferiority. The dimensions on which people are discriminated are many. They can be classified as primary and secondary as shown in Figure 6.1. The primary categories—gender, ethnicity, race, sexual orientation and mental/physical qualities—represent those factors that are either inborn or exert extra influence on early socialisation. These factors make up the essence of who we are as human beings. They define us to others and others react to us because of them. These factors define us to ourselves. They are an enduring aspect of our personality. Secondary dimensions are those features that we learn or have some control over throughout our lives, such as education, marital status, religion, etc.

Employees are discriminated in many ways, particularly in selection process and promotion, rewards, posting and day-to-day dealings on the basis of the above-mentioned dimensions. Certain forms of discrimination are acceptable but others are not, and have been made unlawful. It is therefore necessary to arrive at some definition of diversity.

In its broadest context, diversity is defined as 'recognising, appreciating, valuing, and utilising the unique talents and contributions of all individuals, regardless of age, career experience, colour, communication style, culture, disability, education level or background, employee status, ethnicity, family status, function, gender, age, language, management style, marital status, physical appearance, race, religion, sexual orientation, thinking style, speed of learning, comprehension, etc.'

Equal Opportunities and Managing Diversity—Approaches

There are always certain groups in any society that are discriminated against unfavourably due to the prejudices and preconceptions of the people with whom they have to deal. These preconceptions are sometimes verbalised, but often not, and the people holding these preconceptions may well be unaware of the way that they see and judge things and people.

However, verbalised or not, these preconceived ideas influence the actions of the people who hold them, and the way they deal with others. The effects of this can be seen in the employment arena where disadvantaged groups like women, people from other racial backgrounds, disabled

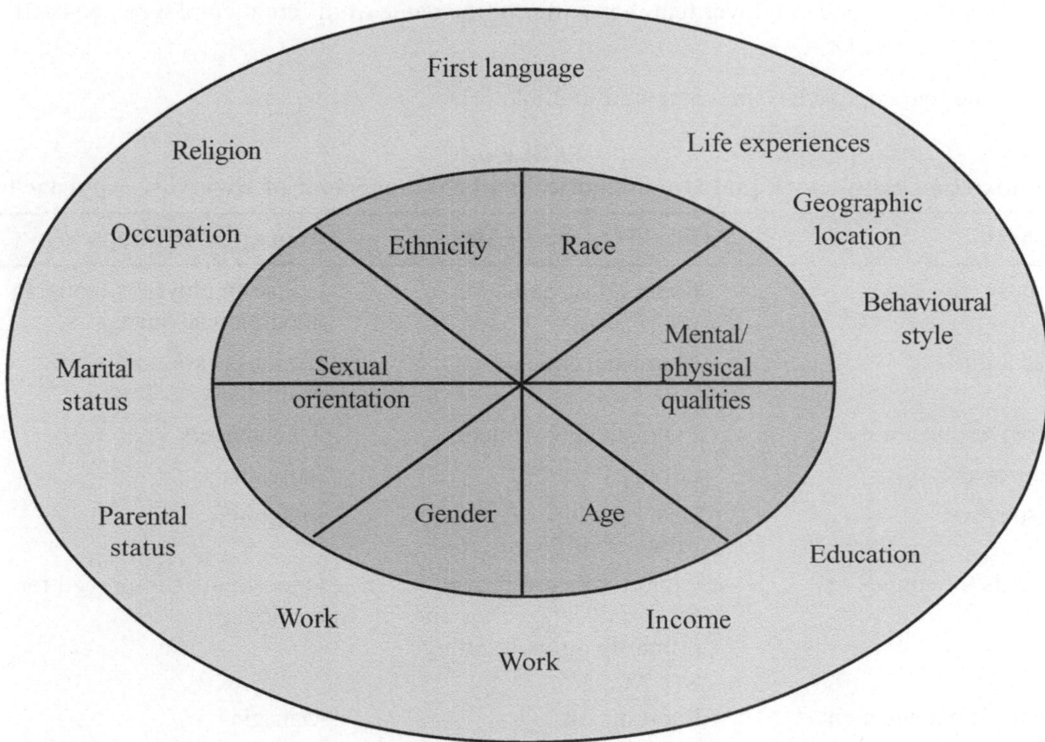

Figure 6.1. The primary and secondary dimensions of diversity

people and older people are discriminated and therefore their rights against discrimination in employment are protected by law in different countries. There is continuing debate concerning the action that should be taken to alleviate the disadvantages that these groups suffer. One school supports legislative action while the other argues that this will not be effective and the only way to fundamental change is to alter the attitudes and preconceptions that are held about these groups. It was hoped that the law will change the attitudes and there was a Year for the Disabled in 1981 and 'Opportunities Year-2000' to encourage employers to increase the quantity and quality of women's participation in the workforce. Hence, two broad approaches emerged, one called 'equal opportunities' and the other 'managing diversity.'

Equal opportunity approaches have sought to influence behaviour through legislation so that discrimination is prevented. It has been characterised by a moral and ethical stance promoting the rights of all members of society. Management of diversity approaches, on the other hand, stresses the economic and business case for equal treatment, offering benefits and advantages for the employer if they invest in ensuring that everyone in the organization is equally valued and given the opportunity to develop their potential and make a maximum contribution. The financial benefits of retaining staff, which might otherwise leave due to lack of career development or the image of the organization as a good employer that may suffer or the value of different employee perspectives, etc. can be stressed.

The two approaches are compared in Table 6.1.

TABLE 6.1
Comparison Between 'Equal Opportunities' and 'Management of Diversity' Approaches

Aspect	Equal Opportunities	Managing Diversity
Purpose	Reduce discrimination	Utilise employee potential to maximum advantage
Case argued	Moral and ethical	Business case—improve profitability
Whole responsibility	Personnel department	All managers
Focuses on	Groups	Individuals
Perspective	Dealing with different needs of different groups	Integrated
Benefits for employees	Opportunities improved for disadvantaged groups, primarily through setting targets	Opportunities improved for employees
Focus on management activity	Recruitment	Managing
Remedies	Changing system and practices	Changing the culture

MANAGING AND VALUING DIVERSITY

A conceptual model of the relationship between quality of opportunity and managing and valuing diversity was developed by LaFasto (1993) as shown in Figure 6.2. Here different types of organisations are termed as 'monolithic', 'plural' and 'multicultural' according to the way they look at and manage diversity. Ellis Sonnefield describes managing diversity as:

> "The challenge of meeting the needs of a culturally diverse workforce and of sensitising the workforce and managers to differences associated with gender, race, age and nationality in an attempt to maximise the potential productivity of all employees".

This brings out three types of organisations:

1. complying type or monolithic ones,
2. managing diversity or plural types, and
3. valuing diversity or multicultural types.

Based on this, LaFasto (1992) has brought out the following conceptual model (Table 6.2):

TABLE 6.2
Differences Between Monolithic, Plural and Multicultural Organisations

Complying Type or Monolithic Organization	Managing Diversity Plural Organization	Valuing Diversity or Multicultural Type
♦ Reacting to the pressure, not to the problem, let alone the opportunity ♦ Compliance and obligation ♦ Keep the law out of our business ♦ Situational ethics ♦ Avoid legal consequences	♦ Diversity is important as a competitive business practice and we are here to run a business ♦ We need to attract the best people ♦ Job stability/continuity is important to success ♦ Turnover costs money	♦ Individual self-esteem is important to performance ♦ People who feel comfortable in their work environment are more likely to feel confident in their ability to contribute ♦ Business, social and moral values are one and the same ♦ Job is part of life and not *vice versa* ♦ The more productive people are those who feel valued for who they are ♦ Productive people = high performance organization

Source: LaFasto (1992). 'Baxter Health Care Corporation'. *Diversity in Human Resource Management,* 31, p. 28. John Wiley and Sons Ltd.

The characteristics of multicultural organisations are:

1. A culture that fosters and values cultural differences.
2. Pluralism as an acculturation process.
3. Full structural integration.
4. Full integration of the informal networks.
5. An absence of institutionalised cultural bias in human resource management systems and practices.
6. A minimum in inter-group conflict due to the proactive management of diversity.

THE CULTURE QUESTION

The roots of discrimination go very deep, and it is culture conditioned. Culture is important in two ways in managing diversity—first, in respect of the whole range of approaches to managing diversity and the way an organization treats its people. Equal opportunity approaches tended to concentrate on behaviour and, to a small extent, on attitudes, whereas managing diversity approaches recognise a need to go beneath this. So changing the culture to one which treats individuals as individuals and supports them in developing their potential is critical, although the difficulties of culture change make this a very difficult task.

Second, depending on the approach to the management of diversity, the culture of various groups within the organization comes into play. Masreliez-Steen (1989) explains how men and women have different perceptions, interpretations of reality, languages and ways of solving problems which, if properly used, can be beneficial to the whole organization, as they are complementary. She described women as having a collectivist culture where they form groups, avoid the spotlight, see rank as unimportant and have few, but close, contacts. Alternatively men have an individualist culture; they form teams, develop a profile, enjoy competition and have many superficial contacts. The result is that men and women behave differently, often fail to understand each other and experience 'culture clash'. However, the difference is about how things are done and not what is achieved. The fact that women have a different culture with different weaknesses and strengths means that they need managing and developing in a different way. They need different forms of support and coaching. A similar argument applies to different ethnic groups and it is generally from this perspective that Jackson *et al.* (1993) propose a series of stages and levels that organisations go through in becoming a multicultural organization.

Level 1, Stage 1: The exclusionary organization

This organization maintains the power of dominant groups in the organization and excludes others.

Level 1, Stage 2: The club

This club still excludes people but in a less explicit way. Some members of minority groups are allowed to join as long as they conform to pre-defined norms.

Level 2, Stage 3: The compliance organization

This organization recognises that there are other perspectives, but doesn't want to do anything to rock the boat. It may actively recruit minority groups at the bottom of the organization and make some token appointments.

Level 2, Stage 4: The affirmative action organization

This organization is committed to eliminating discrimination and encourages employees to examine their attitudes and think differently. There is strong support for the development of new employees from the minority groups.

Level 3, Stage 5: The redefining organization

The redefining organization is not satisfied with being anti-racist and so examines all it does and its culture to see the impact of these on its diverse multicultural work force. It develops and implements policies to distribute power among all groups.

Level 3, Stage 6: The multicultural organization

This organization reflects the contribution and interests of all its diverse members in everything it does and espouses. All members are full participants of the organization and there is recognition of a broader social responsibility—to educate others outside the organization and to have an impact on external stakeholders.

A Process of Managing Diversity

Ross & Schneider (1992) advocate a strategic approach to managing diversity based on their conception of the difference between seeking equal opportunity and managing diversity which is:

- Internally driven, not externally imposed.
- Focused on individuals rather than groups.
- Focused on the total culture of the organization rather than just the systems used.
- The responsibility of all in the organization and not just the personnel function.

Their process involves the following steps:

1. Diagnosis of the current situation in terms of statistics, policy and culture, and looking both at issues and causes.
2. Setting aims that involve the business case for equal opportunities, identifying the critical role of commitment from the top of the organization, and a vision of what the organization would look like if it successfully managed diversity.

   For example, the vision statement of 3M clearly shows the framework of the company to manage diversity. The statement:

   "Valuing uniqueness while respecting difference, maximising individual potential and synergising collective talents and experiences for the growth and success of 3M"
3. Spreading the ownership. This is a critical stage in which awareness needs to be raised, via a process of encouraging people to question their attitudes and preconceptions. Awareness needs to be raised in all employees at all levels, especially managers, and it needs to be clear that diversity is not something owned by the personnel function.
4. Policy development comes after awareness-raising as it enables a contribution to be made from all in the organization—new systems need to be changed via involvement and not through imposition on the unwilling.
5. Managing the transition needs to involve a range of training initiatives. Positive action programmes, specifically designed for minority groups, may be used to help them understand the culture of the organization and acquire essential skills, policy implementation programmes, particularly focusing on selection, appraisal, development and coaching, further awareness training and training to identify cultural diversity and manage different cultures and across different cultures.
6. Managing the programme to sustain momentum. This involves a champion, not necessarily from the personnel function, but someone who continues in his or her previous organization role in addition. Also the continued involvement of senior

managers is important, together with the trade union. Harnessing initiatives that come up through departments and organising support networks for disadvantaged groups are the keys at this stage. Ross & Schneider also recommend measuring achievements in terms of business benefit—better relationships with customers, improvements in productivity and profitability, for example—which need to be communicated to all employees.

It is clear from the above that training for diversity needs to be far more than a one-day event. Experts recommend a series of workshops, which allow time for individuals to think, check their assumptions and reassess between training sessions. Key issues that need tackling in arranging training are ensuring that the facilitator has the appropriate skills; carefully considering the participants mix; deciding whether the training should be voluntary or mandatory; being prepared to cope with any backlash for previously advantaged groups who now feel threatened; and being prepared for the fact that training may reinforce stereotypes. They argue that training has enormous potential benefits, but that there are risks involved.

Organisations have a long way to go before getting to the stage of really valuing diversity and in order for them to continue to strive it is important to reinforce the business advantages. Thompson & DiTomaso (reported by Ellis & Sonnefield, 1994) put it very well:

> "Multicultural management perspective fosters more innovative and creative decision making, satisfying work environments, and better products because all people who have a contribution to make are encouraged to be involved in a meaningful way.... More information, more points of view, more ideas and reservations are better than fewer."

In bringing about this organisational change of mindset, the following framework (Figure 6.2) is useful (source, adopted from 'Cultural Diversity' in *Organisations, Theory, Research and Practices.* San Francisco, U. S. A.: Barrett-Koehler, 1993 (3-10).

Corporate Practices

HP

HP believes that a diverse workforce encourages creativity and innovation. It helps build an exciting, stimulating work environment and provides competitive advantage in the acquisition of new businesses. HP follows the following policies:

- HP has a special committee called Diversity and Inclusion Leadership committee made up of senior business leaders from around the world. The committee meets regularly and reviews HP's progress in the area.
- Regular workshops are organised in order to make the workforce aware of the various policies.
- The best work environment policy gives all employees responsibility for contributing to a positive, productive work environment, free of discrimination, harassment and offensive behaviour.

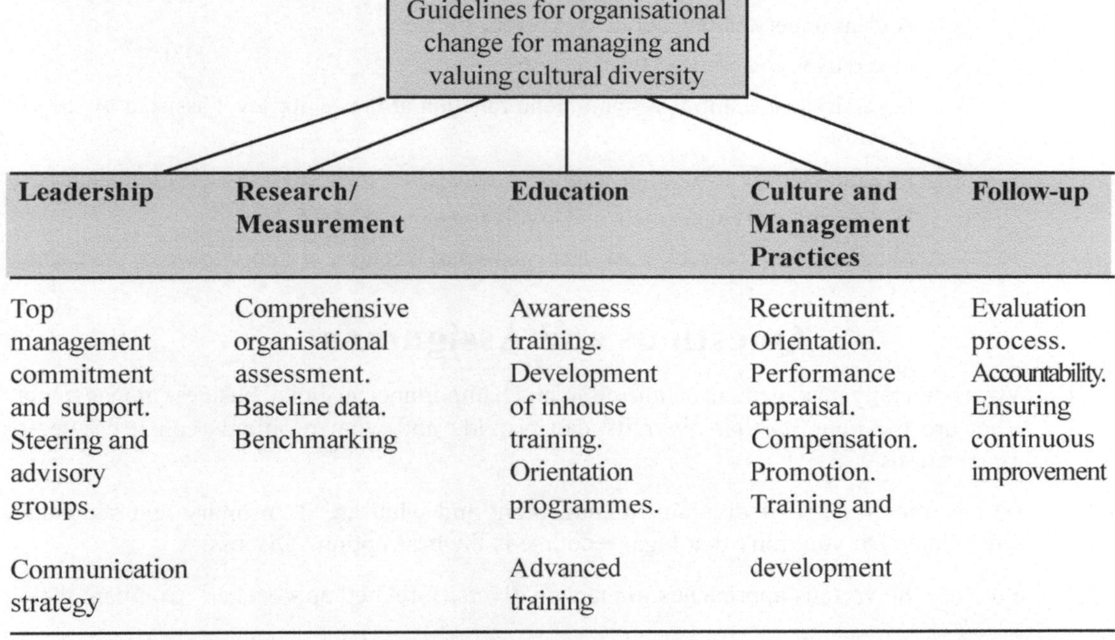

Figure 6.2. Framework for managing change for diversity management

- The equal opportunity policy, states HP, will not discriminate against any employee for employment or promotion because of gender, age, race, ancestry, religion, national origin, physical or mental disability.
- HP encourages employees to report any suspected case of discrimination or harassment, either by using its 'open door' policy or by contacting the Employees Relations Executive. All allegations are investigated promptly and appropriate action is taken.

Deutsche Bank

The bank's annual report informs external stakeholders of the progress and achievements in relation to diversity. A diversity training programme has been developed to provide managers with the necessary tools to build, retain and develop diverse teams which also reinforces the business case for diversity management and encourages managers to be more proactive in creating an inclusive work environment. In addition the bank runs 'managing and working with respect courses' for all employees and managers.

Egon Zehender

This is the world's fifth best HR consultancy organization. It has been a keen associate for managing diversity in various organisations. It considers managing diversity is imperative for longer-term success. An Egon team has recently reviewed some of their practices and found seven key factors for managing diversity effectively, which are as follows:

1. A clear articulation of the business case for diversity.
2. A clear understanding about the current situation.
3. Diversity is championed from the top.
4. Diversity leadership is a stand-alone function at the senior level assisted by the HR function.
5. Programmes are focused on culture change rather than just redressing imbalances.
6. Wide employee engagement and involvement is achieved.
7. Management processes, measuring goals and incentive systems underpin the change.

Questions and Assignment

Q.1. Why is diversity management acquiring so much importance in global business management? What are the benefits that diversity can provide and what problems can it create for organisations.

Q.2. Explain the concept of diversity management and what are its primary and secondary dimensions. Do you think that legal recourse is the best option? Discuss.

Q.3. What are the various approaches to manage diversity-related approaches? Compare them.

Q.4. Explain in detail, with corporate examples, how the organization culture that values diversity at all levels can be changed and sustained.

Q.5. Discuss the process of managing diversity effectively in multinational organisations. What role can HR function play in this?

Assignment

Select any three large companies and research gender discrimination or any other type of discrimination present and suggest how this can be mitigated for better performance.

7 Organization and National Culture

Learning Objectives

After studying this chapter you will learn:

- How to define corporate culture and describe its determining features.
- Understand its impact on the functioning and operation of organizations and people at work.
- Harrison's (1972) typology of organizational cultures prevalent in the various cultural forms.
- The classification of corporate cultures by Trompenaars and Charles.
- Hampden-Turner (1988) on national cultures.
- Understand Professor Dan Denison's work on 'fit' between environment, strategy and culture.
- Understand how national cultural values influence corporate cultures and change management.

INTRODUCTION

Since the industrial revolution, employers have faced a crucial dilemma: on the one hand they had to have tight control over what their staff did and how they did it—to ensure that time, resources, materials are not wasted. On the other hand, they also needed varying degrees of the employee goodwill, creative good sense, responsibilities and commitment of the workforce. Controlling invariably brings in rules, regulations and reporting. No factory can be run by rules and no set of rules can entirely cover all that is required of employees, Efforts to achieve control through rules did not succeed because they were oppressive, intrusive, unpleasant, demanding and risked worker's commitment on which their goodwill and commonsense were dependent.

It is possible to argue that all management philosophies and approaches are nothing but a step in the direction of solving this dilemma—to achieve both control and commitment. Ultimately all solutions fail because they are at two opposite ends.

The only hope to solve this problem is to develop a strong corporate culture, which will generate a high level of commitment and enthusiasm and bring in control through teamwork. This is no doubt a high claim. But a number of studies have established that organization culture is the key to its performance and that it can be changed to ensure that employees are committed and compliant to respond to organisational change.

Defining Organization Culture

Organization culture is very difficult to define. Forehand & Gilmer have defined it as 'a set of characteristics that describe an organization and

(a). that distinguish one organization from another,

(b). that are relatively enduring over a period of time, and

(c). that influence the behaviour of people in an organization'.

Charles Handy (1993) goes further and suggests that cultures are more than just commonly agreed ways of perceiving an organization. He states that 'in organizations, there are deep-set beliefs about the way work should be organized, what authority should be exercised, how people are rewarded and controlled. What are the degrees of formalisation required? How much planning and how far ahead? What combination of initiative and obedience is desired in subordinates? Do work hours matter, or dress or personal eccentricities? Do committees control an individual? Are there rules and procedures or only results? These are all part of the culture in an organization.'

We can also look at some other definitions of culture. 'Organizational culture is the collection of shared (stated or implied) beliefs, values, rituals, stories, myths and specialized language that fosters a feeling of community amongst organizational members (Smirich, 1983). Hofstede (1991) describes corporate culture as the 'psychological assets of an organization, which can be used to predict what will happen to its financial assets in five years time.'

According to Smirich (1993), a strong culture performs five important functions:

1. It gives members a sense of identity.
2. It encourages commitment to the organization's mission.
3. It promotes organizational stability.
4. It influences behaviour by helping individuals to make sense of their surroundings.
5. It expedites organizational processes and ensures controls.

From this, it is clear that organization culture is a major determinant of performance and gives guidelines to employees to understand why others behave in a particular way and how they should behave. It also enables them to interpret and understand organizational activities and processes and happenings.

LIMITATION OF ORGANIZATION STRUCTURE AND IMPORTANCE OF ORGANIZATION CULTURE

The roots of emphasis on culture are several, from empirical research as well as from theory and practice. The recognition of the limitations of organization structure, both formal as well as informal, to act as the social glue or provide a social mechanism for coordination or explain human behaviour at work is quite significant. Empirically, scholars working in the area of organization effectiveness had conducted research to identify its variables and started quantifying a statistical construct of 'climate' by which they meant the profile of values and attitudes which were held in the organization (Payne, Phesysey & Pugh, 1971). In another area, discussion of power and conflict in organizations focused on the extent to which people's beliefs and interests underlie strategic and operational decisions (Abell, 1975). In another area, anthropology had long ago recognized the concept of culture as critical to the understanding of human behaviour. Douglas (1986) placed cultural analysis firmly on the agenda of organizational analysis. Further, it was Western observation of the Japanese 'economic miracle' that stimulated most interest in how culture can be created or changed. It has been argued that the secret of Japanese success lay in a homogeneous national and religious culture, which was reflected in corporate culture. Shared values of dedication, reciprocity, rights and obligations provided a cultural powerhouse as one of the engines of their corporate success.

WHAT DOES ORGANIZATION CULTURE COMPRISE?

Figure 7.1 depicts how culture may be revealed and created in an organization.

Model—First Layer

In the centre of the model there is a core of shared values, beliefs and assumptions and paradigms. The relationship between the values people hold within an organization and the organization's practices, structure, technology and strategy are complex and interactive. A strategy and the values of an organization may be written down, but the underlying assumptions which make up the paradigm are usually evident only in day-to-day conversation or discussions of the people; or may be so taken-for-granted that they can be observed in what people actually do.

Each of the outer rings in the model is the creation of people, the subject of decision-making, the result of action taken or not taken. These actions or inactions are, we assume, to an extent reflective of values; hence the influence from the centre onwards. If there is value diversity within the organization, it is unlikely that everyone's values will be equally represented.

The influence shown in the model is two-way, because each layer, once created has an impact on the way values are subsequently developed. Furthermore, this model represents an incomplete as well as interactive set of influences. In reacting to, and anticipating, events outside the organization, the actions and decisions of its members are not guided by values alone.

There are often significant external environmental influences, which largely dictate internal actions, although of course there is also the possibility of influence coming the other way, from organizations controlling aspects of their environment.

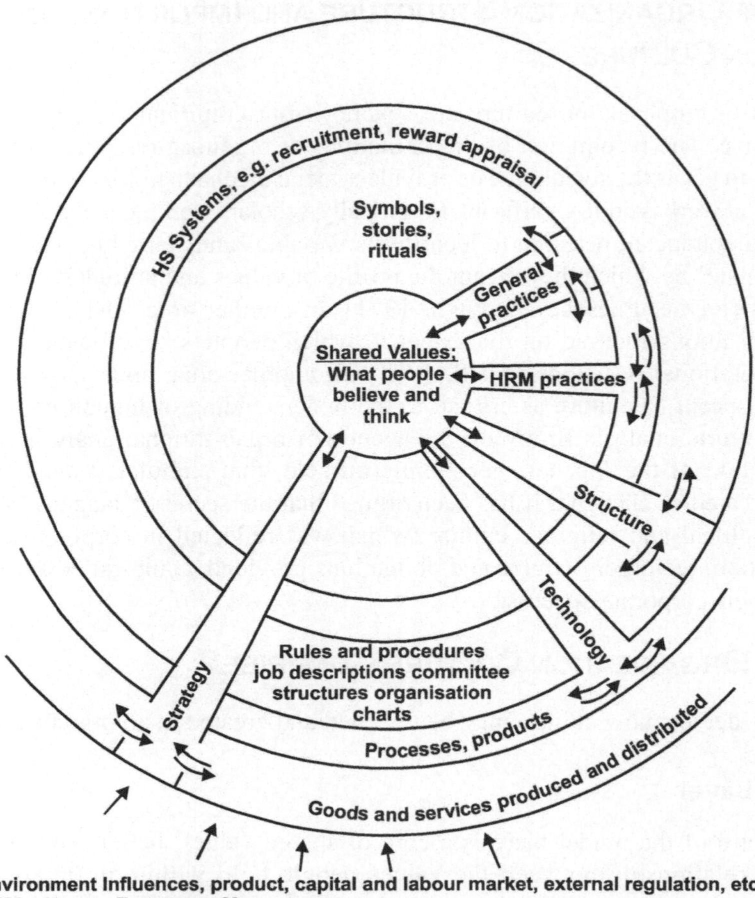

Figure 7.1. A map of the corporate world: how culture may be revealed and created in organisations

Cultural Web—Second Layer—Rituals

An organization's culture is like an 'iceberg', which has both visible and invisible elements. The observable aspects include the physical setting, legends, myths, heroes and heroines, ceremonies, behaviour and dress. The second layer over shared values and beliefs in the model, labelled general practices, includes these visible parts of culture known as the 'Rituals', 'Stories,' 'Language' and 'Symbols' constituting a cultural web.

Values are revealed in these symbols and yet symbols and practices shape values. The search for an appropriate attention-catching logo or signature tune or company song may easily lead to the encapsulation of the value which is either already dominant or else has been selected for serious promotion. The use and development of language reflects values; for example, Garscombke

(1988) shows how, in adopting the language of militarism (for example, defensive strategies, guerrilla marketing and counter-offensive), managers are creating a militaristic culture in their organizations.

The rituals associated with induction, retirement, with the Christmas party, the Annual General Meeting, or the annual cricket match, all reveal things about values as well as being the means by which attempts are made to engineer value changes. The internal and external designs and fittings of buildings, office space and recreation facilities, and the layout design and contents of the annual report are similarly both creatures and creators of corporate values. The following examples illustrate how these rites and ceremonies are used by top managers to reinforce important cultural values.

- In a major bank, election as an officer was seen as the key event in a successful career. A series of activities accompanied every promotion to bank officer, including a special method of notification, taking the new officer to the dining room for the first time, and the new officer buying the drinks on Friday after his or her notification. This is a 'rite of passage'.
- Tupperware sales people hold a weekly rally at which sales people are recognized in reverse order of sales volume. The event is associated with celebration and hoopla. The ceremony reinforces the goal of sales volume held by the company. This is a 'rite of enhancement'.
- An important annual event at McDonald's is the nationwide contest to determine the best hamburger cooking team in the country. The contest encourages all stores to re-examine the details of how they cook their hamburgers. The ceremony is highly visible and communicates to all employees the McDonald's value of hamburger quality. This is a 'rite of renewal.'
- In a major western firm, every Christmas, the chairman comes down from his office on the top floor to walk through every department, shaking hands with each employee. His appearance serves as a ceremony to communicate concern for the organizational family. This is a 'rite of integration.'
- At 3M, top managers keep alive stories that describe innovative projects that were killed by top managements. The hero of the stories worked on a project in secret and eventually proved management wrong by developing a successful new product. These stories are repeated by top managers to enhance the entrepreneurial spirit at 3M and to let employees know that if they feel frustrated and discouraged, they are not the ones to overcome considerable odds in the process of innovation.
- T. J. Watson, Jr., son of the founder of IBM, used the metaphor 'wild ducks' to describe the type of employees needed by IBM. His point was, 'you can make wild ducks tame, but you can never make tame ducks wild ducks again.' Wild ducks symbolized the freedom and opportunity that must be available to avoid taming creative employees at IBM.

HR Practices and Organization Culture—Third Layer

Moving to the next layer shown in the model, the focus shifts to human resource management practices. The operation and contents of the reward system including pay, promotion and fringe benefits, appraisal and performance management, recruitment and selection both reveal and shape values. It is often, here, that disjunctions between practices and values become apparent. On the one hand the company philosophy may talk of treating all employees equally, of placing high value on long service and loyalty, and yet employees may still find separate dining and recreational facilities are maintained for different levels of the firm and that pay and promotions are geared to achievement of short-term performance targets. Similarly, disjunction can occur between expressed values (usually at the top of the organization) and the next layer in the structure. High value may be placed on the maintenance of the internal communication system, the importance of encouraging risk-taking and the development of entrepreneurial flair, and yet procedures for authorising expenditure may remain bureaucratic and stultifying.

Organization Structure and Culture

Organisational structure is likely to reflect the power structure and, again, delineate important relationships and emphasise what is important in the organization. In most companies, there are strong informal networks of individuals and groups, which coalesce around specific issues to promote or resist a particular view.

Charles Handy (1985) a leading writer on organization theory and practices has described the close relationship which often exists between culture and structure. In describing four types of culture, which are covered in detail in this chapter, Handy refers not only to values but also to the shape of the 'host' structure. Thus his 'power' or 'club' culture, with its strong value element of 'watching the boss', is described as a network around a central point. His 'task' culture, with values of 'all hands on deck', is described as an open network without a central point. His 'role' culture, with value placed on following the book/procedures, is described as a pyramid or temple. His 'person' or 'existential' culture, with value placed on human relationships, lacks any focus at all but is a collection of valued individuals or groups. Handy also finds different cultures to be typical of different types of company: for example, he describes how small, family-owned firms and new start-ups have a power culture; how a role culture is most often found in large organizations in stable environments, and the person culture in universities and professional practices of doctors and lawyers. The boundary between history, strategy, structure and culture in this analysis becomes blurred.

Organization Culture and Technology

Moving to the next layer in this model, we can also consider the relationship between values and technology (as evidenced in product and process developments) and strategy (which goods to produce and sell). These decisions and outcomes may well embody and reflect central values, but equally they may reflect values held only by a minority. Indeed they may reflect opportunistic, expedient and thoroughly sensible decisions in terms of achieving strategic objectives, but they may not be in accord with the values.

For example, investments in new process equipment may facilitate lower unit costs and higher quality, and yet require some redundancies. What impact does this have on a cultural change programme, which emphasizes creating a caring family-like atmosphere within the organization?

In this model, culture is shown at the centre of organization analysis. Sometimes culture may be the driving force exerting a major influence on all layers of experience and outcomes. Hence developing an appropriate culture is an essential basis for successful organization development. In other cases, sometimes environment or strategy may be at the centre of the model and culture only operating at the upper layers.

At a general level there is an agreement that culture refers to collection of shared values and common assumptions, which employees may not be even aware of but is reflected in their behaviour, approach and conversation. There is however, less agreement on 'collectivity' and manner and processes by which culture is created or passed on or modalities of change.

Types of Organization Culture (Roger Harrison, 1972)

Power Culture

This type of culture provides excitement and drive for some people and yet is experienced as threatening to others. It depends on a strong leadership from a central power source controlling and manipulating all activities within the organization. This culture functions mainly by subordinates looking to the boss for all decisions and clearances and attitudes of those at the top. In practice, those at the middle and lower levels react quickly to rumours and use the grapevine as the main source of information. Although regulations exist to control and direct behaviour they are not adhered to in practice. Decisions are made largely as a result of political strength rather than logical deduction.

In this type of culture money and status are more highly valued than technical expertise. This has implication for the people who are likely to prosper in such organizations. People strive to get the attention of the boss as all authority flows from him. Members who wish to progress build a network of influential people to increase the information and connections they hold. This culture is usually found in small entrepreneurial organizations and also in companies with bosses of autocratic style.

Role Culture

In this type of culture, great value is placed on functions, job specialization, procedures and rules. Job descriptions, authority relationships and communication procedures are formal and the role of the manager is to coordinate activities between the different functions. Anyone who performs beyond that expected by a particular role is seen to be threatening, and new ideas and creativity are discouraged.

Here everyone sticks to his job-description and role and any unforeseen event is referred higher up. This culture is followed in bureaucratic, mechanistic organizations where the environment is simple and stable. All government and public sector organizations have this type of culture.

Task Culture

This type of culture is job or project oriented; the onus is on getting jobs done rather than prescribing how it should be done.

This type of culture attracts people who prefer to solve new problems. The style of this culture is for people to work in teams on problems or tasks. Great emphasis is placed on the value of group working and individual preferences are sacrificed to ensure the continued life of a team. This culture is adaptable. Unlike the role culture, formal roles and procedures have little meaning and influence, because success is based on expertise, control over an individual's work, easy working relationships and mutual respect for personal competence. The task culture is sensitive to change and adapts quickly to new situations. Control is highly decentralized and exercised by means of allocating projects to group leaders to manage people and resources accordingly. Such cultures are appropriate to organically structured organizations where flexibility and team working are encouraged, that is, where the environment is dynamic and jobs are complex and need high customisation or where speed of action and fast response towards customer or environment is needed.

Person Culture

The primary objective of this culture is to serve the individuals in the group and for this reason the structure, rules, procedures and roles are there only to serve the needs of individual members. Change occurs only to meet their needs and control is exercised by mutual consent of members only. The wishes of professionals are the central focus of this culture. An example of a person culture would be a group of professionals like doctors or members of a voluntary organization. Such cultures will not exist in large organizations except as sub-cultures.

It is clear that, according to Harrison's definition of different cultures, people will show commitment in terms of the extent to which they feel comfortable in a specific culture. To a large extent, people are attracted into a culture, which in some way reflects the values they hold and ways in which they wish to work. Sometimes even when people are comfortable with the role, they may not feel comfortable if the culture does not match their value system.

Strategy and Organization Culture

Strategy and the external environment are big influences on corporate culture. Corporate culture should embody what the organization needs to be effective within its environment. For example, if the organization requires flexibility and responsiveness, the culture should encourage adaptability. The correct relationship between cultural values and beliefs, organizational strategy and the business environment can enhance business performance. Professor Dan Denison conducted a study of culture and effectiveness and proposed that the fit among the strategy, environment and culture is associated with four types of culture, which are described below. These categories are based on two factors:

1. the extent to which the competitive environment requires change or stability, and
2. the extent to which the strategic focus and strength is internal or external.

The four categories associated with these differences are

1. adaptability,
2. mission,
3. involvement, and
4. consistency.

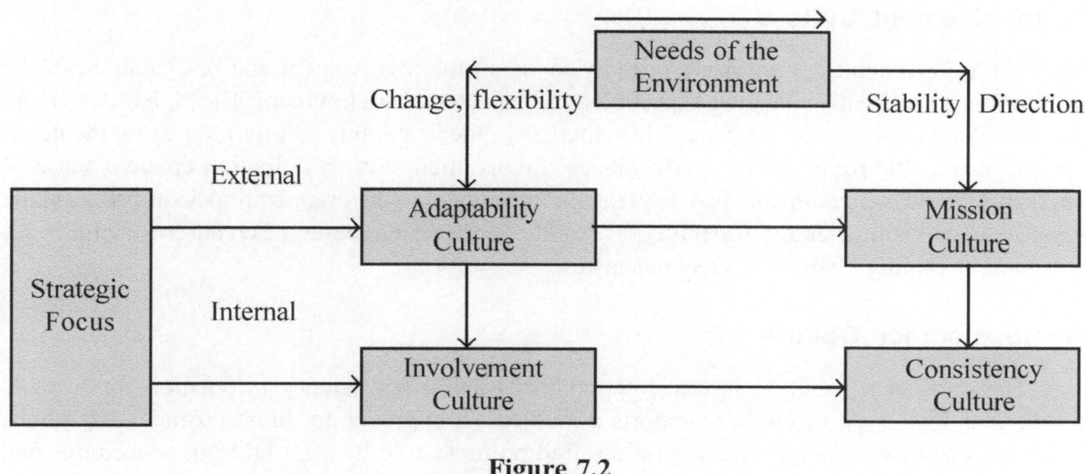

Figure 7.2

Source: Based on Denison, D. R. *Corporate Culture and Organizational Effectiveness*. New York, U.S.A.,John Wiley, 1990.

The Adaptability Culture

The adaptability culture is characterized by strategic focus on the external environment through flexibility and change to meet customer needs. The culture encourages norms and beliefs that support the capacity of the organization to detect, interpret and translate signals from the environment into new behaviour responses. This type of company may need to react to a bid on major new projects and have the capacity to restructure or adopt a new set of behaviours and processes to new tasks. Marketing, electronics and cosmetics companies may use this culture because they must move quickly to satisfy customer needs.

Another example is Detroit Edison which experienced years of predictable growth and suddenly found itself in a decade of rapid change and external demand. The energy crisis, nuclear power and abrupt end of energy demand required a corporate culture that encouraged these demands. The organization had to change its culture.

The Mission Culture

An organization concerned with serving the external environment, but without the need for rapid change, is suited to the mission culture. The 'mission culture' places major importance on a shared vision of organization purpose. The vision provides member's work activities with meaning that goes beyond typically defined jobs and roles. Organization leaders shape behaviour by envisioning a desired future state that is important to everyone.

One example is Medtronics, manufacturer of cardiac pacemakers. Its mission is to contribute to human welfare by application of biomedical engineering. Company employees believe the organization is on a mission to serve people, to make a difference in the medical field. Over the years the environment has changed with respect to government regulation, competition and health care reimbursement, but the organization's mission remains essentially the same.

The Involvement Culture

The involvement culture has a primary focus on the involvement and participation of the organization in the rapidly changing expectations of the external environment. The high involvement culture is like a clan type of structure. More than any other type, this culture focuses on the needs of employees as the route to high performance. Involvement and participation create a sense of responsibility and ownership and hence, greater commitment to the organization. Companies in the fashion and retail industries also use this type of culture because it releases the creativity of employees to respond to rapidly changing consumer tastes.

The Consistency Culture

The consistency culture has an internal focus and a consistency orientation for a stable environment. This type of culture supports a methodical approach to doing business—symbols, heroes and ceremonies, support cooperation, tradition and rule by well laid out procedures and policies to achieve organization goals. Personal involvement is somewhat lower here, but that is outweighed by a high level of consistency, conformity and collaboration among members. This organization succeeds by being highly integrated and efficient.

One example of the 'consistency culture' is Safeco Insurance Company, considered by some as stuffy and regimented. Employees take their coffee breaks at an assigned time and the dress code specifies white shirts and suits for men and no beards. However, employees like this culture. Reliability counts. Extra work is not required. The culture is appropriate for the insurance company, which succeeds because it can be trusted to deliver insurance policies on time and as agreed.

Can Culture be 'Taught' or can it only be 'Caught'?

The 'excellence' literature and much contemporary management consultancy takes the view that it is a key management challenge to create a strong appropriate culture which will facilitate both the development and implementation of a 'winning' strategy. But there is a counter argument which claims that attempts at deliberate cultural creations are, in the long run, doomed to failure. Such a view is based on the assumption that the values people espouse are not open to relatively short-term manipulation. Smircich (1983), Clegg (1990), Turner (1990) and Anthony (1990) are proponents of this approach in which culture is 'caught' and not 'taught'; in which the underlying theme of 'organizational cognition' (Thompson & Wildwsky, 1986) shapes the cognition of individual members of the organizations in what are, to an extent, subconscious processes. Experience is gained and values are formed within the organizational arena. Executive policies and practices have an impact on cultural creations, but their impact is not subject to executive determination.

This perspective has become popular with theorists but as one would expect, from a view which denies deliberate manipulation. Nonetheless one of the reasons for its development has been practitioner concern that attempts to create a Japanese-style situation in organizations in Europe and USA were easier said than done. Even though executives could identify the cultural results they felt were desirable, they have proved very difficult to recreate (Wickens, 1987).

The view of culture as emergent rather than prescribed can most obviously be supported in situations where there is no overarching value consensus, causing sub-cultures (wherein different sets of values and beliefs serve as 'sense making' devices for different groups of workers) to co-exist. In this perspective, values, myths and rituals are not independent artefacts; they are not creatable, but they are generative processes that yield and shape different meanings for different groups. Events, working practices, structures and strategies create the context in which these generative processes grow and develop, but they do not determine them.

The relevance of considering these different perspectives on corporate culture is that each of them has some empirical validity. One can find corporate cultures of Canadian firms, which exactly fit Hofstede's ideas of 'national' imprinting of values. One can find examples of Kanter's 'strong corporate cultures', and one can find examples of diverse and conflicting sub-cultures coexisting in spite of efforts to transform them into a homogeneous culture. Although most organizations have a dominant culture, subcultures may be structured around localized needs of the employees who interact on a daily basis and may have their own heroes and heroines and values. Studies on mergers and acquisitions illustrate the importance of recognizing both subcultures and countercultures (subgroups that strongly resist what the organization stands for). Cultural clashes can and do occur. Understanding the visible and invisible aspects of culture and dominant subgroups in an organization is a first step to managing cultural change effectively.

How Culture Develops and is Transmitted

Change processes are not always of an overt, formal nature: they may also be symbolic in nature. Many of the rituals or rites of organisations are implicitly concerned with effecting or consolidating change. They can be managed proactively: new rituals can be introduced or old rituals are done away with.

Organizational culture, including the invisible elements mentioned earlier, is fostered by a variety of means. Socialization (that is, ways employees learn, adopt and pass on knowledge and culture) is the process by which culture is passed on. Part of the socialization process consists of rites of passage that are designated occasions that reinforce particular values and create a bond among employees and between employees and the organization. Table 7.1 explains such socialization rites, with their roles and examples furnished.

Factors that Influence Organization Culture

Management cannot be conceived of merely in terms of the manipulation of techniques or tools of analysis; it is also about the application of experience built up over years, often within the same organization or industry. This is rooted not only in individual experience, but also in group and organisational experience accumulated over time. These taken-for-granted assumptions, values and beliefs are influenced by several factors, discussed hereunder.

Founders and CEOs

The philosophies, examples and stories about an organization's founder and its CEOs are strong influences on the formation and conditioning of corporate culture. For example, Tisco's

TABLE 7.1

Type of Ritual (Rite)	Role	Example
Rites of Passage	Consolidate and promote social roles and interaction	Induction programmes Training programmes
Rites of Enhancement	Recognise effort benefitting organization Similarly motivate others	Award ceremonies Promotions
Rites of Renewal	Reassures that something is being done Focus attention on issues	Appointment of consultants Project teams
Rites of Integration	Encourage shared communication Reassures rightness of norms	Christmas, New Year and party occasions

culture is very much influenced by the vision and philosophy of Jamshedji Tata (JRD). This is the company where there has been no strike or work stoppage since the last 75 years. Please also see the Case in Chapter 1.

Other examples are Walt Disney's original philosophy which lives on the company's practices and continues to shape its culture: give the people every thing you can give them. Keep the place as clean as you can keep it. Keep it friendly. Make it a fun place to be. Heroes such as Tom Watson at IBM, Ed Land at Polaroid, David Packard at Hewlett-Packard, Lee Iacocca at Chrysler, Bill Gates at Microsoft and Narayanmurthy at Infosys are enduring influences on their company's corporate culture.

National Culture and Organization Culture

Organization culture is shaped not only by technologies and markets, but also by the cultural preferences of leaders and employees. Some international companies have European, Asian, American and Middle Eastern subsidiaries which would be unrecognisable as being the same company except for their logo and reporting procedures.

National culture influences the extent to which leadership, teams and employee activities are socially valued and supported. Studies suggest that directive styles of leadership appear culturally inappropriate in Northern Europe, North America, Australia and New Zeeland. An employee participation programme failed in Russia, perhaps because of the national culture's disbelief and distrust in participation programmes. The cultures of Sweden and Japan strongly support employee involvement in organizational activities.

Trompennars and Charles Hampden-Turner have studied the impact of national culture on organization cultures by distinguishing corporate cultures along two axes: equality—hierarchy and orientation to the person—the task. This gives broadly four types of culture depending on how they think and learn, how they change and how they motivate, reward and resolve conflicts. The four types can be described as follows.

1. The family;
2. The Eiffel Tower;
3. The guided missile; and
4. The incubator.

Each of these types of corporate culture is an 'ideal' type. In practice, the types are mixed or overlaid with one culture dominating (Figure 7.3).

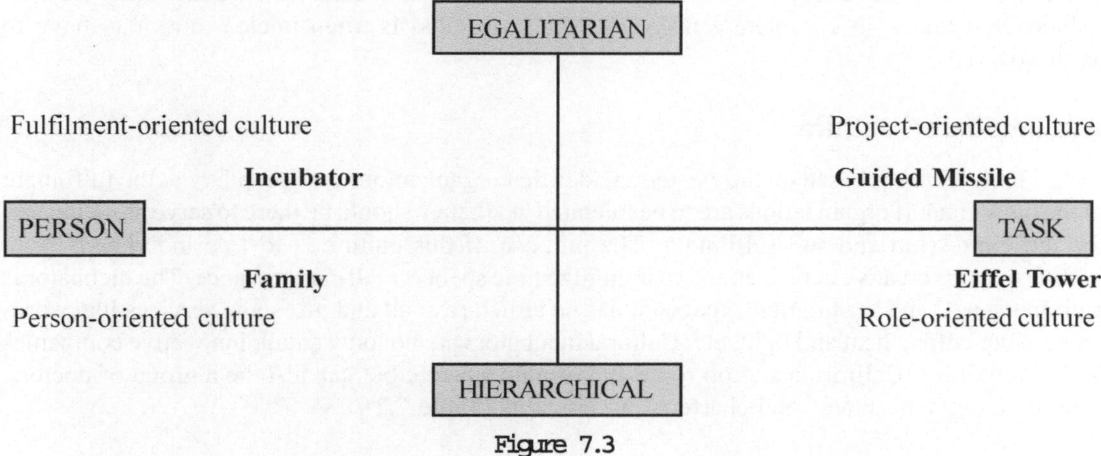

Figure 7.3

The Family Culture

The family culture is one, which is at the same time 'personal', with close face-to-face relationships, and also 'hierarchical' (power-oriented). The main difference is that the leader is not a threatening type but a benevolent one. He is regarded as a caring father who knows better than his subordinates what should be done and what is good for them. The work of the corporation in this type of culture is usually carried forward in an atmosphere that in many respects mimics the home. The Japanese recreate the family type in their corporate culture. The main business virtue is 'amae', a kind of love between persons of different rank, with indulgence shown to the younger and respect reciprocated to the elder. To please your superior is a reward in itself. The main sanction is loss of affection and place in the family. Pressure is moral or social rather than financial or legal. The relationship with the company is long-term and devoted. Many corporations with family-style cultures are from nations like Greece, Italy, Japan, Singapore and South Korea.

The Eiffel Tower Culture

In this culture a bureaucratic division of labour, various roles and functions are prescribed in advance. These allocations are coordinated at the top by the hierarchy. This hierarchy is very different from that of a family. You obey the boss because it is his or her role to instruct you and he has legal authority to tell you what to do. The boss is confined to office only. If you meet the boss on the golf course, you have no obligation to let him play through and he probably would not expect it. Careers are much assisted by professional qualifications. This bureaucracy is depersonalised and tends to a rational-legal system very much prevalent in Austria and Germany.

The Guided Missile Culture

This culture differs from both the family and Eiffel Tower by being egalitarian, but differs also from the family and resembles the Eiffel Tower in being impersonal and task-focused. The guided missile culture is oriented to tasks, typically undertaken by teams or project groups. It differs from the role culture in that the jobs members do are not fixed in advance. They must do 'whatever it takes' to complete a task and what is needed is often unclear and may have to be discovered.

The Incubator Culture

This culture is based on the existential idea that organizations are secondary to the fulfilment of the individual. If organizations are to be tolerated at all, they should be there to serve as incubators for self-expression and self-fulfilment. The purpose of this culture is to free individuals from routine to more creative activities and to minimize time spent on self-maintenance. The incubator is both 'personal' and 'egalitarian'. Indeed it has no structure at all and just some services like word-processing, coffee, heat and light, etc. Cultural incubators are not only small, innovative companies in Silicon Valley, California and on route 128 around Boston, but can also be a group of doctors, legal partners, consultants and chartered accountants (Table 7.2).

Countries and Corporate Culture Fit

Even though the 'pure types' of culture seldom exist, nevertheless in different national cultures one or more of these types clearly dominates the corporate scene researched by the United Nations. The Centre for Intellectual Business with a database of 13,000 respondents from 42 countries and corporates shows very marked distinctions. Figure 7.4 shows the results of this research. It shows the highest scores for guided missile companies in the USA and UK and the highest score for family companies in France and Spain. Sweden scores highest for incubators and Germany for Eiffel Tower. However, in general, smaller companies are likely to take family and incubator form and larger companies needing structure are more likely to take the Eiffel Tower form (Figure 7.4).

Industry Determinants of Organization Culture

Organizational assumptions about an industry's competitive environment, customer requirements and societal expectations also influence a firm's strategies, structure, work processes and its performance and even its survival. Figure 7.5 presents a model of industry-driven culture formation. 'Culture formation is neither a random event nor an action dependent solely on the personalities of founders and current leaders' (Miller). Assumptions regarding the industry

TABLE 7.2
Characteristics of the Four Corporate Structures

Dimensions	Family	Eiffel Tower	Guided Missile	Incubator
Relationship between employees	Diffuse relationships to organic whole is bonded	Specific role in mechanical system of required interactions	Specific tasks in cybernetics system targeted upon shared objectives	Diffuse spontaneous relationships growing out of shared creative process
Attitude to authority	Status is ascribed to parent figures that are close and powerful	Status is ascribed to superior roles that are distant yet powerful	Status is achieved by project group members who contribute to targeted goals	Individuals exemplifying creativity and growth achieve status
Ways of thinking and learning	Intuitive, holistic, lateral and error correcting	Logical, analytical, vertical and rationally efficient	Problem-centred, professional, practical, cross-disciplinary	Process-oriented, creative, ad hoc, inspirational
Attitude to people	Family members	Human resources	Specialists and experts	Co-creators
Ways of changing	Father changes course	Change rules and procedures	Shift aim as target moves	Improvise and attune
Ways of motivating and rewarding	Intrinsic satisfaction in being loved and respected	Promotion to greater position and larger role	Pay or credit for performance and problems solved	Participation in the process of creating new realities
Management	Management subjective	Management by job description	Management by objectives	Management by enthusiasm
Criticism and conflict resolution	Turn the other cheek, save the other's face. Do not lose power game	Criticism is accusation of irrationality unless there are procedures to arbitrate conflict	Constructive, task-related only, then admit error and correct fast	Must improve creative idea, not negate it

Source: Fons Tromenaars & Charles Hampden-Turner, *Riding the Waves of Cultur,*. p. 179. Nicholas Brealy. Pub., 1998.

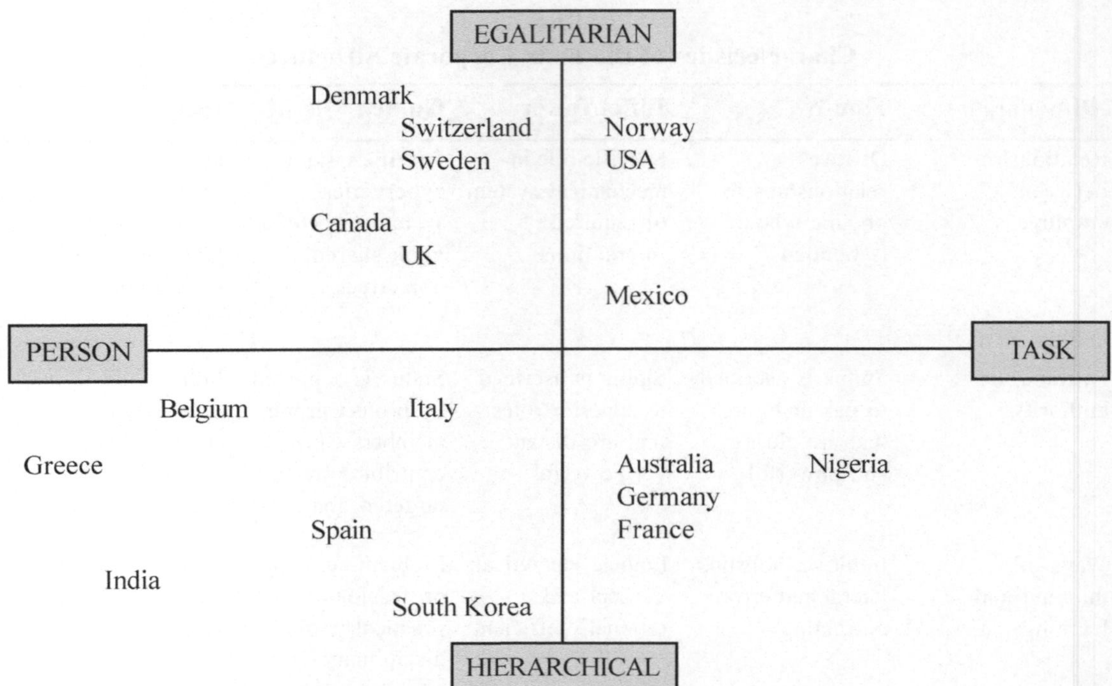

Figure 7.4. National patterns of corporate culture

environment are made and interpreted by an organization's leadership but how the organization responds to customer requirements; competition and societal expectations depend on industry-specific assumptions (Figure 7.5).

Silicon Valley Culture

Silicon Valley project teams are driven by people in their twenties and thirties, close to the knowledge base of recent major university training. The companies in Silicon Valley and companies around Route 128 to Boston take great risks, spend huge budgets and are staffed by young people empowered and at the peak of their early technical competencies. You might also find a dog under the conference table. Even though few senior executives may be more visible, what makes the Valley work is the empowerment of young technical cadres.

As you listen you would sense the group is irreverent towards any existing technology or process. The group's language is both technical and colloquial. There is a high proportion of visual schematics displayed around the room, which seem to be the predominant working 'documents' rather than carefully constructed prose or algorithms. Silicon Valley is a place that thrives on intuitive symbols, which are imprecise, being in a conceptual stage and early development. You will also be impressed by the group's comfort with confrontation. Here is a gathering of youthful, energetic individuals, usually very diverse (in terms of skin colouring, nationality and gender) engaged in intense confronting dialogue with disagreement and differing speculations being

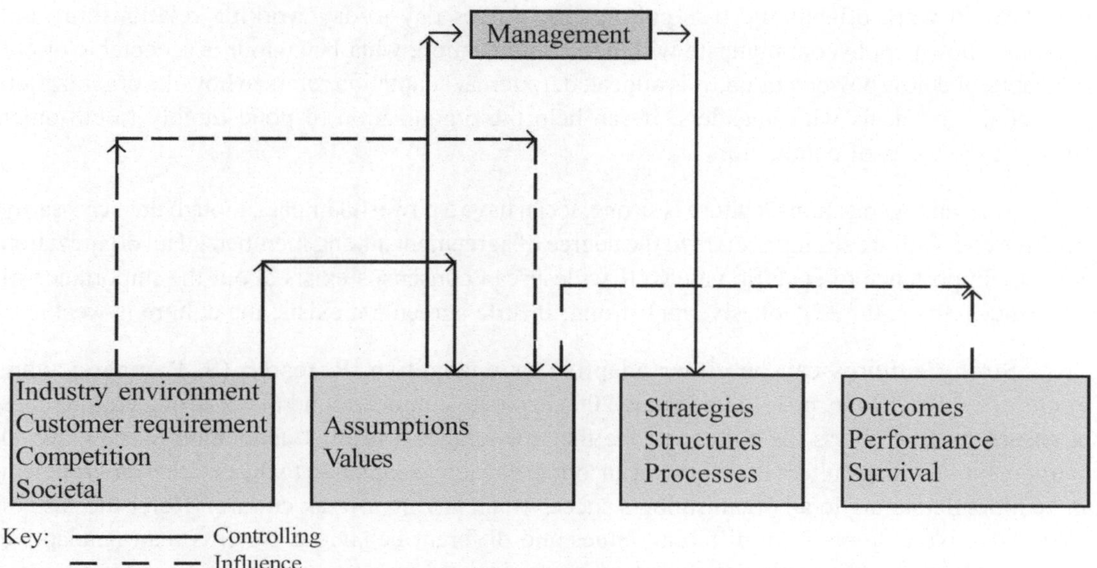

Source: G. Gordon. 'Industry Determinants of Organization Culture'. *Academy of Management Review*, Vol. 16, No. 2 (1991).

Figure 7.5. Industry factors influencing corporate culture

'encouraged' as a humus from which will spring a new approach. And it is always the 'new' that is most reverenced. If an existing approach is seen as efficient and economical, the group searches for ways to incorporate similar features into the 'new' as opposed to sticking with the 'old'.

It is this overriding commitment to change, to incorporating the latest to reaching to new potential designs and approaches, that makes Silicon Valley a special place. The Valley sees itself as the 'incubator' of the future and wealth creating in the Valley is associated with those who obsolete the past, doing so more quickly than their competitors.

Link between Culture and Organizational Performance

The positive correlation between corporate culture and organizational performance is based on the findings that organizational cultures can be assessed, managed, constructed and manipulated in the pursuit of enhanced organizational effectiveness. Employee's norms, beliefs, and values can (and when necessary should) be changed so that they contribute the appropriate behaviour, commit themselves to the organization, support management and its strategy. This view holds that the norms and values shared by members of the organization create consensus, create unity and generate employee commitment.

Organizational culture serves two critically important functions: 1) to integrate members (Meek, 1992) so that they know how to relate to one, and 2) to help the organization to adapt to the external environment. Internal integration means that members develop a collective identity and know how to work effectively. It is culture that guides day-to-day working relationships and determines how people communicate within the organization, what behaviour is acceptable or not acceptable, and how power and status is allocated. External adaptation refers to how the organization meets goals and deals with outsiders. It can help the organization respond rapidly to customer needs or the moves of competitors.

When an organisational culture is strong, it can have a powerful impact, though not necessarily a positive one. Culture strength refers to the degree of agreement among members of an organization about the importance of specific values. If widespread consensus exists about the importance of those values, the culture is cohesive and strong; if little agreement exists, the culture is weak.

Strong cultures can be either adaptive or unadaptive. Research (S. Ramnarayanan, *Organization Behaviour*, p. 338) into some 200 corporate cultures found that a strong culture does not ensure success unless the culture is one that encourages a healthy adaptation to the external environment. A strong culture that does not encourage healthy adaptation to the external environment can be more damaging to an organisation's success than having a weak culture. (Refer the case of IBM). Adaptive cultures have different values and different behaviour patterns than unadaptive cultures. Strong but unadaptive cultures can be detrimental to a company's chances for success. But the adaptive and strong culture is considered 'the managerial formula for success' (Jaggi, 1985). Managers understand the 'elements' that are common in all 'productivity' cultures (Akin & Hopeland, 1986). The 'right' culture may 'reap a return on investment that averages nearly twice as high as those firms with less efficient cultures' (Dennison, 1984). 'Sustained competitive advantage' (Barney, 1986) is expected from the 'right' culture because it is not possible for competitors to imitate it. A strong adaptable culture is described as 'right' (Bleicher, 1983: 495), 'rich' (Deal & Kennedy, 1982: 14), 'healthy, blooming' (Ulirich, 1984: 313), 'consistent' (Hinterhuber, 1986) and 'participatory' (Dennison, 1984; Sackmann, 1990: 119).

Deal & Kennedy (1991: 22) argue, 'since organizational values can powerfully influence what people actually do, we think that values ought to be a matter of great concern to managers. In fact shaping and enhancing values can become the most important job a manager can do. In our work and study we have found that successful companies place a great deal of emphasis on values.' In general, these companies shared three characteristics:

- They stand for something, that is, they have a clear and explicit philosophy about how they aim to conduct their business.
- Management pays a great deal of attention to shaping and fine-tuning these values to conform to the economic and business environment of the company and communicating them to the organization.
- These values are known and shared by all the people who work for the company from the lowliest production worker right through the ranks of senior managers.

Therefore it becomes the primary task of managers to develop a shared system of beliefs and paradigms. Tom Peters (1978: 10), a highly valued management consultant, also supports this new role of the manager.

Strong and Weak Cultures

It is important to clarify here that although various academicians and consultants have identified many common characteristics, there are no 'universal' success factors of corporate culture. Schien stated: 'Do not assume that more or stronger culture is better'. What is better depends on the stage of evolution of the company and its current state of adaptiveness. Instead of implanting a strong culture it is always better to understand and use the strengths of the existing culture. The argument that cultural characteristics, whether imprinted from wider social contexts (as in the case of Japan) or nurtured and developed by management action, can determine or explain corporate performance (or even national economic and industrial performance) would be gross over-simplification. Culture is only one of several human factors associated with corporate performance. Other human factors include staff capability, structure and human resource management practices. Furthermore, there are other factors deriving from technology, market position and national, global, fiscal and economic conditions which profoundly affect performance. The notion, then, that culture and corporate performance are somehow bound together in a one-dimensional way is unrealistic. It is multi-dimensional and culture is one of the several variables influencing, and being influenced by corporate performance.

Nevertheless, researchers have long sought to identify the elements of successful, strong organization cultures and successful cultures are usually defined as strong.

Strong Cultures

Strong cultures have the following elements:

- A strong unifying corporate philosophy and mission;
- Trusted and trusting leaders;
- Open communication channels and access to top management;
- An emphasis on the importance of people and productivity relationships;
- An emphasis on the customer and on service;
- A general sense of accomplishment and belonging by all;
- Commonly shared rites, rituals and ceremonies;
- Uplifting general feelings about employees' work and satisfaction with rewards, performance and efforts; and
- They are also highly ethical in their business ways.

The culture must have a 'fit' with the company's corporate strategy and its external environment.

Cultures that are in Need of Change

Several characteristics of weak cultures that are in need of change can be identified. The managers are more concerned about themselves or some pet projects rather than about customers or employees. The senior members of the organization members are critical of each other and form their own groups and support at the cost of the organization. They do not build on any common understanding about what is important in the organization. The rituals of day-to-day life are either disorganized—that is, everyone 'does his or her own thing'—or are contradictory—'the left hand and the right hand work at cross purposes'. Weak cultures have no clear values or beliefs and cannot agree which are most important. At worst, different parts of the company have fundamentally different beliefs about what constitutes success. Weak cultures also tend to have an inward, short-term focus. Fragmentation, inconsistency and morale problems exist among groups and individuals. Finally, there exist subcultures and clashes flare up occasionally between different groups (Box 7.1).

THE CULTURE-EXCELLENCE APPROACH

A study of the secrets of success of America's 62 excellent large companies by Tom Peters and Waterman (1982) has given rise to much discussion and review both by managers and academicians. Their book *In Search of Excellence: Lessons from America's Best-Run Companys* has become a best selling management book. They studied companies like IBM, Texas Instruments, Hewlett Packard, etc.

The authors argue that there are eight key attributes which organizations need to demonstrate if they are to achieve excellence. They believe that it is the freedom given to managers and to employees to challenge the orthodox and to experiment with different solutions, which distinguishes the excellent companies from the also-rans. This 'autonomy' and 'freedom to challenge the orthodox' and 'empowerment to experiment' is certainly an aspect of strong corporate cultures. Their eight attributes of 'excellence' are as under:

1. A Bias for Action

A preference for doing something—anything—rather than sending an idea through endless cycles of analysis and committee reports.

Bias for action means appropriate and rapid response. One of the methods devised for achieving quick action is 'chunking' which means a problem is first made manageable (that is, broken into chunks) and then tackled by a small group created especially for that purpose. The main reason for the use of such groups, variously called project teams, taskforces or quality circles, is to facilitate organizational fluidity and to encourage action. Key characteristics of these groups are:

- They usually comprise no more than 10 members.
- They are voluntarily constituted.
- The life of the group is usually between three to six months.
- The reporting level and seniority of the membership is appropriate to the importance of the problem to be dealt with.
- The documentation of the group's proceedings is scant and very informal.
- These groups take on a limited set of objectives, which are usually determined, monitored, and reviewed by them.

BOX 7.1
Tandem Computers

At Tandem Computers, Jim Treybig created a culture to fit his vision. At four o' clock every Friday afternoon, employees beer bursts were in full swing at Tandem Computer's offices around the country. Every week, 60 per cent of the company dropped in at beer bursts for an hour, joined by visiting customers and suppliers. Employees at Tandem had neither time clocks nor name tags, but they did have flexible hours, a swimming pool, a volleyball court, and locker room and showers. Despite all the fun, Treybig was serious about his five cardinal points for running a company, which defined the Tandem culture:

1. All people are good.
2. People, workers, management and company are all the same thing.
3. Every single person in a company must understand the essence of the business.
4. Every employee must benefit from the company's success.
5. You must create an environment where all of the above can happen.

Treybig was a hero. He symbolized hard work and concern for people. Without question his culture worked.

Then suddenly, the party at Tandem was over. Growth slowed, profits went flat, and the stock price dropped. The creator of culture had to find a new strategy and change the culture to fit it. At Treybig's behest, Tandem developed a new line of products; even more important, Treybig had to change his style. He symbolized the seriousness of the situation by asking salaried workers to put in 10 per cent overtime without pay, stopped all hiring, froze salary increases and required a vice president's approval for travel. Treybig also became more authoritative and acted no longer like one of the gang. His new style sent signals to tighten up internal controls and focused on getting new products into the market place.

It worked. New products now account for 75 per cent of sales, and administrative procedures are more systematic and suited to a large corporation. Tandem still has the swimming pool and Friday beer bursts to encourage informal communications among people from different departments, as well as other significant elements from the previous culture; but its new culture also fits its new strategy and competitive environment.

Analysis: At Tandem, Jim Treybig used symbols both to create an organization culture and then to change the culture to fit the new environment. Fitting Tandem's culture to its strategy has allowed the company to be extraordinarily successful. The success of Tandem is due to its strong culture, represented by a widely shared philosophy, which stresses its commitment to the importance of the people. This value is 'broadcast by the shirts, bulletin boards and word of mouth'. Another element is the remarkable lack of formal structures, roles and rules which are replaced by their far more effective functional equivalent: unwritten and shared understanding. Tandem seems to maintain a balance between and autonomy and control without relying heavily on centralized or formalized procedures, or rigid status hierarchies.

TABLE 7.3
Adaptive vs. Non-adaptive Corporate Cultures

	Strong-Adaptive Cultures	Unadaptive Cultures
Core Values	Managers care deeply about customers, stockholders and employees. They also strongly value people and processes that can create useful change; for example, leadership initiatives up and down the management hierarchy	Managers care mainly about themselves, their immediate workgroup or some product or technology associated with that group. They value the orderly and risk-reducing management process much higher than leadership initiatives
Common behaviour	Managers pay close attention to all their constituencies, especially customers and initiate change when needed to serve their legitimate interests, even if it entails taking some risk	Managers tend to be somewhat isolated, political and bureaucratic. As a result, they do not change their strategies quickly to adjust to or take advantage of changes in their business environments

- 'Chunking' is just one example, what is intended and encouraged is to innovate and experiment. These companies' philosophy for action is simple: 'Do it, fix it, and try it, by small teams'. Achieving smallness induces manageability and a sense of understanding, and allows a feeling of ownership.

2. Close to Customer

Excellent companies really do get to the customer, while others merely talk about it. The customer dictates product quantity, quality and service. The best organizations are alleged to go to extreme lengths to achieve quality, service and reliability. There is no part of business that is closed to customers. In fact, many of the excellent companies claim to get their best ideas for new products from listening intently and regularly to their customers. Such companies are more driven by their direct orientation to the customers rather than by technology or by a desire to be the low cost producer. They seem to focus more on the revenue-generation side of their services.

3. Autonomy and Entrepreneurship

Perhaps the most important element of excellent companies is their ability to be big and yet to act small at the same time. It means breaking the corporation into companies/units and encouraging them to think independently and competitively. This inculcates an entrepreneurial spirit among the people because autonomy is pushed far down the line. Product champions are allowed to come forward, grow and flourish. The champion is a pragmatist who latches on to someone's idea and doggedly brings something concrete and tangible out of it. Other champions are the executive champion who has earlier been a product champion himself and a Godfather who backs the team and is a role model for other champions. These champions are provided their 'sub-optional divisions', which are independent business units. These are further supported by strong reward systems. Entrepreneurship is further encouraged by 'no-holds barred' communication, which is both informal and supported by physical and material resources. Given this support, the communication between and amongst workers is not only informal and spontaneous but also intense.

4. Productivity through People

It is creating in all employees the awareness that their best efforts are essential and that they will share in the rewards of the company's success. They treat their workers with respect and dignity; they refer to them as partners. This is because people, rather than systems or machines are seen as the primary source of quality and productivity gains. Therefore, there is 'tough-minded respect for the individual and the willingness to train him, to set reasonable and clear expectations for him, and to grant him practical autonomy to step out and contribute directly to his job'. There is closeness and family feeling. The slogans of such companies tend to reflect this view of people: 'respect the individual', 'make people winners', 'let them stand out', 'treat people as adults'.

5. Hands-on, Value-driven

It means that executives keep in touch with the firm's essential business and promote a strong corporate culture. Excellent companies are value-driven; they are clear about what they stand for and take the process of value-shaping seriously. There is an implicit belief that everyone in the organization, from top to bottom, should be driven by the values of the organization. 'These values are almost always stated in qualitative, rather than quantitative, terms. When financial objectives are mentioned, they are always ambitious but never precise. Furthermore, financial and strategic objectives are never stated alone. They are always discussed in the context of the other things the company expects to do well. The idea that profit is a natural by-product of doing something well, and not an end in itself, is almost always universal.'

Implanting these values is a primary responsibility of managers. They set the tone by leading from the front. Coherence and consensus must first be created in senior management by regular meetings, both formal and informal. The outcome of this is that management should speak with one voice. They are passionate in preaching the values of organization. They unleash the excitement, not in their offices but mainly on the shop floor. Inculcating these values, however, is a laborious process and persistence is vital in achieving the desired goals.

6. Stick to the Knitting

This means remaining with the business the company knows best. Acquisition or internal diversification for its own sake is not the choice of excellent companies. But when they do acquire, they do it in experimental fashion by first dipping a 'toe in the water'. If the water does not feel good, they get out fast. Acquisitions are always in fields related to their core competency.

7. Simple Form, Lean Staff

This means few administrative layers, few people at the upper levels, and one structural dimension, either product or function or geography, should have clear primacy.

The core structure remains fixed while work is done through teams, *ad hoc* groups that keep on changing. Such a simple structure requires a small, lean staff at top and middle levels. There are more doers and fewer administrators.

8. Simultaneous Loose-tight Properties

This means fostering a climate where there is a dedication to the central values of the company combined with tolerance for the idiosyncrasies of employees who accept those values. A paradoxical combination of central direction and individual autonomy. It means that they control everything tightly, as well as allow individual innovation and risk-taking. This is possible only by developing a strong organization culture.

Review of Culture-Excellence Perspective

The companies cited by Peters & Waterman (such as RMI, with its emphasis on the value it places on the happiness and smiling faces of its workforce, and McDonald's with its emphasis on 'Quality, Cleanliness and Value') were notable for the consistency they had developed between the values, practices, structures and strategies. However, they only gave 'snapshots' of successful companies, whereas evidence of disjunction between the levels is more likely to emerge from a longitudinal study.

Articles started appearing suggesting that excellent companies were sliding from grace. HP was said to have fallen in the microcomputer and super mini-computer markets, and its ' technology-driven, engineering oriented culture, in which decentralization and innovation were a religion and entrepreneurship was the god, is giving way to a marketing culture and growing centralization'. Hitachi 'was so out of touch with its markets that it failed to realize that its customers were losing interest in video-game players and switching to home computers'. Interestingly, as their success begins to fade, far from emphasizing their 'excellent' attributes they reverted back to more conventional forms of centralized structural response.

Questions have been asked about whether the Peters & Waterman prescriptions could also withstand the voyage across the Atlantic. In a debate reported in the *Financial Times* of 26 November, 1984, between Waterman and De Woot (Belgian Professor from Louvian Institute), De Woot questioned whether European firms were ready to embrace all the elements of excellence. In response, Waterman stressed that he and his co-author had not seen people, innovation, and values as alternatives to structural solutions, but that they were concerned to revive interest in the soft 'Ss' (style, skilled staff, and shared values) on the assumption that the hard 'Ss' (Strategy, Structure and Systems) were already well established as preconditions.

De Woot's six-year study of management at all levels within nine French and Belgian corporates showed that where there is little concept of strategic management, there is no basis for developing a Peters & Waterman scheme.

Not withstanding the criticisms that have been made, there is no doubt that Peters & Waterman have struck a very popular note with practitioners. It is commonplace to hear of companies requiring all their senior executives to read and act on the book.

CORPORATE PERFORMANCE AND JAPANESE MANAGEMENT APPROACH

Reduced to ashes at the end of the Second World War, Japan has now become an industrial power second only to the USA. There are many reasons for its success, but the most important one is its management approach even though there are differences in management of large and small enterprises and treatment of full-time workers and part-time workers and female employees. Hence, some argue that there is no such thing as Japanese Management (Dale, 1986). Nevertheless, a vast majority of observers do seem to agree that it does exist (Pascale & Athoes, 1982; Holden & Burgess, 1994).

The Japanese approach to management broadly revolves round teamwork, quality-consciousness and flexibility (Wickens, 1987). McKenna (1988) believes that the key elements are: lifetime employment, the seniority principle with pay and promotion, and enterprise unionism. Pang & Oliver (1988) also draw attention to training and education, company-based welfare schemes, quality circles and methods of manufacturing, such as just-in-time production. Keys & Miller (1984) point to long-term planning, lifetime employment and collective responsibility. All these factors and more can be separated into two categories: those relating to personnel/industrial issues and those related to business/manufacturing practices.

Personnel Issues

The dedication, commitment and ability of Japanese workers are seen as major factors in the success of Japanese companies. Though much credit for this is given to the culture of Japanese society, especially its Confucian tradition of obedience and loyalty, respect and sacrifice for family, etc., similar levels of motivation have been reproduced in Japanese companies operating in the West (Wickens, 1987), which would imply that other factors are also at work. Chief among these is the crucial role played by personnel policies prevalent in many Japanese enterprises, especially the larger ones. The core of the Japanese approach to personnel comprises a group of practices and policies designed to socialize and bind employees to the organization, and promote their long-term development and commitment. The principles, practices and policies are:

Lifetime Employment

Many employees are recruited straight from school or university, and expect and are expected, to spend the rest of their working lives with the same organization. This 'guarantee', based on mutual obligation, creates an intense sense of loyalty to and dependence on the organization. Akido Morita, founder of Sony used to write a personal letter to every new employee: 'Since you are going to spend most of your life in this company why not make it a happy place to work'. Indeed, Holden & Burgess (1994) observed that while a Japanese worker might survive the loss of his family, the collapse of his employing organization would be unbearable. No wonder that some Japanese workers have died due to extreme hard work without ever complaining and not due to any particular disease. Therefore, lifetime employment gives rise to a stable workforce and stable culture. However, if any worker is fired for any reason, it is difficult for him to find another job.

Internal Labour Markets

Most positions are filled from inside the company, which demonstrates to the employee that satisfactory performance will bring promotion and it eliminates the potential for tension, which can be brought about by the recruitment from outsiders.

Seniority-based Promotion and Reward System

Employees are ranked and rewarded primarily but not exclusively on their length of service, and independent of the precise nature of the job they perform.

Teamwork and Bonding

Although Japanese employees are made to feel part of the organization and see it as some sort of extended family, they are first and foremost a member of a particular workgroup or team. The group is developed as a single entity, which takes collective responsibility for its performance. Japanese companies use a variety of techniques, both at work and social setting, for bonding team members to each other and to the organization.

Enterprise (single company) Unions

Unlike in the West, Japanese companies allow only one union to represent the interests of the workforce. Indeed, they are not trade unions but associations where senior executives at some stage in their career are expected to serve as union officials.

Training and Education

Extensive and continuous training and education form an integral part of Japanese personnel policies. This emphasis on the continual development of employees to enable them to carry out their work better and prepare them for promotion represents a significant investment by Japanese companies in their human capital. Much of the training is done on the job and is always geared to the twin aims of improving organizational performance and individual development. The employees are also encouraged to take responsibility of their own self-development.

Company Welfarism

Many Japanese companies provide a wide range of welfare benefits for their employees. These cover medical treatment, housing, education to children, etc. Some of the large companies are almost mini welfare states in themselves.

Job Rotation

Most employees have to work in different departments like marketing, purchase or production before promotion to senior posts. This makes them appreciate better the demands of other employees and results in better coordination.

Many other practices and policies can be added to this list, but these appear to be at the core.

Business Practices and Work Systems

The Japanese ability to satisfy the customers, and thereby capture markets, by developing and producing products to a higher specification and lower cost than their competitors is staggering. Some of these methods that are used have, quite naturally, Japanese names (such as Houshin Kanri, policy development; Genba Kanri, workshop management; Kaizen, continuous improvement; Kanban, a paperless form of scheduling). Leaving aside the jargon, Japanese business practices and work systems can be characterized by three interrelated elements: long-term planning, timeliness and quality, with the involvement of Japanese workers in decision-making. More details of their manufacturing practices will be available in any textbook on Operations Management.

Review of Japanese Management Approach

It is not the merits of individual practices which has given the Japanese their competitive edge; it is the integrated and mutually supportive way of all the personnel policies combined with hard (strategy, structure and systems) aspects of management that has worked. However, from the Western standpoint, Japanese companies appear to operate very oppressive and authoritarian regimes where workers are more like slaves. Whatever the merits and demerits of the Japanese approach, there is little doubt that it had a very significant impact on corporate performance; consequently attempts are being made to introduce 'Japanisation' into many Western companies (Ackroyd *et al.*, 1988; Hannam, 1993; Pang & Oliver, 1988; Pascale & Athos, 1982; Schonberger, 1982; Turnbull, 1986).

Culture and Ethics

Of the values that make up an organization's culture, ethical values are now considered among the most important. Ethical standards are becoming part of the formal policies and informal cultures of many organizations. Ethics is the code of moral principles and values that govern the behaviour of a person or group with respect to what is right or wrong. Ethical values set standards as to what is good or bad in conduct and decision-making. Ethics is distinct from behaviour governed by law. It goes beyond the law. It does not mean simply following the law. Much behaviour is not codified and managers must be sensitive to emerging norms and values. The notion of 'social responsibility' is an extension of this idea. It refers to management's obligation to make choices and take action so that the organization contributes to the welfare and interest of society (management is an organ of society created to serve its interests—Peter Drucker) as well as to itself. A few examples of need for managerial ethics are as follows.

- The project manager for a consulting project wondered whether some facts should be left out of a report because the marketing executives paying for the report would look bad if the facts were reported.
- A retail store has planted hidden cameras to capture shoplifting and thefts. The cameras also revealed employees criticizing management and making love while on duty. Should it take action against the employees?

These issues are exceedingly difficult to resolve and often represent dilemmas. An ethical dilemma arises when each alternative choice or behaviour seems undesirable. Right or wrong cannot be clearly identified. These choices can be aided by establishing ethical values within the organization as part of the corporate culture.

The standards for ethical or socially responsible conduct are embodied within each employee as well as within each organization itself. The forces that impinge on ethical decisions are shown in Figure 7.6. Organization culture shapes the overall framework of values within the organization.

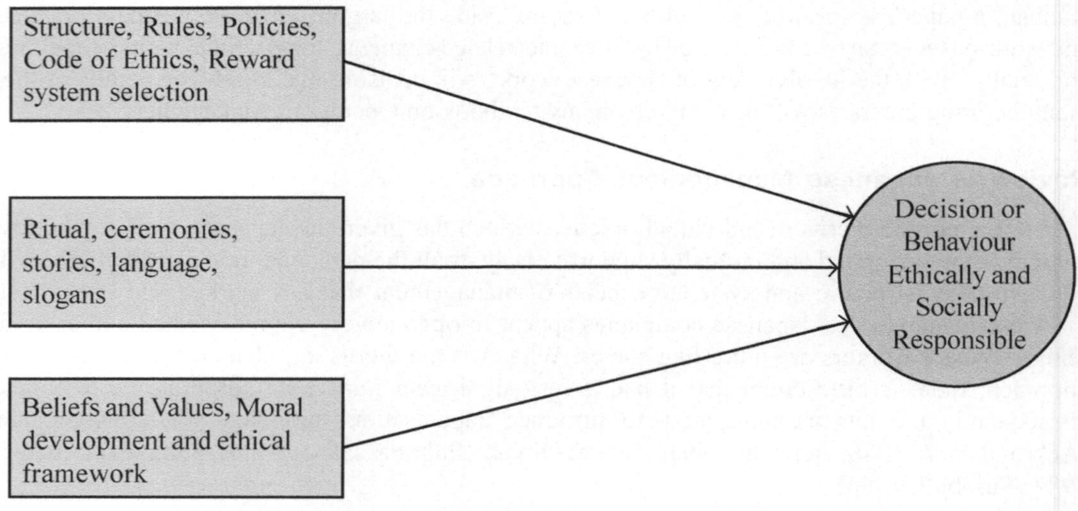

Figure 7.6

Personal Ethics

Every employee brings a set of personal beliefs and values into the workplace, which gets translated into behaviour. The behaviour of individuals is an important aspect of ethical decision-making in organizations. The family backgrounds and spiritual values of managers provide principles by which they carry out business. In addition people go through stages of moral development. The first stage is to obtain rewards and avoid punishment. The second stage is expectations of good behaviour as defined by colleagues and society. Most managers are at this level. At the highest level of development, people develop an internal set of standards and are driven by their conscience. These are self-chosen ethical principles that are more important than external expectations. Only few people reach this high level, which can mean breaking laws if necessary including self-sacrifice to sustain higher moral standards.

The other personal factor is whether the managers have developed an 'ethical framework' that guides their decisions. Utilitarian theory, for example, argues that ethical decisions should be made to generate the greatest benefits for the largest number of people. This framework is quite consistent with business managers when they take disciplinary action against some employees. The personal liberty framework argues that decisions should be made to ensure the greatest possible freedom of choice and liberty for individuals. Liberties include freedom to act on one's conscience, free speech and due process and right to the privacy. The distributive justice framework holds that moral decisions are those that promote equity, fairness and impartiality with respect to the distribution of rewards and the administration of the rules, which are essential for social cooperation.

ORGANIZATION CULTURE AND ETHICS

Rarely can ethical or unethical business practices be attributed entirely to the personal ethics of a single individual. Since business practices reflect the values, attitudes, and behaviour patterns of an organization's culture, ethics is as much an organizational issue as a personal one. Enron is one example and Johnson & Johnson another. Though Johnson & Johnson's handling of the Tylenol-poisoning crisis has sometimes been attributed to the ethical standards of then CEO James Burke, the decision with that crisis actually reflected a shared set of values and guiding principles that have been deeply ingrained throughout the company since its early days. In 1989, Johnson & Johnson won a business ethics award for sustaining ethical decision-making over four decades. Infosys under the leadership of Narayanmurthy has won an award in India for Corporate Governance and Social Responsibility.

ORGANISATIONAL SYSTEMS AND ETHICS

The third category of influence that shapes managerial ethics is formal organizational systems. This includes the basic architecture of the organization such as its policies and rules; whether an explicit code of ethics is available and issued to members; whether organizational rewards, including praise, attention and promotions are linked to ethical behaviour; and whether ethics is a consideration in the selection and training of employees. These formal efforts can reinforce ethical values that exist in the informal culture.

Today more and more companies are establishing formal ethical programmes. HP works hard to familiarize all employees with its high standards for business practice, which cover every thing from conflict of interests to accepting gratitude. HP salespeople are instructed to refrain from commenting on a competitor's character or business practice. At Northup, managers are rated on their ethical behaviour by peers and subordinates through anonymous questionnaires.

HOW LEADERS SHAPE CULTURE AND ETHICS

A report issued by the Business Roundtable, an association of chief executives from 250 large corporations, discussed ethics, policy and practice in 100 companies from the Fortune Five

Hundred list. In the experience of the surveyed companies, the single most important factor in ethical decision-making was the role of top management in providing commitment, leadership and example for ethical values. The CEO and other top managers must be committed to specific values and must give constant leadership in tending and renewing those values.

Values can be communicated in a number of ways—speeches, company publications, policy statements and especially personal actions. Top leaders are responsible for creating and sustaining a culture that emphasizes the importance of ethical behaviour for employees every day. When the CEO engages in unethical practices or fails to take firm and decisive action in response to unethical practices of others, this attitude filters down through the organization. Formal ethics code and training programmes are worthless if leaders do not set and live up to high standards of ethical conduct.

An organization's top manager should keep these guidelines in mind:

1. Pay attention to corporate culture. Understand the underlying values, assumptions and beliefs on which culture is based as well as observable manifestations. Evaluate corporate culture based on rites and ceremonies, stories and heroes, symbols and language.
2. Make sure corporate culture is consistent with strategy and environment. Culture can be shaped to fit the needs of both.
3. Take control of ethical values in the organization. Ethics is not the same as following the law. Ethical decisions are influenced by management's personal background, by the organization's culture and by organizational systems.
4. Act as a leader, for the internal culture and ethical values that are important to the organization. Influence the value system through symbolic leadership, including the use of ceremonies, slogans, symbols and stories. Communicate important values to employees to enhance organizational effectiveness.
5. Use the formal systems of the organization to implement desired cultural and ethical values. These systems include an ethics committee, ethics ombudsperson, disclosure mechanisms and a code of ethics, a mission statement and training in ethical decision-making framework.

Concluding Remarks

Culture captured the imagination and, for a time, appeared to promise the basis for a universally acceptable recipe for success. A closer look at its definition and origin and presumed association with performance, however, shows that conceptually it is so fuzzy that it is unlikely to be able to deliver success in these terms. This is not to say that values and beliefs are not important in analysing organizations, they are often central to our understanding of processes and outcomes in organizations, but they have to be considered within the context of other characteristics.

Questions and Assignment

Q.1. Describe the elements of an organization's culture.

Q.2. What determines the "effectiveness" of an organization's culture?

Q.3. Describe how organizational culture is transmitted. Why has culture become so important?

Q.4. Describe national, regional and industry determinants of culture.

Q.5. Describe different types of organization cultures and their traits.

Q.6. Discuss different types of culture that characterize different nations.

Q.7. From where do managers derive ethical values? Do you think managers use ethical decision frameworks as part of their decision making? Why?

Q.8. Discuss how a strong corporate culture can be negative as well as positive for an organization.

Q.9. Discuss the Peters & Waterman's Culture Excellence Perspective. Can it be universally applied?

Q.10. Discuss the Japanese Management approach. What difficulties do you expect if an Indian organization desires to implement it?

Assignment

Select any organization and identify and analyse the culture of this organization and discuss if it is a strong or weak culture.

CASE

FALCON COMPUTERS

A small group of managers at Falcon Computers met regularly on Wednesday mornings to develop a statement capturing what they considered to be the 'Falcon Culture'. Their discussions were wide-ranging, covering what they thought their firm's culture was, what it should be, and how to create it. Other firms in their environment probably influenced them, since they were located in the Silicon Valley area of California.

Falcon Computers was a new firm; having been created just eight month's earlier. Since the corporation was still in the start-up phase, the managers decided that it would be timely to create and instil the type of culture they thought would be most appropriate for their organization. After several weeks of brainstorming, writing, debating and rewriting, the management group eventually produced a document called 'Falcon Values,' which described the culture of the company as they saw it. The organizational culture statement covered such topics as treatment of customers, relations among work colleagues, preferred style of social communication, the decision-making process, and the nature of the working environment.

Peter Richards read over the Falcon Value statement shortly after he was hired as a software trainer. After observing managerial and employee behaviour at Falcon for a few weeks, he was struck by the wide discrepancy between the values expressed in the document and what he observed as actual practice within the organization. For example, the Falcon Values document contained statements such as this: 'Quality: Attention to detail is our trademark; our goal is to be right for the first time', 'We intend to deliver defect free products and services to our customers on the date promised'. However, Richard had already seen shipping reports showing that a number of defective computers were being shipped to customers. And his personal experience supported his worst fears. When he borrowed four brand new Falcon computers from the shipping room for use in a training class, he found only two of them started up correctly without additional technical work on his part. Another example of the difference between the Falcon Values document and actual practice concerned this statement on communication: 'Managing by personal communication is part of the Falcon way. We value and encourage open, direct, person-to-person communication as part of our daily routine'. Executives bragged about how they arranged their chairs in a circle to show equality and to facilitate open communications whenever they met to discuss the Falcon Values document. Richards had heard the 'open communication' buzzword a lot since coming to Falcon, but he hadn't seen much evidence of such communication. As a matter of fact, all other meetings used a more traditional layout, with top executives at the front of the room. Richards believed that secrecy and communications that followed the formal chain of command characterized the real organizational culture that was developing at Falcon. Even the Falcon Values document, Richards was told, had been created in secret.

Richards soon became disillusioned. He confided in a co-worker one afternoon 'the Falcon Values statement was so at variance with what people saw every day that very few took it seriously'. Employees quickly learned what was truly emphasized in the organization—hierarchy, secrecy and expediency—and focused on those realities instead, ignoring many of the concepts incorporated in the values document. Despite his frustration, Richards stayed with Falcon until it filed for bankruptcy two years later. 'Next time,' he thought to himself as he cleaned out his desk, 'I will pay more attention to what is actually going on, and less to what top management says is true'. Furthermore he thought to himself, 'I guess you just can't create values.'

Questions

Q.1. What is more important? The statements in a corporate culture document or actual management behaviour?

Q.2. Why did Falcon executives act as they did? What type is Falcon culture?

Q.3. Discuss the statement of Richard "I guess you just can't create values". Do you agree or disagree?

Q.4. How can executives go about changing the old values and culture that govern an organization?

Q.5. Why didn't the employees like Richard blow the whistle on Falcon, challenging the inconsistency between values and behaviour?

Part 2

INTEGRATED HR PROCESSES

8 Human Resources Planning

Learning Objectives

- To understand the broad objectives of Human Resource Planning (HRP).
- How HRP integrates and synergizes with other HR processes.
- How HRP can provide sustainable competitive advantage and help in achievement of organizational objectives.
- How HRP can enhance organizational flexibility, diversity and management of change.

INTRODUCTION

Human resource planning is crucial not only for organizational effectiveness but also for the economic development of any nation. At the national level it is necessary for equitable distribution of resources and estimation of developmental growth needs in various sectors and industries in different regions. At this level it encompasses all aspects of human resource development, from population planning, investments required in health, education, housing and so on.

At the organizational level, it constitutes an integral part of corporate strategy. In a services-dominated knowledge economy, people and processes provide the core-competency. Organizations must leverage them to gain sustainable competitive advantage. While processes are relatively static, human resources are dynamic due to continuous replacement and shift in the level of competencies required. Every firm has to ensure that it has the right kind of people at the right time and place. But this requires accurate forecasting and continuous adjustment, which is not an easy task. Further in an era of large-scale rationalizations, redundancies, restructuring, mergers and acquisitions, early retirements, plant closures and globalization of most firms, HRP has acquired new meaning and a different perspective. Focus has also shifted from hard data to soft data and manpower planning has now become human resource planning.

DEFINITION

HRP has been defined by Geisler (1967) as a process of forecasting, developing and controlling human resources in an enterprise. This process helps the enterprise to ensure that it has the right number of people and the right kind of people at the right place at the right time, performing tasks for which they are most effective. Similarly, Wilkstorm (1971) defines it as a process involving; forecasting of future requirements, inventorying the present resources and assessing the extent to which these resources are optimally utilized and also planning of necessary HR programmes

Thus HRP involves five areas of activity:

1. Demand forecasting
2. Supply forecasting
3. Determining HR requirements
4. Action planning
5. Monitoring and control, as shown in the Figure 8.1.

DIFFERENCE BETWEEN HRP AND MANPOWER PLANNING

In the current pursuit of SHRM, many organisations appear to be practising HRP as opposed to Manpower Planning. How are we to understand this change? Is it one which is best described as old wine in new bottles and hence simply a matter of semantic change, or is something more fundamental happening in the process, techniques, ambitions and outcomes of resources planning? This is best described in the words of Bramham (1989).

> "At its most radical human resource planning claims to abandon the 'them and us' attitudes of the past, based on control systems and disciplines, budgets and bureaucracy. Today, the emphasis is all on fairness and flexibility, integrity and development, creativity and commitment. The organisations are taking a longer view and valuing softer aspects of human personality including issues like dual career and burnout including development of a class of international managers or expatriates."

At this stage, it is probably easier to recognise that empirically it is a mixed picture with some organisations claiming to be fundamentally charging the way they plan, develop and regulate human resources, while for others it appears that a simple name change has taken place.

HRP attempts a more strategic planning of employees by getting involved in deciding the corporate and Board level strategy, like new product, market ambitions, growth and diversification, merger and restructuring plans rather than inform the manpower planners to 'pick up' the pieces and alter the employee resource patterns accordingly (tactical level).

HRP attempts more radically to address the individual needs for progression and change as well as fostering quality, commitment and productivity in the workforce.

ISSUES THAT CORPORATES SHOULD PONDER AND DECIDE

Every organization has to seriously examine the following issues and reach an understanding at the highest level for designing and utilising an effective HRP system. These issues are:

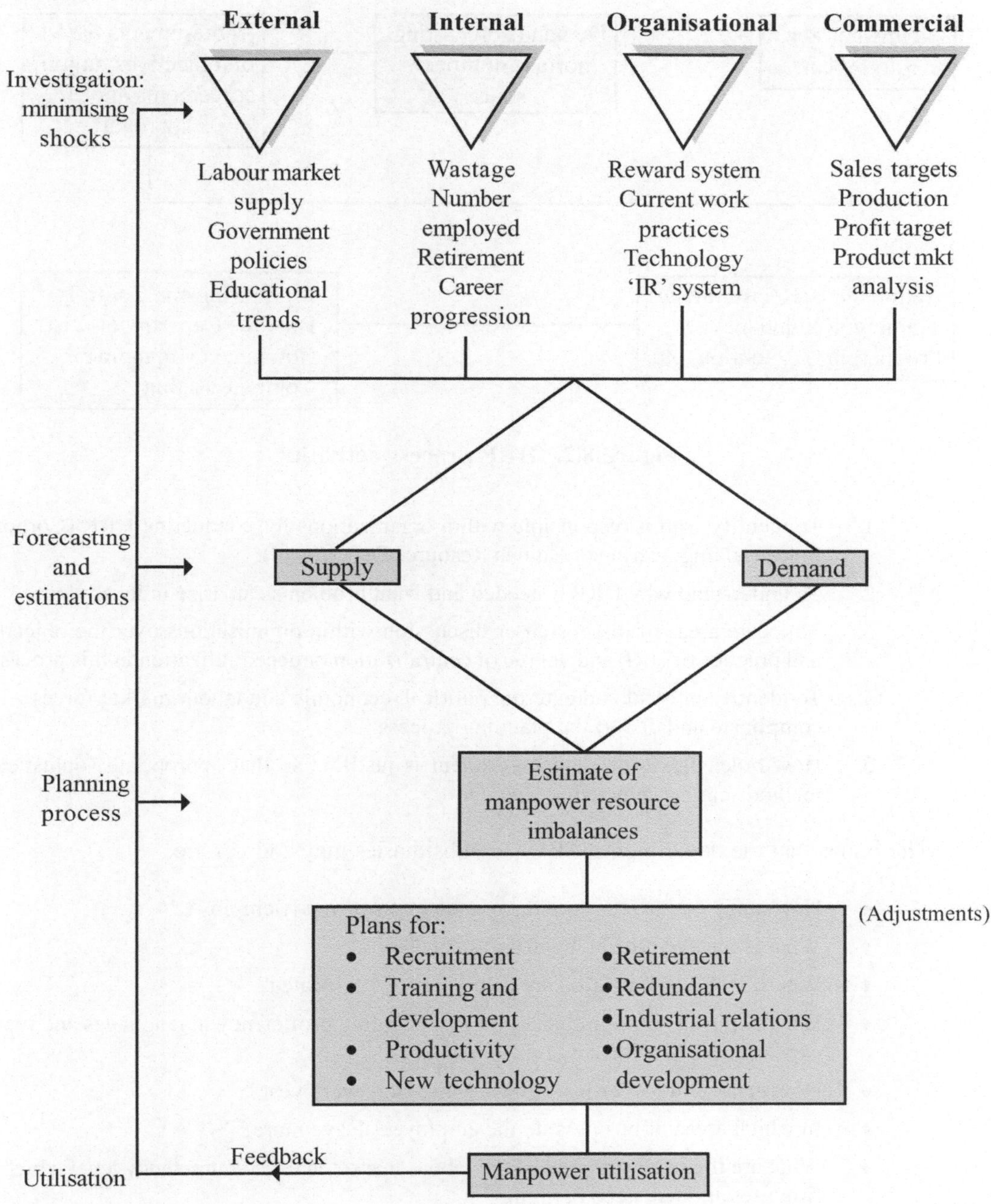

Figure 8.1. A typical manpower planning Process

(Adapted from Bramham, 1989).

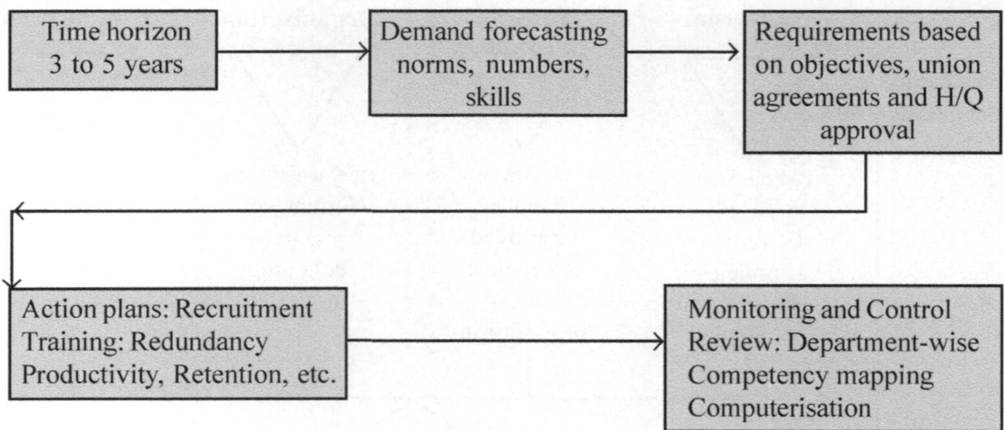

Figure 8.2. HRP process activities

1. To identify who is responsible within organizations for conducting HRP. (Corporate Industrial Engineering or Human Resource Department).
2. To understand why HRP is needed and what problems can arise in its absence.
3. To locate areas of dissension or discussion within organisations over the objectives and practice of HRP and degree of centralization or decentralization in this process.
4. To identify internal and external political, economic and labour market forces which complicate and distort the planning process.
5. How much flexibility and investment is justified so that appropriate sophisticated methods can be selected.

The issues that the departments, SBUs or subsidiaries may address are:

- How many employees does the organization currently employ?
- What is the age profile, by departments?
- Where in the organization are these employees located?
- What skills do our employees possess including proficiency in languages and type of experience in previous organizations?
- How many employees leave the organization every year?
- In which areas of business do the employees leave more?
- What are the characteristics of the labour market in each competency level which the firm uses and will need in future?

In sum, there are both quantifiable and qualitative dimensions in the successful planning and management of human resources requiring careful coordination between corporate and unit levels as well as between the 'external' product and labour markets and the 'internal' organization of processes.

CONFLICTS THAT NEED RESOLUTION

There are several points that need to be decided at the organization level. Firstly where in the organization should responsibility for HRP be vested? At the corporate headquarters or at divisional/ unit level? The trend today is that the headquarters may decide controlling parameters or standards of performance and productivity norms.

Based on these and the nature of demand foreseen, units project and decide their own plan. The production function is playing an increasingly active role in sharing this responsibility. Next, the most critical issue relates to outsourcing of various services and procurement of parts and components from outside vendors. The corporate strategic plan addresses this issue.

Next, a decision is required about proportion of employees to be engaged as temporary hands, trainees, part-timers, consultants or in permanent positions.

This composition is an evolutionary process for the firm and is closely related with the nature of environment which the industry is facing. It can be simple and static or complex (many factors affect it) and dynamic. The product-life-cycle stage of the product also has an influence on the decision.

In the growth stage, a firm would tend to increase permanent resources and in others it should favour the non-permanent ones, unless union pressures and governmental laws restrict it. Hence these pressures and other political and economic forces need to be assessed.

Again, there are competing demands; ambitions and values of employees and top-management need to be reconciled. For example:

- Employee demands for wages over and above what employers are prepared to offer.
- Employee demands for terms and conditions of employment which expect greater rewards than employers are prepared to offer, like:
    - shorter working week
    - increased holiday allowances
    - increased overtime rates or refusal to work overtime
    - job enrichment and job rotation
    - Employee/managerial demands for more promotion and career advancement.

At times the employers are not prepared, or are not in a financial position to meet these demands. Equally, employers may also demand increased productivity, restructuring and upgradation of technology or increased use of short-term contract staff. All these factors require consideration and answers for realistic HR planning. Organisational vision, mission and values become important for this purpose. If the organization believes in a pluralistic approach, then a dialogue with unions and employee representatives is necessary to evolve win-win solutions. This means that long-term adjustments will be made for redundancies, restructuring, mergers and technology changes. On the other hand, a unitary approach means that the firm's HR planning is geared to meet shocks and disturbances by providing for reserves and flexibility and short-term adjustments through outsourcing or overtime payments.

Employee Turnover Analysis

It is necessary to estimate overall employee turnover ratio and also their department-wise, category-wise, age-wise and skill-wise presence, because it is necessary to understand which trade, age or department is more vulnerable to employee turnover. This is done as follows:

$$\frac{\text{Number leaving in one year}}{\text{Average number of employees}} \times 100 = \times \%$$

An alternative to the employee turnover ratio is the Labour Stability Index (Bowey, 1974).

$$\frac{\text{Number of employees with more than one year's service}}{\text{Number of employees employed one year ago}} \times 100 = \times \%$$

This calculation lays emphasis on those who stay and hence is known as the stability index. Its significance can be seen by the following example from two companies' data.

- Company X employs 2,000 in January and from which 800 have voluntarily left that year. This gives a turnover of 800/2000 × 100 = 40% and stability index 60%.
- Company Y also employs 2,000 in January, but only 100 have left voluntarily, although they have been replaced eight times that year. This also gives a turnover ratio of 40% but the Stability Ratio or Index is 95 per cent, which is an impressive figure and calls for a different solution in planning.

Further from Figure 8.3 it is possible to identify three distinct phases in employee turnover. The first is within one year, known as 'induction crises'. During this time the relationship between employee and organization is not settled. He is also subjected to stress of organizational rules, discipline and demands. No doubt, absenteeism from work and accident rate is also high. This turnover could be as high as 40 per cent unless managed through socialization and training. The next phase comes, around the third year or so. This is career related when the employee does not see career prospects in the firm or finds better prospects outside. This highlights the importance of career planning in the firm, which should also go along with HR planning. The third phase comes around the age of 50, when the employee can not rise further for a variety of reasons.

Hence, proper analysis through statistical records of turnover rates in various age groups, trades, departments along with stability analysis, taking into account other variables like absenteeism rate, sickness rate, accidents, training durations, projected retirements and so on are necessary for proper HR planning.

Productivity

Today, firms are competing on the basis of quality, cost or service to the customer. In this regard, productivity plays a central role. Therefore, it is necessary for HR planning to estimate current productivity norms and likely productivity in the planning years. This again requires employee

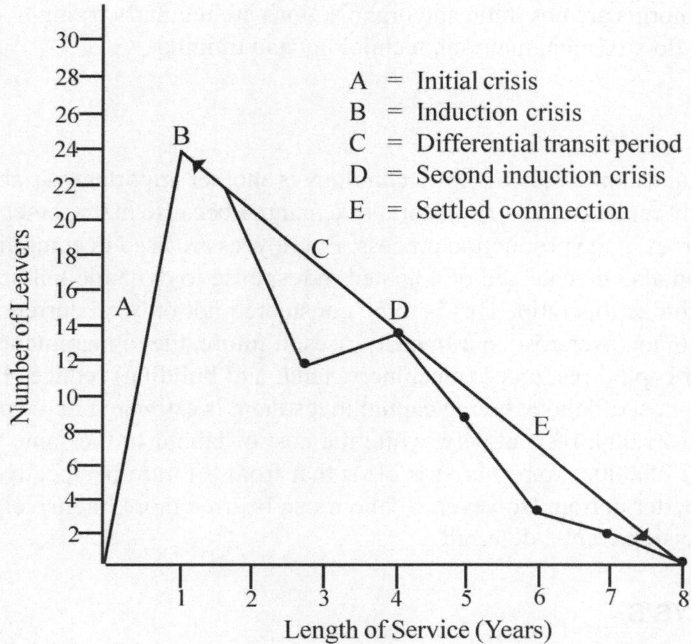

Figure 8.3. Frequency of distribution leavers by length of service

participation and a pluralistic approach. Productivity and capacity utilization are key variables in HR planning. Every organization is trying to be lean and efficient. But productivity norms and available production hours differ widely across industries and countries, as shown in Table 8.1.

TABLE 8.1
Labour Productivity (tonnes per man-year)

Italy	435	
US	429	• It takes two workers to process 100 kg yarn in Indonesia
Belgium	389	
Japan	351	• It takes three workers to process the same yarn in Thailand and Philippines
UK	346	
Spain	328	• It takes seven workers to process the same yarn in India
Germany	316	
France	247	
Brazil	142	
India	50	

Source: N. Kaushal & S. Ghosh, 'Axing 4 Million Jobs', *Business Today*.

Productivity norms are not static and organisations are regularly trying to enhance the same by rationalising the flow of men, material, technology and training.

Technology

Introduction and application of new technology is another important variable. Employees do not have to be simply replaced in some quantitative manner because management does not rely on the employee resources in the production process. Employees are used in combination with capital resources, which can also be changed or adjusted in response to dynamic market pressure. Every firm wants it to optimize this ratio. This is to be considered not only on current costs but also on future costs. While manpower cost continuously rises in future due to increments, salary revision, DA, etc. the cost of capital resources (machinery, land, and building) reduces progressively. For example, the annual cost of labour saving capital investment is estimated in the next 3 years as Rs. 22,000, 21,800, and 21,000, respectively, while the cost of labour in the same years may be Rs. 21,000, 21,500, and 25,000. From this, it is clear that from a future perspective, replacement of labour may be the better option. However, if labour can be used more intensively or productively, the replacement decision can be deferred.

Markov Analysis

The Markov model helps in the analysis of internal factors, which need to be considered in the development of manpower plans. It attempts to model the flow of individuals within the organization; based on the assumption that wastage pattern can be predicted according to length of service and can be judged early on in an individual's career. Once survival rates have been calculated, and barring no future shocks, a fairly stable pattern of progression and replacement needs over time can be calculated for both wastages and promotions. From this a planner can predict the probability and the likely time span of the individual progressing from one grade to another further up the hierarchy. This provides valuable data for the recruitment and selection process and for training needs so that the firm does not suffer from supply shortages. For this, career histories of individuals need to be maintained and used for analysis of movement probabilities. Both Eaton Corporation and Weyerhaeuser have used Markov analysis successfully for manpower planning, as shown in Table 8.2. However, external factors, like labour market, business objectives, competitive position and environmental changes, must also be factored in to be effective.

Business Objectives and Corporate Strategy

This has the most important influence on HRP. A business may be expanding or contracting in response to product-market pressures. If an organization is experiencing rapid market growth as it launches a new innovative product, the requirement of new staff will increase substantially. In the short run, the organization can adjust to shortages by making some adjustments to supply within the organization itself. The most obvious ways in which an organization adjusts its manpower in response to increasing demand are to increase the use of overtime, to temporarily extend the working hours or to use temporary workers. These measures have their cost and quality impact on business. Hence, if manpower planning is integrated with product planning, it would provide time

TABLE 8.2
Markov Analysis at Progressive Tools

Category of Workers	Staffing Levels	Assembler	Mechanist	Foreman	Supervisor	Exit
Assembler-A	Probabilities	0.70	0.10			0.20
Mechanist-M	of remaining	0.05	0.80	0.10		0.05
Foreman-F	in position		0.10	0.75	0.05	0.10
Supervisor-S				0.05	0.90	0.05
Assemblers-A	250	175	25			50
Machinists-M	120	6	96	12		6
Foremen-F	40		4	30	2	4
Supervisors-S	20			1	13	1
*Forecasted supply		181	125	43	20	61

* The upper part of Markov table shows probabilities of remaining on same post and for promotions and exits. In the lower part, the numbers have been worked out by multiplying with staffing level at the begining of the year giving the forecasted numbers at the end of the year.

for HR function to make the adjustment more effectively, avoiding the delays in order fulfilment, customer dissatisfaction and overtime costs. Similarly, if an organization is contracting or restructuring into new business areas there may be need to temporarily reduce the number of staff in old business areas. It may be that retraining and relocation packages are insufficient to resource the new plant or project and there will be need for downsizing in one area of business and expanding in the new business area which may need a different set of competencies.

This is the case currently with Indian public sector banks, which are surplus in old routine clerical staff but short in new technology-based processes and investment banking expertise. This shows the importance of integrating business objectives and corporate strategy with HRP.

Industrial Relations and Labour Statutes

The restrictions imposed by labour policies and statutes of respective governments need to be complied with. There are provisions regarding layoffs, terminations, working hours and leave and holidays and so on. There are guidelines for expatriate appointments and Board level positions. Anti-discriminatory laws in employment and promotion are also gaining ground, including provisions for employment of handicapped and 'sons of the soil' at lower levels.

The pressure exerted by unions for filling up vacancies, making temporary workers permanent and following agreed policies for internal promotions, also has to be built into HRP.

Managing Dynamics and Change

The essence of good HRP is to use it to manage shocks and disturbances within the employment pattern due to resignations, retirements and career-related movements, employee sickness, accidents and unauthorized long absence including study and maternity leaves. These flows are shown in Figure 8.4.

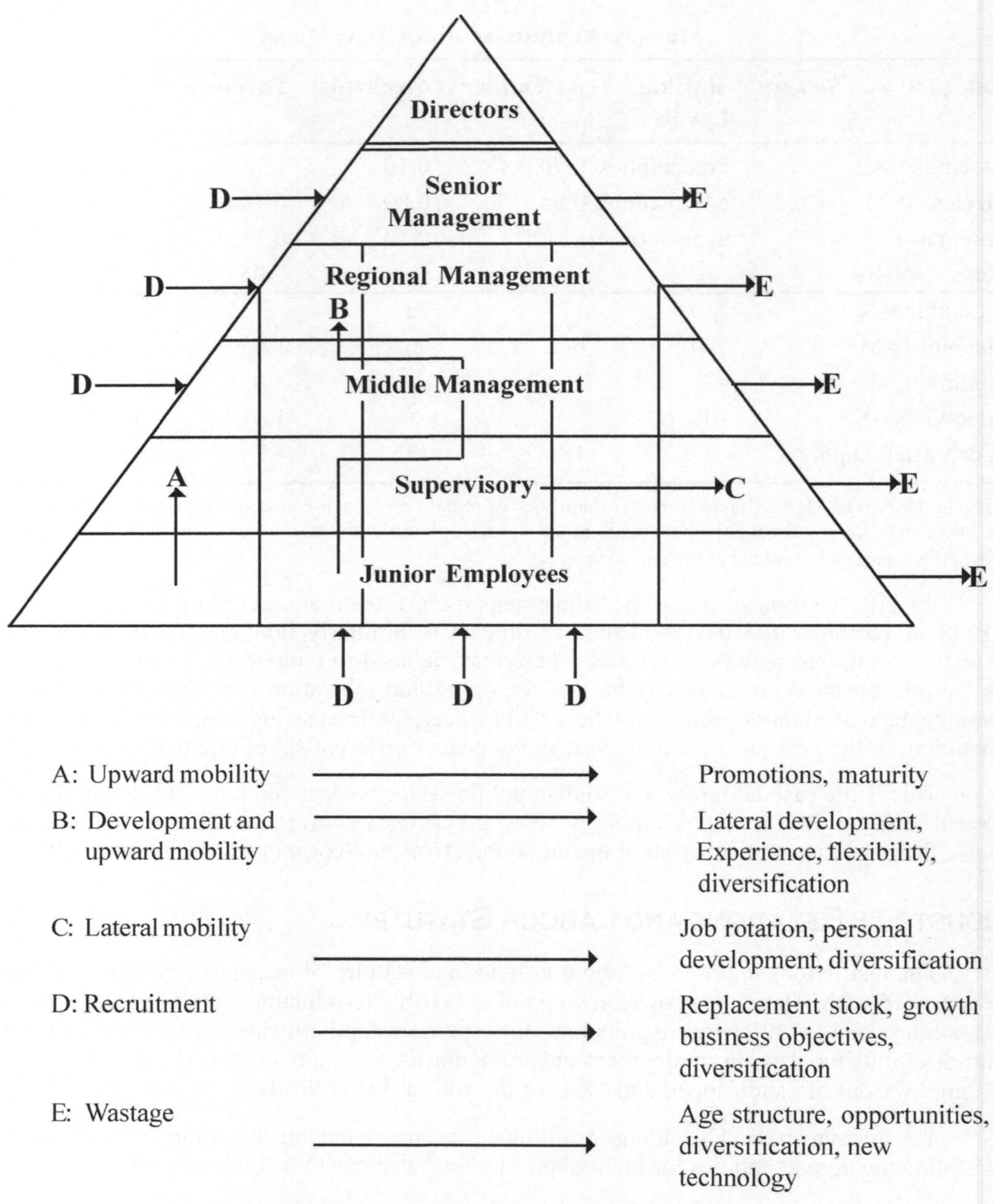

Figure 8.4. Employee 'movements' in an organization

HRP PLANNING: A REVIEW

HRP will not serve its full purpose if it is dealing statistically only with numerical elements like forecasting, supply-demand matching and control of people. It then becomes mere manpower planning. For it to become HRP, it must be concerned with motivating people, developing skills, quality and culture change through succession planning and career planning.

Further, it must anticipate change and respond rather than react to shocks. This requires active participation of line managers. In many companies it is handled mainly by industrial engineering departments as a staff function.

It is the prime duty of HR function to ensure wide participation and active integration with corporate strategic planning, which should take into account demographic changes in society like increasing retirement age and education levels.

In a survey of 245 respondents, more than 60 per cent claimed that they were practising proper HRP.

A good HRP should ensure organizational flexibility and change management. This can be done by providing for job rotation, job enrichment, employment of part-timers, female returnees, consultants and employment of retired personnel (if found fit) and outsourcing of services and contracts based on annualized hours, ensuring availability during peak demand. This requires an enlightened employee relations policy and cooperation of unions.

Questions and Assignment

Q.1. How can investment, both capital and revenue, on HRP be justified? Discuss.

Q.2. What are the various external factors that need to be considered in designing an effective HRP? Discuss in detail.

Q.3. What are the various internal factors that influence HRP that need to be considered in designing and using the HRP?

Q.4. Explain VRS, and downsizing. As an HR executive in a large organization how will you carry out VRS and downsizing if the organization has become overstaffed over the years and is ready for technology upgradation.

Q.5 Write short notes on the following:

- Markov analysis
- Productivity

Assignment

Study Human Resource Planning in any organization. Estimate Turnover and Stability Index of various departments or categories. Also find out how the organization copes with normal and cyclical absenteeism in the workforce. Compare the employee cost with similar organisations.

CASE

RELIANCE RETAIL

Even as Reliance Retail ramps up its nationwide rollout plans, the company is developing a comprehensive manpower policy to streamline recruitment and retention strategy. The new policy will focus on critical areas like talent acquisition, talent transformation, talent design and talent concept of the human resources (HR) function within the company.

Confirming the development, a senior Reliance Retail official said: "The company's HR team has been given the mandate to chart the blueprint by December 2007." The entire exercise is being spearheaded by Reliance Retail president and chief people officer Bijay Sahoo.

The move assumes significance primarily as Reliance Retail plans to have some 5 lakh employees on its rolls by calendar 2010. Increasing competition and shortage of seasoned retail professionals has also taken a toll on the company with some of its top and middle management executives joining competitors like Bharti Walmart and Aditya Birla group's retail venture.

"The HR policy will not only formulate a detailed recruitment and manpower plan for the company, but will also work out a comprehensive retention strategy." Incidentally, the company runs 89 retail outlets and plans to ramp it up to 120 stores by April 2007. While the talent acquisition vertical has the mandate to recruit talent across functions, talent transformation will play a key role in providing necessary skills required by the company, and the talent design team will draw specific profile for the employees. "We may have lost 7-8 guys in the war for talent, but the proposed HR policy will aim to stop attrition in the senior and middle management level," the company official said. Reliance Retail now has some 6,000 employees on its rolls. The company is also firming up plans to use the pool of some 30 senior executives recruited from Walmart's global operations to train its workforce. "These executives will provide training to fresh graduates and professionals recruited from non-retail sectors. We want to handle the entire employee training process internally," the official said.

Source: *The Economic Times*, March 24, 2007

9 Strategic Resourcing, Retaining and Outsourcing

Learning Objectives

After studying this chapter you will learn:

- The limitations of traditional methods and how they need to be upgraded.
- The linkage of recruitment and selection processes (re-sourcing or staffing), to other HR change interventions like organization structure and culture, human resource training and development, compensation and performance management.
- The concept of strategic staffing and its linkage with corporate strategy.
- How to select and retain motivated employees, people who fit the unique culture of the organization must be identified.
- Distinguishing key selection practices based either on achievement orientation or on their potential.
- Evaluate strategic issues in re-sourcing the organization, like temporary employees or permanent, through internal or external sources and the assessment centres.
- How employee turnover, which produces both costs and benefits, can be effectively managed during various stages of organizational growth.
- Implications of outsourcing.

INTRODUCTION

Organisations are made of people and it is they who make and implement policies and strategies, serve customers and relate to stakeholders. Hence recruitment and selection processes (resourcing or staffing), and retaining key personnel, have the potential to make significant contributions either to the organizational effectiveness, success or even to its failure. This strategic HR process can influence both planned and unplanned change. When integrated externally with corporate strategy and internally with other HR levers as shown in Figure 9.1, they represent powerful tools for achieving sustainable competitive advantage. The traditional approach of resourcing and retaining which is most common in organizations has limited applications for gaining competitive advantage or managing change. The narrow focus of the traditional approach on immediate job demands and the tendency to preserve the *status quo* represent the antithesis of what is required from resourcing and retaining when strategic priorities are changing and the future is uncertain.

Increasingly, recruitment and selection processes need to be responsive to a changing and uncertain business environment, values and culture of the organization, changing labour markets, demographic shifts and internationalization of business. The process should be responsive to mergers and acquisitions, restructuring, downsizing and de-layering in a team-based flexible organizational environment. Organisations are moving towards self managed, cross functional team structures with emphasis on roles rather than on jobs. In services and knowledge creating companies, people make all the difference. Finding and retaining the right type of people and motivating them is the most important challenge before HR executives when competitors are ready to pay higher and higher salaries for deserving ones.

The high rate of turnover, as is seen in some industries like BPO, can have a high impact on the bottomline, particularly in high-technology companies. Turnover can also be beneficial to some extent. There are other issues of legal compliance and affirmative action requirement being increasingly questioned. All this makes the staffing process the most important HR lever. The companies are also increasingly resorting to outsourcing the function.

Concept of Traditional Resourcing

Even though most organizations profess that 'people are our most important asset' and it is expected that they will develop carefully considered recruitment and selection methods to meet their dynamic external environment, evidence suggests that recruitment and selection practice is conducted in an *ad hoc*, haphazard manner or reflects the traditional model shown in Figure 9.1. The main features of the traditional approach are:

- It is geared to filling specific job vacancies with a bureaucratic process of sanctioning the recruitment.
- The process continues with the production of a job description, either using or updating a previous one, which is usually translated into a personnel specification.
- Recruitment is predominantly through advertising but with significant usage of agencies or web sites.
- A limited number of selection methods are used and invariably include short listing, using application forms/CVs, interviews and references. About 50 per cent of the organizations use testing for some vacancies.
- Finally, interviews are used for decision making assessing the candidates against the personnel specification or job description forms with test results.
- It concludes with offer/reject letters and candidate acceptance/rejection with, increasingly, some negotiation of terms.

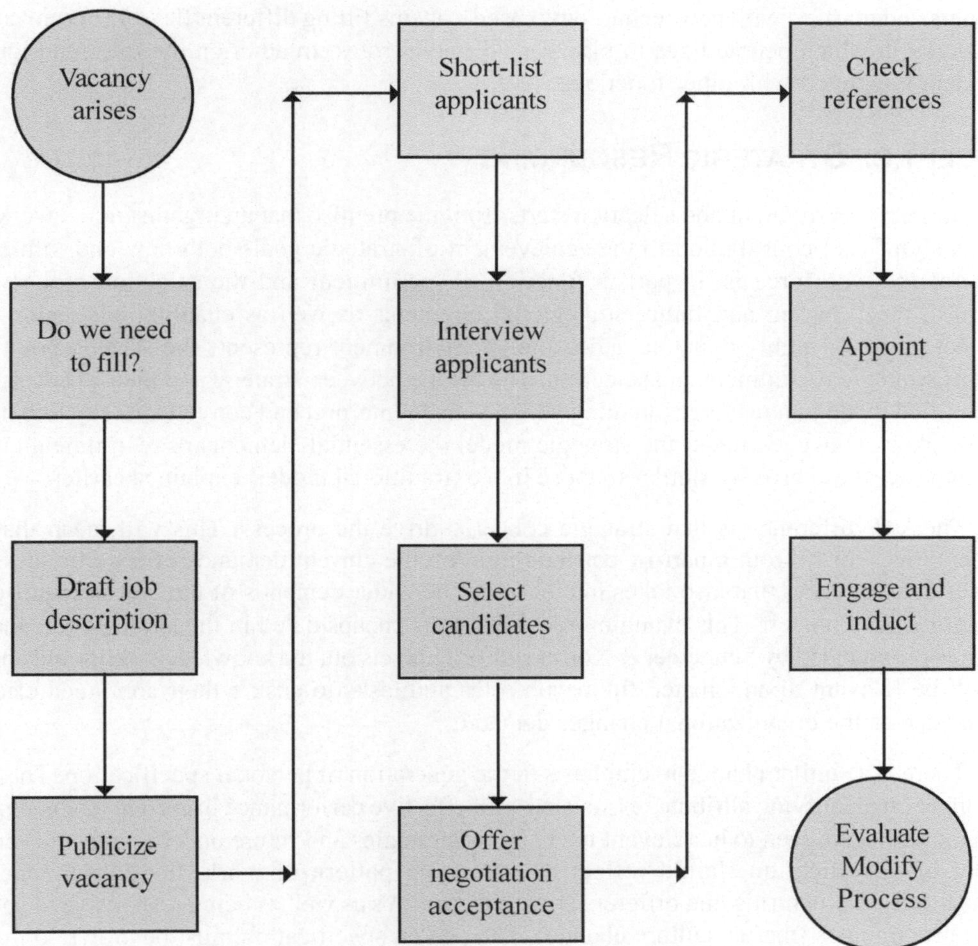

Figure 9.1. Traditional process of recruitment and selection

The traditional model is basically designed to fit people to available jobs, which do not serve the strategic purpose because it is not linked to corporate strategy, nor even to human resource planning, culture and values and the potential in the person. Hence, the traditional approach is static with its focus on present requirement rather than on shaping the future of the firm and its broader future requirements. Further, emphasis on the 'interview' as the key selection method provides ample opportunities for line managers to manipulate the process in order to select in their own image or matching that of the selectors. Also, the interviews are poor predictors of future job performance (Lundy & Cowling, 1996). Finally, the traditional method has a narrow focus in terms of stakeholder involvement. It is a replenishment process meant for steady-state bureaucratic organizations.

The strategic approach is more proactive and looks for finding human resources who can take the company where it wants to be in the future and are able to meet the demand of new customers and markets with new technology-based systems fitting different flexible organizational frameworks in which people have to play very different roles. In addition the roles and jobs are very much integrated with other functions.

Concept of Strategic Resourcing

Strategic recruitment and selection starts from the premise that an organisation's workforce makes a significant contribution to the achievement of strategic goals both now and future. The quality of the workforce is, in part, a function of recruitment and the selection process. The concern to meet current and future strategic requirements as well as enabling adaptation to an imperfect future or highly dynamic and complex environment represents the starting point for a model of strategic recruitment and selection. The bridge between strategy and the staffing process is often filled by human resource planning which aims to interpret and convert strategy into human resource plans. However, under the strategic model the essential elements of recruitment and the selection process are broadly similar to those in the 'traditional model' explained earlier.

The key difference is that strategic concerns drive the process. This will mean that job-analysis moves away from a narrow concentration on the current demands of specific tasks to a future oriented process that also takes into account the wider demands of the unit or teams or the whole organization itself. This changing requirement is encapsulated in the strategic job analysis technique propounded by Schneider & Konz (1989). This sets out the knowledge, skills and abilities that will be relevant to anticipated future job roles and tasks to ensure their continued effective performance as the organizational changes demand.

There is a similar change in emphasis in the generation of personal specification. The focus is no longer on identifying attributes associated with effective performance in current job incumbents but on those that are seen to be relevant to changing strategies and future uncertainties. It is critical that person-specification should reflect the changing pattern of work, the consequences of organizational restructuring and different strategic priorities as well as being responsive to specific change programmes (that is, culture change). The person specification must be drawn to provide sufficient detail for recruitment and the selection process must be targeted specifically at locating, attracting and assessing the desired attributes, whatever they are.

The strategic approach requires a front-loaded investment strategy where there is a concern to recruit the right competencies the first time rather than invest later in rectifying poor selection. Another difference is that much more emphasis is placed on securing active participation of candidates within an open decision-making framework, giving the candidates equal space.

It also demands direct involvement of service providers, subordinates, peers and others concerned in the selection decision. We can therefore understand strategic recruitment and selection process in the words of Lundy & Cowling (1996: 240): 'If organization selection is informed by the organisation's environment, linked to strategy, socially responsible, valid, periodically evaluated and maintained by the leading theory of knowledge and practice, then such selection is indeed strategic.'

Please refer to Figure 9.2 representing core dimensions of strategic recruitment and the selection model.

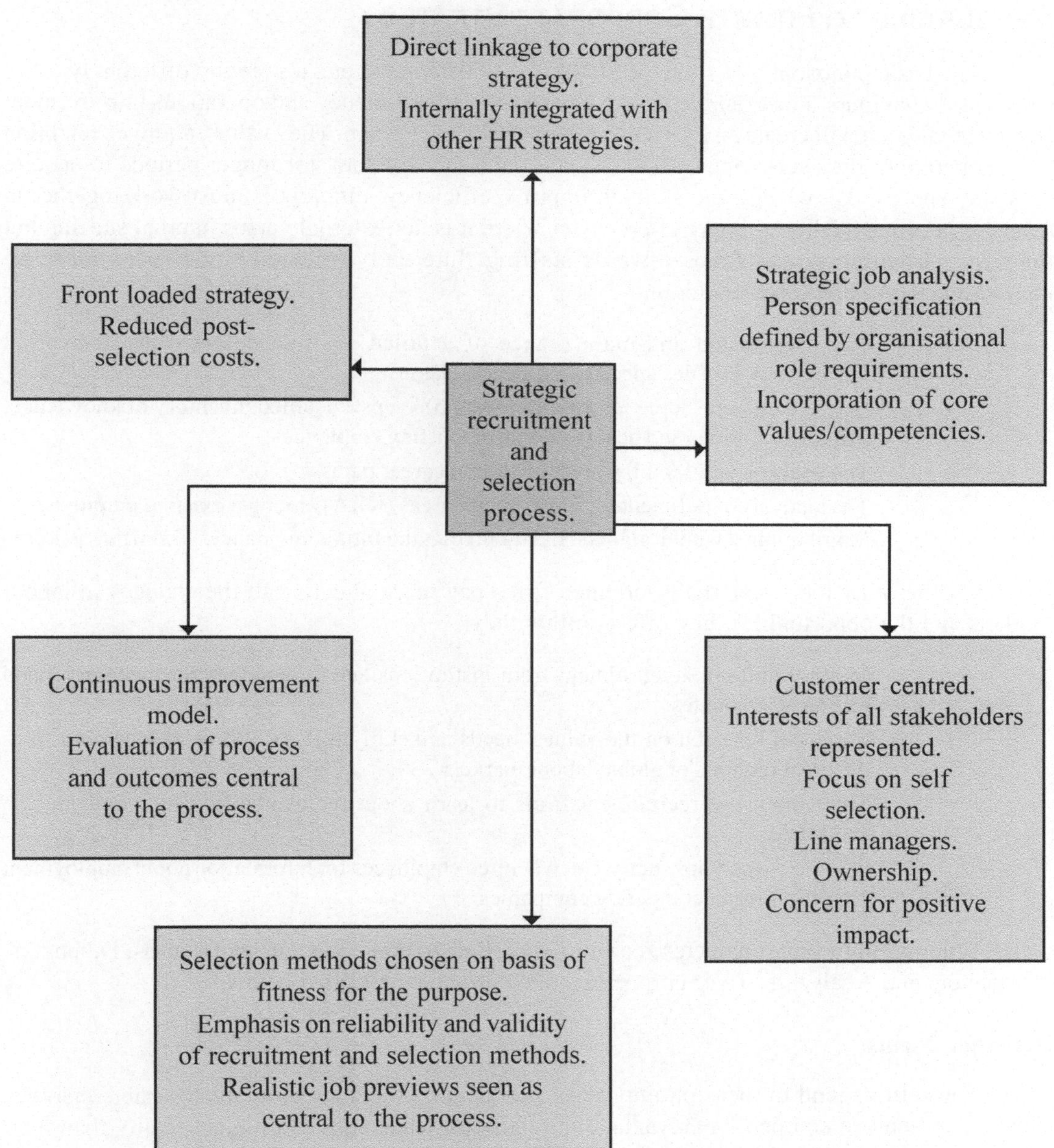

Figure 9.2. Core dimensions of strategic recruitment and selection

RESOURCING TO FIT WITH CORPORATE STRATEGY

The basic philosophy of strategic HRM is that different strategies require different types of employee behaviours. For example, a firm concerned with efficiency and operations improvement and cost reduction will create an internally-oriented staffing system. They value employee retention and cooperation; they seek employees who stay with the company for longer periods to acquire company-specific knowledge and skills to improve efficiency. Employees must work together in teams to improve quality or improve processes. Here it is not external versus internal staffing but the firm's orientation and focus towards staffing. Internally-oriented firms focus more on measurement and processes, including:

1. The preparation and maintenance of detailed position descriptions or explicit competency profiles specific to key job/classes.
2. HRIS (human resource information system) keeps a detailed inventory of knowledge, skills and abilities and achievements of existing employees.
3. The analysis and establishment of formal career paths.
4. The analysis of deficiencies in key result areas (KRA) amongst existing employees.
5. Maintaining a well designed HRP to predict the future imbalances in staffing pattern.

On the other hand, externally-oriented firms pay more attention to the changes in labour markets and the opportunities they offer. Further they:

1. Monitor and utilize enrolment from institutions and universities for managerial and technical graduates.
2. Carry out research on the values, needs and skill levels of individuals coming from different regional or global labour markets.
3. More often use recruitment firms to learn about the availability of promising job candidates.
4. Question—perhaps subtly—newly hired employees for information about employment opportunities in competing companies.

Miles & Snow have characterized firms according to their strategic approach as: Defenders, Prospectors and Analyzers. Their corporate strategies are exemplified below:

Defender Firms

These firms tend to focus on improving production efficiency in relatively stable markets. They try to achieve competitive advantage through cost leadership and higher quality than their counterparts. Their objective is to do better and better at whatever they currently do. Examples are oil, steel or other manufacturing companies.

Prospector Firms

They want to be product and market leaders. They rely on innovation, flexibility and speed. They exploit new markets and product opportunities. Companies like Lucent Technologies and 3Com and Dr. Reddy's Lab. are good examples.

Analyzer Firms

Analyzers are hybrid firms that closely monitor their more innovative competitors for new ideas and then quickly move to develop their efficient production methods for those ideas that appear to be most promising. For example, IBM was at the forefront at designing a PC but firms like Dell and Compaq devised more efficient ways of production and distribution.

Olian & Rynes (*IR* 23, 1984; pp 17-83) and others establish the link between the HR practices of these three types of firms, including their staffing practices. These are presented in Table 9.1.

Resourcing to Fit with the Organization

Conventional selection practices focus mostly on hiring people whose knowledge, skills and abilities provide the greatest fit with clearly defined requirements of specific jobs. Traditional selection techniques rarely consider characteristics of the organization in which the job resides. Traditional methods also ignore characteristics of persons which are irrelevant to immediate job requirements. We can therefore say that the organization hires only 'hands' or a 'part' of people. The new method of selection that is emerging makes it possible to select people who fit the 'culture' of the organization and the whole person and not just the 'hands'. This is in line with the 'role' concept of competencies because the performance of the individual depends on how successfully he carries out different roles while doing any job. And this depends on the type of organizational characteristics and culture (see Box 9.1).

These companies have not ignored the job requirements but have gone further to select people who fit the characteristics and culture of the organization and will not leave easily when inducted. This is particularly important for companies where the employees' personal characteristics,

BOX 9.1

- Sun Microsystems is the fastest growing US company with annual growth averaging more than 100 per cent. Filling open jobs is critical to Sun's effectiveness, phenomenal growth and profitability. Yet the hiring process is extremely time-consuming and labour intensive. Potential hires at all levels are brought into the organization from four to seven times for interviews with up to 20 interviewers. The process is full of ambiguity, lacks formal rules, and demands that all employees engage in problem solving to get themselves hired.

- Toyota (USA) screens 50,000 applicants for 3,000 factory jobs. Each employee hired invests at least 18 hours in a selection process that includes a general knowledge exam, a test of attitudes towards work, an interpersonal assessment centre, a manufacturing exercise designed to provide a realistic job preview of assembly work, an extensive personal interview and a physical exam.

TABLE 9.1
Business Strategy and Attributes of Staffing Policies of Three Types of Firms

Defender Firms	Analyzer Firms	Prospector Firms
Successful defender firms are likely to meet most of their key staffing needs from internal labour markets. The key knowledge skills and abilities sought by such firms will tend to be concentrated in the areas of production and finance.	These firms will use a mixture of recruitment methods, including cross-divisional and cross-product transfers. The key knowledge, skills and abilities sought by analyzers will tend to be in applied research, marketing and production.	Successful prospector organisations are likely to meet most of their staffing needs from external labour market sources. The key knowledge, skills and abilities sought by prospector organisations are in the areas of applied research and marketing.
Because defender organisations hire into lower level positions and then provide planned upward mobility, selection criteria gives major weight to aptitude and future potential and minor weight to achievement.	More like defenders in stable areas of the business; more like prospectors in change-oriented sectors.	Prospector firms, because they hire directly into upper-level positions, will focus on selection criteria that demonstrate given achievement in desired knowledge, skills and abilities.
Selection criteria are likely to reflect a narrow range of specialised skills because defender organisations are often highly specialised along functional lines.	Like prospectors, analyzers require a wider range of aptitudes and abilities for adapting to their more rapid production of service shifts.	Because they must quickly adapt to much more rapidly changing technical and business environments, prospector firms will require a wider or more general range of aptitudes and abilities.
Individuals with high need for security and structure and low tolerance for change and ambiguity will be relatively better suited with defender firms than prospector companies.	More like defenders in stable areas of the business and more like prospectors in the change-oriented sectors.	Individuals who are independent and creative and who prefer risk-taking are likely to be better matched to prospector firms than defender firms.
These firms are likely to use selection devices that assess applicants' future aptitude	More like defenders in stable areas of the business and more like prospectors	Prospectors are more likely to use selection devices that emphasize applicants' work

Continued...

...Continued

Defender Firms	Analyzer Firms	Prospector Firms
and potential, e.g., cognitive ability test or graduates from highly selective universities.	in the change-oriented sectors.	histories or techniques that directly measure current skills and ability tests like managerial simulation or work samples.
	Sonnefeld and Peiperl's Career System	
The career system priority for defender firms is the retention of organization members who have acquired firm specific knowledge and skills.	The career system priority here is the development of firm-specific functional specialists.	The career system priority for prospector firms is the recruitment of celebrity and specialist talent to address innovation as needed.
Defenders emphasize early career entry and organizational exit at retirement.	For analyzers there is exclusive entry and early career and exit at retirement.	Entry at multiple career stages and exit resulting from either poor individual performance or the pull of external opportunities.
Loyalty, length of service and age or advancement at planned life stages; drive movement within the defender.	An internal competition drives advancement through the position hierarchy.	Internal and external contest for advancement.

Source: J. D. Olian & S. L. Rynes. 'Organisational Staffing: Integrating Practice with Strategy.' IR 23 (1984).

skills and attitudes are important and the organization has less control on the nature of jobs (unstructured jobs). It may also be stated that it is difficult to describe or determine the characteristics of the organization in this context but enough is known about the organizational culture.

The new selection model is presented in Box 9.3, which differs from the job-fit traditional model that focuses entirely on the knowledge, skill and ability fit for the job concerned. Here, in addition to job-fit analysis, analysis of work environment and organization characteristics are also introduced. This analysis identifies the behaviours and responsibilities that lead to organizational effectiveness along with personal traits that are associated with such behaviours and responsibilities. Organizational analysis is also important because job-analysis data may become outdated rapidly due to changing of products and technologies. The organisation's overall philosophy and values are likely to be more stable, and consequently, stress the more important long-term focus for fit.

In the new model, focus is on the person's personality that is tailored to work setting; for example, if organizational success requires teamwork, a person's social and interpersonal skills become important. Further, the technical skills are not only those needed to do a job but also the person's capacity to learn new ones and upgrade himself quickly are explored. This capacity can be evaluated in work simulation exercises in real organizational settings. The new approach requires more resources and effort. Is it worth the cost? The potential benefits certainly justify the approach (Boxes 9.2 and 9.3).

The merits of the organization-person fit approach are:

- More favourable employee attitudes with greater job satisfaction, organization commitment and team work.
- More desirable organizational behaviours such as low absenteeism, low turnover and better job performance.
- Reinforcement of organizational design and desired organization culture.

The system also creates problems, such as:

- Greater investment of resources in the hiring process.
- Relative undeveloped and unproven selection technology.
- May be difficult to use the full model where pay-offs are greatest.
- Lack of organizational adaptation.

Resourcing Decisions

Every firm has to take some critical decisions before going about recruitment and selection of employees. A good human resource plan (HRP—see Chapter 3) provides broad guidelines and framework for these decisions. However, within this framework also, some decisions are required at the operational level, as discussed below:

In-house versus External Recruitment

The decision to recruit internally can cause much debate and is particularly embroiled with the issue of promotion and equal opportunities.

One view is that a vacancy provides an opportunity to promote from within, particularly in times of flattening hierarchies and fewer opportunities to move up the organization ladder. The position may have been one meant for succession planning processes arising out of retirement with a successor identified and developed. Other organizations believe that all vacancies should be advertised in-house, thus creating the image that existing employees will always be considered. This is beneficial for the morale and motivation of employees. In times of recession and restructuring, it provides an opportunity to redeploy the employees providing for their security needs. Further, the organization already has their performance profile, their work habits, skills and capabilities to work with others and the fit with the organization culture. Next, in-house promotion reduces training and socialization time because the existing employees know the work procedure, customers and politics of how things are done.

BOX 9.2
Chase Manhattan Bank and Corning Glass

During the 1980s the Bank underwent major managerial change. A key to the bank's successful turnaround was its careful strategic level selection and placement of executives. Historically at Chase, as is the case with banking in general, senior level positions were filled based on historical precedent: the old-boy networks played a major role. Furthermore, the tradition was to reward those with banker skills and not those with managerial skills, which were considered less important. But under the stress of serious performance problems, Chase had to re-examine these practices. As a result, a very systematic effort was launched to strategically manage senior selection decisions. For example: 'When the trust manager retired, corporate management decided that the department, whose operation had been essentially stable, should focus on a more aggressive growth strategy. Instead of seeking a veteran banker, Chase hired a man whose experience had been with IBM because it was felt that he would bring a strong marketing orientation to the trust department, which the new strategy required.

Corning Glass Company

At Corning an extensive effort is underway to assess the company's top 100 executives for such qualities as entrepreneurial flair. The goal is to have a clearer profile of the organisation's pool of executive talent specified in terms of capabilities for managing different parts of BCG matrix.

BOX 9.3
Methodology for Selection for Organisational Fit

Steps:

1. Assess the overall work environment
- Job Analysis
- Organisational Analysis

2. Infer the Type of Person Required
- Technical knowledge, skills and abilities
- Interviews by potential co-workers and others
- Personality traits

3. Design 'Rites of Passage' for organization entry that allows both the organization and the applicant to assess their 'fit
- Tests of cognitive, motor and interpersonal abilities
- Interview by potential coworkers and others
- Personality tests
- Realistic job previews, including work samples

4. Reinforce Person-Organization Fit
- Reinforce skills and knowledge through task design and training
- Reinforce personal orientation through organization design.

Although internal recruiting has advantages, there are also some disadvantages. First, internal recruiting can become very political and competitive, creating conflicts and groups. Interpersonal relations may suffer. Second, those employees not selected can suffer from diminished morale and performance, particularly when they feel equally or better qualified than the candidate selected. Next, continued in-house recruitment may turn the organization stale with an inbred culture which may not remain competitive enough. It will also cause multiple vacancies and promotion of some employees who do not have enough experience on the job.

Hence, internal recruitment is better in times of stability, and for firms pursuing a strategy of internal growth, efficiency improvement and cost reduction. On the other hand, when companies are in the growth phase, facing a volatile and uncertain environment and diversifying, integrating, or facing high competitive forces, finding talent from outside may be beneficial. External recruiting can be expensive and time consuming but will allow the firm to expand its knowledge base, help in compliance of equal opportunities and affirmative action. There is always the chance that the candidates may have a past outstanding performance record but may not succeed in the new position and in the new organization culture.

Temporary versus Permanent

Again, a good HRP can provide an answer to this question. But the issue always remains: how long will this vacancy last? Temporary employees may cost less per day if the labour market is surplus and may cost more if employees are taken from some agency. Temporary employees are not provided with benefits and thus provide flexibility and are non-unionized.

Their productivity is also more because they are trying to justify themselves but it may be at the expense of quality. A high proportion of temporary, casual or those hired through contractors can create labour problems because of dual standards of HR policies in the firm, more liberal for permanent ones and tight for temporary employees (strike in Hero Honda and Maruti Ltd. in India).

Scheduling for Recruitment

Two important questions need to be answered while scheduling the recruitment process: 1) how large an applicant pool is needed, and 2) when should the recruitment effort begin. For answering the first question, a recruitment pyramid as shown in Figure 9.3 can be constructed by reviewing the past data about similar efforts. As shown in the pyramid, the organization will need a pool of 120 applicants to fill the 10 vacancies.

An organization has also to finalize the scheduling of activities involved in the process. Table 9.2 presents a schedule for fixing the time plan for initiating the action so that candidates are available when needed. If candidates have to wait after the final selection, it causes great anxiety in their minds or the organization has to pay them for the waiting period.

On the other hand, candidates take time for joining as they have to resign from their companies which may require a 3-month notice period or less. People also need time to make their travel plans, arrange reservations, etc. Information also sometimes reaches late or people react late to advertisements.

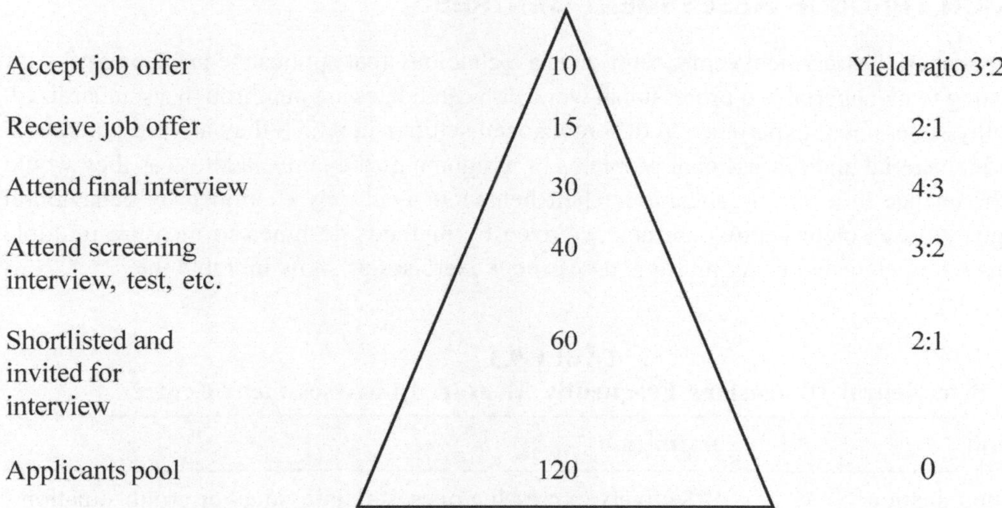

Figure 9.3. Recruitment pyramid

TABLE 9.2
Recruiting Timeline

Stages of Recruiting Process	Normal Time Taken to Complete
Authorisation of vacancy by HQ	3–4 weeks
Advertisement finalisation for release	1 week
Ad publication on the due date	2 weeks
Time taken by candidates to apply	4 weeks
Shortlisting of candidates and despatch of call letter for interview	1–2 weeks
First screening interview/test	1 week
Second final interview/negotiation of terms	2 weeks
Getting approval of HQ	1 week
Receiving acceptance, negotiation and joining time	4–12 weeks
Total time	18–30 weeks

SELECTION THROUGH ASSESSMENT CENTRES

A managerial assessment centre represents a technology that applies the principles of work sample testing to managerial and professional work. Job candidates are put through a standardized, often lengthy, assessment experience in different social settings in which they are presented with simulated managerial and professional problems or assignments they must address as they would if given the chance in a real organization. Their behaviour is closely examined by behavioural psychologists. Assessment centres are characterized by methods designed to measure multiple dimensions (competencies) using multiple assessment exercises as show in Table 9.3.

TABLE 9.3
Behavioural Dimensions Frequently Measured in Assessment Centres

Dimension	Definition
Oral communication	Effectively expressing oneself in individual or group situations, including gestures and non-verbal communication
Planning and organization	Establishing a course of action for self or others to accomplish a specific goal; planning proper assignment of personnel and allocation of resources
Delegation	Utilizing subordinates effectively; allocating decision- making and other responsibilities to appropriate subordinates
Control	Establishing procedures to monitor or regulate the process, tasks or activities of subordinates and job activities and responsibilities; taking action to monitor the results of delegated assignments or projects
Decisiveness	Expressing a readiness to make decisions, render judgements and take action or commit oneself
Initiative	Actively attempting to influence events to achieve goals showing self-starting actions rather than passive acceptance; taking action to achieve goals beyond those called for; originating action
Tolerance for stress	Maintain stable performance under pressure or opposition
Adaptability	Maintaining effectiveness in varying environments, with various tasks, responsibilities or people
Tenacity	Staying with a position or plan of action until the desired objective is achieved or no longer reasonably attainable.

Source: Thornton, G. and Byham, W. *Assessment Centers and Managerial Performance*. New York, U.S.A.: Academic Press, 1982.

These dimensions are assessed by observing the behaviour of the candidates as they complete the exercises like:

- The analysis and resolution of papers typically found in a manager's in-basket.
- The leaderless group discussion: a hypothetical group of managers must reach business decisions or allocate a scarce organizational resource.
- A case analysis: a series of business decisions must be made taking account of an organization's history and environment.
- The role-play exercise: a manager must interact with another manager, customer, or subordinate and solve a problem or attempt to influence the other individual's behaviour.

The most well known research on the assessment centre method comes from AT&T. In fact, the concept of assessment centres was first started in Germany where soldiers were selected and trained under simulated war conditions.

The Cost and Benefit of Retention

Turnover is costly because replacement must be recruited, selected and trained. A high voluntary turnover rate can also disrupt the completion of projects and social and communication patterns among 'stayers'. It increases 'stayers' workload and stress. It is estimated that turnover cost may be approximately one year's pay of an employee who is leaving (one technology company estimated it at $ 20,000 per employee). But certain benefits also can be associated with turnover. For example, newcomers might perform at higher levels than leavers and might bring to the firm an infusion of new ideas about strategy and technology and customer relations and preferences. There will also be times when firms may like to exit people who do not fit the culture of the firm.

While the cost and benefits of turnover must be balanced, a third dimension to this problem also must be considered. Changes in HR systems designed to reduce employee turnover can have major cost consequences of their own, such as increased wages, redesigning jobs or modifying selection systems to better identify individuals who would not resign. These costs of retention must be compared to the overall cost of turnover to find out the optimal turnover rate.

The optimal rate is one that minimizes the sum of costs of turnover plus the costs associated with separation and replacement of employees. This is shown in Figure 9.4 where retention costs are RC and turnover costs are TC. The two curves when combined give the U-shape curve and the point of intersection of two curves which gives lowest overall turnover cost TTC, which gives the optimum rate of turnover for any firm.

Strategic Approach to Manage Turnover

Both voluntary and involuntary turnover can be managed strategically to allow the company to maximize the benefits of turnover and minimize the costs. Table 9.4 presents a Performance-Replaceability Strategy Matrix that was developed by Martin & Bartol.

The model on which the matrix is based argues that turnover is either functional or dysfunctional depending on two factors: the individual employee's performance level and the difficulty

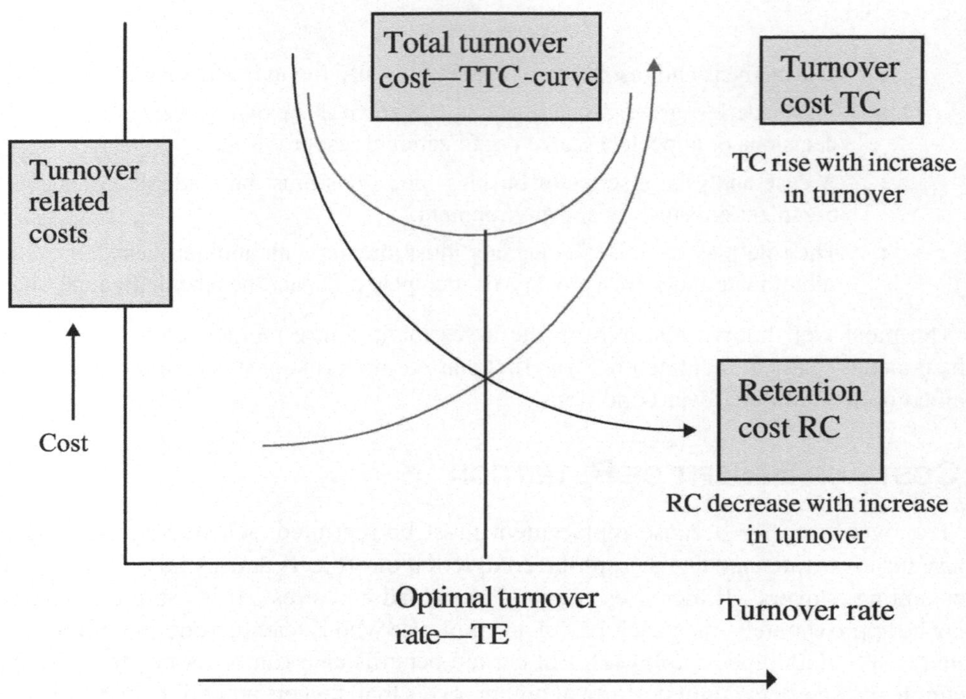

Figure 9.4. Rate of turnover model

the organization will have in replacing the individual. In Table 9.4, replaceability is shown along 'X-axis' and performance along 'Y-axis'. Each of six cells is then classified as resulting in functional or dysfunctional turnover, and appropriate strategies for managing employees who fit into each of these cells are provided. Obviously, the more dysfunctional the turnover, the greater is the attention that will be required by management to retain the employee. Retention strategies for such employees might involve additional career development opportunities, greater compensation and rewards or innovative benefits that are tailored to the needs of the employee. Regardless of the performance level, back-ups should be developed by the organization for any employee who is difficult to replace.

Ideally, the strategy for managing turnover involves keeping high performers rewarded through innovative compensation and recognition and reward programmes while engaging in human resource planning to ensure that as few employees as possible occupy positions that will make them difficult to replace.

Figure 9.5 presents the eventual outcomes of a successfully managed employee turnover and retention programme. All employees whose turnover would be disruptive would be reclassified as easy to replace once appropriate backups had been trained. At the same time, performance incentives and counselling should be provided to low performers to encourage and motivate them to become high performers. If the low performers do not improve in time, they should be terminated.

TABLE 9.4
Performance-Replaceability Strategy Mix

		Replaceability	
		Difficult	**Easy**
Performance	High	High performance—difficult to replace Highly dysfunctional turnover Retain, invest in employee Motivate and develop backup	High performance—easy to replace Turnover dysfunctional Retain, invest in employee
	Average	Average performers Dysfunctional turnover Retain, provide performance incentives Develop backup	Average performers—easy to replace Turnover dysfunctional High if replacement is costly Motivate Retain provide performance incentives
	Low	Poor performers—difficult to replace Short term dysfunctional Improve performance or terminate Develop backup	Poor performers—easy to replace Turnover functional Improve performance or terminate

Source: Martin, David C. & Bartol, Kathryn M. 'Managing Turnover Strategically.' *Personal Administration,* vol. 30, p. 63 (1985).

HUMAN RESOURCE OUTSOURCING

The increasing trend of outsourcing of HR activities (35 per cent in 1996 in the USA with total market size of up to $ 200 billion by 2000; source: Hewitt Associate's Survey) not only to developed countries but even to developing countries like India and China, may create the fear that there will be no need of the HR function in future. Is this phenomenon a short-term extension of the downsizing movement started in the 1990s or a permanent solution for organizational effectiveness? How are HR executives reacting to this: supporting it or resisting it? These are some interesting questions. Outsourcing is defined as 'the performance by outside parties on a recurring basis, of tasks (in this case, HR) that would otherwise be performed in-house' (Charles, *et. al.*, *Academy of Management Executive*s, 1996).

The authors mentioned above, after interviewing leading organizations, identified five competitive forces that are driving outsourcing, which are: downsizing, rapid growth or decline, globalisation, increased competition and restructuring. The increased focus on HR function by top

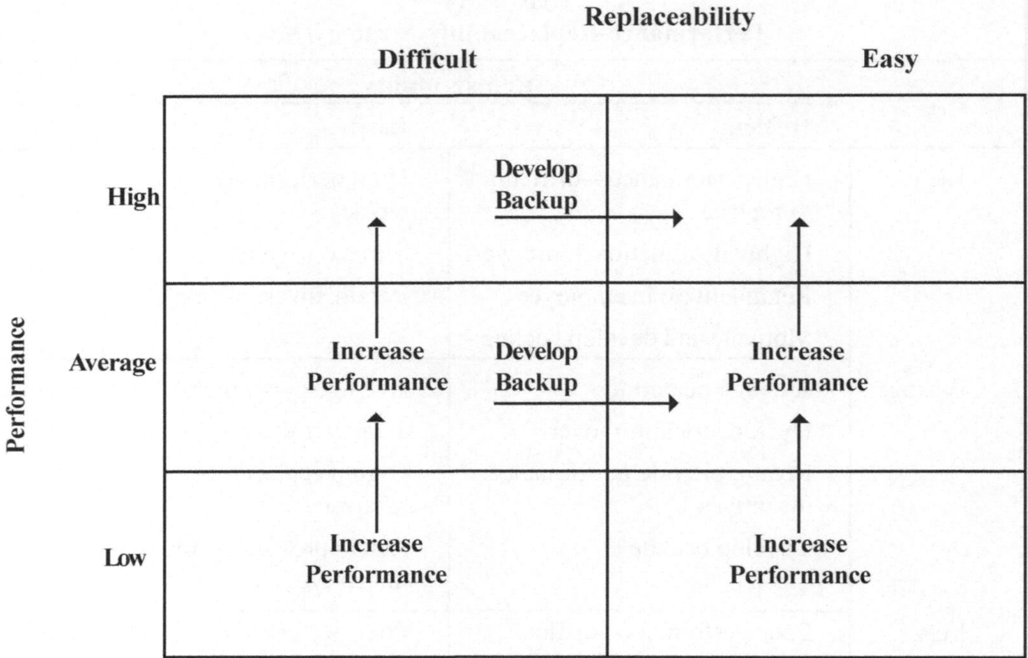

Figure 9.5. Strategic management of turnover and retention

Source: Jefffrey A. Mellow, *Strategic HRM,* p. 379.

management is forcing them to align HR practices and policies with corporate strategy, work more closely with line managers to deliver more value added services at a lower cost and to further reduce their service response time to both external and internal customers. In short, top managements are examining which HR activities are needed and who can best provide them.

Many firms have also undergone changes related to restructuring, mergers and acquisitions where some HR activities have to be done in a time bound manner by specialist outside consultants. Companies resorting to retrenchment or firms in decline face huge pressures to reduce costs, while high-growth firms resort to it for maintaining growth pace and also to control costs. Multinational firms setting up their operations in foreign countries who have little knowledge of the foreign culture find outsourcing very attractive. The choice of activities that can be outsourced depends on whether they are deemed to be in the core competency of the HR function or not. Companies like GE and other multinationals are increasingly looking for customer satisfaction, cash-flow and employee satisfaction improvement and HR function is under pressure to deliver the same and help in achieving competitive advantage. Hence, the HR department has to perform its tasks more efficiently than outside service providers; for example, team-building activities, leadership development activities, compensation management, etc. The following areas which need specialised knowledge are amenable to outsourcing: operation and maintenance of HR information system;

compliance with regulatory requirements; organization development; obtaining data about external labour markets or about competitor benefits and reward policies. Other areas are competency mapping, training and development of mostly off-the-job types and also services in head-hunting and assessment centre related.

Sometimes activities which are overwhelming in nature and with which the HR department is unable to cope, are also outsourced; for example, during wage negotiations or in the event of a strike. Outsourcing is also beneficial in conducting salary negotiations without disclosing the credentials of the firm.

Box 9.4 provides guidelines for managing the outsourcing process. Except for such core competencies as performance appraisal or employee relationship, most HR activities can be considered for outsourcing where maintaining confidentiality or control or maintaining trust with employees is not very important.

One solid argument given by some companies is that outsourcing stimulated the employees' thought processes and kept them in contact with consultants who had current and specialized information that could accelerate their progress on the learning curve. Outsourcing provides a big-picture perspective. Another company thinks that use of vendors improves the HR gene pool and produces new capabilities and out-of-the- box thinking. There is no doubt that outsourcing reduces career development opportunities for HR staff. Hence outsourcing is creating opportunities, threats and challenges with the message that HR staff should deliver value added services and become a specialist function.

Questions and Assignments

Q.1. Explain the differences between traditional and strategic approaches of recruitment and selection.

Q.2. Why does an organisation's investment in recruitment and selection acquire so much importance?

Q.3. Is it more important for an employer to establish a person-job fit or a person-organization fit? Can you think of situations where one would be preferable to the other?

Q.4. Explain. Why retention is dysfunctional as well as beneficial? As a senior executive of an MNC formulate a strategy for optimum retention, explaining the model that you have used.

Q.5. Why is outsourcing of HR activities increasing? What challenges is it posing for HR executives? Suggest guidelines for effective outsourcing.

Assignments

As an HR executive in a large firm you are asked to investigate the data in the table on page 203 and make recommendations regarding cost effectiveness. What other information is required?

- Column A gives the number of initial enquiries which resulted in complete application forms received.

BOX 9.4
Guidelines for Human Resource Outsourcing

Making the Outsourcing Decision

- Don't allow sacred cows. Except for core competencies, all other HR activities should be considered as candidates for outsourcing.
- Determine whether the desire to outsource an activity is driven by its low contribution to core competencies, influences from external environment, or poor management of the activity.
- Recognize that performance is more important than low HR department headcounts or lower costs.
- Beware of vendors that supply off-the-shelf solutions that do not fit the company's needs.
- Avoid excessive reliance on vendors.
- Decide how much control is needed for various HR activities and whether control can be retained with outsourcing.
- Identify critical personal benefits of outsourcing.

Selecting and Negotiating with Outsourcing Vendors

- Assign a high weightage to vendor's knowledge of the industry.
- Perform reference checks of potential vendors.
- Understand the costs involved in switching vendors for outsourced services.

Managing the Outsourcing Transaction

- Expect the external HR team to resist outsourcing and develop ways of managing this resistance.
- Anticipate the conflict and develop a plan for resolving it in a manner that supports the relationship with the vendor.
- Anticipate change to HR culture and careers.

Managing Vendor Relationships

- Develop long-term relationships with outsourcing vendors where such continuity is critical.
- Develop staff members to become effective managers of vendor relationships.
- Maintain stability of the in-house staff who oversee vendor relationships and understand the performance expectations originally negotiated.
- Require competitive bidding for each outsourced service at regular intervals.

Monitoring and Evaluating Vendor Performance

- Establish expectations, measures and reporting relationships up front for both outsourcing parties.
- Insist on high-quality performance by HR vendors.
- Insist on accurate and frequent status reporting by HR vendors and immediate notification when problems arise.
- Establish performance targets for vendors with the assistance of outside consultants when necessary.
- Consider internal customer surveys to evaluate vendor performance.

Source: C. R. Greer & S. A. Youngblood, *Academy of Management Executives.*

- Column B gives the number of candidates called for interview.
- Column C gives the number of candidates recruited/trained after six months.

Recruitment Sources	Advertisement Cost in US $	A	B	C
National newspaper 1	2,000	150	10	1
National newspaper 2	1,500	2	2	Nil
National newspaper 3	1,250	50	3	1
Local newspaper	250	22	7	3
Specialist journal	600	8	5	1
Local radio	350	33	10	2

CASE

RECRUITMENT AND SELECTION AT PROTECTION ROYALE

Protection Royale, a leading player in the composite business, has consolidated over time to become one of the largest direct insurers in the UK. Its headquarters, based in Dorking, reported a turnover of over $ 7,000 million and its future strategy is directed towards becoming the undisputed market leader in the UK insurance market. The company is organized divisionally around its four core business areas.

This case traces developments in recruitment and selection within one of these divisions—Financial Consultancy Services—which is acknowledged as having an increasingly important role to play in pursuit of corporate objectives. This division employs sales consultants whose primary role is to market Protection Royale's insurance products to insurance brokers. These brokers then consider Protection Royale's products along with those of other insurance companies when making recommendations to individual customer's purchasing insurance through this medium.

The basic job description and person specification (dealing with those attributes associated with effective role performance) had remained much the same since the 1990s. Labour turnover amongst the staff was very low at approximately 4 per cent and when vacancies arose, little difficulty was experienced in recruiting replacements, as a relatively undemanding person specification meant that many people in the labour market matched the company's requirements. Replacements were found using a well established recruitment and selection process which, in brief, comprised the following:

1. Advertising in financial services media.
2. Use of specialist recruitment agencies.
3. Recommending from existing staff.

4. Short listing from application forms/CVs.
5. Interviews.
6. Role plays.
7. Psychometric testing.
8. References.

Despite its growing strategic importance, concerns over the division's business began to surface in 1997 eventually leading to a review of its operations. During the early 1990s the division's product lines had proliferated, partly in response to the growing technical complexity of the financial services industry. The resultant lack of product specialization was undermining customer confidence and contributing towards a deterioration of Royale's market standing.

These developments promoted a reappraisal of the division's work and resulted in a major shake-up of staff and a precipitation of a staffing crisis. This necessitated the development of improved recruitment selection and retention strategies designed to address the immediate crisis and at the same time support long-term strategic priorities. What began to appear was a need for a smaller and more focused product range and high performing staff who were able to project their products on to the 'best advice lists' of brokers.

Of these, the latter were seen as crucial and prompted a detailed assessment of existing staff against a much more demanding personnel profile. An emerging Person Specification for Sales Consultants began to coalesce around excellence of product knowledge; interpersonal skills associated with influencing and persuasiveness and the negotiation skills involved in anticipating and countering broker reservations.

An added complication had been introduced in 1994 by the Financial Services Act, which required financial sales practitioners to hold a Financial Planning Certificate. This represented a potential threat to the staffing base as current employees might be unwilling or unable to obtain these qualifications.

In addition these qualifications needed to be built into the emerging person specification for new recruits resulting, almost overnight, in a substantial reduction in the number of people within the external labour market who could meet the requirements of the revised specification.

The reappraisal of the division involved an assessment of current staff against the transformation in the role and profile of Sales Consultants. Assessments resulted in staff being rated as 'suitable', 'unsuitable' or 'possibles', that is, those who, following training and development, might meet the grade. What resulted was a significant and rapid reduction in the workforce through resignations, redundancies and transfers that seriously undermined the ability of the division to meet its performance targets.

At first this was not perceived as a crisis because the line managers believed that they could personally head-hunt replacements despite a radically altered labour market and their lack of experience. However, after their failure to make a single appointment through this route, the situation assumed crisis proportions. Not only was immediate business performance being undermined but also threats to longer term objectives quickly became apparent. The reputation of Protection Royale amongst brokers was steadily deteriorating and this was also making the company less attractive to potential applicants.

At the initiative of the HR department alternative recruitment and selection strategies were devised and implemented in 1998 with the managers and HR specialists working in concert. These comprised the following steps:

- Identification of recruitment champions charged with developing and driving through the strategy and reporting back regularly on outcomes.
- Adoption of recruitment objectives as key performance indicators for line managers and HR staff. As one employee put it, 'any failure to deliver would result in those responsible losing their heads.'
- Introduction of dual recruitment and selection strategy. The first continued the practice of direct recruitment from the external market but this now involved the use of a professional search agency. The role of the agency was to identify suitable candidates who were positively oriented towards joining Protection Royale. At this stage, the Protection Royale took over the process and put the candidates through a selection process designed to assess fit with the organizational culture and job competence. The second, responding to the contraction in the labour market, involved the recruitment of a cadre of trainees who would follow a 15-18 month training and induction programme leading, if successful, to their appointment as Sales Consultants.
- For strategies, recruitment and selection was geared to a revised job description and person specification of the 'ideal candidate'. The latter was extrapolated into a series of competencies and became the main driver of the recruitment and selection process for both direct entrance and trainees following its adaptation to provide greater emphasis on 'potential' and 'trainability'.
- For direct entrants multiple selection methods were adopted for assessing referrals from search agency. Methods were chosen for their relevance to the competencies being assessed. A matrix was produced identifying which method would be used to assess each competence. Selection methods included completion of a competency-based application form, situational testing (that is, based on samples of required job knowledge, skills and attitudes) and psychometric testing to assess aptitudes, competency-based interviews, role-play simulation exercises, presentation and references.
- Recruitment of trainees driven through national advertising. Advertising invited respondents to telephone in for a brief interview and lines were staffed all week including Sunday. Selection began at this stage through assessment of responses to standardized questions and, for successful and interested parties, led to the arrangement of a

screening interview. Recruitment was supported by a detailed information pack for candidates.

- Selection of trainees via assessment centres. These employed similar selection methods to those described earlier for direct entrants.
- Thorough induction of trainees following appointment. A dedicated manager was appointed to support trainees who were also able to maintain regular contact with their designated managers to discuss their progress or any other concern.
- Extensive training for all line managers involved in any aspect of recruitment and selection. Training was supported by a very detailed (54 page) pack providing step-by-step guidance on all aspect of the process. There was emphasis throughout on standardization, including interview questions.

Following the introduction of these procedures an initial cohort of 18 trainees was recruited and they all successfully completed their training programme during 1999. On 'graduation' from the training programme each trainee was placed in his or her designated regional sales office.

10

Performance Management System

Learning Objectives

After studying this chapter you will learn:

- The concept of the performance management system and its elements.
- The objectives and uses of measures of employee performance.
- Aligning performance management system with the corporate strategy.
- Behaviour Anchored Rating System and 360 degree appraisal system.
- Design of performance system for a professional institute.
- Competency mapping.
- How performance management can lead to organizational change.
- Some key principles for making performance appraisal as effective as possible.
- Linking performance management with other important management themes like organization culture, structure and the search for employee commitment.

INTRODUCTION

Managers are not born effective, they become effective. A lot of effort goes in making a manager effective. Performance management system (PMS) can help the managers to become effective and contribute to organizational growth. It has become increasingly clear that sustained effectiveness of organizations depends in large measure on their ability to manage performance and develop capacities of their human resources. Long term competitive advantage of corporations, for example, depends on their ability to attract, manage, develop and retain high quality talent.

Effective performance management systems require employees and supervisors to work together to set performance expectations, review results, assess organizational and individual needs, provide on-going feedback and counselling and plan for the future. Organizations cannot afford to have weak links or unproductive employees. More than ever, organizations need broader measures of employee performance to ensure that development programmes meet the changing needs of the organization and its markets. For this to happen, employee behaviours must be channelled in the appropriate direction towards performance of specific objectives that are consistent with the work unit and organisation's strategy. It is equally important that employees are provided with appropriate and specific feedback to assist their career development.

Concept of PMS

Clark (1995: 187) indicates that 'there is no single universally accepted model of performance management in use'. It is a term originated in the USA to describe an integrated set of activities which are designed to improve the performance of employees. Storey & Sission (1993) emphasise the three basic activities that constitute PMS are:

1. Setting clear objectives for individual employees which are derived from the organisation's strategy and departmental strategies.
2. Formal monitoring and review of progress towards these objectives.
3. Using the outcomes of the review process to reinforce desired employee behaviour through differential rewards and identifying training and development needs.

Clark (1995) stresses one additional PMS activity: that of feeding back to the employee the results of the formal monitoring. PMS is a set of processes and is operated in a cycle, see Figure 10.1. In Clark's cycle there is a stage which is placed after the four stages of setting objectives, measuring performance, feeding back results and rewarding based on results. This stage entails the possible amendment of objectives and changing the objectives which contributed to the performance measure. This creates a direct feedback loop to the setting of objectives. Another feedback loop is needed for amendment of objectives prior to measuring the performance about possible amendment of objectives in the light of departmental and individual strengths and weaknesses. After the formal review and monitoring of progress towards those objectives take place, the outcomes are used for identifying training and development needs and offering of differential rewards. Another feedback loop is introduced here to allow renewed individual objectives so that department or unit may adjust its mission in the light of results achieved.

A major study of PMS by the Institute of Personnel Management claims it offers several advantages, namely:

1. The employees are able to meet increased product market competition more effectively.
2. A greater opportunity is provided to employees to share and participate in setting organizational objectives and mission.
3. Pushing the key decisions down the organization structure to line managers and supervisors.
4. A greater acceptance of accountability by line managers of the necessity to make required decisions.
5. Reward structures forge a clear link between individual or group performance.

BOX 10.1
Guidelines for Performance Feedback Sessions

1. Prepare thoroughly for the review. Be able to discuss specific incidents of effective and ineffective performance.
2. Schedule the review session at a convenient time and in an appropriate place. Arrange to be free from interruptions.
3. After establishing rapport with the employee, clearly communicate important strengths and weaknesses.
4. Encourage the employees to participate in the discussion and listen attentively to what is said.
5. Use problem-solving methods to improve areas of performance that significantly reduce work effectiveness.
6. Jointly set goals for improvement and communicate your confidence in the employee's ability to improve.
7. Conclude by summarizing your evaluation and the goals set during the session and the scheduling of the follow-up meeting.
8. Performance diagnosis and coaching are integral parts of PMS. When it is determined that an employee is falling short, it is important to determine why the problem occurred by identifying the problem areas. The employee and the manager can then work together to remove barriers to performance.

Uses and Design of the System

An organization faces five strategic decisions in establishing its PMS as shown in Figure 10.2. As explained by Jeffery A. Mello, the first is the determination of the purpose of the system and how it will be used. PMS can serve multiple purposes and it is important for the organization to strategise why the system is being used before further design decisions are made. The organization also needs to ensure that, if the system is developed to meet several purposes, they should not be at odds with each other and any purpose should not undermine the data collection for another.

One purpose of PMS is to facilitate employee development by assessing deficiencies in performance levels and skills so that an organization can determine specific training and development needs. In fact, the performance feedback process can be designed to provide information to support the organisation's performance programmes. Assessing individual and team strengths and weaknesses can allow employees and team development plans to be established. A reciprocal relationship exists between the two as the desired outcomes of T&D initiatives to be incorporated into the PMS.

A second purpose of PMS is to determine appropriate rewards and compensation. Salary, promotion, retention and bonus decisions are frequently based on data collected as part of

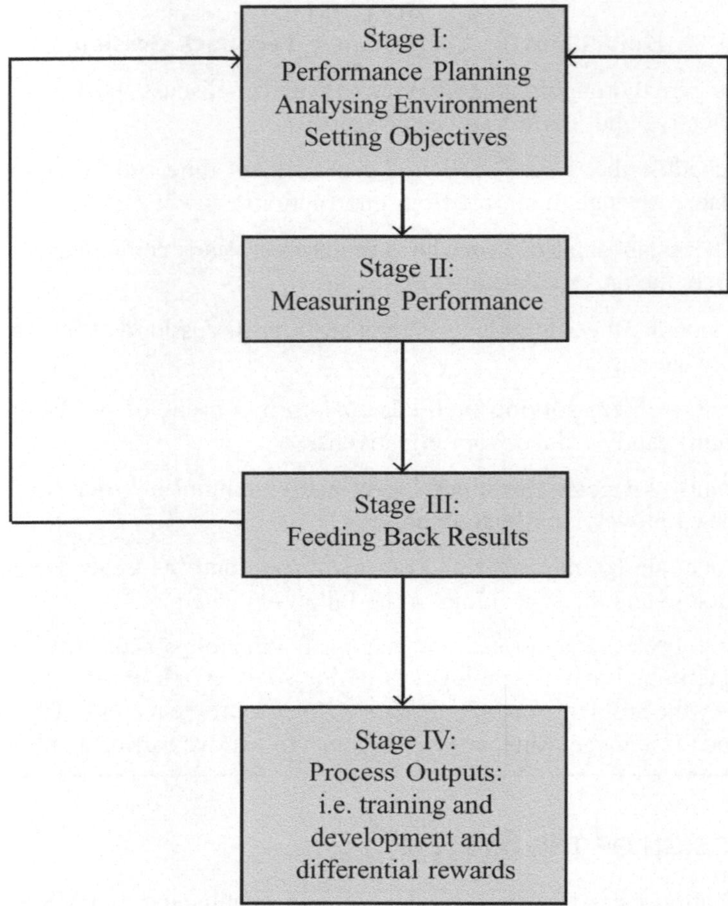

Figure 10.1. The Performance Management System

performance measurement. Therefore, employees must understand and accept the performance feedback system as a prerequisite for accepting decisions made relative to the reward and compensation. Any perceived unfairness of the performance feedback system on the part of employees will result in a perceived unfairness of the compensation system.

A third purpose of PMS is to enhance employee motivation. A formal process that allows employee acknowledgement and praise can reinforce the behaviour and outcomes. They can be told specifically what the organisation's expectations for them are, and employees can inform their employers of the types of job assignment and responsibilities they desire.

A fourth purpose of PMS is to facilitate legal compliance. Claims of unfair dismissal or demotion are best supported when the organization has the necessary documentation of performance deficiencies and reviews. Such information is often admitted into court to prove non-discrimination against employees and to justify termination of employment. Data showing unacceptable

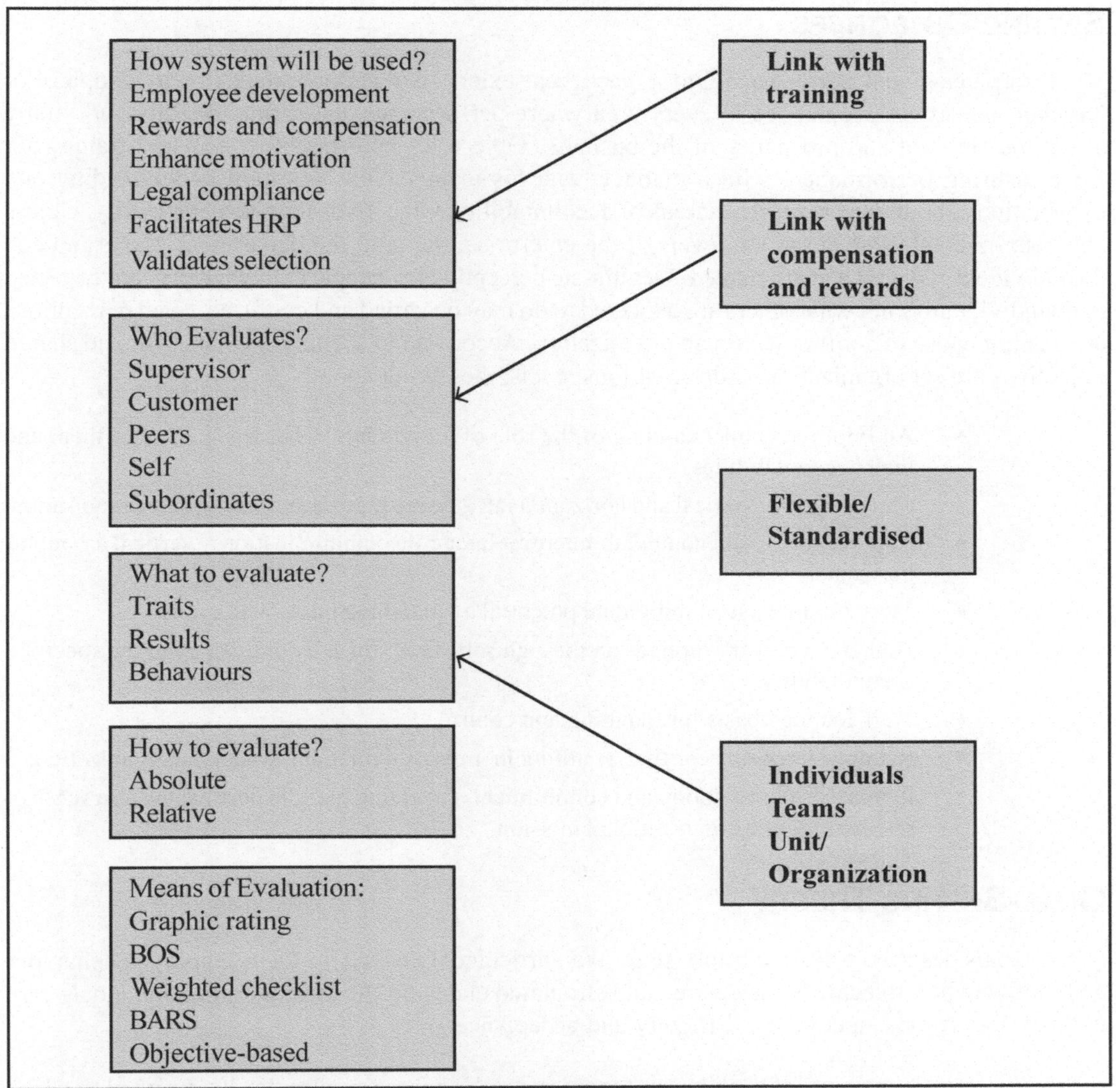

Figure 10.2. Strategic choices in PMS

performance, particularly over a period of time, is a strong defence against charges of unlawful bias.

Finally, PMS supports HRP (human resource planning). Performance data can alert the organization about impending skill shortages and can be used for staffing: recruitment and selection. PMS is also used to validate the selection process and results of various psychological tests. First validation of tests can be done with existing employees and later for the selected ones. Because PMS can serve multiple functions it must determine in advance for what purpose it is going to be used and data is accordingly organised and classified (Figure 10.2).

SETTING OBJECTIVES

Organisational performance, to a very great extent, is the performance of its people. For Drucker, objectives are needed in every area where performance and results directly and vitally affect the survival and prosperity of the business. Objectives help establish a shared framework for measuring performance, with a manager and his team having common understanding and expectations about their respective areas of accountability. Objectives help achieve clarity. Unless concrete objectives are set at the levels of the enterprise, the unit, the department, the group and the individual—shared and articulated—legitimate perceptions of people as to what they are expected to do individually, and what others are expected to do may be varied and confused. Such perceptions are a major cause of conflict within an organization. According to Wehirich, when clear and shared objectives are set organization-wide at various levels, they bring about:

- An improved understanding of the role of individuals: what is expected of them and their accountabilities.
- More effective vertical and horizontal integration of goals and tasks in the organization.
- Concrete and valid context to interpret inter-role communication—vertical as well as horizontal.
- More optimal use of individual potential by matching goals with capacities.
- Higher-level work motivation through self-direction and control within the specified accountability.
- Well-founded basis for planning and control.
- Reduced inter-role conflict, resulting in improved relations across the organization.
- Increased subordination and commitment, providing the role occupant with a sense of relevance to the organizational mission.

GOAL-SETTING THEORY

Goals describe a desired future state. Well articulated goals help focus employee behaviour and motivate him to achieve the desired and stipulated end state. According to Gordon, goals vary in three dimensions: specificity, difficulty and acceptance.

- Specificity of goals means the extent to which these are clear to all concerned, to which their accomplishment is observable and measurable.
- Goal difficulty is the level of performance desired in relation to the employee's capability: it can vary significantly.
- The employees' acceptance of the goals that have been set, will determine his commitment to accomplish it. Imposed or assigned goals are generally less likely to be owned by an employee, compared to those that are jointly set. An employee will accept the goals if he considers them reasonable, is self assured, and has previous successes in fulfilling goals. Acceptance of goals increases the chances of their being achieved and fulfilled. Commitment to goal fulfilment is, however, only partly influenced by employee participation in goal setting. Relationships with superiors, peer group pressure, as well as support to accomplish the goal, organizational work culture and values, the

reward contingent on goal performance, the expectancy of success, etc., are some of the other factors that influence goal commitment and achievement.

- Research suggests that goals that are specific, moderately difficult and accepted by employees are more likely to be motivating than those which are not.
- Research has also shown the value of planned feedback as a necessary condition for goal accomplishment.
- According to Lock, goals that are challenging and specific, and if accepted, result in higher performance than easy goals, not the approach to your best goals are no goals.
- The creative and problem-solving abilities of human beings and their growth potential suggests that self-directed changes occur as natural life processes. The likes of Norman Vincent, Peale and Dale Carnegie rely heavily on the concept of the human will—the ability to control and change one's own behaviour—rather than the belief that man reacts to stimuli and is controlled by the environment.

Communicating the Organisation's Mission

The pursuit of employee commitment to the organisation's mission is something which has dominated people management thinking in recent years. Beer *et al.* (1984) specified commitment as one of the 'HR outcomes'. Guest (1987) identified commitment as one of the four goals of HRM together with strategic integration, flexibility and quality. Legge (1995) suggests that the orthodox interpretation of commitment is operationalised in terms of three factors: a strong desire to remain a member of the organization; a strong belief in and acceptance of the values and goals of the organization; and a readiness to exert considerable effort on behalf of the organization. We have seen in the closing case that the mission of Siemens to be a world leader greatly influenced the employees. Guest argues that organisational commitment will result in high employee satisfaction, high performance, longer tenure and a willingness to accept change.

Appraisal of Performance

According to Heathfield (copyright: 2000 about.com, downloaded from internet), 'second only to firing an employee, managers cite performance appraisal (PA) as the task they dislike the most'. She believes that the process of PA, as traditionally practised, is fundamentally flawed, for the following reasons:

- It is incongruent with the value-based, vision-driven, mission-oriented, participative work environments favoured by forward thinking organizations today.
- It smacks of an old-fashioned, paternalistic, top-down, autocratic mode of management which treats employees as possessions of the company.
- Most of the time, PA reflects what the manager can readily recall, usually the most recent events.
- Almost always PA is based on hunches and opinions as 'real' PA takes time and follow-up to do well.
- Many managers are so uncomfortable in the judgement seat that PAs are often months overdue. Despite the fact that annual raises are usually tied to PA, managers often

BOX 10.2
Appraisal of Performance—What?

A corporate president put a senior executive in charge of a failing operation. His only directive was 'get it in the black' within two years of that injunction. The new executive moved the operation from a deficit position to one that showed a profit of several million. Fresh from his triumph, the executive announced himself as a candidate for a higher level position and indicated that he was already receiving offers from other companies.

The corporate president, however, did not share the executive's positive opinion of his behaviour. In fact, the president was not at all pleased with the way the executive had handled things. Naturally, the executive was dismayed, and when he asked what he had done wrong, the corporate president told him that he had indeed accomplished what he had been asked to do, but he had done it single-handedly, by the sheer force of his own personality. Furthermore, the executive was told, he had replaced people whom the company thought to be good employees with those it regarded as compliant. In fact, by demonstrating his own strength, he had made the organization weaker. Until the executive changed his authoritarian manner, his boss said, it was unlikely that he would be promoted further.

Implicit in this vignette is the major fault in performance appraisal and management by objectives—namely a fundamental misconception of what is to be appraised.

Source: Harry Levinson.

avoid doing them as long as possible. This results in an unmotivated employee who feels his manager does not care enough about him to facilitate his annual raise.

- The manager knows he may have to justify his opinions with specific examples when the staff member asks and, lacking skill in providing feedback, often provokes a defensive response from the employee who may justifiably feel he is under attack. Consequently, managers avoid giving honest feedback, which defeats the purpose of the review.
- Disagreement about contribution and ratings can create a conflict-ridden situation that festers for months. Most managers avoid conflict that will undermine workplace harmony.
- The staff member whose performance is viewed below becomes defensive as he perceives his manager as punitive.
- In today's team-oriented environment, it is also difficult to ask people who work as colleagues, and sometimes even friends, to take the role of judge and defendant.
- With salary increases frequently tied to the numerical rating or ranking, the manager knows he is limiting the staff member's pay if he rates him less than 'outstanding'. No wonder in one unit 96 per cent were rated as 'outstanding'.

Many more defects can be added to this list. Some people might argue that these problems are deficiencies of managers, not of the system. But even if that were altogether true, managers are part of the system. PA needs to be viewed not as a technique but as a process involving both people and data, and as such the whole process is inadequate.

One of the main sources of trouble with the PA system is that the outcome of behaviour rather than the behaviour itself is what is evaluated (as shown in the case in Box 10.2). In fact, most people's jobs are described in terms that are quantitatively measurable; the job description itself is also one of the roots of the problem. In most instances the appraiser is asked to do an overall rating with a five-point scale or some other device. Finally, he is asked to make a statement about the person's potential for the next step. Nowhere in the set of questions or in most of the appraisal systems, is anything asked about 'how the person is to attain the ends' he or she is charged with reaching

Every manager has multiple obligations, not the least of which are certain kinds of relationships with peers, subordinates, suppliers, consumers, financial institutions and government and the public. Some of them are more important than others, and some need to be handled with much greater skill and aplomb than others. Because static job descriptions define behaviour in gross terms, crucially important differentiated aspects of behaviour are lost when performance appraisals are made. In a progressive company's PA, the manager works out his own job description, prepares a mission and role statement of what he is supposed to do according to the guide which specifically directs him to concentrate on the what and the when, not on the why or how. The guide instructs him to divide his mission into four general areas:

1. innovation.
2. problem-solving,
3. on-going administration, and
4. personal.

In another company, a manager appraising a subordinate's performance is asked to describe an employee's accomplishments, neglected areas, goals and objectives. The manager is told to recognize good work, suggest improvement, get agreement on top priority elements of the task, clarify responsibility, verify and correct rumours and talk about personal and long-range goals.

In another company's outstanding performance appraisal guide, which reflects great detail and careful consideration, the categories are: work, effectiveness with others, problem-solving, decision-making, goal setting, organization planning, developing subordinates, attending to self development and finding initiatives. Each of these categories is broken down into example statements such as:

- Exhibits high level of independence in work.
- Identifies problems and deals with them.
- Appropriately subordinates departmental interest to overall company goal.
- Gives people genuine responsibility, holds them accountable, and allows them freedom to act.

Some experts have suggested role analysis techniques to cope with static job description. Even these techniques are of limited use because they do not specify required behaviours. Nowhere the individual is told what behaviour is expected of him in a range of contexts.

Who are the sensitive people with whom certain kinds of relationships have to be maintained?
What are the specific problems and barriers?
What have been the manufacturing blunders or frictions?
How should union relationships and union leaders be dealt with?
What are the specific integrative problems to be resolved and what are the historical conflicts?

These and many more similar pieces of behaviours will be the true bases on which a person will be judged, regardless of the questions an appraisal form asks. This is the background of techniques like Behaviourally-Anchored Rating Scale (BARS) and Behaviour Observation Scale (BOS). An example of these techniques is given in designing the PMS for a professional institute by the author in the final section of this chapter.

In order for PA to be effective for coaching, teaching, and changing those aspects of an employee's behaviour that are amenable to change, an employee needs to know about each piece of behaviour that is good as well as that which for some reason is not acceptable or needs modification. Hence the need for keeping the appropriate data.

Reinforcing Core Competencies

Some firms are using PMS for enhancing their 'core competencies'. Such competencies define for all members of the organization the behaviours, skills, attributes, performance factors and proficiencies that every organization member is expected to possess and display. They are limited in number and critical to organisational success.

The PMS plays several roles here. First, it is the mechanism that helps the organization highlight and communicate the small number of critically important behaviours and skills against which every single employee will be assessed. In addition, creating a new performance appraisal system may help force the organization to define just what attributes or factors are actually at the organisation's core.

Finally, the appraisal system can guarantee that these competencies are fully understood and institutionalised. For example, the senior management of the Minnesota Department of Transportation defined its mission, vision and values and identified seven core competencies and a dozen individual characteristics expected of every employee. The PMS was built around them.

These competencies were: leadership, learning and strategic system thinking, quality management, organisational knowledge, technical knowledge and people management. Instead of defining what each of these terms meant, they instead described the behaviour one would likely see exhibited by a true master performance.

Another innovation in PMS was displayed by the 'City of Irving'. As annual appraisal time approaches, each city employee is asked to fill out a short questionnaire that kicks off the process.

The form consists only of four open-ended questions so that at the end of the appraisal one does not feel that the accomplishments were ignored. These questions are:

1. In appraising your performance, are there any other persons you work with or around with whom your supervisor should speak to get a more complete picture of how you do your work/get results?
2. Of what accomplishments and skills acquired during the last appraisal period are you particularly proud?
3. What can be done to make you more effective in your job?
4. What can be done to help you provide better service to your customers?

In short, PMS can significantly impact organisational performance and processes. However, there is no one optional way to develop and design an effective PMS, Organisations face a number of strategic choices as to how they measure performance and provide employees feedback on the process.

THE 360 DEGREE APPRAISAL

The three hundred and sixty degree feedback programme can involve feedback for a targeted employee or manager from four sources:

1. downward from the target's supervisor,
2. upward from subordinates,
3. laterally from peers or co-workers, and
4. inwardly from the target himself.

Studies show that about 12 per cent of American organizations are using full 360 degree programmes, 25 per cent are using upwards appraisals and 18 per cent are using peer appraisals (Antonioni, D., 1996. 'Designing an Effective 360 Degree Appraisal Feedback Process.' *Organisational Dynamics* 25(2): 24-38). Furthermore, the trend is increasing. The most reasons for this growth include the desire on the part of the organizations to enhance management development, employee involvement, communication and culture change.

A key process driving the present use of this process is the desire to encourage leadership development. Providing feedback to managers about how they are viewed by subordinates, peers and customers should prompt behaviour change. Many managers have not received as much honest feedback as is necessary for an accurate self-perception. When this is compared with self-evaluation by a manager, it may form a real picture of his strengths and weaknesses. This may prompt behaviour change if the weaknesses identified were previously unknown to the manager, especially when there are problems in the introduction of this process and firms are advised to use it initially for development purposes until managers get used to it and have less fear about the possible adverse rating. As is true for all performance assessments, 360 degrees should be congruent with the organisation's strategy and should measure important targets such as accomplishment of the organisation's goals. In Table 10.1 is furnished a format used for customer feedback.

TABLE 10.1
Format for Customer Feedback

Quality		
I had to wait an unreasonable amount of time for my requests to be met 1 2 3 4 5?	Was cooperative in meeting my requests 1 2 3 4 5?	Kept me informed about the status of my requests 1 2 3 4 5? 1 = strictly disagree 2 = disagree 3 = neutral 4 = strongly agree 5 = very satisfied
Customer Satisfaction		
The products I have received have met my expectations 1 2 3 4 5?	Communicated with me to understand my expectations for products 1 2 3 4 5?	How would you rate your overall level of satisfaction with the service you have received? 1 = very dissatisfied 2 = dissatisfied 3 = neutral 4 = satisfied 5 = very satisfied
My requests were met on or before the agreed upon deadline 1 2 3 4 5?	Was uncooperative when I asked for revision/ additional information 1 2 3 4 5?	
The products I have received have generally been error-free 1 2 3 4 5?	Told me when my requests would be filled 1 2 3 4 5?	What specifically could be done to make you more satisfied with the service?
Service, attitude		
When serving me, this person was helpful 1 2 3 4 5?	When necessary, he explained to me why my expectations could not be met 1 2 3 4 5?	How would you rate your overall length of satisfaction with the products 1 2 3 4 5?

TABLE 10.2
General Electric 360 Degrees Leadership Assessment Chart

Characteristic	Performance Criteria	MGR	Peer	Subord-inates	Others
Vision	• Has developed and communicated clear, simple, customer-focused vision/direction for the organization • Forward-thinking, stretches challenges and imagination • Inspires and energises others to commit to vision. Captures minds. Leads by example • As appropriate, updates vision to reflect constant and accelerating change impacting the business				
Customer quality focus	• Listens to customer and assigns the highest priority to customer satisfaction including internal customers • Inspires and demonstrates a passion for excellence in every aspect of work • Strives to fulfil commitment to quality in total product/service offering • Lives customer service and creates service mindset throughout the organization				
Integrity	• Maintains unequivocal commitment to honesty in every facet of behaviour • Follows through on commitments, assumes responsibility for own mistakes • Practises absolute conformance with company policies embodying GE's commitment to ethical conduct • Actions and behaviour are consistent with words. Absolutely trusted by others				
Accountability Commitment	• Sets and meets aggressive commitments to achieve business objectives				

Continued...

...Continued

Characteristic	Performance Criteria	MGR	Peer	Subord-inates	Others
	• Demonstrates courage/self confidence to stand up for beliefs, ideas, co-workers • Fair and compassionate, yet willing to make difficult decisions • Demonstrates uncompromising responsibility for preventing harm to the environment				
Communication influence	• Communicates in open, candid, clear, complete and consistent manner—invites response/dissent • Listens effectively and constantly probes for new ideas • Uses facts and rational arguments to influence and persuade • Breaks down barriers and develops influential relationships across teams, functions and layers				
Shared ownership boundaryless	• Self-confidence to share information across traditional boundaries and be open to new ideas • Encourages/promotes shared ownership for team vision, goals • Trusts others; encourages risk-taking and boundaryless behaviour • Champions workout as a vehicle for everyone to be heard. Open to ideas from anywhere				
Team builder empowerment	• Selects talented people; provides coaching and feedback to develop team members to the fullest potential • Delegates whole tasks; empowers teams to maximise effectiveness. Is personally a team player				

Continued ...

...Continued

Characteristic	Performance Criteria	MGR	Peer	Subord-inates	Others
	• Recognises and rewards achievements. Creates positive/ enjoyable work environment • Fully utilises diversity of team members (culture, gender,, race) to achieve business success				
Knowledge Expertise Intellect	• Possesses and readily shares functional/technical knowledge and expertise. Consistent interest in learning • Demonstrates broad business knowledge/perspective with cross-functional/multicultural awareness • Makes good decisions with limited data, applies intellect to the fullest • Quickly sorts relevant from irrelevant information, grasps essentials to complex issues and initiates actions				
Initiative/speed	• Creates real and positive change. Sees change as an opportunity • Anticipates problems and initiates new and better ways of doing things • Hates/avoids/eliminates bureaucracy and strives for brevity, simplicity and clarity • Understands and uses speed as a competitive advantage				
Global mindset	• Demonstrates global awareness/ sensitivity and is comfortable building diverse global teams • Values and promotes full utilisation of global and workforce diversity • Considers the global consequences of every decision. Proactively seeks global knowledge • Treats every one with dignity, trust and respect				

Questions and Assignment

Q.1. Why do you think stage 3 of the performance management cycle shown in Figure 10.1 (feeding back results) is so important?

Q.2. What skills do you think line managers have for effective functioning of PMS in any firm? Also outline the role of HRM in this process.

Q.3. Individual employees are likely to be more critical of themselves than their managers would be. Why do you think this is the case?

Q.4. It has been argued that performance management may allow a better understanding of the contribution of the business unit to overall organizational performance. What assumptions underpin the two ways in which this may be achieved?

Q.5. Conventional wisdom suggests that including pay and training in the same appraisal process is not a good practice. Why do you think this is so?

Q.6. Visualize yourself as HR manager of a firm where you have experience and your PA is due and your superior has asked you to prepare your performance plan for the next calendar year; prepare the same.

Q.7. Prepare the format for role analysis for a manager in any function in which you have some experience.

Q.8. What recommendations can be provided to an organization considering the implementation of the 360 degree appraisal system?

Q.9. Explain the impact of PMS on other areas of HR. Explain the impact that PMS can have on an organisation's culture.

Assignment

Individually or in small groups, select one occupation and design a PMS for this position.

- University professor
- Retail sales person
- Software engineer
- Priest
- Attorney.

DEVELOPMENT OF PERFORMANCE APPRAISAL SYSTEM, FOR FACULTY OF PROFESSIONAL INSTITUTES: BARS APPROACH

Synopsis

Teachers are expected to shape the values, inculcate learning, impart knowledge and help in building the character of students. Since learning is primarily a cognitive process, evaluation of faculty performance is very important, yet it remains one of the most frustrating and mismanaged tasks for college and university administrators. Communicating strengths, weaknesses and areas of improvement to highly educated, critically thinking professionals is challenging and intimidating. Therefore it is often neglected.

In this paper an attempt has been made to design the performance appraisal process based on current ideas of BARS (Behaviour Anchored Rating Scale) to change the existing confidential reporting system, prevalent in an institute. Critical behaviours that contribute to faculty as well as to an institute's performance have been identified and anchored on a scale and appropriately quantified to generate objective data about faculty assessment. An attempt has been made to make the system:

1. Open, rather than closed. It is transparent and students, peers and senior members of the institute provide information.
2. Democratic rather than authoritarian. It is participatory and equitable. The role of higher authorities in subjective appraisal has been minimized.
3. Developmental: it goes beyond assessment of past performance and encourages improvement by providing self feedback.
4. Customizable: the behaviours and their weightings can be altered to suit the culture, teaching requirements and other factors prevailing in any institute.

It is necessary that rewards should be specifically linked to performance and be explicit as well as provide choices to improve probability of valence and instrumentality for ensuring motivation. For this, the support and prior approval of owners of colleges is a must as well as discussions with faculty members and incorporating their suggestions in the system. Current issues in performance appraisal have been highlighted.

INTRODUCTION

Why companies do not drop their annual performance review systems? This question was asked in a *Wall Street Journal* article, 'Annual Agony', which amply conveys the grumblings of employees and management about performance appraisal as practised today. Most feel that it is just a ritual because ultimately what the boss thinks goes into the final assessment and rewards are distributed not on actual performance but on perceived notions of performance by superiors. It is also acknowledged that 'most of us don't like to sit down and hear where we are lacking and where we need to improve'. One survey even found that 98 per cent of managers reported aggression after giving employees negative appraisal.

With all this being partly true, performance appraisal is critical for any firm to achieve its objectives. Welch (ex CEO of GE) reports that his most important task, and the one he devotes more time to than any other, is motivating and assessing GE employees.

When it comes to appraisal of performance of knowledge workers like faculty of professional institutes, the task is all the more difficult because quantitative targets are few if any and assessment is mostly subjective.

What is to be Appraised?

Performance appraisal has three basic functions:

1. To provide adequate feedback to each person on his or her performance;
2. To serve as a basis for modifying or changing behaviour towards more effective working habits; and
3. To provide data to managers with which they may judge future job assignments, rewards and compensation.

The performance appraisal concept is central to effective management. Millions of dollars have been spent by companies in redesigning the system again and again to meet their changing organizational goals. In fact, HR consultancy largely survives on meeting this business need. Yet, present systems of appraisal in most institutes do not serve any of these functions well. In most cases, the appraisal system purports to evaluate what has been achieved. But in practice, people are really appraised on 'how' they do things, which is never described in setting up their objectives. Although managers appraise the ends, yet actually they give greater weight to the means and employ a static job description base which does not describe the 'how'; hence widespread dissatisfaction with performance appraisal is bound to continue.

Inadequacies of the Appraisal System

It is widely recognized that there are many things inherently wrong with most of the performance appraisal systems in use particularly in professional institutes. The most obvious drawback is that judgements are subjective and impressionistic. The rewards are arbitrary and not linked to performance for which enough information is neither gathered nor available. Ratings by different managers may be different for the same person. When salary increases and promotions are based on perceived notions of performance and impressions, many hard working but not so smart employees are highly demotivated. Although managers are urged to give feedback freely and often, they avoid it and are not able to do so effectively for lack of evidence or data or courage. Individuals who have acquired political skills usually get away with better appraisal and rewards. In case of faculty, there is not even the static job description or targets prescribed except the workload and the syllabus. There is some advice given or even pressure applied to publish papers or do similar activities, but what quality they present is never prescribed.

Some people might argue that these problems are deficiencies of directors, not of the system. But even if that were altogether true, directors are part of the system. Performance appraisal needs to be viewed not as a technique but as a process involving people, their activities and behaviour on the job and performance data. The whole system needs a radical rethink.

BARS (Behaviour Anchored Rating Scale)

BARS is a variation of the basic graphic rating scale. Here we focus on the meaning of the numbers on the scale. What does it mean when an employee is rated '1; versus '3'? Again, every one in the organization should share a common conception of the meaning of the scale anchor points. These scales are custom designed for each job-class. BOS (Behaviour Observation Scale) is another variation. Here again, desired behaviours to achieve the best results on the job are listed on a graphic scale. These behaviours should be observable to the superiors. BOS, is about how often such critical behaviours are displayed by the ratee.

These recent developments in performance appraisal have been used in developing the faculty appraisal system. 'BARS' converts organizational objectives into specific behaviours that can be prescribed for individuals. Such behaviours are anchored on a rating scale with suitable weights given according to the importance of behaviours for achieving organizational objectives to different anchor points. Systems are developed and put in place to collect information and data about such anchors and a mechanism is developed to regularly monitor the prescribed behaviours and record the data at suitable intervals for self, supervisory and peer review.

This, of course, requires lot of research in deciding for each position, which behaviours have a positive impact on organizational performance and which have a negative impact. Similarly, research is also required to decide which behaviours are essential, desirable and which ones are more important than others. The system is very useful for generating data to provide feedback. Since rating is done on the basis of data, subjectivity of judgment is minimized though not completely eliminated. Since the data is collected from students, peers and supervisors, it is a 360-degree appraisal system as well.

Based on the research done, through the case study method and from discussions with students, with the director, with my own experience and insights, a system of performance appraisal has been evolved for faculty appraisal in professional institutes, which is presented here. It is yet to be implemented. What difficulties arise in implementation and how much success is obtained in achieving organizational objectives remains to be studied. But the idea is sound and needs careful consideration of all concerned in professional institutions. The system is presented hereunder.

PROPOSED PERFORMANCE APPRAISAL SYSTEM

Evaluation of faculty performance and the subsequent determination of rewards is quite important, sensitive, and a potentially divisive process. Therefore, any effective system of faculty performance evaluation and distribution of rewards, as far as possible, should be:

1. Open rather than closed. It must be transparent, while respecting sensitive personal information.
2. Democratic, rather than authoritarian. It must be participatory and equitable.
3. Developmental, not only evaluative. It must go beyond thorough assessment of past performance and encourage improvement by identifying goals, avenues and resources for new work. It must motivate the individual to identify his or her potential.
4. Achieve organizational objectives. The institute must be clear about where it wants to be and how it wants to reach there.
5. Create a climate of cooperation and academic pursuit in the institute. It must be simple and supportive of the student's personality development and learning.
6. Make the appraisal process completely transparent to remove suspicion and mistrust among faculty members.

7. To recognize and reward the deserving faculty members and discourage negative culture.
8. To provide precise ratings based on overall performance (composite index) and to link rewards with the ratings so obtained.
9. 360 degree appraisal where self, students, peers, coordinator and the director are involved in providing the rating.
10. Provide a basis for factual feedback for future development of the faculty concerned.

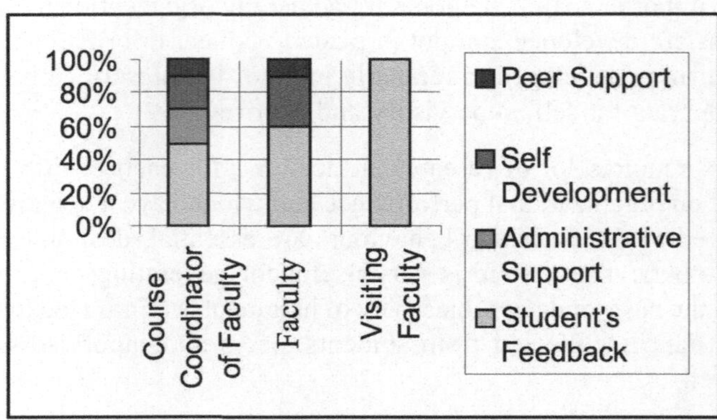

Figure 10.3. Proportionate weights in percentage to be given for students' feedback

The graph explains proportionate weights in percentage to be given for student's feedback, administrative support, self-development and peer support for a Course Coordinator, Faculty and Visiting Faculty.

Stage I (Preliminary Analysis)

In Stage I, various critical behaviours and activities were identified—based on students' response analysis, discussions with senior faculty members and with the Director—for outstanding, very good, good, and satisfactory performance classification. They are listed as under:

Students' Feedback (Stage I)

1. Outstanding (Marks 50)

- Makes the subject interesting and involving.
- Encourages discussions.
- Open to ideas.
- Adjusts to both weak and brilliant students.
- Gives regular feedback.
- Is unbiased.
- Uses current knowledge from different books, journals.
- Always regular.
- Very punctual.

2. Very Good (Marks 40)

- Outlines objectives at the beginning of every class.
- Invites questions and queries.
- Uses practical examples.
- Provides reference material.
- Maintains discipline of the class.
- Mostly regular and punctual.

3. Good (Marks 30)

- Uses practical examples.
- Gives feedback on assignments/projects.
- Knows most of the students.
- Generally punctual.

4. Satisfactory (Marks 20)

- Finishes syllabus in time.
- Uses very few practical examples while teaching.
- Follows one book mostly.

5. Not Satisfactory (Marks 10)

- Does not encourage queries and questions.
- Very few or no practical examples.
- Makes the subject dull.
- Is biased.
- Not regular.
- Not punctual.

Administrative Support (Stage I)

1. Outstanding (Marks 20)

- Coordinator of the courses or in charge of any specific activity of the management such as hostel, library, etc.
- Excellent PR with faculty, staff and students.
- Takes initiative with responsibility in many major academic, administrative or management areas.

2. Very Good (Marks 16)

- Active participation in management of activities such as placements, examination, admission, etc.
- Cooperative and helpful.

3. Good (Marks 12)

- Carries the responsibilities on his own in routine manner without much initiative.

4. Satisfactory (Marks 08)

- Carries the responsibilities but requires guidance and support.

5. Not Satisfactory (Marks 04)

- Needs to be reminded about work.
- Creates friction with staff or faculty.
- Misses deadlines.

Self-Development (Stage I)

1. Outstanding (Marks 20)

- Has done Ph.D., authored a book with a reputed publisher, or published two or more articles/research papers in internationally accredited journals or is member of three or more professional bodies.

2. Very Good (Marks 16)

- Published any article/research paper in any internationally accredited journal, has done two or more books/paper reviews, is member of two professional bodies, or has completed any professional/academic degree/diploma.

3. Good (Marks 12)

- Has published two or more articles/research papers in any Indian journal.

4. Satisfactory (Marks 08)

- Has participated in two or more seminars and given presentations.

5. Not Satisfactory (Marks 04)

- Has participated in one seminar or published any article/research paper in any Indian journal, or is not a member of any professional body.

Peer Support (Stage I)

1. Outstanding (Marks 10)

- Has published any joint paper/article with a peer in an important journal.
- Has helped colleagues/coordinator in doing their job.

2. Very Good (Marks 08)

- Active and productive participation in faculty/management meetings and is proactive and pro management.

3. Good (Marks 06)

- Inactive in regular positive interactions with peers.

4. Satisfactory (Marks 04)

- Talks lightly.
- Dominates discussions.
- Lacks courtesy and grace in behaviour.

5. Not Satisfactory (Marks 02)

- Indulges in gossip and in criticizing management/peers.
- Negative attitude.

Stage II (Final Selection and Development of Scale)

In Stage I, several behaviours were found to be common in outstanding, very good, good, and satisfactory anchors. It would have been a rather general assessment without getting composite indices for each individual and comparative data for providing feedback. Hence, a four-point Likert's scale was developed for precise and appropriate behaviours to be anchored on the scale. This is presented below:

Students' Feedback (Stage II)

1. Makes the subject interesting and involving
   *Always *Mostly *Rarely *Never
2. Encourages discussions, invites questions and queries and is open to ideas
   *Always *Mostly *Rarely *Never
3. Adjusts to both weak and brilliant students
   *Always *Mostly *Rarely *Never
4. Is unbiased
   *Always *Mostly *Rarely *Never
5. Uses current knowledge from different books and journals and does not follow one book mostly
   *Always *Mostly *Rarely *Never
6. Is regular and punctual in the class
   *Always *Mostly *Rarely *Never
7. Outlines objectives at beginning of every class
   *Always *Mostly *Rarely *Never
8. Uses practical examples
   *Always *Mostly *Rarely *Never

9. Provides reference material

*Always *Mostly *Rarely *Never

10. Gives regular feedback on assignments/projects and on class performance

*Always *Mostly *Rarely *Never

Marking
Students' Feedback

50 Marks—Given by 15 students chosen randomly.
On the four-point scale, the marking has been done as follows (out of 10):

1. 10 marks
2. 8 marks
3. 5 marks
4. 3 marks

Questions 1, 2, 3, 4 and 5: 20 marks each [actual marks obtained to be multiplied by two (2) for score on '20'].

Questions 6, 7, 8, 9 and 10: 10 marks each

Total: 150 marks

150 marks/3 = 50 marks

Administrative Support (Stage II)

1. Cooperation with faculty, staff and students

*Excellent *Good *Bad *Very bad

2. Active participation and vital contribution in management of activities such as placements, examination, admission, etc

*Always *Mostly *Rarely *Never

3. Provides vital contribution to the placement activities carried out in the campus

*Always *Mostly *Rarely *Never

4. Needs to be reminded about work

*Never *Rarely *Mostly *Always

5. Does the work assigned with involvement and dedication

*Always *Mostly *Rarely *Never

6. Creates friction with staff or faculty

*Never *Rarely *Mostly *Always

7. Misses deadlines

*Never *Rarely *Mostly *Always

8. Requires constant guidance and support
   *Never *Rarely *Mostly *Always

Marking
Administrative Support

20 Marks—10 marks given by the Director, 10 by Coordinator.
Questions 1 and 2: 20 marks each. Actual marks obtained to be multiplied by two (2).
Questions 3, 4, 5, 6, 7 and 8: 10 marks each
Total: 100 marks
100 marks/5 = 20 marks

Self Development (Stage II)

1. Has done Ph.D.
   *Yes *No
2. Authored a book with a reputed publisher
   *Yes *No
3. Published articles/research papers in internationally accredited journals
   *4 or more *3 *2 *1 *None
4. Member of professional bodies
   *4 or more *3 *2 *1 *None
5. Has done book/paper review
   *4 or more *3 *2 *1 *None
6. Has completed any professional/academic degree/diploma
   *Yes *No
7. Published articles/research papers in any Indian journals
   *4 or more *3 *2 *1 *None
8. Participated in seminars and given presentations
   *4 or more *3 *2 *1 *None
9. Organized any seminars
   *4 or more *3 * 2 *1 *None

Marking
Self-development

20 Marks—10 marks given by Subject Head, 10 by self.
Questions 1, 2 and 3: 20 marks each (to be multiplied by 2)
Questions 4, 5, 6, 7, 8 and 9: 10 marks each
Total: 120 marks
120 marks/6 = 20 marks

Peer Support (Stage II)

1. Published any joint paper/article with a peer in an important journal

   *Yes *No

2. Helps colleagues/coordinator in doing their job

   *Always *Mostly *Rarely *Never

3. Active and productive participation in faculty/management meetings, that is, proactive and pro-management

   *Always *Mostly *Rarely *Never

4. Active in regular positive interactions with peers

   *Always *Mostly *Rarely *Never

5. Listens with empathy

   *Always *Mostly *Rarely *Never

6. Lacks courtesy and grace in behaviour

   *Never *Rarely *Mostly *Always

7. Indulges in gossip and in criticizing management/peers

   *Never *Rarely *Mostly *Always

8. Has a negative attitude

   *Never *Rarely *Mostly *Always

Marking
Peer Support

10 Marks—Given by the Course Coordinator
Questions 1-8: 10 marks each
Total: 80 marks
80 marks/8 = 10 marks

Guidelines

- To be taken twice a year.
- Average of these two appraisals at the end of the year to be taken as final for all purposes.
- Feedback after each evaluation by Director/Professor/Course Coordinator. This gives an opportunity to the faculty to improve his rating in the second appraisal.
- For non-coordinators of courses and for non-in-charge positions like hostel or library responsibilities and only teaching responsibilities: Students' Feedback to be of 60 marks; Self Development of 30 marks and Administrative Support to be of 10 marks.
- For Visiting Faculty only Students' Feedback to be full 100 marks.

REWARDS

Performance appraisal should distinguish between outstanding and average performance and rewards should be designed accordingly. Vroom's expectancy theory is specifically helpful in providing this linkage. It is suggested that faculty and governing management should be involved in deciding relative rewards. Industry information does not exist in this regard for any guidance. However, a tentative scheme is presented for further discussions.

Based on Composite Index of Faculty, motivation can be provided with the following rewards:

I. >90 for two consecutive years—Promotion
II. >70—Two increments
III. Between 70 and 50—One increment
IV. <50—No increment

CURRENT ISSUES IN PERFORMANCE APPRAISAL

Performance management and appraisal system have become very important tools to integrate human resources with the organisation's wider strategy. The process links five policy elements: setting objectives, converting objectives into activities and behaviours, measuring performance, feeding back results, setting rewards and amending objectives and activities. Although the system is based on a rationalist approach, complexity and ambiguity may arise due to social and political factors at work in the organization concerned. These principles of performance appraisal are based on goal setting theory, and Vroom's expectancy theory of motivation. Employee performance is multi-dimensional, and as such there are always multiple roles and behavioural requirements. All such roles and behavioural requirements should be effectively identified and communicated before incorporation in the appraisal system. It is also necessary to reach a composite index as some faculty members may be higher in some dimensions and weak in others. The composite index is also useful for distributing rewards.

If properly designed and implemented, it can change the culture of the institute and put it on the path of progress. Needless to say that implementation is more important than design. Success will depend on effective implementation and participation by all. The implementation would be more effective in the institutions where open culture prevails.

CASE

PERFORMANCE MANAGEMENT AT SIEMENS STANDARD DRIVES (SSD)

Based in Cheshire, Siemens Standard Drives is the global headquarters for the variable speeds drive business of the German electronics giant Siemens AG. It employs 430 people in the design and manufacture of specialist electronic control equipment used in a wide range of electrical equipment. In 2003 it had 5 per cent of world market dominated by Japanese competitors Fuji, Mitsubishi and Yaskawa. Its target is 8 per cent by 2008 and to be the market leader with 10 per cent by 2010.

To achieve this ambitious objective Siemens embarked on a 9-month business process re-engineering project. It was clear that significant process improvements would be required. The company adopted a programme called 'World Class Siemens', the aim of which was to benchmark with other manufacturers and adopt the best processes in all areas and thus engender a culture of world-class practices. These include:

- A zero defects culture;
- Cellular and team-based manufacture;
- Daily cell meetings to discuss and agree on targets;
- Minimum stock at all stages of manufacture;
- JIT, Kanban delivery from suppliers direct to cell;
- Visible and agreed performance measures which form the basis of regular performance feedback;
- A multi-skilled and highly skilled workforce; and
- Total satisfaction of customer demand.

Much was made of the ability of process re-engineering to bring a new start for the company. The adoption of this approach was made easier through the commencement of a new production management team and a new HR manager. The first task of this team was to restructure the manufacturing operation to align personnel roles with the new structure.

The company had been structured on traditional functional lines. This meant that there were too many layers of responsibility, decision-making was slow and HR's responsibility was unclear and therefore ineffective. In order to meet the new operating strategy the structure was changed radically. The new structure is built around two main production segments. One of these manufactures PCBs and the other assembles and tests final products. Each production segment adopts a cellular manufacturing approach with 20-strong production arms headed by a group leader who has total responsibility for all aspects of the team's operation. The production groups are product based and have all the constituent parts of an autonomous cell (operators, a technician, a line feeder, and a test operator).

The group is responsible and accountable for its output and operation. The issue of accountability is crucial to success. If a team member is not performing adequately the team leader is empowered to remedy the situation. Initially this would be by giving assistance to the individual to improve performance. If this fails, the group leader has the power to terminate the individual's contract and recruit a replacement. This new approach was well received by production staff. However, in the early stages, approximately 10 per cent of employees decided they could not meet the new principles and left by mutual agreement.

The role of the group leader is vital. A few of the nine group leaders had been supervisors previously. However, they all accepted that with the new role carrying full operational responsibility and accountability the job could not have been more different. Most of the group leaders had previously been PCB or mechanical assemblers. They were selected for the new group leaders post on the basis of their business awareness and people management skills. Their training for new roles emphasized team building abilities. The senior management hope that the enthusiastic example they set to their team members will be infectious. Group leaders hold their own quality control meetings to discuss important issues for the day. They select, train and appraise team members. SSD is also adopting an annualized hours system whereby team members work a differing amount of hours weekly with an annual target that must be reached. The group leaders plan staffing levels as part of this system.

The key aspects of team working are shared ownership of objectives, skills training, performance feedback, communication meetings and, most importantly, 'no secrets'. Part of the culture change which the company has sought is the generation and publication of shared values. The values agreed by the teams are: openness, honesty, trust and respect.

Performance management is the vital aspect of a group leader's job. It has three elements. The first entails setting of individual performance objectives. This is done six-monthly by group leaders. Siemens uses the MBO approach where objectives are cascaded from overall business objectives through the four-tier company hierarchy to operators. These objectives are clearly displayed at the entrance to the production area. The criteria emphasize the quality, efficiency, attitudes (particularly flexibility) and attendance. The link between these criteria and overall business performance is obvious and demonstrable.

Dialogue between group leaders and the member is the second element. This has two components: an assessment of the member's performance against objectives set and a discussion of the member's training and development and career planning needs. Managers stress the need for a dialogue characterized by 50 per cent input from both group leaders and members. A crucial part of this dialogue is the view of the team members on the ways in which he or she thinks the company may be managed more effectively. This dialogue is seen by the managers to be a vital aspect of the 'open and honest' values they are seeking to create.

The third element is the output of the process. SSD is currently in the process of designing a performance related pay system which will be based on performance objectives. In the recently adopted appraisal system, the group leader makes it clear to each team member how progress through the pay structure can be achieved. This conversation is documented and owned by the team member.

All employees are clear that in a PMS driven by business objectives those employees who do not add value to their team through achievement of their individual objectives are held accountable for such failure. In such cases, improvement targets are agreed by the team member with the group leader and the implication of failure to meet these targets is made clear. In most cases the necessary improvement is forthcoming. But in some cases team members have been the subject of the disciplinary procedure, with some dismissals. The new approach has had considerable success in the twelve months since it was introduced. Labour efficiency has increased from 58 to 78 per cent and delivery performance from 72 to 94 per cent.

11

Strategic Compensation Management

Learning Objectives

After studying this chapter you will learn:

- Main issues and concerns in framing corporate compensation policy.
- The state's policy and legal framework about wages and salaries.
- The role of compensation and rewards in an organization.
- The concept of minimum wage, fair wage and living wage.
- The issues of compensation in team-based operations.
- Issues and concerns in CEOs' pay.
- Appreciate the elements of compensation structure and their rationale.
- How competency-based pay is managed.

INTRODUCTION

Compensation policies, practices and reward systems constitute a key strategic area for all types of organizations. They influence the cost structure of a firm and therefore decide the net profits on which depends the growth and survival of the firm. Besides the cost structure, they also decide the company's capacity to attract top professionals, to retain gold collar employees and its capacity to motivate the employees to give their best which, in turn, decides the overall performance, productivity and the total revenue. In the long-run, employee competencies and their decisions decide the future of the company.

However, the compensation policy and compensation structure of any organization is set and greatly influenced by the prevailing economic and social environment in the country where it is located. The wage policy of the country reflects the status of workers in society and their commitment to the industry and attitude towards management, their morale and motivation towards productivity, their living standard, extent of unemployment, etc. The wage policy of any country is also influenced by the prevailing competition and consumer expectations. In short, wage policy is a determinant of the share of rival claimants to the corporate profits, be they the shareholders or employees or the government.

In this chapter we will study the elements of compensation structure and how to frame compensation strategy and reward systems to achieve both short-term and long term strategic objectives of a firm so as to gain sustainable competitive advantage.

National Compensation Policy

The government is the largest employer (public sector and government departments, police and army, etc.) and also regulator and its wage policy influences the budget deficit, inflation rate and national income. Private sector companies are expected to pay more compared to the public sector to cover the relative security of public sector employment. In India, the Pay Commission is appointed to make recommendations. In today's globalised and hyper-competitive economy every organization has to carefully decide its corporate compensation policy within the national legal framework and design the compensation structure accordingly.

The main factors of national wage policy are:

1. Capital alone cannot generate goods and services. And as the world is moving towards a knowledge economy, old paradigms have to change to end exploitation of labour and provide for fair returns to both capital and labour such that the interests of consumers and primary producers are fully satisfied.
2. The corporate tax should be designed to prevent excessive profits but ensure that reasonable reserves for growth are maintained.
3. Try to achieve a living wage and fix statutory minimum wages in running in loss or start-up industries and a fair wage in more organised industries.
4. Ensure equal pay for equal work so that discrimination of any kind is discouraged.
5. Provide for wage differentials so that employee motivation to achieve performance and skills is encouraged.
6. Reduce undue disparities to minimize social tensions in society.
7. Link remuneration to productivity to enhance national competitiveness.
8. Compensate for rise in cost of living so that real wages are not reduced due to inflation.
9. 'The capacity to pay' should be given due weight for deciding a fair wage above the minimum wage (Supreme Court judgement).
10. To regulate the pay of top executives, board members and expatriates so that the gap in the pay of lowest employees and top executives is not excessive (Company Law).

To achieve the above objectives, the state has framed several Acts and Laws. Corporate compensation executives are advised to carefully monitor national wage policy and make adjustment in their organisation's compensation structure from time to time.

Corporate Compensation Policy

The term 'compensation' is used to indicate the employee's gross earnings in the form of financial rewards and benefits as part of the employment relationship. Compensation may also be viewed as:

1. A system of rewards that motivates employees to perform;
2. A tool used by organizations to foster the values, culture and the behaviours they require, and;
3. An instrument that enables organizations to achieve their business objectives.

As discussed earlier, the compensation policy of the firm will have serious impact on its competitiveness and profitability. The important factors to be taken into consideration are:

1. Community Concerns: Compensation policy cannot be conceived in isolation of community goals and environment. These concerns are price stability; improving standards of living; generating more employment and meeting the demands of competitiveness to attract global business, social equality and harmony.

   Incorporating these goals requires several trade-offs, with emphasis on wages being linked with cost reduction or increase in productivity and quality. This means preferring merit-based pay and fair wages so that workers are motivated and give their best.
2. The pay policy and company objectives, including shareholders' interests, need to be harmonized. It is necessary to align the company's compensation structure and reward systems with business strategy. It is necessary to link some portion of the employees pay to employee performance, skills or seniority. It is also necessary to offer benefits comparable to competitors and employees should have a say in choosing them.
3. Management has to decide whether it wants to lead, lag or meet the market. The market is defined as the average pay level offered by companies competing for employees with similar skill profiles. One common option is to meet the rates of competitors for the reasons that employee dissatisfaction will occur from failure to match and the firm's ability to attract bright employees will be limited by lower pay rates. Again, it is not easy to compute the average market pay because there are so many surveys available. A second option is to lag the market, which gives a cost advantage but makes it difficult to retain and attract the bright employees. If the labour market offers opportunities of good supply of required skills and product is standard, not requiring very sophisticated technology, a firm competing on cost can opt for this strategy. If the company is competing on quality, innovation, customization with sophisticated technology, it has to follow the policy of leading the market by paying higher pay levels.
4. The organization should ensure that in designing the compensation structure, both external and internal equity is achieved as much as possible for motivation of employees. Internal equity is described as the assessment of pay of an individual or of a group by reference to the contribution made or capacities required in respect of such factors as effort, qualification, experience, aptitude, etc. External equity is described as the assessment of pay by comparison with the incomes of other individuals or groups.

These individuals may be inside or outside of the company, in the same or different occupations. The equity criteria not only consider pay levels but all aspects of the employment package. This emerges from the 'equity theory of employee motivation.'

Internal Equity

- Internal equity will imply that wage differentials are structured in such a way that they correspond to relative differences in job contents as well as in different units. The absence of such structured differentials can be a major source of conflicts and grievances. Job evaluation is used to ensure internal equity.
- Consideration of team building, employee empowerment and flat flexible organization structures have led to 'broadbanding'. Internal equity in the process should not be given a go-by.

External Equity

- External equity can affect seriously an employer's ability to recruit suitable candidates and retain them. This may also lead to de-motivation amongst employees.
- External equity is ensured by conducting wage and salary surveys.
- Pay-roll analysis and policy correctives should be done regularly, supplemented by projections of wage and cost trends and monitoring of disparities.

From the above discussion it is clear that for organizations to achieve company objectives and avoid dissatisfaction among employees, it is desirable to ensure rationality of pay packets, internal equity, and external equity which requires that:

- The bulk of remuneration is linked to the job and its outcome.
- Basic wage is a predominant element in the pay packet.
- The basket of fringe benefits is determined by employee needs.
- The firm remains competitive in the global market and transfers between jobs and countries or locations are facilitated.
- The system of wage calculation is simple to understand by workers.

Thus designing the corporate structure and keeping it in alignment with business strategy demands intensive communication with unions, workers and different levels of management and shareholders. Therefore, this position requires in-depth knowledge of HR discipline, economics, and statistics with involvement in the company's corporate policy formulation at a very senior level.

Concept of Minimum, Fair and Living Wage

The deliberations in the 15th session of the Indian Labour Conference, 1957 and the Committee on Fair Wage (1948), have given the concept of wages as shown below. It may be noted that these are country specific.

TABLE 11.1
CEOs Salary Growth as Percentage of Company Profit Growth

Name	Company		Annual Pay Rs./Crore	Salary Hike %	Co. Sales Growth %	Profit Growth %
Sunil Bharti Mittal	CMD	Bharti Airtel	12.68	78.34	58.74	100.45
Pawan Kant Munjal	MD	Hero Honda	15.22	15.74	13.61	–11.68
Rajiv Bajaj	MD	Bajaj Auto	2.08	362.20	24.16	10.13
Naveen Jindal	MD	Jindal Steel	13.54	248.00	36.00	23.00
B.Muthuraman	MD	Tata Steel	2.20	13.40	15.36	20.41
K. V. Kamath	CEO	ICICI Bank	2.48	35.51	60.73	22.45
Aditya Puri	MD	HDFC Bank	1.28	–1.5	53.93	31.08
P. R. Patel	CMD	Cadilla Health	9.93	32.4	13.47	24.14
Malvinder M. Singh	CEO	Ranbaxy	2.62	–2.23	15.13	70.11
Azim Premji	CMD	Wipro	2.53	–1.93	33.49	40.66
Gajendra Patni	ED	Patni Computers	2.00	26.58	13.96	5.84

Sources: 2005-06 Reports; Sales/Profits 2006-07; Balance Sheets.

The Concept of Minimum Wage

This refers to the provisions under the Minimum Wage Act, 1948. It varies from state to state and also from industry to industry in India and is declared by the respective state governments or wage boards.

1. The subsistence or minimum wage is a wage which would be sufficient to cover the bare physical needs of the worker and his family—a rate which has got to be paid to the worker irrespective of the capacity of the industry to pay. ILC-1957 proposed the following norms:
   - The standard working class family should be considered as four consuming units and the earnings of family members are to be excluded.
   - The minimum food should provide 2700 calories for a normal adult.
   - Clothing needs at 16.62 metres per person per year.
   - House rent at minimum of the government industrial housing scheme.
   - Miscellaneous expenditure on lighting, fuel at 20 per cent of total minimum wage.
   - The Supreme Court in a judgement further added children's education, medical requirements and minimum entertainment, old age and marriages at 25 per cent of total minimum wage.

The Concept of Fair Wage

According to Pigou, a fair wage is fair once it is equal to the rate payable to identical workmen in an identical trade.

BOX 11.1
Rising CEO Salaries—What Directors Should Do

Ask any thoughtful corporate board member what he is most concerned about these days, and it is not Sarbanes-Oxley. It is CEO pay. Directors worry because shareholders continue to express outrage, and the media attention to the issue will not go away.

Directors are right to be concerned. The long-term trend has been for CEO pay to rise along with the pay for other senior executives, and it is now twice as much as that of CEOs in major European countries, according to Towers Perrin, a global consultancy. A recent study published by the National Bureau of Economic Research indicates that the increase in pay of senior executives and superstars in other fields has been a major source of the rising inequality of wages in the USA. Rising income inequality is political dynamite and damages the reputation of American business, already scarred by recent corporate scandals. Criticism of CEO pay has two related themes: It is too high, and it is not closely related to corporate performance.

These problems persist for complex reasons even as directors worry about them. The most significant reason is that board compensation committees face pressures to keep raising CEO pay. One pressure is the fear of losing an adequately performing CEO. To make sure this does not happen, compensation committees rely on surveys by compensation consultants about CEO pay in similar companies but without regard to company performance. These surveys report compensation by quartiles, and no compensation committee wants to admit that its CEO is below the median. In fact, most want to place their CEO in the upper quartile. As a result, CEOs are like the children of Lake Wobegon—all are above average.

Another upward pressure occurs when boards are trying to attract a new CEO from outside the company, and they make deals that guarantee the executive will come aboard. This means not only high pay, including incentives for performance, but also guaranteed 'good-bye' payments if things do not work out. These are one of the biggest sources of concern. The only existing pressure to keep CEO pay 'reasonable' other than the directors' conscience is concern about shareholders' reaction to excess compensation. But even well-meaning directors find it difficult to focus on shareholders. Shareholders are a changing and abstract group to the directors, while the CEO who has to be attracted and motivated is real and has an office right down the hall from the boardroom. Not surprisingly the upward pressure wins out.

If there were a silver bullet to relieve these pressures, they would not be so persistent. There are however, few steps a compensation committee can take.

Continued ...

...Continued

First, they should recognize that consultants' surveys are flawed and are a huge source of the problem. In this regard, directors should at a minimum insist on surveys that reflect company performance. Second, as former Dupont CEO Ed Woodlard has suggested, it is helpful to gauge CEO pay in relation to what the next echelon of management is being paid, thus placing the focus on internal equity. Finally, the compensation committee should focus more on what the shareholders will accept. As CEO pay rises, it becomes, along with other executive compensation, a larger portion of the wealth that otherwise would be available for shareholders. And ignoring shareholders' concern will continue to exacerbate the problem.

The SEC's recent attention to greater disclosure, while producing more information for shareholders, is also likely to resolve these problems.

Source: Jay W. Lorch. *HBR*, 13 September, 2006.

- The lower limit of the fair wage is obviously the minimum wage and the upper limit is the capacity of industry to pay, which depends not only on its present economic position but also on its future prospects.
- Between these two limits the actual wage will depend upon:
  1. productivity of labour,
  2. prevailing wages in similar occupations in the same locality,
  3. the level of national income and its distribution, and
  4. the place of the industry in the economy.

The Concept of Living Wage

According to the courts: 'Fair wage is one which is adequate to cover the normal needs of an average employee, being regarded as a human being in a civilised society.' Living wage is one which provides not only for most essential items like clothes and food, but also takes care of frugal comforts, in terms of the present standard of living and future needs.

- Article 43 of the Constitution has adopted the following as a Directive Principle of State Policy: 'The state shall endeavour to secure, by suitable legislation or economic organization or in any other way, to all workers, agricultural, industrial or otherwise, a living wage, conditions of work ensuring a decent standard of life and full enjoyment of leisure and social and cultural opportunities.' This is the ideal wage that unions are trying to achieve.

Corporate Compensation Structure

Corporate Compensation Structure means a single integrated plan for all levels in the whole organization. It is generally observed that:

- Often workers' wages are treated differently than managerial remuneration.
- Elements of managerial remuneration are not identical and tax considerations have led to various perks like maintenance of flat allowance, entertainment and club allowance, rent subsidy, medical allowances, LTC, etc. Further, there are faster opportunities for growth and promotion than provided to workers.
- This disparity requires adopting a comprehensive system approach to compensation management.
- This has added significance to the move towards a flat, flexible matrix organization.

The compensation structure of any firm indicates its preference towards internal and external equity and the degree of harmonization between different grades and jobs. It also indicates how the firm intends to attract, retain or motivate its employees and how much importance it gives to team work and long term performance of executives.

A Salary Scheme comprises progressive levels of responsibility; status and authority with corresponding pay increments; and relates effort to these rewards through a system of rules and procedures. The rules and procedures define what is required to move from one level to another level in the hierarchy and how that promotion decision will be made. Organisations however, will differ greatly in the extent to which the pay and job hierarchy is formalized and proceduralised, and the extent to which managers have discretion in pay and promotion decisions or whether the progression takes place automatically by the application of certain fixed rules. Hence, characteristics of a compensation system are:

1. A hierarchy of pay levels.
2. A hierarchy of jobs.
3. A set of rules and procedures that define relations between 1 and 2.
4. What qualities are necessary for movement from one level to another.
5. Who makes the choices, or by what processes are they made, when there is competition for promotion.

An organisation's compensation system usually consists of three separate components as shown in Figure 11.1.

Each element of the compensation system has a link with an individual's need hierarchy. For example, every individual desires safety and predictability in his pay, so that he plans his life style around it. Further, his pay in money terms should not be eroded due to inflation: for this dearness allowance pay is incorporated which is linked to the Cost of Living Index. Base pay and dearness allowance is provided to serve this purpose and also to distinguish the hierarchy of jobs. All allowances are linked to basic pay. When individuals are young they give their life to organizations, hence organizations should take care of them in their old age or sickness. Legal provisions take care of this part. Although every employee is expected to work, yet to motivate them and get their best effort for achieving various objectives rewards, incentives, merit pay, etc. are incorporated. To make employees share in the profits of the company, bonus and profit-sharing schemes are provided. To get long-term commitment and retain employees, stock option plan and annual

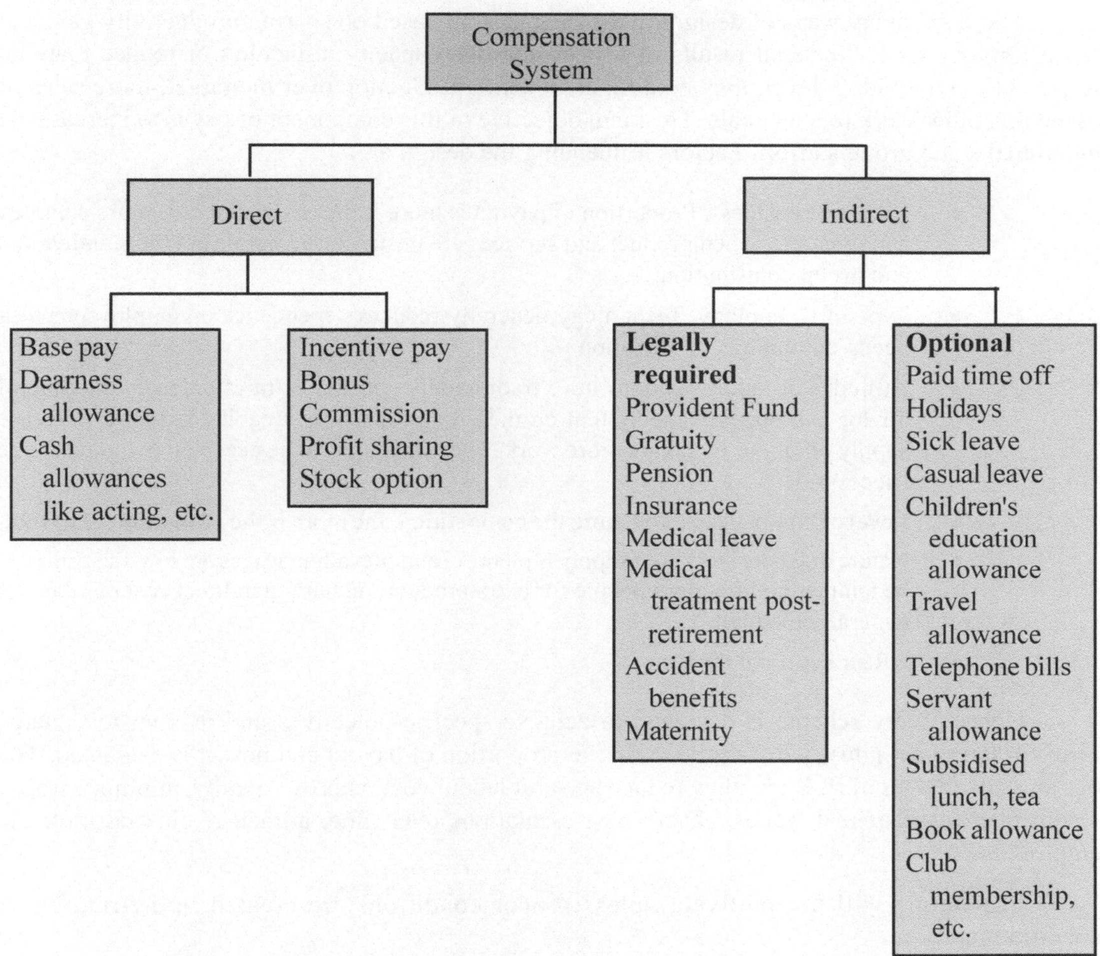

Figure 11.1. Corporate compensation structure

increments and promotions from one grade to another are provided. Other allowances to attract the best talent and improve the quality of life are included.

REWARDS, INCENTIVES AND MERIT PAY

What makes the difference between two organizations' performance in the same industry with nearly similar products? It is the level of their employees' commitment and motivation. Hence, how they reward their employees is a vital component of HR strategy. The performance linked pay or reward (PLR) system involves rewarding the employees according to their performance, or results achieved or contribution to the organisation's goals as individuals or as a part of a group. The reward system cannot be seen in isolation. It must be part of the overall compensation policy and corporate strategy.

There are many ways of designing the PLR system based on sharing productivity gain and profit improvement. Financial results of a firm improve capacity utilization or reduce material waste. At the individual level, they could include extra production over the target, more sales or exceeding other work related goals. The main objective of this component of pay is to increase the individual's and group's effort. Factors influencing the design are:

- Nature of business. Proportion of payout is more if the environment is more complex and dynamic, when product and services are unstructured, requiring more individual and group contribution.
- Type of technology. Technology generally reduces dependence on employees but it needs continuous upgradation.
- Attitudes of unions. Unions have traditionally resisted extra effort from the time of Taylor and opposed the system on the ground that it is a capitalist tool to increase supply of labour by taking more work. The system has to be accepted by unions to be successful.
- Level of competition. The more the competition, the more is the proportion of payout.
- Nature of labour market. If supply is plentiful and prevailing wages are low, the firm may be tempted to hire more people for extra production, but the indirect cost of labour is generally too high.
- HR strategies of the firm.

Hence, every scheme is designed to achieve specific objectives and it is custom made. Firms in the same industry differ greatly in the proportion of payout and how it is evaluated. The obvious advantages of PLR are: they reduce per-unit labour cost, improve quality, minimize waste, result in increase of real wages, absorb cost escalations over time, attract, retain and motivate employees.

PLR alone will not motivate unless proper conditions are created in a firm. These conditions are:

- Proper Information System for timely data collection and fair evaluation, introduced after due deliberation and consultation with unions.
- The scheme is simple and communicated effectively.
- Training and development of employees is organized so that they can complete the assigned tasks properly.
- Developing proactive attitudes amongst employees and supervisors regarding its fairness.
- Establishing a culture of team work.
- Money can never replace non-monetary rewards.
- Success will very much depend on a proper performance management system in the company.

Output-based incentive schemes are appropriate where tasks are repetitive and measurable. It is not suitable for high technology and service activities. Its objectives are:

- To encourage long-term commitment and loyalty to the company.
- To ensure employees benefit from the company's profitability and share in the wealth they help to create.
- Tax efficient rewards for employees.
- Tax efficient means of reward for the company.
- To help keep wage increase demands down and prevent strikes.
- To ensure that labour costs are responsive to the performance; hence profits of the company.
- To attract and retain employees, particularly senior executives.
- To reduce the role and therefore the need for unions.
- The assumption of PBR is that by paying workers directly for effort, employees will work harder—the proportion of PBR varies from high to low.

Types of PLR (Performance Linked Rewards) Systems

Various PLR schemes can be broadly classified as under:

1. Merit pay.
2. Schemes based on individuals, or small groups to contribute more in achieving desired results.
3. Piece rate or sales commission.
4. Incentive schemes which relate pay to increase in production or cost reduction on the basis of a pre-determined formula.
5. Bonus schemes based on contribution to productivity and profitability and plant utilization at the unit level or company level, taking into account the annual performance ratings of employees.
6. Productivity bargaining or gain sharing at unit level or plant level.
7. ESOPS (Employee Share Option Plans).
8. Competency-based reward system.

Merit Pay is the traditional method of salary increase by increments or bonus payments on the basis of the annual performance rating of employees. It is suitable for office staff and for other white collar employees whose work turnout cannot be easily estimated. To make the scheme more transparent and objective, the criterion of rating should be clearly spelled out.

This involves, first, the identification of job factors and their relative importance, the formulation of scale of rewards and collection of data about standards and actual performance and the distribution of rewards. For example, in a marketing department for salesmen, the job factors are: sales orders; realisation of outstandings; goodwill calls; attention to customer complaints.

These tasks differ in their degree of importance with the weights assigned (through job analysis) as 5, 3, and 2, respectively, to the above tasks.

- Suppose it is decided to give 24 per cent of basic pay as bonus/increment/incentive. Let there be 20 points, 1 point means 1 per cent of basic wage. If each identified job factor has a 4-point scale, then 20 points are distributed as shown.

Job Factors	Scale Unsatisfactory	Values Satisfactory	Fair	Good
Sales Task	0	3.0	6.0	10.0
Realisation of outstandings	0	1.8	3.6	6.0
Goodwill calls	0	1.20	2.40	4.0
Total	0	8.0	12.0	20.0

Scale values:

1. Unsatisfactory (sales target not achieved).
2. Satisfactory (sales target achieved).
3. Fair (3 per cent sales target up).
4. Good (5 per cent up).

Total rewards are distributed in the ratio of 2:3:4 for satisfactory, fair and good performance. No increment or rise in pay is given for unsatisfactory performance.

The demerits of this system are that the employees continue to benefit from their best performance in a particular year even if it remains below standard in the future. High rating of some employees may evoke jealousy and friction and thus may affect cooperation and goodwill.

The Piece Rate System or Sales Commission

The salient points of piece rate payments or sales commission are:

- Generally performance and payment are linked by a formula.
- Sales commission generally does not consider other parameters like realisation of outstandings or selling high margin products.

In the piece rate system it is not easy to reach agreement about per unit rate or quality rates. Frequent changes are required in standard output due to changes in layout or technology or other factors. This creates conflict with unions and labour. Conflict may also arise between different work groups when one group is dependent for work upon another.

Productivity Linked Group Schemes

Under this plan, productivity gains are shared in accordance with an agreed, pre-determined formula. Profit sharing gives a share of profits. Sometimes the quantum of bonus is determined on the basis of profits as well as productivity improvements according to a pre-determined benchmark value for each of them. For example, for a firm, calculation of benchmark productivity is decided by taking the average of the past three years' figures, say, 1998 (2.1), 1999 (2.6), 2000 (2.4)—the benchmark productivity is 2.3 and bonus is calculated for every point gain both in base profits and base productivity plotted on a chart. Profitability is defined as the ratio of operating profit before bonus to operating capital which is current assets + fixed assets. Productivity is also defined as the ratio of value added (margin) to labour cost. Sometimes bonus is distributed based on profitability, productivity and the performance rating of employees.

The problems with group schemes are:

- The motivational impact is limited as the link between effort and reward is remote and affected by many other factors.
- A seemingly minimal and infrequent reward and long intervals between effort and reward erodes its value.
- The illusory concept of these schemes and *bona fide* employee participation in decision-making.
- Problems with accurately calculating and allocating profit for distribution.
- Problems of setting of trigger points.
- The widening of gap in employees ranks.

Prerequisites of a successful scheme are:

- The cooperation of workers in the implementation is essential, particularly in deciding methods used to measure the results or output, and the methods followed in setting wage rates for different classes of work and also appropriate safeguards concerning earnings, job security.
- The scheme must be based on scientific work measurement. The standard set should motivate neither too little nor too much.
- Workers must be provided all tools, equipment. material in time so as to enable them to achieve the standards.
- Indirect workers like foremen, helpers, storekeepers, canteen staff, etc. should also be covered by incentives.
- There should be management commitment to the cost and time necessary to administer and plan schemes properly.

Payment by Time

In some organizations, payment is made entirely on the basis of time spent on the job. The reasons for this could be as follows:

- Attempts to encourage cooperation and recognise people's desire for a constant and predictable income.
- Performance in many occupations cannot be measured and linked to pay.

- With the advance of highly mechanised technologies, the need for effort being replaced by a need for reliable monitoring using cognitive and judgmental skills.
- Conflict over pay rates is confined to certain mechanisms such as collective bargaining and to a certain number of years.
- One implication is that it needs more responsibility for supervisors and managers that standards of performance are met (Shaw & Shaw, 1982: 305).

Payment and Results are Linked in Several Ways

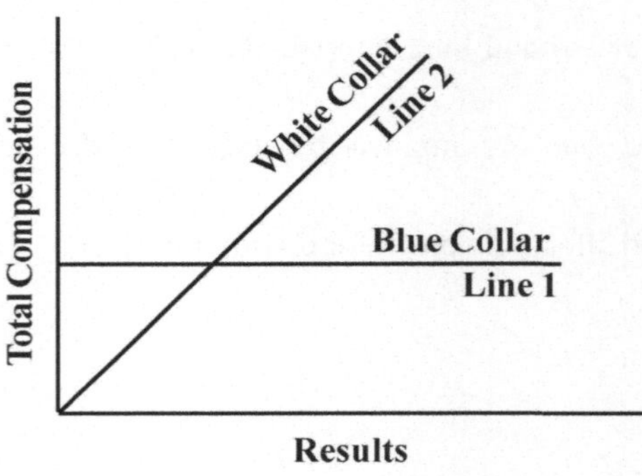

Figure 11.2. Leverage in the payment formula

Total Compensation

Results

Figure 11.3. General shape of payment line

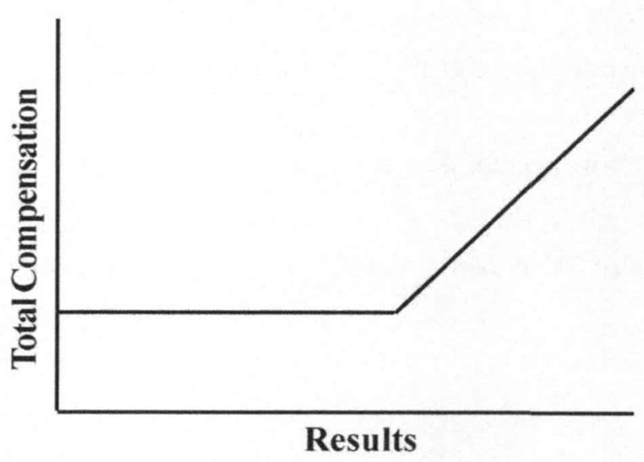

Figure 11.4. Threshold for bonus

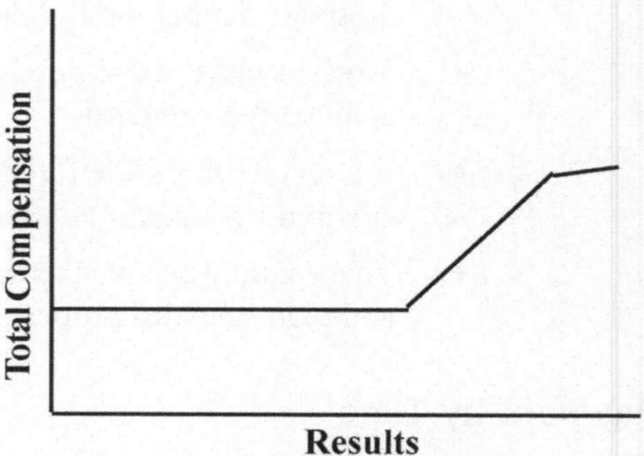

Figure 11.5. Maximum amount of bonus

Source: Rowland and Greene (1987: 57).

Payment is linked with results in several ways:

— Line 1: Base rate is high and extra payment is not highly rewarded, that is, reward and risk are low.

— Line 2: Here the base rate is low but increased performance is rewarded highly, thus amount of risk and reward is low (Figure 11.2).

— Linear: A straight reward represents a belief that each successive level of performance is as difficult or as important as the previous unit.

— Accelerating reward line with upward curve assumes that extra performance is increasingly more difficult or important or decelerating reward line with downward curve assumes that next unit or level of attainment is easier to achieve (Figure 11.3).

— Threshold point is a decision about at what level to begin bonus. It is important to ascertain what sort of return or benefit is expected before making the reward decision (Figure 11.4).

— A decision is also required to place or limit the maximum amount of incentive which can be paid particularly when future conditions are uncertain (Figure 11.5).

Advantages of PLR (Performance Linked Reward)

Most management experts believe that PLR results in:

- Increase in management control—as outlined in Porter & Lawler's model. Managers are able to enhance their control over pay and performance. A 1990 survey found that workers paid on the basis of output were less likely to clock in or out, tending to suggest that PLR enables managers to supervise lightly.
- Less supervision and greater freedom for employees means that workers will be after management to provide tools, materials and prefer to be left alone. This means that they exercise more discretion and more freedom.
- Opportunities to earn high earnings. They decide how to balance the wage-effort bargain.
- Create a joint appreciation to increase profit so as to benefit both the company and the worker.

Disadvantages of PLR

PLR is not entirely problem free and suffers from the following shortcomings:

- The incentive system may be distorted by provision of special allowances when breakdown of machinery occurs or other external factors affect it.
- Performance standards become slack for ex-employees who use the learning curve or discover new ways of doing work inflating unit labour cost.
- Sometimes management may also relax standards when there is shortage of labour.
- Workers might interfere in work allocations to seek their own notions of equity.
- Poor quality and more rejects to raise costs unless they are factored.
- Workers might resist changes in work practices if they perceive that it will affect their earnings.

TEAM-BASED PAY

Today in the globalised services-oriented knowledge economy, firms are making increasing use of teams because they can generate greater gains in productivity and quality even as employees earn psychic rewards from team involvement. They widely employ special-project, product-development, cross-functional, self-managed and ad-hoc teams to cut cost, realign production processes, and engage in all sorts of problem spotting and solving activities.

In compensating the teams for sharing in financial gains and motivating members, the following questions demand answers for better performance:

- How to evolve team performance?
- Should members be paid on individual basis or as a team?
- Should they be paid with money or 'recognition'?
- If it is cash, how much is enough?
- When should they be paid? At the end of a project or during its stages because some projects go on much longer.
- Should members know in advance how much they will be getting?
- Should every member get an equal share or be paid according to his or her contribution? And how to assess relative contributions?

Answers to these questions are not easy. Some firms are still using the traditional method of performance evaluation to compensate teams. As David Goodall, Corporate Director of Compensation at Motorola Inc., puts it: 'Organisations of the '90s are trying to manage with compensation tools of the '50s and '60s'. These firms believe that the motivation comes from within the individual, not from the group, and the development of skills and behaviours is an individual undertaking. Difficulty also arises because people are not assigned full time to teams and often are members of several teams. Today most executives spend considerable work-time in teams. Yet only some firms compensate teams through small group incentives (16 per cent to 19 per cent from 1995 to 1996; *Compensation Survey of 2500 Companies.* William M. Mercer Inc.).

At TRW Inc., additional incentives and recognition are always added for team participation. A significant portion of their pay is tied to the accomplishment of team and organization goals ranging from 10 per cent for the lowest paid to 25 per cent for those at higher levels. The lower level workers get less because they should not be exposed to high risk.

The traditional thinking is to link payment with results or targets. But it is very difficult to quantify results. Again, teams are supposed to take the organization forward by taking risks and they may not always succeed. Hence, they should be rewarded for team behaviours and activities displayed by members. And this can be best judged by the team members themselves or peers through the 360 degree appraisal process.

Teams work best when the head of the team has reward power over members for the time they work together. Further, it is important to ascertain the nature of team activity: is it like a soccer team or a relay race team? If it is a highly interactive team, it is best to reward the team as a whole; also recognize the most valuable team member additionally. It is also suggested that members of the team can divide the bonus amongst themselves.

Money is not everything when you are rewarding teams and managers and consultants agree that various other ways of saying 'thank you' constitute the best incentive over the long run. In this regard, a research into individual taste and background can help in selecting the best way of rewarding. Recognition should not be delayed and first expressed in private and then given in public.

True commitment to the team process starts with allowing the team to determine how it will accomplish its objectives and to suggest, if not to determine, how recognition will be distributed to members and other contributors. Which only stands to reason: After all, to really support the team process, teams have to be given autonomy.

COMPETENCY-BASED COMPENSATION

The competency-based compensation system is based on the premise that the possession of appropriate competencies is highly correlated with superior performance. Acquisition and demonstration of competencies relevant to the role assigned to the employee can therefore be taken as a surrogate measure of performance for the purpose of compensation. There are three building blocks of the system:

The Concept of Competencies

The Hay/McBer definition describes a competency as a characteristic of an individual that has been shown to drive superior job performance. The competencies manifest themselves as a complex of knowledge, skills and personal traits that drive superior performance. In other words, competencies describe what makes people effective in a given role. While the knowledge and skill components of the competencies are clearly visible, the personal attributes like self image, traits and motives are hidden components and are difficult to understand and influence.

The language of competency provides a common framework to describe jobs, people and systems that bring people into roles, reward them and pass them to the next role. Competency defines what kind of roles and behaviours can and should be used to satisfy objectives most effectively.

For individual employees, it means understanding not only what essential objectives are to be achieved but also what skills, knowledge and behaviours are needed to achieve these objectives. It also makes it clear that while knowledge and skills are necessary for top performance, they are not sufficient to guarantee it. The underlying competencies often suggest behaviours that lead to long-term success and ensure that key objectives are achieved.

Concept of Career Stages

Career stages or competency levels define the broad complex of knowledge, skills and personal attributes that an employee is expected to acquire and demonstrate as he grows in his career. There are normally four stages or levels:

Stage 1: Stage of Dependency

- Willingly accepts supervision.
- Demonstrates competence on a portion of a larger project.
- Competent at detailed and routine tasks.
- Shows directed creativity and initiative.
- Able to perform well under time/budget pressure.
- Learns the 'how' of doing things.

Stage 2: Stage of Independence

- Assumes responsibility for definable projects.
- Relies less on supervision, works independently and produces significant results.
- Develops credibility and reputation.
- Increases his technical competence and ability.
- Builds an internal network.
- Develops as an innovator.

Stage 3: Stage of Contribution through Others

- Stimulates others through ideas and knowledge.
- Involves himself as a mentor or idea leader in developing others.
- Increases in technical breadth.
- Represents the organization effectively to clients and external bodies.
- Builds a strong internal and external network, communicates significance of external developments.
- Leader in team performance.

Stage 4: Stage of Leadership through Vision

- Provides global technical direction to the organization.
- Influences decisions and participates in securing resources.
- Represents the organization on critical strategic issues.
- Sponsors technology initiatives.
- Champions significant technology and products.

Broad Pay Bands

The base pay structure that best serves a system of compensation based on competencies comprises a few broad bands. Each band has a sufficient range to accommodate pay steps from entry to a level where the employee acquires and demonstrates competencies for his promotion to the next band. Bands are fewer in number than traditional pay grades. Here, movement between levels is totally dependent on the jobholder acquiring the necessary competencies and do not depend upon the availability of vacancies. Therefore the jobholders progress from one level to another as soon as they acquire and demonstrate the necessary competencies.

It is thus possible for an entire team to start at the lowest level and steadily progress to reach the highest level. Secondly, there is an upper limit to progression. At some stage, structure becomes necessary and then further progression becomes dependent on the availability of vacancies.

This kind of structure has significant implications for controlling wage and salary costs. As each level of competency carries its own pay levels and progression is not constrained by vacancies, there is real risk of paying for inputs without a strong linkage to the output. This problem is minimized by judicious selection of criterion for defining competencies. To be effective, the competency model must be:

- Based on competencies that really drive superior performance.
- Clear about the requirements to move to the next level so that there is real improvement in performance.
- Based on competencies that reflect the real needs of the organization.

360 Degree Feedback

The fourth building block of competency-based compensation system is 360 degree feedback. Instead of confining the feedback to the immediate superior, data relating to the demonstration of the task's critical competencies is also gathered from peers, fellow team members, subordinates and internal and external customers.

Linkage Between Competencies and Reward

In the competency-related model, the contribution of employees is evaluated in terms of the level of competencies demonstrated during the assessment period. This evaluation is done by explicitly expressing the achievement or the level of attainment on each competency and then aggregating it across the entire set of competencies critical to the attainment of key or strategic business objectives. If the competencies in the concerned set widely differ in importance, specified weights are applied to each competency and then the weighted aggregate is calculated as shown in Table 11.2.

The aggregate score can then be either expressed as a percentage of the highest competency level of the relevant set or an absolute value. Assessment of achievement of individuals is made using a table which gives a clear definition of each level of achievement.

An example is given in Table 11.3 in respect of influencing skills as a constituent of a relevant set. It involves clear written and verbal communication, understanding of others' viewpoint and demonstrates packaging practical business ideas. This competency is built on personal reputation and internal selling skills necessary to influence decision makers and drive projects important to the business.

TABLE 11.2
Assessment of Achievement

Competency	Level 1	Level 2	Level 3	Level 4
Knowhow				
Analytical thinking				
Strategic vision				
Influencing				
Organisational awareness				
Team management				
Achievement orientation				
Self-confidence				

TABLE 11.3
Levels of Achievement

Level 1	Level 2	Level 3	Level 4
Under some supervision and/or guidance. Effectively uses written or verbal communications. Reports findings and recommends immediate to short term action for self and direct contacts. .	Independently maintains excellent communication with all appropriate parties. Has strong credibility within the group. Uses well written and persuasive verbal skills to convince others to adopt recommendations.	Communicates effectively across functional boundaries to add value to business and gain support for recommendations. Uses strong verbal and written skills to bring about technical decisions that affect both his function and multifunctional efforts.	Uses communication skills and personal credibility to shape long-term technical direction and other significant business decisions. Credibility within SBU and/or company has been established by a history of recommendations that resulted in significant contribution to business.

Linking Basic Pay to Achievement

In the traditional approach, evaluating the job in terms of factors like skill, responsibility, effort and working conditions arrives at the differentials in pay for different jobs, which constitute the job content. In the competency-based model where the job is replaced by a loosely defined role in a team-based environment, the differentials are calculated for each employee on the basis of acquired and demonstrated competencies assessed in a manner as explained. These differentials are then organized in career stages or competency levels that are linked to broad pay bands.

Traditional vs. Competency-based Model

The total reward strategy required for the competency-based workplace to function effectively is quite different from traditional workplace pay practices. The differences are shown in Table 11.4.

The competency-based model is becoming common in knowledge- and service-based organizations although other traditional industries are also adopting this model if extensive use of

TABLE 11.4
Traditional vs. Competency-based Model

Reward Component	Traditional System	Competency-based Model
Basic pay	Based on internal job evaluation and external market survey comparisons	Based on competency levels demonstrated by employees
Basic pay progression	Represents one more year of service	Represents greater width and depth an employee adds to his value to the core business processes
Variable pay	Privilege of membership of the group	Share of employee as a partner in the success of the business
Total cash compensation	What an employee is entitled to under contract of employment	Amount he has already earned through contribution
Benefits	Company decides as a matter of policy	Employees' share of undertaking risk and accountability as a business collaborator
Quality of work life	Does what the employee is told. His labour is important, not his ideas	Employee is empowered to make decisions and use his mind and involvement
Career opportunity	Job for life for loyalty	Employee and employer are mutually responsible for career. Employer offers an opportunity as business demands and employee has to keep his competencies in line with demand
Total reward	Based on entitlement as per the contract	Share of success as a business partner

IT and business process re-engineering has been incorporated in their operations. The use of this model is not culture specific and hence is being adopted even in newly industrialized countries.

Appropriation of Competency-based Compensation

It is more appropriate where the following conditions exist:

1. Uncertain environment where the results are not within the control of employees.
2. Qualitative and process jobs where competency behaviours are more important for delivering customer satisfaction.
3. Self-managed teams where individual results are less important than contribution to the group process.
4. Developmental jobs where jobs are designed to grow.
5. Changing organizations where employees' potential to contribute to the organization in future may be more important than their past performance.
6. Hospitals, consultancy companies, etc. are best suited for this model.

EVALUATING JOBS AND ROLES

As explained earlier 'internal equity' is achieved through job evaluation (JE). Job evaluation is defined as the systematic method of establishing the relative worth of jobs within an organization. It establishes the rational differentials between jobs leading to a compensation structure by attaching grades and pay-scales in an organization along with carrying out pay/wage-surveys (external equity).

Jobs and Roles

Is job evaluation concerned with jobs or roles, or both? The terms 'job' and 'role' are often used interchangeably, but there is an important difference:

- A job consists of a group of finite tasks to be performed (pieces of work) and duties to be fulfilled in order to achieve an end result. In describing the job, the traditional approach has been to concentrate on why it exists and the activities to be carried out. The implication is that the latter are fixed and carried out by the jobholder as prescribed. Jobs are the same whoever carries them out. There is no room for flexibility or interpretation of how best to carry it out. Jobs are the same whoever carries them out.
- A role describes the part played by people in meeting their objectives by working competently and flexibly within the context of an organisation's objectives, structures and processes. The concept of role is much wider because it is people- and behaviour-oriented—it is concerned with what people do and how they do it; rather it concentrates narrowly on job content. When faced with any situation—for example, doing a job—individuals have to enact a role in order to perform it effectively in that situation. In fact they are interpreting the situation and, according to their perceptions, playing a role.
- Role definition covers the behavioural aspect of work—the competencies required to achieve expected results and completion of tasks. The role stresses the need for flexibility

and multi-skilling, and for adapting to the different demands that are made on the people in project and team-based organizations where emphasis is on processes rather than on hierarchical structures. While doing a job, people are enacting a role—not simply reciting the lines.

By focusing on jobs, rather than roles, traditional JE deliberately avoids considering the value of people. But this view is untenable. It is equally misguided to accept the universal assumption that people adapt to fixed specifications of their jobs rather than that jobs should be adapted to the characteristics of people doing them. It is people who create value, not jobs. By focusing on jobs rather than on roles, JE deliberately avoids considering the value of people.

Objectives of Job Evaluation

1. To establish relative the wage level of different employees within a plant.
2. To bring new jobs to their proper hierarchical position.
3. To facilitate negotiations with unions for job rationalization.
4. Provide a rational basis for design and maintenance of an equitable and defensible pay structure.
5. To determine job specifications for employee selection.
6. To determine criteria for merit rating and promotions and design of incentives.
7. To train new supervisors and find scope for automation/improvement.
8. JE helps in generating and motivating organization climate and culture.

Basic Methodology

- Identify which jobs are to be examined and the total number of jobs to be evaluated.
- Should there be one scheme for all employees or different ones for different levels?
- Select a particular method.
- Select the representative benchmark jobs which will be used for comparison.
- Decide on factors to be used in evaluating the jobs.
- Analyse the jobs and roles.
- Develop pay structure: this usually means designing a grade structure and then deciding on the rates or ranges of pay in the structure through internal comparisons and 'market pricing'.
- Obtain approval of management and unions.
- Set-up a grievance procedure; sort out anomalies.

Methods and Systems of Job Evaluation

Job evaluation schemes can be divided broadly into the following types:

- Non-quantitative Ranking: Paired Ranking and Classification.

- Quantitative or Analytical: Points-factor-rating method; Factor comparison method; Skill or Competence related; Internal benchmarking.
- Market pricing through job surveys.
- Non-conventional: Time span of decision method; Decision band method; Direct consensus method; Guide chart profile; Urwick Orr profile method.
- Proprietary brands of consultants' methods —Hay Management consultants, KPMG management consulting; Price Waterhouse; Saville & Holdsworth; Towers Perrin and Watson Wyatt—for details please see Neathey (1994).

Job ranking is simple and easy—in fact, all JE methods involve ranking. Here job descriptions are made and sorted in sequential order of their worth as a whole. The jobs common in various organisations are identified and all other jobs in an organization are ranked in the order of difficulty, complexity and responsibility. Ranking is made easy by first identifying those jobs that come at two extreme ends of the scale and locating the rest in the middle region. The ranking is best done by a committee and final ranking is circulated for management approval after getting the consent of unions. The work is often repeated in the light of new facts.

No attempt is made to quantify judgements—whole jobs are ranked, they are not broken down into factors or elements. Statistical methods like paired ranking can be used with scoring done as in sports. It avoids multi-comparing which is rather difficult. Finally jobs are put in a grade structure.

Job Classification (JC) is done by slotting whole jobs into predetermined grades. JC is based on an initial definition of number and characteristics of the grades into which jobs will be placed. The grade definition refers to such factors as key tasks carried out, skill, competence, experience, initiative and responsibility. The number of grades is usually 4-8, with clear difference in demands placed on the employee. More than eight grades become unmanageable due to defining clear differences between successive grades. Less than four differences are again hard to distinguish—unless the corporate strategy is to broadband the jobs.

Merits and Demerits of JC

The merits of JC are that it is easy and cheap to implement and easily understood. The standards for making grading decisions are provided in the form of the grade definitions in which explicit account can be taken of the training, experience, level of responsibility and specific demands of a job in comparison with other jobs.

The demerits are that it can not cope with complex jobs which do not fit neatly into one grade. The grade definitions tend to be so generalized that they may not be of much help in evaluating borderline cases, especially at more senior levels. It often fails to deal with evaluating and grading jobs in dissimilar occupational and job families where the demands made on job holders are widely different, for example, technical and administrative job families. Further grade definitions tend to remain inflexible and unresponsive to the technological and organizational changes affecting role and job content. It is said that the grading system can perpetuate inappropriate hierarchies. Because it is not an analytical system, it is not effective as a means of establishing comparable worth and is unacceptable in equal value cases.

This method is suitable for small firms believing in broad-banding the jobs.

Point-Factor Scheme

The point-factor scheme operates as follows:

- In this method the whole job is analysed through 5-8 factors like skill, responsibility and effort and over 20-50 sub-factors.
- These factors/sub-factors are given points which total out as the overall position of the jobs.
- It involves job-analysis through interview, questionnaire and actual observation.
- Writing job descriptions from the data collected and verifying it from department supervisors.
- Next a plan is developed for identifying skill, responsibility and effort.
- The levels or degrees at which these factors can be present in the company jobs are defined.
- Each factor may be assigned a percentage weight to indicate its relative worth and hence its value in the job.
- This weighting is equal to the maximum points that can be given for any factor and the sum of scores for each factor indicates the maximum score that can be allotted to any job.
- The maximum points for each factor are divided between the levels or degrees for that factor. Thus each level has a point score.
- The level at which each of the factors is present in the benchmark jobs is determined by reference to the factor plan.
- Scores are allotted for each factor in accordance with the factor plan and the total score calculated for benchmark jobs and ranking is done with these values.
- A grade structure is developed which divides the rank order into a number of grades which are defined in terms of point-slabs.
- The remaining non-benchmark jobs are then evaluated and slotted into the grade structure.
- The job grades are also priced with reference to market rates or existing rates and relativities.

Merits and Demerits of the Point-rating Method

The point scheme provides evaluators with defined yardsticks that should help them to achieve a degree of objectivity and consistency in making their judgements. Evaluators are forced to consider a range of factors which, as long as they are present in all the jobs and affect them in different ways, will reduce the danger of oversimplified judgements which can be made when using non-analytical methods. The system adapts well to computerization.

It is complex to develop, install and maintain. It gives a somewhat spurious impression of scientific accuracy. It is still necessary to use judgement in selecting factors, defining levels within factors, deciding on weights, and interpreting information about the job in relation to the definition of factors and factor levels. It assumes that it is possible to quantify different aspects of jobs on the same scale of values and then add them together. But the attributes and job characteristics cannot necessarily be added together in this way.

However, it is the most popular method in use.

FACTOR COMPARISON METHOD

Here important factors or elements of a job are evaluated in terms of monetary value and relative jobs are positioned in terms of those factors in terms of their values. The factors usually considered are five: mental requirement, skill, physical requirement, responsibility and working conditions. The system involves detailed job analyses, ranking of jobs in respect of pre-determined factors, apportioning the total money paid to the different factors of the job and fitting key jobs into the system and locating all other jobs in relation to key jobs (Table 11.5).

Factors and degrees defined for education—this factor appraises educational requirements necessary to perform the job satisfactorily.

- Degree 1: ability to follow verbal instructions in the local language for performing manual tasks of either repetitive or closely supervised non-repetitive nature or count numbers.
- Degree 2: ability to read and write words in English and to perform simple arithmetical calculations. Some trade knowledge in paper making equal to primary education.
- Degree 3: ability to read and write simple English, perform arithmetical calculations involving fractions, decimals; use shop tools and understand simple drawings, good trade knowledge.
- Degree 4: ability to read and write, perform mathematical calculations; understand detailed sketches, proficiency in trades like welding, etc.
- Degree 5: background education suitable for understanding all aspects of trade which may be considered equal to ITI course certificate.
- Similar degrees of factors are prepared for all other factors in the plant.

For each job an appropriate degree for each factor is determined and point values are assigned for each degree. The total of these point values represent the worth of each job. All types of jobs are finally grouped into classes having minimum and maximum values for each cluster.

The point values are than converted into money values. The resulting wage structure will reflect the true differential in the worth of jobs.

MANAGERIAL JOB EVALUATION

Time Span of Impact of Decision

This system uses the concept that everyone makes decisions in their work and the effect of such decisions on the work or organization is felt after a certain period for taking up follow up

TABLE 11.5
Job Evaluation Plan for Daily-rated Workers

Factors	No.	Sub-factors—Degree of Points	1	2	3	4	5
Skills 42%	1	Education	14	28	42	56	70
	2	Experience	20	40	60	80	100
	3	Initiative, ingenuity	8	16	24	12	40
Effort 18%	4	Physical effort	10	20	30	40	50
	5	Mental and visual demand	8	16	24	32	40
Responsibility 20%	6	Responsibility for product/process/ materials	8	16	24	32	40
	7	Responsibility for tools and equipment	8	12	16	20	25
	8	Responsibility for work of others	4	8	12	16	20
	9	Responsibility for safety of others	4	8	12	16	20
Working	10	Surroundings	12	24	36	48	60
conditions 20%	11	Hazards	8	16	24	32	48

action. Here the criteria, 'the longest possible time for which the impact of discretion' fructifies is considered, as the key factor in determining the levels of hierarchy. For example, the impact of a decision by Junior Supervisors is felt in a few days. Similarly, decisions by Marketing Managers are felt in a few months and by top Managers in a few years and by Board members in 10 years.

Introduction of Integrated Incentive Scheme in a Plant

The following steps are needed in designing and introducing an incentive scheme: every scheme is custom tailored and no one plan will work for all. First, the objectives must be formulated both short run and long term. Objectives are needed to guide the selection of performance measures, specifications of bonus calculation formula reaching a common understanding about size of the bonus. The potential for performance improvement may change over time, which may be taken care of when the scheme is revised.

Selection of performance measures must encourage the required type of behaviours like increasing output, quality, timeliness of delivery, service to customers and reducing cost, waste of

TABLE 11.6
Job Evaluation Factors

Factors	Sweeper-degrees	Points	Turner-degrees	Points
Education	1	14	4	56
Experience	1	21	3	60
Initiative and ingenuity	1	8	4	32
Physical effort	2	20	2	20
Mental demand	2	16	4	32
Responsibility for material/production/process	1	8	3	24
Responsibility for tools and equipment	1	4	4	16
Responsibility for work of others	1	4	2	8
Responsibility for safety of others	1	4	2	8
Surroundings	3	36	3	36
Hazards	2	16	3	24
Total points		150		316

materials, etc. The performance measures should not contradict and must be under the control of employees and not influenced by external factors. The unit of the performance being measured should be easily understandable and verifiable by workers. They should see clearly the relation between their effort and reward.

The objective of this incentive scheme is to improve performance of the unit by improving production capacity utilization, securing optimum manpower utilization and reducing the consumption of major process materials through better operations, process control, maintenance of equipment and also to provide opportunities to employees to improve their earnings. The scheme will be a composite one based on the following factors:

1. Production capacity utilization.
2. Manpower utilization.
3. Material utilization efficiency.

The scheme will cover all employees up to the level of Assistant Manager, except apprentices, casual employees and employees placed under suspension and those working in marketing.

The Scheme

The incentive payment will be based on:

1. Productivity Index which is a multiple of the Production Index and Manpower Index.
2. Material Utilization Index based on specific consumption of selected inputs for production.

$$\text{Productivity index} = \frac{\text{Actual daily production of urea}}{\text{Base production daily of urea}}$$

No incentive will be paid if actual production is less than base production.

Base production will be 70 per cent of annual related capacity.

$$\frac{\text{Say: } 0.7 \times 511500}{365} = 981 \text{ tons urea/day}$$

$$\frac{\text{Manpower Index} = \text{Standard strength of group/department}}{\text{Actual strength} + \text{equivalent of overtime} + \text{casual labour}}$$

The maximum and minimum limits of manpower will be 1.2 and 0.6 for a period of six months. After that standard strength will be reviewed.

$$\frac{\text{MUI} = \text{Material Index} = \text{Standard specific consumption of input material}}{\text{Actual specific consumption of the input}} \times 100$$

The incentive will be paid for improving MUI beyond base index. The maximum MUI will be 100; the incentive corresponding to the MUI for each raw material will be multiplied by the corresponding weight of that material. Incentives corresponding to each raw material will be multiplied by PL (Production Level) as follows:

$$\text{PL} = \frac{\text{Actual production of the month}}{\text{Standard production of the month}}$$

The maximum PL will be 1.

Attendance: to reduce absenteeism, incentive will be paid only for the days employees are present and not for leave or absence.

Incentive payment is calculated as follows:

% Incentive = (% incentive at Productivity Index + % incentive at MUI).
The payment is calculated as percentage of standard salary (Basic + DA).
All employees will be divided into two groups, Direct and Indirect.

Direct includes those directly concerned with the production activity and the rest, including canteen staff, etc., will be treated as support staff or indirect labour. All direct employees will be paid 100 % and indirect ones 80 % of the rates payable to direct staff.

Note: All differences in production and despatches will be adjusted and shortage or excess of material consumed will be ignored up to 0.5 per cent and the rest will be adjusted in the following month's consumption.

If the production is below quality no incentive will be paid. And materials returned will also be deducted.

This incentive will be in addition to the statutory bonus.

CONCLUSION

It is clear from the above discussion that compensation policies and structure of any organization directly influences the performance and implementation of strategy. These HR processes are closely linked with performance management, recruitment and selection and employee relations in any firm and therefore an integrated HR approach is required.

Questions and Assignments

Q.1. Explain the objectives of the national wage policy. How does it affect the compensation structure and policy of individual firms?

Q.2. Discuss the role of Direct and Indirect compensation structure in an organization.

Q.3. Review the different methods of job evaluation and bring out their merits and demerits.

Q.4. Experts are of the opinion that we must pay the individual and not the job. Comment.

Q.5. Discuss the various changes that are taking place in executive remuneration. Do you agree with very high salaries that CEOs are getting? Justify your choice.

Q.6. Discuss the main components of the competency based model of pay. Where is it appropriate and how does it differ from the traditional system?

Assignments

1. Study the compensation structure at the workers and executives' level in an organization and compare it with the organisation's main competitors.
2. Prepare a write-up on the trends and compensation profile in the IT industry.
3. A manufacturing organization has 10,000 employees on its rolls in four units located in different parts of the country. The company faces many complex problems related to compensation. It also wants to use its compensation policy and structure more actively to influence employee performance and organization culture. In pursuit of these objectives they want to appoint a compensation manager. Please answer the following questions.

1 What kind of person should they look for? Prepare his job profile.
2. List the main function and responsibilities he should be charged with as compensation manager.
3. What are the objectives of a compensation policy?
4. What factors go into determination of pay in an organization?

CASE

REWARD MANAGEMENT AT MIDLAND MAIN LINE

Midland Main Line (MML) is one of the 25 new train operating companies created upon the privatisation of the rail industry following the 1993 Railways Act. It operates the high-speed service between London, Derby, Nottingham and Sheffield. The company employs approximately 900 people including drivers, train maintenance workers, station staff/train crew and office staff. MML is owned by National Express.

The strategic challenge facing MML is similar to those facing many other organisations. Put simply, it has to achieve higher income, lower costs and a better quality service. The company faces an enormous challenge. During the period of the seven-year contract, which MML has been awarded it has to increase passenger income by two-thirds. This is no easy task when set against the maximum 3 per cent annual growth rate which was achieved under British Rail. Operating costs have to be reduced by one-third during the same period. In facing this challenge, MML, in effect, has to satisfy two masters. The parent company, National Express, has its profit expectations of MML. At the same time, the government, which has traditionally heavily subsidised the railways, will cease to provide subsidy by the year 2000. MML's task is made even more daunting by the government edict that regulated fares should not rise by more than inflation minus 1 per cent (Brown, 1997).

Faced with the triple challenge of achieving higher income, lower costs and a better quality service, MML has radically altered its employee relations strategy in which reward management plays a significant role. However, before describing the changes which have been implemented, it is necessary to examine the situation which MML inherited.

The pay structure in British Rail, was, to say the least, exceedingly complex. There were over 100 different staff grades in six different groups. Added to this there were in excess of 300 components of remuneration (Greenhill, 1997). These consisted mainly of allowances which had grown up over this century. For example, drivers were paid only for the time they were actually on driving duty so allowances were important because they were a significant addition to drivers' wages. In another example, fitters were paid an allowance for work performed which was normally part of another craftsman's job. The complexity of this system created a 'mini industry' in British Rail where a considerable expertise was needed to interpret all the pay arrangements. It was a highly centralised national system with little autonomy given to local line managers. This was in part due to the necessity for the British Rail Board to report direct to the Department of Transport.

The creation of MML has simplified collective bargaining arrangements. There is now local company-level bargaining. Pay and other major terms and conditions of employment are negotiated by the MML company council, which consists of management and representatives of the four recognised trade unions sitting around a single table. Company-level bargaining means that MML can not negotiate arrangements, which are tailored to its specific operating requirements. For example, under the new bargaining structure MML has negotiated a deal whereby drivers can complete two return London-Sheffield journeys in a day. Under the national hours agreement it was possible to achieve only 1.5 return journeys.

The root cause of this complex system of pay allowances was the low basic wage paid by British Rail which employees boosted by overtime and allowances. Examples of drivers and electricians illustrate the point. Prior to the creation of MML, drivers were earning average annual pay of £ 11,440 and electricians £ 9,765. This provided an inbuilt incentive for employees to create overtime although this may not have been strictly necessary had their duties been performed expeditiously. It is not difficult to imagine how this situation may have been to the immediate detriment of customer service, since the driver, and other on-train staff, were being rewarded with overtime in the event of trains running late. The new pay structure negotiated with the trade unions has abolished overtime and introduced a far higher basic wage. Drivers at MML now have a basic wage of £ 30,850 for a normal working week of 37 hours although this could be increased to a maximum of 48 hours. The result of this change is that there is now incentive for drivers, and other grades, to get the job done as quickly and safely as possible, with consequent advantageous effects on train punctuality.

The key concept underpinning the new pay arrangements at MML is employee flexibility. It is this, added to the abolition of overtime, which has enabled MML to offer a high basic salary and provide a better customer service. Flexibility at MML impacts upon the duties employees perform and when they perform these duties. Two examples illustrate the concept. The first relates to depot staff at Leeds and Derby. Here work has been arranged in multi-skilled teams consisting of various crafts that maintain trains. The teams consist of skilled and semi-skilled who, as far as possible, perform each other's duties. In addition, the teams operate an annualised hours system. In this system, the company may require the teams to work a potential annual maximum of 1,800 hours (equivalent to 37.5 hours × 48 weeks) spread throughout the year. In some weeks it may be necessary to work more than 35 hours, in other weeks less. The key point here is that it is not necessary to work all of the 1,680 hours. Under this system, there is clearly an incentive to get the job done quickly and go home. The productivity gains made have allowed an anticipated 20 per cent reduction of jobs in the depots.

The second example relates to train crew staff. MML has restructured the on-train teams. There used to be eight grades including senior conductor, chef, guard, senior steward and ticket collector. This has been reduced to three grades: train manager, senior customer host and customer host. There is a higher basic salary for each grade: £ 18,500 for the train manager, £ 15,000 for the senior customer host and £ 11,500 for the customer host. Once again the aim is complete flexibility between roles, which has meant a major training programme.

Clearly, reform of the reward strategy has not taken place in isolation. It is part of a wider set of initiatives which have a clear strategic intent. As can be seen there has been wide-ranging structural change. Training and development have also been very much to the fore. Almost two-thirds of the staff have been through training programmes, which are designed to change the old British Rail culture. The values which these courses are seeking to inculcate are personal ownership of problems empathising with the customer, teamworking, thinking of new ideas, recognition of the value of individual contributions and continuous improvement. Attention has also been paid to performance management. For example, performance criteria for on-train staff are competence-based and emphasise customer service delivery team development and fulfilment of on-train specification. There is an element of 360 degree appraisal in that performance feedback on customer service is elicited by consultancy which does three-monthly surveys with 1,000 customers.

The future may see MML make further reward management changes. Customer Services Director Barry Brown would like as much as 20 per cent of the pay packet to consist of variable pay. This would comprise a profit-related bonus (there is already a profit-related pay scheme in which 99 per cent of employees participate, and a share purchase scheme) and team performance bonus. A significant part of this team bonus could be paid as a cash bonus not consolidated into the employee's salary until the second year provided that performance was sustained. It is thought that this will be difficult to negotiate with the relevant trade unions. They would see it as a return to a lower basic wage with supplement. But in this case, the supplements would be related to organisational and employee performance. It is all a far cry from the pay arrangement which MML inherited from British Rail.

12 Strategic Approach to Training and Development

Learning Objectives

After studying this chapter you will learn:

- Why HRD is such a vital part of HRM and HR strategy.
- The domain and concept of strategic training and development (HRD).
- Designing an HRD plan and carrying out organization need analysis.
- Evaluation of training and development programme effectiveness.
- Integration of training and development with other HR processes.
- Hierarchies of knowledge, skill and competency.
- Competency mapping.
- The attributes and concept of the 'learning organisation'.

INTRODUCTION

In these times of globalization dominated by information technology, multinational operations and services-based knowledge-economy, all functions of management are undergoing a metamorphosis and HRM is no exception. For organizational effectiveness, HRD must become a strategic tool for achieving business goals and objectives and its present and future needs justify itself as a value added function.

Now in the age of mergers and acquisitions, restructuring, downsizing and de-layering, competitiveness demands up-to-date skills and competencies and a diverse workforce which can work well in teams and cope with culture shock. The free market belief in 'buying-in' skills has proven inadequate, even in times of high unemployment. HRD goals include treating people as investment and proactive action towards skill availability in advance of need.

HRD has been identified as the vital component of HRM (Keep, 1989). It could also be argued that HRD lies at the heart of managing change through people because the consequence of any change process is that people will need to think and/or behave differently. This will apply whether the change is incremental (adjustment in work processes) or radical and pervasive, needing a culture change. From this we can see that different behaviours will be required either at the level of individual employees, work groups or units or even potentially, the whole workforce. Irrespective of the degree or scope of change, some types of HRD processes will be inevitable to move staff from where they are now to where the organization wants them to be. The same is true when acquiring sustainable competitive advantage.

HRD Agenda for Companies and HR Executives

In her 'model company statement', Kanter (1992: 39) expresses the need to develop people as a key lever in 'human resource management' making the connection between the learning of organizational members and the survival and effectiveness of the organization.

> 'Our company faces competitive world markets and rapidly changing technology. We need the flexibility to add or delete products, open or close facilities and redeploy the workforce. Although we cannot guarantee tenure in any particular job or even future employment, we will work to ensure that all our people are fully employable—sought out for new jobs here and elsewhere. We promise to:

- Recruit the potential to increase in competence, not simply for narrow skills, to fill today's slots.
- Offer ample learning opportunities, from formal training to lunch-time seminars—the equivalent of a month a year.
- Provide challenging jobs and rotating assignments that allow growth in skills even without promotion to higher jobs.
- Measure performance beyond accounting numbers and share the data to allow learning by doing and continuous improvement.
- Retrain employees as soon as jobs become obsolete.
- Recognize individual and team achievements, thereby building external reputations and offering tangible indicators of value.
- Provide three-month educational sabbaticals or external internships every five years.
- Find job opportunities in our network of suppliers, customers and venture partners.
- Tap our people's ideas to develop innovations that lower costs, serve customers and create markets—the best foundation for business growth and continuing employment.

According to Barrow & Loughlin (1993: 198), these are the abilities organizations will be expecting of their employees:

1. A high level of professional education, so that employees can operate new technology, and understand the contribution of their role to the company and take decisions appropriate to their jobs.
2. The ability to learn new skills and adapt to new circumstances by taking responsibility for their own learning, keeping their skills up-to-date, learning new processes.
3. The ability to work in organizations with flatter structures and fewer layers of management—to work without supervision, set own objectives, monitor own performance, correct failures.
4. The ability to manage the interface with customers and between departments, requiring a good level of interpersonal skills.
5. The ability of problem solving, creative thinking about future possibilities, and contributing their own unique ideas.

In today's information society, managers will have to find ways of developing people and mobilizing the intelligence, knowledge, and creative potential of human beings at every level of organization. They have to be skilled in placing quality people in key places and developing their full potential. It will become increasingly important to recruit people who enjoy learning and relish change and to motivate employees to be intelligent, flexible and adaptive.

Toyota has put the same thoroughness into training as it has into recruitment. It spent a huge sum and 100 man-years on off-the-job training before starting production in its UK plant. It uses the cascade approach. The company took 350 group and team leaders on a 5-week round trip to Japan, USA and Canada to absorb the Toyota philosophy and production techniques and learn the firm's approach to training. It then trained team members.

Maintenance workers were sent to specially commissioned courses at local colleges and at their training centre. They then trained at computer controlled rigs specially commissioned by Toyota UK, which simulated production machinery. This was rounded off by on-the-job training. Their efforts were vindicated when a Toyota quality engineer from Japan approved the first cars off the line as being up to Japanese standards.

THE CREATION OF AN HRD PLAN

There are no set procedures which organizations can follow in creating a human resource development plan; the eight basic steps listed below should act as a guide. This is also shown diagrammatically in Figure 12.1.

1. Assess the training and development requirements from the organizational strategy and business objectives.
2. Analyse the training requirements for effective work performance in organizational functions and jobs.
3. Analyse the existing qualities and training needs of current employees by 'competency mapping.'
4. Formulate an HRD plan which fills the gap between organizational current and future needs and the present skills and knowledge of employees.

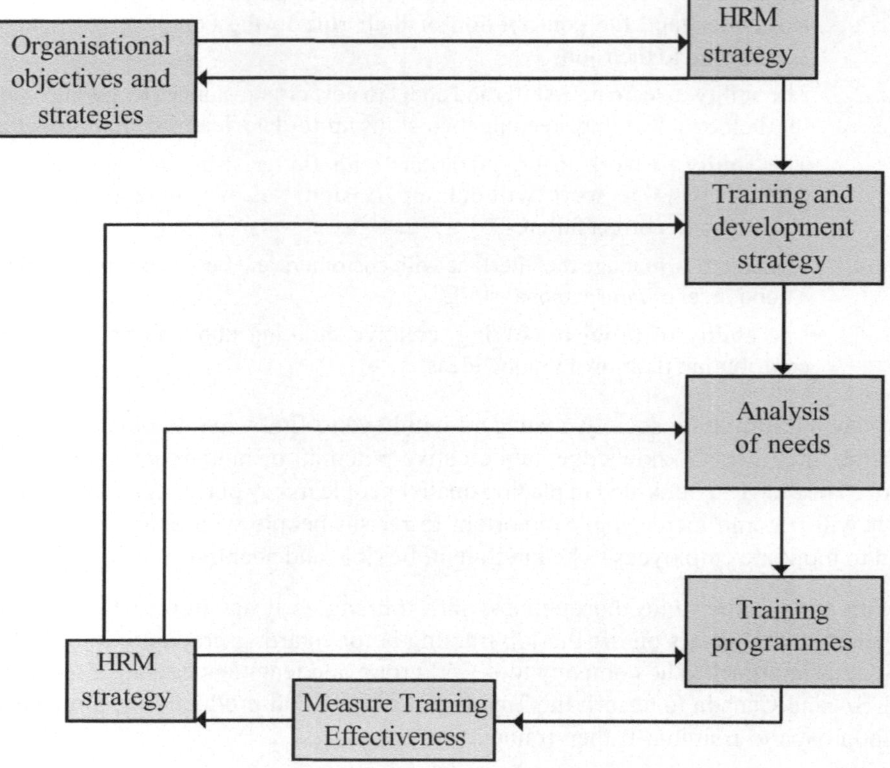

Figure 12.1. A training cycle-based HRD plan

5. Decide on appropriate training and development methods to be used for individuals and groups.
6. Decide who is to have responsibility for the plan and its various parts.
7. Implement the plan and monitor and evaluate its progress.
8. Amend the HRD plan in the light of monitoring/evaluation and changes in business strategy.

This is a system approach for formulating an HRD plan for a firm which serves its purpose of achieving long-term and short-term objectives. It is, however, advised that the plan needs constant monitoring and adjustments so that training schemes which are patently not working due to changes in personnel, personal relationships, business plans, economic performance and other factors should be shown up (Figure 12.1).

Analysing Organisational Needs

The first step of need assessment involves determining why the specific training programmes are required and adapting them to meet appropriate organizational objectives and strategies, both long and short term. This requires identification of needed competencies and areas where employee

BOX 12.1
Summary of Three Levels of Training Need Analysis

Organisational Level

- How does the training relate to organization objectives?
- How does the training impact day-to-day workplace dynamics?
- What are the costs and expected benefits of the training?

Task Level

- What responsibilities are assigned to the job?
- What skills and knowledge are needed for successful performance?
- Should the learning setting be actual work/job setting?
- What are the implications of mistakes?
- How can the job provide the employee with direct feedback?
- How similar to or different from training needs of other jobs are the needs of this job?

Individual Level

- What knowledge, skills and abilities do trainees already have?
- What are the trainees learning styles?
- What special needs do the trainees have?

learning is vital and involves three levels of analysis: organizational, job or tasks, individuals and teams. Researchers are very doubtful whether managerial hierarchies and bureaucratic systems recognize the importance of this criteria and required analysis.

Bernhard & Ingolis (1988) in studying training and its strategic implementation in American companies noted that a considerable amount of money is thrown away mainly because fundamental issues such as analysis of training needs in relation to short-and-long-term business plans had not been addressed. Hall (1984) also comments that many organisations invest considerable resources in T&D but never really examine how training and development can most effectively promote organizational objectives, or how developmental activities should be altered in the light of business plans.

Organization Level

At the organization level the training is considered within the context of the organisation's culture, politics, strategy and structure. This analysis considers how the training will assist the unit to achieve its objectives and how it will affect day-to-day workplace dynamics between and among different units. It also considers the cost-benefit analysis of training and the opportunity cost of forgoing the training.

Job and Task Analysis

Task-level assessment involves looking at specific duties and responsibilities assigned to different jobs and the types of skills and knowledge needed to perform each task. This level also considers whether the learning can or should take place on or away from the job, the implication of mistakes and how the job can be designed to provide the employee with direct feedback on his or her performance. This level also involves determining whether the training needs of certain jobs are similar to or different from the training needs of other jobs in the training organization. Since the purpose of training is to match job requirements with person requirements, it is necessary to study both. Various techniques like job description, job analysis, interview with job-holders and managers and supervisors, study of performance objectives, analysis of competencies and finally study of characteristics of people required (person specification) can be carried out.

Individual Level

The individual level of assessment considers the people to be trained. It requires an analysis of their existing levels of knowledge and skills as well as factors relating to their preferred learning styles, personality, interpersonal styles in interacting with others and any special needs individual employees might have, such as physical or mental condition that might need to be addressed in the design and delivery of training.

Conflict Between Organizational and Individual Level Needs

Another important consideration is the reconciliation of the training and development needs of individuals with the organization. Unfortunately it may be easier to accommodate for professional and managerial employees than for the workforce lower down the organization. The relationship between the two needs can be shown by means of a matrix as in Figure 12.2.

Quadrant 1 High Individual Low Organization	Quadrant 2 High Individual High Organization
Quadrant 3 Low Individual Low Organization	Quadrant 4 Low Individual High Organization

Figure 12.2. Relationship between individual and organisational training needs

The ideal situation is shown in quadrant 2, that is, high individual and high organizational needs being met. The situations in quadrant 1 and in quadrant 4 are much more rare but both have a distorting effect on HRD strategy. The situation in quadrant 3 is, unfortunately, probably the most common, but least desirable situation.

Need Analysis Methods

Much information about employees can be obtained from organizational records including original application forms and other bio-data bases. The following records can be useful:

- Personal profiles which include information concerning career aspirations of employees.
- Performance appraisal records if well done can reveal much about the strengths and weaknesses of individuals in terms of their performance and point out areas where training and development could improve performance.
- Assessment centre techniques where variety of methods using psychometric tests are rather elaborate and expensive but the most thorough way of analyzing individual strengths and weaknesses.
- Survey questionnaires and training audit methods to collect data when far reaching changes are planned.

It is important that training need analysis should be cost-effective in relation to outcomes expected.

Setting up Training Objectives

After training needs have been assessed, objectives for the training activities must be developed. These objectives must directly flow from the assessed needs and be described in specific measurable terms. Measures should be stated in terms of both desired employee behaviours as well as the results that are expected to follow such behaviour. A common problem at this stage is that the organisation's objectives are so vague that success in achieving them cannot be accurately measured or the organization may have no plans for measuring these objectives. Training programmes that cannot be evaluated are of little value to the organization in the long run. Questions that help in setting training objectives are listed in Box 12.2.

Evaluation of HRD Plan

The final stage in the HRD plan is the evaluation and monitoring of training. It is one of the most important but often most neglected activities to be carried out. While it is relatively easy to evaluate a formal off-the job course, much on-the job training often takes place in an informal way, which is usually subjective and open to wide interpretation. The data for evaluation can come from the following sources:

1. Questionnaires (feedback forms) are a common way of eliciting trainee responses to training programmes.
2. Tests are common on formal courses both during and at the end of courses.

BOX 12.2

Del the Delegate

Such training criticisms are illustrated by the sad but familiar story of Del the Delegate, who returns from a course full of new ideas, anxious to implement them. He is confronted with skepticism and cynicism from both his bosses and fellow employees. The friction set up between Del and his company undermines his enthusiasm and exhausts all his energy. Del's behaviour reverts to what is (and it always was) reinforced by the company.

Fairbrains (1991) rightly indicates that an integral part of analyzing training needs is the recognition of what will 'fit' the company culture, as well as the company strategy and objectives. In other words, the training scheme which may fit one company may not fit another and these company differences can only be ignored at great cost. Again this is part and parcel of the organic approach to HRD.

3. Projects are initially seen as learning methods but they can also provide valuable information to instructors.
4. Structured exercises and case studies are opportunities to apply learned skills and techniques under the observation of tutors.
5. Tutor reports. It is important to have the opinions of those who deliver the training. This gives valuable information from different perspectives.
6. Interviews of trainees post-course or during instruction period. These can be formal and informal, individual or group.
7. Observation by those devising training strategies in the training department can be very useful.
8. Participation and discussion during training.

Kirkpatrick & Donald's Four Step Model

A highly regarded model has been developed for training evaluation that suggests that evaluation can take place at four levels and that these levels form a hierarchy, meaning that success in lower levels is a prerequisite for higher levels. In other words, if one of the lower-level measures is not affected, then those measures that follow it will not be achieved. These levels are: Reaction, Learning, Behaviour and Results as shown in Table 12.1.

Reaction measures whether the employees liked the training and the facilities. It is usually measured by a questionnaire. If employees have less-than-favourable reactions, it is unlikely that other employees will have an interest in the training or that the trainees attending the training received anything of value from it. A favourable reaction by itself, however, does not ensure that the training was effective.

Learning measures whether the employees know more than they did prior to undertaking the training. Knowledge-based training can be measured by tests. Skill-based training can be measured

TABLE 12.1
Four Levels of Training Evaluation

Level	Questions Being Asked	Measures
Results	Is the organization or unit better because of training?	Accidents, quality, cost, production, productivity, turnover, morale, profits, etc.
Behaviour	Are trainees behaving differently on the job after training? Are they using the skills and knowledge they learned in training?	Performance appraisal by superiors, peers, clients and subordinates
Learning	To what extent trainees have greater knowledge or skill after the training programme than they did before?	Written tests, performance, tests, graded simulation
Reaction	Did the trainees like the programme? Do they think the course was useful? What improvements can they suggest?	Questionnaire

through demonstration or simulation. If employees did not learn anything, then we cannot expect any change in their behaviour on the job. For any change to occur in behaviour, the trainee must have learnt something.

Behaviour measures what employees do on the job after the training. This enables assessment of whether employees can solve problems, think differently and work differently to give better results. Behavioural impact is usually measured through performance appraisal, which is done by those who are able to witness and observe the employee. If there is no change in behaviour, we cannot expect the employees' performance to have been enhanced.

Evaluation of results looks at the overall outcomes of the training and the impact that the training has had on productivity, efficiency, quality, customer service, etc. This can be measured through budget and cost reports, sales figures, production, customer surveys or any other means that correspond to the organization's performance measures. However, results of training are not immediately available. Training programmes may be on-going or involve employees' developing a level of proficiency which takes time to achieve and master.

Although the result based measures are the most significant, undue reliance on them may cause key decision-makers to abandon programmes that do not produce immediate results. Thus, the evaluation of training should consider all four levels in conjunction with the organisation's overall strategic objectives.

When are the Conditions Right for Training?

When is it appropriate to invest in employee training and development and when are such investments likely to produce disappointing results? A careful review of Goldstein's Framework (1974) can help in deciding this aspect. For training to give the best results all the conditions mentioned should be in place, if not, either the proposed training should be abandoned or steps taken to remedy the situation.

Is There a Need for Training?

Unless the knowledge, ability and skill set has been determined to be critical for successful job performance and also if they are possessed at below if acceptable levels by a meaningful number of job holders, there is apparently no need for training.

Are Employees Ready for Training?

Even if there is a training need, there is little likelihood that training will be effective if learners are not 1) motivated to learn, and 2) prepared and ready to learn. As brought out by expectancy theory, motivation has to do with the belief that effort will lead to success (success in training) and the belief that this success (acquiring new knowledge and skills) will lead to valued outcomes (promotion, salary increase or labour-market mobility). If learners do not exert efforts to master new skills, they will not benefit from training.

Is there Method-Purpose Congruence?

As discussed in the next section, training methods can range from instructor-centred to learner-centred to generation of new knowledge. Similarly, a vast array of technologies including internet and distance learning, etc. can be utilized across these basic learning categories. It is necessary to carefully review the proposed methods, asking if they are the best way to meet the targeted training objectives.

Will the Training Generalize?

Whether the proposed training would be regularly used while performing the job, and would the display of these new skills, knowledge and abilities, be reinforced and supported by management and co-workers are some pertinent questions to explore.

Can Training Effectiveness be Evaluated?

It may be that unless there is a way to evaluate training effectiveness at a reasonable cost, it should not be undertaken. This is because the evaluation may provide the clues that lead to ideas about how to improve training over time.

If all the five conditions are present, there is very good likelihood that investment on training will be justified and provide the desired results.

Selection of Right Type of Training Methodology

The three basic categories of training such as instructor-centred, learner-centred or team-based exploration of new knowledge have been mentioned in the previous section. For each method many options are available as illustrated in Table 12.2 and each method and option is best suited for a limited set of objectives. This congruence is important for getting results from training. Further, training can be divided into off-the-job or on-the-job, and there is place for both types and each can be effective at meeting certain training requirements.

TABLE 12.2
Some Illustrative Training Methods

	Dissemination of Knowledge			Sharing of Knowledge		Creation of Knowledge
	Instructor-centred			Learner-centred	Team-centred	
Learning Outcomes	**Lecture**	**Presentation**	**On-the-Job**	**Simulation Role Play**	**Task Force Assignment**	**Collective Exploration**
Information transfer	*	*				
Beliefs/attitudes	*	*		*		
Interpersonal skills				*	*	
Problem-solving skills			*	*	*	
Creativity					*	*
Motor skills			*	*		
Self-insight				*		
Problem identifaction skills					*	*

Integrating Training with Other HR Processes

In the human resource cycle presented by Tichy, Fombrun & Devenna, 'Selection Process' is the main variable influencing directly the 'Performance' and also directly influencing the 'Employee Development Process'. The four generic processes; selection, performance-appraisal, rewards management and human resource development reflect sequential managerial tasks. The dependent variable in this cycle is performance and other elements in the cycle are designed to impact performance at both the individual and the organisational level. Performance, in other words, is a function of all the human resource components: selecting people who are able to best perform the job defined by the structure; motivating employees by rewarding them judiciously; training and developing people for future performance; and appraising employees in order to justify the rewards. In addition, performance is a function of organisational context and resources surrounding the individual. Thus, strategy and structure also impact performance through the ways the jobs are designed, through how the organization is structured and through how well services and products are planned to meet environmental threats and opportunities. These basic human resource processes can be done at three levels: the strategic level which deals with policy formulation and goal setting; the managerial level which is concerned with the availability and allocation of resources to carry out the strategic plan; and at the operational level to carry out day-to-day activities.

It is necessary therefore to reinforce and integrate strategic training with other HR activities so that the other HR processes are benefited from it and, in turn, provide support to training. According to Beer, this type of internal integration is required for calling it strategic. We have already discussed external integration of training with organizational objectives.

When employees are asked to learn critical new skills or absorb important new knowledge and apply this in their jobs, their performance assessment must reflect these changes. The more critical the skills and knowledge are to the organisation's strategy, the greater the emphasis that should be placed on assessing them in the firm's performance management system. Further, the PMS should provide areas of improvement for individuals, groups and units as well as furnish organizational objectives and how they are being evaluated.

Similarly compensation should reflect the results of training. If employees have learned new skills and knowledge and successfully implemented this learning to enhance the performance of the organization, they should be compensated accordingly in a way that is significant to them. In fact, many firms are resorting to a 'competency-based' compensation system which has been discussed in another chapter of this book in great detail. Several organizations are positioning important development programmes for executives prior to their promotion. If the candidate is aware that his performance in training will be a factor considered in the promotion decision, he will no doubt take the training more seriously.

Even when the recruitment and selection is done to acquire desired competencies, it is rare that all candidates have in them all the required competencies. Certainly, all of them need cultural orientation, apart from providing them with needed skills through training. Other processes like career planning, HRP and employee relations are also influenced by training and development processes. This internal integration represented by the Human Resource cycle is discussed next.

Competency Mapping

There are several outcomes of learning that are of concern to HR managers: skills of various kinds and levels; knowledge of various kinds and levels; and attitudes, habits, motives, traits, intelligence; comprising the competence in a person to deliver superior performance.

Skill

Skill has been defined as 'the performance of any task, which for its successful and rapid completion, requires an improved organization of responses making use of those aspects of the stimulus which are essential to satisfactory performance' (Ribeaux & Poppleton, 1978: 53-54). Borger & Seaborne (1966: 128-129) define it as, 'an appearance of ease, of smoothness of movement,

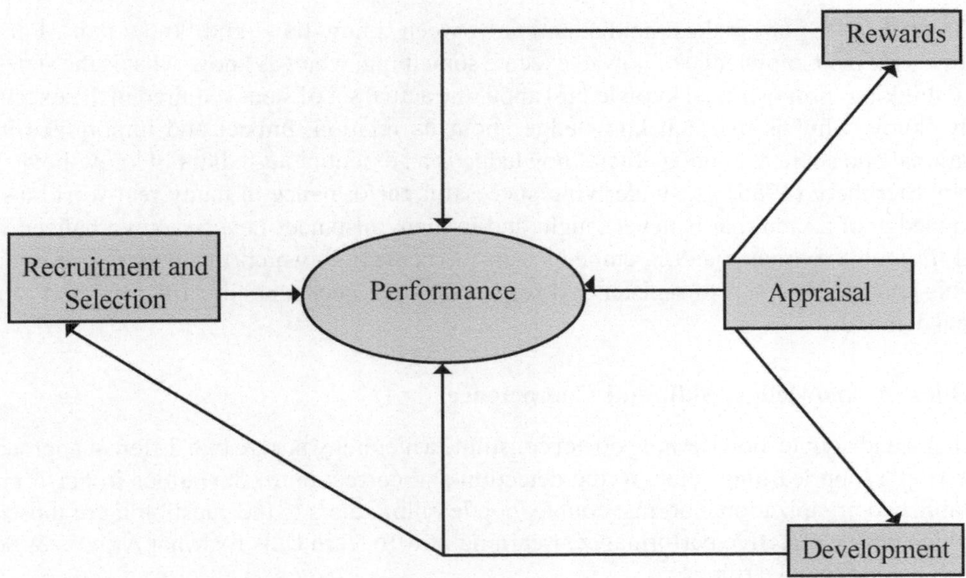

Figure 12.3. The human resource cycle
(by Tichy, Fombrun and Dwenna)

of confidence and the comparative absence of hesitation; it frequently gives the impression of being unhurried, while the actual pace of activity may of course be quite high.... Increasing skill involves a widening of the range of possible disturbances that can be coped with, without disrupting the performance.' These definitions are particularly appropriate to perceptual-motor skills which involve physical, motor responses to perceived stimuli in the external world. Such skills are needed at every level of an organization from operating computer software, conducting negotiations or even in teaching, mentoring or counselling, as well as floor scrubbing or investing company's funds. This shows that there are many kinds of skills needed by an organization—cognitive, linguistic, social and interpersonal. However, their complexity suggests that we need to recognize various levels of skill or hierarchies.

Competence

Competence has now become a major consideration in important decisions like recruitment and selection, compensation and training and development. It is defined as: '...an underlying characteristic of a person which results in effective or superior performance in a job' (Boyatzis, 1982).

The core of the definition is an ability to apply knowledge and skills with understanding to a work activity. The concept of competence integrates knowledge and skill with positive attitudes, which is assessed through job performance.

Know-how and Tacit Knowledge

Gardner (1985: 68) makes the distinction between 'know-how' and 'know-that'. For him, know-how is the tacit knowledge of how to execute something, whereas know-what is the statement of formal thinking (propositional knowledge) about the actual set of steps required in the execution. Similarly 'know-why' is the tacit knowledge about its relation, impact and importance in the organizational and societal context. Tacit knowledge is an essential ingredient of know-how and is defined by Sternberg (1985) as, 'underlying successful performance in many real-world tasks is tacit knowledge of a kind that is never taught and in many instances never even verbalized'. It is acquired through experience and is embedded in the context in which this experience is taking place. This enables a person to register and read contextual cues and adjust the method to meet situational demands.

Hierarchies of Knowledge, Skill and Competence

Single and double loop learning do not constitute a hierarchy but are two different approaches. Whereas single loop learning refers to the detection and correction of deviations in performance from established organizational norms, double loop learning refers to the questioning of those very norms which define effective performance. Learning how to learn calls for what Argyris & Schon (1978) call double loop learning.

Dreyfus & Athanasion (1986) set out a five-stage model of the process of acquisition of skill that moves from the effective performance of lower to higher order thinking and skills.

1. Stage 1: The novice:

   Follows context free rules, with relevant components of the situation defined for him; hence lacks any coherent sense of the overall task.

2. Stage 2:

   The advanced beginner: Learners begin to recognize the contextual elements of their task through their practical experience in concrete situations; they begin to perceive similarities between new and previous experiences.

3. Stage 3:

   The competent: They begin to recognize a wide range of cues and be able to select and focus upon the most important of them. Their reliance upon rules lessens; they experiment and go beyond the rules, using trial-and-error.

4. Stage 4:

   The proficient: Those who arrive at this stage achieve unconscious, fluid, effortless performance. They think analytically but can now read the evolving situation, picking up new cues and becoming aware of emerging patterns; they have an involved, intuitive and holistic grasp of the situation.

5. Stage 5:

   The expert: At this stage, highly experienced people seem to be able to recognize whole scenarios without decomposing them into elements or separate features. They have a multi-dimensional map of the territory; they frame and reframe strategies as they read changing cues. With this intuitive understanding of the implications of the situation, they can cope with uncertainty and unforeseen situations.

Competency Mapping

Competency mapping consists of breaking a given job into its constituent tasks or activities and identifying the competencies needed to perform the job successfully and smoothly. It is about identifying preferred behaviours and personal skills, which distinguish excellent and outstanding performance from the average. An example is provided below for mapping the competency of the HR training manager of a large organization.

The competencies of the training manager can be mapped by using a four-point scale to indicate the expected competency level, that is, Expert (E), Competent (C), Familiar (F) and Novice (N). This exercise will help in identifying his competencies that need to be developed for impacting organizational capability of training function.

TABLE 12.3
Four-point Scale to Indicate Expected Competency Level

1. Training Needs: Identifying competency gaps from performance process.

N	F	C	E
		*	

2. Identifying individual competency strengths aligned to organization competencies.

N	F	C	E
			*

3. Scanning the environment for technology shift/business area. Cascading the technology shift to technology competencies/business area.

N	F	C	E
		*	

4. Assimilating organization strategy/business area.

N	F	C	E
		*	

5. Identifying performance gaps/expectations with respect to personnel in key positions.

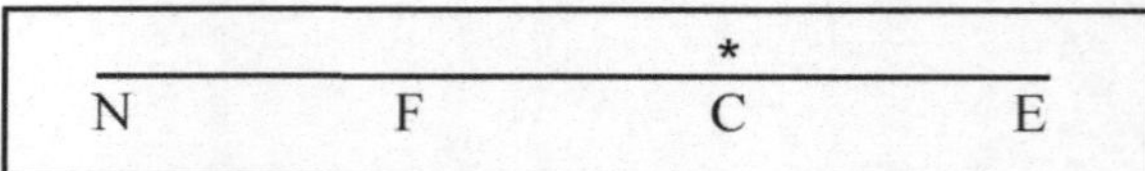

6. Designing a database with respect to competence development areas along with associated competencies.

7. Clustering the competencies together and formulating competence development areas.

8. Designing the process of competency development with cost benefit analysis.

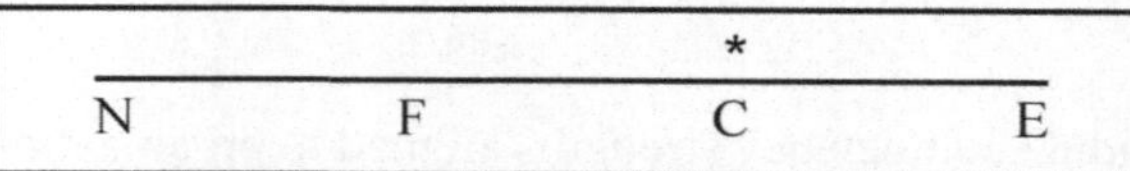

9. Design the appropriate feed-forward and feedback process.

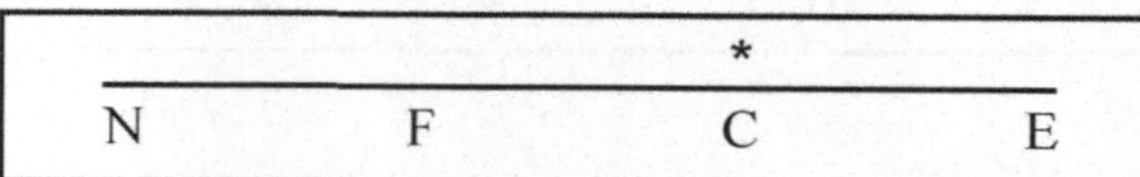

10. Facilitating the analysis and synthesis of success/failure pattern of application/ competency development area.

11. Developing a database of programmes and trainers for competency development.

*

N F C E

12. Scanning the environment and identifying all places for conducting the programmes. Doing a cost-benefit analysis.

13. Facilitating the identification of learning objectives.

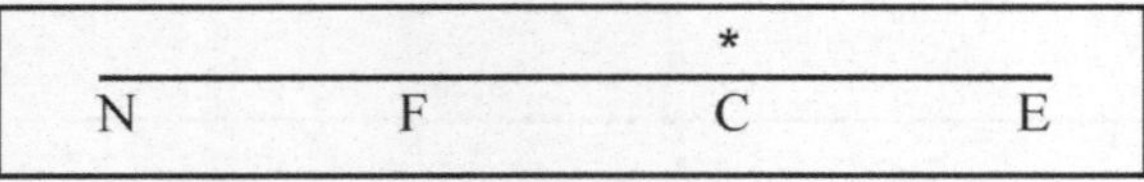

14. Training follow up and assessment: administering a certification process which assesses the participants with respect to level of competency.

15. Collecting data with respect to the competencies developed and the level of development, thereby calculating ROI in terms of competencies/Rs. 1000.

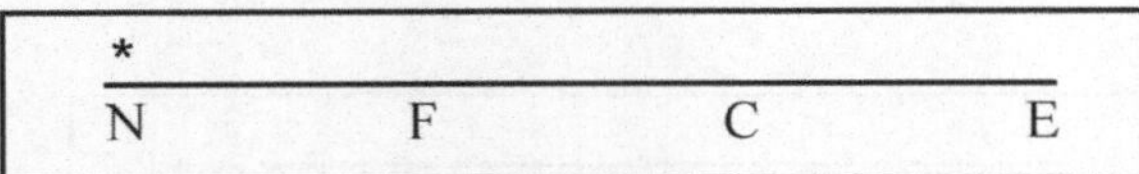

16. Facilitating learning transfer sessions wherein the participants share success/failure patterns with respect to the in-focus competencies, facilitating project reviews in case projects were taken up as application points at the end of competency development areas.

17. Designing a feedback form for assessment of programme effectiveness to become a basis for ascertaining competencies developed and their levels.

18. Facilitating changes on the basis of participant's feedback and data collected during certification processes.

19. Mapping the key business/work process in the organization.

20. Identifying and classifying the key competencies/business process/key positions.

21. Assimilating e-learning technologies.

22. Designing e-learning modules with respect to each stage of competency development.

23. Mentoring: designing and developing a mentoring process to enable learning in the real business environment by observation and analysis of mentors by employees and interaction between them.

*

N F C E

24. On-the-job training: deploying on-the-job training which is aligned to competency development process.

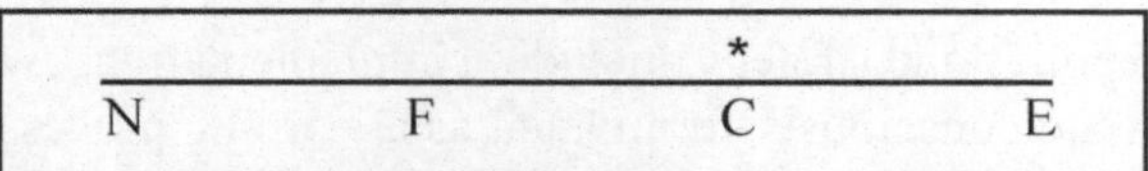

25. Facilitation: facilitating the competency development process with respect to all competency development programmes.

LEARNING ORGANIZATION

The concept of learning organization has emerged from the need of knowledge development and competitive advantage. A learning organization can be described as one which facilitates the learning of all its employees and continuously transforms itself as a whole (Pedler *et al*., 1991: 1). It has skills in creating, acquiring and transferring knowledge and at modifying its behaviour to reflect new knowledge and insights. The concept of learning organization has the underlying idea of transforming an organization through an open learning approach to present and future performance. It refers to an organization's adaptability to changing an environment, particularly when it is complex and highly dynamic. Underpinning the definition by Pedler is the creation of a learning climate where everybody is encouraged to learn and the company as a whole organization develops a capacity for learning. Box 12.3 illustrates the characteristics of a learning organization.

Drawing on the literature about the learning organization concept, it is possible to distinguish a number of features of learning organization (Pettigrew & Whipp, 1991; Storey & Sission, 1993; Mabey & Salman, 1995; Lundy & Cowling, 1996):

1. Learning can be derived from all experiences—successes and failures—and used to shape future behaviour.
2. Learning is valuable in its own right and learning how to learn is an important part of the process.
3. Learning from both the internal and external environment takes place at all levels of the organization and there is a premium on sharing knowledge across organizational boundaries.
4. Learning is a continuous process and at its most powerful when it becomes habitual and internalized.
5. Unlearning and the reconstruction and adaptation of an organisation's knowledge base is a key managerial task.
6. Learning is used intentionally as an enabling mechanism for organizational transformation.

BOX 12.3
Characteristics of the Learning Organization

1. Organization policy and strategy, including implementation, evaluation and improvement are consciously formulated as a learning process.
2. Wide participation and identification in the debate over policy and strategy:
   - Differences are recognized.
   - Disagreements are aired.
   - Conflicts are tolerated and worked within the decision-making process.
3. Management systems for accounting, budgeting and reporting are structured in order to assist us to learn from the consequences of decisions.
4. Information systems should inform as well as automate. Staff should be able to:
   - Question operating assumptions.
   - Seek information for individual and collective learning about the organisation's goal and processes.
5. Information on expectations and feedback on satisfaction should be exchanged by individuals and work units at all levels to assist learning.
6. Employees with external links—such as sales representatives—act as environmental scanners, feeding information back to other staff.
7. There is a deliberate attempt to share information and learn jointly with significant others outside the organization, such as key customers and suppliers.
8. The organisation's culture and management style encourages experimentation, and learning and development from successes and failures.
9. Everyone has access to resources and facilities for self-development.

Learning, however, is difficult to evaluate. It becomes measurable only when it results in some distinguishable behavioural outcomes. Some of them are listed in Box 12.3.

Argyris & Schon (1978) distinguish two ways in which this interaction between learning and outcome can occur. They are labelled single loop learning and double loop learning. These concepts are already explained in an earlier section. Learning organizations use mostly double loop learning, that is, they attempt to construct new conceptual pictures of organizational processes through challenging existing values, procedures and knowledge or more simply 'the way things are done around here.' This double loop learning can be used to examine all processes including HR processes and training programmes which have not yielded results.

Next, the underlying hypothesis where learning takes place all the time in the whole organization must be better able to cope with change and uncertainty (Lundy & Cowling, 1996). Again, where the continuous development of employees is inextricably linked to the process of strategic management they 'become a major source of competitive ability, positioned to take advantage of every opportunity, while taking positive stance when confronted with adversity (Harrison, 1993). Others have gone further to argue that people are the only source of competitive advantage within a complex environment (West, 1994) and that organizational learning may be the only competitive advantage for firms in the future.

From this perspective the learning organization concept, indeed, seems to be a 'pot of gold' (A. Thornhill, P. Lewis & M. Millmore: 2000). However, against this, the concept may present no more than an idealized construct rather than a practical working model (Storey & Sission, 1993). For example, conditions conducive to learning may not be readily found in practice. These conditions include

1. employees who are committed to and capable of managing their own continuous development,
2. the presence of mechanisms that support mutual learning and which capture, share and disseminate learning,
3. an appropriate culture that supports experimentation, risk-taking and independent thinking and toleration of discord, and
4. authority based on expertise rather than status and (a pluralist ideology). Organizations based on bureaucracy, control, status and unitarism are mostly the reality.

Another difficulty is that the very concept of continuous transformation (Pedlar) is open to criticism. How many times has an organization transformed itself? Mumford (1998) argues strongly that learning should be incremental rather than transformational. He questions whether employees can be equipped with the capacity for double loop learning when our HRD system is not able to deliver even single loop learning. We can perhaps conclude that the learning organization 'as now' is an illusive concept.

Questions and Assignments

Q.1. Why is training such a critical issue for organizations? How is training likely to change in future?

Q.2. What key factors influence the success of training programmes?

Q.3. Formulate an HRD plan for any organization, making your own assumptions, as a chief of T&D. How will you assess your own performance?

Q.4. What is 'competency mapping'? How is it done? Why has it become so important an HRD tool today? Prepare a plan for mapping competencies of sales persons.

Q.5. What makes any organization to be known as a 'Learning Organisation'? What is the role of HR in a learning organization? Discuss.

Q.6. Discuss methods of training evaluation. And also how training need analysis is done?

Assignments

1. Visit *'virtuallearn.com'* which has thousands of products from nearly 100 vendors and publishers. Select a subject module and evaluate the opportunities for training with the following media: Web, Book, Live, Video, Audio, and CD-ROM. What mode of delivery appears to be most popular for various subjects? Also explore '*www.astd.org*' and review what these sources include.
2. In small groups, develop a tool to evaluate the learning/training you had in your summer training and also evaluate the learning you are getting in any two subjects in your course. Keep all the factors and objectives in your mind.

Human Resource Development at Xerox—Case Study

The document company at Mitcheldean is a part of the Xerox Corporation. The site manufactures digital document office products. Approximately 2,300 staff is employed on site of which 1,800 are directly employed in production work. For a number of years, Xerox has sought to gain competitive advantage through the relentless pursuit of customer satisfaction. Exceeding customer requirements in every part of business is seen as the route to increased productivity growth, stability and investment. This strategic commitment has prompted the development of a management model (XMM).

For manufacturing 'Business Units' the ever changing demands of customers involved an early commitment to team working which is evolving over time into the X team. Under 'Team Xerox', traditional flow line systems were reconfigured into manufacturing teams in the early 1980s. Subsequently, higher productivity demands led to their development into 'Self Managed Work Groups' (SMWG) at the beginning of the 1990s. However, employees signalled through the regular 'Employee-Motivation and Satisfaction' surveys (EMSS) that greater emphasis on effective team performance as an important part of continuous improvement was desirable. This led in the mid-1990s to the X-team initiative where the focus was on empowerment, leading to high performance.

While manufacturing continues to be organized around teams, grouped into 'Business Units', this evolutionary process has transformed roles and responsibilities. Earlier, Section Managers heading the team were responsible for various managerial functions—daily communication, disciplinary process, identifying development needs, allocation of work, etc. The underlying concept of team-working was to move decision-making progressively to the point at which the decisions are likely to have most impact, that is, those who do the job. X-teams are really a process that enables production teams to take far more responsibilities for the day-to-day running of their working area, ownership of their performance and results, and setting targets, monitoring and formulating actions for improvement.

Progression to an X-team is voluntary. An existing team seeking this designation must first find a sponsor. This is usually their line manager. The team itself can be any identifiable group of employees with a common purpose/output and may include their direct line manager. The process starts with the team conducting a self assessment exercise against four sets of criteria: customer assurance; process management; team motivation and satisfaction, and empowerment. Once the assessment has been done by the sponsor, it is validated by an 'assessor' which leads to an official rating between 1–7 where 7 indicates that the team is operating as a 'world-class team'. Subsequent assessment takes place as the team improves its performance against the four sets of criteria.

Currently, 36 teams have been enrolled and 10 have qualified as X-teams (that is, they have achieved an official rating). One of the teams has already progressed to a rating of 5 and another six to rating 4. Each criteria set has a 7-point scale and initial measurement against these provide teams with information on where improvement can be made. The team then can decide on what and how it will improve upon, that is, through re-engineering work processes, improving skills or obtaining better understanding of customer requirements. The sponsor supports the team by helping with self-assessments, providing clear direction, goals, understandable performance measures and agreed work boundaries; coaching the team to help make its own decisions, effectively use the tools available and to achieve its goals including diagnosing development needs.

In total, these developments are changing the management environment. A natural corollary of empowerment within X-Teams has been that organizational practice is challenged by everyone. Section managers now place greater emphasis on the management of their staff through coaching and facilitating with less time personally dedicated to managing operational issues. However, although more teams are seeking X-Team status the concept is still in its infancy. Nevertheless, they represent a long-term commitment that is integral to planned changes to the management style and culture of the organization which, of course, will not happen overnight.

The evolution of team working should not be seen in isolation. It consistently stresses the same key values of XMM-Customer first and Employee Satisfaction. It is regarded as a significant conduit for translating these into reality for shop-floor teams and helps them drive actions which also support the direction of the company—to have world-class standards with high profitability and customer satisfaction.

The progress movement of X-teams has inevitably impacted the skills, knowledge and attitudes required of the workforce. From what has been said so far, it is clearly evident in three groupings of employees: production operatives, section managers and sponsors. Changes to the structure of jobs have simultaneously involved the vertical integration of tasks, the exercise of interpersonal skills and movement to an empowered culture. This has involved successful integration of new team members; and the translation of strategy into operational activities.

Underpinning Xerox's approach to managing its HR is a framework of 23 'Leadership Attributes and 9 'Cultural Dimensions' (Table 12.4). These drive the HR processes of HR development, recruitment and selection and performance review.

From its inception the move towards team working has been supported by a series of training interventions. To support 'Team Xerox', team building days were held and supported by formal training courses. The productivity-focused SMWGs and X-Teams were underpinned by NVQs and multiskilling which was mapped on a learning matrix for each team. The HRD activity within the organization is, however, also clearly moving with the evolving needs of its customers. The launch of 'Skills Partnership' is a measure of how the integration of the HR function is needed

TABLE 12.4
Xerox Case Study: Leadership Attributes and Cultural Dimensions

Leadership Attributes	Cultural Dimensions
No. 5: Decision Making • Take decisions in a timely manner • Wherever possible manages by facts • Uses best sources of information available as a basis for decisions in uncertain situations • Assumes responsibility for the results of decisions made • Takes calculated risks to seize opportunities	No. 7: Open and Honest Communication • Sensitive to concerns and feelings of others • Does not treat disagreement as disloyalty • Encourages feedback, dialogue and information sharing • Fosters openness and trust through personal behaviour • Confronts conflicts openly
No. 6: Quick Study • Understands processes, technologies and issues quickly • Identifies causes/effect relationships • Generates original ideas • Reduces complex situations to essential elements • Fully understands problems and recognizes their implications	No. 8: Organization Reflection and Learning • Sees problems as learning opportunities • Role model in self-development • Encourages others to learn from success and failure • Treats ideas with respect • Encourages sharing of knowledge

to support the modern learning organization. This team is an amalgamation of traditional functions of resourcing as well as training and development. The boundaries between them are blurred in this new service organization. Their mission is to provide the service that helps their business centre customer teams and individuals acquire the skills they need to be successful in world markets. They therefore support any activity that helps in people development and learning and look to the introduction of new skills from outside the organization to provide continuous freshness in that learning process. Driven by the HR manager, the physical infrastructure looks like a high-street shop which sends powerful signals about the *modus operandi* of the HR function. It represents an accessible service committed to meeting the needs of internal customers. While previously the approach was not entirely prescriptive, the ethos now is very much based on consultation leading to many of the training needs being identified from the bottom up.

The development needs of X-Team members are likely to be met through three different routes. First, there are companywide initiatives such as customer service training and TQM that all employees undertake through off-the-job formal courses. Second, product training operates to ensure new developments and progress through multi-skilling. This could be met in part or in full through on-the-job training. However, whereas the first two routes are mandatory the third is optional and is driven by the employees themselves.

The third route focuses on self development as a means to address identified needs. These may well be identified through the annual performance feedback and development review process which is underpinned through the 'Leadership Attributes' and 'Cultural Dimensions' and uses the 360 degree appraisal approach. There is onus on all team members to recognize the importance of development to organizational success; serve as a role model for personal and professional growth; coach teams to achieve high performance and self managing capability. The identification of individual and team development needs can, therefore, be driven by the team itself and often arises directly from operational issues or the continuous improvement process.

Teams can draw on the support of the Team Facilitator—a post specifically created to service X-Teams. All through the emphasis is on team members, the sponsors, and 'Skills Partnership' working in concert to analyse gaps and identify appropriate development strategies. These may be met through a variety of methods including formal education, training courses, shadowing, special projects, mentoring, etc. In this way the whole principle of empowerment underpinning the X-Teams also becomes an important dimension of the HRD process which in itself is an important vehicle for progressing towards the designation of a 'world-class' team.

Questions

Q.1. Discuss how HRD can help in achieving the mission of any organization.

Q.2. How can HRD help in changing the culture of a firm? What difficulties and challenges are faced? Discuss.

CASE

Mahavir Polyester Limited

Mahavir Polyester Limited (a pseudonym) was established in the early 1980s and manufactured chips, yarn and film, with industrial alcohol being a by-product. Its sole plant was located in the upper reaches of eastern Uttar Pradesh while its head office (including marketing and finance departments) was in New Delhi. For many years, the company enjoyed the benefits of the 'licence-permit' raj and posted good profits. But with the opening up of the economy came stiff competition, both domestic and foreign. While the cost of raw material and key inputs rose sharply, and in some cases up to three times, the sale price of film (the chief cash earner for the company), fell steadily. In short, the company had to more than run to stay in the same place, and in the emerging competitive environment that was insufficient.

Market conditions apart, the organization carried the burden in two distinct areas. Managerial turnover was so rapid that most managers stayed not beyond 2-3 years, with top plant management leaving at an even faster pace. Between 1990-95, there were three chief operating officers at the plant, the last one staying on a few months. The other feature was the turbulent industrial relations scenario. Work stoppages, gherao and assault on managerial personnel were regular features, not to speak of loitering, abandoning work site for long periods and defiance of managerial authority. The flashpoint came in January 1991 when the workers effected such a complete gherao of the factory premises that food packets had to be air-dropped in the officers' colony!

It was during this turbulent phase that effective control passed from father to son in this essentially family controlled organization. The son's educational background and operating style were in juxtaposition to his father's feudal style. Around this time too, senior management personnel joined the plant, significant ones being the Executive Vice President (the CEO of the plant), General Manager (Personnel) and General Manager (Film). These senior plant recruitments were brought about by the President of the company who himself was a new appointee having worked in a leading organization in the U.S.A. for about two decades. Also inducted was the Vice President (P&A) at the head office in New Delhi who was to play a vital role in the turnaround exercise.

By November 1995, there were about 600 permanent workmen and 125 staff at the plant. There was one recognised union with which the management negotiated and entered into the usual three-year wage agreement. While membership verification is a disputed and ticklish issue, over 75 per cent of the workmen were believed to be unionised under its banner. Excepting the President and the General Secretary, all office bearers of the union were permanent workmen of the plant. The President and General Secretary were former workmen of the plant who were dismissed during the afermath of the January 1991 gherao and violence.

It is in the areas of general upkeep and workplace governance that many things were amiss. The whole plant appeared dirty and unkempt, with huge piles of waste stockpiled. The toilets were unclean and stinking and the canteen, even after a facelift, remained shoddy. But workplace governance was the greatest casualty. Shoddy workmanship, refusal to work, littering, and defiance of managerial authority were the order of the day. Shop floor supervisors were diploma engineers, whose technical knowledge and supervisory skills were considered crude by middle management and workers alike. On the other hand, shopfloor supervisors felt they operated against great odds, caught as they were between demanding superiors and difficult and defiant workers. While senior managers were only interested in production at any cost, they extended little support when it came to taking even minimum disciplinary action against erring workmen. Abrasive worker behaviour at the shopfloor and specific incidents of assault outside the factory gate were cited as evidence of their helpless situation. Workers in turn found little cause to behave otherwise. While the company prospered and the management got their hefty annual increments and rapid promotions, workmen did not even get a grade change. Demoralisation, helplessness and apportioning blame were the organisation's characteristics.

The Beginning of Transition

To the new management, it appeared that conditions were not conducive to meet the challenges of a competitive environment. What was possibly called for was an overhaul of operational outlook. The organization had to get its act together, and quickly. A leading consulting firm from South India was hired and Vision and Mission statements worked out and prominently displayed. Another Delhi-based consulting firm having an international tie-up was hired to impart TQM training to each and every workman. Kaizen activities were also initiated. Sustained efforts were made in the areas of housekeeping and waste reduction. A year after these activities were started, wastage had gone down and productivity and quality had improved. There was also a noticeable improvement in housekeeping. Nonetheless, to the top management, the degree and pace of change were not sufficient to be pleasing, and specially so considering the effort, money and time invested. To the top management, work culture somehow did not appear to be right.

It was in this context that a team of two consultants was brought in. The consultants, as a prelude to any interventional role, embarked on a two-day diagnostic study of the organisational climate by conducting interviews and having a dialogue with the management, staff and workmen. The findings indicated

(a). a great divide between and mistrust amongst the management hierarchy, and between individuals in the same group;

(b). non-utilisation of existing strengths, seeking ideas for OD low, and no process for seeking contribution;

(c). individual orientation, compartmentalisation and little recognition for difficulties of others; and

(d). lack of rapport with the workforce, poor workplace discipline and difficulty in getting work out of reticent workmen.

As a consequence of the report submitted to the Vice President (P&A), it was decided to tentatively commence a series of attitudinal/behavioural training programmes that were to address the issues and concerns expressed during the organisational climate survey. The first three-day training programme was so tentative, that it did not even have a title other than being referred to as a management development programme. While a loose structure was drawn up on the basis of the diagnostic study, the consultants' understanding was that they would be able to firm up the outline only after a couple of programmes. Indeed, it was also a question of testing their assumptions about organisational reality gleaned through the diagnostic study.

The Training Programmes

The first training programme commenced in mid-December 1995 with 14 participants, with two of them trooping in well after the inauguration. (They said they were told to join the programme only "this morning" at the shopfloor). The Vice President (P&A) who had come down from Delhi for the inaugural session, informed the participants about the basis and nature of the ensuing programme. When the Executive Vice President was asked by the VP (P&A) to say a few words, the former very reluctantly agreed, saying he had, till that moment, no idea of the programme's objective, contents or methodology but, going by the VP (P&A)'s introductory remarks, he 'wholeheartedly' agreed with the necessity of such a training programme. He was to later ask the consultants if they had a spare copy of their diagnostic study report.

Beginning with a micro-lab, the programme sought to draw out the participants' perception of organisational culture. The small-group-activities (SGA), through pictorial presentations and skits, presented a scenario that could be classified under the following heads:

- **Organisational:** top management remote; no bonding between departmental heads, lack of organisational focus; absence of work culture; adhocism in the absence of established policies and clear guidelines.
- **Work-Related:** adhocism; lackadaisical attitude towards work; poor work discipline; poor coordination between departments.
- **Individual:** low identity with organization; uncertain about growth and future.

Through a series of games, exercises and role plays that was to constitute experiential learning, the group tried to come to grips with the causative factors of such a situation, as well as to examine their own role and work behaviour. The objective was to move from a position of apportioning blame on external factors to a position of what the participants could do to increase their own contribution; how they could help themselves; what constituted team work and the work behaviour needed to improve team work for task completion, efficiency and improvement in quality.

As the programme drew to its end, the participants examined the efficacy of the three-day exercise. The novelty of the experiential learning method apart and the intense feelings that it generated, it was felt that the programme had touched a "raw nerve", a "critical aspect" governing organisational functioning and proceeded to give a title to the training programme, *Transforming Work Culture*. This went ahead to set up two study groups to go through readings pertaining to work culture.

After conducting three such programmes for the management, the first training programme for the workers was held. This was similar to the ones conducted for the management except in two respects: the medium was Hindi and the programme was for two days. In terms of participant response, these programmes were distinctive in terms of display of intense emotions pertaining to working conditions and welfare related matters, distribution of promotions and rewards between workmen and management, and their own contribution to productivity and profitability in spite of poor calibre of diploma engineers who formed their front-line supervisors. The union, too, was a touchy matter. At the same time, workmen identified many strengths of the organization.

As more programmes were conducted, the discordant notes grew louder, until a participant questioned the utility of SWOT exercises in the absence of any organisational response. He went on to say that these training sessions were meant to brainwash workers and keep them in a lulled state. The trainers, though not in the least surprised, placed the participant's opinion to the whole group and wanted to know if they agreed with the opinion expressed. The participants took pains to point out that they had the utmost respect for the faculty and were sure the faculty harboured no mala fide intention. They said the impact of training was very visible: there was all round improvement in the way work was done. But the fact remained that the organization did not care about the workmen. One participant opined that the only way to make the management listen was to use strong-arm tactics.

Surely, the OD interventions had reached a critical stage. It was necessary for the organization to respond meaningfully to various systemic issues being raised. Ignoring them would not only negate the gains but jeopardise the OD interventions. Based on worker feedback from these programmes, and the linkage that OD intervention has with systemic responses, the consultant-trainers presented an unsolicited report to the top management for appropriate organisational responses.

The management was soon to introduce:

(i). lateral promotions on a large scale;

(ii). Rs. 500 cash award to every worker in appreciation of significant improvement in productivity and housekeeping;

(iii). additional leave;

(iv). leave encashment; and

(v). increased bonus.

Committees were also formed to actively pursue Mahavir's funding proposal with the electricity department to provide street lights from the factory gate to the heart of the town so that the workmen could safely cycle the three-km stretch. Negotiations also began with a small school whereby the company could fund infrastructural development provided the school management extended free or subsidised education to workmen's children. While the organization was itself unable to provide a housing loan to workmen, it was willing to stand as guarantor to organisations like LIC or HDFC, if the workmen formed a housing cooperative.

Parallel Development

Meanwhile, the management introduced electronic card punching system for marking time. To begin with, only management and staff were required to mark their entry and exit into the plant. Data was now available if any manager took too long a lunch break or was absent for a long duration without authorised permission. Although such incidents were rare in any case, people did come to know which errant manager was talked to by his senior. As the GM (P&A) put it, it was necessary for people to know that corrective action was being taken at the top. About two months later, the system was made applicable for workmen too. Habitual late comers were at first warned and then served memos. The introduction of this system reduced the incidence of late coming significantly

Bolstered by the success of card punching, the administration declared the plant premises to be a tobacco-free zone. Smoking, *pan* and tobacco chewing were banned after giving a short notice period. Many heads of departments and senior managers switched to chewing gum and toffees or had to go out of the plant premises for a smoke which was naturally an onerous exercise. Even the President of the company, who was a chain smoker, would grumble but abide by the no-smoking ban on his visits to the plant from Delhi. Stray incidents of violation by management, staff and workmen were talked about, but the administration took a benign view and limited itself to counselling.

The organization also introduced joint councils as an interactive form for workmen and management to discuss work-related issues. While the union was not formally represented in the council, many union office bearers were members of this council. The introduction of the council was preceded by the circulation of a draft document, and a two-day training programme for the union. Since the President and the General Secretary of the union were terminated employees, the training programme was organised in a nearby resort.

The focus was on how to manage the union better, and the qualities and skills required to discharge the union role. The functioning of the joint council also figured prominently in the training programme. Back at the plant, a special training programme was organised for the members of the joint council. While the council constitution formed the basis of discussion, the programme focused on the qualities and work methods required to make the council a working proposition.

INCIDENTS OF DISQUIET

Although the canteen was spruced up, workmen were generally unhappy with the quality of food and service. There would be some trouble every other day, and even replacing the canteen contractor did little to alleviate the situation. Management's proposal to workmen to take over the canteen management through a committee remained a non-starter. One day, the workmen boycotted the canteen food over an unpleasant, but not unusual incident. The management, in spite of the boycott, kept the canteen operational for three days and much food was wasted. The impasse was broken when worker representatives approached the management to pay the workmen a monthly sum of Rs. 100 per worker in lieu of the subsidy that it was providing for canteen facility. The management agreed, although they were to acknowledge the measure as a bad solution to a vexing problem. The canteen closure issue was invariably raised by workmen participants in the training programmes. The money was grudgingly welcome, but they said many found it difficult to do without the canteen. Tea and snacks in any case continued to be served at the work site, an arrangement with which the workers were unhappy as fine ash from chimneys settled in the cup.

There was, however, real trouble on the industrial relations front. In April 1995, the then Senior Manager (P&A) had agreed to give a bonus of 18 per cent. This understanding was reached with a faction of a union that is no longer recognised by the management. The then management had initially offered the statutory 8.33 per cent, later increased the offer to 15 per cent, and ultimately declared 18 per cent. The Security Officer was assaulted during the course of talks on bonus. The 1995-98 agreement with the recognised union provided for regularisation of 30 casuals and by January 1996, 28 of them were regularised. On 3 February 1996, the leader of the faction that had wangled the 18 per cent bonus, instigated stoppage of film slitting operations to force the regularisation of a casual. While other departments kept functioning, it was only a matter of time that other departments of a process plant had to come to a halt. There was however no violence. The GM (P&A) maintained a "hands-off" stance, telling the workmen and staff who approached him that it was their plant and if they wished not to work or to remain silent spectators, what could he do? He even refused to ask the men in the slitting section who had stopped production to resume work. By 11-o-clock that night, the night shift started as usual. The following day, three workmen including the leader of the faction were issued termination orders. There was no violence, no work stoppage or overt unrest of any kind.

Seven months later, another incident occurred, and once again in the film plant. A worker, who also happened to be a leader of the recognised union, manhandled the DGM of his department. The administration promptly suspended the worker-leader for 10 days pending inquiry. The DGM, apprehending closure of the film plant, asked the GM (P&A) to withdraw the suspension order. The latter declined to relent, even when other union office bearers interceded on the workman's behalf. When the worker-leader turned up at the factory gate during shift time, he was promptly stopped. There was no untoward incident and the workman had to serve his 10-day suspension and tender a written apology.

Soon thereafter, the GM (P&A) was himself at the receiving end of violent behaviour. The incident that triggered off the fracas was in itself quite a trivial one. A worker-leader (though not of the recognised union, yet a blue-eyed boy of the administration) could not be provided a company car for marriage purposes for the simple reason that none was available at that time. The worker came to the GM (P&A)'s chamber in a drunken state, abused him roundly, flung the files from the table and smashed the table-top glass. The dismissal that followed was a tame affair and there was not even a whimper, except that some people made entreaties for forgiveness and leniency.

The net effect of the processual and structural-systemic interventions coupled with work practice changes resulted in significant improvements in Mahavir. A year after the various interventions were set in motion, production of film had increased by 37.5 per cent from 400 tons to over 550 tons per month, quality improved and wastage and costs reduced. There was a significant drop in managerial turnover alongwith the return of some staff and workers from competitors. Dysfunctional activities like late coming, absenteeism, loitering and abandoning work stations reduced, and worker unrest, violence and defiance of managerial authority gave way to improved workplace discipline. The plant premises, which for years resembled a huge dumpyard, now looked almost picturesque. Large scale lateral promotions were accorded to workers, wages improved and higher bonus given. Moreover, every worker was granted Rs. 500 cash and gift; additional leave and leave encashment were introduced for the first time, along with other benefits and facilities. Finally, the company was able to add another state-of-the-art film plant within its existing premises and able to shift many 'surplus' workmen and staff to the new unit. The workmen did not lose jobs and the organization was able to reduce its manning ratio in the older unit and at the same time recruit tried and tested workmen without having to add to its wage bill.

Questions

Q.1. To what extent do you think processual (training) interventions alone could have contributed to managing performance at Mahavir?

Q.2. It appears that it was matter of pure chance that Mahavir blundered along the right path of development. What role did leadership play in managing industrial relations and performance at Mahavir?

Q.3. The training programmes were labelled "transformation of work culture". How appropriate is this label? What relationship does it have with performance management (was it transformation of work culture or changes in work culture or improvement in work culture)?

Q.4. D you think that strict enforcement of work practice changes, including disciplinary actions, endangers peaceful IR and thus affect performance management efforts? Why did Mahavir escape the consequences given its history of IR?

Q.5. Can you categorise the organisational interventions at Mahavir that led to significant improvements as those involving Industrial Relations Strategy?

Q.6. What distinctive features of Indian industrial relations are discernible from the developments of HR and management of human resources at Mahavir?

13 Employee Relations and Management of Change

Learning Objectives

After studying this chapter you will learn:

- The significance, need and concept of employee relations in organizations.
- The reasons for workers to join trade unions and the reasons for the declining membership the world over.
- The strategies of unitarist employers to get employee commitment and involvement.
- The role of HRM in organizations where union activity is absent or on the wane.
- The types of EI strategies and likely problems in implementation.
- The planning, implementation, people's involvement and maintaining momentum of change in organizations.
- Employee burnout, reasons, process and prevention.

INTRODUCTION

An organization comes into existence when the efforts of people are pooled to complete some tasks to achieve these objectives. Some of the basic elements of an organization are its ownership and sources of authority; the purposes it is intended to achieve; the tasks that flow from these; the people who constitute it; the relationship between them, and between them and the tasks, tools or technology, its boundary and relationships with what lies outside. The very nature of organization, therefore, generates a number of significant tensions: between people with different stakes in the organization, and therefore different perspectives and interests in it; between what owners and other members of the organization may desire and what they can feasibly achieve; between the needs, capabilities and potentials of the members and what the environment demands of and permits them. Management is the process and the relationships between members and stakeholders are its vital components that keep the organization together, preventing it from flying apart due to these tensions and that which makes it work to survive and grow. Thus the study of employee relations is the study of management itself or the management of tensions between the stakeholders, which naturally come into play as soon as the organization is formed.

Although the organization of tasks packages people into organizational roles, individuals are larger and more organic than those roles tend to be. The organization, writes Bernard (1938) 'pays people only for certain of their activities.... But it is whole persons who come to work'. Unlike other resources people interact with those who manage them and among themselves; they have need for autonomy and agency, they think and are creative, they have feelings, they need consideration for their emotional and therefore physical needs and protection. Their characteristics of being human greatly complicate the tasks of management and managers who can only work with and through people to ensure that the organization survives and thrives in the pressures from the environment.

Again the environment, both external and internal, undergoes continuous change: sometimes slow and at times at very fast pace. Organizations being organic entities take all their inputs from it and give the value added back to it. Hence when environment or any of the internal components like technology, ownership or tasks change the 'relationships' which experience new tensions and get disturbed, at times leading to violence. But without relationships, work cannot go on. This process of cooperation, conflict and cooperation, called 'employee relations and management of change' is the subject matter of this book.

Employee relations are a key strategic issue for organizations because the nature of the relationship between employees and employer can have a significant impact on morale, motivation, and productivity.

EMPLOYEE RELATIONS

The subject 'employee relations' deals with all the formal and informal relationships of an interpersonal nature that arise from management/employee interactions in working situations. Where the workforce is unionized, it deals with managing them for gaining their support to achieve organizational objectives of increased productivity, cost reduction and gaining flexibility. The subject also covers broadly employee communications, participation in decision-making and gaining the employees' commitment and involvement for improving quality and customer satisfaction.

The modern approach to management of employee relations is to emphasize cooperation rather than conflict and to integrate employee relations policies into the overall corporate strategy of the firm. This requires that managements recognize the critical importance of harmonious relations with its workforce in different units, and relate its employee relations policies to the achievement of increased competitiveness. Major decisions that have to be taken when formulating an employee relations strategy include:

- Whether to recognize trade unions, unless the law demands it.
- Managerial approaches to personnel policies and procedures that affect employee relations (recruitment and promotions, selection, training, redundancy and performance appraisal).

- Whether management is prepared to use external bodies to arbitrate and help resolve disputes. If there are recognized trade unions, disputes are not resolved amicably; the dispute resolving mechanism (Industrial Disputes Act 1947 in India) is to be followed as prescribed.
- The basic formula to be applied in the division of the firm's profits between the owners of the business and workers.
- The methods to be used for communicating with the workers in addition to what is required by law.
- The degree to which employee representatives are to be involved in management decision-making.
- Should the company follow a standardized approach in all units or customize it according to conditions prevailing in each unit?
- What needs to be decided at headquarters and what can be negotiated at unit level?

Generally the headquarters staff is likely to fill an advisory role and will advise on:

1. The company's overall philosophy on management/worker relations, the role of trade unions and so on.
2. Alternative solutions to employee relations problems that might be pursued.
3. Cost constraints necessitated by overall company strategy.
4. Updating units on employee relations policies with success stories and benchmarking it with competitors and others.
5. Productivity improvement measures introduced in other countries/units.
6. Intervene if relations deteriorate beyond a certain point.
7. Select the top HR executives for different units and rotate them for greater experience. The aim is to apply consistent policies in all units and dovetail them into an overall company plan for employee relations.

Why Employees Unionize

Employees usually form or join unions because of the perceived benefits that unionization might provide them. These benefits can be economic, social and/or political. Economic benefits can result from a union's ability to negotiate higher wages, better or expanded benefits, greater job or employment security and improved working hours and conditions. Social benefits can be derived from the affiliation and sense of community that workers share when they are unionized. Their personal issues and needs relating to their jobs can be integrated within the union agenda, with corresponding support gained from co-workers. Unions often sponsor social events for the members and their families. Political benefits can be gained through the sense of power in numbers. In negotiations with management, individual employees are relatively powerless. Management may be able to do without individual employees but they cannot do without their entire workforce.

Trade unions have a long history of struggle for worker's rights in all countries. They have held their grip on organized industry and the public sector. HR executives have spent all their time and energies to maintain harmonious relations with them. However, with the rise of MNCs and capitalism, the collapse of communism and outsourcing of work, unions are losing their strength and power.

HRM AND UNIONS

Developments in HRM and the adoption of new economic policies have drastically lowered the degree of unionization. Employers the world over are strenuously trying to prevent union formation at new worksites so as to discourage union influence at existing plants. MNCs are known to shift the plant to another country and location if unionization prevents achievement of objectives. Unions in most countries are in deep crisis as they are considered the biggest obstacles to efficiency, competitiveness, new technology and labour flexibility (the exception being Tata Steel and other group companies). In the USA, a flourishing class of labour consultants is emerging to stall union-organizing campaigns. The Dunlop Commission estimated that 70 per cent of US employers used outside consultants in regard to labour-management relations. At 40 per cent of workplaces, employees were not able to secure a collective bargaining agreement with their employers even after winning certification for collective bargaining (US Department of Labour, 1994). Employers are increasingly resorting to contingent, non-permanent employment in the form of part-time, *ad-hoc*, temporary and contract workers. In the post-Reagan USA, union membership has dropped to below 16 per cent from 35.4 per cent in 1985. In India, presently only 8.5 per cent of the Indian workforce is unionized (*Economic Times*) and a major section of the unionized workforce belongs to the public sector.

ILO's World Labour Report provides information on trade union density for 65 countries, which shows that 33 countries saw a decline of union membership by more than 20 per cent. Several factors have contributed to the steep decline of unions. These include declining employment, changing technology leading to increasing employment of white collar workers who are reluctant to unionize, the general decline of liberal politics and pursuit of hard HRM policies by employers.

Employers use these policies as tools for individualizing workplace relations and thus for weakening unions. HRM, whether hard or soft, co-opts the individual workers and integrates them into the organizational goals. It is posing challenges to trade unions that they had never faced in the past. States are also collaborating in this by relaxing labour laws and standards.

Studies have also found that employees now espouse a more unitarist view of employment relations. Individually and collectively, they feel that unionization is not in their interest. This category of workers is referred to as 'gold-collared' or 'pink-collared'. They command a high price in the employment market because they possess rare skills which are in great demand. The high performers, in particular, think that union demands relate more to securing standard benefits for all rather than to higher benefits related to performance.

The younger workers immensely value personal advancement, greater organizational involvement and higher social status. In order to survive in the new scenario, unions will have to cater to the needs of these workers. With SHRM in the saddle, trade unions will have to compete with management for worker loyalty, which they can only do by offering a more dynamic and innovative programme.

CREATING A UNITARY WORKFORCE

As discussed in the previous section, SHRM has to play the role that unions have been playing to meet the needs of employees if it aims to integrate them with the goals of the organization by developing a more enthusiastic and committed workforce through fostering better employee relations. A unitary workforce is 'an integrated group with a single authority/loyalty structure and a set of common values, interests and objectives shared by all members of the organization' (Salmon, 1998: 5).

Whether it is possible or even desirable, opinions may differ, but this is the rhetoric that underpins the philosophy of SHRM. Even governments also desire that both workers and management work closely for society's sake. One of the ways this can happen is to create a partnership agreement between unions and management. The contents of the agreement may vary but the common features found are as follows:

- New consultation and communication agreements.
- Setting up of joint working groups.
- Increased employee flexibility and team working.
- Employee commitment to business goals.
- Long-term pay deals.
- An umbrella of employment security. Sharing of information.
- An emphasis on training and development.
- Greater focus on local problem-solving activities.
- A move towards harmonization and single status.

The creation of partnership agreements has a lot to offer all parties. If redundancy is necessary, partnership agreements commonly give employees 'employability training' or a golden handshake. A good example is agreement in Tata Steel mentioned in the case of Chapter 1.

EMPLOYEE INVOLVEMENT (EI)

Some employers managing employee relations without trade unions (The proportion of UK workplaces in which there are no unions at all has risen from 36 per cent in 1990 to 47 per cent in 1998—source: Cully *et al.,* 1998) have developed alternative methods of generating the support of employees by adopting employee involvement approaches.

TQM or ISO 9000 can not be implemented without employee involvement (EI). These strategies are potential means of bringing change into employee behaviours. EI means that people get involved in the work that they do.

EI is defined as 'a range of processes designed to engage the support, understanding and optimum contribution of all employees in an organization and their commitment to its objectives' (Kesseler & Bayliss, 1998). The claims made about the relationship between EI and various facets of organizational and individual effectiveness are summarized in Table 13.1.

TABLE 13.1
EI Types and Purpose

Main Categories of Employee Involvement	Examples of Methods Used	Brief Intended Rationale
Downward communication	Team briefing, other briefing groups, newspapers, journals aimed at employees, videos, emails, recorded telephone briefings	To provide information; uniform messages; to be educative or re-educative
Problem-solving, involvement and upward communication	Quality circles; quality action teams; suggestion schemes; employee surveys	Explicit access to employees' experiences and skills; gain cooperation and opinions
Consultation	Joint consultation committees; working groups, staff forums, works council	Providing information and testing reactions
Involvement through structural changes at job and work organization levels	Job redesign, job enlargement; job enrichment, work reorganisation; team working; autonomous working groups; empowerment	To be re-educative; providing greater levels of motivation and satisfaction; empowering
Financial involvement	Employee share ownership plans; profit-related pay; bonus schemes	To be re-educative; providing incentives and promoting effort
Managerial style and leadership	Participative managerial style; being visible, accessible and informal; creating credibility; ensuring actions in line with key messages	To provide support; encourage positive working relationships and trust; reduce barriers

It has been claimed that effective EI should:

- Improve employees' business awareness.
- Generate employees' commitment to the objectives of their employee organizations.
- Foster trust by employees towards those who manage them.
- Improve product quality.
- Promote greater acceptance of organizational change.
- Lead to employee flexibility.

- Encourage more effective working relationships.
- Generate employee empowerment.
- Improve employee relations.
- Improve job satisfaction and employee morale.

These claims raise a number of issues. They based on the assumption that this strategy will not lead to any conflict with other organizational or personal goals, but this unitarist view is not completely possible. EI may be conceived as a range of communication techniques or allowing employees to give their ideas and suggestions for improvement. The broad impact of EI suggested above suggests a major change in the operating processes embedded in deep culture change. Various writers have identified several employee involvement methods. Guest *et al.* (1993) and Marchington (1992) have grouped these methods into related categories as shown in Table 13.1.

Problems in Relation to the Realization of EI

1. The following organizational characteristics and prevailing strategies may act to prohibit or promote EI:
   - Organizational performance, prospects and corporate direction.
   - Organizational culture.
   - Organization structure and restructuring.
   - Training human resource development and career management.
   - Performance management and compensation.
   - Other strategies such as those relating to health and safety and employee relations approaches.

   For example, a mechanistic structure may inhibit EI while a project-based structure may serve to encourage EI. Other factors will include organizational performance and perceptions about job security, prospects for development and advancement in careers and the prevailing employee relations climate. The impact of these basic factors are perhaps more capable of inhibiting or promoting EI than the use of many specific techniques designed to achieve this type of outcome.

2. Implementation issues in the use of EI as a change strategy. A simple stakeholder analysis reveals conflicting factors that are capable of influencing EI. It is the role and response of groups of managers, employees and trade unions. Line managers are likely to play a central role in implementation of EI, but if they feel that this type of strategy is wasteful of their time because it may cut down their powers and discretion to act, they may not promote it or may even inhibit it directly or indirectly. This type of managerial behaviour is seen in some organizational cultures. Further, functional goals of managers (finance and production) may also create conflict with respect to EI. Further, the line managers may not subscribe or support EI strategies for lack of proper understanding. They may require skills training and orientation in implementing EI.

3. Although EI may be seen as a positive development from the employee's perspective, it is not always so. A number of factors will affect employee perceptions about particular

attempts to introduce EI strategies. One such factor may relate to employee experiences of any previous attempts to introduce EI strategy. Previous attempts that have been seen to fail, or which were perceived as attempts to increase managerial control over employees rather than to increase their involvement, are likely to increase employee resistance and cynicism.

Some groups of employees who may be used in an environment in which they have not been involved may reject EI. Employees are likely to resist EI if they see other threats from the organization and perceive inconsistencies in the policies.

4. Trade unions, unless offered an inclusive role in EI, may also try to sabotage it.

THE CHANGE PROCESS

From the Industrial Revolution to the present day, we can see that the history of organizations is one of change and upheaval. In fact organizations have hardly operated in stable or predictable environment. Whether because of economic fluctuations, the development of new products and processes, social change or war, organizations and entire industries tend to face recurrent bouts of upheaval.

Some industries emerge leaner and fitter from this process but others shrink to a shadow of their former selves and appear doomed to be relegated to the back stage. In managing change, the HR role is crucial as people are the most complex beings and major resistance comes from them and they are also the change agents.

The change process comprises three interlinked elements: Objectives and Outcomes; Planning the Change, and People.

Objectives and Outcomes

Studies show that a high proportion of change efforts end in failure. Burns & Weeks (1989) found that change projects failed because their original objectives or the desired outcomes were poorly thought-out. Organizational change is basically a political process driven by sectional interests rather than organizational needs. It also results in redistribution of power. Burns (1989) suggested an approach with four phases to assess the need for any type of change. These are:

- The trigger
- The remit
- The assessment team
- The assessment

The Trigger

The organizations should investigate the trigger for change in the company's vision/strategy, highlight it if the need for improved performance arises or if current performance or operation indicates that severe problems or concerns exist. It can also examine the suggestions or opportunities if they offer significant benefits.

The Remit

This should state clearly the reasons for the assessment, its objectives and timescale, and who should be involved and consulted. The remit should stress the need to focus as much on the social aspects as the technical considerations involved. It must make clear that those who will carry out the assessment must look at all options rather than merely considering one or two alternatives.

The Assessment Team

In most cases this should be a multi-disciplinary team consisting of representatives from managers and staff, specialist staff and, where appropriate, an outside consultant or change facilitator (HR executive). It may also require the involvement of senior managers.

The Assessment

The first task of the assessment team is to review the remit and if necessary amend it. It is carried out in four steps:

1. Clarification of the problem or opportunity. This is achieved by gathering information from those concerned. In some situations the problem or opportunity may not exist, or it may need redefinition.
2. Investigation of alternative solutions. A wide-ranging examination should take place to establish the range of possible solutions with their cost-benefit analysis and selecting the one with the greatest benefit.
3. Feedback. The definition of the problem or opportunity and the range of possible solutions should be discussed with interested and affected parties, to obtain their views and to establish the criteria for selecting the preferred approach.
4. Recommendations and decisions. Recommendation should include not only the type of change but also the mechanics and time-scale for making such change and the resource implications as well as performance targets.

Planning the Change

Whether the need for change arises from an organization's needs or in some other way, it is necessary to plan how this will be achieved and followed by implementing the plan. This process comprises six interrelated activities:

1. Establishing a change management team. This must include some, if not all, of those responsible for the original assessment of the need for change, including the assistance of an outside consultant or change facilitator. Sometimes, for large change projects, a sub-group comprising primarily those affected by the change is established to handle the day-to-day implementation issues.
2. Management structures. Because original transition tends to be ambiguous and needs direction, special structures, for example, in order to establish appropriate reporting

relationships to senior management, may need to be created to support and guide the change management team. These management structures should include people who have the power to mobilize resources to promote change.

3. Activity planning. This involves constructing a schedule for the change programme, citing specific activities and events that must occur if the transition is to be successful. Activity planning should also gain top management support, should be cost-effective, and should remain adaptable as feedback is received during the change process. It must therefore determine the final and intermediate objectives tied to a specific time-table.
4. Commitment planning. The activity involves identifying key people and groups whose commitment and support is needed for change to occur and deciding how to gain their support.
5. Audits and post-audits. It is important to monitor progress and to see to what extent objectives are being met. The more uncertain and unclear the change process, the greater the need for periodic review. After change or when a particular milestone is achieved a post-audit should be carried out to establish that the objectives have really been met, and what lessons can be learnt for future projects.
6. Training. This is a key part of any change project and takes a number of forms. The obvious one is in relation to new skills that might be necessary. Training can also be given to the staff to undertake the change themselves. One aspect of this might be team building sessions. Furthermore, there is a need to give general awareness training to those in the organization who might be indirectly affected. To ensure that the various types of training are targeted at the right people or groups, a training programme—starting before implementation and continuing after completion should be established, showing who needs training, the form of training, and when it will take place.

Though planning change is in some way a 'technical' issue, it is also about involving and motivating the people concerned and those whose support is necessary.

People

Organizational change takes many forms. It can be of a structural or technical form which requires little of individuals in terms of behavioural or attitudinal change. On the other hand increasingly it requires individuals and groups to reconsider radically their attitudes towards how work is performed and how they behave towards both their colleagues internally and their counterparts externally. Whatever form it takes, however, there are three people-related activities that need to be undertaken:

- Creating a willingness to change;
- Involving people; and
- Sustaining the momentum.

Creating Willingness to Change

Even when change is purely technical or structural in nature, there has to be willingness among those concerned with change. There are organizations which are putting a great deal of effort to make change a norm; still many are at the stage where they have to convince the staff of the need for change. For many people, organizational change involves moving from known to the unknown, with the possibility of loss as well as gain. Companies therefore need to create a readiness for change among their employees at an early stage. This can be done in four ways:

1. Make people aware of the pressures for change. They must be informed on a regular basis about the plans for the future, the competition the firm is facing, customer requirements and the performance of its key competitors. Obviously, promoting the vision and explaining the strategic plan are vital components in this. Through this approach, members come to appreciate that change is not only inevitable but being undertaken to safeguard rather than threaten their future.
2. Give regular feedback on the performance of individual processes and areas of activities within the organization. This allows a company to draw attention to any discrepancy between actual performance and desired present and future performance. It allows those concerned to begin to think about how this situation can be improved and prepares them for the need to change. It is seen that companies with open information are easily amenable to change compared to those where information is guarded.
3. Publicize successful change. In order to create a positive attitude towards change, the company should publicize the projects which are seen as models of how to undertake a change and the positive effects they can have on employees. This does not mean that mistakes should be hidden or poor outcomes ignored. These should be examined, explained and lessons learnt. However, staff should be encouraged to expect and set credible and positive outcomes for change programmes.
4. Understand people's fears and concerns. One of the major mistakes made by management, where change has failed, is not to recognize the real and legitimate fears of staff and not take appropriate measures to address them. Organizations need to recognize that change does create uncertainty and those individuals and groups may resist or may not fully cooperate with it, if they fear the consequences. Furthermore, resistance should be seen as a signal that there is something wrong with the change process rather with those who are resisting. From this perspective, resistance can be viewed as positive: it reminds the organization that it has not considered all the consequences of its actions, and forces it to review its plans. There is no doubt that it needs special attention of change champions.

Involve People

Achieving a successful change can be and usually is a long and complex process. There will be difficult obstacles to overcome, not all of which can be anticipated in advance. To overcome them and to develop commitment and support of those who are most closely affected, it is necessary to involve them. In effect, these people are required to take ownership of the process so that it is 'their' project and it is 'their' success. This involvement can be achieved through:

Communication

One way to avoid the uncertainty that change can promote is to establish a regular and effective communication process. The purpose of this should be to inform those who will be affected by the change process from the early stages of what is happening, how it might or will affect them and to give them reports on the progress being made. It is important to give both the context for proposed changes as well as the details and consequences. Communication should be regular rather than a one-off exercise. This has a number of benefits. The change team will very quickly pick up any worries and concerns and can respond to them. Communication means seriously listening to the people who are affected. This will make them aware of aspects which have been overlooked that need to be taken into consideration.

Getting People Involved

Communication does help to overcome fears and does encourage those concerned to assist rather than resist change. However, one of the most vital initiatives an organization can take with staff is not to treat them as objects of or obstacles to change, but to involve them in it and make them responsible for it. Though not everyone can be involved in planning and execution, it may be possible to ensure that all those most closely affected are involved in some, if not all, aspects. Where possible, responsibility for aspects of the change project should be given to those who will be directly affected by the results.

Sustaining the Momentum

Even in the best-run organizations, the initial enthusiasm for change wanes and in the face of normal day-to-day pressures, progress becomes slower and can grind to a halt. In organizations which are less well run, the momentum may not even be present in the beginning.

In such situations, people will return to the methods and types of behaviours with which they are familiar. Given that momentum does not arise of itself, nor continue without encouragement, organizations need to consider how to build and sustain it. The points already made about planning, implementation and involvement are clearly part of this. In addition, however, organizations should:

Provide Resources

To achieve any change will require additional resources, both capital and human. In cases where staff is required to keep up the same level of output during the transition phase, it may require considerable additional resources to achieve this.

It is important that these extra resources are budgeted for and allocated as necessary, whether for the provision of training, senior management time or whatever. Nothing is guaranteed to be more demoralizing than having to make changes without the necessary resources or support.

Give Support to Change Agents

An enormous responsibility falls upon the change management team. They have to not only plan and oversee the change project, but also to motivate others and deal with difficulties, sometimes very personal problems. Just as they have to support others, however, so too must they receive support themselves. Otherwise they may be the ones who become demoralized and will no longer be in a position to motivate others.

Develop New Competencies and Skills

Change frequently demands new knowledge, skills and competencies. Increasingly, managers have to learn new leadership styles, the staff has to learn to work as teams and all are expected to be innovators and improvers. This requires more than just training and retraining. It may also include on-the-job counselling and coaching. Therefore, organizations need to consider what is required, who requires it and—the difficult part—how to deliver it in a way which encourages rather than threatens staff.

Reinforce Desired Behaviour

In organizations, people generally do those things which bring rewards or avoid criticism. Consequently, one of the most effective ways of sustaining momentum for change is to reinforce the kinds of behaviour required to make it successful. Sometimes this may be monetary linking increased pay or bonuses to particular types of activity or progress. Sometimes it may be symbolic like tearing down walls and elimination of personal desks. Sometimes it may be through recognition, whereby senior managers openly single out individuals or groups for particular praise. Such activities are particularly important during the early stages of change, when achieving an identifiable and openly recognized success helps participants develop a positive attitude about the change project.

The lessons from experience in change management show that:

- While managers do seek to align their organisations with the external constraints they face, they can also influence and restructure them as well.
- Depending upon the circumstances and objectives being pursued, organizations tend to use a combination of planned and emergent approaches to strategy development and change management.
- Radical and rapid organizational transformation could be incorporated within the planned/emergent spectrum and also any lack of employee involvement in such situations does not necessarily constitute a rebuff to either approach.

PLANNED CHANGE	EMERGENT CHANGE
♦ Stable environment	♦ Turbulent environment
♦ Small scale	♦ Organization-wide
♦ Localised change	♦ Behaviour/attitude focus

The actual change process, therefore, is a complex blend of objective-setting, planning and people. It is the most important challenge if not *the* test for HR executives in these times, which are the 'best of times and the worst of times' to quote Charles Dickens in *The Tale of Two Cities.*

EMPLOYEE BURNOUT

Pines & Aronson (1988) defined burnout as a state of physical emotional and mental exhaustion caused by long-term involvement in situations that are emotionally demanding. The emotional demands are caused by a combination of very high expectations and chronic situational stress. Burnout is accompanied by an array of symptoms that include physical depletion and feelings of helplessness, hopelessness and lack of enthusiasm about work and even life in general. People who burn out develop negative self-concepts and negative attitudes towards work and towards other people (dehumanising others). Burnout appears to be a major factor in low morale, absenteeism, tardiness, and high job turnover. Burnout usually affects those who go into helping professions with a strong desire to give themselves to others, who are highly motivated and idealistic, and who have expectations that their work will bring a sense of meaning into their lives.

Maslach (1982a; 1982b) and Maslach & Jackson (1981, 1984a, 1984b, 1986) have defined burnout as a syndrome of emotional exhaustion, depersonalisation and reduced personal accomplishment that occurs among individuals who work with people in some capacity. Emotional exhaustion refers to feelings of being emotionally overextended and drained by one's contact with other people. Depersonalisation refers to an unfeeling and callous response towards these people, who are usually the recipients of one's service or care. Reduced personal accomplishment refers to a decline in one's feeling of competence and successful achievement in one's work with people, low morale, depression, withdrawal and inability to cope.

Maslach & Jackson (1984a) have stressed the importance of viewing burnout as a multifaceted concept.

Another comprehensive definition of burnout is the tendency of committed supervisors and workers to lose enthusiasm for their work and to become less effective in managing the stress of physical and emotional contact with colleagues and work situations. The following are the symptoms of burnout:

- fatigue
- withdrawal from work and colleagues
- cynicism
- irritability
- difficulty relaxing off the job
- physical manifestation of anxiety and depression
- feelings of diminished enthusiasm and effectiveness at work.

Burnout has its roots in people-oriented, helping professions. That is where the term originated and that is where the vast bulk of research, both past and current, has been done. Virtually all jobs involve some sort of interpersonal contact (for example, those with co-workers or administrators, if not with clients or patients of some kind), and thus all of them involve some level of interpersonal tensions. However, probably none have as high a potential for emotional strain as do those jobs in which the worker deals continuously with other people and their problems. It was for this reason that initial researches were done with the helping professions, since this seemed to be the best place (but not necessarily the only one) to study how people managed to handle strong arousal. But as research continued, it was asserted that there are many other occupations in which interpersonal stress occurs. Examples are personnel managers, middle managers, supervisors, secretaries, etc., and to which the application of the burnout concept might prove useful. And this realisation has backed this research and many other such researches carried out for occupations other than human service personnel and to all levels in the organization and from work to non-work spheres of life. Presently, it is being considered as an ongoing process which is multidimensional, with a developmental sequence.

Models of Burnout

The model in Figure 13.1 summarises the burnout process. Individuals bring their own personalities, self-concepts, goals, ideals and levels of commitment to the work situation. They also come with some idea of how to respond to stress. The environment applies stress to the individual both inside and outside the work setting. It then becomes necessary to handle this stress through some type of coping mechanism. Individuals will be able to dissipate some or all of the stress at this point by means of personal or organisational strategies. Osipow & Spokane (1983) indicate that stress becomes negative, resulting in strain if the individual is not able to deal (cope) with stress well and restore stability. Prolonged instability, or intense and extreme instability, is likely to produce negative results. One of these negative results is burnout.

With a view to these consequences the gravity of the problem of burnout can be realised. But burnout is not a disease and it can be dealt with by individuals alone or with the help of family members or friends and within a corporation, the management has to reconcile concerns for productivity and the profit motive values with concern for people.

Coping with Burnout

Coping is primarily a psychological concept. In psychological usage, there are many definitions of coping but all share a central theme, namely, the struggle with external and internal demands, conflicts and distressing emotions.

Coping refers to a person's active efforts to resolve stress and to create new ways of handling new situations at each life stage (Erikson, 1959). This idea emphasises the importance of the personal resource and competencies that are used to deal with new challenges.

The term 'coping' has two meanings in literature. The term has been used to denote the way of dealing with stress, or the effect to master conditions of harm, threat or challenge when a routine or automatic response is not readily available (Lazarus, 1974). Coping refers to efforts to master conditions that tax or exceed adaptive resources (Monel & Lazarus, 1977). At a general level, coping has been broadly defined as "any effort at stress management" (Folkman & Lazarus, 1980). The term 'coping' is viewed as a stabilising factor that may help individuals maintain psychological adaptation during a stressful period (Folkman & Lazarus, 1985).

The Individual	The Environment and its Potential Stressors	Processing of Stressors	Strain	Burnout
Personality	Work	Stressors are processed through the person and his/her coping skills	Strain results from stress that is not handled appropriately	Accumulated strain to the point of reducing a person's effectiveness
Self-concept	Physical environment			
Ideas/goals/ level of commitment	Emotional environment			
How he/she views and responds to stress	Load			
	Role			
	People contact			
	Collegial social support autonomy outside work			
	Physical environment			
	Emotional environment support			
	Overall balance			
			Some stressors are handled and dissipated without strain	

Figure 13.1. Model for burnout

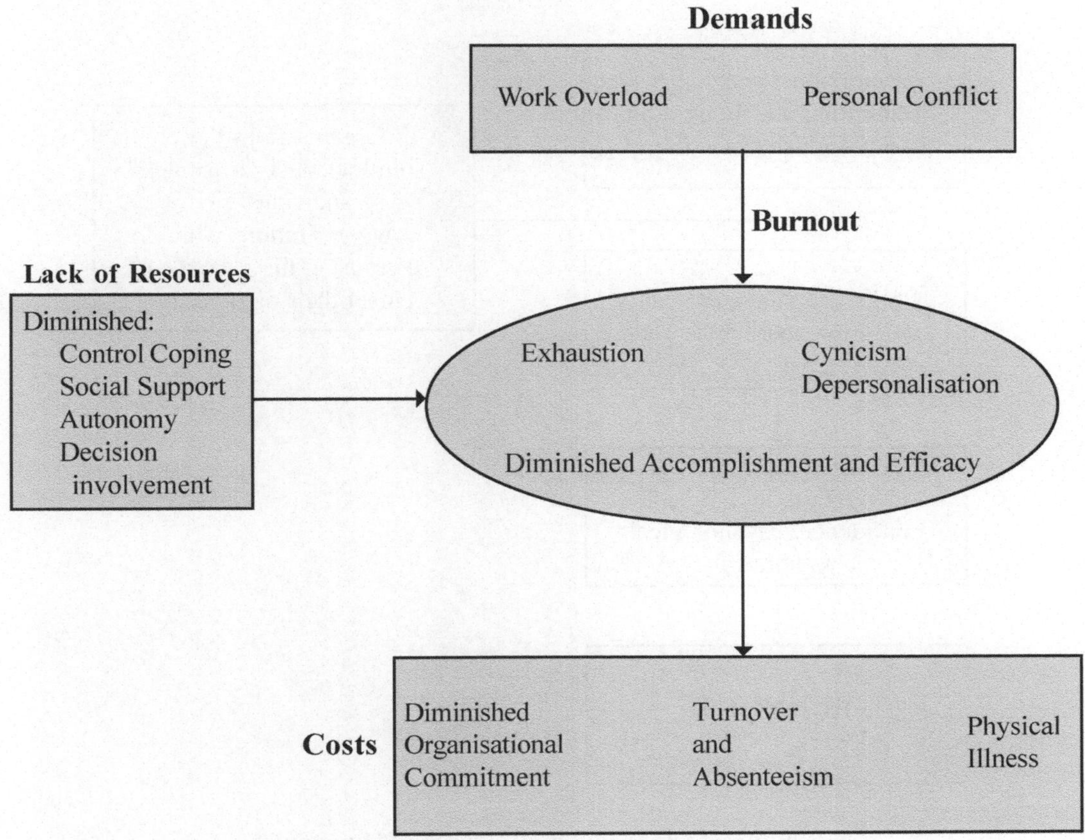

Figure 13.2. Structural model of burnout

Pinkerton, Trauer, Duncan, Hodson and Batteon (1985) have defined coping as the minimisation of emotional distress.

This places coping as the dependent variable and loses the notion of different coping cognitions/ behaviours being enacted in an attempt to limit the effects of stress.

The most commonly used definition of coping is put forward by Folkman & Lazarus.

They see coping as a psychological mechanism for managing psychological stress (Lazarus & Folkman, 1984). This mechanism may be both action-oriented and intrapsychic and is intended to avoid or mitigate the consequences of stressors (Cohen, 1987).

Pareek (1983) proposed two types of coping strategies which people use as the ways of dealing with stress. One way is that the person may decide to suffer, accept or deny the experienced stress or put the blame on somebody (self or others) for being in that stressful situation. These are passive or avoidance coping. Another way is that the person faces the stress consciously and takes

The Process of Burnout

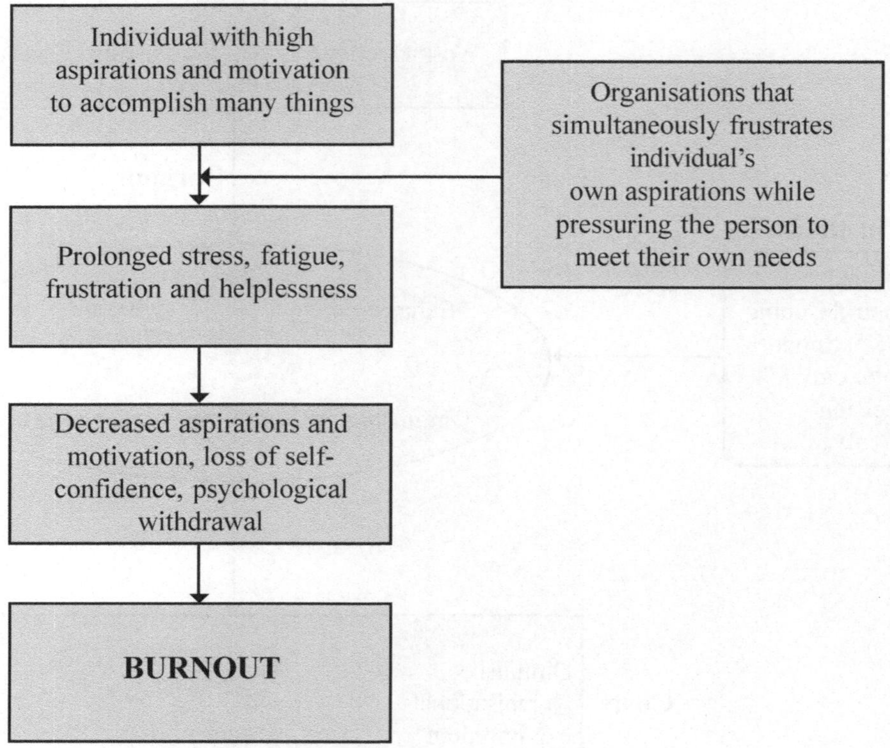

Figure 13.3. Sequential process of burnout

action to solve the problems himself or with the help of other people. These are active approaches of coping and are termed as "functional" styles of dealing with stressful situations. Pareek (1983) has proposed eight coping strategies and styles: (1). impunitive; (2). intropunitive; (3). extrapunitive; (4). defensive; (5). impersistive; (6). intropersistive; (7). extrapersistive; and (8). interpersistive. These strategies can be categorised into two types: dysfunctional and functional.

Finally, we are faced with the difficult question of what to do with the burned out individual. According to Freudenberger & North (1982), many of these individuals can be saved and can continue to contribute productively within organisations. They are not mentally ill and do not require intensive counselling and psychotherapy. The more productive emphasis is short-term counselling oriented towards reality issues and personal perceptions. This is an important alternative to the traditional and expensive solution of terminating the burned out employee.

A wide variety of specific techniques and strategies have been proposed to deal with burnout. Almost all can be grouped by primary goal and site of intervention. The primary goals are:

1. Identification: These are techniques for the analysis of the incidence, prevalence and characteristics of burnout in individuals, work groups, sub-unit or organisations.
2. Prevention: These include attempts to prevent the burnout process before it begins.
3. Mediation: These include techniques for slowing, halting or reversing the burnout process.
4. Remediation: These include techniques for individuals who are already burned out or are rapidly approaching the end stages of this process.

Interventions can also be targeted at specific sites or levels. The four important sites are:

1. Individual: These are interventions designed to strengthen an individual's ability to deal with job-related stress.
2. Interpersonal: These include attempts to strengthen interpersonal relations or work group dynamics either to decrease stress or to support an individual's ability to deal with stress.
3. Work Place: These include modifications in the immediate work environment intended to reduce stress or ameliorate it in some way.
4. Organisational: These include changes in policies, procedures, or structure intended to deal with organisational factors related to burnout. However, in the present day, the single largest area of intervention involves techniques intended to help individuals manage personal stress. These include everything from yoga to meditation, from aerobics to Zen.

Coping successfully with stress is the key to avoiding burnout. An extensive review of the literature by Nusbaum (1983) indicated the following individual/social strategies as the most common functional methods:

Site of Intervention	Identification	Goals of Intervention		
		Prevention	**Mediation**	**Remediation**
Personal	Self-evaluation	Professional training orientation	Stress management	Individual counselling
Interpersonal	Peer feedback	Support groups	Creative supervision	Group counselling
Workplace	Formal surveys	Professional development	Job redesign	Job/career changes
Organisational	Performance monitoring	Organization development	Quality assurance	Employee assistance

Figure 13.4. Illustrative burnout interventions

1. Develop a realistic picture of yourself—know what you are feeling and why.
2. Set realistic goals for yourself.
3. Recognise the symptoms of stress and burnout.
4. Ask for help when it is needed.
5. Develop a structural and personal support system.
6. Retain hope.
7. Develop a detached concern for recipients of your efforts.
8. Maintain an active personal social life outside of work.
9. Take time-outs when you need them.
10. Maintain a regimen of proper nutrition and physical exercise.
11. Develop a sense of organisational involvement.
12. Be willing to accept counselling when needed.
13. Develop self-therapies such as meditation, biofeedback or relaxation response.
14. Accentuate the positive.

Of these, the most important is the first. Individuals must be aware of their own feelings and physical condition to realise problems that exist and thus seek the proper coping strategy.

Maslach provides an excellent overview of burnout when she states: If all of the knowledge and advice about how to beat burnout could be summed up in one word, that word would be 'balance'. Balance between giving and getting, balance between stress and calm, balance between work and home—these stand in clear contrast to the overload, understaffing, over commitment and other imbalances of burnout.

Questions and Assignments

Q.1. What factors encourage or inhibit the employee relations strategies in organizations?

Q.2. What role do line managers play in improving employee relationship and their involvement?

Q.3. Why do workers join trade unions and why is their density declining all over the world?

Q.4. What role does SHRM play in promoting the unitarist philosophy in organizations?

Q.5. If you are an HR function head entrusted with the responsibility of steering a major change initiative, discuss the steps and how you will carry it out.

Assignments

1. Select any two organizations and study the state of EI in them. Present your findings to the class and compare your notes with other groups on similar assignments. Then make your recommendations.
2. Study as a research project the relationship between employee empowerment and employee involvement. Which influences more?

CASE 1.

Employee Involvement at ENGCO

Engco manufactures components used in a range of domestic equipment. It is a subsidiary business unit of a larger organization which is, in turn, a division of a MNC employing 28,000 people across 17 different countries. The head office of this particular division is based in Germany. Operating policies stem from this Divisional Head Office, although they frequently cause problems for business units based in other countries, such as those based in the UK and USA because of different cultural and operational expectations.

Because of the threat of closure of Engco and its relocation of work to a business unit based in another country, its management realized that they had to improve its performance. They were also concerned about the possibility of having to implement an employee involvement strategy emanating from the Divisional Head Office which they felt would threaten their freedom to manage in the way that they had in the past. Consequently they devised an EI strategy which they would work towards placating both of these threats. This was called 'Focus on Quality and Service'. It became known as 'FQS programme' or 'Focus' programme.

The Focus programme was introduced across the various parts of Engco through a series of workshops. In all about 250 people were employed in Engco. A four-day workshop was devised for senior and line managers. Other grades in Engco attended a two-day weekend workshop. The intention of the workshops was to introduce the employees to the need for the Focus programme, what it intended to achieve and the techniques to be used to involve employees in helping the organization achieve its goal of improving quality, service and performance.

During their four-day workshops managers received additional training intended to equip them with the skills to implement the techniques to be used. Employees attending the two-day workshops generally reported enjoying the experience of a weekend away at the employer's expense and a couple of these workshops quickly entered the 'folklore' of Engco for the drinking events that apparently took place into the early hours of the morning. More enthusiastic Focus programme participants were identified and offered the opportunity to become Focus Champions in their groups.

A number of employee involvement initiatives were devised for introduction and all of these were clearly identified with the aims of the Focus programme. Improvement in communications was intended to be realized through the 'Focus briefings'. Employees were being encouraged to become involved in the improvement of quality through the introduction of 'FQS Suggestion Scheme' and 'FQS improvement teams'. The work pattern was also reorganized through the introduction of 'Focus work teams' to promote employee involvement. The announced intention of this initiative was that production processes would be remodelled to replace traditional clusters of engineering operations (for example, machining or assembly operations being clustered together) to create 'production cells' that would be able to take more responsibility for producing particular components or sub-components. Management was also encouraged to become much more visible through 'walking the shop' and by attending Focus briefing groups and FQS improvement team meetings.

Focus briefings were arranged as a cascade with information emanating from the Managing Director. These briefings were also used to include key messages from the parent organization and from the Divisional Head Office. However, the downward focus of the information provided was often felt to be threatening and to lead to frustration; the operating climate for the Division was reported as being highly competitive and the particular circumstances of Engco were portrayed as 'being under review'. This had the effect of creating a high level of uncertainty for employees and some reported that they felt 'very stressed' after attending a briefing session. Some managers made particular efforts to obtain supplementary information and answers to the concerns voiced by those who attended their particular briefing sessions. Senior managers had been encouraged to attend these briefing groups to raise their visibility and to show that all employees in Engco were facing the same issues and aiming at the same goal. However, their presence in the situation in evident uncertainty led to mixed reactions. Some employees turned their questions on the senior manager attending their briefing group. Other groups felt that the presence of a senior manager at the briefing group was like having a 'spy in the camp'. The result was that these groups received the information with very little discussion. Soon senior managers stopped attending these briefing groups.

The 'FQS suggestion scheme' was launched with a poster campaign around the site offering different types of prizes for individual and group suggestions that would improve performance in any part of Engco. This scheme led to a significant and quick response from some parts of Engco. This took the management by surprise and led to the setting up of a panel to establish some criteria against which to evaluate the suggestions being submitted. Some of the suggestions were thought to be not viable and these were rejected with an accompanying explanation. Other suggestions were felt to be potentially viable and were entered into a further round of evaluation. A small number without cost implications was implemented within a few weeks. However, the initial stream of suggestions soon ceased with few following in the subsequent period.

The introduction of 'FQS improvement teams' followed the campaign for the 'FQS suggestion scheme'. The Focus Champions were used to lead teams specifically set up to examine a particular process or business problem that had been identified. In some parts of Engco, these improvement teams were seen to work well and to involve employees in working out solutions to the problem identified for them to examine. The use of these teams was also felt to develop team workings and the competencies required for this to be successful attendance at these teams was initially introduced as being on a voluntary basis, within a particular part of work time. After initial high level attendance in those areas where these teams were established, attendance in some of these areas began to fall off. This led management to require attendance at these improvement teams. However, this compulsory strategy did help to promote the advancement of problem-solving solutions and, in some cases, it inhibited the work of these teams. Consequently this requirement was soon withdrawn. These improvement teams continued to operate in some parts of Engco, where they were valued by both the organization and those who participated. In other parts of Engco, they were rarely used, if at all in particular sections.

The introduction of the 'Focus work team' was associated with the implementation of various forms of job redesign and work reorganization. The exact nature of these forms varied between the different sections within Engco. In some sections, work was reorganized to allow for the use of job rotation and some form of job enlargement. In other sections, work was more substantially reorganized to allow for the introduction of semi-autonomous work groups that encouraged multi-skilling and job enrichment. The level of involvement was seen by those managers who took an interest in this development to be higher in those sections that adopted a more radical approach to reorganizing work. The nature of the jobs that resulted in these sections allowed for greater employee influence and opportunities for development. However, those managers who took an interest in the outcome of these attempts to introduce EI still felt that even in these sections, as well as elsewhere in Engco, the introduction of this strategy 'still left a lot to be desired'.

Questions

Q.1. How effective was the introduction of EI in Engco?

Q.2. What factors affected the level of effectiveness of EI in Engco?

Q.3. How would you approach any attempt to encourage EI in this organization?

CASE 2.

MORRO GROUP: FROM DIVERSITY TO UNITY

Arindam Basu was at the end of his tether. The mind-boggling matrix before him was just not making sense. Basu was trying to see if there was a common thread in the work cultures of the various groups he was dealing with. But no matter how much Basu, the training manager at Morro Industries, juggled the variables, there were no signs of any similarity among the brands, product categories, geographical regions and market dynamics in which the various members of the sales force operated before they were brought under the Morro umbrella.

Twenty years ago, Morro had been an oil manufacturing company with a small presence in dairy products. Over the years, Morro diversified and acquired skin care, food and fabric care businesses. Morro's hair oil brand Kesha had a steady market in the south. Its managing director, Shantanu Grover, felt that hair care was a natural complement to Morro's cosmetic care business. So, in the mid-nineties, when liberalisation forced companies to review their portfolios, Morro bought Satin, a regional herbal shampoo brand, from the Karnataka-based Suraksha Enterprises. Morro also bought Suraksha's mass detergent brand, Ujjwala, which fitted well with the company's fabric care business. Likewise, Morro picked up an Uttar Pradesh-based fruit processing company, Favor India. With Favor came a fruit drink brand Fruitola, and a range of jams and canned fruit.

In 1997, Morro decided to merge all its acquisitions under one umbrella. Grover wanted a lean organization, both in terms of numbers as well as costs. He reckoned that the merger would enable him to end duplication of functions in finance, sales and administration and to plough the savings into developing the supply chain and beefing up sales and distribution.

The merger brought together five sales teams from different companies and Basu's task was to make them work as one. His training programmes were derived from a continuous evaluation of need gaps in the various divisions and touched upon aspects like functional skills, interpersonal behaviour, negotiating abilities and team building. It was this attention to training that had brought success to Morro during the lean 'eighties.

But bringing together the sales staff of five different companies was not an easy task, and Basu was beginning to realise this. The acutely differing cultural viewpoints of the five teams worried Basu. For instance, Charu Vardhan, the area sales officer of (the erstwhile) Suraksha Enterprises, said: "I wouldn't really try to drive a hard bargain. The intention is to ensure a cordial long-term relationship with the stockist; it doesn't matter if you are giving him an extra per cent." Vardhan's gentle approach was, in all likelihood, based on his two decades in the Suraksha system which had always been very considerate towards the trade and rather soft in its orientation.

On the other hand, Vikas Malik of Morro's Kesha team sought visibility and high growth. "I don't waste my time on retailers who give me less than 15% growth. I leave them to the stockist. The ones that clock more than 15% are easier to convince and deal with", he said. Today, both Vardhan and Malik were part of the same team since Morro had brought all hair care products—including Kesha and Satin—under one profit centre.

But the stark differences in the antecedents was evident. Kesha had been bred by Morro, while Satin had grown under Suraksha in the conservative south Indian market. So, while the Satin salesmen had the fair and forgiving culture of the south, the Kesha marketers, who had worked in the fiercely competitive metro markets, were quite the opposite. To some extent, the aggressive culture of Maadhyam, the edible oils brand, had rubbed off on the Kesha salesmen. The edible oils managers were very aggressive marketers, who pushed till they surpassed targets. Kesha and Maadhyam operated from the same office, had a common management and shared a distribution network. In fact, the edible oils business had opened the rural markets for Kesha.

But there were disparities even within the Maadhyam team. To the rural stockist, the man supplying Maadhyam was more of an adviser than a salesman. He virtually decided what—and how much of it—he should stock. Therefore, he was a dominant influence on the stockist's business. The situation was just the opposite in the metros, where the stockist called the shots. If he did not agree with the sales officer's stocking plan, he spoke to the Morro bigwigs who shopped at his outlets.

There were differences in the other categories also. In skin care, for instance, size did not matter in the rural context. Market penetration was so critical that even a Rs. 15,000 per annum stockist was valuable to the sales officer. But in the mature metro markets, penetration was not the issue. Instead, the sales officer was more concerned about his brand getting pride of place in the retail outlet amidst the crowd of rival brands.

Likewise, more than three kinds of salespersons pushed Morro's fabric care range. The salesman who handled the liquid detergent had a mindset very different from the salesman who sold the mass detergent powder brand Alayn. He, in turn, was poles apart from the salesperson who pushed the mass market washing bars. Not only were the markets in which they operated different, the segments they targeted were also vastly different.

Then again, the teams looking after the rural markets for all these products were also different from their metro counterparts. The metro salesman interacted in English and was probably a business school product. The rural salesman was more comfortable in the local dialect and his sales pitch was not so aggressive. The men who sold the popular brands and those who sold the premium brands were also very different.

Flummoxed as he was by the variety before him, Basu could see that each category and every market required a different approach. The relationship with the trade in each market was based on very different factors. Whether it was discussing the width of coverage with the stockist or shelf space with the retailer, the approach adopted by the salesperson depended on the kind of business he was representing and the culture of his erstwhile company. For instance, the conservative Favor salesman was used to a nominal 2-3% growth, unlike the edible oils, fabric care or skin care salesmen who were forever chasing high growth targets. Yet, he was not soft in his approach like the Satin shampoo man in Karnataka.

As he sat in his office wondering how to tackle the problem, the word 'culture' flashed in Basu's mind. It took him back to his days at the Indian arm of an American soft drinks company. The parent company had invested vast amounts in integrating the cultures of the top management that was drawn from four different companies. In comparison to the challenge before him, that appeared as simple as blowing a bubble. At Morro, he was facing 25 men from five different businesses.

During the tea break, Basu decided to think afresh. "Yes, the physical organization has changed, but the business dynamics have not," he reminded himself. "Or have they, by virtue of the merger?" Yet, there was something incongruous about five teams with distinct attitudes to selling, attitudes that were more than market-oriented. Basu decided that he had to first identify a common dialect of sorts that would deliver the same value to each of them.

Basu tried a small mental ploy. He put himself in the shoes of a sales officer who sold Taru skin care and imagined walking into a retail outlet. He was trying to see what kind of information he must have with him when he met the retailer or stockist. He repeated the same exercise for Kesha oil and Satin shampoo.

The results were unsatisfying because, though the situation was the same, the responses were different each time. "God!" he sighed. "He may be selling a Morro product. So where is Morro in all this?"

Ironically, the same differences had cropped up at a negotiation skills programme Basu had held for the personnel of each of these companies two months ago. However, at that time Basu had not perceived it as cultural diversity. Kartik Rajan, a Morro man and the personnel manager for the northern region, had cited the example of how the union had accosted him and asked for coolers on the shopfloor. "In the north, 20 union members barge into the industrial relations manager's room and talk with unbridled aggression about their demands. It is certainly a very provocative approach", he said.

"So, how did you respond?" Basu had asked.

"I adopted strategy for strategy," said Rajan. "I didn't get provoked. Instead, I asked why so many of them were away from the shopfloor. The first thing I did was to send 10 of them back immediately, thereby splitting their strength."

The personnel manager from the south, an erstwhile Suraksha man, was amused. "At the Satin plant, probably just one man will come and very politely tell you about their demand. Later, maybe, six of seven union members will come and say that they need to discuss the matter in detail, or there will be a problem."

Basu knew that this difference in approach was essentially regional, which a company could not change. But he realised that Morro needed to adopt a uniform approach in handling aggression or union demands, irrespective of the region.

He recalled when the western region industrial relations manager at Favor had said: "Oh, we have very strong unions which have a strategy for every thing. The union leaders are good psychologists. They can pre-empt a move even before it takes shape in your mind. They will not get involved in small issues and will straightaway talk of a court settlement. But they are typically split into rival camps."

Basu felt that the human resource function had to be tailored to suit regional differences. The problems at any branch or factory were largely dictated by the situation in the state in which it was located. But he also believed that there had to be a common corporate strategy for intervention and negotiation. The experiences of the personnel team and the sales team were not very different, he reckoned.

Basu also saw how regional differences manifested themselves in behavioural patterns. For instance, managers from Delhi were brash and noisy. In stark contrast, the Chennai managers were polite and would not think of interrupting a conversation.

Also noteworthy was the fact that their erstwhile corporate ethos was imprinted on the minds of the Chennai team. They came from a company which was very personalised in relationships. Asking about the family's welfare, for instance, was common among colleagues. This attitude was mirrored in the way the sales force dealt with their customers.

Also, there was a certain element of generosity. When the Satin team came for a quarterly sales review, the sales head distributed samples of the new shampoo. But the sales head of Morro, which was headquartered in Mumbai, exploded: "What? Free samples? Who is bearing the cost?"

With such a varied menu, Basu wondered whether he should seek a unified cultural approach for Morro. If he did that, what would happen to the regional culture that had driven the business till now? Should it be intra-company integration, functional integration or national integration, he wondered. Transnational companies worked on integrating global cultures, but here he was finding it difficult to evolve a common culture among five Indian companies. He wrote out a note to Chandrasekhar Bangur, the human resources director. "We need to have an integrated approach. A business may vary according to region, but there has to be a single culture that governs the company. That is going to affect the way we negotiate, the way we build teams, and the way we deal with markets. If we have a common mission, the message reaches across the company and the country."

Bangur and Basu discussed the matter in detail and finally approached Grover. He heard them out and said: "We need to find a common thread which would stand for the culture that we want in Morro. We cannot reject what these people from these five companies have brought in. We cannot say that since Morro is very successful, it need not change the way it looks at things. These companies were bought because they are very good, and they are that because of a culture they have had all these years. So, we take some, and leave some, of their attitudes. Why, we are going to reject some of our own attitudes. Such a review is necessary, given the diversity of the brands in Morro's portfolio and the differences in values and practices. Maybe we are deriving our corporate personality from this very diversity of products and brands."

Basu agreed. He had met the head of each category and realised how much their brands influence their perception of Morro as a company. For instance, the edible oils division head believed in the health platform for the Maadhyam brand. That attribute spawned the other qualities linked to Maadhyam: trustworthy, enduring, edible.

Likewise, the highly successful and trusted Kesha hair oil stood for ancient ayurvedic wisdom. Or the hugely popular detergent brand Ujjwal, which was touted by the company as a lost-cost and high-performance product. The fruit processing company Favor epitomised steady growth that was derived from Fruitola's success.

But confusion continued to dog Basu. "What should Morro's new personality be," he wondered. Cost-effective and reliable, like Ujjwal, mature, like Fruitola or gentle and secure like Kesha? How could a brand's personality have an effect on the corporate personality? Yet, Sudhir Dalvi, a Satin sales officer, had said: "When a customer thinks about Satin, the attributes that come to his mind are gentleness, caring and reliability. That makes him think about the company as caring and trustworthy." Dalvi's thought process worked in the same manner. "Suraksha is a caring, fair and honest company. It looks after its employees very well," he had said.

Basu had also asked a Morro salesman to define his company. "Morro is task-oriented and aggressive. It delivers value, cannot do wrong and is bottomline-oriented. Working here is a stimulating, challenging experience," he said confidently.

A remark by a Favor sales officer intrigued Basu. "As long as we were on our own, we stood for innovation, research and new products. I don't know whether that still applies," he had said when asked to describe his company.

Elaborating on his anxiety, he said: "When I joined Favor, they put me through a series of orientations, workshops and training. They took me around and introduced me to everyone. At Favor, we gave a new entrant nearly six months to find his feet in the organization. But here, a new man gets over with that in just two days. After that, he has to find out the names of people and their designations on his own."

Pritam Singh, the senior sales manager at Morro's edible oils division, had said: "At Morro, if you cannot help yourself, it is bad news. It is the survival of the fittest. You get down to business quickly," he said with an air of authority.

A debate ensued. "I have seen how our meetings work here," said the Favor man. "At Favor, when presentations were made, the audience observed complete silence. But here, the speaker is bombarded with all kinds of interjections."

"But that's how we are," countered Pritam Singh. "You guys are used to a very careful, cautious, risk-averse style—just like your erstwhile company. You take 18 months to launch a product from the time you go into research, during which time others would have launched and even withdrawn products." Then, addressing Basu, he asked "We don't want that kind of work culture, do we?"

Excusing himself for the interjection, the Favor man said: "Neither do we want the aggressive Maadhyam style. That needs to be toned down."

"There can be no other style," declared Pritam Singh with an air of finality. "The market is so ruthless that we can't afford to be soft."

Later, Basu narrated these exchanges to the managing director. Grover thought for a while before speaking. "We have a presence all over the country. We can't look at the businesses as Kesha or Satin or Fruitola or Maadhyam. We have to look at these as different markets. In a physical sense, too, the head office of these companies and everyone must have a single driving force. But integration can not mean a conglomeration of five cultures," he said.

"It has to be a serious integrated approach to get everyone to think that this is his company. Otherwise, we will have a scenario where Satin and Fruitola may feel they have been bought over. As it is, when the merger or acquisition was announced, the middle-level management at Suraksha felt that Morro would decimate them and they would have no role to play," he continued.

Basu was all ears as his managing director poured forth his plans. "The sales effort must be based on a common cultural fabric. Therefore, it will be contradictory to reject their cultures entirely. After all, even the Morro culture is not sacrosanct. But there should be a buying-in of the new culture where the constituents see that we, too, want to recast our culture. There will be a wall as long as they act as 'you versus me' or 'them versus us'. Our real culture lies in the marketplace and that is where the real integration will take place."

The task before Basu was daunting. Strategising a merger or an acquisition was tough, but the post-merger adjustment strategies were far tougher. He had read somewhere that it took seven years to form a habit or break away from one. Morro would have to accomplish the process in a much shorter time. "But where should I begin?" he wondered.

Part 3

Current Issues in HRM

14 Organisational Restructuring and Empowerment

Learning Objectives

After studying this chapter you will learn:

- The role organisational structure plays in organisational effectiveness.
- The significance of organisational environment on the design of structure.
- The influence of stakeholders in the design of structure.
- The design of structure for different types of technologies.
- The nature of work and its design.
- The rationale for team-based structures and problems that teams experience.
- Employee empowerment.
- Management of teams so that they work effectively.
- Understand the problems and people's reactions in the event of retrenchment.

INTRODUCTION

In the opening case we have seen that globalization, liberalization and other environmental forces are affecting organizations in a major way. Some organisations are able to grow globally while others become sick. Corporate strategy which tries to steer the organization through changes is implemented by restructuring organizations (structure follows strategy), culture change and right HR policies and practices. According to the Maybey & Salman model, the desired HR outcomes and behaviours are pursued through the HR strategy which consists of three 'key levers' (structural, cultural and personnel strategies). These are intended to subsume all aspects of organization which have an impact on organizational effectiveness, its survival, growth and decline.

The way the organizations use human resources and technology to transform inputs into outputs determine how much value is created by them and this depends very much on how they are organized, integrated, coordinated, differentiated, controlled, staffed and led. The HR function is primarily responsible for design and regular changes and periodic restructuring of organizations.

In this chapter, the issue of organisational restructuring is being approached from both micro and macro perspectives. Macro perspectives are stakeholders' interest, environmental complexity, nature of technology, national cultures and corporate strategy. The micro perspectives are design of jobs and work-systems to meet the need of today's workplace and times. If organisations are not structured from time to time to respond to the environment they become sick and may be taken over or liquidated as happened with the TransAsia firm (see Box 14.1).

How Structure Affects Organisations

Structure is a social creation of roles and relationships, which facilitate effective control

BOX 14.1
Sick Birla TransAsia Retrenches 75% Staff

Birla TransAsia Carpets Ltd, the sick Yash Birla group company, has retrenched around 75% of its employees in an attempt to reverse its sagging fortunes. The company's staff strength has come down to 140 employees from 560 employees as a result of this pruning exercise. It has retrenched 344 workers as well as another 55 employees. Another 20 employees have left the organization on their own.

According to Mr. D. K. Mittal, Director of the firm, the company was paying Rs. 3 crore as compensation to the workers. Each worker is getting 32 days salary for each year of service he has put in as gratuity and retrenchment compensation. He said that Rs 3 crore was contributed by the promoters. Mr. Mittal said that excessive manpower had constituted a major problem for the company.

Manpower cost accounted for as much as 26 per cent of the company's turnover and with this large-scale retrenchment, it is expected to come down to about 5.5 per cent of turnover. The company had declared a lockout at its plant in UP last year. However, following an agreement with the union, the lock-out had been lifted from September and the plant will commence commercial operation from October.

The unit manufactures woollen carpets and has a capacity of 36 thousand square metres per month. Birla TransAsia Carpets, which is the only publicly held carpet company in the country, was referred to the Board of Industrial and Financial Reconstruction (BIFR) for the second time a few years ago after its net worth of Rs. 4.5 crore was eroded by accumulated losses. For the last year the company's losses amounted to Rs. 8 crore. Mr. Mittal attributed the losses to excessive manpower and interest cost.

and coordination by clarifying authority-responsibility-accountability and role-clarity both vertically and horizontally across the boundary of the organization. If organizations are appropriately structured, they provide a climate of cooperation, job satisfaction and innovation. An inappropriate structure can create conflict; lack of teamwork and obstacles to change and people may resist control or pursue their own agenda at the cost of the organization. As a result, many multinational organizations are restructuring themselves regularly in response of local and global competition, joint ventures, mergers or acquisitions, divestment, diversification and integration, and strategic alliances.

The organization structure is important because it influences:

1. The nature and fulfilment of organization strategy.
2. Organizational responsiveness to environmental opportunities and threats.
3. Scope for innovation.
4. Organisational capability to cope with uncertainty.
5. Organisational performance and effectiveness.
6. Product and service quality.
7. The organization of work and job design.
8. The location and exercise of power and control.
9. The nature and channels of communication and work-related stress.
10. Formal and informal relationships and effectiveness of coordination.
11. Group processes, team working and network relationships.
12. Career paths and scope for development and employees' psychological contracts.

Some more items can be added to this list and some forms of structure have direct influence on people's behaviour; for example, a vertically decentralized multi-divisional structure may become more concerned with meeting financial targets established for them rather than on focusing on corporate HR issues, even when these have been identified. We can see from the example of the NIIT case (Box 14.2), that successful achievement of strategy depends on the right type of structure.

STAKEHOLDERS' CLAIMS AND ETHICS

Organisations exist because of their ability to create value and acceptable outcomes for various groups of stakeholders, people who have an interest, claim or stake in the organization, in what it does and in how well it performs. In general, stakeholders are motivated if they receive rewards that exceed the value of the contributions they are required to make. There are two main groups of organisational stakeholders: external and internal. Their contribution to organization and their expectations are shown in Table 14.1.

There is no room to assume that all stakeholders will be equally satisfied with the balance between rewards and their contributions. This means some stakeholders have priority over others. But it must satisfy minimally each group because contributions from all are needed. When all stakeholders are minimally satisfied, the relative power of a stakeholder group to control the distribution of rewards determines how the organization will attempt to satisfy different stakeholder

BOX 14.2
NIIT (India's Global IT Solutions Company)

NIIT, India's global IT solutions company, is nurturing an ambitious growth plan to allow it to increase its sales eight-fold within six years, and to reach its target of becoming a Rs. 10,000 crore ($ 2,200 million) company. The company undertook nine months of intense planning, during which the top management team examined the firm's business processes, organization structure, and employee aspirations and beliefs. The result was the 'Fast Forward' plan. A key element of the plan is to change the organization structure.

The proposed organization structure will consist of Independent Business Units (IBUs), and a Corporate Centre. The Independent Business Unit Heads (IBHs) would be accountable to the NIIT Board for strategy, targets and performance, and will be equipped with an advisory board. The Advisory Board, to be constituted by IBH, would be responsible for providing external inputs and cross business linkages. Advisory Board members from NIIT (typically from other businesses) would enhance the synergy unique to the NIIT business model, while outside members would enforce the crucial outside-in perspective. The IBUs will have their own staff functions like Human Resources, Finance and Commercial. The IBHs will have increased independence coupled with increased accountability.

The Corporate Centre will pursue NIIT's long-term strategies. It will have a few highly experienced heads of staff functions, and will act as the brains trust of the organization and would be available to the IBHs to draw upon NIIT values, wisdom, and experience.

This restructuring is the third phase in NIIT's organizational evolution. In its first phase, in 1989, the company had adopted a divisional structure. That restructuring allowed it to grow from a Rs 169 million ($ 3.7 million) revenue organization to a Rs. 1,670 million ($36.8 million) one by 1995. In the second phase, in 1995, NIIT adopted the global matrix structure and achieved a turnover of Rs. 12,370 million ($ 272.7 million). In the press release, NIIT says it expects the new structure to help NIIT scale the Rs. 100 billion ($ 2,200 million) revenue mark it has set for itself for the next six years, just as earlier structures helped NIIT achieve new revenue levels. As the NIIT example shows, when companies grow large in size, and shift strategy, there is a need to change their organizational structure.

For an organization to successfully implement its strategy, it should be designed appropriately. One of the most important reasons why organization design is so vital isthat it often determines what people in an organization pay attention to and, thereby, determines what sort of decisions are made. As we will

Continued ...

...Continued

see in this chapter, if an organization is group-based on functions, the needs of the function are focused upon; and when it is grouped by customer, the needs of the customer take priority. Organization design also plays an important role in determining how quickly the organization can respond to its environment, and how innovative it can be.

How an organization is designed also has cost implications—some designs are efficient while others have duplication of personnel. Obviously there are important trade-offs. At the micro level, organization design influences the motivation of employees. When an organization is designed poorly, strategic initiatives go astray because no one is responsible for them, information and knowledge is not shared resulting in all sorts of coordination problems and turf wars take place. Costs may increase, or innovation may decrease.

This case also shows that structure plays a key role in influencing organisational performance and human resource outcomes.

groups and what criteria they will use to judge the organisation's effectiveness. An organization structure should facilitate how to allocate organisational rewards and minimally continuously satisfy all stakeholders, managing conflicting goals and balance between short-term as well as long-term goals. These organisational responsibilities are vested with top management and constitute an hierarchy. At the top are shareholders followed by the Chairman of the Board, CEO and Executive Directors, General Managers and Functional Heads.

The CEO is responsible for setting the organisation's goals and designing its structure. He selects key executives to occupy the topmost positions; he determines rewards and incentives for them. He controls and allocates resources and attracts resources from outside. He thus has a major role to play in the success of any organization. The structure should support the efforts of the CEO while at the same time providing internal controls to prevent misuse of power and should be able to throw him out if necessary. This depends upon the corporate governance practices and constitution of a professional Board with adequate independent members.

Apart from stakeholders influencing structure and its working, it is also influenced by their social background, beliefs and association with other bodies and education level. They can hold a radical perspective, or pluralist perspective, or unitary perspective. The organization will have conflicts and assume a distinct political system depending upon the majority view prevailing from time to time. It is very necessary to understand that structure alone cannot deliver unless people are selected and socialised into a coherent group with shared mission and values.

One of the main responsibilities of the HR function is to take care of workers, unions and middle management stakeholders. The HR function should ensure two-way communication, their participation and involvement for maximising their contribution and ensuring that they are rewarded adequately. The HR function is a bridge between these stakeholders and top management.

TABLE 14.1
Contributions and Expectations of Various Stakeholder Groups

Stakeholders	Contribution to the Organization	Expectation of Rewards for Contribution
Inside		
• Shareholders	Money and capital	Dividends and stock appreciation
• Managers	Skills and expertise	Salaries, status, power and bonus
• Workers	Skills and expertise	Salaries, bonus, job security and promotion
Outside		
• Customers	Revenues	Quality, prices of goods and services
• Suppliers	High quality inputs	Revenue from purchase of inputs
• Government	Rules governing good business practices	Taxes and growth, employment Free and fair competition
• Unions	Free and fair collective bargaining	Equitable share of rewards and growth in employment
• Community	Social and economic infrastructure	Revenue, taxes and employment
• Public	Customer loyalty and reputation	National pride and clean environment

Environment and Structure

An organisation's environment is a complex network of changing forces that affect the way it operates. The environment is a major contingency for which an organization must plan and to which it must adapt. Furthermore, it is a source of uncertainty that an organization must try to control. Environmental complexity is a function of the strength, number, and interconnectedness of the specific and general forces that an organization has to manage. The greater the number, and greater the difference between them, the more complex and uncertain is the environment and more difficult to predict and control. The more interconnected the forces in an organisation's specific and general environment are the more uncertainty the organization faces. For example, depreciation of the rupee will influence the imported input price from all suppliers causing disruption and delay in getting inputs.

Environmental dynamism is a function of how much and how quickly forces in the specific and general environment change over time and thus contribute to the uncertainty an organization faces. An environment is stable if the forces affect the supply of resources in a predictable way. An environment is dynamic and unstable if an organization cannot predict the way in which the forces will change over time. Environmental richness is a function of the amount of resources available to support an organisation's domain. In rich environments, resources are plentiful and uncertainty is low because organisations need not compete for resources. Environments may be poor because either they are located in a poor country or there is a high level of competition between them. These three forces constitute the level of uncertainty for firms as well as for industries. Diversity relates to the range of activities of an organization, so that a business would be likely to face a greater uncertainty where it had diversified into a number of different markets.

These environmental dimensions will interact between themselves affecting the type of organization structure that will be appropriate in particular combinations of circumstances, according to contingency theory. Table 14.2 shows the interaction between only two of these environmental dimensions, namely complexity and stability and the structural implications of these interactions that are believed to result according to this contingency approach.

J. Galbraith (1973, 1977) analysing complexity due to technology suggests that complexity faced by any organization is a function of its division of labour, required level of goal performance and goal diversity, which in turn reflects capital, labour and product markets and technologies in its environment. Any organization in which there is a complex pattern of specialisation, with a strong emphasis on high performance and with a wide range of products and associated goal diversity

TABLE 14.2

Structural Types Relating to Interaction Between Complexity and Stability

Environmental Stability	Environmental Complexity Simple	Environmental Complexity Complex
Stable	The stable environment promotes a bureaucratically-based structure and the limited environment interaction encourages centralised decision-making	While the stable environment promotes a bureaucratically-based structure, the environmental complexity requires decentralised decision-making linked to a divisional structure
Dynamic	Environmental variability requires a structure that encourages flexibility, adaptability and responsiveness. Limited environmental interaction makes centralised decision-making possible while the dynamic nature of the environment means that this is also desirable	Environmental variability requires a structure that encourages flexibility, adaptability and responsiveness. However, environmental complexity also requires decentralised decision-making. This will result in an organisational structure with a high level of internal complexity

faces a large amount of uncertainty. This uncertainty, in turn, requires a large amount of information that has to be acquired and processed and transmitted to the right place and at right times. It is also possible that some information may not have been discovered as yet. The difference in the amount of information required and available at the right place and right time is the measure of degree of uncertainty that an organization faces.

Galbraith suggests that faced with a degree of uncertainty people in an organization can adopt some strategies to seek its reduction. Figure 14.1 depicts them. Attempts to increase the amount of information within the organization can be approached in a variety of ways according to resource availability or structural modifications. Here comes the rationale for effective knowledge management in organisations and the strategic role of HR functions in seeking, processing and transmitting to the right place and at the right time the information required by the organization to meet the uncertainty. The strategies suggested by Galbraith are not exclusive.

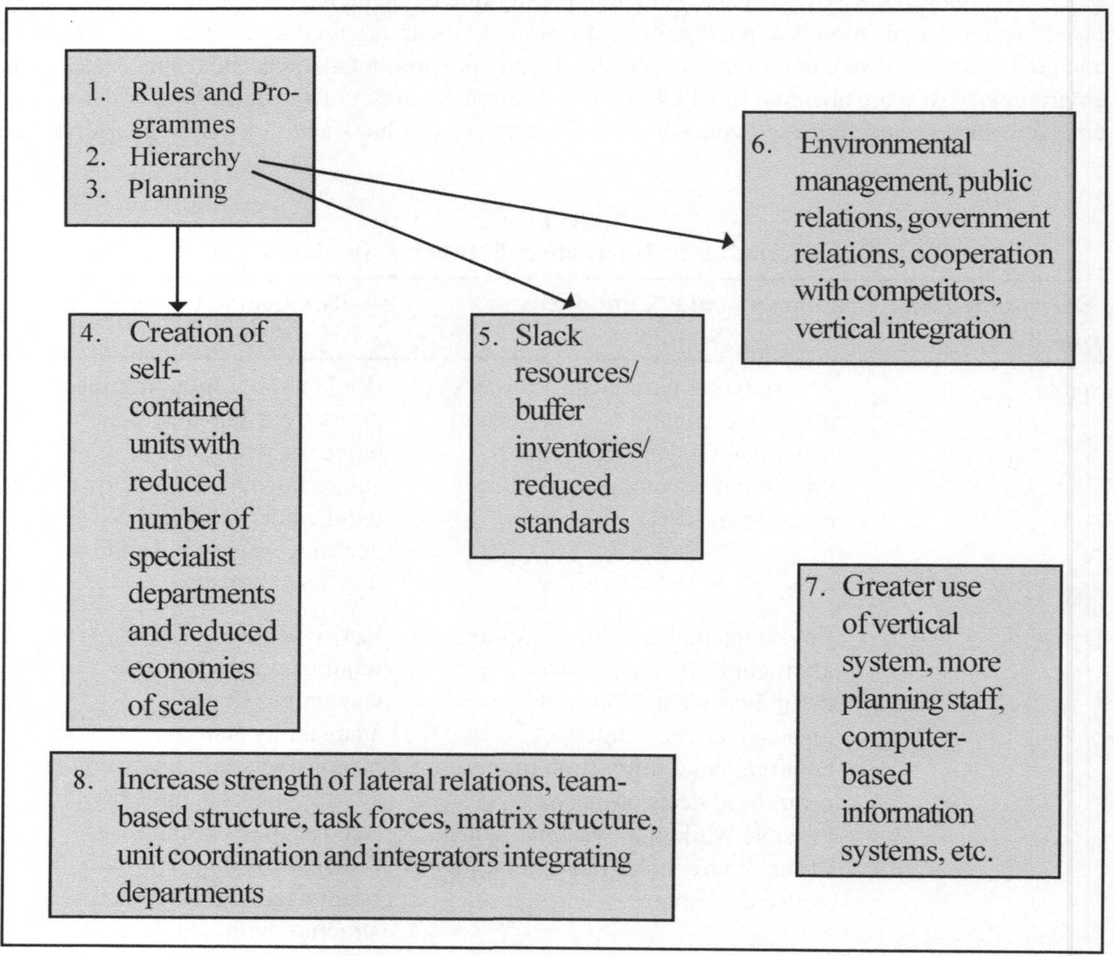

Figure 14.1. Galbraith's suggested strategies for coping with uncertainty

Structure Design Dimensions

Differentiation is the process by which an organization allocates people and resources to organisational tasks and establishes the task and authority relationships that allow the organization to achieve its goals based on specialisation or division of labour. The basic building blocks of differentiation are organisational roles. Roles are task-related desired behaviours with boss, peers, subordinates and others.

Vertical differentiation looks at the roles in terms of authority and rank. Horizontal differentiation is the way an organization groups organisational tasks into roles and roles into sub-units. It makes the departments become more specialised. For a structure to be effective, it is necessary to balance differentiation with integration, centralization with decentralization and standardisation with mutual adjustment. The HR's main role is to work for this balance to be achieved by various HRM strategies. Integration is the process of coordinating various tasks, functions and divisions so that they work together and not at cross purposes. Centralization is the process whereby the authority to make important decisions is retained at the top of the hierarchy and, in decentralization, authority to make decisions is delegated to lower levels of the hierarchy. Formalization and Standardisation refer to conformity to set rules and norms that are considered proper in a given situation. Mutual adjustment is the process through which people use their judgement rather than standardised rules for solving problems and decision-making.

The right balance makes some actions predictable so that basic organisational tasks and goals are achieved, yet it gives employees the freedom to behave flexibly so that they can respond to new and changing situations (uncertainty) creatively (Box 14.3).

Mechanistic and Organic Structures

As early as 1961, Burns & Stalker had suggested that, through a judicious design of organization structure, firms could greatly increase their ability to secure their position within their environment. Their research is an empirical study of electronic firms in Scotland, suggesting that mechanistic structure is more suitable in stable and simple environments where uncertainty is low.

Mechanistic structures are designed to induce people to behave in predictable, accountable ways. Decision making authority is centralized, subordinates are closely supervised and information flows mainly in a vertical direction down a clearly defined hierarchy. In this structure the tasks associated with a role are also clearly defined. Each person is individually specialized and knows exactly what he or she is responsible for, and behaviour inappropriate to the role is discouraged or prohibited. At the functional level, each function is separate and communication and cooperation among functions are the responsibility of some one at the top management level. Hierarchy is the principal integrating mechanism. Tasks and roles are coordinated through standardisation. Formalization is strong. Given the importance of the vertical command structure, the organization is very 'status' concerned. Promotions are slow and related to performance and seniority.

Organic structure is the opposite end of mechanistic structures. They promote flexibility, so people initiate change and can adapt quickly to changing conditions. They are decentralised and 'roles' are loosely defined and people continuously develop new skills in new activities. Many tasks are performed jointly. Employees from different functions work together to solve problems.

BOX 14.3
Amazon.com—Bezos Obtains the Balance

How did Jeff Bezos address these design challenges given his need to create a structure to manage an e-commerce business which operated through the internet and never saw its customers, but whose mission was to provide customers great selection at low prices? Since the success of his venture depended upon providing high quality customer responsiveness it was vital that customers found Amazon.com's one-click (SM) information system Internet software easy and convenient to use and service reliable. So his design choices were driven by the need to ensure his software linked customers to be served most effectively.

First, he quickly realized that customer support was the most vital link between customer and organization. So he decentralised control and empowered his employees to find a way of meeting his customers needs quickly. Second, realizing that customers wanted books quickly he moved to develop an efficient distribution and shipping system. Essentially, his main problem was handling inputs into the system (customer requests) and outputs (book distribution). Hence he developed information systems to standardise work, to increase efficiency, but also encouraged mutual adjustment at the input or customer end—employees were able to manage exceptions such as lost orders or confused customers as the need arose. The information system helps in integrating across functions and is the backbone of value creation activities.

Third, because the company employs a small number of people—about 2,500, world wide—Bezos was able to make great use of socialization to coordinate and motivate his employees. Employees are very carefully selected and socialized by other members of their functions so that they quickly learn their organisational roles and, most important, Amazon's important norm of providing excellent customer service. Finally, to ensure Amazon's employees are motivated to provide the best possible customer service, Bezos gives all employees stock in the company. Employees currently own 10 per cent of their company. Amazon.com's rapid growth suggests that Bezos has designed an effective organisational structure.

As a result, a high level of integration is needed so that employees can share information and overcome problems. The integration of functions is achieved through complex mechanisms like task forces and teams. Coordination is achieved through mutual adjustments. In an organic structure informal norms and values develop that emphasize personal competence, expertise and the ability to act in innovative ways. Status is conferred by the ability to provide creative leadership, not by any formal position in the hierarchy. Sony Corporation has become a successful giant by maintaining an organic structure within a highly complex and dynamic environment (Table 14.3).

TABLE 14.3
Choices and Results of Mechanistic and Organic Structures

Mechanistic organization results when organisations make following choices	Organic structure results when organisations make these choices
• Individual specialisation. Employees work separately and specialise in one clearly defined task	• Joint specialisation, employees work together and coordinate their actions to find best way of performing a task
• Simple integrating mechanisms. Hierarchy of organization is clearly defined and is the major integrating mechanism	• Complex integrating mechanisms. Task forces and teams are the major integrating mechanisms
• Centralisation, authority to control tasks is kept at the top of the organization. Most communication is vertical	• Decentralisation, authority to control tasks is delegated to people at all levels in the organization. Most communication is lateral
• Standardisation. Extensive use is made of rules and SOPs to coordinate tasks, and work process is predictable	• Mutual adjustment. Extensive use is made of face-to-face contact to coordinate tasks, and work process is relatively unpredictable

TECHNOLOGY AND STRUCTURE

It is important for HR executives to understand the nature of technology being used or proposed to be introduced in the near future and which organisational structure is the best 'fit' with it. This is because the technology subsystem and the human subsystem are interdependent and interlinked. One influences the other significantly. Technology is defined as the combination of skills, knowledge, abilities, materials, machines, computers, tools and equipment, processes, manuals, etc., that people use to convert or change raw materials into valuable goods and services. Inside an organization, technology exists at three levels: Individual, Functional or Departmental and Organisational. At the individual level, technology is the personal skill, knowledge and competencies that individual workers possess. At the functional or departmental level, the procedure and techniques that groups work out to perform their work creates competencies that constitute technology and the way an organization converts inputs into outputs is often used to characterise technology at the organization level.

Some kinds of technology are more complex and difficult to control than others. The ones that can be programmed or made predictable are highly complex than those that are not so programmable and depend upon people. Joan Woodward had identified 10 levels of technical complexity which she associated with three types of production technology: 1) small-batch, 2) large-batch and mass production, 3) continuous or process technology, as shown in Table 14.4.

TABLE 14.4
Woodward's Classification of Technology

	1. Production of simple units to customer orders	Low technical complexity
	2. Production of technically complex units	
	3. Fabrication of large equipment in stages	
	4. Production of small batches	
Group I: Small batch and unit production	5. Production of components in large batches, subsequently assembled diversely	
	6. Production of large batches, assembly-line type	
Group II: Large batch and mass production	7. Mass production	
	8. Process production combined with the preparation of a product by large batch or mass production	
Group III: Continuous process production	9. Process production of chemicals in batches	
	10. Continuous flow production of liquids, gases and solid shapes	High technical complexity (computers)

Woodward wanted to see whether effective organisations had structures that matched the needs of their technologies. When she compared the structural characteristics of organisations pursuing each of three types of technology, she found systematic differences in the technology-structure relationship. Table 14.5 shows some of her findings.

Using Task Variability and Analysability matrix, Parrow divided organisations into four types: Craftswork, Non-routine research, Routine manufacturing and Engineering production as shown in Table 14.6. Task variability is the number of new or unexpected situations encountered while performing the task. It is high when such situations are many. Variability is low when the task is standardised and workers encounter the same situation time and again. Task analyzability is the degree to which the search activity is needed to solve a problem.

TABLE 14.5
Woodward's Technology—Structure Relationship of 'Fit'

	Technical Complexity Low	Technical Complexity Medium	Technical Complexity High
Structural characteristics	Small batch	Mass production	Continuous process
Level in the hierarchy	3	4	6
Span of control of CEO	4	7	10
Span of control of first-line supervisor	23	48	15
Ratio of managers to non-managers	1:23	1:18	1:8
Organisational form	Relatively flat with narrow span of control	Relatively tall with wide span of control	Very tall with very narrow span of control
Type of structure	Organic	Mechanistic	Organic
Cost of operation	High	Medium	Low

TABLE 14.6
Task Variability and Analysability Matrix

	Task Variability Low	Task Variability High
Task analysability is low	Craftswork, e.g., manufacture of customised products like furniture, clothes, etc.	Non-routine research is most complex and least routine, e.g., high tech research and development
Task analysability is high	Routine manufacturing. Tasks routine, programming possible, e.g., McDonald	Engineering production. Existing procedures are used to make many kinds of products, e.g., engineering firms

The more analyzable the task is, the more routine it is, because, the procedures for dealing with it have been worked out or programmed in advance. Analyzability is low when procedures for carrying them out and dealing with exceptions cannot be worked out in advance. Parrow has suggested that an organization should move from a mechanistic to organic structure as tasks become more complex and less routine.

J. D. Thompson (1967) suggests that the higher the level of task interdependence, the more likely an organization is to use mutual adjustment rather than standardisation to coordinate work activities. From this discussion we can see that the organization structure has to be adjusted for the selected technology and HR policies and processes to fit with the structure.

Structure Follows Strategy—Types of Structures

In fact, corporate strategy emerges or is formulated in response to the environmental opportunities and threats so as to gain long-term competitive advantages. In the formulation of corporate strategy, factors like stakeholder interest and nature of technology have already been considered. Other factors like nature of products and markets, size of the firm, its internal strengths and weaknesses, and nature of competition further significantly influence it. As the firm grows, the nature of its products and services and markets change and, to implement the strategy, structure changes accordingly. Chandler's (1962) work charted the development of organisational structures that were used in the USA to meet changing needs of strategy. These are:

Simple Organization Structure

This is suitable for small organisations supplying a single product, or a set of related products, within a defined market. This structure is centralised with one person or a few people exercising control and direction. The main constraints are getting the resources and the main focus is to find the customers and markets. Roles and responsibilities cannot be defined clearly and further growth depends upon the vision, leadership and style of its leader.

Functional Structure

This structure is designed to overcome the inability of a simple structure to respond to an organisation's increasing internal complexity resulting from its growth. In this structure, specialised roles, functions and departments are created, such as production, marketing, finance and HR. Here also power and control is vested with senior line managers and it is a mechanistic or bureaucratic type structure as described earlier. Here the CEO is only responsible for profits and inter-functional coordination and problem solving. There is often conflict between functions and departments but efficiency and job satisfaction is high and it is the most economical structure.

Divisional Structures—Product-based

When organisations have to meet complex and diversified environments, a divisionalised form of structure is most appropriate. The basis of divisionalisation could be geography, products, customers or processes. Here, different units, departments or even companies are made self-managed with a common mission and corporate strategy coordinated by the centre. The product-

BOX 14.4
Sony Magic Touch

Product engineers at Sony turn out an average of four ideas for new products every day. Despite the fact that Sony is now a diversified organization employing over 115,000 employees world wide, the company continues to lead the way in innovation in the consumer electronics industry. Why? A large part of the answer lies in the way the company uses its structure to motivate and coordinate employees. First, a policy of 'self promotion' allows Sony engineers, without notifying their supervisors, to seek out projects any where in the company where ever they feel they can make their contribution. If they find a new project to which they can make a contribution, their current boss is expected to let them join the new team. Sony has 23 business groups composed of hundreds of development teams, and this movement of people cross-pollinates ideas throughout the organization.

Sony deliberately emphasizes the lateral movement of people and ideas between design and engineering groups. The "Sony Way" emphasizes communication between groups to foster innovation and change. Sony has a corporate research department full of people in integrating roles, who coordinate the efforts of business groups and product development teams. It is their responsibility to make sure that each team knows what the others are doing, not only to share knowledge but to avoid overlap of efforts. Once a year, the corporate research department organises an in-house three-day special event, where each product development team can display its work to its peers only.

That Sony's organic structure works is evident from the company's success in the market place and from the number of innovative products Sony turns out. Like many other large Japanese companies, Sony has a policy of lifetime employment, which makes it easy for its engineers to take risks with ideas and encourage the development of norms and values that support innovative efforts. Moreover, Sony rewards its engineers with promotion and more control of resources if they are successful.

Sony is hard-headed, however, when it comes to making the best use of its resources. Top management takes pains to distance itself from decision making inside a team or even a business group, so that the magic of decentralised decision-making can work. But it does intervene when it sees different groups duplicating one another's efforts. For example, when Sony made a big push in computers it reorganised the relationship among its audio, video and computer groups so that they improved the way they coordinated new product developments. Once again, however, Sony takes a lateral view of the way the organization works, and its vertical chain of command is oriented towards finding ways to decentralise authority and still make the best use of resources. This lateral approach to decision making contrasts dramatically with the old IBM's vertical, centralised product development system, in which getting a decision made was according to one engineer, like wading through a tub of peanut butter.

based divisional structure treats each of its major products as distinct strategic business units (SBUs). Product Divisions at corporate office are given worldwide responsibility for production, finance, marketing and management of supply-chains for each product or product line. These product based divisions also have internal functional support. The structure is shown in Figure 14.2.

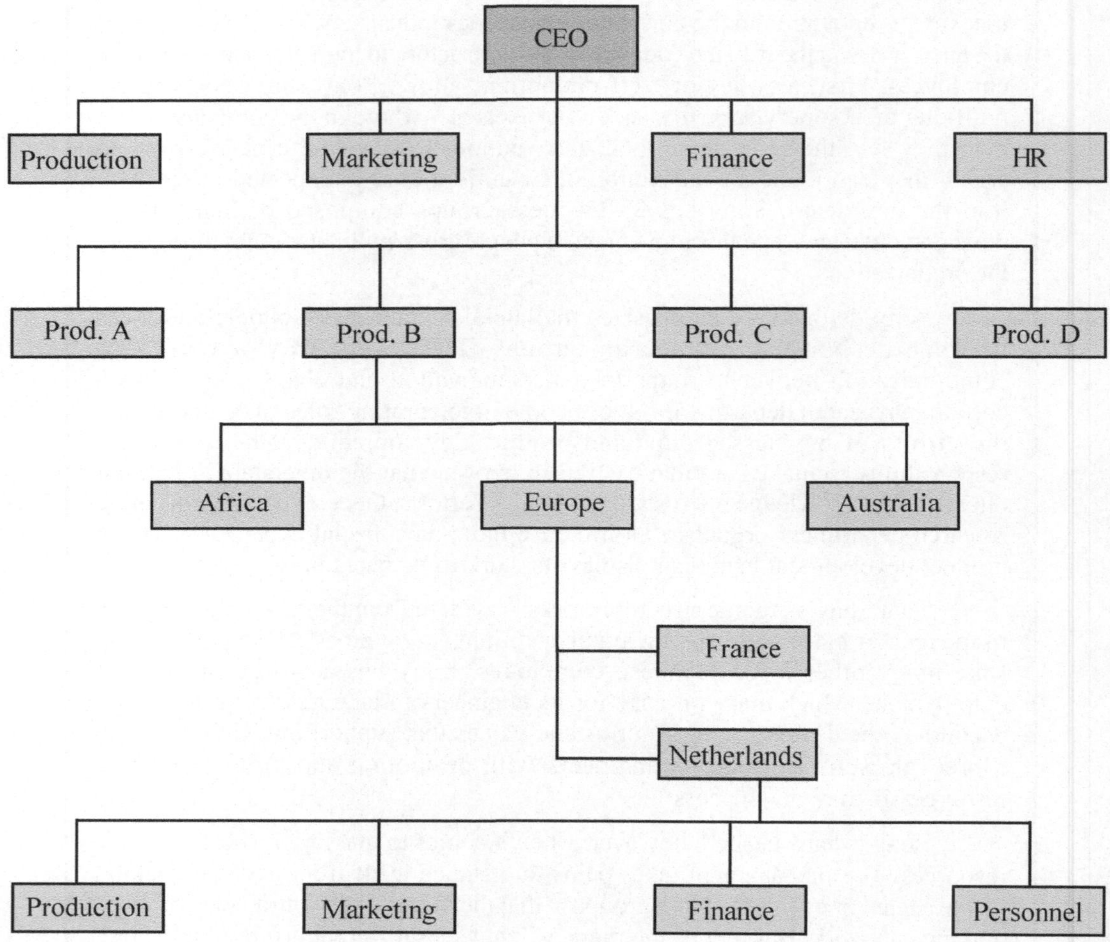

Figure 14.2. A global product-based structure

It also helps to integrate marketing, production and finance globally on a product basis. Further, a firm can strategize shifting of products as they reach different life cycle stages from one market to another according to their acceptability and scope. For example, if colour TVs have reached maturity in advanced countries, then it can shift them to developing countries for promotion and black and white TVs to underdeveloped countries. A major advantage is that this structure provides a link direct from customers to policy makers and directs research and development of products that serve the need of global customers.

The logic behind this type of structure is that products and services of the company should be sufficiently distinct in production technologies, requiring different marketing skills to deal with different types of customers and markets. Each product division is treated as a separate profit centre for accounting and finance purposes. The products are generally in the growth stage of the product life cycle stage, hence they need to be carefully promoted and marketed. The corporate headquarters will usually maintain control in terms of budgetary constraints, approval of certain decisions like launching of new products, total profit and contribution.

This structure has certain advantages. If the firm is very diverse (for example, if it produces products using a wide variety of technologies or has wide variety of customers), the need to customise the product to the specific demands of the buyer becomes important. It can lead to client satisfaction because product responsibility and contact points are clear. Different units can adapt to differences in products, cultures and market practices in various regions. This structure also helps to integrate the supply chain globally on a product basis.

The disadvantage of this structure is duplication of personnel within each division, making it expensive. A second disadvantage is that product managers may pursue currently attractive markets and neglect other areas with better long range potential. A third is that many country managers spend too much time trying to tap their local markets rather than the international markets because it is more convenient and easier as they become more experienced with local operations.

Area-based Structure

In this arrangement, a multinational prefers to divisionalise the foreign operations on the basis of geography, rather than on a product basis. The corporate structure at headquarters remains the same as in the case of product-based divisionalisation. This signifies a major change in the thinking of the company because the international operations are now put on the same level as domestic operations. This structure offers advantages when the economic and political environment in different countries where the firm is operating is fast changing and requires the operations to be adapted to the pressures of the environment and government in those countries.

This structure is also useful when the product range is not very different and therefore common resources in a country can be shared to support all the operations. The headquarters is responsible for transfer of excess resources from one country to another as required and to establish coordination and control among different countries for achieving synergy and overall goal achievement.

This arrangement is also suitable when products are in the maturity stage and have narrow product lines. These product lines are often differentiated on the basis of geographic area or when they have large demands concentrated in some countries and much less in others. This structure allows the area manager to integrate marketing, production and finance functions in a given area to achieve economies of scale and scope. Firms that are producing automobiles, beverages, containers, cosmetics, food or pharmaceuticals often use such a global area structure.

The main disadvantage of the global area structure is the difficulty encountered in reconciling a product emphasis with a geographic orientation. For example, if a product is sold worldwide, a number of different areas are responsible for the sales. The lack of centralized management and control can result in increased cost and duplication of effort. A second disadvantage is that divisional groups often ignore development efforts because they are selling goods that have reached the maturity stage. Their focus is not on the latest technologically superior goods that will win in the market in the long run but on those that are proven winners and are now being conveniently marketed worldwide.

Matrix Structure

When a multinational is trying to integrate its operations across more than one dimension, such as product as well as geography, or customers or technology; it resorts to the matrix structure. As shown in Figure 14.3, both the product division and area division share joint responsibility. This means both executives jointly decide allocation of resources and other important matters but the matrix manager is held responsible for results.

In this structure, there are pressures from horizontal matrix managers for equal allocation of resources; however, the vertical managers are supposed to balance this by taking into account the relative importance of products or projects based on organizational priorities and other long-term considerations. This structure reflects the process of decision-making and results in a higher quality of decisions. It also results in better customer focus or on final results or response to local needs.

However, there are several shortcomings associated with the matrix. First, as the design complexity increases, coordinating the personnel and getting everyone to work towards common goals often becomes difficult. Second, some employees experience dual authority, which is frustrating and confusing. Matrix managers need excellent interpersonal and conflict-resolution skills. The matrix also forces managers to spend a great deal of time in meetings. If managers do not adapt to the information and power sharing required by the matrix, the system will not work. Managers must collaborate with each other rather than rely on vertical authority in decision-making. Proliferation of communication channels creates information logjams and barriers of distance, culture and language make it virtually impossible for managers to resolve conflicts and to clarify the confusion.

J. Barlett & Ghoshal conclude that the most successful multinationals today focus less on searching for the ideal structure and more on developing the abilities, behaviour and performance of individual managers. This creates 'a matrix in the minds of managers' where individual capabilities are captured and the entire firm is motivated to respond cooperatively to a complicated and dynamic environment.

New Types of Multinational Structures

The structure has so far been viewed from the headquarters-subsidiary relationship, from coordination and control, flow of resources and information, and decision-making and problem-solving perspectives. However, in large, mature multinationals, these flows are multidimensional:

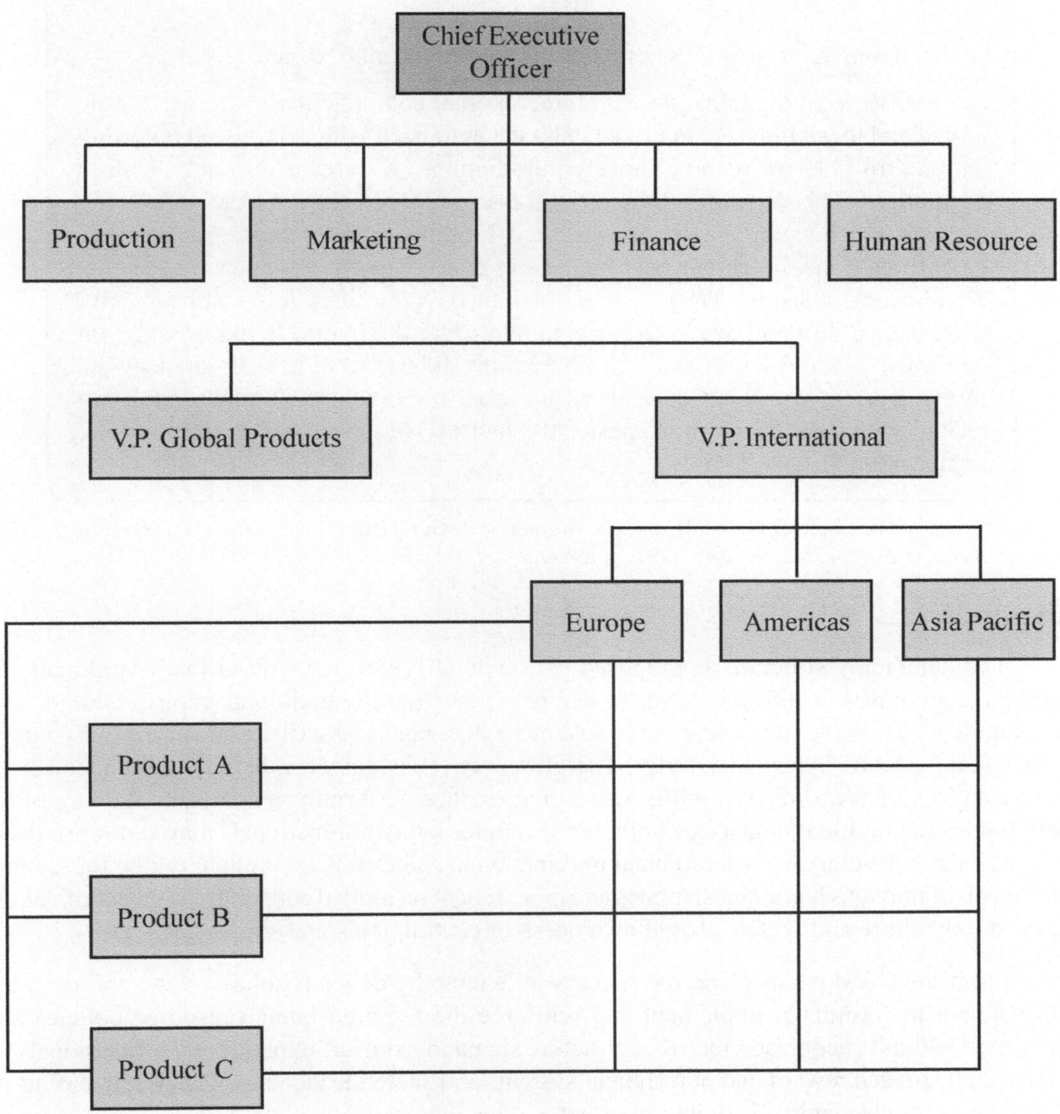

Figure 14.3. The matrix structure

from headquarters to subsidiary and from subsidiary to other subsidiaries and also from subsidiary to headquarters. Mergers, takeovers, joint ventures and strategic alliances are also giving way to newer variations in organization structure design. These can be considered under four types: the heterarchy, the transnational, the network firm and the *Keiretsu*.

BOX 14.5

Bernevic, former CEO of ABB discussing the matrix, said:

"ABB is an organization with three internal contradictions. We want to be global and local, big and small, radically decentralized with centralized reporting and control. If we resolve those contradictions, we create real organization advantage. This is where the matrix comes in. The matrix is the framework through which we organize our activities. It allows us to optimise our business globally and maximize our performance in every country in which we operate. Some people resist it. They say that the matrix is too rigid, too simplistic. But what choice do you have? To say you don't like the matrix is like saying you don't like factories or you don't like breathing. It is a fact of life. If you deny the formal matrix, you wind up with an informal one—and that's much harder to reckon with. As we learn to master the matrix, we get a truly multi-domestic organization."

Source: 'The Logic of Global Business: An Interview with ABB's Percy Bernevik', *Harvard Business Review*, March-April 1991, pp. 95-96.

Heterarchy

The heterarchy structure as proposed by Hedlund (1986) recognised that a multinational might have a number of different kinds of centres apart from the traditional centre referred to as "headquarters." He argues that competitive advantage does not necessarily reside in any one country, rather it may be found in many countries. Therefore, each subsidiary centre may simultaneously be a centre and a global coordinator of discreet activities, thus performing a strategic role not just for itself, but for the multinational as a whole. For example, some multinationals may centralise R&D in a particular subsidiary. In heterarchical multinationals, control is less reliant on the top-bottom mechanism of previous hierarchical modes and more reliant on mutual cooperation and coordination, organization culture and widely shared awareness of central goals and strategy.

From the HRM perspective, the success of heterarchy depends solely on the ability of the multinational to formulate, implement and reinforce the required human resource policies and practices. Hedlund recognises that this structure demands skilful, experienced professionals as well as sophisticated reward and punishment systems and shared leadership. The use of staff as an informal control mechanism is quite important.

Transnational

The term 'transnational' has been coined to describe a new organisational structure that is characterised by an interdependence of resources and responsibilities across all business units, regardless of national boundaries. The transnational copes with large flows of components, products, services, resources, people and information among its subsidiaries, while simultaneously recognising the specialised resources capabilities of each business unit. It demands a complex process of coordination and cooperation involving strong cross-unit integrating devices, a strong corporate identity, and a well-developed worldwide management perspective. The human resource's role is once again very critical and similar as in matrix or heterarchy. There is a need for transnational or global managers who can think and act across national and subsidiary boundaries. Staff transfers also play a crucial role in integration and coordination. Unilever, for example, is more like a transnational organization today.

Bartlett & Ghoshal aptly define transnationals in the following words:

> Among the companies we studied, there were several that were in the process of developing such organisational capabilities. They had surpassed the classic capabilities of the multinational company that operates as decentralised federations of units able to sense and respond to diverse international needs and opportunities: and they had evolved beyond the abilities of the global company with its facility for managing operations on a tightly controlled—worldwide basis through its centralised hub structure. They had developed what we termed transnational—capabilities—the ability to manage across national boundaries, retaining local flexibility while achieving global integration. More than anything, this involved the ability to link local operations to each other and to the centre in a flexible way, and in doing so, to elevate those local and central capabilities.

Networked Firms

Some scholars [like U. Anderson, M. Forsgren, C. Pahalberg and P. Thilenius (1990)] suggest viewing certain large and mature international firms as a network, in situations where:

- Subsidiaries have developed into significant centres for investments, activities and influence and cannot be regarded as at the periphery.
- Interaction between headquarters and each subsidiary is likely to be dyadic, taking place between various actors at many different organisational levels and covering different exchanges, the outcome of which is important for effective global performance.
- Such multinationals are loosely coupled political systems rather than tightly bonded homogeneous, hierarchical systems. This runs counter to the traditional structure where linkages are described formally via the organisation's structure and standardised procedures, and informally through interpersonal contact and socialisation.
- One subsidiary may act as a nodal unit linking a cluster of satellite organisations. Thus, one centre can assume responsibility for other units in its country or region.

The management of multi-centred networked organisations is complex. Apart from the intra-organisational network (comprising headquarters and the numerous subsidiaries), each subsidiary also has a range of external relationships with local suppliers, customers, competitors, host governments and alliance partners (Figure 14.4). The efficient management of both intra-organisational and inter-organisational spheres, and of the total integrated network, is crucial to global corporate performance. It involves a less hierarchical structure featuring five dimensions: delegation of decision-making authority to appropriate units and levels; geographical dispersal of key functions across units in different countries; de-layering of organisational levels;

(Partial Organisational Chart)

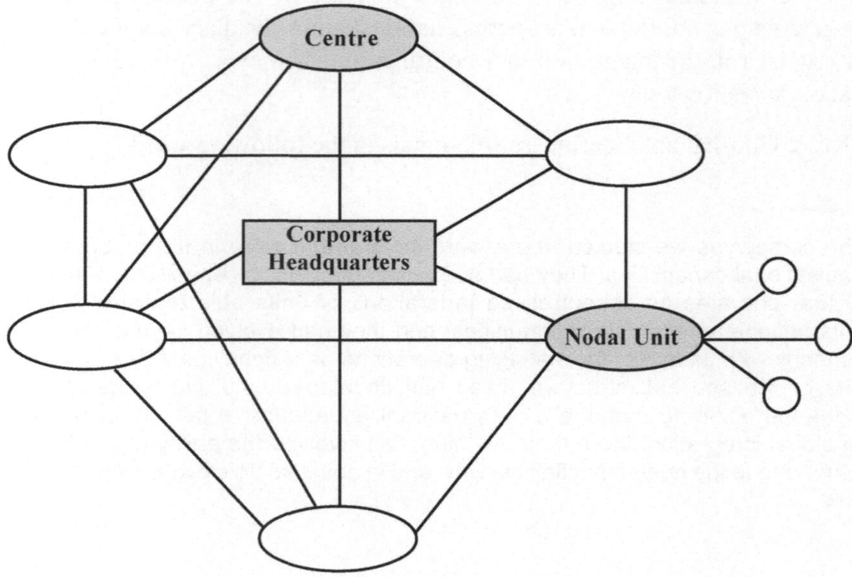

Figure 14.4. Beyond the matrix—a networked firm

de-bureaucratisation of formal procedures; and differentiation of work, responsibility and authority across the networked subsidiaries.

Keiretsu

Still another type of newly emerging organisational arrangements is the *kieretsu*, which is a large, often vertically integrated group of companies that cooperate and work closely with each other. A good example is the Mitsubishi group, shown in Figure 14.5. This *keiretsu* consist of 28 core members who are bound together by cross-ownership, long-term business dealings, interlocking directorates, and social ties (many of the senior executives are college class mates or family members and relatives). There are three flagship firms in the group: Mitsubishi Corporation, which is a trading company; Mitsubishi Bank, which finances the *keiretsu*'s operations; and Mitsubishi Heavy Industries, which is a leading worldwide manufacturer. In addition to the firms, as shown, there are hundreds of other Mitsubishi-related companies that contribute to the power of the *keiretsu.*

This form of organization has been cited by some international analysts as the reason why Japanese multinationals are so successful For example, although *keiretsu* companies in Japan account for less than 1 per cent of all Japanese firms, they account for 78 per cent of the value of all shares on the Tokyo Stock Exchange, and 68 per cent of all Japanese investments made in the US high-tech firms. Quite obviously, these *keiretsus* are very powerful. However, the Japanese are not the only ones using this organisational arrangement. The Birla group can also be thought of as an

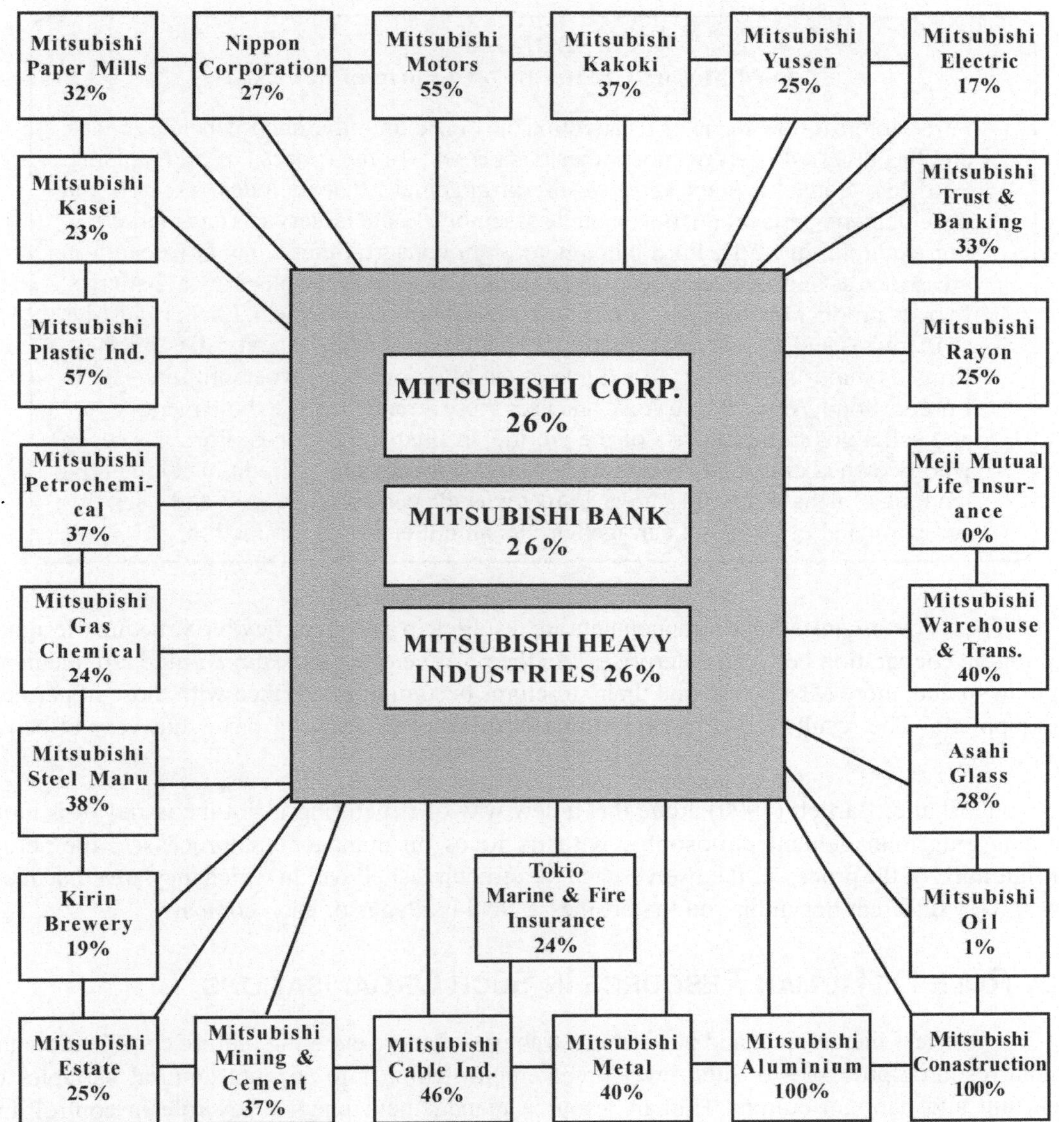

Note: Percentages refer to shares of each company that are held by other members of the group.
Source: Adapted from information in William J. Holstein *et al., Mighty Mitsubishi is on the Move.* Business Week, Sep. 24, 1990, pp. 98-104.

Figure 14.5. The Mitsubishi *Keiretsu*

Indian *keiretsu.* Reliance Industries was developing on the line of becoming an Indian *keiretsu* and that is the reason why demerger of the company into separate entities between Mukesh and Anil Ambani had become so difficult. Even large American multinationals are creating their own type of *keiretsus* (see Box 14.6).

BOX 14.6
Ford Motors Creates its own Form of *Keiretsu*

Ford Motors is now focusing its attention only on automotive and financial services, and has divested itself of most other businesses. In the process of reorganising, Ford has created a giant *keiretsu*-like arrangement that includes research and development, parts production, vehicle assembly, financial services and marketing. For example, in R&D, Ford belongs to eight consortia that conduct research in areas such as improved engineering techniques, materials and electric-car batteries. In parts production, Ford has equity stakes in Cummins (engines), Excel Industries (windows), and Decoma International (body parts, wheels) and relies on these firms as major suppliers. In vehicle assembly, Ford has ownership interests in Europe, South America and Asia, and uses these arrangements to both manufacture and sell autos in these parts of the world. In financial services, Ford has seven wholly owned units that cover a wide gamut from consumer credit to commercial lending. In the marketing area, Ford owns 49 per cent in Hertz and uses this company and other rental car agencies as an outlet for its production.

These new organisational arrangements are resulting in a need for flexible structures designed to promote cooperation between enterprises. As the positive effects of *keiretsu*-like arrangements begin to spread, more MNCs will find their structures becoming interlinked with those of partners and suppliers. The result will be a design that is difficult to draw on paper but very effective in practice.

Ghoshal & Bartlett (1990) argue that a new way of structuring is not the issue—it is more the emerging management philosophy, with its focus on management processes: the actual configuration of the processes themselves, and the structural shell within which they are embedded, can be very different depending on the businesses and heritages of each company.

Key Role Of Human Resource In Such Organisations

These less hierarchical and networked structures that are evolving require coordination and human resource processes of high-level involvement, taking into account cultural variables of each unit and national culture. Human resource management plays a key role in control and coordination processes:

- Ghoshal & Bartlett (1995) argue that the key means for vital knowledge generation and diffusion is through personal contact. This means that networked organisations need processes to facilitate contacts. Training and development programmes held in regional centres or at headquarters become an important forum for the development of personal networks that foster informal communication channels, as well as for building corporate cultures.
- Network relationships are built and maintained through personal contacts. Therefore, staffing decisions are crucial to the effective management of the linkages that the

various subsidiaries have established. Nevertheless, staffing decisions are made without regard to their effect on relationships. As a rule, very high importance is given to communication and interpersonal relationship ability in the selection process.

- The management processes in a networked multinational rely heavily on the ability of key staff to integrate operations to provide an environment and culture that fosters the required level of cooperation, commitment and communication flows between functions and subsidiary units.
- Staff transfers are also an important part of the required management processes, particularly that of soft control.
- Expatriates are used to instil a sense of corporate identity in subsidiary operations and to assist in the transfer of corporate norms and values as part of corporate cultural control.
- The visit of the CEO to different countries also helps in integrating relationships and developing strategic focus.

JOB DESIGN

So far we have discussed macro factors in organisational restructuring. The micro factors like job and role analysis, design of jobs and processes (business process re-engineering) and taking into account employee needs and expectations, are very important for structuring to be effective. Work systems need to be constantly assessed and evaluated to ensure that the organization has assigned workers tasks and responsibilities that assist in achieving organisational objectives.

Job design concerns and approaches were first studied by Taylor in his seminal book, *Scientific Management* (1891), followed by other classical management experts like Galbraith and others. This industrial engineering approach is basically concerned with products, process, tool design, plant layout, operating procedures, work measurement, standards and human-machine interactions. It has also been closely associated with CAD (computer aided design), and CAM (computer aided manufacturing). These computer systems had a positive impact by reducing task and work-flow uncertainty. Top management could readily perceive the immediate cost savings from job engineering, but certain behavioural aspects like quality, absenteeism, job satisfaction and turnover were generally ignored.

In the 1950s, different methods were being adopted by practising managers, For example, IBM had introduced job-rotation and job enlargement programmes, which reduced boredom and stress at the workplace and were supposed to have motivated the workers. Boredom and stress at the workplace are still important problems due to increased use of advanced technology, downsizing, frequent restructuring and changes in products and business environment. To assist organisations in designing enriched jobs, a model was developed for ultimate performance and behavioural outcomes by J. R. Hackman and G. R. Oldham (1974) (see Figure 14.6).

The model suggests that five core job characteristics can impact certain employee psychological states that will, in turn, impact certain work-related outcomes. These five core job characteristics are: skill variety, the extent to which the work allows an employee to use a variety of acquired skills; task identity, the extent to which work allows an employee to complete a 'whole'

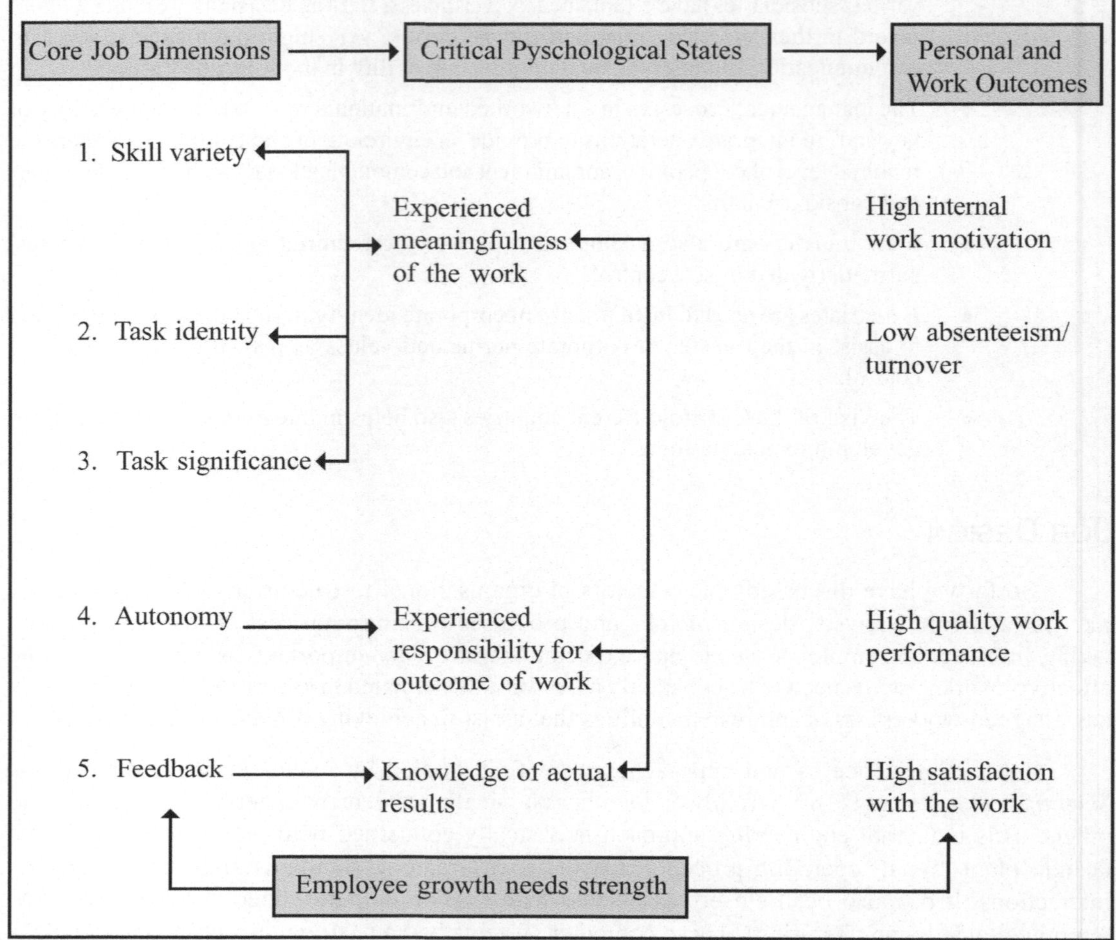

Figure 14.6. Job design model

or identifiable piece of work; task significance, the extent to which an employee perceives his or her work is important and meaningful to those in the organization or outside; autonomy, the extent to which an employee is able to work and determine the work procedure at his or her discretion without supervision; and feedback, the extent to which work allows the employee to gain the feedback on his efforts. The model argues that work systems can be designed to provide satisfaction, motivation and performance.

The model has been used extensively in cellular manufacturing where groups of workers assemble or make complete products or components collectively without a supervisor. For example, at Motorola's Communications Division, workers assemble, test and package paging devices whereas previously these tasks were performed on an assembly line with a 100 workers performing a hundred different steps.

THE CHANGING WORKPLACE

The design of work systems must also consider what 21st century workers (knowledge workers) need and want in order to carry out their job responsibility. Certainly all employees do not work for the same reasons, nor do they expect the same thing from their employers. The workplace today is characterised with increasing diversity with wide differences in age, gender, race and culture, and family backgrounds. Organisations must realise that employees no longer have generic needs. They expect their employers to understand their needs and respect them. This theme is discussed in this book separately in the chapter on 'Diversity Management'.

The issue of 'work-life balance' has acquired much significance. Employers who design work systems that do not allow employees to have the balance they desire in their life activities will find workers who not only are less committed to the work but also suffer from burnout and perform at less than optimal levels. Many forward-looking employers are establishing stress management programmes and physical health and wellness programmes with the help of external agencies to ensure that employees retain an essential balance among their life activities. Preventing burnout at work is a major corporate responsibility. There is another important area concerning employing both husband and wife, particularly in overseas assignments and the education of their children.

All employees, particularly younger ones, are far less loyal than they were a generation ago. They want some form of representation or 'voice.' Highly skilled and knowledge workers do not want to be micro-managed. They expect to use their training and experience to make the contribution to the organization, and they expect their organization to listen to their concerns. Getting employee inputs in work-related matters is not only highly motivational but helps the organization to utilize human capabilities to the maximum. In unionized organisations the employee voice is highly centralised and formalized. But with unions in decline, or with many craft unions in action, listening to employee 'voice' and their involvement and participation in work related decisions is one of the major challenges for the HR function and for employers generally.

Ensuring workplace safety is increasingly becoming important and with major disasters like the 'Bhopal Tragedy', not only whole organisations are liquidated but also directors may find themselves behind bars. New types of occupational diseases are appearing from watching computer screens, exposure to radiation. With long hours at workstations or desks, it is important to design the ergonomics of the work place.

WORKING IN TEAMS

In search of excellence for quality and performance in the midst of competition, organisations are turning to 'teams' for many activities such as project management, problem solving, product development, innovation and so on. This reliance on teams is appropriate for several reasons. First, organisations are now so complex that it is virtually impossible for an individual to have all the information necessary to make a good decision. Second, improvement efforts are often focused on process flow and cross functional teams can provide both needed information and 'buy-in' to process improvements. Third, managers believe that if they put people into on-going teams, they will be better motivated and more productive. Fourth, recent models of 'learning organisations' further suggest that teams are natural ways to gain and share the new information vital to organization growth and flexibility. Fifth, organisations even see teams as a way of assuring quality 'in process' by making teams responsible for internal quality control and innovation. Finally, the success of companies from Japan and Sweden was attributed primarily to their team culture and a large body of research indicates that groups can be highly creative and effective if teams are made self-managed and responsible for large tasks. Honda assigned to a cross-functional team of young professionals (average age 23) the design of a car for their generation, with only one caveat: that the car should be economical and fuel efficient. The famous Honda City model was the result.

The early uses of teams were focused in quality circles (QC) which addressed specific organisational issues, and on project teams. While these QC teams were worthy efforts at developing teams in the organisations, the teams needed for restructuring and re-engineering processes which form main organisational units in many leading companies now, are quite different. The success rate of teams had been uneven. There are reports that teams were poorly trained and poorly supported and were not integrated into the organisation's main hierarchy. A survey of 4,500 teams across 50 firms (*Training and Development Journal*, 1991), reveal inappropriate compensation and rewards as well as problems faced by teams in the inability of employees to change. It also comes out that teams are rare in top management. The time spent in developing trust and agreement does not translate easily into high creativity and performance. Individual stars feel that contributions in a team environment dilute their personal success. However, this picture from America, India and several other countries, is very different from Japan and Sweden where teams have performed outstandingly well. This only shows that national cultures play a significant role in the success of teams. Notwithstanding these mixed outcomes, the potential benefits of working in teams are great and organisations must create conditions for teams to flourish.

THE FOUR KEYS TO SUCCESSFUL TEAMS

The four keys of success in team working are:

1. value and endorse dissent;
2. encouraging fluidity in team structure;
3. encouraging teams to make decisions and value their work; and
4. the relationship of teams with senior management.

Once these are implemented, higher performance from teams is possible. Without active dissent, it is easy for managers and employees to consider 'our' way is the 'right' way or to focus on incremental improvement rather than innovation. Since many in the organization have a vested interest in maintaining the *status quo*, few will argue. Controversy is therefore discouraged. Such thinking can be a pathway to failure. The decline of many major companies, for instance GM and IBM, can be partially attributed to their inability to tolerate deviation from what was considered to be the 'right' product or strategy. To value and endorse dissent, organisations and teams must learn the techniques of productive controversy and constructive thinking. The teams should be trained in how to bring up controversial issues, explore alternatives and reach consensus while focusing on the outcome. The teams should also be trained in constructive thinking.

The second key is increased flexibility in team membership. It is not clear whether stability of team membership is better or not for team working. In fact, too much stability and cohesion may be detrimental. A team structure would have three components. First, a stable core of three to four members who stay with the team until the task is done. These members would have the technical, problem-solving and interpersonal skills necessary to address issues and to generate and consider new ideas. They also provide continuity and stability to the team. The second component will be resource people with specialized skills and experience, who enter and exit the team as needed. These members play many roles and bring new ideas and differing perspectives to problems, thereby preventing complacency and lack of creativity. Resource people can include both customers and suppliers. The third component is made up of temporary or part-timers. These members are called upon at special times for some tasks. These members play a key political role by advocating and championing its work and can be used for sending up trial balloons.

The third key to building an effective team is to empower them with decision-making authority. It is also to be seen that their task is not tied to strategic plans and initiatives which will prevent them from addressing fundamental issues in the organization. They are often asked to seek permission before implementing their recommendations thereby minimizing timeliness, ownership and innovativeness of their ideas. Effective teams empower themselves. They decide their own goals and their area of impact. The team should consider organisational politics and understand others' needs and perspectives before reaching optimal solutions. Finally, teams must adjust to the cultural background of its members.

With so much more accountability being delegated to teams, establishing effective relationships with senior management requires special mechanisms. Senior management needs to retain the ability to guide the team while empowering it to lead and act, a responsibility usually taken by an executive sponsor—typically the vice president of the engineering, marketing or manufacturing function. This sponsor becomes the coach and mentor and seeks to maintain close, ongoing contact with the team's efforts. In addition, the executive sponsor serves as a liaison. If other members of top management have concerns, or inputs to voice, or need current information, these are communicated through the sponsor. This reduces the number of mixed signals received by the team and clarifies to the organization the reporting and evaluation relationship between the team and top management. It is important to settle in advance the area of responsibility that lies with the executive sponsor. In one electronics company, the following was agreed between the executive sponsor and team:

1. Resource Commitment—head count, fixed costs, and major expenses outside the approved plan.
2. Pricing for major customers and major accounts, potential slips in major milestone dates with recovery plans.
3. Plans for transitioning from development projects to operating status.
4. Thorough reviews at major milestones or every three months, whichever occurs sooner.
5. Review of incentive rewards that have company-wide implications for consistency and equity.
6. Cross-project issues such as resource optimization, prioritization and balance.

Identifying such areas at the outset can help the executive sponsor and core team to better carry out their assigned responsibilities. It also helps other senior executives feel more comfortable working through the executive sponsor, since they know these 'boundary issues' have been articulated and jointly understood.

Employee Empowerment

Teams are a powerful means of employee behaviour change. A critical feature of successful teams in modern organisations is that they are invested with a significant degree of decision-making authority. Empowerment is not a programme. It is a culture change. Empowerment is the process of enabling or authorising an individual to think, behave and take action, and control work and decision-making in autonomous ways. It is the state of feeling self-empowered to take control of one's own responsibility. It is defined as "employee empowerment refers to management strategies for sharing decision-making power" (Brown & Lawler, 1992) and it is predominantly about encouraging front-line staff to solve customer problems on the spot, without recourse to management approval (Goldsmith *et al.,* 1997). In short, empowerment is finding new ways to devolve power in the hands of the people who need it most to get the job done—putting authority, responsibility, resources and rights at the most appropriate level for each task. The key ingredients of empowerment are:

- Sharing information about the organisation's performance;
- Rewards based on the organisation's performance;
- Knowledge that enables the employees to understand and contribute to organisational performance; and
- Power to make decisions that influence organisational direction and performance.

Empowerment comes from the individual The organization has the responsibility to create a work environment, which helps foster the ability and desire of employees to act in empowerment ways. Empowerment as an instrument of strategic approach tends to be unitarist but can be practised to some extent in pluralist management. Why is it gaining so much attention? The reasons are

1. Time to respond to environmental opportunities and threats is much shorter today and change is happening at an exponential rate.
2. People at the boundary of the organization sense the change and they are required to act, otherwise competitors are going to do it for them.
3. According to theory 'Y' people have great untapped potential.
4. Empowered employees are more committed, have more job satisfaction and stay with the organization longer.
5. Employee empowerment changes the manager's mind set and leaves him with more time to engage in broad-based thinking, visioning and nurturing.

How is empowerment achieved in practice? It can be done in a variety of ways, such as:

- Express confidence in the employee's abilities.
- Hold high expectations concerning their performance.
- Provide information about the job, department and company and enable them to use the information.
- Allow employees freedom and autonomy in how they perform their jobs.
- Accept mistakes as normal and try to learn from them without victimising employees.
- Provide extensive training about the job and enhance communication and leadership skills.

BOX 14.7
The Trident Group

The company with a Rs. 56-crore turnover in 1993 rose to reach an impressive Rs. 2,000 crore mark now with a formidable presence in yarns, terry towels, paper, pharmaceuticals, power generation and IT. At Trident, people just do not follow the rules; rather they create their own and rewrite the books. The basic philosophy about people at Trident is to let them "face and create challenges". It is a group that created a new history of innovative HR practices which include the following:

- Total trust and openness (attendance marking, leave applications, etc.) are replaced by self-declaration of salary due at all levels including the factory operator.
- Compulsory open house for 3,000 employees once in six months and any one can raise any issue just by raising one's hand.
- Modification of appraisal by 360 degrees including that of MD.
- Harnessing human potential through job upgradation/rotation scheme.
- No designation allowed—all to be called Trident members.

Stages in Empowerment

1. Suggestion involvement represents a small shift away from the control model. Employees are encouraged to contribute ideas through formal suggestion programmes or quality circles, but their day-to-day activities do not really change. Also they are only empowered to recommend; management typically retains the power to decide whether or not to implement any ideas they generate.
2. Job involvement represents a significant departure from the control model because of its dramatic opening up of job content. Jobs are redesigned so that employees use a variety of skills. Employees believe their tasks are significant; they have considerable freedom in deciding how to do the work. They get more feedback than employees in a command and control organization and they handle a whole, identifiable piece of work. However, despite the increased level of empowerment, this does not change higher level strategic decision-making about structure, power or rewards.

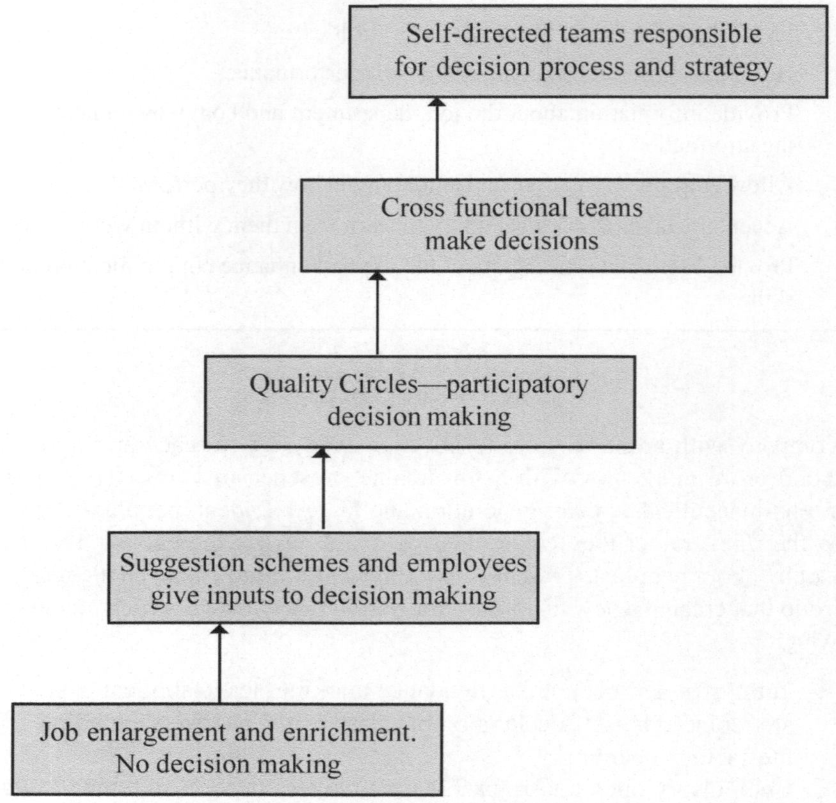

Figure 14.7. Empowerment continuum

3. High involvement organisations give their lowest level employees a sense of involvement not just in how they do their jobs, or how effectively their group performs, but in the total organisation's performance. Virtually every aspect of business performance is shared horizontally across the firm, as well as up and down the delayered structure. Employees develop extensive skills in team work, problem solving and business operations. They participate in work unit management decisions. High involvement organisations often use profit-sharing and employee ownership. Managers in empowered companies must take a number of new roles, like:

    1. counsellor or coach
    2. articulation of vision
    3. goal definer
    4. creator of challenge
    5. developer of talent
    6. resource obtainer
    7. leader

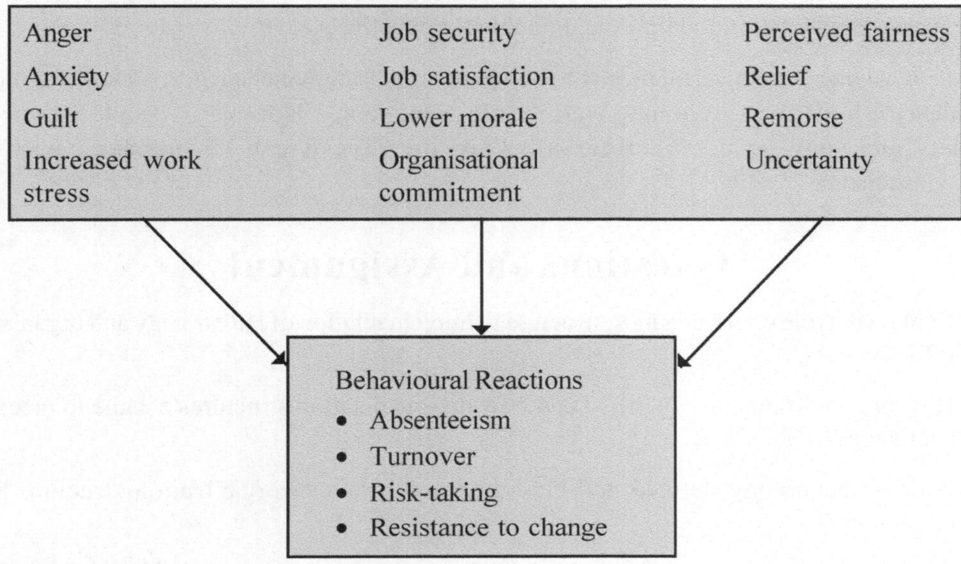

Figure 14.8. Emotions, psychological states and work attitudes

Employee empowerment can also be a major problem for an organization, if employees are given large increases in responsibility with preparation. Successfully instituting even a lesser degree of empowerment requires preparation. The results of empowerment have been mixed. In some companies dramatic improvement has been observed while in others success is limited.

RETRENCHMENT (DOWNSIZING)

Restructuring is usually accompanied by downsizing or some retrenchment and it is necessary to understand the process and reactions of those who remain and manage the process successfully. The intended goals are, of course, to increase profits or reduce cost or improve efficiency. The need for organizational commitment and loyalty is likely to be more significant after the advent of downsizing since those who remain become more important to the functioning of the organization. However, this is likely to be threatened if the organization does not purposefully intervene to foster commitment, and its employees maintain some sort of third-party relationship with its customers. In this regard, studies in the USA show (Misra & Misra, 1994), that just one quarter of the surveyed organisations had realised their objectives after downsizing. This is primarily due to psychological and behavioural reactions from those who survive the process.

This suggests that downsizing needs to be managed as a 'bottom-up' process as well as a 'top-down' one. This means that if objectives of downsizing are to be achieved, it will be necessary to consider and manage the process from the perspective of affected individuals and work groups and the stress which this event creates. The nature of these reactions is summarised in Figure 14.8. Please study Box 14.1 in this chapter (the case of TransAsia) which has done repeated downsizing resulting in its decline. Also read the case in Chapter 1 (Tata Steel) about how to conduct a successful downsizing. Tata's have reduced manpower by half over the last 10 years and increased production three times and doubled productivity.

Downsizing is a powerful means to generate organisational change. As a structural change its incidence is highly pervasive and adversely affects the people. However, if people are considered as assets and long-term objectives are kept in view, it can be managed with much lesser consequences.

Questions and Assignment

Q.1. Explain the role of organization structure in implementation of HR strategy and organisational effectiveness.

Q.2. How are environments classified and how do organization structures change to meet future challenges?

Q.3. How is technology defined and classified and how can organization structure best fit technology?

Q.4. Distinguish between mechanistic and organic structures. In what conditions is one preferable to the other? If you are an HR executive in these two types of organisations, how will your role change?

Q.5. Discuss the statement, 'structure follows strategy'. Can structure also influence corporate strategy? If so how?

Q.6. What are the needs of today's workplace? Discuss Hackman's model of work design.

Q.7. What are the challenges in the working of teams and how can their performance be enhanced?

Assignment

Select any organization where you have worked or taken training and study the changes it has undergone over the years in its structure, product and market profile. Interview some senior people about their experience in going through the change process.

CASE

RESTRUCTURING AT FLEXCO

Flexco commenced as a business unit of a large private sector organization which had a number of operations in the IT sector. Flexco was originally set up as a service function to some of these operations. The parent organization had experienced very rapid growth over a number of years. In the mid 1990s, its senior management decided to undertake a programme of internal rationalisation because it was felt that management control systems were inadequate and that it had exposure in a very wide range of operations. This review of operations led to a policy to outsource some non-strategic operations and spin-off or divest the internal operating units associated with these operations. Flexco was one of these operations. Its senior managers decided to 'engineer a buyout', and having raised the finance largely through an investment company it commenced operations as an independent company in its own right.

As a business unit of the original parent organization Flexco had operated with a simple functional structure. The GM of the unit, who became the MD of Flexco, had undertaken an overall coordinating role but with specific responsibility for the financial management of the unit. Each of the two other central business unit managers had specific functional responsibilities. One was responsible for arranging contracts and coordination of service provision across the parts of the parent organization that composed its business at that time. The other manager was responsible for service development and training. Other functional requirements were contracted from the corporate service provision of the parent organization. In this way, personnel services were brought in from the parent organization. The HR department was aware of its image as being a cost. Over the life time of the organization it had followed a strategy to counter this by developing a professional image as a provider of value in the work that it did for the respective parts of the business. Flexco had therefore been able to draw on this central HR function whenever it required support in this area. A somewhat paternalistic ethos had developed across the business, despite its outward appearance of having an entrepreneurial approach, with one outcome of this being that the organization 'looked after' its employees and provided them with employment security.

The transformation of Flexco to an independent organization therefore heralded further change for this business and those who worked for it. It would no longer have what had been in practice a guaranteed supply of contracts, nor the old parent organisation's financial backing and support of its corporate service provision. It expected to continue to work for parts of the old parent organization but had been told that it would not be given preferred status in relation to other providers. The strategy of outsourcing was seen as an opportunity to test the market place to a greater extent than had been the case previously.

This exposure to market forces led to a number of changes. These were driven by a desire to cut costs, maximise the utilization of those that worked for Flexco and increase the level of managerial control. The strategy of the new organization was now focused outward towards its market place and competitors rather than just inward towards the old organization for which they had traditionally worked. Thus, the new situation they found themselves in was seen to offer a series of threats and opportunities. Although the old business had a simple functional structure, the organization of work under three central managers had developed around the use of bureaucratic procedures. This had been encouraged by the stable and generally repetitious nature of the work carried out within the old organization. Because the old parent organization had operations in a range of locations around the country, there were also a number of regionally based service centres, staffed by a regional manager and service support staff.

The structural changes that occurred were focused on these aspects of Flexco. The senior managers wished to see the development of a much higher level of functional flexibility. This was accompanied by a review of staffing levels in different functional and sub-functional areas and a consequential downsizing of the workforce. This particular process utilized voluntary severance and some compulsory redundancies. Indeed, in some areas more than the numbers of staff that needed to leave wished to do so and a decision was taken to let them go. However, this also occurred amongst the support staff and it was agreed that these staff would be 'paid off' but re-engaged on a flexible contract basis. Several of these staff members were happy to proceed on this basis. This proved to be a more costly exercise than was first anticipated but was seen to offer significant cost savings after initial severance costs are absorbed. The result of this was a reduction in the total staffing to about 70 per cent of the buyout number and the creation of a core group of staff supported by other staff consisting of flexible workers. Those who remained in the core were expected to absorb much of the work of those who left and there was a desire to introduce some sort of performance management system, although ideas about this were rather hazy.

The managers in the regional service centres were also affected by these strategic and structural changes. While in most cases they retained their jobs, the nature of their work changed significantly. Previously these managers had had a fairly comfortable existence coordinating the delivery of the contracts agreed with the old parent organization for locations within their region. Now they were expected to maintain these contracts against commercial competition in the new market place and to win new work from other businesses. In addition, they were expected to assume responsibility for the management of the people that Flexco either employed or contracted to work in the region for which they were responsible in the past. HR issues of almost any nature had been referred up to the personnel function of the old organisation's service provision. Now, of course, this option did not exist.

Questions

Q.1. How do you think Flexco's workers will react to its changing organisational structures and the strategies used to implement these changes?

Q.2. How do you think these reactions will affect Flexco's ability to realise its intended strategies?

Q.3. What recommendations would you make to the senior management of Flexco in relation to the scope for and nature of HR strategies in this organization?

Q.4. Would you suggest some other way of restructuring Flexco and manage the change process?

15

Human Resource Processes in Multinationals

Learning Objectives

After studying this chapter you will learn:

- The concept of International HRM (IHRM)
- The quality required in international managers.
- How to select the right type of expatriates for overseas assignments.
- How multinationals organize cross-culture training for expatriates.
- How international companies evaluate expatriate performance and reward it.
- What are the causes of expatriate failure and how to minimize such failures.

INTRODUCTION

The twenty-first century is dominated by multinationals. The role of the HR function in international business has significantly changed because these organizations work as a network of subsidiaries operating in different country environments and in diverse cultures. As international trade continues to rise, the number of people working as expatriate managers is also on the rise. The direct cost of employing an expatriate manager is around 3-4 million dollars per annum and their cost of failure is very high taking into account indirect cost from business loss. Literature has also demonstrated that the failure rate is high, or that some of the expatriates work ineffectively on international assignments and are often recalled. Research has also found that the demand for expatriates is increasing. Although a lot of MNCs intend to stabilize or reduce their number of overseas assignments, the expatriate workforce is growing because there is a steady increase in small and medium-sized companies entering the international marketplace.

Firms operating in international markets face very different kinds of conditions and competition. Multinationals are characterised by an interdependence of resources and responsibilities across all business units regardless of national boundaries. These companies try to cope with the large flows of components, products, resources, people and information among its subsidiaries, while simultaneously recognizing the distributed specialized resources and capabilities. Management of multinationals demands a complex process of coordination and cooperation involving strong cross-unit integrating devices, a strong corporate identity and a well-developed worldwide management perspective.

This chapter is about how MNCs select the best expatriates for the job and how they provide cross-cultural training, evaluate their performance and reward them.

Concept of International Human Resource Management (IHRM)

We are now in a position to understand and look into different approaches to IHRM and how it is different from domestic HRM, including its definition. There are three broad approaches to international HRM. Early work in this field emphasized a cross-cultural management approach and examined human behaviour within organisations from an international perspective. The second approach focuses on human resource management processes, policies, procedures and strategies of multinational companies. The third approach is developed from the study of comparative industrial relations and employee management in different countries.

Multinationals employ three types of employees (PCN, HCN and TCN) and operate in different country environments with a view to obtain maximum synergy in the organization as a whole. There are some additional activities that are required to be performed in the course of international management, over and above those of domestic companies. 'International human resource management is the interplay among these three dimensions—nationals of different countries, country environments and additional responsibilities—with basic human resource management processes remaining same' (Morgan).

Differences between HRM and IHRM

Some would say that there is not much difference between HRM and global HRM and that essentially it is doing the same things, but doing them in a wider arena. But the truth is not quite so. The international dimension brings with it a host of issues with which the domestic HR function would not normally be involved. The practice of HRM in the international context is different from its domestic counterpart in a number of ways. These include:

- Being responsible for a greater number of functions and activities, such as the selection, training and management of international assignees.
- Having to expand one's area of expertise to include a much broader knowledge of foreign country employment laws and global organization designs.
- Having to get much more closely involved with employees' lives as the firm moves employees to foreign assignments. For example, collecting and furnishing information to visa authorities about the marital status of employees, etc.
- Being involved with a greatly expanded and constantly changing mix of employees (from the host country and foreign locales), adding considerable diversity and complexity to the HR tasks.

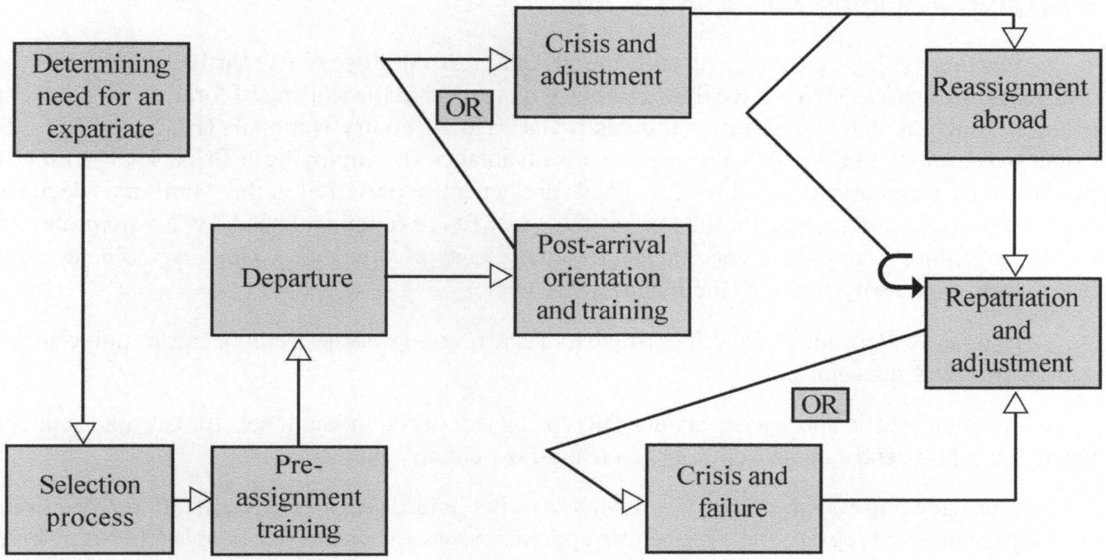

Figure 15.1. The expatriate assignment life cycle

- Having to cope with even more external influences, for example, having to consider the impact of foreign cultures and laws.
- Having to face greater exposure to problems and greater liabilities (for example, making mistakes in expatriate assignments, which can cost as much as US$ 4 million per assignee). The accumulated direct and indirect costs can be huge.
- Additional responsibilities like translation of language both at headquarters and at subsidiary levels, organizing schooling and housing for expatriates and providing administrative services.
- Management of differential compensations due to a variety of allowances and adjustments.
- More emphasis on activities like international relocation and orientation, both pre-departure and post departure cultural training.
- Knowledge of international taxation, rate of inflation and cost of living, including currency fluctuation.
- Diversity management like managing people from different cultural and political backgrounds, gender differences and variety of jobs and skill requirements.
- More contacts with government officials for obtaining visas, tax certificates, fixing meetings and so on.
- More coordination and travel to assess performance of expatriates and solve problems.
- More risk management as threats from terrorists, kidnappers and in protecting intellectual property rights of the firm.
- More public relations work to enhance the multinational's image and deal with human rights and other NGOs and interest groups operating in different countries.

STAFFING POLICIES AND APPROACHES

Staffing policy is concerned with the selection of employees for particular positions in different subsidiaries. MNCs have three options with respect to the staffing of foreign management positions, such as Parent-Country Nationals (PCN), Host-Country Nationals (HCN), and Third-Country Nationals (TCN). Advantages and disadvantages of employing a PCN, HCN or TCN executive are summarized in Table 15.1. PCNs are generally preferred in the 'start' and 'decline' phase of business and usually for the top positions as CEO or functional head. HCNs are preferred where the culture is very different and also to satisfy local governments which may coincide with the growth or maturity phase of the business life cycle.

Heenan & Perlmutter have identified four staffing approaches: ethnocentric, polycentric, regiocentric and geocentric.

An ethnocentric approach is about MNCs using parent country nationals for key management positions; a polycentric approach refers to using host-country nationals.

The egocentric approach is when MNCs utilize and develop regional staff for positions anywhere within the region; and a geocentric approach is one, when the best people from anywhere in the world are selected and posted to key positions. Combinations of these approaches can possibly apply in different functional areas.

In Onrack's study, he discovered that all the MNCs surveyed use a combination of geocentric coordination for some control functions such as finance and product groups; and polycentric for market oriented functions such as marketing and personnel. The geocentric approach seems to be a new trend in staffing policies; however, there are several factors which constrain its achievement, such as staff availability, time and cost constraints and host government requirements.

While the advantages and disadvantages of employing local managers (HCN) are the opposite of those employing expatriates (PCN), employing third country nationals runs the risk of either getting the best or worst of both worlds! Therefore, researchers discovered that the MNCs use either local nationals or parent-country nationals, although there is an increasing trend to use third country nationals.

MNCs tend to use PCN expatriates for transfer of corporate technology and management skills in the early stages of international operations. The use of TCNs occurs in the later stage of internationalization. For example, Japanese MNCs did not use third country nationals at any level of management in their overseas assignments during the 1980s. But the situation almost 20 years later; Japanese MNCs nowadays employ third-country nationals in management positions in overseas assignments.

COMPETENCIES REQUIRED IN INTERNATIONAL MANAGERS

A successful international business manager would need all the skills that are required in the domestic business operations. He or she must have operational knowledge of the different facets of the industry in which they operate. Each country having its own ethos, values, business and social culture, managers have to be 'generalising specialists' as well as 'specialising generalists'

TABLE 15.1
Advantages and Disadvantages of Employing PCNs, HCNs and TCNs

	Advantages	Disadvantages
PCN (Parent Country National)	• Familiar with the headquarters' goals, objectives, policies and practices, hence ensuring transfer of business/ management practices	• Problems of adapting to the foreign language and the socio-economic, political, cultural and legal environment
	• Technical and managerial competence	• Extra cost of selection, training and supporting expatriates and their families abroad
	• Easier to exert control over the subsidiary's operation	• Family adjustment problems, particularly regarding the unemployed partners of the expatriates
	• Effective contact and communication with headquarters' personnel	• High expatriate failure rate
	• Establishment of pool of internationally experienced executives	
HCN (Host Country Nationals)	• Familiarity with the socio-economic, political and legal environment and with business practices in the host country	• Difficulties in exerting effective control over the subsidiary's operation
	• Lower cost of employing HCN compared to PCN and TCN	• Communications difficulties in dealing with head-quarters' personnel
	• Provides opportunities for promotion to local nationals and hence increases their commitment and motivation	• Omission of opportunities for the parent-country nationals to gain international and cross cultural experience
	• Reacts effectively to the host country's demands for localisation of the subsidiary's operation	

Continued ...

...Continued

	Advantages	Disadvantages
TCN (Third Country Nationals)	• Perhaps the best combination of ensuring needed technical and managerial expertise and adapting to a foreign socio-economic and cultural environment	• Host country's probable respect for nationals of specific countries
	• TCN are comparatively less expensive to support than PCN	• Local nationals are obstructed in their efforts to upgrade their own ranks in the multinational subsidiaries

adding depth to the breadth of their knowledge and ability to synthesise specialist functions into general management, as one moves from one country to another.

In international business there is room for both cooperation and competition. More than a series of mechanical tasks, managing is a set of human interactions. Global managers operate in a matrix-like structure that demands cross-functional, cross-cultural, cross-product/service and international, often multi-regional, interactions.

Knowledge of One's Own Country

To understand the culture of other countries better, one should know one's country well. Appreciation of one's history and cultural values, understanding of current social and political issues and business situation and a reasoned future scenario is necessary. To gain respect from others, one has to have respect for oneself. Self-esteem as an individual, a citizen, a representative of the country and a business manager is essential for positioning oneself in the competitive global business.

A Global Perspective

The world is often referred to as a global village. Notwithstanding many differences in the shades of culture and value systems, many issues and concerns are global. We live in an interconnected, interdependent world economy. A global business manager must have a global business perspective and an understanding of how the world works.

Learning, unlearning and relearning activity is an integral part of the knowledge-intensive global business. Besides acquiring thorough knowledge of the business operations in their chosen field of operations, a global manager must be willing to listen and learn in the global arena.

Aspiring global managers have to be mentally ready to cope with surprises, mistakes, misunderstandings and even blunders in their cross-cultural interactions. Some mistakes are avoidable but some are a part of the hands-on learning of international business operations. Differences in cultural nuances often crop up at the most unexpected and critical times. Mistakes may occur in any area of business interaction, ranging from selection of cross-cultural partners to location of international business sites; name of a product or translation of business promotion messages to choice of management strategies. Mistakes in international business may occur due to ignorance or carelessness; over-enthusiasm or attaching additional meaning to spoken words, tone or gestures; improper use of idiom, or telling a wrong joke at the wrong time to the wrong person.

Cross-cultural mistakes may also occur in simple things such as use of personal or family names or doing simple translation; giving wrong gifts at the wrong time to a wrong person; in accepting or in rejecting a cup of tea or an invitation. At times the mistakes or misunderstandings may prove to be embarrassing and very costly. Knowing what to do in another country is as important as knowing what not to do.

Global Mindset

A global manager must develop a global mindset—the capacity to appreciate the beliefs, values, behaviours and business practices of individuals and organizations from different parts of the world. Cross cultural mistakes cost money and may cause long-term damage to the company. Global managers have to constantly deal with the other cross-country, cross-culture business managers. The ability to speak the language of the host country, adapt to the given environment, motivate his team, negotiate and understand other cultures is a competitive advantage in the global market place.

Knowledge of Other Countries

It takes two to communicate. As stated earlier, listening with the ears as well as eyes is an integral part of communicating and learning in the international business arena. To communicate effectively, one must have knowledge of the culture of the country in which one is going to operate. Not just business practices but also a good understanding of the country in areas such as its history, arts, human relationship, values, political system, social issues and cultural sensitivities including their ways of thinking, living and working. A curiosity to know and understand the other country and its people and thus educate oneself about the social, cultural and business environment of the country where one is going to play the business game is essential.

It is important to remember that cultures are not right or wrong, good or bad, just different. Perception is a person's view of reality. How people see reality varies with the position of their individual culture. Sometimes, international success is hindered by failure to understand how cultures differ. It is necessary to monitor how the trade pattern of countries is changing and reasons for the same; how politics is changing in different parts and how it is going to affect the trade pattern and business rules.

Understanding of the International Business Environment

To do business in other countries, one must know the rules of the market; one must acquire in-depth knowledge of the stated and prevailing practices of business. One must acquire thorough knowledge about the other country in areas such as their tax rules, labour laws, social benefits to be provided to the employees, government and public attitude towards foreign business executives and workers, foreign business investment and foreign business ownership.

To be successful in global business, one has to have a clear understanding of global business rules and develop a global business mindset.

Understanding International Business Partners

Business relationships are held together by mutual confidence. For confidence building, it is essential that one should be able to communicate effectively and for this one should know the subjects of interest of the other party and what he/she likes to listen and talk about most. Each relationship has to be carefully cultivated by inviting business partners to the home country on the occasion of important occasions. One should keep in touch with their development goals and strategies.

Knowledge of Customers

Like individuals, customers differ in their experiences, outlook, expectations, purchasing methods and decision-making. Each set of customers in each country must be understood from their individual economic, social and cultural background. Markets have to be redefined for each segment of each individual country.

Knowledge of the Silent and Spoken International Languages

Silence is a form of speech. Spoken silent languages are the main channels of communication in any culture. While each country may have one or more official languages, there are many variations in the use of spoken and silent languages within the regions of most countries.

Knowledge of Business Etiquette of the Host Country

This has been covered earlier in detail for most of the cultural regions of the world. Business units operate in a social-cultural milieu. Each country has its own social, historical and cultural sentiments. Each business representative has his or her own values and sentiments about one's own culture. A good business opportunity may be lost because of a wrong social act. In general, all managers domestic or expatriate require the competencies described later.

Developing Global HR Strategies

The various tasks that need to be addressed by a company's international HRM division, for creating global strategies and business synergies are as under:

- Building an organization which encourages the shared mindsets and attitudes to develop an integrated, networked organization for coping with global customers and global transactions.
- Developing the global leadership and management capability and structure to support strategies and operations.

- Gaining management support and involvement for implementing progressive HR policies.
- Ensuring sufficient quality and depth of managers to serve global customers.
- Ensuring that managers have the technical and managerial skills to work effectively at a global level as a team with shared vision and mission.
- Identifying and retaining highly qualified managers.
- Developing a global and local approach to training and development.
- Ensuring management succession.
- Sustaining and improving performance at all levels in all areas of the company.
- Establishing a total quality culture, and changing people's attitudes to quality.

Recruitment and Selection of Expatriates

In terms of recruitment and selection, the main issues are whether to recruit externally or internally and in what way the criteria used for selecting expatriates should differ from that used for domestic staff. Brewster discovered that most MNCs prefer to recruit expatriates amongst their own employees rather than externally, but they understand that this may not always be possible. For instance, technical specialists may have to be recruited externally.

Hamill's survey revealed that all the companies believed that the correct selection of individuals was crucial to successful performance abroad. Torbiorn identified eight selection criteria, namely:

1. Adaptability
2. Language skills
3. Motivation
4. Level of education
5. Social manner
6. Family adaptability
7. Medical status
8. Status of job

However, Borg & Harzing stated that four major groups of criteria have been mostly used, which are:

1. Technical competence at work.
2. Personality traits/relational abilities.
3. Ability to cope with environmental variables.
4. Family situation.

In Teagarden & Gordon's survey, they found 16 selection criteria related to expatriate success in the international HRM literature; they grouped these criteria again into four categories, which are:

1. Technical abilities
2. Relational skills
3. Family situation
4. Motivational state

Zeira & Banai proposed another facet of selection. They criticised that most of the selection of expatriates is a closed system rather than an open system. They believed that an open system approach is definitely needed and proposed that selection should be widened to include an analysis of the expectations of the host environments in addition to those of the MNCs. It is important that MNCs base the selection of their expatriates on the expectations and analysis of the real environment where expatriates operate, with which they have ultimately to cope.

Although there is consensus amongst scholars that personal characteristics are important, there are differences on how to evaluate them. A Price-Waterhouse study reports that only 12 per cent companies used assessment centres. Further selection tests that may be valid for one culture need to be validated for other cultures. They also found that the current selection tools used by MNCs are not enough for identifying right candidates who have the characteristics desired by a host country environment.

Generally speaking, the list of selection criteria currently used by MNCs is listed below. It may be noted that different MNCs assign different weights to these factors.

- Technical abilities.
- Managerial talent.
- Administrative skills.
- Knowledge of domestic operations.
- Relational skills.
- Cultural empathy, flexibility, intercultural communication competence.
- Language skills.
- Family situation, adaptive and supportive family members, stable family relationship.
- Motivational state, interest in working abroad, interest in specific host culture and belief in international assignment or career move.

Further components of these criteria are shown in Table 15.2.

Technical skills indicate the person's ability to perform the required tasks with ease. These can be evaluated from his past performance and records as well as through suitable tests. But past performance in one culture may not always guarantee success in another culture.

The main reasons for the high expatriate failure rate is the inadequate selection criterion used and insufficient attention paid to details. A study by Phatak discovered that none of the American companies seem to have any sophisticated methods for selecting expatriate candidates for international assignments. It is believed to be one of the reasons for the high failure rate of American expatriates. Selection methods generally used are:

TABLE 15.2
Main Factors Influencing Expatriate Selection

Technical Abilities	Relational Skills
• Managerial talent	• Cultural empathy
• Administrative skills	• Flexibility
• Technical expertise	• Intercultural communication competence
• Knowledge of domestic operations	• Language skills
Family Situation	**Motivational State**
• Adaptive and supportive family members	• Interest in working abroad
• Stable family relationship	• Interest in specific host culture
	• Believe international assignment is career move

1. An examination of past performance.
2. A battery of tests.
3. Interviews with senior managers.
4. Candidate's qualifications, experience on similar type of jobs or experience in that country.

By and large, selection criteria and selection procedure will differ from job to job and from company to company. Before designing any criteria and procedure, it is very important for MNCs to review and understand their needs and strategy first.

COMPENSATION AND REWARDS MANAGEMENT IN MNCs

Compensation decisions are strategic decisions and play a key role in achieving performance and sustainable competitive advantage for international firms. These policy decisions should be first consistent with the overall strategy, structure and business needs of the multinational. Second, the policy should attract and retain the best staff in those areas where the firm has the greatest needs and opportunities and core competency. Third, the policy must facilitate the transfer of international employees in a cost-effective manner. Fourth, the policy should take into account due consideration to equity and ease of administration. It should reduce the cost of operations and enhance commitment. It should facilitate international posting and transfer of employees.

These policy decisions regarding compensation and benefits require knowledge of employment and taxation laws, customs, cost of living index, environment, employment practices of many countries so as to avoid double taxation, to reimburse actual costs and provide incentives to employees to take up foreign assignments.

In addition, the knowledge of labour markets and industry norms regarding benefits and compensation is also necessary. Labour markets are the availability of required skills and demand for those skills and competencies and the going rate at which they are available for hiring in each country or globally. For higher levels of skills and competencies, international firms tap international labour markets, and for lower levels of skills, local markets provide the required resources. Hence, knowledge of both labour markets is necessary. In order to ensure equity with parent country nationals, the salary of expatriates has to be adjusted for foreign currency fluctuations of the two countries unless they are paid full salary and allowances in the home country currency only. If the expatriates are paid in local currency, then their salary should also be adjusted for rise in cost of living in that country from time to time. Hence, HR managers have to continuously watch these foreign exchange rate fluctuations and monitor the rate of inflation or cost of living index in different countries. It should also be kept in mind that all currencies are not free floating and some countries keep their currencies pegged at controlled rates.

It is also necessary to find out which locations are relatively difficult and throw up challenges of living and managing there, that will qualify for hardship allowances. These are locations where the climate is hard or modern facilities for living are not available.

One should also be aware of the vision and mission of the company, its corporate philosophy regarding managing human resources and its corporate strategy of growth or stability and strategy of its business units regarding cost leadership, differentiation and innovation. The life cycle stage of each unit in each country also plays a part in taking compensation decisions. One should also factor the strength of local unions and their pressure on compensation decisions. Finally, all these decisions are to be adjusted according to changing political, economic and social conditions in different countries of the world. Hence, these decisions may require services of specialized consultancy firms or experts.

Constitution of Total Package

How a total package of compensation is constituted is also significant. For example, executives can be paid higher basic salary with lower benefits and incentives; this may not motivate an employee to achieve high performance if taxes are high and will take away a major portion of pay. On the other hand, lower basic pay and a large portion in benefits and incentives related to performance may also not encourage the employee if his net savings remain low. Then there are options and choices regarding issuing company stocks for encouraging employees and senior managers not to sacrifice long-term objectives of growth and profitability for earning bonuses and incentives which are linked to short-term targets and objectives. Thus there are many complexities in international compensation programmes as all objectives are difficult to meet and therefore require a high degree of expertise.

Paying Expatriates

The structuring of a compensation system for expatriates presents some unique problems. These are listed below:

- Discrepancies in pay between parent-country, host-country and third party-nationals.
- The need to vary expatriate compensation, depending on the 'life cycle' of the expatriate's family (for example, young children and children in college).

- Compensation issues related to re-entry into the parent country organization.
- Using compensation programmes that have not changed sufficiently over time to deal adequately with the new international business environment.

Most expatriate compensation plans are designed to achieve five major objectives:

1. Attract employees who are qualified and interested in international assignments.
2. Facilitate the movement of expatriates from one subsidiary to another, from home to subsidiary and back from subsidiary to home.
3. Provide a consistent and reasonable relationship between the pay levels of employees at headquarters, domestic affiliates and foreign subsidiaries.
4. Be cost effective by reducing unnecessary expenses.
5. Should be easily understood and easy to administer.

Approaches to Expatriate Compensation

Basically there are two approaches, one is 'the going rate approach' (also known as market rate) and the other is 'balance sheet approach' (also known as the build-up approach). They are discussed below:

The Going Rate Approach

In this case the base salary on international transfer remains linked to the salary structure of the host country. For this, required information is obtained through compensation surveys and published information from the host country. The firm then has to decide whether local nationals (HCNs), or expatriates of same nationalities or expatriates of all nationalities will be the reference points in terms of benchmarking. For example, a US company operating in India has to decide whether its reference point will be local Indian salary, other US companies operating in India or all foreign companies operating in India. With this approach, if the location is a low-pay country, the multinational usually supplements base pay with additional benefits.

The advantages of this system include:

1. Equality with local nationals.
2. Approach is simple in administration and easily understandable for expatriates.
3. Expatriates are able to identify with the host country.
4. There is often equity among expatriates of different nationalities.
5. It attracts nationals of PCN and TCN if the location is a high-pay country like the USA or Japan.

There are also some problems with this system particularly with transfers from a developed country to a developing country where the salary differences as well as tax rates make a substantial difference to one's salary. Further, there will be differences between persons of the same nationality working in different countries in the same firm. This will create politics for getting favourable postings and resistance to low-pay country postings, defeating the company's strategic objectives and needs. Further, there will be problems when the expatriate is repatriated back to the home country. This is a problem for developing countries when their nationals return from the USA or other high-pay locations after a few years' service and are likely to be de-motivated with salaries in the native country. For example, a survey by Towers Perrin of total compensation for CEOs around the world reported the following results:

U.S.A.	$ 901,801
Singapore	$ 572,414
France	$ 523,511
U.K.	$ 489,710
Australia	$ 476,700
Germany	$ 423,898
Malaya	$ 342,151

This policy, however, is very much favoured by polycentric organizations where subsidiaries are given autonomy to decide compensation for their employees according to local laws, custom and economic conditions.

The Balance Sheet Approach

This is the most widely used approach for international compensation. Its main objective is to 'keep the expatriate whole' which means maintaining the relativity to PCN colleagues and compensating for the costs of international assignments and maintaining home country living standards. Thus, it links the salary of expatiates and TCNs to the home country salary structure. The key assumption is that foreign assignees should not suffer financially due to transfers and this is accomplished through the 'balance sheet approach'.

The salary package is divided into four parts:

1. Goods and services: home-country outlays for items such as food, personal care, clothing, household furnishing, recreation, transportation and medical care.
2. Housing: major costs associated with host country.
3. Income taxes: parent-country and host-country income taxes.
4. Reserve: contributions to savings, payments for benefits, pension contributions, education expenses, social security taxes, and so on.

When costs associated with the host country assignment exceed equivalent costs in the parent country, both the firm and the expatriates need to ensure that parent-country equivalent purchasing power is achieved to meet these costs.

For example, if a US national is posted in India, as an employee of a US multinational, and suppose the dollar exchange rate is $ 1=Rs. 50.00 and Mack Index or Cola Index is 5 then the break up of his annual pay will be as shown in Table 15.3.

TABLE 15.3
Expatriate Compensation when Host Country Costs are Higher

Item	Amount in $ per Year in USA	Paid in $ in India	Paid in Rs. in India
Basic Pay	100,000	60,000	2,000,000
Cost of Living Allowance	10,000	Nil	500,000
Overseas Allowance	20,000	20,000	Nil
Hardship Allowance at 5% of base	5,000	5,000	Nil
Housing Deduction at –10% of base	–10,000	–10,000	Nil
Income Tax Deduction @ 30%	–30,000	–30,000	Nil
Total	95,000	45,000	2,500,000

Thus he gets a total compensation of $ 45,000 and $ 2,500,000. The US firm pays for housing in India on actual basis. The US firm will also pay differences in taxes if the expatriate has to pay a higher tax rate in India.

The premiums for overseas service can be paid in several ways. In some cases, a one-time payment of 30-35 per cent of salary is made to encourage the employee to move abroad. In other cases, a constant premium is paid each year, or the premium is paid in decreasing amounts until it is phased out after a certain number of years.

When an employee takes an assignment in an undesirable location, a hardship allowance is often paid, with the amount varying according to the level of hardship. Determining this level is not easy. ICI, a British MNC has used the services of Employment Conditions Abroad (ECA) to determine the amount of hardship amount to be given. ECA has used the following dimensions:

1. Distance from Britain.
2. Ease of travel to and from Britain.
3. Difficulty of learning the local language.
4. Climate.
5. Health consideration (for example, the types of diseases that are prevalent).
6. The quality of local health care facilities.
7. Availability of English language schools.
8. Quality of education.
9. Availability of goods and services and recreation facilities.
10. Risk to expatriates and their family, such as terrorism or crime.

To mitigate the hardship, the firm may also provide two home trips per year or paid holidays for the family. Finally, there is a group of allowances provided to cover differences in the cost of living between home and foreign countries and to cover additional expenses associated with setting up a home in a new location. Paying a one time allowance of a certain amount covers this. Housing costs vary a great deal in different parts of the world. A recent survey indicated annual housing costs in US dollars in different cities:

- Tokyo $ 118,200
- Hong Kong $ 84,645
- Paris $ 71,359
- London $ 51,634
- Frankfurt $ 46,083
- Rio de Janeiro $ 38,195
- Chicago $ 28,894

Since public schools are not suitable for the children of expatriates, companies often provide funds to allow expatriates to send their children to private schools where they can get a proper education. Similarly, packaging, shipping and storage costs are also paid.

Advantages of Balance Sheet Approach

There are several advantages to the balance sheet system. First, it provides equity between foreign assignments and between expatriates of the same nationality. Second, no problems arise when he returns back to his home country and finally it is easy to administer and communicate. Further, it facilitates easy transfers from any country to any country.

The main disadvantage is that considerable disparity may arise between nationals of the host-country and the expatriate, resulting in de-motivation. Second, there may be differences in pay among the different nationals working on the same type of jobs because their basic pay is decided according to their country by their firms. Similarly, Americans may be paid higher for the same job by American firms than an Indian posted in the USA and paid by an Indian firm.

Cultural Impact and Compensation Policy

MNCs have to take into account national cultural differences while designing their compensation and reward policies.

- National cultural differences also play a significant role. For example, Linchon Electric, one of the first companies to successfully implement the productivity-linked incentive system in the USA, has attempted to transfer the system of piece-rate, end-of-year bonus and continuous employment to its operations in other countries. While this was successfully implemented in Australia and partly in Mexico, it met stiff resistance in European countries.
- In high power-distance cultures, the compensation system should reflect the hierarchical divisions in the firm. Pay should reflect status and job difference between

different levels. Compensation for local managers, pay and benefits, should be tied to the manager's position.

- In low power-distance cultures, the salary system should be more egalitarian and group based. Pay and compensation should reflect the seniority as well as consideration of family needs.
- Similarly in individualistic cultures, rewards should be given on individual basis and in collectivist cultures, they should be team based.
- In cultures with masculinity, MNCs should pursue a compensation strategy that recognizes and rewards competitiveness, aggressiveness and dominance. In cultures with low masculinity, compensation should focus on social benefits, quality of work life and equity.
- In cultures with high uncertainty avoidance, structured and consistent pay plans are preferred. Salary and benefits decisions should be centralized, with no variable plans or discretionary allocations. Where uncertainty avoidance is low, pay should be linked to performance. In addition, the salary of the local manager should be competitive to retain talent.
- In high uncertainty avoidance cultures, it is better to have centralized pension systems with multiple controls and safeguards.
- Low uncertainty cultures would be more open to defined contribution pensions with flexible plan implementation.
- In masculine cultures with moderate to high uncertainty avoidance, policies designed to protect job security would be welcome.
- Employees with feminine cultures with moderate to high uncertainty avoidance would prefer policies designed to protect income security.
- Employees from feminine cultures prefer family-friendly practices as well as other policies designed to maximize quality of work life.
- Employees from low-individualistic and low-power distance cultures will prefer flexible benefits programmes.

Termination of Contract

One aspect of compensation that varies from country to country and has important implications for both subsidiary HR managers and HQ-based managers is the issue of what happens if the MNC decides to leave a foreign country or another firm takes over the management, which is not interested in doing business in this country. When such a decision is made, termination liabilities may result in significant payoffs to employees. By tradition, or law, or union contract, the MNC may be required to pay up to two years' salary to employees who are involuntarily terminated. In some countries, firms intending to close down operations may be required to develop a systematic plan to deal with severance payments, relocation expenses, retraining and other services for employees who are laid off.

PERFORMANCE APPRAISAL OF EXPATRIATES

A multinational company has a global strategy and goals. In this strategy, the role of foreign subsidiaries is to help achieve the overall goals of the firm, which may include supporting another subsidiary at its own cost. Therefore, individual subsidiary performance and expatriates posted therein, are evaluated according to expectations, outcomes and behaviours that contribute to attainment of organizational goals. Evaluating the performance of expatriates linked to the subsidiaries is difficult as it is influenced by the following factors:

- Non-comparable data. Different countries have different accounting standards, account closing periods, currency fluctuations, etc.
- Volatility of the international environment. Economic, social, and political changes may occur rapidly in the world, affecting the performance of subsidiaries and the corporate office should take into account such factors, which often it does not.
- Headquarter-subsidiary interdependence. A subsidiary's performance will depend on the support provided by headquarters, which depends on their goal congruency and resource matching.
- Separation by time and distance. Senior executives at headquarters may not be able to visit a subsidiary often and may not appreciate local problems and low productivity norms or non-availability of skilled resources or lack of infrastructures, etc.
- Motivational problems like poor compensation, incompatibility with local culture and family problems of expatriates. Problems may also arise if there is no role and goal clarity.

EXPATRIATE FAILURE

Expatriate failure is the premature return of an expatriate to his or her home country; however, some researchers argue that failure rates include both premature returns and those who perform under par on international assignments.

For example, Tung defines expatriate failure in her survey as the inability of an expatriate to perform effectively in an overseas country and, hence, the employee is either dismissed or recalled home. Most publications define and measure expatriate failure as the percentage of expatriates returning home before their assignment contract expires. The reasons for the same are listed below:

1. Poor performance in foreign assignments.
2. Personal dissatisfaction with the experience (expatriate or family).
3. Inability to adjust to the local environment.
4. Not accepted by local nationals.
5. Rewards are not commensurate with the responsibilities.

Hiltrop & Janssens pointed out that once the selection process is completed, companies should provide formal training programmes to prepare expatriates and their families for their international assignments. Even the most rigorous and careful selection does not eliminate the need for training. According to Forster & Johnsen, training can increase an individual's ability to cope and work in a foreign and unfamiliar environment. In addition, Forster & Johnsen found that although MNCs might feel uncertain about the effectiveness of expatriate training, expatriates and partners are positive about formal expatriation training.

Expatriates who receive more training and support are more likely to have lower failure rates. Mentors are individuals who support, guide and counsel less experienced colleagues, particularly newcomers, in order to enhance their career development. In the study of Heimann & Pittenger, they reported that mentoring can have its most dramatic impact soon after new members join the organization. As Feldman & Bolino stated, mentoring helps newcomers decrease their uncertainty about the new environment. In addition, it helps newcomers imbibe the organisation's culture and they feel more comfortable with the work group.

Therefore, mentoring during expatriate assignments could be positively related to expatriate socialization. It could be expected that more sophisticated social networks help the expatriates adapt to and work more effectively in a new environment.

Appropriate HRM policies also have an effect on a family in coping and adapting (Figure 15.2).

Expatriate Training

Pre-departure Training

Once a candidate has been selected for an expatriate position, pre-departure training is considered to be the next necessary step so that the expatriate could work effectively and successfully abroad. In Oddou's survey, it was discovered that over 65 per cent of the expatriates reported receiving no training at all. The results were not surprising as most MNCs doubt the effectiveness of the training programmes. There are a number of other reasons for not providing any pre-departure training, four of which have been summarized by Mendenhall & Oddou:

1. There was past dissatisfaction with the training programmes on the part of expatriate trainees.
2. The time between selection and departure is short and there is inadequate time for the expatriate to become exposed to in-depth acculturation training.
3. As the expatriate's assignment is sometimes for a short-term purpose, it is not worth spending resources on training.
4. The dimensions of acculturation are simply not well enough known to formulate practical training programmes.

As highlighted earlier, training is of crucial importance for expatriates, particularly in helping to establish cultural empathy. Forster & Johnsen state that training in cultural empathy can be broadly described as any procedure intended to increase an individual's ability to cope and work in an unfamiliar environment. Tung proposed that the cross-cultural training programmes designed for expatriates should be classified into six major categories:

1. Environmental briefings. Information should include geography, housing and schools.
2. Cultural orientation. Information about the cultural institutions and value systems of the new country should be mentioned.
3. Cultural assimilation. Information consists of brief episodes describing intercultural encounters.

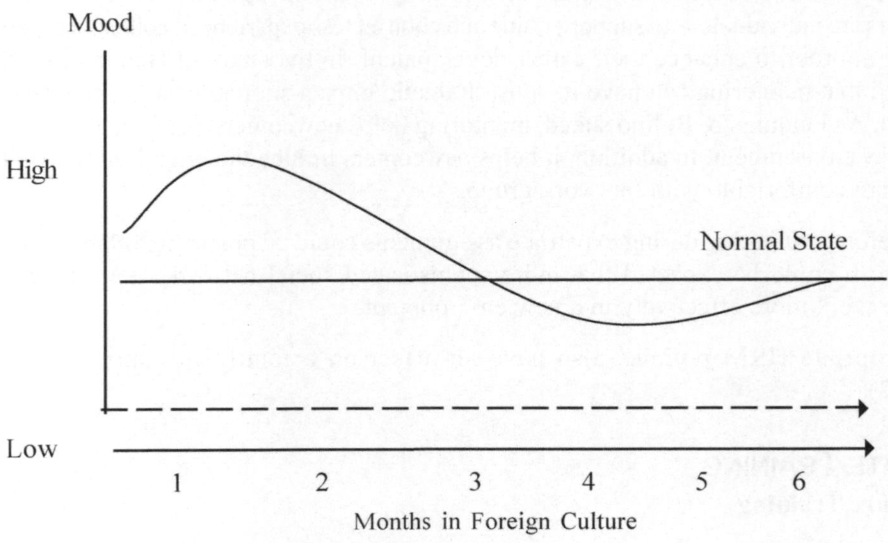

Figure 15.2. Expatriate adjustment cycle

4. Language training.
5. Sensitivity. Training to develop attitudinal flexibility should be included.
6. Field experience. Where candidates are sent to the country of assignment or to a micro-culture where they can undergo some of the emotional stress of living and working with people from different cultures.

Brewster also suggested that expatriates' training should be divided into six categories:

- Shadowing
- Look-see
- Informal briefings
- Overlap
- Formal training courses
- Language training

Shadowing means that the potential expatriate acts as a headquarters link with responsibility for a particular country prior to moving there on foreign assignment. It may involve developing an intimate knowledge of the overseas country, meetings with current expatriates at headquarters and sometimes visits to the country. Whilst it seems to be very useful training, Brewster found that not many MNCs offered it, as it was difficult to organize.

A look-see visit means a pre-visit to the country of the assignment, which is not a common form of training either, and relatively few organisations use this for all their expatriates. Although a look-see visit could be a very powerful form of preparation, it is costly and potentially problematic.

It is also not realistic enough as, while visiting, the expatriates and their partners are likely only to encounter all the good sides of the host country. They would stay in the best hotels, meet important people and be on their best behaviour. It is sometimes not possible to notice and understand foreign business practices and other cultural differences while on a short visit.

Informal briefing was the most common method of training. Informal briefing could take many forms, such as a short meeting with personnel specialists, or consist of casual conversations with a colleague who has recently spent time in that particular country. It also could consist of discussions with a range of experts, locals, and returned expatriates. Owing to the low cost of these informal briefings, it could remain the prime source of preparation.

Overlap means having one expatriate who has started a tour of duty before the previous one left. Brewster found that it was not a common method of training, and that it was costly but potentially effective. It was costly, as the company needed to retain two expatriates at the same time, and might entail the involvement of two families as well. Furthermore, the method was sometimes impossible to practise, as some postings are the result of an emergency.

Formal training courses are especially designed to help the expatriate to settle into, and operate in, a foreign country. Some companies provide training by their own staff, while others use outside providers, such as university experts, specialist consultants and specialist expatriate training colleges. Julius recommended that expatriates and their partners should both attend training sessions.

Language training could be vital, not only for practical purposes but also in creating a constructive attitude to cultural adaptation. However, Brewster believed that training in the language of the host country was arguable. For example, he stated that US companies seldom provide any language training as, in some industries such as airlines, petroleum and banking, English is the universal language. In addition, some languages are so different from English that even a three-year course would prove insufficient for many to become fluent.

For example, it is difficult for English expatriates to learn Cantonese (one of the dialects of Chinese). Fitzgerald-Turner observed that many small- and medium-sized companies provide language training for expatriates. Further, the expatriate's partner and children do not have any language skills, which often prevented them from communicating with locals in daily life, thereby making it difficult for them to adapt to the new environment.

Apart from the six types of training already described, cultural awareness training is also very important for expatriates and their families. The benefits of cultural awareness training include:

- Maximum utilisation of business opportunities.
- Reduced expatriate failure rates.
- Increased expatriate efficiency on arrival.
- The reduction of mental and physical health problems.
- Better coordination of work and motivation of expatriates.

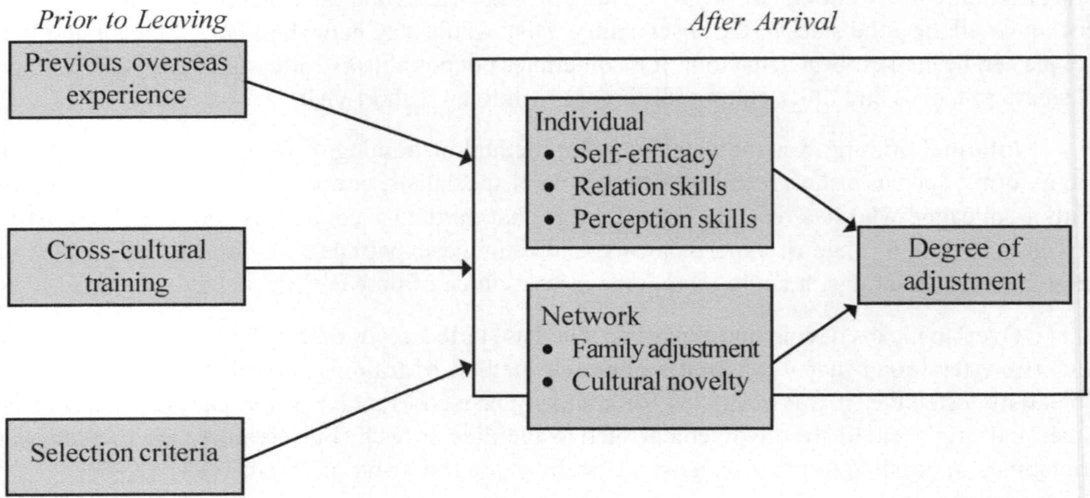

Figure 15.3. Factors influencing adjustment: International adjustment

Expatriate Adjustment

After going through a series of selections and training, the expatriates move on to the next stage: the assignment period abroad. This is the most important stage of the international career cycle. The period of expatriate adjustment is traditionally thought of in terms of a U-shaped curve of adjustment, known as the culture shock. Culture shock is defined as the emotional disturbance that occurs when individuals find themselves in an uncertain environment, where previous learning or training is not enough for coping.

Expatriates arriving in the new environment will have a short honeymoon period where the excitement of the new environment is the predominant feature. This is followed by a long culture shock period where disillusion with the new country settles in and morale declines. In a third stage, the expatriate learns to act appropriately in the new environment.

Other traditional views of the process describe it as a learning curve in which adaptation increases rapidly at first, then starts to fall in a journey marked by increased self-insight and reduced ethnocentrism as the expatriate moves from the margins towards the centre of the foreign culture. Next, after a few months of learning, expatriates find they understand more and find it easier to react appropriately in the foreign country. The pattern of the adjustment curve is different for each individual. Therefore the expatriate's family members will experience culture shock at a different intensity and at different times.

Individual skills, which are important from the adjustment perspective, have been categorised into three dimensions: the self-dimension, which includes skills that enable the expatriate to maintain mental health, psychological well-being, etc.; the relationship dimension consists of the interpersonal skills for fostering relationships with the host nationals; and the perception dimension, which involves the cognitive abilities that allow the expatriate to perceive and evaluate the host environment and its actors. According to Black, Mendenhall & Oddou, cultural novelty can be referred to as cultural distance, it is agreed that the more culturally different a host nation is from an expatriate's own, the more difficult it is for him or her to adjust .The adjustment of the spouse and family of the expatriate is an important factor.

Although expatriates might have all the necessary skills for adjustment, if the spouse or family do not possess these skills, expatriate failure can still happen, as the spouse or family member cannot adjust to the new environment.

REPATRIATION

Repatriation is the opposite of expatriation. It involves the move of the expatriate back to the headquarters and home country from the international assignment. Coming home is now identified as one of the most difficult moves of all because repatriation has received far less attention than expatriation in both academic and practitioner literature. However, recently more attention has been drawn to the adjustment problems, and the importance which managing repatriate careers plays in international staffing.

According to Feldman, the reasons for the increased interest in repatriation were two-fold. First, there is much evidence that returnees are having difficulties in re-adjusting and getting back to high levels of productivity. These reintegration problems are costly for both MNCs and individuals. Second, surveys suggest that only four per cent of MNCs felt that an international assignment has a positive long-term effect on a manager's career. Consequently, MNCs seem not to be fully utilising the skills and experiences gained from overseas assignments, which could result in many repatriates leaving their companies after their return.

Re-entry experiences frequently surprise returnees. As claimed by Forster, evidence shows that returnees experienced 'reverse culture shock'. Returnees describe stages similar to those of culture shock, that is, first being in a very high mood, but then very quickly turning into a low mood and then slowly rising to their normal mood. The lowest time is usually the second and third months of their return. Returnees also experience significant problems with careers, their family and financial issues.

Approximately 20 per cent of the returnees leave their companies within six months after return. Harvey concluded that MNCs have not developed a sense of awareness as to the need for repatriation programmes. This lack of attention to repatriation may have a long-run impact on the performance of these organisations as a result of the problems for returned executives, and the corporations. It could also be predicted that the problems that are experienced by the repatriates could influence the willingness of future managers to accept international assignments.

Questions and Assignment

Q.1. Discuss the characteristics of three categories of employees employed by multinationals. What are their advantages and disadvantages?

Q.2. Outline the main characteristics of ethnocentric, polycentric, regiocentric and geocentric approaches to international staffing practices.

Q.3. What are the main important criteria MNCs should use when selecting expatriates? What factors may influence these criteria?

Q.4. Discuss the reasons for failure and success of expatriates.

Q.5. Explain the types of training imparted to expatriates and what factors can ensure their success.

Q.6. Write short notes on: a) Repatriation; b) Expatriate adjustment model; c) language training.

Assignment

Interview any expatriate manager in any MNC and find out the challenges he is facing and also his unique experiences, if any, in India. If it is possible to interview expatriates from other countries find out what is common between them and what is different in their service in India.

CASE

SEIKO INSTRUMENTS

The Seiko group established in 1937 consists of three distinct companies—Seiko Corporation, Seiko Instruments Inc. and Seiko Epson Corporation. They operate independently but function as a cohesive unit in the design, production and marketing of the timepieces that established the Seiko name. The company has around 70 subsidiaries worldwide with over 10,000 employees. Through its global network, Seiko Corporation markets the timepieces produced by SII and Seiko Epson. In 1988, Seiko completed the world's first automated assembling system for multipurpose, small-lot production of watch movements.

The organisation's structure is constrained by British standards in some respects, in common with other Japanese companies operating in the UK.

HR STRATEGY

The General Manager (GM), who is Scottish, has worked on the site for over 10 years and in all these years there have been only two visits by a personnel representative from Japan. The main objectives of the visits was for the HQ to survey the Japanese employees working overseas.

> The Corporation's stance is basically that in the overseas countries, the personnel function should operate entirely autonomously. It's fairly bizarre to have identical policies and procedures in sites in as diverse locations as Japan, China, Thailand, Malaysia and the UK. Generally the company tries to treat its employees fairly well and it's left up to local personnel to follow local standards.
>
> 'If it wasn't for Mr X (a Japanese senior manager) you wouldn't know you worked for a Japanese company. There isn't really anything Japanese about it at all. I say to people: you will probably find this company is not like your typical Japanese company.'

Most personnel policies of the Scottish site are made locally; the site is given targets and a free range to achieve them 'the Scottish way'. The company's policy is to respect local ways—they try to adapt to local management practices 100 per cent within the Scottish location. People management is designed locally, mainly by the General Manager. They have constructed a policy manual and handbook containing mostly local practices. They are first written in draft, involving all the managers at this stage, agreed upon, and then formalised. Then they are placed on notice boards and employees are notified. Revisions are initiated as required by legislation, for example, changes in working practices. The GM has spent some time working in the USA (California) with Seiko and has introduced some Californian practices into the site.

Recruitment

All practices are driven from the Scottish site. In Japan they select school leavers for operators. Initially, the Japanese Manufacturing Manager had a preference for school leavers and teenagers and wanted the Scottish site to recruit them. He was involved in the recruitment of the first 90 employees who fulfilled this age criterion. When these 90 young recruits were assessed on, for example, how they behaved against their elders on site, they were considered unreliable and 'unaccustomed to this kind of work'. Absenteeism was a problem at this stage. He believed that 'they had no work ethic at this age'. The Personnel Manager at the time was the only personnel manager of a Japanese company in Livingston to say: 'I will not employ school leavers and teenagers'. He thinks the policy of recruiting school leavers works in Japan because youngsters are more obedient and better educated.

Overseas Training

Watch manufacturing has been in operation for over four years. A lot of initial training was done in Seiko's subsidiaries in Singapore and the Far East; a lot of overseas trainers came over, and worked with the operators for about three months. The on-site practices have been refined over the years. Production supervisors go over to Japan every year to learn new processes. If the Scottish site had a disastrous manufacturing problem, a Japanese would come over. Recently, they have had an engineering design problem in the printers section and quality people came over from Japan. They stayed for three days to sort things out.

What has been brought from overseas is mainly knowledge. When the watch manufacturing was set up there were no processes in existence. Twenty four employees were sent over to Japan to learn how to operate the equipment. They came back and eventually increased the number of people in the area and developed their own systems. The senior manufacturing engineer goes to Japan for training and looking at business opportunities, and to Singapore for transfer of production lines and further training. Generally, no one goes over to Japan to train, although things are changing—they are becoming more interested in what Scotland is doing with regard to technical processes. Scotland has taken Japanese ideas and is now running some of their machines more efficiently.

Training Differences between Japan and Scotland

In Scotland, the company encourages people to develop at operator level, both in-house and in colleges and other educational establishments, and finances their further education.

In Japan, because employees remain in the company a long time, they have large, established internal training and recognised formal qualifications. They have extensive support resources, for example, engineering and technical support. Rank-and-file employees do not go to college or university, because they are not available to everyone at the company's expense, but sometimes managers do attend short courses in these establishments. However, the company will pay up to 50 per cent of the cost of out-sourced English classes if employees wish to learn the language.

Team Working

The subsidiary management has introduced the Japanese way of teamworking. The local managers know the Japanese practices such as total quality management and quality circles, and use them in a modified way. The management does not push Japanese quality initiatives; they are happy for the employees to apply the tools they prefer. Also, in Japan, they run quality circles after working hours on a voluntary non-paid basis but the Scottish managers would not be able to implement them here because the operators would want to be paid overtime. In addition, the managers believe that such practices as twice daily exercises in the office, customary in the Japanese sites, would not work here 'because the company is not a school or army'.

Consensual Decision Making

The GM's observation from working in Seiko plants in Japan is that Japanese style consenual decision making offers unsatisfactory compromises. He says decisions take more time to be made. Also, if junior Japanese managers are involved they will not speak their mind because they feel inhibited, for cultural and traditional reasons. In the Scottish site, employees are more frank.

'I would imagine that having worked here for a number of years our boss probably prefers what he may have initially interpreted as a fairly antagonistic discourse—it's a bit more stimulating and actually more things are aired and moved forward.'

Pay and Benefits

These are decided locally. There is considerable competition for skilled local staff. Seiko in Livingston competes against the likes of Motorola and Sky for employees. Consequently, their pay is competitive, with rewards for hard work. They also offer paternity leave, pensions, life assurance and sick pay.

Industrial Relations

The Scottish site is not unionised, but the Japanese sites have company-based unions. Moreover, in Scotland there are grievance procedures in place to enable the employees to file claims against their boss, but such a system does not exist in the Japanese sites. Senior managers believe that the history of local trade unions still make the employees suspicious of management, even today. The management has to work harder to gain trust and get people to buy in and get them to come up with ideas and work on problems themselves.

In Scotland, they make employees redundant if they have to. In Japan, Seiko does not do this. The company offers jobs for life, and if need be, transfers employees to holding divisions rather than make them redundant.

Questions

Q.1. Why has the parent company adopted an HRM strategy which would allow overseas subsidiaries to perform their personnel function autonomously?

Q.2. In what respect is the Scottish subsidiary's recruitment policy different from its Japanese parent company, and why?

Q.3. Why has the local management team decided not to implement some of the Japanese parent company's practices in Scotland?

Q.4. In what ways have the local environment enabled the subsidiary to act locally as they see fit and thereby go against the HQ's current HR policies?

16 International Mergers and Acquisitions-HR Perspective

Learning Objectives

After studying this chapter you will learn:

- The reasons for the spate of M&As.
- The reasons for failure of M&As.
- The stages involved in M&As.
- The HRM issues involved in successful implementation of M&As.
- The stages in the successful completion of M&A activity.
- The cross-cultural issues in cross-border M&As.
- Corporate examples of M&As.

INTRODUCTION

In today's globalised economy, mergers and acquisitions (M&As) have become the preferred strategy for organizational growth and survival. Organizations today compete on the basis of their supply-chain. M&As are the means by which firms enhance their control and market power on the supply-chain through backward and forward integration. M&As are also used for related and conglomerate diversification.

The increasingly volatile global business environment poses a threat to the existing business organizations' survival and success. Mergers and Acquisitions are evolving as the most effective and innovative strategies to consolidate and strengthen their positions to grow in this hyper competition and challenging scenario.

Subodh Verma in *TOI* Headlines (4 March 07) reports that 'over $ 3.8 trillion worth of deals were struck, according to Thomson Financial'. This represents a 38 per cent increase over the previous year. Nearly 37,000 deals were hammered out globally in 2006, of which 157 were hostile takeovers, worth just under $ 500 billion. Joint ventures, strategic alliances and other modes of market entry also raise similar people-related cross-cultural issues.

The saga of mergers and acquisitions is replete with many instances of success and failure. Many of them encounter massive obstacles in the path of reaching stated outcomes. There are many reasons for this but the main reason is poor integration of culture, selection of target company and the price and strategies of the firms involved.

Some mega mergers are Hewlett Packard-Compaq; Daimler-Chrysler; Chase-JP Morgan; McKinsey-Envision; UBS-Pain Webber; SKB-Glaxo; Nations Bank-Bank of America; Nestle-Purina; GE-Honeywell; Deutsche-Telecom-Voice Stream; AOL-Times Warner and Barclays and ABN Amro Bank.

India is emerging at the top as a vibrant player in the world of mergers and acquisitions. Be it Mittal's acquisition of Arcelor or Tata's acquisition of Corus, the list is endless. In this chapter we will study M&As and what international companies should do to be successful. This strategy of international expansion and growth is being increasingly adopted by most organisations across the globe supported by financial institutions and banks.

Why M&As? Reasons

There may be seven reasons that drive M&As. These are as under:

1. Accessing new markets.
2. Maintaining growth momentum.
3. Acquiring visibility and international brands.
4. Buying cutting-edge technology rather than importing it or building it.
5. Developing new product mixes.
6. Improving operating margins and efficiencies and taking on global competition.
7. Consolidation of markets, players and production capacities.

UNCTAD's *WIR 2006* pointed out four factors that drive developing nations to go global. They are:

First, it helps market penetration. MNCs looking for niche markets—such as IT services and pharmaceutical products—gained substantially through outbound investments.

Second, rising labour costs at home push MNCs abroad.

Third, competitive pressures in the domestic economy force MNCs to invest abroad.

Fourth, home government policies of liberalizations stimulate outbound investments.

In 1990, only six developing and transition countries had made any outward investments. In 2005, the number had increased to 25 and the share of global M&As by MNCs from developing and transition countries rose from 4 per cent to 13 per cent in value terms and the share in greenfield and expansion projects exceeded 15 per cent in 2005.

STAGES INVOLVED IN M&As

M&A activity can be classified into the following stages:

1. Pre-deal Stage. It involves identification of reasons, priorities, compatible companies with similar views and business philosophies. This involves critical evaluation of internal resources including competencies and identification of resources and competencies required to achieve the mission and objectives of the company. It also involves identification of possible consultants and bankers whose services will be useful.
2. Due Diligence Stage. It involves identification of reasons, priorities. All cultural, financial, legal and other issues related to M&A are analysed so that the deal makes win-win sense from strategic, economic and implementation perspectives.
3. Compliances. Prior consultation and compliances of governmental approvals, competition law, SEBI and other institutions is obtained.
4. Proper Integration. This stage calls for preparation of a comprehensive work plan to integrate various functions and units to obtain synergies.
5. Implementation. This stage calls for final concretization of idea into action which requires serious involvement of senior management to maintain business continuity and momentum.
6. Post Deal. After the implementation of M&A, the senior management needs to address some key issues that may result in serious problems if not handled carefully, such as stockholders' concerns, transparent communication, identification of core competencies, etc. Thus the post deal stage should be professionally managed.

The motive behind discussing these stages involved in M&As has a serious implication upon the success and failure of any such activity. Also, it helps to understand better whether the business in a merger makes strategic sense holistically as experience has shown that many mergers failed not due to poor integration but because of poor conception of how the mergers fit the strategy of the firms involved. Further, each stage requires different types of expertise and leadership to handle it.

WHY DO M&As FAIL?

As per the research done by The Bureau of Business Research at the American International College, 1996, many obstacles and drawbacks lead to failure of M&As. These are as follows:

- Inability to manage targets and effectively implement change.
- Objective not well understood.
- Overestimated synergies.
- Excessive premium for acquisitions: A problem in many cases has been the unrealistically high price paid for the acquisition. It may be due to deficiencies in the valuation.

Further the valuations are often based on certain assumptions, which may not hold true. Bidding high to win over competitive bidders also sometimes causes unrealistic prices.

- Incompatible cultures.
- Poor integration strategies.
- Lack of strategic sense.
- Loss of key talent.
- Inability to maintain financial performance.
- A clash of management styles or egos.
- Means of financing: financing takeovers by debt may create problems. What landed many companies in trouble is the acquisition leveraged by high cost junk bonds.
- Hidden Liabilities: These are like product injury liability for hazardous products, expenses for pollution abatement, etc.

HR Issues in M&As

When financial and performance results of merger and acquisition activity fall short of plans, the reason usually rests with people management systems rather than operational or financial systems. Human Resource Management processes play a key role at different stages of mergers like pre-merger assessment of human capital, organizational culture, organizational processes and structure. These factors, in turn, are influenced by national cultures. Hence study and research is needed how best the cultures of two companies can be best integrated to obtain the required synergy.

Similarly in the second stage of combining two companies into one unit with one structure there is need for assessing the competency profile of executives from different cultural backgrounds for staffing various positions according to the proposed organization structure. Training modules are required to be specially designed, which are culture-conditioned.

In stage three, it is necessary to integrate two diverse organization cultures into one homogenous strong culture so as to remove 'they and us' thinking in carrying out roles, responsibilities and decisions in groups and teams. The cross-cultural dimensions that can be used in the process are those of Hofstede and Andre Laurant and others. Greater focus is given to studying the influence of national cultures on the organization culture and design of HR processes and organization structure, which is an essential activity in every merger or acquisition. Needless to say, effective communication contributes immensely to a successful merger which is again very much conditioned by the cross-cultural aspect.

The Influence of National Cultures

M&As and JVs give rise to new organizations that bring together individuals and groups from different national and organizational cultures. In the process, as Andre Laurent (1986) puts it, 'unprecedented cross-cultural puzzles get created that may result in the most confusing disasters or lead to highly creative synergies'.

There are important people-related issues in the areas of exercising control, structure design, implementation of corporate strategy, human resource policies, facilitation of knowledge management across the network, corporate culture change, management of diversity and integration of diverse cultures for successful mergers, acquisitions and joint ventures that need to be addressed from the cross-cultural perspective.

In the case of MNCs, there is need to address the fit of corporate culture with the different national cultures of their subsidiaries to assure strategy implementation, particularly HRM strategy.

Corporate culture in part is managed through HRM practices (Evans, 1986). Some of these practices, however, may not be appropriate given the beliefs, values and norms of the national culture wherein the subsidiary is embedded. Further, the HRM practices of one company evolved in one culture may not be effective in another culture as brought out by Mendonca, Kanungo & Aycan (1999).

Problems arise in transferring corporate culture through these practices in an effort to achieve synergy and congruence of individuals with the organizational vision, mission and goals across diverse national cultures.

This is because the objectives of two entities are different in seeking merger, acquisition or joint venture partnership.

Cross-Culture and HR Processes

In the above mentioned business areas, for successful implementation, MNCs can choose from a menu of HR practices that concern planning, selection, staffing, appraising, compensating, and socialization. Within the menu there are several options which need to be in line with the overall corporate strategy and culture. There is also need to take into account differences in the national cultures where they are to be implemented. Some examples are given here:

Planning, Staffing and Selection

Planning can be considered along several dimensions such as formal/informal; and long-term/short-term. Career management systems represent formal, long-term human resource planning. These systems are inappropriate in cultures where man's control over nature/future is considered minimal, for instance, Islamic belief, 'Inshallah' (God willing).

Some career management systems assume that people can be evaluated, that their abilities, skills, and traits—their net-worth to the company—can be quantified and fed into computers. Derr (1987) found that the French used highly complex and sophisticated computerized systems. This may reflect a humanistic vs. engineering approach or social vs. task orientation. Some companies assume that databanks can be created of specific skills and matched to 'jobs'. Olivetti, on the other hand, says 'potential not skills is most important'. IBM says it hires for careers, not jobs. In Japan, job descriptions are left vague and flexible to fit uncertainty and strengthen the bond between the individual and company. In the USA and France job descriptions are detailed so as to reduce uncertainty and permit more job mobility.

Skills Importance

In France and Germany, mathematics and science diplomas have status and engineering is the preferred course for advanced studies. This system encourages narrowly focused specialists which makes functional mobility more difficult. In the USA and UK, psychology and human relations is valued and more generalists are preferred. Knife-and-fork tests, assessments of table manners and conversation skills as well as personal appearances are considered to be more important criteria for selection in the UK.

Performance Appraisal

In cultures where 'Doing' rather than 'Being' is the norm, the evaluation system is based on the belief that past performance reflects future performance, while in other cultures 'who you are' (character, loyalty, integrity) is more important. Similarly, geographic mobility is culture-related. Europeans are more internationally oriented than Americans as they stay longer abroad and expatriate failure rate is higher with US multinationals compared to European multinationals, and is least in Japanese companies because of adjustment capabilities (Tung, 1987).

In this regard, two examples serve to support the point. First, in Western cultures, it may be appropriate for feedback during a performance appraisal review to be in confrontational mode; but such a mode would be inappropriate in non-Western cultures where face-saving is regarded as more important than learning from the appraisal review. Second, job autonomy is a highly valued non-economic reward in Western societies, but this is not necessarily the case in non-Western societies where rewards that satisfy the social and security needs are valued more.

Problems with transfer of MBO to other cultures have been discussed in detail by Hofstede, 1980; Laurent, 1983 and Trepo, 1973. Tying performance to rewards is also suspect in some cultures while it is logical in others. In one MNC's Danish subsidiaries, a proposal for bonus to sales people was turned down because it favoured specific groups, that is, it ran counter to their egalitarian culture. Needless to say that HR practices are highly culture sensitive.

Three Stages of Mergers and Acquisitions

The experiences of companies in merger and acquisition suggest a model of M&A activity which has three stages:

1. pre-combination;
2. combination—integration of the partners; and
3. solidification and advancement.

These stages are also applicable in the management of joint ventures and strategic alliances.

Stage 1—Pre-combination

There are several human resource issues in the first stage of the M&A, activity. In the Pre-combination stage the most significant HR issues and their specific implications are illustrated in Table 16.1:

TABLE 16.1
Stage I: Pre-Combination

Issues	HR Implications and Measures
• Identifying reasons for M&A • Forming M&A Team/Leader • Searching for potential partners/target • Selecting a partner/target • Planning to manage the process of M&A • Learning from the process • Competency mapping of both acquirer and target organizations	• Knowledge and understanding need to be disseminated, competencies needed for growth to be outlined and explored. • Proper leadership needs to be in place, which is strategic and understands the organization environment and stakeholder inter phase • Composition of cross functional top level team which is able to analyse large amount of data and take decisions • Systematic and extensive search and proper selection is important, with clear goals in sight • Conducting thorough due diligence is vital • Training and experience in audit of all kinds vital • Cultural assessment • Planning for combination to minimise problems later

As highlighted in the table, an important HR issue in the Pre-combination stage of any M&A activity is identifying the reasons to initiate the activity. Of the many possible reasons for an M&A, a substantial number are human resource related, for example, acquisition of key competencies or talent. At companies like Cisco and GE, retention of key talent is often the number one concern. Here the M&A is announced because a major reason for the combination is to obtain that talent which is needed to enter a new market or to introduce a new product in an existing market or to develop a new product or to master a new technology.

In carrying out due process for identifying reasons, the period for which financial and economic analysis is to be done is influenced by national cultures. Japanese companies take a much longer perspective as compared to US companies. The latter are guided mostly by hard economic logic and external environmental analysis while their counterparts in eastern cultures focus more on internal dimensions and place more value on gaining reputation or building an image disproportionate to its economic logic. For example, in the Mittal-Arcelor case, winning had become more important for L. N. Mittal and many economists and financial experts had commented that the deal is over-priced.

Another important HR issue is the creation of a dedicated senior executive, such as Michael Vulpine at Cisco, as the Integration Manager, and a team to head the M&A process. As suggested earlier, a key reason for M&A failure is the lack of a capable leader who can focus completely on all the aspects of the M&A process, one of which is seeking out potential companies to merge with or acquire. If cost of cultural integration and culture distance are not built into the decision-model, the choice may not be right. It is not easy to assess such costs accurately but one should be more conservative in case of wide culture distance of countries and companies involved.

Then, after the identification of potential companies, comes the selection of the CEO. From which cultural background to choose? Regardless of how well the two other stages may be planned for and implemented, selection of the wrong partner and leader is likely to diminish the possible success of the combination. Alternatively, selection of the right partner and leader, without a well thought-out plan for managing the rest of the M&A process is also likely to diminish the possible success of the combination.

An immediate HR implication of this last HR issue is that firms that have a better understanding and knowledge base of the M&A process are likely to be more successful in their M&A initiative. This understanding and this knowledge base, however, have to be shared and disseminated to have maximum impact because M&A activity is likely to affect everyone in the company, particularly if the combination results in extensive integration of the two companies. A dedicated and skilled leader with a cross-functional team for M&A activities is likely to be best served through the use of a variety of HR practices in accord with the national culture to suit the beliefs, values and norms of merged entity.

Stage 2—Combination and Integration of Companies

For Stage 2 to be effective, it is important that planning for the integration activities is skilfully prepared in Stage 1 itself. Lack of integration planning is the main reason for 80 per cent of the M&As that have under-performed. It is suggested that Kurt Levin's ideas can be effectively used to identify the forces that are resisting the change and forces that are helping the change to fructify. Use of Ralph Kilman's ideas (*Managing Beyond the Quick Fix*) about total system change through five critical leverage points can also be very effective. Kilman's five tracks are:

1. the culture track;
2. the management skill track;
3. the team building tract;
4. the strategy-structure track; and
5. the reward system track.

Based upon a study of several cases and research of M&A processes, it is suggested:

1. A systematic, explicit integration planned process is at the heart of a successful acquisition.
2. All acquisitions require some degree of integration in both the area of day-to-day systems and processes in achieving key synergies.

TABLE 16.2
Integration of Companies

HR Issues	HR Implications and Actions
• Selecting an Integration Manager • Designing the composite structure for synergy and performance • Competency mapping for strengthening core competency • Instituting training and development strategies • Retaining key employees through compensation design • Motivating the employees through performance linked reward system • Managing the change • Communicating with and involving the stakeholders • Deciding HR policies and practices in an integrated framework	• Selecting the appropriate candidates based on past performance records and new challenges through a transparent system • Creating teams for rationalising major HR policies, like compensation grades, leave rules, perquisites, performance standards, etc., are critical for the transition success • Communicating the above is essential • Deciding on who stays and who leaves • Establishing a new culture, structure and HR policies is essential • Managing increased diversity

3. It is important to tailor what is integrated and how it is done to the specific strengths and weaknesses of the acquired company.
4. Integration processes and priorities will differ depending on the company's characteristics.
5. Maintaining the ability to focus on the few key value drivers is a critical part of the integration process.

Structure and Cross-culture

Perhaps the most critical HR issue for the success at this integration stage is to design and implement a new organization structure including various work processes. In this exercise some cross-cultural dimensions of Gert Hofstede (1987) are quite relevant. In countries with greater power-distance, the structure should have more levels and shorter span as status is more valued and communication is mostly formal. In cultures with low-power distance, the structure should be flatter and individuals provided more autonomy. Communication in such countries is informal and explicit.

Similarly, in collectivist cultures like Japan, work units in groups are more effective with group goals and rewards, while in individualist cultures, they should be individual based. Role and job clarity should be made more specific in high-power distance and high uncertainty avoidance cultures.

Trompenaars & Hampden Turner in their work *Riding the Waves of Culture* (1998); (pub. Nicholas Brealey), have divided the organization cultures in the context of national cultures, which vary considerably in how people think, how they change, and how they motivate, reward and resolve conflicts. These four types are

1. the Family,
2. the Eiffel Tower,
3. the Guided Missile, and
4. the Incubator.

They have placed countries and organization cultures most prevalent in them into a grid which has two axes represented by egalitarian and hierarchical; person and task. Japanese companies have a family type organization culture, Western firms are well structured with roles and responsibilities, Eiffel Tower type professional bodies and consultancy organizations have the Guided Missile type organization culture which is highly task oriented and small organizations have an Incubator type where individuals are most important and every thing is built around them. They conclude:

> We have defined four broad types of corporate culture, which are closely related to the national differences.... Just as national cultures conflict, leading to mutual comprehension and mistrust, so corporate cultures collide. Attempts to 'dice' the family with a matrix can cause rage and consternation. Getting cozy with subordinates in the Eiffel Tower could be seen as a potentially improper advance. Asking to be put in a group with a special friend is a subversive act in the Guided Missile culture. Calling your boss 'buddy' and slapping him or her on the back will get you down from the Eiffel Tower, while suggesting in an Incubator that everyone fill out time-sheets will be greeted with catcalls.

Hence cultural sensitivity is required in carrying out cultural integration and restructuring. It is also recommended that if cultures are so extreme then the two companies should rather function as separate units and integration be attempted gradually, starting from the top level and only in key functions.

It is again suggested that a team of experienced top level persons with cross-cultural sensitivity is formed under an expert leader for reorganization and re-structuring.

The Role and Traits of the Integration Manager

The integration manager performs these roles to manage change:

1. Sorts out a plan for combining the operations of two companies, so that the integration meets its deadlines and performance targets.
2. Educates the new people about the parent company and *vice-versa.*

3. Forges the social connections between the two organizations.
4. Often acts like a lightning rod for many people's emotions. At the time of merger or an acquisition, employees often want to make sure that things are being done in a right way. So the IM checks that people are satisfied and are not hurt.
5. The IM speeds up the organization through the two important phases of merger and acquisition—first, the time between the deal's announcement and its close and secondly, the starting 100 days after the close.
6. Finally, the IM is responsible to orchestrate tangible success rapidly that could not have been achieved before the companies came together. Such success generally achieved within the first 100 days not only starts to pay for the deal but also builds confidence in the minds of managers and staff that the 'change' makes sense.

Traits of the Integration Manager

1. Deep knowledge of the acquiring/merging company.
2. No desire for credit.
3. Comfortable with chaos.
4. Emotional and cultural intelligence.

Assisting the integration manager are integration teams (Marks & Mirvis, 2000). DaimlerChrysler created over 100 integration teams. Specific teams were assigned to various functional areas and organizational levels within the two companies. Johnson & Johnson found that integration teams should be first focused on key priorities or value drivers:

1. One of the first steps in the integration planning process that happens between signing and closing is to better identify those few key value drivers that will significantly impact the performance of the new acquisition.
2. Recognize that there will be a number of day-to-day systems and processes that must be integrated in order to support efforts to attain synergies. Examples are sales reporting systems, certain IT systems, access to the global e-mail network and the distribution chain.
3. It is important to limit these activities to areas that are required to support the achievement of key synergies.
4. One J&J executive has stated: 'We only attacked things that would bring benefits to the business. We did not integrate just for the sake of integrating'.
5. Once these key areas are identified, it may help to make sure that each one of these value drivers has a team of people associated with it and those teams are tracked for their progress.

The other critical HR issue is the selection of a leader who will actually manage the new business combination. At the lower end of the organization the person should be, as far as possible, from the same culture but at the top end the individual should be selected entirely on merit from any of the organizations or even from outside.

If the business has unclear or absent leadership at different levels, the result will be crippling uncertainty, lack of direction, stalled new product development and the postponement of important decisions. Strong leadership is essential to acquisition success— perhaps the single most important success factor. A strong leader's influence will be quickly recognized and felt. The integration process, restructuring and change management activities involve staff selection, training. performance appraisal, compensation and communication HR processes which require cross-cultural consideration.

The other important HR issue is the need to create policies and practices for learning and knowledge sharing and transfer. Forums for information sharing and creation of Intranet are tools amongst others that companies can use to facilitate the sharing of knowledge. HR policies and practices that appraise and reward employee sharing, flexibility, development and long-term orientation are incorporated.

Overall, this second stage of integration in an M&A activity is extensive and complex. Whereas Stage 1 activities set the scene for M&A activity, those in Stage 2 are the ones that make the activity come to life. Clearly there are differences here between a merger and an acquisition, differences between a merger of equals and non-equals, and differences between an acquisition with inclusion and an acquisition with separation including industry types.

Stage 3—Solidification of Culture of the New Entity

Particularly for a merger of equals with high levels of inclusion and in the case of joint ventures, usually a new entity is created. As the new combination takes shape, it faces issues of readjusting, conflict resolution, solidifying and fine-tuning. These issues take on varying degrees of intensity, although not importance, depending upon whether it is a merger of inclusion rather

TABLE 16.3
Solidification and Assessment

HR Issues	HR Implications and Actions
• Leadership and high managerial qualities • Assessing new strategies and structures • Setting up shared vision and customer focused new culture • Assessing new HR policies and practices for flexibility and investment orientation • Leveraging teams • Learning from the process	• At this stage leadership styles needed are different. The focus is on retention of key people and redressal of grievances of many • Time for rationalization of manpower and focus on efficiency in every thing • Blending two cultures needs large scale visioning exercises • Training, compensation and performance management to focus on harmonizing grades, team-based rewards and orientation

than one of separation or an acquisition of relative equals versus unequals. DaimlerChrysler, an acquisition of relative equals, provides an example. DaimlerChrysler went through this for more than two years after the formal combination was completed.

At the beginning of 2001, Dieter Zetsche, a veteran Daimler executive took over Chrysler's leadership, replacing a former Chrysler head, James Holden. Zetsche in turn had created his own top management team composed of one Daimler veteran and five Chrysler veterans. All these changes were made because the earlier top management team of former Chrysler veterans failed in its efforts to stop the 'breathtakingly' fast decline of the bottom line. Similarly, the strategy and structure had to be assessed and revised. The new top management was given more control over the Chrysler Group largely because a senior Daimler executive was running it. He and his team developed a new strategy of cost cutting by reducing supplier costs and reducing product offerings. Instead of running the Chrysler Group as a cash-rich growth business, management managed it as a turnaround. Consequently, staff was reduced and the culture was also changed to reflect the new strategy and the new leadership. Zetsche and his team being much more egalitarian reshaped the culture and structure with focus on performance appraisal and compulsion to cut costs, improve supplier management, increase flexibility and enhance employee morale.

The issues of human resource management and cross-culture are being seen as major ones by the Tata group which recently acquired steel major Corus, as shown below.

TATA'S ACQUISITION OF CORUS

Tatas Hope to Bridge Cultural Divide to Win Over Corus Workers

Soon after Tata Steel announced its acquisition of Corus at a packed press conference, its Managing Director B. Muthuraman talked about other pressing issues to be handled, as described by L. N. Mittal, chairman of Arcelor Mittal, the world's largest steel company: 'The biggest challenge ahead of the Tatas would be how to integrate these two companies, these two cultures, how to work with a new type of management and how to work in a matured market as opposed to working in a developing market.'

'Work on those fronts started last year', he says. That was when, in anticipation of the acquisition, Muthuraman started to meet key people from Corus worker unions in both the UK and Netherlands. But it is work-in-progress. Now that the acquisition has actually happened, the unions want to know if the new bosses will implement job cuts. 'Any change involves a certain amount of apprehension', he says. 'One of the most important jobs of leadership is to clarify such apprehensions and that is what we will be doing from now,' he added.

'It is important for us to get the respect of people, get the motivation levels high, to make every single employee in the Corus organization understand the strength of this partnership. We will make them comfortable that their livelihood will be safe with us,' says the man who had spent 30 years in the steel business. He has invited key union members at Corus from UK to India to visit Jamshedpur. 'They can see our practices first hand and experience how we deal with our people here. That will give them the much needed comfort level. We are not in the acquirer mode, we don't go around asking for bigger rooms. We don't throw our weight around. That is not the Tata style,' he says.

As far as cultural barriers are concerned, conflicts usually come to the fore in cross border mergers and acquisitions. L. N. Mittal had to face it when his bid got mired in an ugly battle that drew in even governments in the EU and India. But Muthuraman thinks that Tatas have it in them to handle these differences.

'Tata group companies have handled Korean, Malaysian, Chinese, Singaporean, Thai and English cultures so far. One of the most important things of handling people from other cultures is to be sensitive about what they believe in, how they behave and how they react to situations,' he says.

'We respect them for what they are doing and we want to learn from them just like they need to learn from us. You can't nurse a superiority syndrome. It is the merger of two entities which will result in 1 + 1 = 3 or 4 rather than 2,' added Muthuraman.

Acquisition Strategy of GE Capital

GE Capital uses a successful model called 'pathfinder' for acquiring firms. The model distinguishes the process of M&A into four categories, which are further divided into subcategories. The four stages incorporate some of the best practices for optimum results. The pre-acquisition phase of the model involves due diligence, negotiations and closing of deals. This involves the cultural assessments, devising communication strategies and evaluation of strengths and weaknesses of business leaders.

An integration manager is also chosen at this stage. The second phase is the foundation building. At this phase the integration plan is prepared. A team of executives from GE Capital and the acquiring company is formed. Also a 100-day communication strategy is evolved, the senior management involvement and support made clear.

The needed resources are pooled and accountability is ensured. The third is the integrating phase. Here the actual implementation and correction measures are taken. Processes like assessing the workflow, assignment of roles, etc., are done at this stage. This last phase involves continuous feedbacks and making necessary corrections in the implementation. The last phase involves the assimilation process where integration efforts are reassessed.

The stage involves long term adjustment and looking for avenues for improving the integration. This is also the period when the organization actually starts reaping the benefits of acquisition. The model is dynamic in the sense that the company constantly improves it through internal discussions between the teams that share their experience, effective tools and refine best practices.

(*Source:* Ashkensas, R. N., DeMonaco, L. J. and Francis, S. C. (1998). 'Making the Deal Real: How GE Capital Integrates Acquisitions.' *Harvard Business Review*, Jan/Feb. 1998, Vol. 76, Issue 1, p. 165).

Acquisition Strategy of Cisco

The acquisition strategy of Cisco is an excellent example of how thorough planning can help in successful acquisitions. After experiencing some failures in acquiring companies, Cisco devised a three-step process of acquisition.

This involved analyzing the benefits of acquiring, understanding how the two organizations will fit together—how the employees from the organization can match with the Cisco culture and then the integration process. In the evaluation process, Cisco considered whether there is compatibility in terms of long-term goals, work culture, geographical proximity, etc.

For example, Cisco believes in an organization culture which is risk-taking and adventurous. If this is lacking in the working style of the target company, Cisco is not convinced about the acquisition. No forced acquisitions are done. And the critical element is in convincing the various stakeholders of the target company about the future benefits. The company insists on no layoffs and job security is guaranteed to all the employees of the acquired company. The acquisition team of Cisco evaluates the working style of the management of the target company, the calibre of the employees, the technology system and the relationship style of the company. Once the acquisition team is convinced, an integration strategy is rolled out.

A top level integration team visits the target company and gives clear-cut information regarding Cisco and future roles of the employees of the acquired firm. After the acquisition, employees of the acquired firm are given 30 days orientation training to fit into the new organizational environment. The planned process of communication and integration has resulted in a high rate of success in acquisitions for Cisco.

(*Source*: ICFAI Centre for Management Research, 'Cisco's acquisition strategy').

Conclusion

As Eric Bouden & Greg Smith have rightly noted, blending organization cultures is an unnatural act—like splicing genes—yet newly merged companies must act quickly to shape the evolving culture into a joint asset. Otherwise they risk creating a nagging and compounding liability. The real HR challenge is how to bring about this change. In this respect, the ideas of John Kotter about bringing about change are significant as brought out in his landmark article in *HBR*, 'Organization Performance and Culture.'

Questions and Assignment

Q.1. Explain the reasons for increase in M&A activity across the world. List the activities that generate synergy between merging entities.

Q.2. Explain the important steps involved in M&As and the role of a leader leading the merger.

Q.3. What are important HR issues involved in different stages of M&As?

Q.4. In what ways do national differences in culture influence cross-border mergers?

Assignment

Organise a structured interview process of people at different levels during and after the merger to find out the impact of anxiety levels on work performance and morale and suggest the steps the management could have additionally taken.

CASE

To Partner or Acquire?

Cross-border alliances between companies are a fact of modern business. Such alliances are particularly relevant today because the ability to create and sustain global collaborations is vital for companies to compete and be profitable. Two commonly recognized forms of collaborations are joint ventures (JV) and acquisitions.

In India a JV is generally understood as a technical and/or financial collaboration between two existing companies to form a third one in which both the firms hold agreed positions in share capital. An acquisition, on the other hand, is a complete takeover of a company either through a purchase of shares, assets of the entire business.

As JVs and acquisitions differ greatly in their utility, one of the most important decisions for any company is whether or not a JV will be best suited to achieve its corporate goals, as opposed to an acquisition or simple organic growth. A company that needs international technology which has not been implemented in India can consider creating a JV with a foreign company that has such technology. On the other hand, an acquisition may be better for a company that seeks to gain market share or an exclusive distribution channel. Structurally, a JV offers significant contractual support in respect of coordination and cooperation with a partner and at the same time, alleviates the integration challenges presented by an acquisition. Instances when a JV is preferred to an acquisition are:

1. **When the assets are difficult to separate.** Assuming that a company manufactures two different products from one factory, if an acquirer wants to buy out such a company, it will be saddled with assets that it does not need. Therefore, if a JV is arranged , the required assets can be structured to flow into the JV company without the other undesired assets.
2. **When a full acquisition will increase the management costs.** In a corporate acquisition, the buyer acquires an existing corps of employees having their own routine and culture. Integrating such employees is difficult.
3. **When valuation is difficult**. A JV is an effective and easy solution when the valuation of the target company is difficult.
4. **When the legal or regulatory constraints make an acquisition difficult.** Generally JVs have lesser regulatory constraints and are easier to put in place.

Assuming that a JV is the preferred mode of alliance, one issue that must be dealt with at the contracting stage is control and management of the JV company. The shareholders' agreement can prescribe the number of directors on the board, the quorum for the meetings, the mode of day-to-day management, the procedure to be followed on the bankruptcy of a JV partner, etc. To prevent a deadlock, the chairman of directors can be given a casting vote.

Protecting confidential information is very important in JVs. For this a confidentiality and non-disclosure agreement must be entered into prior to commencing negotiations. Relevant clauses must also be included in the shareholders' agreement. Indian courts enforce such agreements and grant injunctions on adequate proof of breach or proposed breach.

In many instances, companies route their investments into an Indian JV company through an offshore tax jurisdiction. India has double taxation avoidance treaties (DTAA) with many countries. Many foreign companies route their investments through Mauritius because under the Indian-Mauritius DTAA, a Mauritius resident does not pay any capital gains tax on a transfer of shares of an Indian company. On the flip side, a JV is also susceptible to various hazards such as misappropriation of knowledge, hold-up by the JV partner, etc., which may make an acquisition more attractive.

Structuring an acquisition so as to optimize tax on operational benefits is extremely important. For example, amalgamating two companies by following the procedure under the Companies Act, 1956, can save capital gains tax that otherwise may be applicable on an asset or share acquisition deal. However, the court procedure can be long drawn and requires compliance of a number of procedural formalities. Likewise, although a share purchase transaction can be completed fairly quickly, it requires a much higher level of due diligence on the part of the company because, effectively, the buyer of the shares becomes the owner of the company and inherits all its liabilities also. As such, no compromise should be made on due diligence, and it is imperative to require the seller to resolve all company compliance matters before closing. An asset purchase transaction attracts capital gains tax and VAT on the assets, and is usually the easiest to close.

An acquisition of a listed company can trigger the Securities Exchange Board of India Regulations, 1997 (The Takeover Regulation), as amended from time to time. If this occurs, the takeover regulations have to be followed, and an open offer has to be at least 20 per cent of a target company's existing shareholders. In a buoyant stock market, it can sometimes be difficult to successfully close an open offer. Further, in cross-border acquisitions, it is important to comply with the government's foreign investment regulations. Various industry sectors in India such as telecommunication, banking, insurance, aviation, defence, etc., have restrictions on foreign investment, and compliance of sectoral caps and sector-specific guidelines is imperative. The Vodafone–Hutchison deal is a classic example. It is better that prior approval of government is taken right at the beginning otherwise the foreign investor runs a high risk of post-closing scrutiny.

On the anvil is a Competition Law, similar to the Hart-Scott-Rodino Act in the USA and the EU competition legislation. Once notified, most mega mergers that have an adverse effect on competition or cross a certain turnover threshold in India or abroad will have to be reported to the Competition Commissioner (CC). The CC will have to assess the impact of the merger on competition and public interest in India, and will have the authority to either approve or disapprove it.

Therefore, the decision between a JV and an acquisition should be an informed one based on objective business criteria.

Source: *Economic Times*. Managing Partner, Majumdar & Co.

17

E-HRM

Learning Objectives

After studying this chapter you will be able to understand:

- The concept of Human Resource Information System (HRIS)
- Difference between E-HRM and HRIS
- Goals of E-HRM
- Types of E-HRM
- E-HRM outcomes
- State of E-HRM in organisations

INTRODUCTION

Technological optimistic voices want us to believe that from a technical perspective, the IT possibilities for HRM are endless: in principle all HR processes can be supported by IT. Words are becoming even more provocative when some say that the question whether HR should become digital already is outdated: HR must become digital! According to Trapp (2001), HR departments are not immune from such trends, in particular nowadays when they are being pressed to prove their added value to business performance. Jäger (2001) believes that HRM will acquire a new dimension with the emergence of e-business. Wright & Dyer (2000) present a similar line of reasoning: e-business is emerging, and therefore HR and HR professionals are faced with the challenge of performing in ways that are in line with the business. In their view 'HR functions [can] become critical partners in driving success, but to do so requires that HR changes its focus, its role, and its delivery systems' (Wright & Dyer, p. 52). According to them, in e-business, the application of intranet technology for HR is inevitable.

HUMAN RESOURCE INFORMATION SYSTEM (HRIS)

HRIS is the system used to acquire, store, manipulate, analyse, retrieve, and distribute pertinent information regarding an organisation's human services and the purpose of HRIS is to provide service, in the form of information, to the users. It is needed because in the USA, government regulatory acts like EEO (equal employment opportunity); OSHA (occupational safety and health administration) and Employee Retirement, Omnibus Budget Reconciliation Act require submission of annual and quarterly reports which is difficult for large corporations without HRIS. In India also companies have to file returns under Factory Act, SC/ST, OBC returns, ESIS data, tax deducted at source, professional tax, etc.

HRIS is therefore basically meant for the effective working of HR departments and primarily used by HR executives. HRIS is necessary because of difficulty in maintaining and the shortcomings of manual record systems. The difficulty here refers to the voluminous data on the employees which is unfeasible to track manually and has to be updated from time to time. Manual records also suffer from high cost, less accuracy, fragmentation, duplication and difficulty of analysis.

C. S. Venkataratnam & B. K. Srivastava (1991) have stated the following basic purposes of HRIS:

- To store information and data for each employee.
- To provide a basis for decision-making in day-to-day personnel issues, that is, grant of leave, as also of planning, budgeting, implementing and monitoring various HR functions.
- Supplying data/returns to government and other public.
- Helping settle employees' dues in time, in respect of PF, Retirement, Gratuity, LTC, Earned Leave Compensation, etc.
- Helping the HR to utilize the time saved to undertake other creative functions.
- Records are correctly maintained and easy to retrieve.

The information system proves useful in the following areas:

- Manpower movement status.
- Manpower position, grade-wise, category-wise, etc.
- Promotion and career planning status.
- Training and development planning status.
- One American study cited: a reduction of one-third in the time taken to process new employees.
- Savings of between 55 to 90 per cent of the time taken to provide the routine information.
- Clerical savings of 600 hours per year in providing data to pay-roll, 800 hours in preparing weekly reports and 500 with improved accuracy.

in Cologne. Perhaps one can speak of a cyber-division at the organizational level. What became clear, related to this aspect, is that institutional aspects of the organizational environment are a complicating factor in global e-HRM initiatives. Two examples from the study can illustrate this. At Belgacom, the publication of personnel information through the HR intranet was complicated by the Belgian law on privacy. At Ford, in Germany, the project team hinted at the wide diversity in the nationalities of employees working for Ford; but at the same time warned us not to ask questions that could be related to the issues of different nationalities, cross-cultural differences, etc. Such issues were considered by the Works Council as sensitive.

Guaranteeing the security and confidentiality of input data is an important issue for employees in order that they should feel 'safe' when using web-based HR tools. Information technology and the like have the image that they make it easy for one to be checked upon and observed by 'invisible third parties'. When implementing online HRM tools and asking employees and line managers to input personal data, the question arises as to who is authorized to look at the data and to use them? If employees do not feel comfortable about the confidentiality of certain types of data, they will be hesitant about inputting such data.

Further, a good e-HRM strategy (that is, where are we heading, and how are we going to get there?) is important. Good and clear goals, and a good plan how to achieve them, cannot be avoided if one is to convince users of the usefulness of online HRM. There is also a danger of information overkill through an HR intranet. Without a clear and easy structure, employees and line managers can be afraid of spending excessive time exploring web-based HR tools. As an example, at IBM, employees and line managers felt that the HR intranet site contained too much information in a form that was difficult to comprehend. Therefore they tended to call the HR call centre (Ask HR) to get answers to their immediate HR-related questions rather than search the HR site. Strikingly, the HR call centre assistants would use the same source, the HR intranet site, to find the answers! Although IBM convincingly reported a reduction in costs, the abovementioned observation might question whether this was really due to e-HRM. IBM had outsourced the HR call centre and this in itself may have reduced costs.

The final observation is that employees and line managers' mindsets need to be changed: they have to realize and accept the usefulness of web-based HR tools. They generally feel that they lack the time and space needed to work quietly and thoughtfully with web-based HR tools and so, if there is no real need, they will not do it. E-HRM can become a new destiny in terms of HRM; in the first place because of the opportunities it creates to put employee-management relationships in the hands of the employees and line managers. In the second place because information technology creates possibilities to design HRM tools and instruments that would not be possible without this information technology. A good example is advanced personal assessment and measurement tools that can be used at any moment of the day, and in any location. Employees really can begin to steer their careers with a click of a mouse. HR professionals have to realize and accept this: it will not go away. It is probable that we won't even need to point this out in a few years time: it will be seen as stating the obvious!

- Manpower movement status.
- Promotion and career planning status.
- Training and development planning status.

HRIS requires the use of codes for grades, staff, categories and designations. It will require use of a single identifier for each employee. It can print letters to staff and job applicants, incremental advice, promotion letters, acknowledgement letters, rejection letters, etc. It creates exception reports like employees whose salary increases are overdue, etc. Manpower utilisation can be accessed. It can be developed to work like DSS to help in formulating strategies, negotiations for which 'average' data is used.

Manpower Planning Module of HRIS

This module provides support to Human Resource Planning in the following ways:

- Matching person and job information.
- Manpower forecasting and planning.
- Future replacements.
- Systematic employee search and placement.
- Eligibility list of promotion-worthy candidates.
- Career planning system: identifies surplus manpower for which growth in some functional areas is not possible.
- Succession planning—identifying key posts becoming vacant due to retirement, promotions, etc.
- Generates surplus and deficit reports level-wise, department-wise due to new technology requirement, redeployment conditions, confidential reports.
- Maintains grievances data bank, personnel anniversaries.
- Industrial disturbance data bank.

A booklet containing information about him can be given to each employee. It would include data such as basic biodata, joining date, qualifications, membership, previous employment details, transfer and deputation details, charge sheets, hospitalization records, loss of pay and training details, particulars of nominees and relatives, details about publication details, joining details, promotion details, unauthorised absence data, leave encashment, details of provident fund deductions, deductions in pay if any, and so on.

The HR department maintains the following computer files:

- Special files on recruitments, type of posts, dates, number of applications on file, data about labour market, schools and colleges.
- Induction programmes, numbers, categories, duration.
- Update on wages, fringe benefits, employer contribution on employees statutory benefits like PF and gratuity.

- Leave data, earned leave, casual leave, sick leave, unauthorised absence category/ division wise.
- Training needs data, workers, supervisors, managers category-wise.
- Data on welfare package, canteen, transportation.
- Housing on company lease, company house allotment details, housing loan deductions.
- Collective bargaining details, working out skill differentials, cost of living escalations, enhanced allowances and cost of total package.
- Appraisal and selection data, HRP file, manpower market analysis, data required for statutory requirements like SC/ST, OBC, handicapped persons, women, etc., e-performance rating analysis, rating profiles.
- Potential appraisal data.

HRIS is useful not only for HR executives but also for top management as it gives them access to the following information:

1. Monthly manning, number of staff according to skills/categories/grade/permanent/ temporary/casual, etc.
2. Actual manning against sanctioned strength.
3. Data on grievances, transfers, promotions, discipline and court cases, accidents.
4. Summary table of wages, welfare ratios.
    - Wages as percentage of sales turnover.
    - Wages as percentage of net profit.
    - Wages as percentage of cost of production.
    - Net output per employee.
    - Training expense per employee.
    - Training and development data, titles of programmes for each level, number of participants and duration.

Differences Between E-HRM and HRIS

There is a fundamental difference between HRIS (human resources information system) and e-HRM in that basically HRIS is directed towards the HR department itself. Users of these systems are mainly HR staff. These types of systems aim to improve the processes within the HR departments itself, albeit in order to improve the service towards the business. With e-HRM, the target group is not the HR staff but people outside this department: the employees and management. HRM services are being offered through an intranet for use by employees. The difference between HRIS and e-HRM can be identified as the switch from the automation of HR services towards technological support of information on HR services. There are authors who write about HRIS, or write from an HRIS perspective, but they cross the divide with e-HRM when they start to develop their ideas. For example, the so-called stage-oriented approaches regarding the relationship between IT and HRM make, at a certain stage, a step over to e-HRM. Technically speaking, it can be said that e-HRM is the technical unlocking of HRIS for all employees of an organization.

e-HRM is a way of implementing HR strategies, policies, and practices in organizations through a conscious and directed support of and/or with the full use of web-technology-based channels. The word 'implementing' in this context has a broad meaning, such as making something work, putting something into practice, or having something realized. E-HRM, therefore, is a concept—a way of 'doing' HRM.

E-HRM Goals

What goals drive stakeholders when deciding about e-HRM? All the reasons mentioned so in professionally-oriented sources are 'confirmed' in a scientific article entitled *Human Resource Management Review* by Lepak & Snell (1998). They refer to the four 'pressures' of virtual HRM. First of all, HRM departments are asked to focus on strategic questions. Secondly, these departments need to be flexible in terms of policymaking and practices. Thirdly, HRM departments should work efficiently and be aware of costs ('...a hard line on costs'). Fourthly, HRM departments should be service-oriented towards management and employees. In short, HRM departments must be strategy-focused, flexible, efficient, and client oriented; and all at the same time (Lepak & Snell, 1998). Ruël *et al.* (2002) highlight an aspect that is fairly well covered by the above but that is nevertheless interesting to spell out, namely the changing nature of the employment relationship. With the supply shortage in the labour market (during the economic upturn of the 1990s), the individualization of society, and the increased educational level of citizens (and thus of employees), the power balance in the employment relationship has shifted in the direction of the employees: they want to steer their own career paths. In the view of Ruël *et al.*, a move towards e-HRM can provide the tools to support this development. This aspect fits into earlier-mentioned drivers such as improving service towards internal clients, but has an external societal drive.

The rapid developments in IT, and in its possibilities for HRM, have even led to new journals and magazines especially focused on the integration of these areas. Based upon the above, we can draw conclusions about the reasons or goals of organizations making steps towards e-HRM. The four 'pressures' from Lepak & Snell (1998) were a good start, but we think that they can be reduced to three types of goals, namely:

1. Improving the strategic orientation of HRM
2. Cost reduction/efficiency gains
3. Client service improvement/facilitating management and employees.

This division of objectives is in line with the conclusion of the annual study on e-HRM in the United States conducted by the consultancy firm of Watson Wyatt. The results from their 2002 study show that companies that had invested in e-HRM, and there were many, were driven by the aim of improving the strategic role of HRM, reducing administrative HR work, and improving employees' satisfaction with HRM services. The three types of goals are essentially the building blocks for the e-HRM research model we will develop.

The goals that drive parties, stakeholders and individuals in organizations will set a framework for the real e-HRM applications and approaches to be implemented. In our view, the 'choice' of possible e-HRM approaches can be reduced to one.

TYPES OF E-HRM

E-HRM is not a specific stage in the development of HRM, but a choice for an approach to HRM. Wright & Dyer (2000) distinguish three areas of HRM where organizations can choose to 'offer' HR services face-to-face or through an electronic means: transactional HRM, traditional HRM, and transformational HRM. Lepak & Snell (1998) make a similar distinction, namely operational HRM, relational HRM and transformational HRM.

The first area, operational HRM, concerns the basic HR activities in the administrative area. One could think of salary administration (payroll) and personnel data administration. The second area, relational HRM, concerns more advanced HRM activities. The emphasis here is not on administering, but on HR tools that support basic business processes such as recruiting and the selection of new personnel, training, performance management and appraisal, and rewards. Transformational HRM, the third area, concerns HRM activities with a strategic character. Here we are talking about activities regarding organizational change processes, strategic re-orientation, strategic competence management and strategic knowledge management.

The areas mentioned could also be considered as types of HRM that can be observed in practice. In some organizations, the HRM emphasis is on administration, in others on the application of operational HRM instruments and in a third group the HRM stress is on its strategic role. Within all the types of HRM, choices can be made in terms of which HRM activities will be offered face-to-face, and which will be offered through web-based HR (e-enabled). This question, for the operational type of HRM, provides the choice between asking employees to keep their own personal data up-to-date through an HR website or to have an administrative force in place to do this.

For relational HRM there is the choice between supporting recruitment and selection through a web-based application or using a paper-based approach (through advertisements, paper-based application forms, letters, etc.). Finally, in terms of transformational HRM, it is possible to create a change-ready workforce through an integrated set of web-based tools that enables the workforce to develop in line with the company's strategic choices or to have paper-based materials.

In cases where an organization consciously and in a focused way chooses to put in place web technology for HRM purposes, based upon the idea that management and employees should play an active role in carrying out HR work, we can speak of e-HRM. With this line of reasoning, three types of e-HRM can be distinguished: Operational e-HRM, Relational e-HRM, and Transformational e-HRM; and these three types are included in our model.

E-HRM OUTCOMES

We assume, based upon Beer *et al.*'s ideas about the expected results or outcomes of HRM, that e-HRM also aims to achieve a certain set of outcomes. As stated earlier, e-HRM is a way of carrying out HRM; it is a way of thinking about and implementing HRM strategies, policies, and practices. By following a specific e-HRM direction, an organization expects to achieve certain goals: an improvement in the HR's strategic orientation, an improvement in client focus and satisfaction, and a decrease in costs or increased efficiency.

Besides these goals that can lead to anticipated outcomes, a number of so-called 'overall' organizational goals can be distinguished regarding an organization's 'social capital'. All HRM activities, and therefore also all e-HRM activities, will implicitly or explicitly be directed towards these 'overall' goals. Beer *et al.* (1984) distinguish four possibilities: high commitment, high competence, cost effectiveness and higher congruence. By high commitment they mean that the workforce is motivated and understanding, and that they are willing to interact with the management about changes in the organizational environment and the impact that this can have on the internal organization. For HR itself, this means that it should be able to play the role of change agent, to use Ulrich's (1997) terminology. High commitment implies a high level of trust between management and workforce. High competence points towards the capacities of employees to learn new tasks and roles if the circumstances require it. For HR itself it means, in Ulrich's framework, playing the employee champion role. Cost effectiveness refers to the competitiveness of pay levels and employee turnover rate, and to the acceptability of costs resulting from employee resistance such as strikes. As Ulrich (1997) states, HR itself has to be able to play the administrative expert role in order to contribute to an organization's cost effectiveness. Finally, higher congruence refers to the internal organization, the reward system, and the 'input, throughput, and output' of personnel, which need to be structured in the interests of all stakeholders.

Depending upon the way in which individuals and parties want to be affected by e-HRM, in line with the defined goals, outcomes to some extent will emerge. These outcomes, in turn, may change the state of HRM in an organization, or through individuals and/or groups within an organization, actually result in a new HRM state. This closes the circle.

Consequences of E-HRM for HR Department

The consequences of e-HRM for the HR department will be that e-HRM will assume an active role for line management and employees in implementing HRM strategies, policies, and practices. In terms of the more operational and information processing work, such as administration, registration and information distribution, there will be less demand for HR people. This seems most logical for organizations with an operational e-HRM approach. However, also with a relational e-HRM approach dominating, a smaller HR staff will be necessary if line management and employees pick up and use the HRM instruments provided by the HR intranet. There will still be HR experience necessary for the renewal of instruments and to prepare them for easy intranet-based use. Finally, with a more transformational e-HRM approach, strategic HRM expertise will be necessary in order to formulate adequate strategic HRM plans.

Less administrative tasks for the HR department and therefore less administrative positions, focus more on the strategic goals of the organization and therefore an HRM staff consisting mainly of 'thinkers'; this is, in essence, what HR departments can expect or are already facing and experiencing. Kavanagh *et al.* (1990) actually gave a good 'push' when they wrote about the consequences of HR information systems (which we distinguish from e-HRM) for HRM

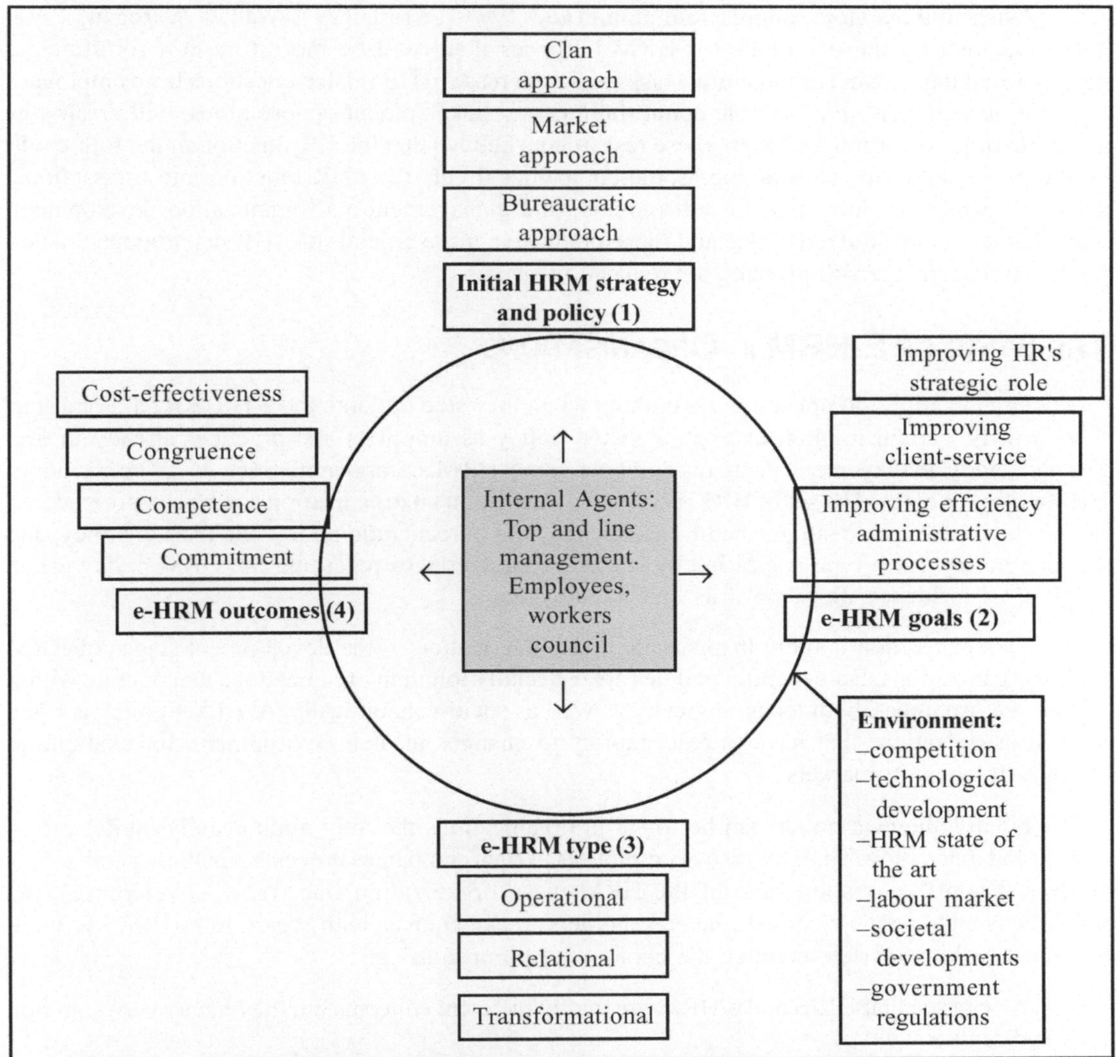

Figure 17.1. e-HRM model

professionals: 'Today and in the future, however, the successful HR professional must be part HR generalist, part HR functional specialist, part consultant, part business manager, and must understand and be comfortable using information systems' (p. 325). More specifically, they state that HR departments will be more involved in strategic planning processes if they are able to provide adequate, accurate and fast information through the use of information technology. A change for HR departments, related to this, is that with an appropriate use of information technology they can improve their client focus. '...the HR group will focus on providing services to employees, line managers, and senior management, often by serving as an internal consultant. This will better enable the HR function to truly support the business.'

Other authors (for example Rampton *et al.*, 1997; LeTart, 1997; Walker & Regan, 1997) also think that by the use of IT for HRM purposes there will be more time left for strategic decision-making. Fewer administrative tasks and a decrease in HR related questions from employees and line management, for example about training and development opportunities, will create this available time According to Trapp, these researchers believe that the HR function in the future will be the prime target for outsourcing. Some companies divide their HR function into transactional activities, which are attractive for outsourcing, and management and organization development, which have a more strategic value and therefore have a more crucial role. HR departments that do not make this change will probably be reduced in size.

The State of E-HRM in Organisations

Organizations do not start with nothing when they step out onto the e-HRM road. For a start there will be certain implicit or explicit HRM policy assumptions and practices already in use. Further, every management decision contains some HRM component. Beer *et al.* speak about HRM policy choices. The set of HRM policy choices within an organization can be categorized into one of the three types distinguished by Beer *et al.*: the bureaucratic policy, the market policy, and the clan policy. Each type is typified by specific characteristics regarding the HRM policy areas: employees' influence, flow, rewards and work systems.

This distinction is more than simply a characterization of the development stages of HRM within organizations. Bureaucratic policies are especially found in organizations that operate within a stable environment, both technologically as well as socio-economically. A market policy is often seen in organizations that have to react rapidly to changes in their environment, for example to strongly fluctuating markets.

Finally, the clan policy can be found in organizations that rely quite heavily on delivering quality and innovation. The expertise of employees in such companies is decisive in the organization's success. From the existing state of the HRM in an organization (the frame of reference), the individuals and groups involved (the stakeholders) make choices with regard to e-HRM. As these are made within a certain context, the choices are purpose-driven.

We can see that HRIS and e-HRM are totally different concepts but they have many common files and reports.

Questions and Assignment

Q.1. Distinguish between e-HRM concept and HRIS.

Q.2. What advantages do you see for companies moving from HRIS to e-HRM?

Q.3. Are both complementary to each other or do they require different software and platforms?

Assignment

Practise on any HR software and learn various applications. Which data is confidential?

CASE

Dow Chemicals, ABN Amro, Ford Motor Company, IBM and Belgacom

The case studies involve the following five large companies (each with more than 15,000 employees): Dow Chemicals, ABN Amro, Ford Motor Company, IBM and Belgacom. All of them have been on the 'e-HR road' for a number of years, and in a variety of ways. In fact, this suggests the first conclusion: there does not seem to be 'one natural way' to get on the 'e-HR road'. Companies are different, operate in different markets and have various structures and cultures.

Results

Starting to work with e-HRM seems to be connected with the process of globalization and aims of the companies. This is one of the more interesting points to emerge from a look at the five companies. Four of them operated internationally, and all of these linked their e-HRM plans with their aim of becoming a global company rather than an internationally dispersed one.

The following quotes illustrate this:

- The goal of the project is to establish a common HR information infrastructure across the band. We try to put in place one package for the whole world (A project manager).
- If [the company] wants to do talent management, if it wants to steer all kinds of HR processes across the world, utilize the skills and competencies you have worldwide in the most optimal way, then [the company] has to do these kinds of things [e-HRM] (A project manager).
- Technology is just a tool, and I experience that IBM wants to present itself more and more as a global player, also internally, and therefore tries to align and make clear procedures, to harmonize and standardize HR processes, across country borders. Because you want to harmonize and to standardize, technology can be used to help, especially because technology offers more and more possibilities and my perception is that these possibilities are applied to the maximum (A personal development manager).

The fifth company involved, Belgacom, is not yet an international company, and therefore would not make this connection.

The four international companies in the study chose to standardize and harmonize HR policies and practices as a precondition for becoming global companies and also to create a sound basis for e-HRM, or because they saw no other option but to achieve globally standardized and harmonized HR policies and practices.

Interestingly, in all of these companies, 'globalizing' HR produced a tendency to centralize HR policy responsibilities at the company headquarters, while responsibilities for applying HR responsibilities were actually decentralized, placed in the hands of line managers and employees. Through the last of these aspects, it seems that with the 'rise' of e-HRM, the responsibility for carrying out HR policies is actually becoming a line responsibility—something that HRM theory has been proclaiming since the mid-1980s!

Further, what we see is that the companies involved have ambitious aims with HR and in implementing e-HRM. The three types of e-HRM goals that we distinguished based upon the literature, namely, to improve administration and efficiency, to improve client orientation and service and to improve HR's strategic orientation, were all selected by the companies involved in this study. However, they all seem to have been selected without any clear priority or, in other words, the three seem to be almost equally important. This is surprising, and actually rather strange, because it is questionable whether an improvement in HR service to employees and line management can coexist with an improved efficiency (for which read decreasing costs). Furthermore, the concept of e-HRM has to be facilitated with web technology, and in all of the involved companies large investments were needed to support their e-HRM technology plans, especially in terms of labour input by project team members, trainers, and so on. The return on investment therefore cannot be seen as quick; it will need several years to 'recoup' the outgoings. In one case this was openly acknowledged. The cost reduction goal is more of a hope than a short-term expectation, and perhaps a way of 'selling' e-HRM plans to the top management.

The complex set of chosen goals in starting out with e-HRM is also surprising because it goes against the general belief that clearly defined goals are a very important precondition for successful project management. In the companies involved in the study it seems to be the case that goals are used pragmatically: if one is not achieved, then at least one of the others might be. Furthermore, only two of the five companies (Dow and IBM) had a clearly defined HRM strategy on which the e-HRM tools were based; the other three (ABN-Amro, Ford and Belgacom) had ideas about where they wanted to go with e-HRM, but the links between the e-HRM content and the overall HRM strategy were less clear.

In Table 17.1 we have placed the companies and the e-HRM goals in a matrix, and made a judgement about the emphasis placed by the companies on the selected goals.

E-HRM Types

This overview is not intended to classify the e-HRM experiences as 'good' or 'bad' but to show the differences between what is available in the technical sense for employees and management, and how it was being used in practice at the time of the study. All the companies were, and still are, working on further developments and further improvements, and therefore this overview has somewhat of a transitory value. However, the goal of Table 17.2 is not so much the labelling of the type of e-HRM in use, but to compare between the technical state of the e-HRM and the 'use-state'. What is clear is that there is a 'gap' between e-HRM in a technical sense (the available functionality) and the use and adoption of it by employees and line managers. The actual usage/adoption lags behind what is possible. An initial response to this observation could be that this is natural: real use always follows behind technical implementation. At Dow Chemicals, the time taken for the adoption of e-HRM by users to catch up with the technical possibilities can be around three years! The main explanation for this is that starting with e-HRM does not mean that users simply have to learn to work with a new version of a familiar system, but rather that employees and

TABLE 17.1
The Companies and their HRM Goals

	Dow Chemical	ABN Amro	IBM	Ford	Belgacom
To globalise the company, (Standardise, harmonize HR policies and processes)	***	***	**	*	
To improve HR's strategic orientation	**	**	**		**
To improve internal client orientation and service delivery	**	**	**	***	***
To improve administrative efficiency/achieve cost reduction	**	***	***	***	**

*** = strongly emphasized; ** = moderately emphasized; * = slightly emphasized.

line managers have to be ready, able and willing to pick up responsibilities that were previously someone else's. This really does require a change in mindset!

E-HRM Outcomes

Cost reduction and a reduction of the administrative burden are in most cases mentioned as an effect of e-HRM. However, no exact figures exist regarding the size of these reductions.

Most concrete is the reduction in (HR) staff levels, but to give the whole picture we have to calculate the extra time that is needed by middle-managers and employees to keep up their own HR-administration and to search for their own possibilities at the intranet. For instance, at Dow we

TABLE 17.2
Comparison Between e-HRM in a Technical Sense (Available Functionality) and e-HRM in Practice

	e-HRM Technical Sense	e-HRM Practice
Dow Chemicals, Benelux	Transformational	Relational Transformational
ABN Amro, Luxembourg	Operational/Relational	Operational
Ford Motors, Germany	Operational/Relational	Operational
IBM, Netherlands	Transformational	Relational
Belgacom, Belgium	Relational/Transformational	Operational

saw the development of a new function, namely an assistant for management and employees to help them with the use of e-HRM. There is a danger of information overkill through the HR intranet. Without a clear and easy structure, employees and line management can be afraid of spending time on exploring web-based HR tools. For example, at IBM, employees and line managers felt that the HR intranet site contained too much info in a non-easy way. Therefore they called the HR call centre ('Ask HR') to get answers to their immediate HR related questions instead of searching the HR site. Strikingly, the HR call centre assistants use the same source, the HR intranet site, to give the answers! Although IBM reported a convincing reduction of costs, the abovementioned might raise questions. As was known, IBM outsourced the HR call centre and this itself may have reduced costs.

The most important e-HRM effect, however, seems to be the strategic integration of HRM with the (revised) company strategy, structure and culture. In all cases e-HRM is mainly seen as an indispensable instrument to help realize this integration by, on one hand, centralizing and standardizing HR policies and practices and, on the other, decentralizing their execution. This is the same effect we see with IT applications in other fields, like production, logistics, finance, etc. IT makes it possible to combine centralization and standardization on the one hand and decentralization in the execution and operations at the other. Against this background we may expect companies to continue with e-HRM, more or less regardless of the costs.

For the employees, the introduction of e-HRM brings changes in the way they experience HRM in a company and in the HR tools and instruments they get offered. They get the opportunity to be updated in the organizational developments, take part in the online discussions, choose their career path. However, not all employees are willing to pick up the full responsibility for their personal career development through the available web-based HR tools. Some (and the cases suggest a certain group) find that their managers have to come up with career development initiatives. At Dow Chemicals, Benelux, the philosophy was that through the availability of HR online tools employees would become the initiators of their own career development. However, employees in the plants or factory (instead of those in offices) did not even have access to online HR tools because of a lack of PCs or because of cost considerations. This was also the case at Ford Motor Company, Cologne. The availability of PCs in all 'corners' of the company and sufficient PC skills with management and employees are important requisites for the success of e-HRM.

Further, although e-HRM creates new opportunities for line management and employees the organisational practice can be limited in using these opportunities because of a lack of time and the willingness to pick them up. E-HRM is not something technical; it is, in the first place, a change of minds and behaviour of HR, line management and employees. At the second place, it is about facilitating through IT. In these cases, it seemed that IT played a very big role. Selection of the right package, implementation of pieces/parts of the package got a lot of attention. The fact that the philosophy behind the usefulness of the technology had to be 'sold' and made possible to incorporate it into day-to-day working life was, at first, forgotten. An example of this was the ABN-Amro case, where line management and employees did not have a good understanding about the 'story' behind the online HR tools that were made available. Employees and line managers felt that they hardly had time to even explore the tools. The HRM department did a good job by starting marketing campaigns a number of times per year to stimulate use, with success actually. Employees'

TABLE 17.3
E-HRM Outcomes

Dow	ABN-Amro	Ford	IBM	Belgacom
Cost effective growth in employee competencies, more 'open' culture, transparent and flexible internal labour market	Hardly yet, especially not at the level of employees. For line managers first administrative support. For HR departments less administrative work load	HR-intranet site (HR online) became global internal brand for HR services. 80% consider HR-online as primary source for HR. High client satisfaction with e-HR service. HR site most visited internal website. ROI in the long term, not short term	Cost reduction (57%). Organis-ational climate change: more flexibility, better balance work/ private life. Communications improved. Support risk-taking and innovation. Emphasizing flexibility over bureaucracy. Client-satisfaction strongly improved	67% of all HR data entries go through the employee self service. Improved employee satis-faction with HR service, from 4.39 to 4.93. (on five point scale) in one year. ROI in 2006

and line managers' minds need to be changed; they have to realize and accept the usefulness of the web-based HR tools.

They usually experience a lack of time and space to work quietly and thoughtfully with web-based HR tools, so if there is no real need employees and line management will not easily start to use it.

Implementing e-HRM in international and global companies seems to be difficult in the sense that it is hard to convince the local HRM departments to contribute and to collaborate because it is difficult to make the advantages of e-HRM visible and tangible in the first place.

To make local HRM professionals change their way of working is difficult. When implementing e-HRM globally it can be difficult to get the support of relatively small components of the company. Implementing e-HRM on a global scale is not as easy as to make e-HRM advantageous on a local scale. That makes it harder to get local HRM professionals enthusiastic about it. ABN-Amro is the best example of this point in our study.

Good and clear goals and a good plan on how to achieve them cannot be ignored in order to convince users of the usefulness of online HRM.

KEY FINDINGS

- E-HRM seems to be providing an important 'push': to put HR responsibility in the hands of the line manager. After 15 years of 'preaching', an administrative component of HR is becoming a task for the line management. The introduction of e-HRM is accompanied by the decentralization of HR tasks and by the harmonization and standardization of HR processes.

- In order to become a 'real' global company, HR policies and practices need to be the same in 'all the corners of the globe' where a company is present. Differences in cultures and languages between continents and countries are a hurdle in the acceptance of newly introduced web-based HR facilities.
- For the HR department, introducing e-HRM shows itself to be a 'push-factor' for changing HRM within an organization: from a bureaucratic approach towards a market/clan approach.
- Introducing e-HRM will be accompanied by a reduction in HR staff levels, especially in terms of administrative staff. If implemented well, it provides an opportunity for an HR department to get a clearer profile and a better image.
- Turning to the employees, the introduction of e-HRM brings changes in the way they experience HRM in their company and in the HR tools and instruments they are offered. They acquire the opportunity to become updated in terms of organizational dynamics, take part in online discussions, and choose their career path. However, not all employees are willing to accept full responsibility for their personal career development through the available web-based HR tools. Some (and the case studies suggest a specific group) require their managers to come up with career development initiatives. For example, at Dow Chemicals, Benelux, the philosophy was that through the availability of HR online tools, employees would become the initiators of their own career development direction. Unfortunately, this did not always occur.
- Further, although e-HRM creates new opportunities for line management and employees, the organizational practice in using these opportunities can be limited because of a lack of time and the willingness to pick them up. What tends to be forgotten is that e-HRM is not primarily technical; it is first and foremost a change in the mindsets and behaviours of HR personnel, line managers, and employees. Only secondly is it about facilitating the above through IT.

In the companies studied it seemed to be the case that IT played a very large role: selection of the right package, and implementation of pieces or part of the 'package', received a lot of attention. The fact that the philosophy underpinning the usefulness of the technology had to be 'sold' and incorporated into the day to-day working routines was, in the first instance, forgotten. An example of this occurred in the ABN-Amro case where the line managers and the employees did not have a clear idea about the reasoning behind the online HR tools that were being made available. Further, the employees and line managers felt that they hardly had any time to explore the tools. In response, the HRM department (at ABN-Amro, Luxembourg) did a good job by starting 'marketing campaigns' a number of times per year to stimulate use and these were quite successful.

Interestingly, in those companies that had an 'industrial' nature, PC availability in all 'corners' of the company and the PC skills of employees was found to be a crucial element in successful switching to e-HRM. Employees in the plants or factory (unlike those in offices) tended not to have access, or at best only limited access, to online HR tools because of a lack of PCs or because of cost considerations. This was the case at Dow Chemicals, Benelux, and at the Ford Motor Company

18 HRM and Quality

Learning Objectives

After studying this chapter you will learn:

- The concept of quality.
- The philosophy of TQM and the critical elements in its implementation.
- The concept and practice of Six Sigma.
- The implementation of Six Sigma in any organization.
- The role of HRM in implementation of TQM and Six Sigma.
- Implementation of TQM or ISO 9000 within the HR department itself.
- The ingredient of employee employment.

INTRODUCTION

Quality improvement is a highly desired objective in the fiercely competitive international business world, yet it remains elusive to many organizations. Improved quality is commonly believed to reduce cost, as doing things right the first time eliminates waste (Juran, 1989). TQM helps in eliminating waste, reducing variations and ensures continuous improvement. TQM is an integrative philosophy of management for continuously improving the quality of products and processes to achieve customer satisfaction. The TQM practices have evolved from traditional statistical controls originally proposed by Shewart. These have diversified since the 1950s into a host of fields, including supplier management and employee involvement by the writings of Juran & Gryna, Deming and Crosby & Ishiwaka.

The study of the literature on this subject shows that the performance of an organization system is composed of seven inter-related criteria: effectiveness, efficiency, total quality, productivity,

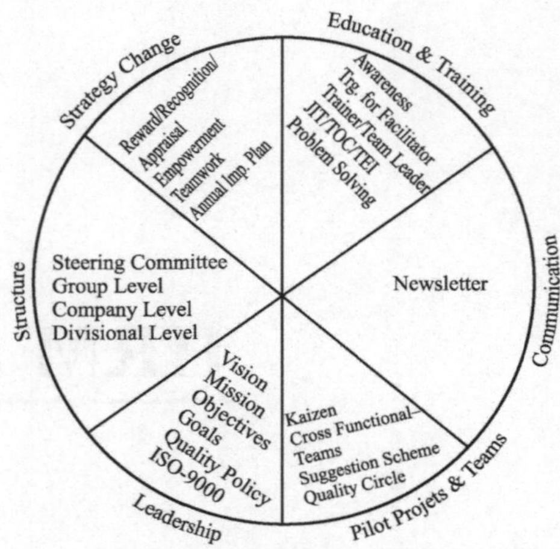

Broad Elements of TQM

Comprehensive Approach in TQM Implementation

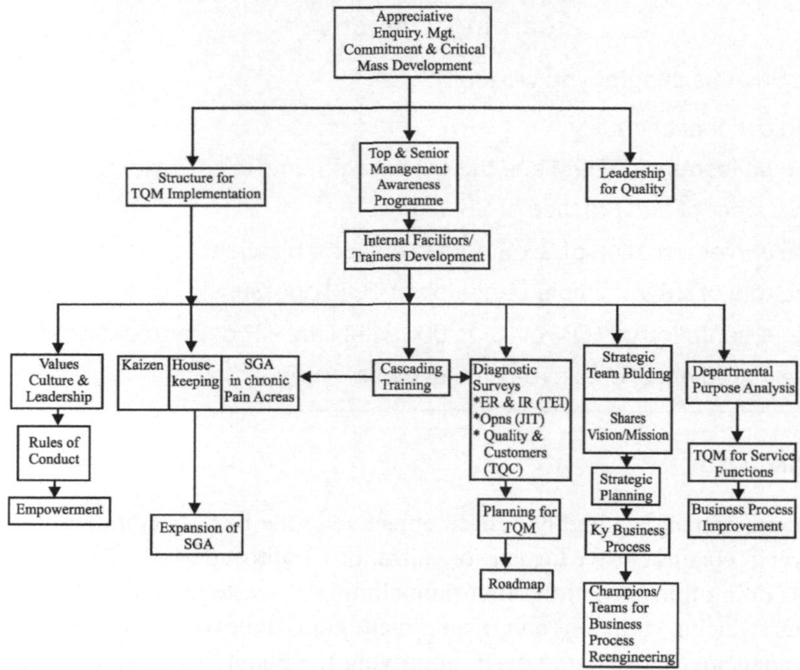

quality of work life, innovation and financial performance. In achieving these goals and transforming the culture of any organization to one in which TQM or Six Sigma thrives, HR function plays a critical role. We explore this HRM role in implementation of TQM or Six Sigma or ISO 9000 in any firm.

WHAT IS QUALITY?

In order to understand TQM, one must first understand quality. When pressed to define, someone commented that he couldn't define it but knew it when he saw it. One way to understand quality as a consumer-driven concept is to apply such criteria:

quality as a consumer-driven concept is to apply such criteria:

- Service
- Response Time
- Environment/atmosphere
- Price
- Selection.

The concept is that quality is the resultant aspect. Does the product or service meet or exceed the customer expectations? But it is a much broader concept which includes 'processes, environment and people.' It has been defined by several authorities differently, as under:

- Fred Smith, CEO of Federal Express, defines quality as, 'performance to the standard expected by the customer'.
- GSA defines it as, 'meeting customer needs the first time and every time'.
- Boeing defines quality as, 'providing our customers with products and services that consistently meets their needs and expectations'.
- In his landmark book, *Out of the Crisis*, W. Edwards Deming has this to say:

> 'Quality can be defined only in terms of the agent. Who is the judge of the quality? In the mind of the production worker, he produces quality if he can take pride in his work; poor quality to him means loss of business, and perhaps of his job. Good quality he thinks will keep the company in business. Quality to the plant manager means to get the numbers out and to meet specifications. His job is also, whether he knows it or not, continual improvement of leadership.
>
> The products, services, people, processes and the environment element is critical. It makes the point that quality applies not just to the products and services provided, but also to the people and processes that provide them and the environments in which they are provided. In the short-term, two competitors who focus on continual improvement might produce a product of comparable quality. But the competitor who looks beyond just the quality of the finished product and also focuses on the continual improvement of people who produce the product and the processes they use and the environment in which they work will win in the long run and, most frequently, in the short run also. This is because quality products are produced most consistently by quality organizations.

TQM Philosophy Explained

TQM is seen by some as an extension of scientific management, by others in terms of systems theory and by still others as an altogether new paradigm. The case at the end provides the essence of TQM philosophy.

The US Department of Defence defines the total quality approach as: Continuous improvement activities involving everyone in the organization—managers and workers—in a totally integrated effort towards improving performance at every level. This improved performance is directed towards satisfying such cross-functional goals as quality, cost, schedule, mission need and suitability. TQM integrates fundamental management techniques, existing improvement efforts and technical tools under a disciplined approach focused on continued process improvement. The activities are ultimately focused on increased customer/user satisfaction.

TQM is also defined as: A management approach that focuses on the organization as a system, with an emphasis on teams, processes, statistics, continuous improvement, and delivering products and services that meet and exceed customer expectation. Six Sigma is a disciplined extension of TQM.

Not many organizations have been significantly benefited by TQM, primarily because of poor implementation. The critical dimensions affecting TQM implementation are given in Table 18.1.

These factors can be evaluated in a research assignment to ascertain the efficacy of TQM implementation.

Six Sigma Explained

The Six Sigma story began in the 1980s at Motorola, where it was first developed and proven. In 1983, reliability engineer Bill Smith concluded that if a product was defective and corrected during production, then other defects were probably being missed and later found by customers. In other words, process failure rates were much higher than indicated by final product tests. His point? If products were assembled completely free of defects, they probably wouldn't fail customers later. This is where Six Sigma took off. Mike Harry, the founder of the Motorola Six Sigma Research Institute, further refined the methodology to not only eliminate process waste but also turn it into a growth currency—regardless of the specific type of service, product or market sector.

Six Sigma statistically measures and reflects true process capability, correlating it to such characteristics as defects per unit and probabilities of success or failure. Its value is in transforming cultural outlooks from complacency to accomplishment across the spectrum of the industry. Any repetitive action—be it in a transactional, manufacturing or services environment, can be improved through the Six Sigma technique. This methodology collects data on variations in outputs associated with each process, so that it can be improved and those variations reduced.

Most companies function at Four Sigma—tolerating 6,210 defects per million opportunities. Operating Six Sigma creates an almost defect-free environment, allowing only 3.4 defects per million opportunities: products and services are nearly perfect (99.9997 per cent). Eliminating defects eliminates dissatisfaction.

Sigma c is a term used in statistics to represent standard deviation, an indicator of the degree of variation in a set of measurements of a process. Six Sigma is a statistical concept that measures a process in terms of defects at the Six Sigma level where there are only 3.4 defects per million opportunities. Six Sigma is also a philosophy of managing that focuses on eliminating defects through practices that emphasize understanding, measuring, and improving process. The

TABLE 18.1
Critical Dimensions Affecting TQM Implementation

No.	Item	Definition
1.	Organization size	Size of organization in terms of employees and turnover, spread, etc.
2.	Top management support	Commitment to implement TQM by investing time and money and providing coaching and guidance to all in the organization
3.	Team-building approach	Extent to which quality circle, total employee involvement and cross-functional deployment is used
4.	Communication	The channel of communication and degree of transparency and feedback support
5.	Flexibility	Degree of responsiveness to change systems and procedures
6.	Organisational goals	The long and short goals of the organization
7.	Structures of planning framework	The extent of strategic quality planning and connectivity across the organization
8.	Infrastructure	The extent of service and support systems compatible with the company requirement
9.	Management risk-taking ability	The degree to which management can take financial risks
10.	Competitive strategy	Extent of competitor scanning and active perusal of benchmark performance
11.	Technology policy	The degree of aggressiveness of the company's policy on technology adaptation, transfer and assimilation
12.	Customer interaction	Extent of supplier-customer interaction
13.	Product design	Degree of emphasis on reliability, manufacturing ability, maintainability, etc.
14.	Vendor relations	Degree of participation of vendors in quality assurance, value engineering and inventory control

Continued ...

...Continued

No.	Item	Definition
15.	Compatibility and coordination	Compatibility and coordination of quality management policies and programmes within the company between various levels and layers
16.	Financial position	Ability of the organization to invest in different resources
17.	Recognition and reward systems	The policies and practices towards recognition and rewarding good work
18.	Role of HRM	How much importance HR function gets and understands its role in TQM implementation

Source: R. L. Shrivastava and others. *Linking Performance Measures with TQM Factors & Practices.*

central idea is that if you can measure the defects in a process, you can systematically figure out ways to eliminate them. So, in short, it can be described as:

- ***Define***: determines the project goals and deliverables to customers (internal and external).
- ***Measure***: identifies one or more product or service characteristics, maps the process, evaluates measurement systems and estimates baseline capability.
- ***Analyze***: evaluates and reduces the variables with graphical analysis and hypothesis testing and identifies the vital few factors for process improvement.
- ***Improve***: discovers variable relationships among the vital few, establishes operating tolerances and validates measurements.
- ***Control***: determines the ability to control the vital few factors and implements process control systems.

The Six Sigma methodology uses statistical tools to identify the vital few factors: the factors that matter most for improving the quality of the process and generating profits. It basically consists of the following five steps (DMAIC):

The Six Sigma methodology is not rigid. Approaches vary significantly. We should first understand and measure process capability to eliminate likely defects in the process. Process capability is a statistical measure of inherent variation for a given event in a stable process.

It is usually defined as the process width (normal variation) divided by Six Sigma and quantified using capability index (CP). More generally, it's the ability of the process to achieve certain results, based on performance testing. Process capability answers the question, what can your process deliver?

The next important step is to realize that people are assets and unique investments. Once

BOX 18.1
Both People and Processes are Important

Managers often tend to focus just on people in their organizations. When something goes right or some thing goes wrong, they look for a person to congratulate or to blame. The fact is that work gets done through processes executed by people; both success and problems are usually the result of what lots of people do, not just one person. If you don't pay enough attention to both people and processes, improvement will not happen.

you are thinking in terms of 'human assets' it is equally important to realize the underlying monetary value of investments in people. This is another aspect of the Six Sigma approach.

An easy way to understand the concept of human assets is to calculate their individual return on investment (ROI); for example, if an employee costs the business $ 50,000 a year and his or her activity produces revenue of $ 100,000, the employee has covered the costs and raised an additional 100 per cent the profit or return. So, the annual ROI for that employee is 100 per cent. By calculating employee ROI, you can focus on making the most of them as assets invested in your business.

A CEO of a major corporation was once asked, 'what's the 30-second elevator speech that explains the Six Sigma?' His answer went like this:

> 'Six Sigma is a problem-solving technology that uses human assets, data, measurements and statistics to identify the vital few factors to decrease waste and defects while increasing customer satisfaction, profit, and shareholder value.'

Six Sigma is frequently perceived as a statistics and measurement programme. This is not the case. To achieve a high level of quality requires not just statistics but also changes in the culture of the organization. Culture is the vital factor in implementation of both TQM and Six Sigma. It refers to the beliefs, expectations, ways of operating, and behaviours that characterize the interactions of people in any organization. It's about 'how things are done around here' in an organization. Culture evolves over a long period of time and it often reflects the beliefs and behaviours of top management. Because Six Sigma affects the way things are done, its successful implementation will require a change in culture, which may be profound. Essential to this culture change are key players known as 'champions' and 'black belts', who act as agents to facilitate that change.

A Champion, generally selected from the ranks of upper management, is a senior-level manager who promotes the Six Sigma methodology throughout the company and especially in specific functional groups. The champion understands the discipline and tools of Six Sigma, selects projects, establishes measurable objectives, serves as a coach and mentor, removes barriers and dedicates resources in support of belts. A champion 'owns' the process—monitoring projects and measuring the savings realized.

A Black Belt leads a defined project on a full time basis, working strictly on defining, measuring, analyzing, improving and controlling processes to reach desired outcomes. He is a full-time change agent trained in the methodology to solve product and process defects, project by project, with financially beneficial results. A black belt does Six Sigma analyses and works with others (often teams) to put improvements in place.

Green Belts assist Black Belts part-time. After gaining experience, they can become Black Belts in future projects.

BOX 18.2
Six Sigma in GE

General Electrics has encouraged its executives to promote Six Sigma by linking it to compensation. Forty per cent of the bonuses for the top 7,000 executives is tied to Six Sigma implementation. That incentive sends the message about the importance of Six Sigma and ensures commitment from the top levels down.

Jack Welsh called Six Sigma 'a part of the genetic code of future leadership at the company'.

Regardless of the designated role each participant plays in the Six Sigma initiative, they must all have full responsibility for their individual areas. Simply put, to be responsible is to be accountable, trustworthy and dependable. It is important that all your participants recognize this as their charter: from green belt to executive, they need to exercise responsibility in all that they do to achieve optimum outcomes.

HR Role in Quality Management

Traditionally the predominant focus in the quality movement has been on upgrading of technical systems. The attention to products, manufacturing processes and information technology have been found necessary and productive in quality improvements. The recognition of human resources as a key and clinching variable in the quality equation has come up only gradually although they have been always there. For example, the widely cited 'fourteen points' of quality guru W. Edwards Deming focus on the following HR related directives:

- Institute training on the job.
- Breakdown barriers between departments to build team work.
- Create a climate of 'kaizen' at the workplace.
- Drive fear out of the workplace.
- Create conditions that allow employees to have pride in their workmanship, including abolishing annual reviews and merit ratings.
- Institute a programme of education and self improvement.

Richard S. Johnson in his book *TQM: Leadership for Quality Transformation* elucidates four specific steps that can identify an organization's progress towards TQM:

1. Awareness
    - Directive leadership
    - Vision creation
    - Process audit
    - Determine process and equipment requirements
    - Educate quality concepts
    - Communicate the need.
2. Involvement
    - Coaching leadership
    - Develop a support structure
    - Develop a mission
    - Review process capability
    - Determine asset requirements
    - Develop training
    - Conceive a quality environment
    - Communicate the vision.
3. Commitment
    - Participative leadership
    - Demonstrate commitment
    - Develop goals
    - Promote change
    - Develop teams
    - Develop a recognition system
    - Solve problems
    - Implement suggestions
    - Energise quality environments.
4. Ownership
    - Delegate leadership
    - Empower the workforce
    - Encourage team improvement

BOX 18.3
Elements of Employee Involvement (EI)

- Problem solving at the lowest level.
- Meet conditions of empowerment.
- Revised organizational structure (flattened hierarchy).
- Congruence/design—(Value-Action-Measurement-Reward).
- EI is a misnomer as it also is pertinent to others like suppliers.

- Recognise achievements
- Reward success
- Share benefits.

It is evident from his list that the route to TQM is replete with HR processes.

Implementation of TQM in HR Function

Most HR functions are so specialized and cut off from the rest of the organization that department members lack the breadth of perspective necessary for TQM. Indeed, these specialists may view the demands of a full scale quality improvement as a threat to them. In some cases, even though the number of top HR executives attending CEO meetings is increasing, the HR people may not be having full access to the company's overall competitive position.

HR departments are frequently autocratic and hierarchical, with strict definitions of responsibility and authority.

From this discussion, it is clear that the HR function cannot inspiringly contribute to the quality movement in the organization before it convincingly presents its own credentials to quality.

So, the HR function has little option but to change their perspective to include quality orientation. How then can they do this? They have to throw themselves open for either TQM or ISO 9000, like any other department.

Alan Fowler outlines the issues this way: there are two types of customers for the HR services and the HR specialists and therefore two different aspects to the definition of quality. First, there is the organization as a whole with its mission statement, the core values which it requires from all its members to support its corporate objectives. Secondly, there are the individual managers of business units who have their own more detailed operation needs and aims. Hence, the HR department must not only contribute to TQM implementation but also itself become a TQM unit.

Bowen & Lawler argue for redesigning the complete HRM department to fit the following TQM principles and create what they call TQHRM:

1. Quality work the first time. The HR executives must insist on and support by giving the time needed to 'do it right the first time' even when line managers are pressing for a quick fix.
2. Focus on the customer. The HRD programmes should be more service-oriented and less production oriented.
3. Strategic holistic approach. Quality improvement may require changes in mission, structure, job-design, management practices and every other facet of the HR organization.
4. Continuous improvement a way of life. The HR department should adopt values and practices to support continuous, incremental improvements in quality throughout the organization, including within itself.
5. Mutual respect and teamwork. If HR is to champion such issues as employee involvement and cooperation throughout the organization, it must first champion them internally.

The quality of the HR function is likely to be seen more in terms of the expectations of internal customers with emphasis on factors like speed of response to requests for assistance, the accuracy and reliability of information and records, the unit cost of transactions such as recruitment and the specific outcomes of selection and training programmes. The ISO 9000 approach insists that relevant, efficient and effective systems and processes are in place and are operated intelligently.

HRD and OD Interventions that Support TQM

Once the HR department has inducted quality into its own functioning, it can assume the expanded role of steering and supporting the quality organization efforts in the organization. The following steps are suggested:

1. Identification of need for quality, and appreciation of TQM or ISO 9000. The process of registration must necessarily begin with top and senior management appreciation of the standards with subsequent commitment to the idea of acquiring the certification.
2. Selection of model and planning. The next step is to select the most suitable model and decisions-related goals and targets; formulation of implementation plan and strategy; constitution of a steering committee and core groups.
3. Formulation of quality policy. Top management commitment to the chosen quality standards along with its overall orientation to total quality will have to be articulated through its Quality Policy. The HR department may find itself appropriately involved.
4. Creating awareness. It is necessary to undertake company wide communications through seminars, workshops and other means on these standards, which may also include dissemination of Quality Policy for all junior and front-line managers.
5. Support facilities. This means creating facilities for changing existing practices by bringing in new equipment and tools and corresponding manpower.
6. Preparation of quality manual, procedures and work instructions.

BOX 18.4
Four Key Requirements for Success of TQM

Mckinsey and Company's survey of CEOs of the top 500 European corporations found the following relation to the key requirements for success in TQM.

- Top management attention 95% agreement
- People development 85% agreement
- Corporate team spirit 82% agreement
- Quality performance information 73% agreement
- Top management capability building 70% agreement
- Sense of urgency 60% agreement

7. Preparing for change. At this stage, it is necessary to change the attitudes of employees and to inculcate new skills. This would call for quality awareness training and training for improvement in work processes, statistical tools and other behavioural skills.
8. Safety and motivation. Motivation is essential for any enterprise-wide effort.
9. Selection. TQM organizations require individuals who are problem solvers, knowledgeable about statistical process control, Pareto analysis, etc. Secondly, because of the emphasis of group processes in TQM, selection methods must identify candidates who can function well in group settings.
10. Performance management. Traditional performance appraisal systems are more supportive of individual effort than they are of a system-oriented focus on quality. HRM should change this process.
11. Reward systems. In case of TQM, it would be specifically necessary to create reward systems that not only reward quality improvements but also create a team environment and group orientation.
12. Collaboration with the unions. There would be little room for generating participation, problem solving and system solutions that quality management programmes emphasise if unions do not become constant partners in the quality improving endeavours.
13. Continuous communication of varying on-going quality improvement efforts in the organization, information about the strategy and direction of the organization, feedback on the problems across the units are some of the major activities which will become a part of HR interventions.

Questions and Assignment

Q.1. Why are organizations increasingly adopting quality enhancement through TQM or ISO 9000?

Q.2. Explain the concept of Six Sigma.

Q.3. As an HR functional head, how will you proceed to implement TQM in your company?

Q.4. What is the role of HR in implementing Six Sigma and TQM?

Q.5. Why is the quality movement so successful in Japan but not in India? Comment.

Assignment

Study any two organizations and determine the state of TQM with respect to all critical elements mentioned in this chapter. Compare the same and explain the differences.

CASE

TQM IN AN INDIAN SETTING

The organizational system includes all stakeholders, that is, customers, employees, suppliers and shareholders. The relationship of various stakeholders to each other and to the outside world is a complex one, interacting in limitless ways. Thus, the response of the organization to any internal or external intervention is very complex. Change in one part of a system affects all the parts. Further, the system encompasses both external and internal environments, receiving inputs and providing outputs.

Tom Peters wrote: 'Most quality programmes fail for one or two reasons. They have system without passion, or passion without system. You must have both.' TQM stands on this philosophy. TQM rests on the pillars of customer focus, continuous improvement and team work. All this requires a culture change. In order to predict the amount of adaptation that is required to make the quality movement a success in India, we have to understand the cultural distance between India and the West, from where the TQM model was borrowed. Cultural distance is the measure of difference between two social systems. Cultural distance affects the response of all involved in business, resulting in problems. These problems get magnified if the cultural distance is large.

In order to understand the possible impact of Indian socio-cultural variables on the TQM movement, we have to analyse the organization structures prevalent in India, the prevailing systems and processes, and the existing culture and the beliefs of the people. Possible reasons for failure could be a lack of realization of the need to dramatically transform company culture, which is dependent upon people.

Socio-cultural Issues

The issues to be addressed while developing a coping strategy in an Indian organization should consider the following:

- The nature of the Indian workforce, its historical background, personality traits, attitudes, beliefs and values.
- The interpersonal and intra-personal behaviour of the Indian workforce in work situations.
- People's socializing behaviour pattern and its impact on an organisation's effectiveness.
- The strength and weaknesses of management at various levels.

The major obstacles to the success of the TQM experiment are two-fold. First, the TQM culture may not have been properly defined or not properly understood, or the management commitment may not be real. In order to make the change effective, both are essential. It is felt that an organization:

- Must understand and define the company culture properly and adequately in a language understood by one and all.
- Must demonstrate top management commitment by example.
- Bring awareness of company culture to one and all.

In order to build awareness, management gurus are of immense help. If the problem is one of understanding only, then it works provided the message is convincing and the right one. But the problem comes when, after understanding the concept, the managers underestimate the complexity of changing the culture by example. This requires a multi-disciplinary collaborative approach.

Company Culture

It refers to a set of values, beliefs, folklore, guiding norms and attitudes of people working in the organization. It is strongly influenced by:

- How decisions are made.
- How human resources are used.
- How the external environment is used.

A leader creates and turns a vision into reality by defining the company culture and integrating the vision in it. The culture of an organization governs its capacity to implement its strategy. The strategic responses of the company are to be matched by its ability to position them quickly and effectively in a coordinating manner. Such a matching represents an important competitive advantage for the organization. An organization culture and strategy need to be mutually supportive and aligned.

The basis of its alignment and synergy, however, rests on a set of values and shared beliefs in the form of inspiring vision. In the absence of a strong cultural support system, effective implementation of TQM may not be sustainable in a highly dynamic and volatile environment. Company culture can be described in words, but is only recognized when people experience it. It has to be created. One has to indoctrinate employees from the start in the culture. The vision and culture of the company should be shared and properly understood by all. The management has to make sure that everyone understands and knows how to behave consistently.

To bring about acceptance, the management should reward the people who do behave consistently. Just as external environments are important, internal ones are equally important. If we ask a number of people 'how things are done here' the response will indicate everything about company culture.

If it is consistent, that means the culture is good and accepted by all. If it is inconsistent, that means there is no company culture and individual culture is predominant. In fact, if nobody tells people what to do, then people take decisions considering what they perceive the company culture to be.

Here is an example: suppose somebody is fabricating a tank for a power transformer and finds that the quality of welding is poor but will not be critical immediately. It will create quality problems after some time.

What is to be done? In such circumstances, people base their decision on what they perceive as company culture. If the culture is one where quality is important, they will do something about the poor welding. But even if the culture is quality-oriented but managers are inconsistent in their response, people will keep quiet and let someone else sort out the problem.

This is the difference between companies devoted to TQM culture and those which are not. Organization culture has tremendous effect on its effectiveness. The extent to which the set of values, norms and beliefs of its people is widely diffused and shared throughout the organization will be revealed in the results.

A company's culture strengthens and integrates the company's strategy, policies, structure and operation and results in excellent performance. A strong and integrative culture provides the basis for the innovative *élan* and ethos of an organization.

A confused, dissonant, divisive and parochial value system will result in poor quality, disharmony, low productivity, a poor work ethic, low morale and dismal performance. Thus, for the success of TQM in Indian organizations, we should have a strong integrative culture.

Effective leadership to move the organization towards achievement of organizational goals, in the face of uncertainty and challenges from the external environment, is a pre-requisite for the success of TQM.

Prerequisites

1. **The 'can do' attitude**

   Our culture is one of evasiveness. Our reaction to complaints about products or service is merely saying: 'It is not my job', 'It is not my fault', 'It is the system', 'We cannot do anything about it', etc. These phrases are examples of a 'can't do attitude' while the success of TQM requires a 'can do culture' in the company. This change has to come sooner or later. The management has to make sure that everyone is a part of the 'can do culture'. A 'can do 'attitude means more openness and freedom to act and getting rid of bureaucracy.

2. **Redefining the customer**

In a Total Quality culture, the definition of customer is also changing. It is not just the external customer but includes internal customers too. Understanding the needs of the internal customers is more important.

In TQM implementation, the internal-external customer-supplier relationships are well defined and clearly communicated. In TQM implementation, it is the individual contributor whose value addition is important.

Surrounding the individual is the process—how to do the job. The organizational system is socio-technical and to be effective in such a system one has to be patiently impatient, consistent and persistent.

Interactions occur as the product flows from one person to another for value addition, then to a third person for further value addition, eventually reaching the customer. There are expectations and responsibilities of each person in the organization, which results in working relationships.

In this framework, the individual plays the roles of a craftsman, connoisseur or an entrepreneur. Figure 18.1 shows the value addition relationship in the organization.

3. **The cost of controlling quality and people**

Most organizations are in fact unconsciously spending an astronomical amount on poor quality. Instead of developing their employees' skills and confidence to deal with quality problems and taking preventive action, they are spending more in delaying the tackling of these quality problems.

In the TQM environment, it is considered that a systems approach helps in generating a tremendous awareness about quality cost and eventually results in lower costs. Phillips Crosby stated: 'Quality is free' in the opinion of others, Quality is free but it is not a gift, one has to work for it.'

4. **Responsibility and ownership for quality**

The employees should own responsibility for quality and the management should nurture them to see how they can improve things. It's easy to tell someone that quality is his or her responsibility but to make the atmosphere congenial to achieve quality is difficult. This is where more sincere efforts are needed.

This is where company culture comes in, especially in terms of freedom to act. Most companies employ people to work for them, but expect them to deposit their brains in their lockers before they start and collect them while leaving each day.

Freeing people to tackle everyday quality problems by themselves is at the heart of the TQM empowerment process.

5. Teamwork

To achieve revolutionary instead of evolutionary quality improvement, teamwork is absolutely essential. In a total quality environment, the organization has to get a critical mass of enablers within the organization. People should work as team members and the team has to perform consistently better than the sum total of individual performances. TQM encourages participation by all to provide a stimulus and a continuous learning environment.

In TQM, ignorance about ideas and concepts is accepted and discussions are encouraged. Through discussions, the cross-fertilisation of ideas takes place and this makes them evolve better and more effective solutions to problems.

6. Positive mental attitude

The TQM environment requires that employees get the right signals and adopt a positive mental attitude. This is necessary to be aware of the existence of quality problems and to appreciate the need for continuous quality improvement.

7. Impact of socio-cultural variables

When attempting to implement TQM in the Indian context, we have to do so in a given cultural and social heritage. The Japanese quality programmes have been successful within their cultural and social framework, such as lifetime employment, the homogeneity of the Japanese people, the paternalistic and collective nature of the Japanese, their labour management relationship and managements' concern with the long term objectives of the company, rather than being overly concerned with the quarterly profits.

In the Indian context, for the success of the TQM movement a change of culture and employee attitude needs to be effected. Indian work culture is 'soft'. The attributes of our soft culture are as follows:

- Planning is neglected in general.
- Short-term considerations take precedence over long-range planning.
- Non-adherence to laid-down systems and procedures, standards and norms are acceptable.
- Consciousness of time as money is lacking.
- Low individual credibility, as no one believes anyone.
- Roles are unclear and there is lack of accountability.

8. Action plan

To make the TQM movement a success story, more efforts are required. The TQM culture in the Indian environment requires redefining the roles and behaviour of the management and ensuring a continuous feedback as shown in the management system model (Figure 18.2).

The following action plan can be of immense help to initiate the change process.

- **Action based.** Nothing can be done by thinking or talking alone. To reach the goal one has to start moving right now.
- **Obtain sufficient data.** TQM cannot be implemented on theory concepts, philosophies or principles alone. TQM requires action based on facts and data. Hence, collection of adequate data is important.
- **Exceed consumer expectations.** The people in charge in the next process/operation are best equipped to specify the needs. The producer may be satisfied but the customer may not.

  Then the customer may not be aware of his own requirements. To be successful, the focus has to be changed from meeting customer requirements to exceeding his expectations so that he continues to be your customer.
- **Review standards/performance norms.** The available standards and norms may be either too high or vague. High standards mean more cost. Vague standards mean more quality problems.

  One has to check the adequacy and sufficiency of the same, considering the objective of exceeding customer requirements. We may find a lot of problems. One should ensure that they are acceptable to those who use them.
- **SQC Technique.** Statistical (Quality Control) Data can tell us a lot when they are properly analysed. Use of simple SQC techniques makes data a powerful tool. The proper use of SQC techniques depends upon the understanding of basic statistical concepts.

  The main reason Xerox's quality programme stumbled in the 1980s, was the failure of rigorous statistical analysis.
- **Review Controls.** TQM implementation is an organization wide intervention. It requires tremendous amount of integration, coordination, communication and conflict management. In the organization, all existing systems, procedures and controls should be reviewed and amended.
- **Review Activities.** People tend to be carried away by immediate and relatively minor problems due to short-term visible gains and forget more critical ones. Review achievement frequently and make sure that long-term objectives are always kept in mind.
- **Training and Retraining.** Progress stops if people stay within their narrow confines. Individual learning should be encouraged. Listen to what others have done. Discuss with people outside your company and broaden your scope through mutual development.

The route to quality for many firms in India has begun with an emphasis on systems. The simple objective is to have efficient and effective customer–focused processes which everyone can understand and implement. For most firms in India today, the TQM movement started with redefining systems and initiating action for certification to ISO 9000. The second route which organizations are considering is the increased use of SQC. Any of these tools will give the benefits, but maximum benefits will only be realised when they are practised in the right environment.

Everybody works with people and thereby influences the behaviour/quality of life in an organization. The top management has to build a climate in which people are motivated, work together productively and become more effective and result-oriented individuals. TQM is a win-win approach. It creates a reward system in which human, organizational and social objectives are met simultaneously. People find more satisfaction in work when there is cooperation and team work. They are learning, growing and contributing. The organization is also more successful because it operates more effectively. Quality is better and costs are reduced. Perhaps the greatest beneficiary of the reward system is the society itself, because it has better products and services, better citizens, and a climate of cooperation and progress. Thus, there is a third party win-win-win situation with no losers.

For the successful implementation of TQM we have to develop our own indigenous models. We have to devise a mechanism for achieving excellence in the context of poverty, inequality and rapid socio-economic change. The keys to excellence are values, mission, vision, style of management, goals, policy frameworks, management systems, and structures, the revitalization processes and mechanisms such as creativity, effective leadership, action-based research and OD.

We have to change our 'soft' culture to a culture where discipline, hard work, precise work standards and performance effective implementation of laid-down systems, procedures and credibility are respected and maintained.

Management Article

Nature, Scope and Functions of Human Resource Management

—Ms. Shikha Goyal and Dr. Vishnu Bhagwan

It is rightly said that the most fertile land on this earth is the human mind. Among the various factors of production human resource is the most important as the efficient use of physical resources *i.e.*, land, machinery and materials ultimately depends on how the human factor is put to good use on various operations. Human Resource Management is the art of procuring, developing and maintaining competent human minds to achieve the goals of an organisation in an effective and efficient manner.

Human resources may be defined as the total knowledge, skills, creative abilities, talents and aptitudes of an organisation's workforce, as well as the values, attitudes, approaches and beliefs of the individuals involved in the affairs of the organisation. It is the sum total or aggregate of inherent abilities, acquired knowledge and skills represented by the talents and aptitudes of the persons employed in an organisation.

The human resources are multidimensional in nature. From the national point of view, human resources may be defined as the knowledge, skills, creative abilities, talents and aptitudes obtained in the population; whereas from the view-point of the individual enterprise, they represent the total of the inherent abilities, acquired knowledge and skills as exemplified in the talents and aptitudes of its employees.

Human Resource Management: Defined

Human Resource Management has come to be recognized as an inherent part of management, which is concerned with the human resources of an organisation. Its objective is the maintenance of better human relations in the organisation by the development, application and evaluation of policies, procedures and programmes relating to human resources to optimize their contribution towards the realisation of organisational objectives. In other words, HRM is concerned with getting better results with the collaboration of people. It is an integral but distinctive part of management, concerned with people at work and their relationships within the enterprise. HRM helps in attaining maximum individual development, desirable working relationship between employees and employers, employees and employees, and effective moulding of human resources as contrasted with physical resources. It is the recruitment, selection, development, utilisation, compensation and motivation of human resources by the organisation.

Human Resource Management: Evolution

The early part of the century saw a concern for improved efficiency through careful design of work. During the middle part of the century emphasis shifted to the employee's productivity. Recent decades have focussed on increased concern for the quality of working life, total quality management and worker's participation in management. These three phases may be termed as **welfare, development and empowerment.**

Human Resource Management: Nature

Human Resource Management is a process of bringing people and organisations together so that the goals of each are met. The various features of HRM include:

- It is pervasive in nature as it is present in all enterprises.
- Its focus is on results rather than on rules.
- It tries to help employees develop their potential fully.
- It encourages employees to give their best to the organisation.
- It is all about people at work, both as individuals and groups.
- It tries to put people on assigned jobs in order to produce good results.
- It helps an organisation meet its goals in the future by providing for competent and well-motivated employees.
- It tries to build and maintain cordial relations between people working at various levels in the organisation.
- It is a multi-disciplinary activity, utilizing knowledge and inputs drawn from psychology, economics, etc.

Human Resource Management: Scope

The scope of HRM is very wide. The Indian Institute of Personnel Management has specified the scope of HRM as:

- **Personnel aspect**—This is concerned with manpower planning recruitment, selection, placement, transfer promotion, training and development, lay off and retrenchment, remuneration, incentives, productivity etc.
- **Welfare aspect**—It deals with working conditions and amenities

Contd...

PD/July/2009/73
Courtsey: Authors

such as canteens, creches, rest and lunch rooms, housing, transport, medical assistance, education, health and safety, recreation facilities, etc.

- **Industrial relations aspect**—This covers union-management relations, joint consultation, collective bargainig, grievance and disciplinary procedures, settlement of disputes, etc.

The Human Resource Management philosophy is based on the following beliefs:

- Human resource is the most important asset in the organisation.
- Human resource can be developed and increased to an unlimited extent.
- A healthy climate with values of openness, enthusiasm, trust, mutuality and collaboration is essential for developing human resource.
- HRM can be planned and monitored in ways that are beneficial both to the individuals and the organisation.
- Employees feel committed to their work and the organisation, if the organisation perpetuates a feeling of belongingness
- Employees feel highly motivated if the organisation provides for satisfaction of their basic and higher level needs.
- Employee commitment is increased with the opportunity to discover and use one's capabilities and potential in one's work.
- It is every manager's responsibility to ensure the development and utilisation of the capabilities of subordinates.

Human Resource Management: Objectives

The basic objectives of Human Resource Management may be outlined as follows:

- To help the organisation reach its goals.
- To ensure effective utilisation of human resources.
- To generate maximum development of human resources.
- To ensure respect for human beings.
- To ensure reconciliation of individual goals with those of the organisation.
- To identify and satisfy the needs of individuals.
- To achieve and maintain high morale among employees.
- To employ the skills and abilities of the workforce efficiently.
- To provide the organisation with well-trained and well-motivated employees.
- To increase to the fullest the employee's job satisfaction and self-actualization.
- To develop and maintain a quality of work life.
- To be ethically and socially responsive to the needs of society.
- To develop overall personality of each employee in its multidimensional aspect.
- To enhance employee's capabilities to perform the present job.
- To develop and maintain high level of motivation among the employees.
- To equip the employees with precision and clarity in transaction of business.
- To develop employee's capacity for higher work and greater responsibility.
- To inculcate the sense of team spirit, team work and inter-team collaboration.

Human Resource Management: Functions

In order to achieve the above objectives, Human Resource Management undertakes the following activities:

- Human resource or manpower planning.
- Recruitment, selection and placement of personnel.
- Training and development of employees.
- Appraisal of performance of employees.
- Taking corrective steps such as transfer from one job to another.
- Remuneration of employees.
- Social security and welfare of employees.
- Setting geneal and specific management policy for organisational relationship.
- Collective bargaining, contract negotiation and grievance handling.
- Staffing the organisation.
- Aiding in the self-development of employees at all levels.
- Developing and maintaining motivation for workers by providing incentives.
- Reviewing and auditing manpower management in the organisation
- Potential appraisal
- Feedback counselling.
- Role analysis for job occupants.
- Job rotation.
- Quality circle.
- Organisation development.
- Quality of working life etc.

Human Resource Management: Major Influencing Factors

In the 21st century HRM wil be influenced by following factors, which will work as various issues affecting its strategy:

- Size of the workforce.
- Rising employees' expectations
- Drastic changes in the technology.
- Life-style changes.
- Composition of workforce.
- New skills required.
- Environmental challenges.
- Lean and mean organisations.
- Impact of new economic policy.
- Political ideology of the Government.
- Downsizing and rightsizing of the organisations.
- Culture prevailing in the organisation etc.

Human Resource Management: Futuristic Vision

On the basis of the various issues and challenges, the following suggestions will be of much help to the philosophy of HRM with regard to its futuristic vision:

- There should be a properly defined recruitment policy in the organisation that should give its focus on professional aspect and merit based selection.

Index